Cover photo:
Confluence of the Petitcodiac River and Hall's Creek, close to the landing
site of the Petitcodiac Germans on June 3, 1766.

Cover design:
Peter Manchester, Sackville, N.B.

Deutschkanadische Schriften

B. Sachbücher

Im Auftrag des Verbandes für deutschkanadische
Geschichtsforschung (German-Canadian Historical Association)
herausgegeben von
Lothar Zimmermann und Gerhard Friesen
Anschrift der Herausgeber:

Dr. Gerhard Friesen
Department of Languages & Literature
Wilfrid Laurier University
Waterloo, ONT N2L 3C5
Canada

Prof. Lothar Zimmermann
Department of Modern Languages
University of Prince Edward Island
Charlottetown, PEI C1A 4P3
Canada

Band 8

Rainer L. Hempel

New Voices on the Shores

Printed in Canada

ISSN 0832 7750   ISBN 0-921415-08-7

Rainer L. Hempel

NEW VOICES ON THE SHORES

Early Pennsylvania German Settlements in New Brunswick

German-Canadian Historical Association
Toronto, 2000

New Voices on the Shores
Table of Contents

Acknowledgements	vii
Preface	ix
List of Abbreviations	xi
Ferdinand Freiligrath's Poem *Emigrants* (Excerpt)	xii
Introduction	1
Chapter I: Conditions in Europe and the Lure of America	**18**
I.1 The "Push" Factors	18
I.2 The Religious Puzzle	26
I.3 The "Pull" Factors	33
Chapter II: Origins of the Petitcodiac Germans	**43**
II.1 Ricker	43
II.2 Sommer	44
II.3 Wortman(n)	44
II.4 Treitz	47
II.5 Lutz	54
a. The County of Wertheim	54
b. Forefathers of Michael Lutz in Höhefeld and Kreuzwertheim	62
II.6 Stieff	81
a. The Dukedom of Württemberg	84
b. Forefathers of Heinrich and Regina (Stahlecker) Stieff	100
Chapter III: The Journey Westward	**124**
Chapter IV: The Petitcodiac Germans in Pennsylvania	**135**

Chapter V: Northbound to a Vacant Land   152

     V.1   Germantown, N. B.: the Story of an Unsuccessful   157
          Settlement
     V.2   The Petitcodiac Germans in "Monckton"   170
     V.3   The Hillsborough Settlement   196

Chapter VI: History and Stories of the Petitcodiac   227

     VI.1   Land Deeds for "Monckton" and Hillsborough   227
     VI.2   Matters of the Spirit   239
     VI.3   The Spirit of Enterprise   255

Chapter VII: Homesteading and Beyond   318

     VII.1 New Names in a New Province   318
     VII.2 A Blending of Old and New   325

Epilogue   361

Genealogical Reference   373

     Beck   375
     Copple   381
     Jones   382
     Lutz   387
     Ricker   398
     Sommer   404
     Stahlecker   407
     Stieff   409
     Treitz   426
     Wortman(n)   437

Sources   443

     Archival and Unpublished   443
     Published   447

Appendix   468

Index   478

Acknowledgements

On the financial side I am greatly indebted to the German Academic Exchange Service (*Deutscher Akademischer Austauschdienst*) for allowing me to carry out research at the Ruhr-Universität Bochum in Germany, where Dr. Wolfgang J. Helbig of the *Fakultät für Geschichtswissenschaft* provided valuable assistance and many practical suggestions during the initial stage of this project. Dr. Hans-Josef Niederehe of the *Fachbereich II - Romanistik* at the Universität Trier invited me to his university as a base for further research in south-western Germany. The early phase of gathering data abroad occurred during a study leave granted by Mount Allison University. The financial contributions by the City of Moncton assisted in acquiring many of the illustrations and, combined with support from the Michael Lutz (1766) Descendants and Steeves Family Inc., made the publication of this book possible.

My gratitude is extended to Erich Langguth, an archivist in Wertheim, who set up the Michael and Thomas Lutz family tree, furnished important background information about the Lutz family, and continues to show an active interest in this project. As well, archivist Roland Deigendesch in Münsingen provided valuable assistance on the background of Heinrich Stieff, often on very short notice. Dr. Glenys Waldman of Philadelphia was an able and willing resource person in Pennsylvania-German matters. I gratefully acknowledge the time and effort of Mount Allison University librarians, in particular Anita Cannon for the many lengthy searches for elusive texts on the Internet. Without the contributions of the many archivists and assistants at New Brunswick's Albert County Museum, the Provincial Museum, and Provincial Archives, as well as the Public Archives of Nova Scotia, this study would not have been possible. I recognize Les Bowser's unselfishness in sharing his discovery of the origins of the Stieff family at an early stage. Lieselotte Marks, the former secretary of the Department of German at Mount Allison University, typed a good portion of the first draught from rather cryptic notes. My heartfelt thanks also go to my long-time colleagues, Drs. David Beatty and Eric Ross, for reading the manuscript critically and providing helpful suggestions, as well as to Dr. John Stanton for his advice regarding theoretical aspects of local historical studies. Mr. Bernard LeBlanc, the Curator of the Musée Acadien, who drew the maps, has become an invaluable ally in the discovery of early New Brunswick and Moncton history, Mr. V. "Bing" Geldart shared freely on many occasions his extensive genealogical data and knowledge, and Darren Spidell at Mount Allison University's Computing Services digitized, cropped, and computer-enhanced the pictures. Susan Gallant of Charlottetown, P.E.I., rendered invaluable service in formatting the manuscript. The love of good food, conviviality, and caring for their forefathers which I have witnessed and shared on many occasions in the company of Michael Lutz descendants have spurred me on during the writing of this book, as well as the contagious enthusiasm of John Lutz, the President of the Michael Lutz (1766) Descendants. I also gratefully acknowledge the unfailing support of Ricker descendant Councillor Kathryn Barnes of the City of Moncton and Prof. Lothar Zimmermann of the University of Prince Edward Island, President of the German-Canadian Historical Association, who offered his expertise as an editor to facilitate the publication of the book. Finally, I would like to thank all members of my family for their patience and understanding for my long absences from home. Moreover, my wife Adèle has not only encouraged me but taken an active part in all phases leading up to the finished manuscript. Her research in the history of the Treitz Haus, the former Prince-Lewis House, has contributed many valuable details about early Moncton. She also set up new family genealogies for the settler families and assumed the thankless task of critically reading and improving the text.

Preface

As a first generation immigrant, issues of migration, integration, and assimilation comprise a personal component for me. The descendants of Lunenburg Germans provided a historical dimension, in particular after a lecture by Dr. Manfred Richter from the University of Waterloo which he gave at Mount Allison University in 1975 about the Lunenburg dialect and preservation of their mother tongue well into the 20th century. Considering the detailed research of Nova Scotia's German pioneers, relatively little was known about the early German settlers of the Petitcodiac region. Since topics of language preservation, integration and assimilation are part of the wider field of German-Canadian Studies, the settlers in the immediate proximity of my place of residence and work offered a promising avenue for research. In this I was spurred on by their descendants who demonstrated an equal interest and wish to know about their past; some spared no effort compiling their own genealogies. A systematic wider search of available archival material on the settlers in Europe as well as in Pennsylvania was to show the variety of background influences on their North American endeavours. In the early stages of gathering material at the Ruhr Universität Bochum in 1989, I met Dr. Walter Kamphoefner, then at the University of Miami, who discussed with me his similar approach in the study of Westphalians in the Old and New Worlds. His conclusions regarding immigration with a transatlantic perspective were an affirmation of my own approach.

The wealth of publications on central European emigration to North America and its divergent aspects with regard to the sociological, religious, political, and economic environments of the times carries the risk of generalization and superficiality. Yet the dearth of specific information about such 18th-century settlers in local sources necessitated the inclusion of material which might have been ignored in a study of more recent times, where statistics and private and government documents are more readily available. The present study must be viewed as a first attempt to gather and evaluate in one volume information concerning New Brunswick's early German settlers, specifically those who settled along the Petitcodiac River, but also later arrivals collectively referred to as United Empire Loyalists.

The descendants' interest in detailed historical and geographical information about the regions whence their forbears came was taken into account in the subchapters on the Lutz and Stieff families. This background material comes exclusively from German sources, not readily accessible to Anglophone North Americans. This study explores diverse facets of the emigrants' collective European and Pennsylvanian experiences, and topics less commonly found in history books, such as culture, folklore, and ethnicity, should appeal to a more general readership. However, the scope of this study (and its index) allows those interested only in particular aspects or names to choose their appropriate topics. This holds especially true for the genealogy, which was compiled as a reference for Petitcodiac-German names. The detailed narrative and endnotes are also intended to encourage use of this study as a reference tool and basis for further inquiry.

The research for this study was highlighted by a series of memorable moments rewarding the uncertain quest in the archives, such as the discovery of the Harper Ledgers which opened a window to life along the Petitcodiac around 1800. The fact that new information came to light right to the moment of completion of the text underscores the disquieting realization that much more remains to be uncovered. This is particularly true regarding information on the exact origins and family data for some of the settlers in Germany and Pennsylvania. The church records of the Palatinate, for example, are not centralized or indexed, necessitating a village by village search for the Treitz forbears. However, the time has come to make the results of this inquiry more widely available. It is hoped that future research and the ongoing discovery of new sources will provide an ever clearer picture of how this ethnic group fared in New Brunswick.

List of Abbreviations

ACM	Albert County Museum, Hopewell Cape, N.B.
CRO	Cumberland County Registry Office, Amherst, N.S.
HaP	Haldimand Papers, National Archives of Canada, Ottawa, Ont.
HuP	Hughes Papers, Historical Society of Pennsylvania, Philadelphia, Penn.
HSP	Historical Society of Pennsylvania, Philadelphia, Penn.
JP	Jacob's Papers, Historical Society of Pennsylvania, Philadelphia, Penn.
MAUA	Mount Allison University Archives, Sackville, N.B.
MAUL	Mount Allison University Library, Sackville, N.B.
NAC	National Archives of Canada, Ottawa, Ont.
NBM	New Brunswick Museum, Saint John, N.B.
PANB	Provincial Archives of New Brunswick, Fredericton, N.B.
PANS	Provincial Archives of Nova Scotia, Halifax, N.S.
ST	Sackville Townbook, Mount Allison University Library, Microfilm 5331
WPR	Westmorland County Probate Records
WRO	Westmorland County Registry Office, Moncton, N.B.

The Emigrants

I cannot take my eyes off you;
I have to look at you constantly:
As you pass your belongings
To the deckhand with busy hands.

Oh tell! Why did you depart from here
The Neckar River valley has grapes and grain;
The Black Forest is rich in stands of dark firs,
The highlander's horn sounds in the Spessart woods.

When in the woods of foreign lands,
How will the green hills of your homeland,
The yellow wheat fields of Germany,
With its vineyards beckon you to return!

How will events of days gone by
Drift through your dreams in gleaming images!
Like a quiet, pious saga
They will stand before your inner eye.

The riverman signals! - Depart in peace!
God keep you, man, woman, and aged,
And grant you joy in your breasts,
And rice and corn in your fields!

Die Auswanderer

Ich kann den Blick nicht von euch wenden;
ich muß euch anschaun immerdar:
Wie reicht ihr mit geschäftgen Händen
dem Schiffer eure Habe dar!

O sprecht! warum zogt ihr von dannen?
Das Neckartal hat Wein und Korn;
der Schwarzwald steht voll finstrer Tannen,
im Spessart klingt des Älplers Horn.

Wie wird es in den fremden Wäldern
euch nach der Heimatberge Grün,
nach Deutschlands gelben Weizenfeldern,
nach seinen Rebenhügeln ziehn!

Wie wird das Bild der alten Tage
durch eure Träume glänzend wehn!
Gleich einer stillen, frommen Sage
wird es euch vor der Seele stehn.

Der Bootsmann winkt! -- Zieht hin in Frieden!
Gott schütz' euch, Mann und Weib und Greis!
Sei Friede eurer Brust beschieden
und euren Feldern Reis und Mais !

Ferdinand Freiligrath [1]
(1810-1876)

[1] Despite the loss of rhyme and rhythm through translation, the central question of this excerpt from the poem, *Die Auswanderer,* remains: Why did so many Germans leave, in particular from the southern regions of the country, despite its apparent fertility. The poet knew the reasons but did not attempt to furnish an answer. He focussed instead on the emigrants' future sense of loss and longing in a foreign land. Later in life, Freiligrath abandoned his apolitical stance and became critical of the established order, in particular the princes, and as such was at one time closely associated with Karl Marx (1818-1883). Like many politically active writers, he was forced to flee Germany in the 1840's for fear of incarceration. After a general amnesty was declared, he returned as a celebrated poet, recognized for the sufferings on account of his democratic convictions.

Introduction

In a giant leap of faith, a number of settlers sailed north from Philadelphia at the invitation of a group of Pennsylvanian land companies. When on June 3, 1766 Captain John Hall lowered the gangway of his sloop onto the muddy bank of the creek that divides twentieth-century Moncton and Dieppe, a new era of European settlement was ushered in along the shores of the Petitcodiac River. Once the ship had sailed off and the new arrivals sat huddled together in a make-shift shelter for the night, tradition tells of an Acadian by the name of Pierre Belliveau, who stalked the encampment after dark. What Belliveau overheard was not the tongue of his dreaded foe, the English, who had expelled or killed all his kin a mere eight years earlier; these were new voices, conversing in a language unlike any he had ever heard before. He soon learned that they were Germans who had come from a more southern province to settle the fertile lands of the Petitcodiac region. What must have been a surprise and stroke of good fortune in the eyes of Belliveau was, for historians, an event of regular occurrence in the context of British North America, as Germans had been setting out to the New World for years, with as many varied reasons to leave their homeland as one might fathom. Belliveau's forefathers had emigrated from France for their own good reasons, and his fellow Acadians had had to leave their carefully tended lands for, without doubt, even more compelling reasons, namely the threat of British guns.

This is the nature of migration, whether it be called an expulsion, flight, or move away from deteriorating or threatening conditions in the homeland to a more favourable living environment. Neanderthal man may have walked ahead of the advancing glaciers at the onset of the last ice age (c. 35,000 B.C.). The Cimbri and Teutons had to leave their inundated tribal lands in the low-lying areas surrounding Denmark, paying the terrified Romans an unwelcome visit in the 2nd century B.C.. Countless migrations of other Germanic tribes which began five centuries later were triggered by repeated invasions of the ancestral homelands and changed the face of Europe altogether. Such constant wars and movement of large numbers of peoples during the "Dark Ages" solved, if only temporarily, the problem of competition for food and land by reducing Europe's population virtually to half

1

and thus diminishing the necessity to migrate. The stability in Central Europe established by Charlemagne and his successors encouraged the rise of towns and the development of trade and commerce, providing an environment that allowed previous population levels to be restored or surpassed. However, persistent wars and plagues in later centuries once again ravaged Europe to such a level that its population was probably little higher than that of the previous millennium. A phenomenal doubling of this population occurred during the 18th century in the absence of major plagues and as the result of improved sanitation and medical care, relatively limited warfare, and government policies inspired by the doctrine of mercantilism which encouraged high birthrates. Once again, migration was perceived to be a solution for an ever-increasing population, with some people moving at the invitation of Catherine the Great of Russia to the southern Ukraine and the plains of the Volga or at the beckoning of the victorious Habsburgs to the lands vacated by the Turks. At first slowly, but then with ever greater frequency, North America became the preferred destination despite the physical and psychological barrier of the Atlantic Ocean.

By the time of this most recent population explosion, certain countries had been able to coalesce into empires, whereas Germany[1] rarely experienced the benefits to be gained by a strong central government until modern times. In a country with few natural boundaries, its people were less able to defend themselves against the ambitions of united, powerful neighbours who in times of war ravaged the land and in peace kept its inhabitants hemmed in and introspective. This began with the Romans and continued with the Huns, Hungarians, Normans/Vikings, Swedes and particularly the French under Louis XIV and Napoleon. When Germans stood united, as under Otto the Great in 955 A.D., they proved themselves capable of defeating the invading Hungarians, but when they did not -- which was most of the time -- external powers dominated them. This *Angst*, or fear of invasion and of being confined, is an important component of the German psyche, particularly since the Thirty Years' War (1618-1648) and the Treaty of Westphalia (1648), and explains the preoccupation with personal safety on one hand and desire to escape or emigrate on the other. With the exception of the Hanseatic League, Germany before 1900 boasted no strong fleet like the great colonizing nations of Holland, France, Portugal, Spain, and the most successful of all, Great Britain. Although Germans could move freely

2

throughout most of central Europe during their journeys as part of the apprenticeship system, the sea and other continents were not open to enterprising men at that time. Rather they turned to philosophy, music, and the sciences, or became tinkerers in their backyards or houses, laying the foundations for inventions of the latter part of the nineteenth century, like the car.[2]

The dream to go to faraway places, to escape the overcrowding and narrow confines of their lives, to start something new elsewhere and to obtain that ever so elusive security was, and still is, strongly rooted in Germans although today it has taken on different forms. Such longing was expressed in folklore and popular songs which idealized sailing away on long journeys to other continents and life in exotic places, and beneath their love of foreign cultures and languages, especially those of North America, lies an element of this desire to break free. A game German children used to play around the table, which was accompanied by the verse, "We're going to America, and who is going to come along?",[3] shows the depth of this societal preoccupation. Emigration was once the way in which Germans could escape, and a large number over the centuries has at least pondered this possibility, even though many never followed through. And recently, too, when the unification of Germany threatened the earning power of Germans, many expressed great concern that they would not be able to afford their two annual trips abroad to which they had grown accustomed. Today, German tourists are the most numerous in the world alongside American and Japanese, all of whom for their own particular reasons cherish such "temporary emigrations".

If a young man wanted to see the world and make his mark on it, he had to enter the services of foreign masters, which often lead to emigration. Perhaps the first German-speaking person to do so and actually touch the shores of Canada was a man named Tyrkir, in the service of Leif Erikson when the latter explored North America's east coast, predating Columbus by about five hundred years. Tyrkir was reportedly the one who discovered grapes and vines like those he knew in his homeland and who, in his excitement, succeeded only in expressing his astonishment in his mother tongue, German.[4] As a consequence of this discovery, the Vikings called this new land "Vinland". A number of the early pioneers to settle in Quebec were

Germans whom the French had recruited from Alsace-Lorraine and adjacent areas. Hans Bernard from the Mosel River area bought land near Quebec City in 1664, the first record of a German settler in Canada. Many arrived in Quebec as soldiers, but under French rule were required to be Catholic; as a consequence, they can be traced through baptismal records as to when they converted from the Lutheran to Catholic faith. Often they were simply referred to as Pierre or Jean *dit l'Allemand*, and one such *Jean dit l'Allemand* was Hans Daigle, who accompanied Des Grosseilliers and Radisson on their expeditions.[5] More than one hundred years later, a German accompanied Cook on his last fateful journey. Heinrich Zimmermann, who had departed from Wiesloch in the Palatinate as an apprentice harnessmaker, signed onto the *Discovery* as a coxswain. In 1781, he published a German account of the voyage which related among other events contacts with natives on the coast of British Columbia and a visit to the governor in Kamchatka, a German named Boehn, in the service of Russia.[6]

Of great importance to the history of Canada was the founder of the Hudson's Bay Company, Prince Rupert (*Ruprecht*), who was the son of the electoral prince Friedrich V of the Palatinate and Elizabeth, the grandchild of Maria Stuart. Being a cousin of Charles II, he had entered the services of the King and in 1670 became the governor of lands that eclipsed the size of the realms of most European rulers.[7] He is remembered in such names as Rupert's Land, the territories originally granted to the Hudson's Bay Company, the town of Prince Rupert in British Columbia, a Hudson's Bay trading post, and Rupert River.

Baron von Dieskau, a general from Saxony, directed the French war effort against the British in North America. Upon being severely wounded in 1755, he was saved by a prominent settler named William Johnson, who was fighting for the British and prevented natives under his command from scalping their prisoner. For this noble gesture Johnson was knighted by the King. Sir William Johnson married Katharina Weissenbach, whom he had met in one of the many German communities of upper New York province. Their equally gifted son, John Johnson, later led a regiment of Palatine Germans which became famous as the "Royal Greens" in the war against the rebellious American colonies. He fought on the same side as General Baron von Riedesel, who commanded a German force of about 9,000 in the defence of Canada. Most of the Hessian and Brunswick troops commanded by Riedesel accompanied Burgoyne on the latter's ill-fated campaign, and it was General Nikolaus Herckheimer, who, with his fellow German settlers, fought for the American side and prepared the ground for the eventual defeat of the British forces under Burgoyne in the relatively small battle at Oriskany[8] in 1777.

Of direct importance to the Maritimes was Samuel Waldo (a descendant of the Prussian family von Waldow [9]), who was one of the wealthiest men in New England and who wielded enormous influence during the 1740's and 1750's. Waldo brought over 300 Palatine German Lutherans for settlement in Maine, where they founded Waldoboro. Many of these settlers were conscripted into his militia companies for the first siege and conquest of Fortress Louisbourg in 1745, on which occasion Waldo acted as second-in-command. He also drew up the plans which General Geoffrey Amherst followed for the second attack in 1758. Fighting for the French at Louisbourg in 1745 was the Swiss-German Regiment de Karrer which formed part of the garrison at the Fortress between 1721 and 1745.[10] German settlers under French rule on Île Royale, later named Cape Breton, had moved for protection to the fortress at Louisbourg in 1757. Their *Village des Allemands*, comprising about forty mostly Palatine emigrants, ceased to exist after the British victory. It is presumed that the survivors were deported to France along with the remainder of the French inhabitants of Île Royale.[11] Part of the British expeditionary force in the second conquest of Louisbourg was the Regiment Bouquet, comprised of Germans and Swiss from Maryland and Pennsylvania, which also fought the French in the battle for Quebec City in 1760 and belonged to the first English troops to garrison the former French fortresses.[12] On account of the division and weakness of their own country, Germans sought opportunities elsewhere and found themselves fighting on opposing sides.

Not only on the battlefield in the service of foreigners or as settlers under the jurisdiction of such powers did Germans make their impact. They contributed on various other levels: humanitarian, educational, cultural, technical, business, and religious. Examples include the introduction in 1781 of the Christmas tree in Sorel by the Baroness von Riedesel and the influence

5

of Canada's first professional musician, Heinrich Glackemeyer, who taught the Riedesel daughters in 1783, after their departure opened a music business in Quebec City,[13] and in 1820 founded Canada's first symphony orchestra. The German Loyalist Pastor Samuel Schwerdtfeger became the "Saint" of the St. Lawrence for his work among the Loyalists in the Lunenburg district of Upper Canada in the latter part of the eighteenth century[14] and another Loyalist, Michael Grass, founded Kingston, Ontario in 1783.[15] The artist Albrecht Moll, alias William Berczy, became the co-founder of Toronto, and the engineer, Dr. Thomas Keefer/Kieffer, wrote treatises about the advantages of rail travel when this mode of transport was still in its infancy. He became a member of the Royal Society of Canada and co-founder of the Canadian Society of Civil Engineers. Adam Beck, a child of German immigrants, became known as the father of Ontario Hydro for his role in the construction of the first hydro power station at Niagara Falls. There are also well-known artists like Cornelius Krieghoff, Peter Rindisbacher, and writer Fredrick Philip Grove.

Another cultural exchange took place along Canada's east coast that is scarcely mentioned in the history texts of this country. Moravians, or brethren of the *Herrnhuter Brüdergemeine*, who were given a home in the domain of Count von Zinzendorf in Herrnhut, Saxony in 1727, were and still are a Protestant group believing in brotherhood, tolerance, pacifism, and service to mankind, who have distinguished themselves in their active missionary work amongst the native peoples on several continents. These Brethren established ten missionary stations along the Labrador coast between the years 1776 and 1966. The total respect of these missionaries for the Inuit and the Moravians' insistence that they formally purchase the land for their mission is recorded in bilingual documents[16] in the Herrnhut archives both in German and Inuit, with the "signatures" of the Inuit. The story of the missionary station Hoffenthal (plate 1), present-day Hopedale, and documents for other such stations in the Herrnhut archives, provide the Labrador Inuit Association with concrete evidence and precedents in their struggle to resolve land-claims since they can now argue that they must have owned the land in order to have sold small parcels of it to the Herrnhut Brethren. Moravian missionaries and their outlook on life were to influence the "Petitcodiac Germans"[17] during their years in Pennsylvania.

Germany may not have sent ships and men to other lands to colonize, thereby exploiting and subjugating,[18] but by the very outflow of its people -- some historians have called it a "blood-letting" -- its emigrants have contributed at all levels to the development of North America, and this despite their initial impoverished circumstances, through sheer diligence and spirit of enterprise. In New Brunswick in particular, they left their mark in such names as: Erb Settlement, Etter Ridge, Mount Fisher, Franc(k)fort, German Brook, German Creek, German Lake, Germantown, Germantown Marsh, Germany, Gesner Ridge, Grimmer Parish, Hiltz Road, Knapp Lake, Lutes Mountain (Lutesville), Mannhurst, Mann Mountain Settlement, Memel, Ricker's Point, Somers Creek, Steeves Settlement, and Steeves Mountain.[19]

The loss of large numbers of subjects, in particular to Great Britain, alarmed German rulers who attempted subsequently to determine the causes for the departure of so many from their realms. For the student of emigration, such government reports and studies, in addition to emigrant correspondence, are the first documents dealing with the emigration topic. This material has become the object of many lengthy studies especially after the major wave of emigration that occurred around the middle of the 19th century. General sources of information indispensable to this study include Edith Abbott's survey *Historical Aspects of the Immigration Problem*[20] (860pp.), which consists of over two hundred independent essays arranged under such headings as "Causes of Immigration", "Economic Aspects of the Emigration Problem", and "Early Problems of Assimilation", etc., from the perspective of English, Irish, Scottish, Welsh, Swedish, French, and German immigrants. Another important source is Marcus Lee Hansen's study *The Atlantic Migration 1607-1860*.[21] As its title suggests, this book is primarily concerned with immigration in North America. Hansen draws his information from wide-ranging sources such as newspapers, emigration and immigration society papers, unprinted archival records, official and private correspondence, and government reports. There is a wealth of publications about emigration to America from the German point-of-view, the first comprehensive one being Friedrich Kapp's frequently quoted *Geschichte der deutschen Einwanderung in Amerika*[22] ("History of German Immigration in America"). Although primarily concerned with emigration from Germany during the 19th century, Mack Walker's study *Germany and Emigration*[23]

7

is useful as a source for earlier emigration as well because of the parallels he draws, as between prices of staple foods and emigration. Wilhelm Mönkmeier's *Die deutsche überseeische Auswanderung*[24] ("German Overseas Emigration") provides many pertinent tables and statistics, and the book *Auswanderung und Auswanderungspolitik in Deutschland*[25] ("Emigration and Politics of Emigration in Germany") edited by Eugen von Philippovich is devoted to legal and political matters in separate articles about German states like Württemberg and Mecklenburg. Of the sources that concentrate on emigration from specific German regions, those about the Palatinate and southern Germany during the 18th century head the list in sheer numbres. August Rupp's *Pfälzische Kolonisation in Nordamerika*[26] ("Palatine Colonization in North America"), Fritz Trautz's *Die Pfälzische Auswanderung nach Nordamerika im 18. Jahrhundert*[27] ("Palatine Emigration to North America in the 18th Century"), Wolfgang von Hippel's *Auswanderung aus Südwestdeutschland*[28] ("Emigration from South-Western Germany"), and Walter Allen Knittle's *Early Eighteenth Century Palatine Emigration*[29] are the most useful. Mention must also be made of the many source studies on emigration from various German regions carried out by Werner Hacker.[30] The most important and comprehensive source for immigrants' names in North America was edited by William Filby and Mary Meyer,[31] which contains approximately a half million entries. It is a summary of many previous publications, of which the best known on German immigration are by Rupp[32] and Strassburger/Hinke.[33]

The first and only comprehensive study of German immigration and settlement in Canada was carried out by Heinz Lehmann more than fifty years ago during the years 1929-1931 in his book *Das Deutschtum in Ostkanada*[34] ("German Settlement and Culture in Eastern Canada"). His findings regarding the Lunenburg Germans and those who settled along the Petitcodiac River in New Brunswick were kept relatively brief but are still surprisingly accurate.[35] The claim of a sizeable German component among the United Empire Loyalists in New Brunswick, absent in later publications, is found in this work.[36] One of the best-known subsequent studies, more limited in scope than volume, is that by Winthrop P. Bell, entitled *The "Foreign Protestants"*.[37] Bell's book is also valuable because he was able to access German sources directly on account of his fluency in German. Unfortunately, he shows no awareness of Lehmann's research. Such is the importance of Lehmann's work that Gerhard P. Bassler of the Department of History at Memorial University has translated both volumes of this history of German settlement into English. The one for Eastern Canada (pub. 1931), Western Canada (pub. 1939), and three additional related publications by Lehmann are combined in this new English version, entitled *History, Settlement and Culture*.[38] In his introduction, Bassler provides an excellent bibliography that documents the advances in research since Lehmann's publications on ethnic German settlers and their role as one of Canada's founding peoples. In 1990,[39] the most comprehensive bibliography on German Canadiana to date was made available through the efforts of Hartmut Froeschle and Lothar Zimmermann in a special volume of the *German-Canadian Yearbook*. It contains over 6,500 entries, demonstrating the growth of German-Canadian studies as a field of research. Whereas under the rubric of regional studies this bibliography lists 284 Ontario entries, 136 for Manitoba, and 60 for Nova Scotia, the editors were able to find only 5 publications for New Brunswick that mention Germans and only one devoted to German settlers in New Brunswick alone.[40] The present study is intended to fill this gap. Several of Esther Clark Wright's publications, in particular *Samphire Greens*[41] and *The Petitcodiac*,[42] have furthered research into the early German settlers of New Brunswick, most particularly the Stieff/Steeves family, and provided a starting point for this study.

Particularly since the Canadian Centennial Year, an increasing number of scholars has examined a great variety of ethnic communities in Canada. They range from loose collections of names, places, and events as Bruce Ramsay's 69-page booklet, *A History of the German-Canadians in British Columbia*[43] to two-volume essay collections such as *The Untold Story: The Irish in Canada*, edited by O'Driscole and Reynolds,[44] or monographs like Mason Wade's *The French Canadians*.[45] Some convey a broad view of the ethnic group as Kenneth Bagnell's *Canadese: A Portrait of the Italian Canadians*[46] or a narrow view in time and topic like Louis Rosenberg's collection of graphs, maps, statistics, lists, and short commentaries and interpretations called *Canada's Jews: A Social and Economic Study of Jews in Canada in the 1930s*.[47] As a reflection of immigration waves, some studies concentrate on limited periods and specific locations in the Old World such as the Irish around the time of the famine, the Ukrainians from Galicia and Bukovyna around 1900 in Orest T. Martynowych's *Ukrainians in*

Canada: The Formative Period, 1891-1924[48] and Jaroslav Petryshyn's *Peasants in the Promised Land*,[49] the story of Ukrainian settlement in the Canadian prairie provinces during the years 1891-1914, or Johannes Helmut Merz's *The Hessians in Upper Canada.*[50] Other studies concentrate on religious groups such as Frank H. Epp's *Mennonites in Canada, 1786-1920*,[51] B.G. Sack's *History of the Jews in Canada*,[52] and M.J. Dhillon's *The Sikhs in Canada and California.*[53] From the above it is evident that there is no established theory which guides the approach to the topic of emigration/immigration and settlement although most authors keep their remarks about conditions in the country of origin brief to concentrate on the circumstances in Canada. Only recently have studies like A.G. Roeber's *Palatines, Liberty, and Property*[54] confined their focus on cultural transfer of ideas such as liberty and property to America and their redefinition in the latter part of the 18th century. "Transoceanic" studies are now also used by quantitative historians who scour archives for vast bodies of genealogical sources to arrive at conclusions about emigration/immigration and settlement patterns. One such example is Bruce S. Elliott's *Irish Migrants in the Canadas: A New Approach*,[55] a "microstudy" of 775 North-Tipperary Protestant families who came to Canada between 1818 and 1855. Another example is Peter Murphy's genealogical study *Together in Exile*,[56] which traces back a large number of families from the south end of Saint John, N.B., mainly to the Parish of Carlingford in Ireland between 1834 and 1855. The large-scale studies are possible as the result of the relatively recent date of the emigration and the completeness of the archival sources.

A less quantitative approach must be contemplated if archival material has been destroyed as in the case of Württemberg or is incomplete because the emigration occurred a full one hundred years earlier and if the sample is only two families in Germany and seven in Pennsylvania. The nature of this examination demands a versatile, methodological approach[57] in order that information gleaned from German, Pennsylvanian, and Canadian archives, and that from the quantitative historian Mönckemeier or the social historian Walker,[58] for example, can be used to paint a total picture of the regions' histories.[59] With repeated references to the wider context, a micro-historical examination of the Lutz and Stieff family backgrounds in Germany and later in New Brunswick permits the interfacing of economic, social, political, religious, cultural, ethnic, as well as personal factors.[60] Only by limiting these to regional and local history can their interdependence be shown in a more "controlled" environment that involves specific individuals. Macro-history can then base its generalizations on such micro-historical studies.[61] To reach the goal of a quantitative emigrants' biography, Wolfgang von Hippel, the author of the most comprehensive and current study on emigration from Württemberg, recommended in 1984 that researchers first explore the lives of individual emigrants and their families, beginning in the New World and trace them back to their origins in the Old World. The absence of adequate statistical data for Württemberg's 18th-century emigration has led Hippel to suggest that detailed local studies carried out in immigration countries would provide promising new approaches to this subject. The names of immigrant families could then be traced back to their country and region of origin and more general socio-historical and demographic questions be probed in regional examples.[62] Hans Medick's argument regarding "local" history as "general" history is similar in intent and can be shown in the examples of Michael Lutz and Heinrich Stieff. Hippel warns that these are time-consuming studies and, because of the multiplicity of tasks and requirements of expertise in many areas, should only be attempted by a team of researchers. The exemplary character of the Lutz and Stieff emigration studies will assist in the search for reasons why other Germans came to North America and New Brunswick and contributed in the ways they did. Furthermore, the regional approach to history is appropriate for Canada on account of its vast size and varied historical experience,[63] but it is no less so for Germany until 1871, despite this country's small size, on account of its political division. This study combines the micro-historical approach with Hippel's suggestion to trace the immigrants back to their exact regions of departure[64] in order to focus on the various influences from both sides.

The smaller number permits the immigrants to be regarded as a group of individuals, as men and women with names and personalities and not merely as "heads of households" and statistics in a mass. Genealogical information was introduced to attach specific persons to the settlement pattern and development of the community. Although family histories emerge, this study distinguishes itself from the "numerous pieces of family history ... that start with the group's arrival on this side of the Atlantic ... [from which] observations about the nature of migration and about the process of cultural transfer cannot be drawn with confidence ...."[65]

11

The causes of the emigration/immigration, or "push/pull" phenomenon, are traced in the living conditions of Central Europe and contrasted to the lure of North America, which attracted these settlers first to Pennsylvania and later to the shores of the Petitcodiac River. By investigating primary sources in Germany, the personal backgrounds of those who immigrated to New Brunswick are revealed and reasons presented for their later successes. The story of the Germantown settlement in Albert County, N.B., is contrasted with that of the Steeves (*Stieff*), Trites (*Treitz*), Lutes (*Lutz*), Wortman, Ricker, and Somers/Summers (*Sommer*) families. First-hand accounts detail initial phases of the settlements and some of the immense difficulties which arose during the American War of Independence, as well as the highlights of gaining title to the lands they had helped clear, their increasing political consciousness, independence in the religious sphere, and interaction with the United Empire Loyalists after the American War of Independence.

For over two centuries, German-speaking immigrants have settled and left their own, unique mark on New Brunswick's landscape. This study explores numerous facets of their cultural background, folklore, religion, ethnicity, and assimilation, and although scholarly in nature, episodes and original accounts are interspersed throughout to provide variety and bring the grand schemes of colonial history down to a more human level. The initial number of settlers may have been small, but their impact within and outside the region has been significant, and not only as a consequence of their remarkable fertility. Because descendants of these pioneers have spread throughout North America ever since, such a focussed study of the earliest Pennsylvania German migration to the northern provinces not only sheds new light on Maritime history but adds another chapter to Canadian history as a whole.

ENDNOTES

[1] The term "Germany" in the context of this book denotes the areas of central Europe where the German language is spoken. Similarly, the term "German" is used in the context of culture, heritage, and language. Germany as a political entity only came into being in 1871.

[2] Jan P. Norbye, *The Complete History of the German Car*, 1886 to the Present (New York: Portland House, 1987), pp. 9ff..

[3] Any quotes in English from German sources were translated by me

[4] *The Vinland Sagas, The Norse Discovery of America*, eds. Magnus Magnusson and Hermann Palsson (Penguin Classics, Toronto, 1965), p. 57.

[5] Georg Weissenborn, "The Germans in Canada: a chronological survey of Canada's third oldest European ethnic group from 1664 to 1977," *German-Canadian Yearbook*, IV (Toronto: Historical Society of Mecklenburg Upper Canada, 1978), p. 23.

[6] Peter Liddell, "The First Germans in British Columbia," *German-Canadian Yearbook*, VI (Toronto: Historical Society of Mecklenburg Upper Canada, 1981), pp. 74-77.

[7] The importance of Prince Rupert and his family for Great Britain and Canada is only now being fully recognized. Beside being the founder of the Hudson's Bay Company, he became a cavalry general and First Lord of the Admiralty. His acquaintance with William Penn resulted in the latter's visit to the Palatinate and recruitment of Quakers and others which triggered the German mass migration to Pennsylvania. Prince Rupert's nephew, the Electoral Prince Georg Ludwig of Hanover, became King George I of Great Britain in 1714 and thereby founded the British House of Hanover, whose descendants occupy the British throne today..

[8] Friedrich Kapp, *Geschichte der deutschen Einwanderung in Amerika* (Leipzig: Verlag von Quandt & Händel, 1868), pp. 229ff..

[9] David Artiss, "The 'Waldo Scheme': General Samuel Waldo and his 'Long-Shot' Claim to the Territories of Nova Scotia and New Brunswick," *Annalen/Annals/Annales, 8: German-Candian Studies in the Nineties, Results and Projects,* ed. Lothar Zimmermann (Toronto: German-Canadian Historical Association, 1993), 59-65.

[10] Hartmut Froeschle, *Adler auf dem Ahornbaum* (Toronto: German-Canadian Historical Association, 1997), p. 3.

[11] Weissenborn, "The Germans in Canada", p. 24. Cf. also Winthrop P. Bell, *The "Foreign Protestants" and the Settlement of Nova Scotia,* 2nd ed. (Sackville, N.B.: Centre for Canadian Studies, Mount Allison University, 1990), p. 59.

[12] Froeschle, *Adler auf dem Ahornbaum*, p. 15.

[13] Weissenborn,"The Germans in Canada", pp. 25ff..

[14] *Ibid.*, p.58.

[15] F.P.J. Rimrott and W. Eichenlaub, eds., *"Was du ererbt ..."* (Toronto: Deutsche Sprachschulen, 1978), p. 20.

[16] Erhard Treude, "Eskimoische Landabtretung in Nordlabrador im 18. Jahrhundert," *Polarforschung*, ed. Deutsche Gesellschaft für Polarforschung, 47. Jg., Nr. 1/2 (Münster: 1977), pp. 61-71. Cf. also David Artiss, "Cultural Heritage Study in Atlantic Canada", *Proceedings of the Atlantic University Teachers of German Conference 1979*, ed. Rainer L. Hempel (Sackville, N.B.: Mount Allison University, 1979), pp. 72-82.

[17] The founders of Moncton in 1766 and Hillsborough in 1769 are referred to collectively as "Petitcodiac Germans". Other Germans such as Martin Beck from Fort Cumberland and Frederick Burksdorf from Germantown, N. B., later became part of this group.

[18] Germany was a colonial power from about 1885 to 1918 in Africa and the Far East.

[19] Alan Rayburn, *Geographical Names of New Brunswick* (Canadian Permanent Committee on Geographical Names, 1975) and William B. Hamilton, *Place Names of Atlantic Canada* (Toronto: University of Toronto Press, 1996).

[20] Edith Abbott, *Historical Aspects of the Immigration Problem* (Chicago, Illinois: University of Chicago Press, 1926).

[21] Marcus Lee Hansen, *Atlantic Migration 1607-1860* (New York: Harper and Brothers, 1940).

[22] Friedrich Kapp, *Geschichte der deutschen Einwanderung in Amerika* (Leipzig: Verlag von Quand und Händel, 1886).

[23] Mack Walker, *Germany and Emigration 1816-1885* (Cambridge, Massachusetts: Harvard University Press, 1964); Walker drew graphs that are nearly identical regarding the price of rye and the numbers of emigrants at a given time (pp. 45, 156).

[24] Wilhelm Mönckmeier, *Die deutsche überseeische Auswanderung:* Ein Beitrag zur deutschen Wanderungsgeschichte (Jena: Gustav Fischer Verlag, 1912).

[25] Eugen von Philippovich, *Auswanderung und Auswanderungspolitik in Deutschland* (Leipig: Verein für Sozialpolitik, 1892).

[26] August Rupp, *Pfälzische Kolonisation in Nordamerika* (Stuttgart: Eugen Wahl Verlag, 1938).

[27] Fritz Trautz, *Die Pfälzische Auswanderung nach Nordamerika im 18. Jahrhundert* (Heidelberg: Carl Winter Universitätsverlag, 1959).

[28] Wolfgang von Hippel, *Auswanderung aus Südwestdeutschland: Studien zur Württembergischen Auswanderung und Politik im 18. und 19. Jahrhundert* (Stuttgart: Klett-Cotta Verlag, 1984).

[29] Walter Allen Knittle, *Early Eighteenth Century Palatine Emigration* (Philadelphia: Dorrance and Company, 1937).

[30] Separate studies exist for Baden/Breisgau, the northern Lake Constance region, the upper Neckar River, lower Neckar River, Ulm, south-east Black Forst, Speyer, upper Swabia, Palatinate/Saarland, all regions from which emigrants left in large numbers for North America and south-eastern Europe.

[31] P. William Filby, Mary K. Meyer, eds., *Passenger and Immigration Lists Index: A Guide to Published Arrival Records of about 500,000 Passengers who came to the United States and Canada in the Seventeenth, Eighteenth, and Nineteenth Centuries*, 3 Vols. with supplements (Detroit: Gale Research Co., 1981).

[32] Israel Rupp, *Chronologisch geordnete Sammlung von mehr als 30.000 Einwanderern in Pennsylvanien aus Deutschland, der Schweiz, Holland, Frankreich und anderen Staaten von 1717 bis 1776*, rpt. (Hildesheim: Gerstenberg, 1975).

[33] Ralph B. Strassburger, W. J. Hinke, eds., *Pennsylvania German Pioneers*, 3 Vols. (Norristown, Penn.: Genealogical Publishing Co., 1934 and 1966).

[34] Heinz Lehmann, *Zur Geschichte des Deutschtums in Kanada*, Band I: *Das Deutschtum in Ostkanada* (Stuttgart: Ausland und Heimat Verlags-Aktiengesellschaft, 1931).

[35] Only three pages are devoted to the German settlers in New Brunswick, probably because they appeared to have been assimilated by the time he carried out his studies.

[36] *Ibid.*, pp. 38-39.

[37] Winthrop P. Bell, *The "Foreign Protestants" and the Settlement of Nova Scotia* (Toronto: University of Toronto Press, 1961).

[38] Heinz Lehmann, *Immigration, Settlement and Culture*, trans., ed., and intro. by Gerhard P. Bassler (St. John's, Nfld.: Jesperson Press, 1986).

[39] Hartmut Froeschle and Lothar Zimmermann, eds., "German Canadiana: A Bibliography," *German-Canadian Yearbook*, Special Issue, XI (Toronto: Historical Society of Mecklenburg Upper Canada, 1990).

[40] Rainer L. Hempel, "Germantown - die Geschichte einer deutschen Siedlung in Neubraunschweig," *German-Canadian Yearbook*, IX (Toronto: Historical Society of Mecklenburg Upper Canada, 1986), 49-62.

[41] Esther Clark Wright, *Samphire Greens* (Kingsport, N.S.: Clark Wright, 1961).

[42] Esther Clark Wright, *The Petitcodiac* (Sackville, N.B.: The Tribune Press, 1945).

[43] Bruce Ramsay, *A History of German-Canadians in British Columbia* (Winnipeg: National Publishers, 1958).

[44] Robert O'Driscoll and Lorna Reynolds, eds., *The Untold Story: The Irish in Canada*, 2 Vols. (Toronto: Celtic Arts of Canada, 1988).

[45] Mason Wade, *The French Canadians (1760-1967)*, 2 Vols. (Toronto: MacMillan of Canada, 1968).

[46] Kenneth Bagnell, *Canadese: A Portrait of the Italian Canadians* (Toronto: Kenbar Productions Ltd., 1989).

[47] Louis Rosenberg, *Canada's Jews: A Social and Economic Study of Jews in Canada in the 1930s* (Montreal & Kingston: McGill-Queen's University Press, 1993).

[48] Orest T. Martynowych, *Ukrainians in Canada: The Formative Period, 1891-1924* (Edmonton: Canadian Institute of Ukrainian Studies Press, 1991).

[49] Jaroslav Petryshyn, *Peasants in the Promised Land: Canada and the Ukrainians 1891-1914* (Toronto: James Lorimer and Company, 1985).

[50] Johannes Helmut Merz, *The Hessians in Upper Canada* (Hamilton, Ont.: German-Canadian Historical Book Publishing, 1997).

[51] Frank H. Epp, *Mennonites in Canada, 1786-1920 : The History of a Separate People* (Toronto: Macmillan of Canada, 1974).

[52] B.G. Sack, *History of the Jews in Canada* (Montreal: Harest House, 1965).

[53] Mahinder Singh Dhillon, *The Sikhs in Canada and California* (Vancouver: Shromani Akali Dal Association of Canada, 1981).

[54] A.G. Roeber, *Palatines, Liberty, and Property: German Lutherans in Colonial British America* (Baltimore and London: The John Hopkins University Press, 1993).

[55] Bruce S. Elliott, *Irish Migrants in the Canadas: A New Approach* (Kingston and Montreal: McGill-Queen's University Press, 1988).

[56] Peter Murphy, *Together in Exile* (Saint John, N.B.: Peter Murphy, 1990).

[57] "History is not an exact discipline that imposes an explicit body of theory on its practitioners. In contrast to most other areas of scholarly endeavour where paradigms determine the lines of research and help to assess the validity of their results, most historians stand outside such systems." Terry Crowly, *Clio's Craft: A Primer of Historical Methods* (Toronto: Copp Clark Pittman Ltd., 1988), p.6.. Information for this study from 18th century sources was so scarce that a wide range was consulted to arrive at a picture that was as balanced and complete as possible.

[58] Mack Walker, *German Home Towns*: Community, State, and General Estate 1648-1871 (Ithaca and London: Cornell University Press, 1971).

[59] The difference between "most local historical writing" and that which aims for "a wider purpose" has been argued before; Donald Harman Akenson, *The Irish in Ontario: A Study in Rural History* (Kingston and Montreal: McGill-

16

Queen's University Press, 1985), pp. 333f.; cf. also John G. Reid, "Writing About Regions," *Writing About Canada: A Handbook for Modern Canadian History,* ed. John Schulz (Scarborough, Ont.: Prentice Hall Canada Inc., 1990), pp. 84f..

[60] In this context the present study has made use of the *Annales* approach to history by gleaning its information from various sources of local historical records in parish and secular archives . For more on the differences betweeen the "old" and "new/modern" approach to historical interpretation, consult T. Crowly, *Clio's Craft,* pp. 1 ff..

[61] In an exhaustive micro-analytical study (708 pages) of the weaving trade in the small Swabian Highland community of Laichingen, Hans Medick selected this local historical frame to study the interaction of the various forces in isolation while at the same time interrelating the situation in Laichingen with the larger picture of Württemberg. Medick repeatedly stresses the primacy of the micro-historical perspective; Hans Medick, *Weben und Überleben in Laichingen: 1650-1900* (Göttingen: Vandenhoek & Ruprecht, 1997), pp. 13ff..

[62] Hippel, *Auswanderung aus Südwestdeutschland,* pp. 20ff..

[63] John G. Reid, "Writing About Regions," pp. 77ff..

[64] "The development of regional study as a branch of historical enquiry is not confined to Canada. Regional micro-studies have assumed importance in historical fields studied internationally: rural history, migration history, the history of various ethnic groups, and aspects of North American colonial history. In these areas, Canadian regional historians have been influenced by colleagues in France, the British Isles, the United States and elsewhere, and have contributed in turn." *Ibid.,* p. 82.

[65] Donald Harman Akenson, "Foreword", pp. xii-xiv, Elliott, *Irish Migrants in the Canadas.*

CHAPTER I

Conditions in Europe and the Lure of America

I.1 The "Push" Factors

Although many a study has delved into the reasons behind emigration, none can embrace all the variables which bear upon an individual reacting to the unique circumstances of his or her personal world. The historian can try with rigorous objectivity to examine the adverse conditions, but it is the emigrant, ultimately, who makes the subjective decision to leave. If miserable living conditions alone were the automatic trigger to emigrate, then Europe's population might have been cut in half by the time of the French Revolution. Clearly, a factor such as the psychological make-up of the individual, whether one is tolerant, submissive, enterprising, ambitious, introverted, or extroverted, is an important determinant. So is the strength of the family unit in times of crisis and, on a larger scale, the degree of community, cultural, and religious support. Some bear their lot stoically, others content themselves simply muttering about their misfortunes, while still others actually try to turn their lives around altogether.

In times when social status was a question of birth and supposedly part of the God-given order, people were more accepting of their fate, but following Martin Luther's revolt against the authority of the Church of Rome, various groups including the peasants in Germany began to look at their plight in a more mundane way and rebelled in the secular realm. These uprisings were ruthlessly suppressed by the rulers, including the Count of Wertheim, from whose realm the forbears of the Lutz family came. In later years emigration became one of the means by which the socially and economically disadvantaged could extricate themselves from a web of traditions, privileges, societal barriers, guild laws, religious squabbles, political patronage,[1] and above all the restricted use of land in order to seek out a better life for themselves elsewhere. Emigration was a reaction against conditions in a particular realm, and rulers interpreted this often enough as insurrection against their person, something which had to be suppressed. Without suggesting that it was the sole response to dismal economic circumstances and exploitive, repressive governments, it must be acknowledged that the mass exodus which occurred in the middle of the 18th century was triggered by a pervasive feeling of unease, distrust, and despair. Whereas social and economic hardship could trigger rioting in larger urban centres and later in industrial areas, emigration occurred most often in decentralized, agrarian regions of Germany, Ireland, Scotland, and Galicia. Franz Oppenheimer has summed up immigration succinctly: "Men go from the place of highest social and economic pressure to the place of the lowest social and economic pressure by following the line of least resistance."[2]

The "push-pull" scenario of emigration-immigration is a complex issue. An examination of the forces that "pushed" the settlers from their native lands and "pulled" them to North America calls for an examination of German, British and American history. Although in dealing with such a wide field one inevitably runs the risk of over-generalization, certain compelling reasons, or "push" factors, as to why the Petitcodiac Germans left Germany for Pennsylvania and eventually Pennsylvania for the shores of the Petitcodiac River become apparent.

Germany as it is known today did not exist when the forbears of the Petitcodiac Germans lived there. Most of the German-speaking areas of 17th-century Europe were a mosaic of kingdoms, princedoms, dukedoms, city states, and smaller secular and clerical domains.[3] With the notable exception of a few strong leaders who were able to bring divergent parts of the Holy Roman Empire into line, this was a realm in which after 1648 about three hundred rulers tried to maintain as much of their independence as possible, attempting to weaken the central power either by the election of unsuitable candidates as rulers or by contributing to the seemingly endless struggle for power between the popes and kings/emperors. Wars kept the Empire in an almost uninterrupted state of imbalance, with the ultimate victory being handed over to the territorial princes at the conclusion of the Thirty Years' War in 1648. This devastating struggle took place principally on German soil and reduced the population from sixteen million to eight million. Famines and waves of disease also ravaged the continent. It took Central Europe many generations afterwards to recuperate from the devastation and terrible loss of life. Only by the middle of the 18th century did the population recover to pre-war levels and, in the southern half of

Germany, reach a point of saturation for what the land base could sustain. To exacerbate the situation, foreign powers controlled the estuaries of the main rivers, preventing the people from trading with other countries. Such stagnation of trade and commerce severely impeded the activities of the once famous craftsmen and artisans. Even within the German-speaking areas there were hundreds of borders and customs-gates where tolls were exacted from travellers and traders alike, resulting in a population more impoverished than before the Thirty Years' War.[4] Employment in fields other than agriculture was also very limited.

The most precious commodity in this densely populated area, therefore, was land.[5] A person's worth and social status were directly related to the number of acres in his or her possession. A woman became more desirable as a bride if she brought land as a dowry into the marriage; mayors and other officials in the community owed their positions to wealth alone. Possession of land or real estate, whether private or joint as part of a guild, signified membership within the community, a *Heimatschein*, or "certificate of citizenship"[6], and in the last analysis security because the *Heimat* looked after its own people in times of need. It is only understandable that a parent would try to bequeath at least some of this precious commodity to his or her children. In south-western Germany,[7] where most of the emigrants came from, old laws and customs stipulated that inheritances be divided among all the children. This caused fragmentation of the agricultural lands into ever smaller plots, eventually making them too small to sustain families. This process of subdivision was a gradual one and does not explain the actual waves of emigration which took place at specific times. However, when wars, adverse weather conditions, and increased taxation by rulers occurred, either singly or in combination, such marginal farms became especially vulnerable and could no longer sustain their owners. In later years the planting of potatoes helped temporarily to stave off famines. In-dustrialization[8] and the lowering of trade barriers also lessened such dependency on land, but these were 19th-century developments; the 18th-century solution was still emigration, often in large numbers and over relatively short periods of time.

It is astonishing that people could live on such small tracts of land even in good times. Elaborate safeguards were set in place to ensure the protection of land possessions. In order to prevent field marks from being secretly moved, a group of reliable councilors would oversee the setting of markings. Innocuous-looking objects like pieces of broken glass, specially shaped or coloured stones, bones or other such non-decomposable material were buried beneath, or in proximity to, the property posts. Anyone attempting to move these markers would not know their secret configuration, thus making it impossible to increase one's property size by simply "moving the stakes". Needless to say, moving such markers illegally was a serious offence.

In addition to the scarcity of land and the virtual exclusion of Germans from international trade, the political system has to be regarded as one of the main reasons behind German emigration.[9] The bureaucratic status of larger, independent entities such as Austria, Prussia, Saxony, Hanover, and Bavaria was inherently more stable, ordered, and bound by tradition[10] than the often minute territories of south-western Germany -- some no larger than a village -- from where the bulk of immigrants originated. Almost without exception, their rulers tried to imitate the lifestyle of the Sun King, Louis XIV of France,[11] who demanded blind obedience and whose words "*L'Etat, c'est moi*" asserted his bold claim that the State was his personal property. They were rulers *dei gratia*, "by the grace of God",[12] and they used this religious and political dogma to full advantage.[13] Their subjects had few rights, and any criticism was ruthlessly suppressed. Daring but unfortunate individuals could languish in dungeons for years without a trial.[14] History books and literature are filled with accounts of the excesses in princes' lifestyles, the arbitrariness of their rule and justice, their indifference to the plight of the lower classes, and sheer wantonness in personal dealings with their subjects. It is not coincidental that the bulk of German emigration came from areas of worst abuse, for example the Rhenish Palatinate. For many years "emigrants" and "Palatines" were terms used almost interchangeably. In one source[15] there was mention of a "Palatine from Holsteyn", who was an immigrant from the northern region adjacent to Denmark. The proximity of the Palatinate and other principalities to France exposed their rulers to the direct influences of Versailles -- cultural, political, military, and moral. No self-respecting prince, it seems, could do without his own hall of mirrors inspired by the court of Louis XIV, without his own splendidly designed Baroque buildings, numerous lackeys, gourmet foods, and the French

21

language. Even Frederick the Great of Prussia, who died on the eve of the French Revolution, spoke only French to his peers, (German was for addressing servants and horses!) and invited the French philosopher Voltaire to live at his court in Potsdam. Maintenance of the courts and the erection of splendid residences and castles swallowed up unconscionable amounts of money,[16] much of which was raised in the form of taxes levied on an impoverished population. If one considers the sizes of such dukedoms and princedoms, the splendour of their palaces, which can be admired today, the number of servants in their employ and the monies spent on food and entertainment, one has some impression of the lavish, wasteful lifestyle at these courts. The rather dubious compliment by a French courtier that life at a German court was comparable to that in his country[17] confirms these excesses.

An important part of princely entertainment was the hunt. A veritable competition existed among the rulers as to who could provide the best sport. Every effort was made to ensure a sufficient supply of game for each event, and since natural sources were not abundant enough, this was specially reared and tended. Traditionally, the hunt remained the exclusive domain of the aristocracy, and commoners were forbidden to chase stray animals off their fields. The archives are full of petitions in which starving peasants pleaded for protection from the "princely" wild boars which devastated their "submissive" crops.[18]   As part of their obligations, peasants often had to care for the game and, at the time of the hunt, be prepared to act as beaters when they should have been attending to their harvests. How this enter-tainment affected the daily lives of subjects is illustrated in the account of the Stieff family origins in the following chapter.

Warfare was another powerful push-factor. Although there were some minor internal military conflicts after the Thirty Years' War, these pale by comparison to incursions made into the Palatinate and surrounding areas resulting from French aspirations on the territory of the old German Empire. The French continued their military involvement in the German-speaking areas which they had begun in the latter part of the Thirty Years' War. Beginning in 1673, but particularly under Marshall Turenne in 1674 and 1675, this initial wave of devastation continued until the Peace of Nijmegen in 1679. "Whereas individual bands of troops had burned and devastated out of wantonness during the Thirty Years' War, now the ... king continued the murdering and burning in grand style for the glorification of the Grand Nation."[19] With his policy of *réunion*, Louis XIV laid claim to and annexed considerable portions of Alsace, Lorraine, and the Palatinate, including some six hundred villages and towns, one of them being the old German city of Straßburg. The Habsburg emperor could do little to defend this corner of his realm since the French king simultaneously encouraged and supported Turks to launch a second and far greater attack on the south-eastern border of the Empire.

At about the same time, Louis XIV intensified his harassment of the Huguenots, who, under the Edict of Nantes, had in 1598 been granted the right to emigrate, freedom of religion, and a Protestant education.[20] In the 1685 Edict of Revocation of Fontainebleau, he annulled these rights, and when Louis XIV laid claim to the whole of the Palatinate and marched into southern Germany in 1688 as a consequence of his aggressive expansionist policy of *réunion*, Europeans became even more incensed. A grand coalition comprising the Netherlands and England under William of Orange, Austria, Spain, the German Imperial Princes, Sweden, and Savoy formed to challenge him. During this conflict, called the Palatine War, the French succeeded in destroying the Palatinate altogether since Louis XIV's aim was to leave a wasteland on France's boundaries.[21] Heidelberg, Mannheim, Speyer, Worms and countless villages were levelled and burned. The ruins of Heidelberg Castle[22] and persistent accounts of people driven to cannibalism are testimony to the "scorched earth" policy[23] ordered by Louis XIV during the French withdrawal from the Rhineland.[24] Several hundred families resorted to escape and settled in Prussia,[25] as did many Huguenots who also fled the wrath of the French king.[26]

The Palatine War ended in 1697, only to be followed by the Spanish War of Succession in 1701. It saw Louis XIV fighting a new anti-French coalition,[27] with military consequences for the previously pillaged areas of Germany. This time it was Marshall Villars, who "crossed the Rhine unexpectedly in May 1707, terrorized south-western Germany, plundering and requisitioning freely on the Palatinate, Württemberg, Baden and the Swabian Circle."[28] The presence of English military personnel from the coalition on location ensured that the court in London was informed firsthand of the plight of the Palatines. One colonel in the English army wrote that the French withdrew across the Rhine, having "overrun the lazy and sleepy Empire and not only maintained a great army in it all that year, but by contributions, sent money into France to help the King's other affairs".[29] Once the French finally retreated at war's end, the countryside had again been laid waste; by their order, fields had not been cultivated in years, there were serious food shortages, and many Palatines either died or were forced to abandon their homeland. These wars had a direct bearing on the Stieff, Lutz, and Treitz families by imposing hardship and poverty, which triggered their emigration.

Another push-factor was weather conditions. If marginal farms experienced less than favourable growing conditions, tenants found themselves in difficulty. It needed only to be a late or early frost, too much or too little rain, a snowfall during the apple- or vine-blossom season, or certain cyclically occurring diseases or pest infestations. One particularly striking example was the severe winter of 1708-1709, which drove a flood of people from the Palatinate and set the stage for continued emigration during the rest of the century:

As early as the beginning of October the cold was intense, and by November 1st, it was said, firewood would not burn in the open air! In January of 1709 wine and spirits froze in solid blocks of ice; birds on the wing fell dead; and, it is said, saliva congealed in its fall from the mouth to the ground. Most of Western Europe was frozen tight. The Seine and all other rivers were ice-bound and on the 8th of January, the Rhone, one of the most rapid rivers of Europe, was covered with ice. But what had never been seen before, the sea froze sufficiently all along the coasts to bear carts, even heavily laden. Narcissus Luttrell, a famous English diarist of that day, wrote of the great violence of the frost in England and in foreign parts, where ... men were frozen to death in many countries. The Arctic weather lasted well into the fourth month. Perhaps the period of heaviest frost was from the 6th to the 25th of January. Then the snow fell until February 6th. The fruit trees were killed and the vines were destroyed. The calamity of this unusually bitter weather fell heavily on the husbandmen and vine-dressers, who in consequence made up more than half of the emigrants of 1709.[30]

Waves of emigrants from the years 1689-93, 1709, 1717, 1738, 1744, 1750, and following were brought about at least partially by bad harvests.[31] The poor in grape-growing areas were particularly disadvantaged[32] in comparison to those in "beer country".[33] Beer was considered a "staple," intended for daily consumption as a thirst-quencher,[34] whereas wine was more of a luxury, expensive,[35] and therefore dispensable in difficult times. When vines failed to produce, seasonal work was also lost, and this affected the poor segments of society. Even in good years, grain prices in mono-cultural, wine-producing areas, were higher because staples had to be brought in from elsewhere, but in times of war grape-growers and their labourers were particularly hard-hit, and many emigrants from south-western Germany were in some way connected to this industry.

Although population growth was encouraged as part of the doctrine of mercantilism, early marriages, especially of poor people, were discouraged.[36] Money was needed for the ceremony, and proof of one's ability to support a family had to be provided. If one considers the life-expectancy at that time, men married very late.[37] The moral, societal, and material consequences, not to mention the "shame" of fathering or bearing children out of wedlock, were for many a contributing factor to move away from such a restrictive society.[38]

Another push-factor, in particular in times of war, was the fear of being coerced into the military. The memory of the Thirty Years' War was vivid among Germans. Although major conflicts were relatively rare and confined to specific regions in the first half of the 18th century, draft evasion through emigration could nevertheless take on alarming proportions for the princes. Not only were able-bodied male subjects lost to the economy, but so was their potential head value when rulers actually rented them to the English for hard cash. One example of this kind is the presence of so many untrained farm hands who fought as "Hessian mercenaries" in the American War of Independence. Landgrave Frederick III of Hesse-Kassel "sold" 17,000 young men to Britain for a little over 6 million pounds sterling.[39]

I.2 The Religious Puzzle

The last push-factor from the homeland to be addressed here is the one of religious persecution, which has been claimed repeatedly for the Petitcodiac Germans. Although religion did play a role in emigration from Germany at different times in history, persecution at the hands of Catholic princes or clergy was *not* a push-factor around 1750 when the forbears of the Petitcodiac Germans left their homeland. This type of harassment and conflict belonged to the 16th and 17th centuries, when attempts by peasants, Anabaptists, and others to apply Luther's ideas on reform to political, social, and deeper religious levels were ruthlessly suppressed and when the struggle for religious dominance was still contested on the battlefield. However, Louis XIV's attitude toward Protestants as manifested in his treatment of the Huguenots prolonged this strife, with the result that the struggle for political hegemony between France and England took on a religious component. William of Orange and his successors saw themselves as defenders of the Protestant faith against French "papist" aspirations. The escape of approximately one half million Huguenots was a considerable economic, intellectual, and moral loss to the French, and conversely a gain to the English, Dutch, and Prussians. Many Huguenot descendants proved themselves useful as soldiers and administrators in British uniform against the French in North America. The Catholic and Protestant faiths would also become an important precondition, a sign of loyalty and suitability, for both the French and English in their acceptance of foreign immigrants to settle newly acquired territories. Religion thus became another weapon in the arsenal during the continued French-English conflict and would also play a large role among the Petitcodiac Germans, both in Pennsylvania and after their settlement in Moncton and Hillsborough. It is important, therefore, to examine the religious ferment in Europe during the more than two hundred years prior to their North American departure because the ancestors of the Petitcodiac Germans were a part of such developments and bequeathed a collective knowledge of this to their descendants. Delving into this religious background leads to a deeper understanding of the attitudes of the Lutz, Treitz, Stieff, Sommer, Ricker, and Wortman families and of their contribution to the religious history of New Brunswick. This also sheds some light on the apparent puzzle as to why so many ultimately adopted the Baptist persuasion.

The Church had always seen periods of decay and revival, but none was as severe and profound as that which occurred around 1500. The rediscovery of classical principles during the Renaissance, the emphasis on individual and human values, and the discovery of beauty in the physical world during the time of Humanism challenged the medieval Christian church. People began to think for themselves and question the abuses of the Vatican in Rome, which had allowed itself to slip into a deplorable state of affairs. The Pope was not simply a spiritual leader but a leader on the world stage, with all the possibilities of intrigue and corruption coupled to his immense spiritual weapon, that of excommunication. While a good portion of the population struggled at the subsistence level, church officials often lived a life of abundance and moral decadence. The author of the *Decameron*, Giovanni Boccaccio, has provided us with many vivid accounts of the debauchery and decay of monastic life in 14th-century Italy. Constant wars between princes and kings in which the various popes eagerly participated, either directly or indirectly, contributed to the general misery of the masses.

There were attempts to reform the Church before Martin Luther. However, these were ruthlessly suppressed, like the one by Johannes Huss, who was declared a heretic and burned at the stake, but whose followers in Moravia, later in Herrnhut, Saxony, and as German-speaking missionaries in North America, touched the lives of many including the Petitcodiac settlers. Even Luther might not have succeeded if certain princes had not supported him and if Gutenberg's invention of moveable fonts had not made the dissemination of his ideas faster and much more cost-efficient. By the time the Church realized what kind of danger Luther represented, it was too late.[40] His ideas spread like wildfire because they fell upon receptive ears, in particular his attack on the Church's sale of indulgences or donations for the forgiveness of sins. The little rhyme in German says it all: *"Wenn die Münz' im Kasten klingt, die Seele in den Himmel springt"* ("When the coin tingles in the collection box, so shall the soul leap heavenwards"). As Humanism on the secular level focussed on the individual so did the Reformation on the religious level. Now each person was permitted to have a direct, personal relationship with God. No longer was there a need for the Church to act as mediator or arbiter in the confession of sins, the recognition of good deeds, the making of sacrifices, or the granting of atonements. Man was justified by faith, and his good deeds and good behaviour were the result of faith alone. So undermined was the role of the Church that officials fought back vigorously to oppose this turn of events. At the Imperial Diet of Worms in 1521, Luther was invited to defend his 95 Theses, which he had fastened to the portal of the Wittenberg Court Church in 1517, but upon his refusal to recant, an Imperial Ban was pronounced over him. Others soon followed Luther's lead. Ulrich Zwingli in Switzerland separated from the Roman Church in 1522, followed by England's Henry VIII in 1534, and John Calvin in 1541.

At the same time, liberation from Roman oppression was perceived by some as a sign to free themselves from political and social oppression. In the years 1524-1525, peasants in central Germany rebelled against their masters. Going far beyond Luther's aims, the Thuringian theologian Thomas Münzer demanded a more serious effort toward the realization of God's realm on earth and the elimination of poverty in order that mankind be free to study the Bible and work toward its salvation. Such demands were combined with millenarianism and communist ideas of the early Christians. These and other attempts to transfer religious reform to political and social levels were brutally suppressed. Even Luther turned against the peasants[41] when he realized that his teachings and efforts at mediation were being politically misrepresented.

A similar fate befell the Anabaptists, who became active about 1525. Their "... movement arose in Zwingli's own circle as a result of an effort to carry through more consistently the program of restoration of primitive Christianity."[42] The Anabaptists felt, unlike Luther, Zwingli, and Calvin, that the "World", i.e. government and society at large, would always be a partner in evil. Even opponents of the Anabaptists testified that there was "... no lying, deception, swearing, strife, harsh language, no intemperate eating and drinking, no outward personal display, but rather humility, patience, uprightness, meekness, honesty, temperance, straight-forwardness in such measure that one would suppose they had the Holy Spirit of God."[43] Witnesses also noted their abstinence from alcoholic beverages which not even Catholic monasticism demanded. If the Anabaptists demonstrated such exemplary behaviour, it seems puzzling why Catholics and Protestants alike pounced on them in such unchristian manner. They applied an old law, the

Code of Justinian, which maintained that repeated baptism was a capital crime. The Anabaptists' insistence on adult baptism was hardly enough to outweigh their Christian living, nor to justify their horrible deaths; rather this law was revived in the fear that Anabaptists would fundamentally upset the structure of Church, state, and society due to their pacifism and complete abstention from public life:

> Had they become too numerous, Protestants would have been unable to take up arms against Catholics, and the Germans could not have resisted the Turks. And the Anabaptists did become numerous. They despaired of society at large, but they did not despair of winning converts to their way. Every member of the group was regarded as a missionary. Men and women left their homes to go on evangelistic tours ....[44] In some of the communities of Switzerland and the Rhine valley the Anabaptists began to outnumber the Catholics and the Protestants alike.[45]

At the 1529 Imperial Diet of Speyer, Catholics and Protestants alike decided that the death penalty be inflicted on Anabaptists, who were subsequently killed by the thousands. The fact that the Anabaptists/Baptists were all but wiped out stands as a black mark in German history:

> The Anabaptists had been the first sect to make religious liberty a cardinal point of their belief. Had Lutheranism been subject to the stimulus of criticism and competition of the sects, it could never have become so complacent and allied to the established order .... So completely were the Anabaptists exterminated that few Lutherans realized the principles of British dissent originated on German soil.[46]

Without such repression the Baptists would clearly have flourished, as they did more than two centuries later in the freer religious environment of New Brunswick.

The Anabaptists were decimated in Germany and survived mainly in fringe areas where the wrath of the Church and the established order could not follow them, as in Poland, Moravia, Transylvania, and for a while Russia. Since there were no Anabaptists in those areas of Germany where the Petitcodiac Germans mainly originated from, it answers the frequently asked question concerning their religious persuasions prior to emigrating to America.[47] The Petitcodiac Germans were definitely not Anabaptists/ Baptists and also not Catholics, rather in all likelihood Lutherans. This has been verified for the Lutz/Lutes and Stieff/Steeves families and opposes Clark Wright's assertion:

> Heinrich Stief may have belonged to the Plain People, non-conforming groups of devout believers who had developed a simplicity of worship and a communal type of living based on the practices of early Christians .... Although Heinrich Stief carried with him on the voyage to Nova Scotia a German Bible which contained a life of Luther, it seems unlikely that he was a Lutheran. Anything known of the life and practice of the family in their early days on the Petitcodiac suggests that Heinrich and Rachel Stief belonged either to the Plain People or to some sect akin to them. Another family tradition, that they left Philadelphia because of the likelihood of compulsory military service in the near future, tends to confirm this hypothesis. The Plain People and kindred sects believed in the brotherhood of man and the fatherhood of God and took no part in wars. [48]

Clark Wright clearly means the Anabaptists/Baptists when she describes the "Plain People". In her hypothesis she has relied on Stieff family tradition rather than on the fact that, in the Pennsylvania of Heinrich Stieff's day, there was no compulsory military service. Research establishes in a later chapter that the Stieffs were members of Lutheran churches in Germany and Philadelphia and that their early religious activity on the Petitcodiac involved Revs. Paulus Bryzelius, John Eagleson, Henry Alline, and William Black, and not the Baptist faith. Thus, Heinrich Stieff and his family were Lutherans, originating from the area around Münsingen (and not Osnabrück, as substantiated in Chp. II), where no Anabaptist/Baptists were known to have survived.

After eliminating their common Anabaptist enemy, Catholics and Protestants had to come to terms with one another. In the religious Peace of Augsburg of 1555, Catholics were forced to accept Lutherans, who had become too large a group to be simply wiped out. They became equal to Catholics legally, and the two were to live in "eternal peace".[49] Denominations like the Calvinists, Baptists, and other sects were excluded from this agreement. According to the principle *cuius regio eius religio*, the religion in an area was determined by the ruler, and this led to much hardship.[50] Every subject, however, had the *ius emigrandi*, or "right to emigrate", provided he or she was not a serf and able to compensate the ruler for his loss of a tax-payer. Only where denominations were mixed as in Frankfurt/Main was religious freedom guaranteed from the outset. Widespread belief that the Reformation had been stopped short by the Lutheran church's opposition to dissent and renewal fuelled the Pietist movement of the 17th and 18th centuries, which shared and continued many ideas of the early dissenters such as the Moravians and Anabaptists and gave rise to several Protestant groups collectively called Brethren, which in turn exerted a powerful influence on the Petitcodiac Germans in North America.

In the major areas of Europe the struggle between Protestants and Catholics eventually led to blows and not eternal peace as stipulated in 1555. As was seen earlier, Catholics in France fought the Protestant Huguenots from 1562 to 1598. In Central Europe, the devastating Thirty Years' War ended in a stalemate. Religious strife in England lasted from 1642 to 1649. There was a large political component in all these conflicts, and religion as a political tool continued to be deployed in future wars. Widespread outrage against Louis XIV's treatment of the Huguenots, however, underscores the general attitude of tolerance shown most non-traditional denominations by the end of the 17th-century. Support of the Netherlands by the new English king, William of Orange, kept French gains during their expansionary phase to a minimum, thanks also to the cooperation of Catholic Austria and Protestant England and the military genius of Prince Eugene of Savoy and John Churchill, the Earl of Marlborough. Religion by then had become important only if politically expedient. Louis XIV had already moved beyond this when he sided with the Protestants in the Thirty Years' War or incited Muslim Turks against fellow Catholics in Austria 40 years later when it became a question of weakening the Habsburgs.

Queen Anne, who succeeded William of Orange in 1702, was married to a German prince. Like her predecessor, she wanted to support the

Protestant cause against the encroachment of Catholic France. As indicated earlier, Queen Anne became well-informed about the plight of destitute Germans in the Palatinate. The added suffering of these people due to severe weather conditions, chronic exploitation, and above all the ravages of war, moved this monarch sufficiently to act on their behalf. In the years 1708-1709, more than 10,000 Palatines sailed down the Rhine at Queen Anne's invitation to be provided with land in her realm. About one-third of these immigrants turned out to be Catholics, who were unceremoniously sent back since, as Defender of the Faith, she was obliged to look after Protestants only. In the eyes of British authorities these Catholics were no more trustworthy than those Acadians expelled from Nova Scotia for similar reasons 36 years later. From all reports, including their own, it is known that these Palatines did not come on account of religious persecution. In fact, on June 27, 1709, "the council of the Protestant Consistory in the Palatinate issued a statement denying the pretences of emigrants that they were persecuted."[51] Most came from principalities whose declared denominations were their own, including Catholics, so that religious persecution was out of the question;[52] rather they came because of economic circumstances. Nothing was to be lost, however, by posing "as poor German Protestants persecuted for their faith" and claiming the "lustrous prestige equal to that of the Pilgrim Fathers."[53]

Although this mass exodus surprised the Queen's officials and cost the Crown a great deal of money for food and accommodation in London, every effort was made to resettle the Protestant Palatines in areas most beneficial to England. A considerable number of these were settled in Ireland as a counterbalance to the Catholics and in support of English interests there, a fact well known in Germany. Their experiences in Ireland, especially the conflicts between the Catholic Irish and Protestant Palatines, became the subject of the drama *Die Pfälzer in Irland*[54] by the 19th-century German writer Paul Heyse. Many of those who took part in this mass exodus from the Palatinate were eventually settled in upper New York along the Hudson River (and later along the Mohawk River) to produce naval stores such as tar, thereby reducing England's dependency on Sweden.[55] Many later descendants of the Irish and American Palatines did not forget their generous treatment by the Crown. When the American War of Independence broke out, they supported Great Britain and, after the colonies were lost, came to

Canada as United Empire Loyalists.[56] Later waves of German-speaking emigrants from the Palatinate and elsewhere occurred for a variety of reasons, but religious persecution was rarely one of them. Most rulers took pride in their displays of religious tolerance through support of the arts and encouragement of scientific thought and inquiry. The Age of Enlightenment had arrived, in which a writer like G.E. Lessing in his drama *Nathan der Weise* made religious tolerance among Christians, Muslims, and Jews the central theme.

I.3 The "Pull" Factors

Although Queen Anne wanted to help the impoverished Protestants, there was a strong component of power, politics, and commercialism in her move. Mercantilism attached a high value to the size of population in a given country. It is "a Fundamental Maxim in Sound Politics that the greatness, wealth and strength of a country consists in the number of its inhabitants."[57] Hanson concurs: "People were wealth, and a nation in order to prosper must encourage their multiplication, entice settlers and artisans from other lands, and prohibit the departure of its own subjects."[58] In response to entreaties from many sources, the British Parliament passed the Bill of Naturalization proposed by William Penn in 1709.[59] By taking an oath of allegiance and partaking of the sacramental elements in the Anglican communion service, foreigners could become naturalized subjects with the right to own land and engage in business. This was a strong pull-factor and also a tremendous advantage for the British if they could procure such an invaluable commodity, i.e. colonists, who would be of a religious persuasion that could be trusted.[60]

From 1714 until 1901, the House of Hanover occupied the British throne,[61] King George I of Britain was also the Electoral Prince of Hanover. He was a Protestant, of course, and with him the exodus from German principalities continued. These subjects were favoured especially as the King's own countrymen, a fact which also helps to explain the large number of Germans in British North America. Such immigrants came because they were politically and economically deprived, and it was in the interest of the British Crown to continue attracting people eager to better their lot in the newly acquired lands. As a result of the Treaties of Utrecht (1713), Aachen

33

(1748), and Paris (1763), France had gradually been losing most of its North-American possessions. British authorities like Lord Halifax and Governor Shirley of Massachusetts recognized the value of these hardworking German Protestants who had proven themselves in the settlement of Pennsylvania and were prepared to do so yet again.[62]

In the case of Lunenburg, Nova Scotia, which was one in a series of settlement schemes, the land was to be settled through direct recruitment by the British Crown. The Lords of the Board of Trade in London engaged an agent, John Dick, to recruit prospective German settlers for the Crown. It was one of the few times that the British government became directly involved in a settlement scheme rather than leaving it to land companies.[63] Halifax and Lunenburg were established as a counterbalance to the Fortress of Louisbourg, which the French had retained in the Peace of Aachen. The reason for becoming directly involved in such a scheme was undoubtedly the immediate need to protect the English territory there. The British, therefore, needed trustworthy settlers not only to take possession of the land ceded by the French, but also to supply the garrison in the province, if required, with the necessities of life.

Many of the difficulties which John Dick encountered were symptomatic for the whole emigration/immigration business -- and a "business" it was. Its centre was Rotterdam and, although located in the Netherlands, was held firmly in British hands because of stipulations in the Trade and Navigation Laws. Ships sailing from Rotterdam to Philadelphia had to berth at a British port, generally Cowes,[64] on the Isle of Wight, to submit to a customs inspection, levy and to take cargo and provisions on board. Recruitment in Germany and the transportation of settlers to America was big business for shipping companies as well. So was the "sale" of immigrants upon arrival as indentured servants and acquisition of cheap labour by business barons. Land companies, in turn, could take possession of their sizeable land grants only upon fulfilling the conditions of their grants and attracting a certain number of foreign Protestants to their townships. As in any business, promotion played a major role in the success of the venture and became an important pull-factor: "To those Germans dissatisfied with their lot ... came the enticing advertising of English proprietors of the colonies of America. Pamphlets extolling the climate and life in the New World were disseminated throughout the Rhine Valley."[65] One of the earliest examples was a book by Joshua Kocherthal, who worked for a Carolina land company and sang the praises of this province in his *Ausführlich und umständlicher Bericht von... Carolina* ("Detailed account of ... Carolina"), which had undergone several editions by 1708-1709. This "Golden Book", so called because the title pages bore gilt letters, also made veiled promises about help from the Queen. It is interesting to note that the author had never visited Carolina. The British parliamentary committee investigating the causes of the mass exodus found this book to be a strong incentive for Palatines to leave their country. Similar publications extolled other provinces. The founder of Pennsylvania, William Penn, made several trips to the Rhine country to invite Lutherans, Calvinists, Quakers, and others to share in his dream of religious and political freedom. Shortly after 1681, the year of the granting of the Charter of Pennsylvania, a small book entitled *Some Account of the Province of Pennsylvania* appeared in London and was also translated into German and widely distributed in the upper Rhine region. Publications like Pastorius' *Umständliche geographische Beschreibung* ("Detailed Geographical Description") of 1700 and Faulkner's *Curieuse Nachricht von Pennsylvania* ("Curious News from Pennsylvania") of 1702 helped for decades to make Pennsylvania the preferred destination of thousands of German immigrants. John Dick and his agents also used pamphlets and "circulars" or "handbills"[66] to inform Germans and Swiss about Nova Scotia. Competition to attract the best settlers was fierce. A rival recruiter once claimed that Dick's pamphlets had been issued by his own company and that the emigrants who followed their invitation be transported by his shipping company. When the ruse was uncovered, he insisted the pamphlets contained only lies, "that Nova Scotia was a land in which no crops would grow, and where there was nothing but fish and sand ...."[67]

In order to convince prospective immigrants to travel with certain shipping companies, agents were sent into deprived areas to sign up prospective "customers". These *Neuländer* or "Newlanders"[68], who purported to have come back from the "new land", were natives of the region where they recruited. They came in fashionable clothes with watches, gold chains, and rings all supplied by the shipping company, describing in graphic detail and with gross exaggerations the paradise to which they wanted to lead these naïve and gullible Germans. They promised free passage to those unable to pay, even money and clothes for the journey, and claimed to have just come back to let everyone see how good America was and to help others to attain the same bliss. The authorities in many principalities recognized the unscrupulous methods of the *Neuländer* and forbade their activities. Prospective emigrants, however, interpreted this as just another example of the rulers' attempts to stand in the way of their happiness. The tall tales of the *Neuländer*, more about whom will be said later, were a powerful pull-factor, perhaps the strongest. What more evidence would a subsistence farmer need than to see the fine clothes and obvious wealth of someone who had left but a few years previously as impoverished and destitute as he still found himself.

In order to prevent the truth about the cost of the crossing, the dreadful conditions on board, and the ruthless redemption practices from reaching the ears of prospective immigrants, letters from Philadelphia to relatives at home were frequently falsified. Favourable reports by settlers to their relatives and friends were important recruiting tools and a strong pull-factor. In letters to the Board of Trade in 1750 and a year later to Governor Cornwallis, John Dick expressed his hope that "the immigrants arriving in those early years ... be generously treated, assigned fertile tracts for their places of settlement ... because favourable reports written by them to Europe would have the best possible influence in predisposing increasing numbers toward Nova Scotia in subsequent years."[69] Dick was so concerned about the reports of passengers in his first shipload on the *Ann*, that he suggested "... that things might easily [be] arranged that all letters back from these people should first pass through the hands of the Board -- or his own -- to find out if there were any ill-intentioned people sent over on purpose to give a bad account of that place."[70] Prospective emigrants trusted their own family and neighbours more than anyone else,[71] and they also wanted to settle where their kin were. Even *Neuländer* found out that it was "a difficult thing if even practicable to persuade any of these People to go to any part of America but where their Countrymen and Relations already are."[72]

It cannot be claimed that the voyage by ship was a pull-factor. The thought of crossing a big, hostile ocean was forbidding to those unused to the sea. There were other options open to emigrants such as Prussia, Austria, and Russia, and many chose these destinations. The deep reassurance of remaining on the same continent and the possibility of simply walking home in case things did not work out in the new location were reasons why many chose to remain in Europe. Sailing to America was, in most cases, a farewell for ever. Yet the majority of people opted for America in the long run because of the promise of freedom, land, and perhaps something less tangible, an escape from the web of Old Country laws and privileges. Many were simply tired of Europe, its wars, political oppression, and economic hopelessness. The lure of America with its promise of freedom, newness, excitement, a sense of finality in having "burned all bridges", and the hope for a brighter future inspired many thousands to brave the uncertainty and perils of an ocean crossing.

Overcrowding has been cited most frequently as the principal reason for the mass exodus of 1749-1754. However, a certain urgency to leave the precarious situation in Europe during a lull in the fighting should not be ignored. There also appears to have been a backlog of people desirous to leave who could not be shipped to America while the presence of the French fleet was still a threat. The number of arrivals in Philadelphia illustrates this; from 1727-1740 an average of five immigrant ships arrived per year. The European conflict begun in 1740 between Prussia and Austria had drawn Britain in by 1744. Not a single ship arrived in 1745 and only two in 1746. As England gained naval superiority, the number of arrivals increased. Five immigrant ships docked in 1747, eight in 1748, and an average of 17 per year between 1749 and 1754. Virtually no ships arrived for the duration of the Seven Years' War, from its preliminary skirmishes to 1763.[73] The Lunenburg and Petitcodiac Germans, as well as most Loyalists of German descent, probably arrived between 1749 and 1754, when the wave of immigration was at its peak. The Petitcodiac Germans, however, could come to Nova Scotia[74] only after they had worked off their passage costs and other debts as redemptioners in Pennsylvania.

ENDNOTES

[1] Background information in this context can be found in Mack Walter's books, *German Home Towns, 1648- 1871, Community, State and General Estate* (Ithaca and London: Cornell University Press, 1971) and *Germany and the Emigration 1816-1885* (Cambridge, Mass: Harvard University Press, 1964).

[2] Quoted in Eugene Kulischer, *Europe on the Move, War and Population Changes 1917-1947* (New York: Columbia University Press, 1948), p. 15.

[3] Cf. Holger Herwig, *Hammer or Anvil?, Modern Germany 1648-- Present* (Toronto: D. C. Heath and Company, 1994), pp. 2ff..

[4] Kapp, *Geschichte ...*, pp. 8ff..

[5] Even today one third of Germany is forested. For princes the extensive woods were less valuable as agricultural land than as hunting ground and source of wood. Landowners in Germany were not too different from those in Scotland who evicted tenant farmers in the Highlands to make room for more sheep.

[6] A certificate of citizenship, which attested to the birth -- preferably legitimate -- and membership of an individual in a community was called a *Heimatschein*. It was the *Heimat*, or "home community", which had to care for its own members in case of need. A good explanation in English of the German concept of *Heimat* can be found in Alan Watson's, *The Germans, Who Are They Now?* (London: Mathuen, 1992), pp. 54-56.

[7] Mack Walter, *Germany and the Emigration*, pp. 3ff.; also Wolfgang von Hippel, *Auswanderung aus Südwestdeutschland*, Studien zur württembergischen Auswanderung und Auswanderungspolitik im 18. und 19. Jahrhundert (Stuttgart: Klett-Cotta, 1984), p. 108.

[8] The encouragement of trade, commerce, and manufacture in the second half of the 18th century by liberal-minded Prince Carl Thomas did much to counter the urge to emigrate from the County of Wertheim; Erich Langguth, *Wertheims Geschichte in neuer Sicht*, Wertheimer Jahrbuch 1981/82, Stadtarchiv Wertheim, pp. 28-29.

[9] Kapp, *Geschichte ...*, Chapters I (pp. 3-10) and IV (pp. 58-76).

[10] An exception in this context has to be Württemberg, which was the home of the second largest group of emigrants who settled in Pennsylvania. More of the abuse of Württemberg's rulers will be discussed in the chapter on the origins of Stieff family.

[11] Walter Allen Knittle, *Early Eighteenth-Century Palatine Emigration* (Philadelphia: Dorrance and Company, 1937), pp. 5ff..

[12] Cf. Kapp, *Geschichte ...*, p. 9.

[13] These "rights" often extended into the most personal spheres. The "right of the first night" *entitled* the prince to sleep with a bride the first night after her wedding, thus making certain virile rulers real fathers of many of their

38

subjects, in contrast to the figurative designation, "father of the people" (Knittle, *Early ... Palatine Emigration*, p. 5), which the princes claimed for themselves.

[14] The German poet and musician Christian Schubart was imprisoned without trial for ten years for satirical references in his newspaper *Deutsche Chronik* about the Duke of Württemberg and his mistress, Franziska von Hohenheim.

[15] Kapp, *Geschichte ...*, p. 59.

[16] Kapp, *Geschichte ...*, pp. 70ff..

[17] Cf. also Kapp, *Geschichte ...*, pp. 70-71.

[18] The German poet Johann Wolfgang von Goethe found himself caught in a predicament when he had to handle the complaints of peasants in such matters as a minister of the Duke of Sachsen-Weimar, whose interests he represented. Having championed the cause of liberty for all mankind in his famous drama *Götz von Berlichingen*, he did not acquit himself very well, deciding the question 'against' his conviction and conscience in favour of the privileges of his benefactor, the Duke.

[19] *Ibid.*, p. 63.

[20] Ploetz, *Große Weltgeschichte* (Darmstadt: Wissenschaftliche Buchgesellschaft, 1986), p. 672.

[21] Kapp, *Geschichte...*, p. 64.

[22] Knittle, *Early ... Palatine Emigration*, p. 3.

[23] *Loc. cit.*.

[24] Ploetz, *... Weltgeschichte*, p. 674.

[25] Kapp, *Geschichte...*, p. 64.

[26] During this period of French invasions, emigration from the Palatinate reached its first pinnacle.

[27] Ploetz, *... Weltgeschichte*, p. 674.

[28] Knittle, *Early ... Palatine Emigration*, p.3.

[29] *Loc. cit.*.

[30] *Ibid.*, pp. 4f..

[31] Wolfgang von Hippel, *Auswanderung ...*, pp. 60f..

[32] Cf. Ploetz, *... Weltgeschichte*, p. 602.

[33] Hippel, *Auswanderung...*, p. 61.

[34] An average yearly consumption of 300 liters is almost double that of today's Germans, still rated high among world consumers.

[35] There are regions in Germany where wine is the main beverage, but it is still not consumed in the same quantity as beer.

[36] Hippel, *Auswanderung ...*, p. 107.

[37] Herwig, *Hammer or Anvil*, p. 10.

[38] Mac Walker makes a convincing argument in his book *German Home Towns*, that the once flourishing and constructive guild system had turned into a

moralistic, repressive, and restrictive element in German society, stifling work and trade conditions in the aftermath of the Thirty Years' War.

[39] Herwig, *Hammer or Anvil*, p. 8. Some recent studies question whether the Landgrave "sold" his subjects. He was certainly well-paid for their presence in Canada and deployment against the rebellious southern provinces. Cf. Claus Reuter, "Kanada und die Braunschweigischen Truppen, 1776-1783", *German-Canadian Yearbook*, XIII, (Toronto: Historical Society of Mecklenburg Upper Canada, 1993), pp. 268ff..

[40] Martin Luther, *Three Treatises* (Philadelphia: Fortress Press, 1960), p. 5.

[41] Philip Hughes, *A Popular History of the Reformation* (Garden City, N.Y.: Image Books, 1957), p. 142.

[42] Roland H. Bainton, *The Reformation of the Sixteenth Century* (Boston: The Beacon Press, 1952), p. 95.

[43] *Ibid.*, p. 97.

[44] This ability of Baptists to evangelize is one of the possible reasons for their success amongst the descendants of the German immigrants in the Petitcodiac region, a success denied them in the Old Country.

[45] Bainton, *The Reformation ...*, pp. 101-102.

[46] *Ibid*, p. 107.

[47] In the introduction to his book, *Newlight Baptist Journals of James Manning and James Innis,* (Hantsport: Lancelot Press, 1984, p. 57), editor David C. Bell claims that the religious background of the Petitcodiac Germans is unknown. The researcher Karl-Heinz Stief has asserted that all the Stief(f)s were "evangelisch", i.e. Lutheran; cf. letter of May 11, 1990 by Karl-Heinz Stief, Im Vordersberg 23, 6148 Heppenheim, Germany.

[48] Esther Clark Wright, *Samphire Greens. The Story of the Steeves* (Kingsport, N. S., 1961), pp. 3f..

[49] Ploetz, ... *Weltgeschichte*, p. 621.

[50] French and British insistence that settlers in their colonies be Catholic or Protestant, respectively, was an extension of this principle.

[51] Knittle, *Early ... Palatine Emigration*, pp. 10-11.

[52] Most publications in the context of the early German settlers in Moncton and Hillsborough make the erroneous claim of religious persecution by Catholic rulers in their homeland, e.g. John Edward Belliveau, *The Monctonians, Citizens, Saints, and Scoundrels* (Hantsport, N. S.: Lancelot Press, 1981), p. 21; cf. also Clark Wright, *The Petitcodiac*, p. 55. More recent scholarly studies unfortunately perpetuate this claim of 18th-century religious intolerance, e.g. Kenneth Stewart Paulson in his thesis, *Settlement and Ethnicity in Lunenburg, Nova Scotia, 1753-1800: A History of the Foreign-Protestant County* (University of Main: Thesis, 1996), p.7. Dan Soucoup even maintains that, in order to escape

religious persecution, "these ... Germans ... had fled to Pennsylvania from Saxony;" Dan Soucoup, *Historic New Brunswick* (Lawrencetown Beach: Potterfield Press, 1997), p. 54. The Kingdom of Saxony was almost exclusively Lutheran and no Protestant was persecuted on account of his faith there.

[53] Knittle, *Early ... Palatine Emigration*, p. 6. B. Elliott perpetuates this erroneous claim: "The Palatines were Germans who had come to Ireland in 1709 as refugees from principalities torn by political and religious warfare;" Bruce S. Elliott, *Irish Migrants in the Canadas*, p. 134.

[54] Paul Heyse, *Gesammelte Werke,* Band IX (Berlin: Hertz, 1872-1901), pp. 333-406.

[55] Knittle, *Early ... Palatine Emigration*, pp. 123ff..

[56] Joan Magee, *Loyalist Mosaic: A Multi-Ethnic Heritage* (Toronto and Charlottetown: Dundurn Press, 1984), pp. 176-189, 190-199.

[57] Knittle, *Early ... Palatine Emigration*, p. 26.

[58] Marcus Lee Hanson, *The Atlantic Migration, 1607-1860* (Cambridge, Mass.: Harvard University Press, 1945), p. 19.

[59] Knittle, *Early ... Palatine Emigration*, pp. 27f..

[60] It is interesting to note that the British resorted to foreign Protestants. They did not consider their country overpopulated. Rather they needed their people for the industrial revolution and did not want to lose them even to their own possession overseas; cf. also Knittle, *Early ... Palatine Emigration*, p. 19.

[61] With the death of Queen Victoria in 1901, the House of Hanover "died out" and the issue of her Royal Consort, Albert of the House of Saxe-Coburg-Gotha, Edward VII, ascended the British throne. The British royal house changed its name to House of "Windsor" during World War I when it became expedient to bear a less offensive name than that of the German House of "Saxe-Coburg-Gotha".

[62] Winthrop P. Bell, *The "Foreign Protestants" and the Settlement of Nova Scotia*, p. 11. Many details about British plans to attract German and Swiss settlers may be found in Bell's well-researched account (pp. 19ff.).

[63] The mass exodus of Palatines of 1708-1709 and their settlement in North America and Ireland was another example.

[64] Bell, *Foreign Protestants*, p. 87; also mentioned is Gosport.

[65] Knittle, *Early ... Palatine Emigration*, p. 12. Details regarding the publications on Carolina and Pennsylvania, mentioned subsequently, are found in the same source, pp. 14ff., 20, and 20f., respectively.

[66] Bell, *Foreign Protestants*, pp. 133, 138.

[67] *Ibid*, pp. 137f..

[68] Kapp, *Geschichte ...*, p. 289; Bell, *Foreign Protestants*, p. 135; Hansen, *The Atlantic Migration*, p. 51.

[69] Bell, *Foreign Protestants*, p. 108.

[70] *Ibid.*, p. 140.

[71] Letters by relatives, friends, and former neighbours were shown to be an important catalyst in the emigration movement. They created *Wanderketten,* or "emigration chains"; cf. Karl Sieveking, "Unsere Auswanderer aus dem unteren Werretal -- Ihre Gründe, Wege und Ziele --", *Beiträge zur Heimatkunde der Stadt Löhne und Bad Oeynhausen* (Löhne, Bad Oeynhausen: 1985), p. 12.

[72] Bell, *Foreign Protestants*, p. 135.

[73] *Ibid*, pp. 86-87.

[74] The area along the Bay of Fundy and Petitcodiac River where the Germans settled lay in Nova Scotia until 1784 when it became part of the newly created Province of New Brunswick. The name "New Brunswick" for this Province reflects the origin of the British Royal family, the House of Hanover in the Dukedom *Braunschweig-Lüneburg,* and the importance of *Braunschweig* in the dynastic history of the Royal House. The name "Lunenburg", N.S., was chosen for similar reasons.

CHAPTER II

Origins of the Petitcodiac Germans

In spite of much searching, the exact place of origin of the Rickers, Sommers, Trites, and Wortmans has not been determined although the general vicinity is now known for most of these families. Since travel until about two hundred years ago was limited, except for the wealthy and those furthering their training as journeymen in the apprenticeship system, certain names tended to occur in clusters. There was some movement of families within specific principalities, but since most of these were not very large, the spread of names was not wide, especially not in Canadian terms. This principle of name frequency within a given area has served as an important tool in determining the origin of the Petitcodiac Germans. In addition, over one hundred newspapers and publications of genealogical and historical societies were contacted, a summary of which shall follow, together with other source material.

II.1 Ricker

The name Ricker, or Rickers, originated in the northerly part of Germany. It is the Low German version of the High German names *Richard, Reichard, Reichert* etc.. There are other variants of this name, like *Riggert, Riggers, Reckers, Rücker* etc..[1] This surname is derived from a Germanic name meaning "powerful ruler." The name *Rücker* occurs in the region around Limburg[2] on the Lahn River, about 30 km from Koblenz on the Rhine. Many of the bearers of that name originated in Selters, about 30 km from Frankfurt/Main, where this name was common as far back as the 16th century. The Hauptstaatsarchiv in Stuttgart[3] lists a certain Johann Jacob Riecker from Bodelshausen near Rottenburg on the Neckar in the Black Forest, who emigrated to America around 1750 with his wife A(nna) Maria and child Georg, born in 1745. J. Jacob Riecker was a miller by trade. If he was the Petitcodiac German Jacob Ricker Sr., he was born about 1705 and entered into several marriages. Jacob Ricker Jr. (born c. 1730) was the issue of the first, who may have followed his father to North America as a young man in much the same way as Loyalist Peter Etter (Chp. VII.). Jacob Ricker Jr.'s son, Michael (born 1764/1765), is the only male heir among the five probable children of the Moncton branch of the Ricker family. A Jacob Ricker who came to the Petitcodiac River with "Smith & Co. from Penn[sylvania] to Moncton in 1766 ... , moved to Hillsborough ... in 1770, [and] had 8 children by 1770, 2 sons & 6 daughters."[4] In the 1775/1783 "Census", a Jacob Ricker Sr. with a family of four and a Jacob Ricker Jr. with eight dependants are listed as residents of Hillsborough, proving that two men, a father and a son by the same name came with Smith and Co.. These families and the inconsistencies in past attempts to account for the various Rickers of these two families are revisited in Chapter VI.

II.2 Sommer

Less information is available about the name *Sommer*. This is, indeed, the correct spelling of the name and not the myriad of other spellings, like Somer(s), Sum(m)ers, etc.. The signature in the "Articles of Agreement" of January 27, 1766[5] clearly reads Ma[t]thias Sommer. A line over an "m" in German signifies that this letter is doubled, therefore the signature *Som̅er* means "Sommer". The spelling "Summer" in the English text of the same document is the Anglicized version of the name. Other Anglicized names recorded in this Agreement include: Cline/*Klein*, Miller/*Müller*, Criner/*Greiner*, and Trites/*Treitz*/*Tritz*. The name "Sommer" is common and used all over Germany, like the name "Winter". It was often attached to another name to signify that this person was employed during the summer or winter. As a result, the origin of Matthias Sommer could not be determined.

II.3 Wortman(n)

A search of the Wortman family name has led to better results. The name has many variants: *Wordtmann*, *Woortmann*, *Wurthmann*, *Würdemann*, *Wörd(e)mann*, and most commonly *Wort(h)mann*. The name has its origin in the Low German word, *word* or *wurd*, meaning "elevated home", as in a farmhouse surrounded by wet grounds.[6] A *Wortman(n)* was therefore a man who lived on, or owned, a farm situated on elevated land surrounded by marsh or bog. This description fits the type of land

44

from which most of the Wortmans came, namely the areas to the north, south, and east of the Ruhr Valley, called Münsterland and Sauerland. Hundreds of entries can be found in the archives and sources of Soest, Menden, Iserlohn, Arnsberg, Münster (Map 1), but also further north in Diepholz and Holm near Hamburg, and down the River Rhine toward Holland, in Xanten. Some of these families go back to the 15th century. The village of Endorf near Sundern in the Sauerland is reported to be the original place of residence of Wortmans in this region.[7]

An interesting contribution was made by a correspondent from the Netherlands,[8] who reported the occurrence of the name *Wortmann* in regions of his country adjacent to Germany, like Zwolle, Enschede, Hengelo, and Emmen. In Emmeloord there is a *Wortmanlaan* and in Kampen (15 km northeast of Zwolle) a *Wortmanstraat*, suggesting that Wortmans had become important enough to have streets named after them. Whereas the Petitcodiac German, Georg(e) Wortman(n), consistently gave his origin as Germany, there is a family tradition which claims that he came from Holland. This need not be a contradiction but could have several explanations. In order to emigrate, Georg Wortman had to have passed through Holland to reach the harbour from where he could sail to America. He could actually have lived in Holland for some time, perhaps with relatives, before deciding to come to America, or he is another example of the consistent confusion of *Deutsch* and *Dutch*. The area in Germany where most of the Wortman(n)s lived, and still live, is within 100 km of the border between the two countries. The Netherlands have attracted many Germans over the centuries because of their strong navy, trade, great wealth, and good opportunities for young people. The north-western German region and Holland were politically, linguistically and economically closely connected before the end of the Thirty Years' War, and Holland remained an important trading partner for principalities along the Rhine and its tributaries. Without lumber from the Black Forest and Spessart for building its ships, Holland could not have become the naval power that it did. As recently as in the 19th century, many Germans regularly went to Holland as seasonal workers.[9] Considerable numbers of these stayed or continued on overseas using Holland as a springboard. The German governor of the Dutch West Indian Company, Peter Minnewit, is one such example. Like the

Legend:

1 - Freudenberg
2 - Bronnbach
3 - Höhefeld
4 - Esslingen
5 - Heilbronn
6 - Weinsberg
7 - Lauffen
8 - Kircheim
9 - Vaihingen
10 - Pforzheim
11 - Calw
12 - Sindelfingen
13 - Schlaitdorf
14 - Tübingen
15 - Reutlingen

16 - Lichtenstein
17 - Bodelshausen
18 - Honau
19 - Stahleck
20 - Bad Urach
21 - Ebingen
22 - Seissen
23 - Apfelstetten
24 - Laichingen
25 - Hundersingen
26 - Buttenhausen

Map 1

Wortmans, he was born not far from the Dutch border. A native of Wesel, he entered history as the man who bought Manhattan from natives for sixty guilders. It is possible, therefore, that Georg Wortman spent some time in Holland before coming to America. Both Rupp[10] and Strassburger/Hinke[11] list the October 21, 1754 arrival of a single, and presumably young, Georg Wärthmann on the ship *Bannister*. If he is Georg Wortman, he may have been born about 1735.

II.4 Treitz

The *Deutsches Namenlexikon* has no entry for the name Tritz, Treitz, or Treutz, but for Treitzschke, which does not warrant any further scrutiny. The article "Le nom 'Tritz' au fil des siècles"[12] by Alain-François Tritz gives *Tritzmann* as "a person who translates, interprets, and one who brings word (*porte-parole*)." The root of the word has the connotation of "chatter" and "gossip",[13] and the name has many variants: *Tritsch(e), Trutsch, Trütsch, Trötschler, Tritzel, Trütz, Drietz, Treitz, Trietz*. The signature in German script in the "Articles of Agreement" (figs. 1, 1a) allows for the possibilities of the variants *Tritz* and *Treitz* (and possibly *Treutz*), of which examples have been found in archival sources.[14] The 1811 entries on July 14th and 19th by the inspector of troops in New Brunswick, Lieutenant Colonel Joseph Gubbins, consistently spell the name "Tritz."[15] This British officer spent an evening and night at the home of Christian Treitz, son of the original settler Jacob *Treitz*. His spelling is no insurance, however, since the Colonel is known to have misspelled many other names.[16] In the document portion of the "Articles of Agreement"(fig. 2), the name is written "Jacob Trites", which is not surprising since the majority of other names were Anglicized and thus "misspelled". The other Anglicized names, however, phonetically represent the German names, and the same must be assumed for Treitz, i.e. "Trites" for *Treitz*. The frequency of this name in the Saarland and Palatinate furthermore suggests that Jacob's name was *Treitz*, which is the version that will be used here.

While doing research on the name *Stieff* in the Saarland, the name *Treitz* was discovered frequently there, too, as well as in the Rhineland-Palatinate. The request for contributions through genealogical publi-

47

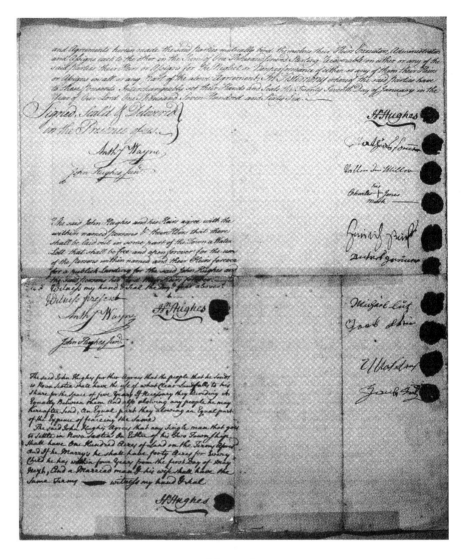

Figure 1
Last page of the Articles of Agreement, January 27, 1766 with the signatures
of the settlers and the representatives of the land companies.

Courtesy: Historical Society of Pennsylvania, Philadelphia
Photo: Rainer L. Hempel

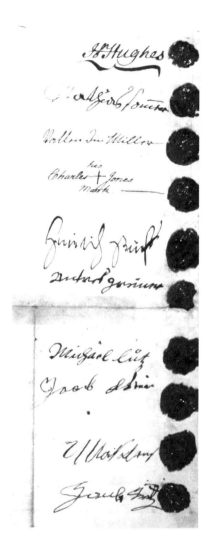

Figure 1a
Detail of Articles of Agreement with the settlers' signatures.

Courtesy: Historical Society of Pennsylvania, Philadelphia
Photo: Rainer L. Hempel

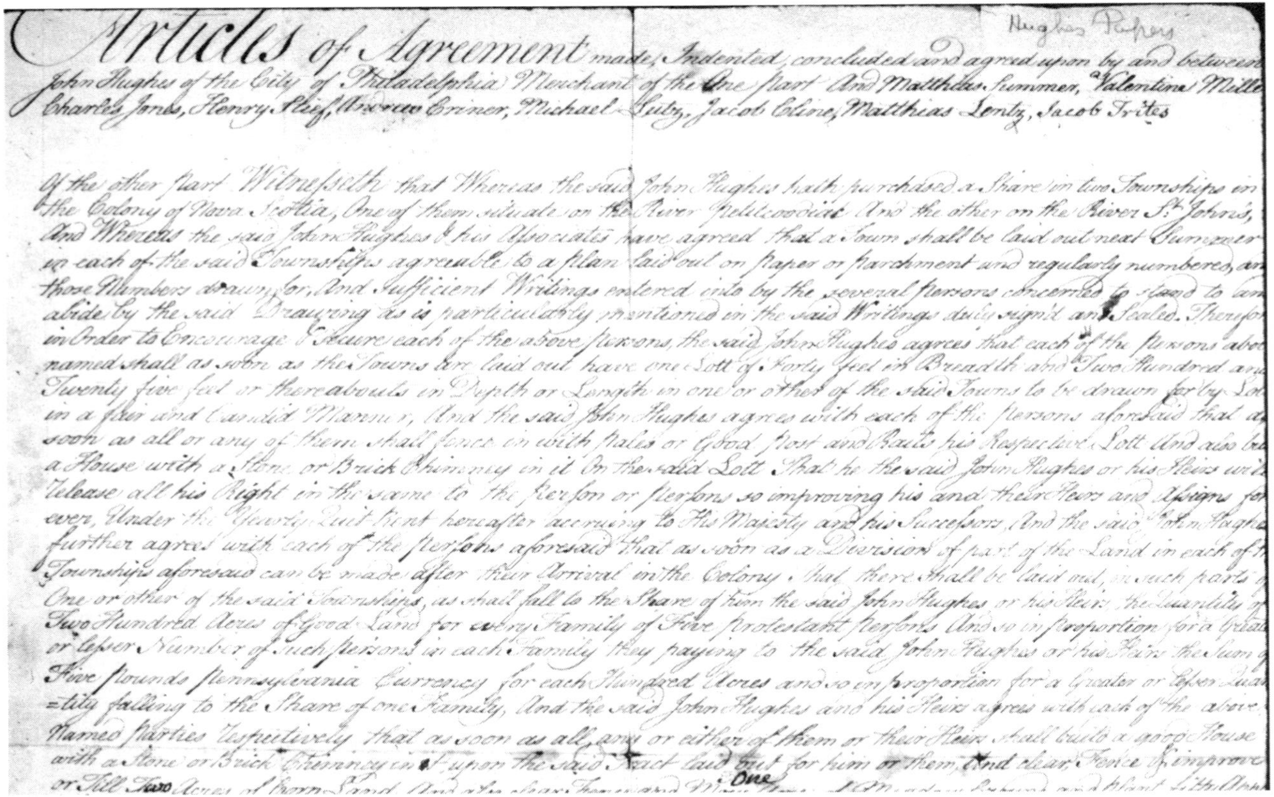

Hughes Papers

Articles of Agreement made, Indented, concluded and agreed upon by and between
John Hughes of the City of Philadelphia Merchant of the One part And Matthias Summer, Valentine Mille
Charles Jones, Henry Steif, Andrew Criner, Michael Lutz, Jacob Cline, Matthias Lentz, Jacob Trites

Of the other part Witnesseth that Whereas the said John Hughes hath purchased a Share in two Townships on
the Colony of Nova Scotia, One of them situate on the River Petitcodiac And the other on the River St Johns,
And Whereas the said John Hughes & his Associates have agreed that a Town shall be laid out next Summer
in each of the said Townships agreeable to a Plan laid out on paper or parchment and regularly numbered, an
those Numbers drawn for, And Sufficient Writings entered into by the several persons concerned to stand to an
abide by the said Drawing as is particularly mentioned in the said Writings duly sign'd and Sealed. Therefo
in Order to Encourage & Secure each of the above persons, the said John Hughes agrees that each of the persons abo
named shall as soon as the Towns are laid out have one Lott of Forty feet in Breadth and Two Hundred an
Twenty five feet or thereabouts in Depth or Length in one or other of the said Towns to be drawn for by Lo
in a fair and Candid Manner, And the said John Hughes agrees with each of the persons aforesaid that a
soon as all or any of them shall fence in with pales or Good post and Rails his Respective Lott And also bu
a House with a Stone or Brick Chimney in it On the said Lott That he the said John Hughes or his Heirs wi
release all his Right in the same to the Person or persons so improving his and their Heirs and Assigns fo
ever, Under the Yearly Quit Rent hereafter accruing to His Majesty and his Successors, And the said John Hughe
further agrees with each of the persons aforesaid that as soon as a Division of part of the Land in each of t
Townships aforesaid can be made after their Arrival in the Colony, that there shall be laid out, in such parts o
One or other of the said Townships, as shall fall to the Share of him the said John Hughes or his Heirs, the Quantity o
Two Hundred Acres of Good Land for every Family of Five protestant persons And so in proportion for a Great
or lesser Number of such persons in each Family they paying to the said John Hughes or his Heirs the Sum o
Five pounds Pennsylvania Currency for each Hundred Acres and so in proportion for a Greater or lesser Quan
=tity falling to the Share of one Family, And the said John Hughes and his Heirs agrees with each of the above
Named parties respectively that as soon as all, any or either of them or their Heirs shall build a good House
with a Stone or Brick Chimney in it upon the said Tract laid out for him or them, And clear, Fence & improve
or Till Two One Acres of ...

Figure 2
Excerpt from the first page of the Articles of Agreement, January 27, 1766, with the prospective settlers' names.

Courtesy: Historical Society of Pennsylvania, Philadelphia
Photo: Rainer L. Hempel

cations like the *Familienkundliche Nachrichten* resulted in contact with the president of a well-established "Tritz" organization,[17] and copious material was submitted. Research suggests that the area from which the *Tritz/Treitz's* came straddles the border between Germany and France.[18] Jost Tritz, the earliest known ancestor of the *Tritz/Treitz* was born before 1580 and lived in Niedaltdorf (Map 1) in Germany. In 1609 he moved to Bisingen, Lorraine, to take over the position of mayor and chief justice of the village. In this position he had jurisdiction over more than a dozen surrounding villages, including his former place of residence, Niedaltdorf, about 12 km away, and the three villages Hemmersdorf, Fürweiler, and Oberesch, all of which lie in Germany today. Jost Tritz's prestigious position ensured that numerous documents concerning his activities got distributed over a large area. More information about him, therefore, survived the ravages of the Thirty Years' War than about other Tritz/Treitz's. The wars which France fought over the old German province of Lorraine between 1552 and 1766 caused a great deal of hardship in the Tritz/Treitz homeland, as detailed in a publication of the French branch of the Tritz family.[19] After being struck by the plague, especially in 1625, and pillaged and burned by the Swedes in 1634-1635, it was assailed by the French:

> *Ce fut ensuite le tour des exactions commises par les troupes françaises, à partir de 1643. Les Français, qui pensaient profiter de la situation, mirent la ville de Sierk en péril, et Louis XIII fit raser plusieurs villages de la région, dont seuls les noms ont survécu .... Après ces destructions et massacres, reflets de la guerre opposant le roi au duc favorable à l'empereur germanique, la région eut à souffrir de la guerre de succession d'Espagne, en particulier en 1705.[20]*

During these upheavals, many Tritz's had to flee their homeland. Some came back after 20 or 30 years, but many never returned and only few families can follow their genealogies through these troubled times because so many archives and churches were destroyed. The terrible winter of 1708-1709, which caused a famine and killed many children and old people, also affected the Treitz's. Most of them in Lorraine became Francophone but, like others of German descent, many, including their president Dr. Louis Tritz, have retained their German and become part of the large proportion of bilingual French who inhabit this border region. This is not likely to change with the diminishing importance of borders in Europe, more enlightened language policies, and the friendship that exists between Germany and France today.

None of the villages in Lorraine which have the highest concentration of Tritz's is further than 12 km from the German border, apart from the many *Tritz/Treitz* who live in the areas adjacent to Lorraine, like the Saarland and Palatinate. The publication *Lorraine-Cradle of the Tritz*, appears in three languages: French, German, and English, the latter for the benefit of those who emigrated to North America.[21] The Tritz/Treitz family has spread over many countries, has many subchapters (e.g. on Martinique) and its own coat of arms (fig. 3). There is no pretense that this family is of noble ancestry; rather the crest is intended as a symbol of common origin and identification. It was decided to take the crest of a neighbouring village, Grindorf (Bising does not have any) near where their forebear, Jost Tritz, was *Hochgerichtsmeyer*[22] or "penal-court judge", as a basis for their coat of arms. The crowned lion on the right-hand side, which reflects a past connection with the Duke of Luxemburg, was replaced by a large "T", the initial for *Tritz*, and the left-hand side retains the symbol of three eagles in memory of Gottfried von Bouillon, the Duke of Lower Lorraine,[23] who had participated in the First Crusade. Toward the end of the year 1099, while he was in charge of the defence of one of the fortification towers of Jerusalem, he saw three strange-looking birds. A prophecy is said to have promised the title of "King of Jerusalem" to the knight who could shoot down these eagle-like birds with a single arrow. The Duke decided to test the prophecy and took aim, killing three eagles with a single shot. He was elected "King of Jerusalem" but refused this title, accepting the less pretentious one, "Baron of the Holy Sepulchre", although his less modest descendants laid claim to the original title. This fabulous deed is symbolized by three eagles, which eventually found their way onto the coat of arms of Grindorf and the dukes of Lorraine, in whose realm the village lay.[24]

The exact home of the Petitcodiac German *Treitz* remains to be determined. If the frequency of occurrence of the name and adverse

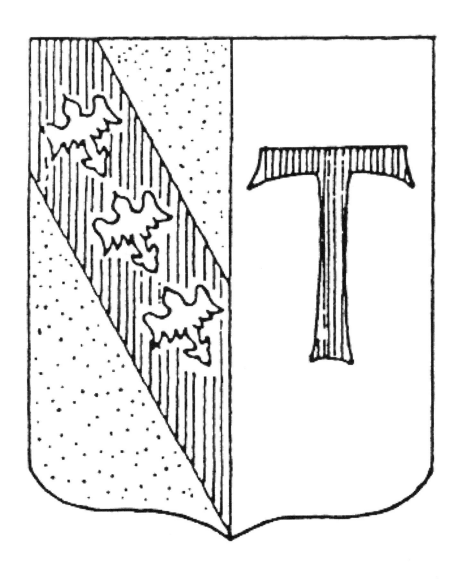

Figure 3
The Tritz Family Crest, proposed by Louis Tritz and designed by Claude Janssens: Three silver eagles on a red diagonal band which crosses on the golden/yellow left half of the crest. A red "T" is on the silver/white right half of the crest.

conditions in the homeland are any indication, then the Jacob Treitz who was born about 1720 emigrated from the Palatinate or Saarland during the main exodus of the late 1740's and early 1750's. He probably took the Rhine as the traditional means of transportation to Holland and from there a ship to America.

II.5 Lutz

The name Lutz is a short form of the name *Ludwig*. It was in its variations favoured as a name of kings, princes, and nobility in general meaning "one who loves glory and battle." The founder of the West-Franconian Empire in 486 A.D., out of which France later evolved, was a *Chlodowech/Ludwig*. The name became so popular in that country thereafter that its rulers, i.e. *Louis* in French, had to be numbered. It was not very different in the various German principalities and kingdoms; however unlike in France, no single dynasty reached the number XVIII. In deference to their rulers, many subjects named their children *Ludwig* or *Lutz*. In Germany these names exist as first names and surnames.

Since the Lutz and Stieff families are the only ones whose actual places of residence and ancestral villages have been ascertained, their histories will be examined in detail, not only as a matter of interest to their descendants but also in order to find out the circumstances and causes which prompted the brothers Michael and Thomas Lutz as well as Heinrich and Friedrich Stieff to emigrate. Although the specific origins of the other Petitcodiac Germans have yet to be determined, the general reasons for their emigration can be assumed to be similar.

II.5 a The County of Wertheim

Thanks to the pioneer work of an archivist in Wertheim,[25] the name *Georg Michael Lutz* in the archives of the Historical Society of Pennsylvania has been connected to the small town of Kreuzwertheim, located at the confluence of the Main and Tauber Rivers (Map 1), not too far from Frankfurt/Main along the south-eastern edge of the Spessart Forest and about 150 km west of the Stieff ancestral area. The town of Kreuzwertheim was called Wertheim up until the Middle Ages, and today's Wertheim is a more recent settlement on the south side of the Main River. Both communities lie north of the fortified boundary, the Limes, which the Romans had built by 155 A.D. to keep out Germanic tribes. The Romans' influence extended much further north when their Empire was still in its expansionary phase. They brought, among other things, grape-growing to the region, of special significance to the forbears of the Petitcodiac emigrants. In pre-Christian times, the region was contested by the Thuringians and Franks, with the final victory going to the latter in the Battle at the Unstrut River in the year 531 A.D.. It is not certain which of these two Germanic tribes settled the north shore of the Main River and gave Wertheim its name. The word *werd* means "elevated land, beyond the reach of floodwaters", and *heim* means "home". This riverside settlement beyond the reach of the Main's high waters was first called *Werdheim* in a document dated 779 A.D., preserved in the Fulda Monastery, to which it belonged at that time.[26] Christianization of its people had taken place about fifty years earlier (722 A.D.) through the missionary work of St. Boniface and his Irish monks, charged by Pope Gregory II with the conversion of Hessians, Thuringians, and East-Franconians. When bishoprics were established and this territory came under the jurisdiction of the Bishop of Würzburg, known for his spiritual and worldly powers, the latter requested that Emperor Henry II grant *Werdheim* the right to hold open markets. This privilege, bestowed on October 22, 1009 A.D.,[27] ensured that this community remain the economic centre of the region. On this occasion, a Celtic cross was erected in the town square as a sign of the new market privilege and testimony to the Irish missionary efforts. Michael Lutz and his descendants reestablished contact between the two cultures, Celtic and Germanic, in New Brunswick and would have considered Celtic crosses a familiar sight, such as that on Partridge Island off Saint John, N.B., erected in later years.

The first reference to a Count von Wertheim appears in the year 1132,[28] when the Archbishop of Mainz mentioned a Wolfram von Wertheim who served as witness in the signing of a document. The right to levy customs on goods and travellers on the Main River and to escort merchants travelling through -- for a fee, of course -- were considerable sources of revenue for the Counts of Wertheim. Several of them played prominent roles at the courts and in the campaigns of Emperors Frederick Barbarossa and Henry VI. Count Poppo I also participated in the Third Crusade, during which his fellow crusader, Emperor Barbarossa, died. Two famous German poets of the Middle Ages, Wolfram von Eschenbach (1170 - before 1220) and Heinrich von Veldeke (1140/50 - 1210) make reference to the Counts of Wertheim. One of them is called Wolfram's liege lord in *Parzival*, and the coat of arms of the Counts of Wertheim is shown in the Berlin manuscript of Heinrich von Veldeke's *Eneide*. This coat of arms was changed subsequently from a single eagle, signifying the closeness of the Counts of Wertheim to the imperial court, to one that included three roses in the lower half. These roses came from the coat of arms of the Countess von Riedenburg, who joined the family as the wife of Poppo I. The three roses are still a part of the Kreuzwertheim coat of arms today, but the eagle has been replaced by the Celtic cross in the top half to represent the *Kreuz*, or "cross", in the town's name (plate 2).

The Celtic cross which figured so prominently in the name of the town stands in the centre of the former marketplace before the church (fig. 4). Many legends tell of its connection to the church. One in particular relates that a heathen knight came galloping out of the Spessart Forest, wanting to snatch up a maiden from beneath the cross during a gathering of the faithful. As the result of a prayer by the minister attending, the horse shied and threw the rider to the ground, killing him. In remembrance of this divine judgement, a horseshoe was nailed to the church door, where it can be seen today. This Holy Cross became the destination of the faithful who wanted to have their horses cured. To this day there is a *Gäulgasse*, or "Horses' Lane", in Kreuzwertheim which derives its name from these times. Thus, the cross after which the village was named was both a pilgrimage destination as well a market cross.[29] The designation *Crucwertheim* was used for the first time around 1300. In subsequent years, it slowly changed to *Cruciswertheim, Creutzwertheim*, and finally to the present spelling of the name.

The church in the centre of the village, appropriately called "Church of the Holy Cross" (*Zum Heiligen Kreuz*) was erected in Romanesque style, probably at a site of heathen worship in pre-Christian times.[30] It is of modest dimensions, 14.5 x 8.9 m, and has undergone several

Figure 4
Celtic cross and Church of the Cross in Kreuzwertheim.

Photo: Rainer L. Hempel

57

changes in the course of the last one thousand years. The tower was built with embrasures for defence purposes in wartime as was customary in early Christian churches, and bullet holes around the portal facing the market square confirm this usage even in later years. Both the church and cemetery surrounding it were protected by a two-metre high wall, torn down in 1827. Most of the changes to the church had been made by the time of the Lutz's departure from Kreuzwertheim, between 1752 and 1755. Both the baptismal font at which Michael and his brother were christened (plate 3) and the organ, dated 1730, can be seen today.[31]

In the latter half of the 12th century, the counts of Wertheim must have decided that *Werdheim* or *Wertheim*,[32] "the home beyond the floods", was perhaps safe from cresting Main River waters but that the much higher land on the southern banks of the Main River was more suitable for a castle and defence. By 1244 the castle and surrounding houses[33] were given the designation of "town" and named Wertheim, whereas the original settlement on the opposite shore of the Main came to be known as *Kreuzwertheim*.

Although the wealthiest and most influential people moved over to the southern side of the river, the village of Kreuzwertheim was still fortified over a period of years. Four massive defence towers were erected at the periphery of the village, two of which appear to have had fortified gates. Although some controversy surrounds the kind of defence structure this was, local historian Peter Hofmann has cited several sources indicating that Kreuzwertheim was surrounded by a wall about 80 cm at the base joining the four towers and forming quite a formidable village en-closure.[34] Two of the original towers are still standing although one of these, a 416-ton structure, had to be moved five meters in 1972 in a daring engineering feat to reduce obstruction on one of Kreuzwertheim's main arteries.

As much as the Main River was a division between the old and new settlements, it was the lifeblood of both. The right to collect customs was a source of wealth and power to the counts. Trade along this important waterway provided employment to many down through the centuries as merchants and shippers, innkeepers, and suppliers for horsemen and their draft animals that dragged the barges against the current upriver, and it allowed the products of the County to be exported cheaply, relatively quickly, and safely. The Main River was their connection to the world, such as it was then. Many famous travellers used this waterway as a means of comfortable transportation. In 790 A.D., Charlemagne passed by Wertheim, as it was called at that time, on his way from Worms via Mainz and Frankfurt to Neustadt on the Saale River, and four years later again after celebrating Christmas in Würzburg. The legendary German Emperor Frederick I, or Barbarossa, often sailed by both towns on his way to and from his favourite residence in Würzburg. He also probably stayed over at the castle of Count Poppo I of Wertheim since the two men knew one another well and became fellow crusaders on their way to the Holy Land. Albrecht Dürer, the famous German painter and engraver, journeyed by Kreuzwertheim in 1520 on his way from his home town of Nuremberg to Leiden in The Netherlands, and in 1745 the villagers saw a splendid armada of ships as the Austrian Empress, Maria Theresia, sailed downriver on her way from Vienna to Frankfurt. It is likely that Michael Lutz and his fellow Kreuzwertheimers stood onshore to witness this major event. This same river made the County of Wertheim easily accessible to troops in war, to trade and commerce in peace, and to new ideas. Early in Luther's confrontation with the Church of Rome around 1522-1523, Count Georg of Wertheim introduced the Reformation to his subjects. Along with this new freedom of religious expression came the furious rejection of older values. Rich pictorial representations of Mary and the saints along with other works of art were destroyed during the iconoclastic rampage that followed, affecting both the County and the Church of the Holy Cross in Kreuzwertheim. Today's Main River is as important as ever before. Visitors to Kreuzwertheim can see vessels of every kind ply these waters, which are now part of the Rhine-Main-Danube Canal system which allows goods to be transported from Amsterdam or Basel to Vienna, Budapest and the Black Sea.

In 1556, the original line of Wertheim counts died out, and Count Ludwig von Stolberg was invested with the County as father-in-law of the last count, but the Bishop of Würzburg contested this claim and involved the County in years of war and strife which extended into the Thirty Years' War and beyond. One of Ludwig's descendants accepted the

59

Catholic faith on marital and political grounds in 1621 and became the founder of the Rochefort (Catholic) line, whereas another was the progenitor of the Virneburg (Protestant) line. Rochefort and Virneburg were smaller counties elsewhere which had been acquired by marriage.[35] The implications of this division of the County along religious lines were only fully realized after the Thirty Years' War.

During the years of turbulence in the County on account of this war and the conflict with the Bishop of Würzburg, yet another devastating blow befell Kreuzwertheim. In 1625, over the course of a single year, the plague killed 165 of its 368 inhabitants. The brave minister Hieronymus Siegfried stayed with his flock during this trying time in spite of extreme risk to himself and the death of his own wife. Some families were completely wiped out, in some cases all the children in a family succumbed to the disease with only one parent surviving. Over 100 children died, 77 of them not old enough to have partaken in the Lord's Supper. It was of little consolation that the "black death" that ravaged Kreuzwertheim in 1344-1345 had killed even more of its inhabitants, 70% of them.[36] How Höhefeld, an earlier ancestral village of the Lutz family, was affected by the plague, is unknown. Perhaps as the result of the frightening loss of life, seven families from outside the village limits, including Georg Lutz, an important link in the Lutz genealogy, were allowed to settle in Kreuzwertheim several decades after the plague had passed.

It was hardly a year after this scourge when a new trial beset Kreuzwertheim: Kronberg troops set up their quarters in the village.[37] The annals of the Thirty Years' War are full of accounts which describe the way such mercenary soldiers pillaged friend and foe alike in search of food and loot. Everyone but five villagers fled the inhumanity of the soldiers, seeking out safety in the forest. In their absence, Kreuzwertheim was ransacked and devastated.[38] The maintenance of troops stationed in the County, whether Protestant or Catholic, remained a heavy burden on the villagers for the rest of the war, a story already familiar from the Tritz/Treitz family history.

The religious differences that prompted the Thirty Years' War became part of the discord of the Counts of Wertheim. Whenever Imperial (Catholic) troops occupied the County, the predominantly Protestant population was put under pressure by the Catholic Count, Johann Dietrich. When the Royal (Swedish) troops were in control, the Protestants received their due protection.[39] Even at war's end, the differences between the Protestant (Virneburg) line and the Catholic (Rochefort) line of the Wertheim counts had not been resolved. An unexpected advantage arose from the fact that there was a Catholic prince in the County whose relatives supported Louis XIV of France. When the latter's troops under Marshall Turenne posed a threat, these relatives interceded and requested that they be spared.[40] The same troops that had devastated the Palatinate under this infamous Marshall left the County of Wertheim relatively unscathed, although not without paying Wertheim a visit and plundering the monastery at Bronnbach.[41] It certainly also helped that Turenne and his officer corps were given substantial quantities of Wertheim wine as a goodwill gift. Before the French beat a hasty retreat in the face of the approaching Imperial army, Germans managed to burn their supply ships anchored just off Kreuzwertheim on the Main River. The famous engraver Matthäus Merian must have witnessed the event, for he made two detailed engravings of it in 1673.[42]

Because of the constant religious rivalry between the counts, it was decreed by the Imperial Court Council in 1690 that the County of Wertheim be divided, but in the end reason prevailed and the plan to divide even the town itself was shelved.[43] Although tensions continued, no longer was there persecution on account of a person's faith. At the time when Michael Lutz was contemplating his emigration, the joint County administration served merely as an irritant to administrators and subjects alike due to the sheer bureaucracy of it all.[44] By 1752, when Michael Lutz emigrated, the good relationship in the County between Catholic Prince Karl Thomas of the Rochefort line and the Protestant clergy is a matter of record.[45]

II.5 b Forefathers of Michael Lutz in Höhefeld and Kreuzwertheim

About 10 km to the south-east of Kreuzwertheim lies the small village of Höhefeld, an earlier home of the Lutz family. Höhefeld, mentioned for the first time in 1303-1304,[46] is the only village in the County situated on a high plateau between the Main and Tauber Rivers. At the beginning of the Peasant Wars in 1525, it was ransacked by its own Count Georg II as a lesson to its inhabitants for having revolted against the established order. In 1606 it suffered a similar fate in the long disagreement between the Bishop of Würzburg and Count Ludwig III of Löwenstein (Wertheim).

An examination of the socio-political history of Höhefeld and backgrounds of its 108 households for the years 1595, 1598, and 1605 reveals that, although a few trades such as smiths and tailors were present, about 85% of the villagers were involved in agriculture, in particular grape-growing. Almost half of these people did not have enough land to sustain themselves by agriculture alone and were required to work as *Häcker*, "cultivators of the soil", or hired hands in the vineyards of wealthy burghers from Wertheim and of monks at nearby Bronnbach Monastery. Full-time farmers made up less than 30% of the population, the wealthiest of whom had properties assessed at 1,426 and 1,843 guilders. As to be expected, these wealthier citizens assumed the positions of leadership in the community, such as *Schultheiß*,[47] or mayor, village elders, jurors, and landmark-witnesses since the wealth they had accumulated reflected their worth, ability, and sense of responsibility. At the same time they were held accountable with their property as collateral for any errors committed in office. No poor person, no matter how able or trustworthy, could provide such a safeguard to the community.

The "wealthiest" in Höhefeld's *Häcker* class was assessed at 238 guilders, and the poorest of these was Christoph (nicknamed *Stoffel*) Lutz, the ancestor of Michael Lutz, the Petitcodiac German, going back six generations. In 1595, the total value of Christoph's possessions amounted to 64.75 guilders, of which 40 guilders were debts, so his assets amounted to a mere 24.75 guilders, little more than the value of a cow.[48] Christoph's situation in life was such that he was forced to work as a herdsman at times, a position of low social and economic status (much like the father of Petitcodiac German Heinrich Stieff). Financially, Christoph ranked just above the poorest of the poor, such as day labourers -- and the village teacher -- who made up 14% of the population. Christoph was a bondman, or serf,[49] and died in 1611, leaving about 60 guilders' worth of property to his widow Anna and children Michael, Johann (Hans), Vei(d)t, Anna and Eva. The County officials reduced Anna's inheritance tax from 3 to 1.5 guilders because " ... [Christoph] was a poor *Häcker*, has also been a herdsman and didn't have much at all."[50]

The three Lutz sons settled in Höhefeld. At that time, disease and death were an ever-present threat. On February 22, 1622, Johann and Veit took the "last rites" in the form of communion, which suggests that a serious influenza was passing through the village. A public prayer was held for Johann a week later and on March 10th a prayer of thanksgiving for his recovery. This close call apparently did not affect Johann's longevity, for he died in 1654 at the age of 81 years, quite remarkable for that time. The third son, Michael (Michel), who did not become ill in 1622, was the great-great-great-grandfather of the Petitcodiac German by the same name. The elder Michael fathered two sons,[51] one of whom was called Nicolaus, the Petitcodiac settler's great-great grandfather. He met an untimely death in 1669 while transporting construction lumber, and his son, Martin Lutz, also died prematurely at age 34, being the father of Johann Georg, called *Jörg*, who escaped the confines of Höhefeld and its vicious cycle of poverty and moved to Kreuzwertheim. Georg was the grandfather of brothers Michael and Thomas Lutz, both of whom left Kreuzwertheim for Pennsylvania in 1752 and 1755, respectively.

Unlike today when Höhefeld lies somewhat off the beaten track, villagers of the past could walk directly into Kreuzwertheim via the "Höhefeld Pass"[52] and did so routinely. Perhaps on one such stroll into town Georg Lutz chanced to meet his future wife, Regina Schöner(t). It did not seem to be an obstacle that she was nine years his senior -- or that she had some financial means. This dowry was not great but enough for Georg to make the move from Höhefeld to Kreuzwertheim upon their marriage in 1688. This move into town, even though it was within the County, was not merely a matter of personal preference. The era of freedom of movement had not yet arrived, and this "neighbourly admission" of Georg into Kreuzwertheim cost 2 guilders and 24 *Kreuzer*[53] (fig. 5), permission for which could be granted only on grounds of marriage or inheritance.[54] In 1699, Georg is listed as a "dragoon", or soldier. There was no conscription, and those who joined the military usually did so for socio-economic reasons. This work away from the family farm suggests that Regina's land and money were not enough to support the family. In the Kreuzwertheim *Lagerbuch*, or "census"[55] of 1710, Georg Lutz is listed as the owner of slightly more than 2 acres of land in total.[56] No family, however frugal, could sustain itself on such a small parcel of land, particularly since it was of such inferior quality. This land was split seven ways and scattered about Kreuzwertheim. The smallest field was twenty "Ruten" (12 x 20 m) and was described as a *Wüstung*, or "arid piece of land". Georg also owned five plots of vineyard of equally minute proportions. All of his land was marked as being of "bad" to "very bad" quality.

The entry in the *Lagerbuch* also gives the exact location of Georg's town property. This was situated at the lower tower, next to one which still stands today (fig. 6), and was bounded by the properties of Philipp and Leonard Amend and by two lanes, called *Haßlocher Gaßen* and *Schafgaßen*. There was a house on the property with a small kitchen garden, but no mention of any barns or stables such as one could find on many of the other properties at that time in Kreuzwertheim. The total size of this property was twenty "Ruten", like his smallest field, or roughly the size of a small house lot in Canada.[57] It was customary then, and still is, for farmers to live in a village next to their livestock and go to their various fields from this base rather than live in the country surrounded by their fields as is more often the case in Canada. If Georg Lutz had no barn or stable next to his house, one can assume he had no livestock of the kind that would require such buildings. Although Regina Schönert had pulled him out of a dismal situation in Höhefeld, the land and house she brought into the marriage were not enough to support a growing family, let alone to provide for the future of their four children.

One of Georg and Regina's children was their son, Johann *Wilhelm*, who fathered seven children including Georg *Michael*, the Petitcodiac

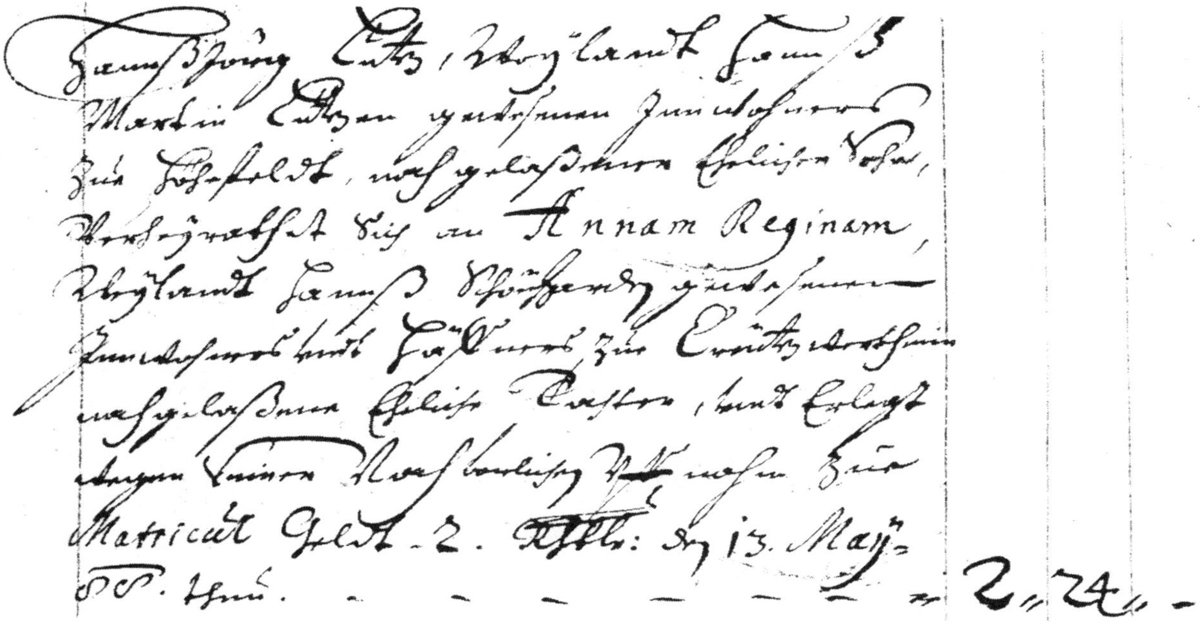

Figure 5

Faximile of entry in Kreuzwertheim townbook under *Einnahm*, "Income" re. the "neighbourly admission"
of Anna Regina's husband Hanß Jörg Lutz on Mai 13, 1688.

The text in old German script reads: "Hannß Jörg Lutz, the bereaved (orphaned), legitimate son of Hannß
Martin Lutz, former resident of Höhefeld, marries Anna Regina, the bereaved (orphaned), legitimate
daughter of Hannß Schönhard ("Schöner[t]" in the Lutz Genealogy is an alternate version), the former
resident and potter/stove fitter of Creutzwertheim, and pays 2 guilders and 24 "Kreuzer" on May 13, 1788
on account of his neighbourly admission [to the community of Kreuzwertheim].

Courtesy: Stadtarchiv Wertheim

65

Figure 6

Opposite this tower on the right stood the modest house of Georg Lutz, Michael Lutz's grandfather.

Photo: Rainer L. Hempel

settler, who was born in 1723. One can easily imagine Wilhelm's situation in life. He could not have inherited much from Georg. At the time of Michael's birth, grandfather Georg was still alive. In 1730, when Michael was almost seven years old, his grandmother Regina passed away at the age of 72, and in the following year his 65-year-old grandfather married Agnes Amend (*née* Schöning), widow of his neighbour Philipp Amend. Agnes was 23 years younger and, a year later in 1732, bore him a son named Johann Georg. Michael Lutz thus had an "uncle" nine years his junior. The last of Michael's own brothers was born in 1734. Since both father and grandfather were producing children at approximately the same time, it is unlikely that this improved the material wealth or chances of an inheritance by Michael or his siblings. Any property that came into the Lutz family by way of Philipp Amend's widow likely went to their son Johann Georg, who remained a bachelor and outlived Michael and probably the other siblings, dying in 1814 at the age of 82. Michael's grandfather Georg passed away in 1737, five years after the birth of his last child. Michael married Anna *Walpurgis* Wießler[58] a decade later, in 1747, and they had two children in Germany, Anna *Catharina* (born 1749) and Peter (born 1751). Michael and Walpurgis' chances of improving their circumstances were no better than those of their parents or grandparents.

Michael Lutz received his education at the local school in Kreuzwertheim between the ages of 6 and 14, probably under Schoolmaster Klein, since three generations of Klein taught in the village throughout the 18th century. Although the school year was adapted to the times when the children were needed on the farms, the quality of education was hardly affected by this. It was generally considered to be better in Lutheran areas because of the profound influence of the Renaissance humanist and pedagogue Philipp Melanchthon (1497-1560), also called *Praeceptor Germaniae*, or "Teacher of Germany". Illiteracy was not a problem, even among the poorest, since school attendance was compulsory, but occasionally, as in Canada today, the mentally challenged or unmotivated could leave school without being able to read or write, as evidenced by the illiteracy of Heinrich Stieff's father, to be discussed shortly, or the crosses given in place of signatures on legal documents and ships' lists.[59] Michael Lutz must have received a good education to judge by the penmanship of his signature in the "Articles of Agreement" of 1766 (figs. 1, 1a). His education, however, did not improve his chances in life at that time. Society and its various levels were much more static than they are today. The strict monopolistic laws of the guilds[60] guarded against intrusion or competition. Only through marriage could one possibly break through the barriers of poverty and low social status, but this was a rare occurrance since people tended to marry within their social order.

One exception to this pattern was Michael's paternal uncle, Johann *Peter* Lutz, who married Anna Catharina of the well-established En(t)z family of Kreuzwertheim (cf. Lutz Family genealogy). Johann Georg En(t)z, for example, was the mayor (*Schultheiß*) of Kreuzwertheim from 1742 until 1762, the official who signed Michael's request for manumission and emigration. Michael's uncle, Peter Lutz, became a "field judge", a position of trust and prestige in the community. This societal step upward benefitted Peter's family, and his son Johann *Nicolaus* also became a village and field judge. On the other hand, Michael Lutz, whose father had not married as "advantageously", felt compelled to emigrate.

The relative poverty of Kreuzwertheim is not surprising as development of the new town Wertheim across the river caused the original settlement to stagnate. Between the years 1380 and 1618, Wertheim experienced a veritable building boom. In one of the engravings by Merian,[61] numerous handsome and substantive buildings in Wertheim are depicted in contrast to the more modest structures of Kreuzwertheim on the opposite shore (figs. 7, 7a). Peter Hofmann makes mention of the similarly modest size of Kreuzwertheim's public buildings like the church, school, and town hall.[62] The construction of a castle in Wertheim must have convinced many of Kreuzwertheim's more affluent and mobile residents to move to this more secure community, enabling them to participate in the economic and cultural activity generated by the court; poorer residents were forced to stay behind in Kreuzwertheim. In spite of the renovated and improved appearance of the houses in Kreuzwertheim today, one can still discern the poverty and modest circumstances of their earlier occupants. Some of the oldest surviving

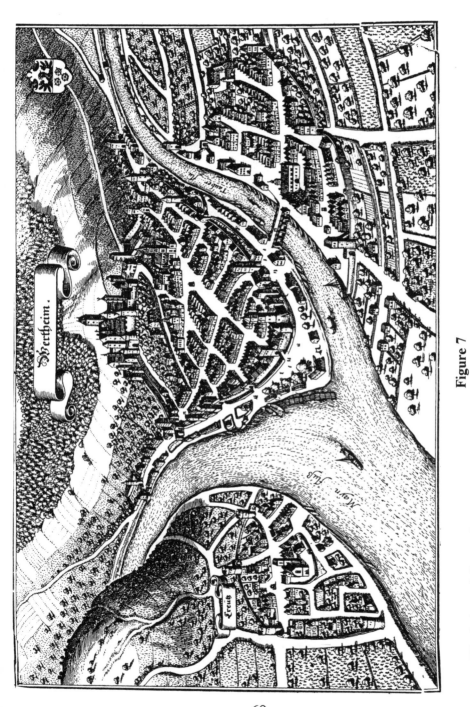

Figure 7

Wertheim and Creütz (Kreuzwertheim), 1648 engraving by Matthäus Merian. The difference between the 800-year-old original settlement and the more recent and affluent town of Wertheim is clearly visible.

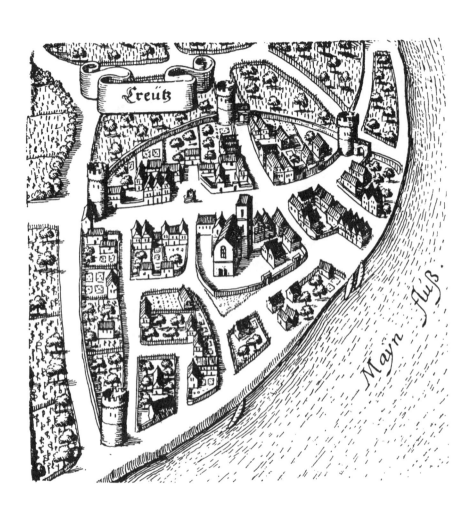

Figure 7a
Detail of the 1648 engraving by Merian, showing the fortifications and
buildings of Kreuzwertheim.

homes can be seen on the *Maingasse, Nebengäulsgasse,* and *Pfarrgasse.* They are one-storey structures with a living room of 12-15 m² (ca. 10 x 15 feet), a kitchen of 7-10 m² (ca. 10 x 10 feet), and another room, most likely the bedroom for the parents, also 7-10 m². Two tiny upstairs rooms with sloped ceilings were the sleeping quarters for the children, an area often shared by ten or more people.[63] In this village, the Lutz's belonged to the poorest. Since a man's worth was measured in terms of his land ownership, Michael's grandfather was valued at a mere two acres of barren land.

Like other principalities of south-west Germany, the County of Wertheim experienced a wave of emigration in the 1750's, particularly by its rural population. Hermann Ehmer suggests: "It was evidently a deep agrarian crisis, which was probably triggered by a series of lean years."[64] Although, as pointed out previously, adverse weather conditions could trigger waves of emigration, it is doubtful that this one was caused primarily by the weather. After consumption dropped off during the financially depressed years, the County's wine-making industry was unable to regain the prominence it had enjoyed before the Thirty Years' War. Furthermore, its population had once again reached a point of saturation. Both are compelling reasons for the high emigration rates.

An article on viniculture in Kreuzwertheim underscores the importance of wine production for this village[65] since at least 1346.[66] The wine from this area, especially on the right-hand bank of the Main River due to its southern exposure, was one of the very best in Germany. This "captured sunshine" of Kreuzwertheim, as the author called it, was served at public functions when noblemen tried to impress one another.[67] What made this wine even more attractive was the distinctive shape of the bottle in which it came, i.e. the *Bocksbeutelflasche,*[68] a tradition carried on to this day. The bottle is shaped, and named after, the scrotum of a ram, which was a traditional source of material for wine-skins. In fact, the road system connecting the vineyards of this region is named after this wine-skin as well: "The *Bocksbeutelstrasse* consists of a series of routes which connect Würzburg with the surrounding Franken vineyards. The route gets its name from Franken's traditional flask-shaped bottle."[69] Kreuzwertheim and Wertheim are important towns along this route. In the 18th century, this wine was also sold by the bucket, equivalent to 64 litres. Johann Wolfgang von Goethe, the prince of German poets, had buckets of this wine brought to his residence in Weimar.[70] In his 1714 treatise *De vino Wertheimensi*, Dr. Johann Leinweber extolled the virtues and therapeutic value of the wine from the confluence of the Main and Tauber Rivers. Among other benefits, this scholar praised its stimulating effects on potency and fertility. Thanks to the local wine, he claimed, it was not uncommon for parents in the area to produce up to twenty children, and he also noted a higher frequency of twins and triplets.[71] Leinweber's findings may not withstand the scrutiny of 20th-century science, but they do underscore the size of families in this wine-growing region, an important factor in overpopulation.

Archival records give an indication of the quantities of wine exported from the County. Within a six-month period in 1574, the County customhouse of Freudenberg, located about 15 km from Kreuzwertheim, recorded the passage of 1,245 *Fuder* of wine. Since a *Fuder* was 800-900 litres, about 13 buckets, approximately one million litres (17,000 buckets) must have left the County. The annual yield, however, could fluctuate, depending on natural or man-made circumstances, such as early or late frosts, insufficient or excessive rainfall or sunshine, hailstorms, and war. All of these, singly or in combination, could harm the sensitive vines and reduce the annual yield. There were years when one litre could fetch as much as half a florin, or guilder,[72] and others when it cost only one-tenth of this. All accounts agree, however, that wine-growing and -trading were the most important source of revenue for Kreuzwertheim. Of the sixty households in the village in 1632, fourteen were directly involved in viniculture. Not only grape-growers, wine makers and merchants lived off viniculture, but others with related skills such as vinedressers, cultivators, barrel makers, and carpenters. The *Häcker*, or "hired hand", was given a breakfast, noon meal and afternoon snack along with a daily ration of wine. This had to be "reduced" to 2.25 litres per worker because there had been complaints about drunkenness and alcoholism among vineyard workers. The wage for this physically demanding work was 27 *Kreuzer*[73] per day during the summer, or less than one-half guilder. Itinerant workers received only 16 *Kreuzer* and a grape-picker 12 per day without the food supplement. These wages have to be compared to the cost of living at that time, when an old chicken cost 12 *Kreuzer* and an old goose 20. According to Langguth, a worker had to toil at hard physical labour for three days from dawn till dusk in order to earn one guilder with which he could buy 12 pounds of beef. No work was available for *Häcker* during the off-season or when a crop was ruined. Although the wine business was very profitable for its merchants, the lower rungs of society were kept at subsistence level and were the most vulnerable during a downturn in the economy.

Since grapes were considered a cash crop, other dietary staples tended to be more expensive. The land allotted to such crops was restricted in favour of vineyards, requiring that food for the commoners be shipped in from outside, all at extra cost. Vineyards in good locations were especially in demand. In 1627 for example, a vineyard the size of about one-third acre sold for 348 guilders.[74] If one considers that the annual income of a master bricklayer was 20-30 guilders, then acquisition of good land was altogether beyond the reach of even the best middle-income earners. That land could command such high prices and wages remain so low, confirms the underlying reason of manpower oversupply. If there had been a shortage of labourers, wine-growers and merchants would not have been able to employ *Häcker* at such low wages. By contrast, at this time in North America the situation was reversed; land was plentiful, therefore inexpensive, and labourers were relatively few and so better paid.[75] Herein lay the big attraction for the potential emigrant. For businessmen and rulers, waves of emigration were a source of concern because of the loss of cheap labour and the threat of higher wage demands. Even in the economy of a small area such as the County of Wertheim mercantilism was in effect.

By no coincidence, tradesmen and other city dwellers were relatively unaffected by burgeoning numbers, but an expanding rural population situated on a diminishing land base could not survive indefinitely on meager resources. In these difficult times, rulers became ever more inventive in their tax-collecting schemes. Otto Langguth identified no fewer than 23 different taxes which country dwellers were required to pay their princes in addition to their obligations as serfs.[76] One subject complained that his dues and taxes amounted to more than the actual revenues from his entire property. In 1754, a resident of Höhefeld, Barbara Adelmann, was so poor that her father could not afford her exit fee, or *Memorial pro Manumissione*, but requested that she be released anyway. She was allowed to leave without payment, so "that we [the officials of the County] may be rid of this worthless girl. She is as poor as a beggar, and dissolute besides."[77] This and many similar submissions were granted because it was of no benefit to a ruler to have his realm burdened with subjects in abject poverty and mental or physical infirmity. At least 15 families emigrated from the village of Höhefeld at this time. According to mercantilism, people represented wealth only as long as they were contributors to the system. Thus, the government of Wertheim gladly turned its back on certain subjects. Payment of 10% and, after 1753, 20% of the value of property which emigrants took with them was levied not only on serfs but also on "free" citizens of Wertheim and nearby Wenkheim. Nobody, free or in bondage, was allowed to emigrate without the permission of the prince and whatever the latter considered to be his fair recompense.

The catalyst in the emigration fever that caused hundreds of families in County Wertheim to leave for Philadelphia was the intrusive activity of professional agents of shipping companies.[78] The most infamous of these was Johann Philip Buch, son of a respectable barge master in Wertheim. Buch Jr. had been in America and knew all too well what hardships lay in store for poor emigrants. After plying his dubious trade for a time, he was arrested and charged with kidnapping and the trading of slaves. He admitted having received 100 guilders from the shipping firm Hoppe in Rotterdam for delivering so many "freights", or adult passengers. There were letters from emigrants who accused him of fraud and other misdemeanours. Buch's aged parents left nothing undone to save him and, thanks to their excellent reputation, were able to prevent his execution. At the end of a long trial he was escorted out of Wertheim under armed guard, banished from the County and prevented from claiming his inheritance forever. At the border, he had to promise under oath never again to entice anyone to emigrate. Buch seems not to have taken advantage of the shipping company's offer of a free return-fare to Pennsylvania because he returned to the County in 1757, ill and in dire straits, and died full of remorse in the same year.

One of the more respectable recruiters was a man by the illustrious name of *Der Kgl.*[Royal] *Großbrittannische Capitain Herr Waldo*, who advertised in a Frankfurt newspaper with a readership in the County of Wertheim as well. He turns out to be the same Samuel Waldo of German-Swedish descent who founded Waldoboro in 1740 and was closely involved in the seizure and conquests of the Fortress of Louisbourg in 1745 and 1758. How many Wertheim citizens this entrepreneur and schemer *par excellence* was able to attract to his lands or conscript for the conquest of Louisbourg is unknown.

It is not surprising that Michael Lutz was touched by the general excitement and hope which many felt on hearing the promises of free land and transportation, of hunting privileges, and relief from the web of regulations, taxes, obligations, and princely rights. It was perhaps also a relative who had started Michael thinking about emigration, for in 1743 a certain Anna Catharina Schaaf (*née* Lutz) had left Kreuzwertheim with her husband for Pennsylvania,[79] and letters from landed immigrants often encouraged other people to leave. The following is a translation of a document (fig.8) in which Michael Lutz petitioned his Sovereign for release from bondage and permission to emigrate. Its language reflects the relationship between lord and serf:

To the most serene Prince and Master, Mr. Carolo, Prince of Löwenstein-Wertheim of the Holy Roman Empire, to my most gracious Prince and Lord, my most submissive memorial, Georg Michel Lutz, subject in Xwertheim [Kreuzwertheim] presented April 21, 1752.

Most high Prince, most gracious Prince and Lord!

Your most serene Highness (would) condescend most graciously to allow yourself to be informed in all and most obedient submissiveness, that I, Georg Michel Lutz, until now subject and citizen of Creutzwertheim, have decided with God, to move from here with [my] wife and two children to go to Pennsylvania in order to settle there.

75

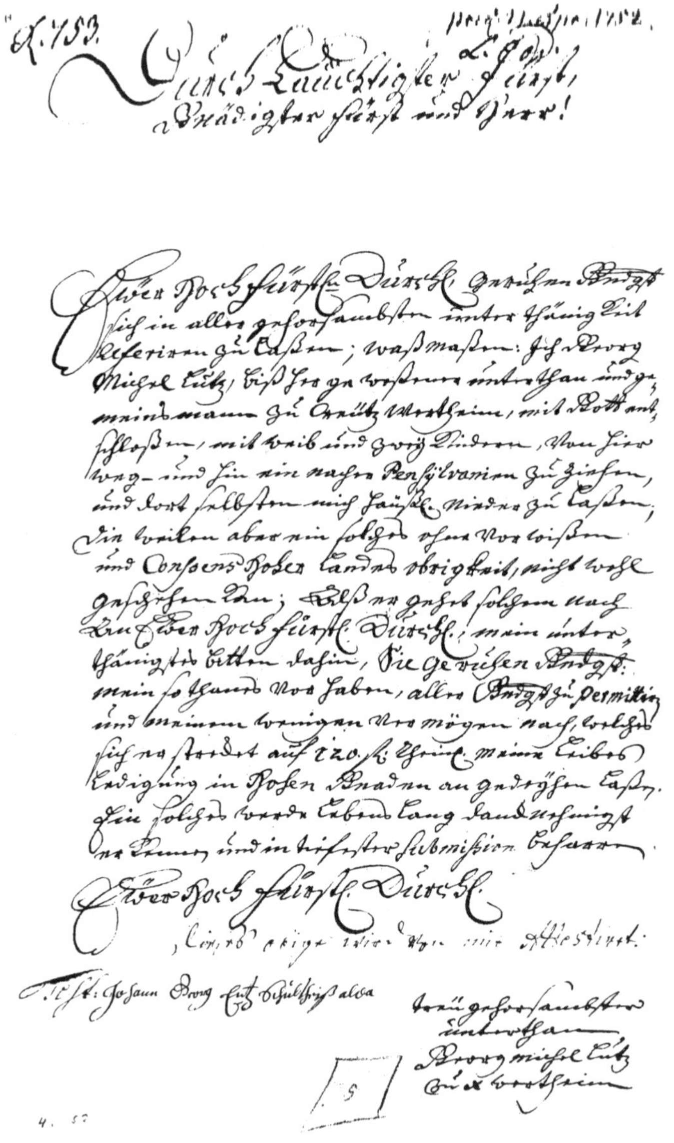

Figure 8
Michael Lutz's letter of application for manumission on April 21, 1752.

Courtesy: Stadtarchiv Wertheim

However, because such an undertaking cannot take place without previous knowledge and consent of the high authorities of the land, my most humble request is directed to your most serene Highness, that you condescend most graciously to permit most graciously my ... intentions and to allow that my freedom from serfdom be graciously bestowed on me in view of my few possessions of 120 guilders in Rhenish currency.

(I) will recognize such most thankfully my whole life long and remain in deepest submission,

Your most serene Highness' most faithfully obedient subject

Georg Michel Lutz of X-Wertheim

The above has been certified by me:

Johann Georg Entz
County Official and Village Elder [*Schultheiß*]

An abstract from the Princely Office of April 21, 1752 confirmed that "Georg Luz [sic] von Creuzwertheim" had pleaded for manumission, or freedom from serfdom, granting Michael Lutz's request upon payment of 10 guilders.[80] This was a sizeable sum of money, considering that Michael's total possessions amounted to only 120 guilders. At about the same time, Anna Catharina Müller of Kreuzwertheim decided to join the emigrants although she was single and did not have a penny to her name because her parents were poor.[81] She was one of many from the County who left at the same time as Michael Lutz. A letter of the year 1780 reported that Catharina Müllerin, the sister of an innkeeper in Kreuzwertheim, had remained in Pennsylvania and settled in well.

Because of the epidemic proportions of the "emigration fever," or "emigration nuisance",[82] as officials in Wertheim referred to it, both ruling houses of the County became increasingly nervous. In the first of several directives beginning in 1752, after Michael Lutz had made his request to leave, the Protestant and Catholic governments of the County issued warnings to the parishioners that two "pedlars of people", or *Neuländer*, had been arrested. The Prince's "praiseworthy, fatherly concern" prompted this warning:

> ... [T]he journey is so dangerous and difficult that hardly one twentieth of the people, especially the aged and children, survive the hardships, apart from the bad and unaccustomed food and water, thus leaving their few belongings to the *Neuländer*. Those with few or no possessions, if they survive the woeful seasickness, ... have to allow it to happen that the high costs for freight, food and recruiting fees are recovered by their sale as miserable slaves until these monies are paid off. Parents and children, husband and wife have to accept service miles apart, and often do not see one another for the rest of their lives. The land is by far not as good, but bad and desolate .... And the goods are very high in price. Religious worship is in the most deplorable condition, insofaras most have no religion at all, but want to be Pennsylvanian, as they call it. Follow the warning for the sake of your and your poor innocent children's well-being.[83]

Such advisories were not motivated by concerns which the *Landesvater*, or "Prince", had for his subjects. Later ordinances become more direct and reveal the true motive like the one of May 23, 1753 by Wertheim's Prince Carl zu Löwenstein, who admonishes his officials not to allow subjects, especially those with property, to be lured away. In the directive of May 20, 1754, both Wertheim governments agreed that the obvious damage and disadvantage of this emigration "nuisance" could no longer be tolerated. Accordingly, they ordered that all sale of property for the purpose of emigration cease and that no bonded subject be henceforth allowed to emigrate except in very special circumstances. The numbers of applications for emigration show how effective this ordinance was. There were 85 applications in the year 1752, 56 in 1753, 49 in 1754, and a mere 4 in 1755, one of them being Michael Lutz's brother, Johann *Thomas*, whose "special circumstance" was Michael's invitation and equal poverty. No one emigrated from the County between 1756 and 1759. For the time being, emigration had ceased from the County of Wertheim. There was, however, the occasional subject who managed to leave after the Counts' ban, e.g. Burkhard Kuch from Kreuzwertheim, a baker, "who left secretly [in 1755] with his wife and children; [had] ... nothing at all in property, but left many debts behind."[84]   A Georg Schober also left the County in 1774 "without manumission".[85]

The counts of Wertheim appear to have learned from this mass exodus, for they tried to attract industry and provide better employment opportunities for their subjects in later years. But for some these, improvements meant little, as in the case of *Johann* Lutz, born in 1872, who lived in the village poorhouse and earned his keep with seasonal jobs. In the winter he gathered up stone remnants for masons, thus earning the nickname *Schrotterhannes* ("Rubble John" *Schrotter* being the stone rubble left behind by masons). During the summer he acted as the last official gooseherd in Kreuzwertheim, looking after 600-800 geese for the entire community. He died in 1935.[86] Although there were special circumstances in *Schrotterhannes'* life, little seemed to have changed for him from the expectations of his ancestors in Höhefeld some three hundred years previously.

There is one story about two Lutz's who did not have to emigrate and who managed to make their fortune at home. Their names were Leonard and Philipp Lutz, father and son, who were brewers and innkeepers at the same time. Between 1887 and 1949, Philipp developed the local brewery into one of the leading enterprises of the village. It was so successful he was forced to close the popular *Gasthaus zum Löwen* in order to make room for the ever-expanding brewery business. Thanks to the *Brauerei Lutz*, the whole village was supplied with electricity even before World War I. The brewery was later renamed *Spessartbrauerei* (fig. 9) and set up its first artificial ice-maker in 1928.

This singular brewing success occurred almost a century and a half after Michael and Thomas Lutz were forced to leave their home and village in the face of abject poverty. They could not have accomplished their moves without help from relatives. Grandparents, parents, and siblings wanted to provide their emigrating family members with as much physical comfort and security for the journey as possible, so all was shared. The departure of extra mouths, on the other hand, eased the

Figure 9

20th-century Lutz descendants in Kreuzwertheim.

Photo: Rainer L. Hempel

80

burden on the family's strained resources at home. In some cases the community at large assisted too, since it would likewise stand to benefit from the reduction in hungry mouths.[87] There were mixed emotions but mostly profound sadness that matters had come to such a pass. History books and literature abound with stories describing the heart-rending scenes and dejection caused by the departure of loved ones under these circumstances. It was as though the emigrants had died before their time, and they often departed like "condemned" people. It is perhaps difficult to imagine in our age of transportation, communication, and affluence that emigration to North America in the 18th century was usually a farewell forever. Even sending a simple letter was an expense which emigrants at that time could ill afford. People had to wait up to a year for a reply. When Michael Lutz made his decision to leave, his older brother Thomas had just recently married and become a father while his younger brother was just eighteen and single, so that there was perhaps some hope of seeing them again. As with many, there must have been verbal agreements that others of the family would follow if stories about the promised land held true. Michael's father, however, was 62 and his mother 56, and at a time of much lower life expectancy this was considered old. The realization that he would probably never see his parents, relatives, friends, or birthplace again, must have made this a sorrowful occasion indeed. As it turned out, Michael Lutz never did set foot in his homeland again although he was fortunate to meet up with Thomas in Philadelphia.

II.6 Stieff

The name *Stief(f)*[88] is derived from the Middle-Low German word for "stiff, rigid, unbending, and stubborn."[89] *Stief* is also used as a prefix meaning "step" in words like *Stiefvater* ("stepfather"), *Stiefmutter* ("stepmother"), or *Stiefkind* ("stepchild").

Studies of name frequencies, information from the *International Genealogical Index*, and contributions by genealogists and private researchers lead to the region just north-east of Nuremberg in Bavarian Frankonia. The small town of Sulzbach-Rosenberg (Map 1) alone has 13 families with the surname Stief. The villages and towns north-east of

Nuremberg[90] also have large concentrations of Stiefs. This area must be considered the family's ancestral region, where they had been living at least since the early part of the 17th century. Kirchensittenbach, which has 42 entries for the name Stief in the *International Genealogical Index*, may be the ancestral village. It is likely that a forefather of Heinrich Stieff departed from there. One Stief descendant[91] contributed information about records of his family as early as 1650 in the Odenwald region, approximately 200 km to the west of Nuremberg. This is not surprising because the ravages of the Thirty Years' War and the resulting famines and diseases depopulated wide areas of the Old Empire. There was considerable migration both in the form of refugees during the war and movement to fill the void in the depopulated regions afterwards.

This branch of the Stief family appears to have had a mind of its own, for the Freiherrlich Wamboltisches Archiv (the Baronial Archives of Wambolt) documented in 1705 the rebellious behaviour of a Johann Heinrich Stief.[92] There had been some disagreement over the payment of shepherds' fees. When the due date arrived, about 20 of the 80 families of Birkenau refused to pay. After several warnings, the authorities decided to impound property for the outstanding amount. Johann Heinrich refused to admit defeat. When the bailiff wanted to arrest him for his recalcitrant behaviour, he threatened him with a knife and ran home "pouring out frequent insults". The ruler's officials then sent several people to take him into custody, but "... they let him go when the delinquent positioned himself with a bare sabre and his pistol on the steps of his house and threatened to shoot or split the skull of the first to come up."[93] Afterwards he is said to have strutted up and down the village streets, even insulting and challenging relatives of officials. Since this insolent behaviour was tantamount to rebellion at that time, six soldiers were ordered to take the house by force, but to no avail since Johann Heinrich had already fled. Only his son, Johann Friedrich, was arrested and later charged six guilders for his part in the conspiracy. A Christoph Stief, presumably another son, was fined three guilders in connection with the same incident. It is tempting to construe this episode as a motive for a disgruntled, uprooted family to emigrate to America as it was difficult within the German states to settle somewhere else or to escape the law, but the emigration of the Petitcodiac German, Heinrich Stieff, occurred almost half a century later. Had the result of a wrongful decision against his grandfather been harboured in the family or sufficiently tarnished its reputation prompting the emigration of Heinrich and his brother Friedrich? If one considers that certain first names run in families, it is noteworthy that all the names of the Birkenau Stiefs occur also in the family of the Petitcodiac German Stieff. However, this is no proof but may be a lead for further research on whether the families are in any way related.[94]

It should be noted here that it is the second of the two given names by which most Germans are usually called, making this the *Rufname*, or "calling name." In the Odenwald region the name *Johann*, or *Hans*, was added as a matter of custom so that the true "calling names" of the Stiefs in question were Heinrich and Friedrich. The same may be observed in the Lutz Family genealogy. The older Lutz brother was *Johann* as well, but his "calling name" was Thomas, i.e. Johann *Thomas* Lutz. A popular name in the Lutz family was Georg, and Michael's full name was Georg *Michael* Lutz. The custom of "first name" and "calling name" frustrates immigrants to this day when people address them by what they consider to be their secondary names.

The claim in the *International Genealogical Index* that Heinrich Stieff and his wife Rachel were residents of Osnabrück in Northern Germany in 1749 is incorrect.[95] This erroneous entry has become a part of the Stieff family tradition and has been repeated in at least a dozen publications, including those by the dean of Stieff research, Esther Clark Wright.[96] Research carried out in this city revealed that there was not a single Stief(f) entry before 1780.[97] Although practically all Stief(f)s were Lutherans, the records for the Catholic churches in Osnabrück were examined as well but to no avail. Clark Wright claims that Heinrich Stieff was born in 1730,[98] but there is no evidence of this, nor for 1749 as the date of marriage.

II.6 a   The Dukedom of Württemberg

Another Johann Heinrich Stieff has been found recently in German archives.[99] Heinrich was the son of a cowherd from Münsingen (Map 1), about 60 km south-east of Stuttgart in the Swabian Highlands of Württemberg, and was married to Regina Stahlecker, a farmer's daughter from the village of Honau, about 20 km west of Münsingen. Their place of origin belongs to one of the oldest, continuously settled regions of Europe since encroaching glaciers from the Alps as well as those from the north during the various ice ages never covered Württemberg.[100] During the 8th century B.C., Celtic peoples migrated into this area, bringing with them the knowledge to melt and forge iron.[101] This resulted not just in better weapons but also superior agricultural implements to cultivate inferior soils and clear-cut thick forests.[102] Since animal husbandry had priority over agriculture amongst the Celts, the Swabian Highlands with their sparse soil became a preferred area of settlement. Large tracts of the *Alb* ("Highlands") became extensive pastures, shaping the landscape to this day with their anthropogenic heath that would revert to forest if not grazed regularly.[103] Herding cattle and sheep in this region remained an important occupation for its inhabitants, including Heinrich Stieff's father. Beginning in approximately 80 A.D., the flourishing culture of the Celtic Helvetians was disturbed by advancing Alemanni, a Germanic tribe of Swabian origin, who entered Roman territory in 211 A.D. and eventually took possession of the Württemberg region in 454 A.D., destroying the Roman farms and taking over the cultivated land.

The origin of the town name Münsingen can be traced to this early period of permanent settlement by Alemanni/Swabians, which was carried out around 630 A.D. mainly by units of one hundred soldiers (and their families), the so-called *Huntari*,[104] such as the *Munigiseshuntari*[105] ("Münsingen Hundred"). The name of this group, however, was not that of its leader, as was often the case, rather it derived from a previous settlement founded by a man called *Munigis*.[106] The name *Munigisingen* comprises this man's name plus the Germanic suffix *ingen* which denotes the dative plural, meaning "(belonging) to the men/people of Munigis".[107] Place names ending in *ingen* and *heim* represent some of the oldest Germanic settlements.[108] Although a firm date for the founding of Münsingen has

84

not been determined, it is believed to have occurred by 550-600 A.D. From 769 A.D. on, the area around Münsingen was called *Munigesingen marca* and the settlement itself *villa Munigesinga*.[109]

Toward the end of Germanic migrations throughout western Europe, the Franks asserted their leadership over other tribes, including the Alemanni/Swabians. An attempted conquest of portions of Italy in 534 A.D. initiated at the behest of a Frankish king ended in utter defeat when malaria decimated the troops. Feeling their gods to be ineffectual and finding themselves surrounded by tribes which had accepted Christianity, the Alemanni soon embraced this new faith as part of a higher culture. Because of the Frankish influence, the early churches were often dedicated to St. Martin of Tours, a popular saint of the Franks, inlcuding the one in Münsingen, in which Heinrich Stieff and several of his forbears were baptized or exchanged their marriage vows. The origins of this church go back as far as 804 A.D.[110]

The *Lex Alammanorum* [111] ("The Alemannic Law"), dated about 720, is a reworked collection of earlier laws that reflects the Christianization of the Alemanni/Swabians. It determined among other changes that oaths no longer be sworn over arms but at an altar and that marriage and divorce were not a matter of the Church as in Heinrich Stieff's time. The close connection between the Franks and the papacy probably explains why the Anglo-Saxon monk Wynfrith, better known as St.Boniface (675-754) also became active in the Alemannic area and established many monasteries which became centres of education, art, and agricultural innovation. These brought forth such men as Albertus Magnus (1220-1280), a Dominican monk who taught in Paris and Cologne and became well known for his rediscovery of Aristotle and as the mentor of Thomas Aquinas. With the weakening of Frankish power, Swabia rose in prominence, culminating in the rule of the Staufen dynastic house, the most famous member of which was Emperor Barbarossa (1152-1190). With him the Holy Roman Empire achieved its pinnacle. During this period many new towns were founded by the granting of certain rights, such as for holding markets and fortifying settled areas around castles.

Beginning in 1246, the Counts of Württemberg emerged from the struggle between the Pope and the Staufers as the dominant rulers of the region. Münsingen came into their possession and was mentioned as a town for the first time in 1339. As such, it was fortified by a wall and served as a fortress, suffering destruction in 1378 and 1449.[112] Between the 14th and 16th centuries, German towns were at the height of their power as centres of trade and commerce. Trades people united in *Zünfte*, or "guilds", which challenged the aristocracy for power, whereas the increasing rural population with its agricultural base was forced, as in the County of Wertheim, to subsist on an ever-decreasing land base. Most peasants were serfs required to deliver a yearly *Leibhuhn* ("chicken") as a sign of subservience and, in case of death, surrender the *Besthaupt* or "best" of everything in the deceased's household (e.g. the best animal, the best coat, etc.). The Counts and later Dukes of Württemberg were rather typical princes for their time. One of the more outstanding was Eberhard V im Bart von Württemberg (1459-1496), whose mother, Mechthild von Österreich, had a deep appreciation of art and literature. Eberhard's court, not unlike that in Wertheim, was open to humanistic influences, and men such as Johannes Reuchlin (1455-1522), father of early German humanism, and his nephew, Philipp Melanchthon, later friend of Martin Luther, were drawn to Württemberg. In 1468, Eberhard im Bart undertook a pilgrimage to the Holy Land. He founded the University of Tübingen in 1477 and, in the Münsingen Treaty of 1482, reunited the County of Württemberg after a 41-year-long branching of dynastic lineages. Since Duke Eberhard[113] left no heir, his cousin Ulrich (1498-1540) became Duke at Emperor Maximilian's behest. A peculiar connection was established between the Dukedom of Württemberg and the County of Wertheim when, during the Bavarian War of Succession in 1504, Ulrich supported his mentor, the Emperor, by invading the Palatinate and thereby also taking over the possessions of the Counts of Löwenstein, who were to inherit the County of Wertheim toward the end of the 16th century. In 1514, Duke Ulrich signed the Tübingen Agreement in which he surrendered some of his absolute powers to the *Stände*, a body of representatives consisting of knights, abbots of monasteries, and the upper levels of urban society. The Tübingen Agreement is understood today as a precursor of constitutional government, a sort of *Magna Carta*, for it wrested from the ruler the rights to declare war, levy taxes, and limit the movement of his subjects, rights which were largely ignored during the absolutist period of the 18th century. The Reformation encountered fertile ground in the ruling circles and Imperial cities of Württemberg although a temporary rule by Austria restricted the spread of this new religion to rural areas until the return of Duke Ulrich in 1534. After this date, Württemberg became the largest Protestant region in a predominantly Catholic Southern Germany, providing a territorial connection between the Lutheran regions of North and Central Germany and the reformed cantons of Switzerland, through which many Swiss later emigrated to the New World.

Württemberg's rural population understood Luther's and Zwingli's reformation as a social movement and demanded a "natural law based on divine justice",[114] which found its expression in Twelve Articles written in 1525 by a journeyman in Memmingen, about 60 km south-east of Münsingen. This important document of the Peasant Wars, initiated by no mere coincidence in Swabia, demanded: the abolition of serfdom, the reduction of service to a prince, the right to hunt and fish, access to the forest, and freedom to choose their own pastors and, thus, religion -- all privileges the Petitcodiac Germans were to attain only as settlers in New Brunswick. The revolt spread quickly from Swabia to Franconia, including the Tauber and Main valleys. In unprecedented bloodbaths, the princes routed the peasant armies, killing around 100,000. Between Böblingen and Sindelfingen, about 50 km north-west of Münsingen, the Württemberg peasants were defeated and 2,500 of them massacred. Several villages were burned as a lesson, just as the Count of Wertheim had done in the case of Höhefeld.

The Thirty Years' War brought much suffering to Württemberg, as it was the only Protestant territory in Southern Germany. Until January of 1632 it was occupied by Catholic Imperial troops. The early death of the Swedish king Gustavus Adolphus in November of that year augured badly for the fortunes of the recently liberated Protestants. In the September 1634 battle of Nördlingen, about 90 km north-east of Münsingen, the Protestants were defeated, the greater part of the Württemberg militia killed, and the land devastated. As a result of this victory, the Catholic Habsburgs appeared to be on the ascendancy, and

87

Catholic France, casting aside religious considerations, sided with Protestant Sweden. The last two major battles of this conflict were likewise fought on Württemberg's soil. The destruction of crops resulted in famines, and the effects of dysentry, typhoid fever, and worst of all the plagues of 1626 and 1634-1639, when combined with the losses in fighting, reduced the region's population from 450,000 to 100,000.[115] Even four years after war's end, one-third of all agricultural land had not yet begun to be recultivated. Viniculture, as in the Wertheim region, never regained its pre-war importance.

Münsingen had established itself mainly in agriculture and animal husbandry and in the 16th and 17th centuries developed some trades, especially weaving. During the Thirty Years' War, many from the surrounding villages fled to the protection of the walled town, at times doubling the population with serious consequences. In 1631, Protestant Münsingen was plundered by Catholic troops.[116] In 1635, almost 500 inhabitants and refugees died of the plague. Again in 1643, Catholic Bavarian mercenaries plundered the town. As a result of stress, hunger, and disease between 1642 and 1644, two-thirds of all infants did not survive. In 1646, marauding Swedish troops paid the town a visit. From a pre-war total of about 200 families (i.e. about 500 inhabitants)[117] only 40-50 people remained after the plague and last plunder. A loss of subjects of such magnitude could only be replenished by immigration.[118] In order to repopulate the empty towns and devastated countryside, the Duke promised new settlers free land and freedom from taxes for several years. One of those who accepted the Duke's offer was the grandfather of Petitcodiac settler Heinrich Stieff. Although Württemberg was a land open to immigrants in the years following 1648, it took less than one hundred years before overcrowding, lack of work, excessive taxes, and the Dukes' passion for the hunt left this land ripe for a mass exodus.

A measure of the population increase has been made in a study of the female fertility rate of married women in Württemberg. Between 1654 and 1749, the average for women who entered into marriage at age twenty and still had their husbands by age fifty was twelve children.[119] Although this statistic pertains to the village of Laichingen, about 20 km north-east of Münsingen, it can be regarded as typical for the region. Such population growth, however, was reduced by an alarmingly high infant mortality rate.[120] About one-third of all babies did not survive their first year, particularly in poor households where families depended largely on contributions made by child-bearing women. A widespread custom in Württemberg, which lead to the highest mortality rate in Europe, was the substitution of mother's milk with cow's milk and cereal-based pablum. When the devastating effects of the *Schwäbische Mehlbrei* ("Swabian pap") finally came to be acknowledged around 1850, even ministers preached from the pulpit against this *Mordbrei*[121] ("murder-pap"). This method of feeding babies must be regarded as the regrettable attempt of a society to come to terms with its challenging social and economic conditions when women worked to supplement husbands' incomes from marginal farms and/or cottage industries, at a time when mothers in other regions could afford to provide better care for their new-borns.[122] Despite a mortality rate calculated to be over 50% to the age of five, the renowned fertility of Swabian women who stopped nursing early had made up for the human losses of the Thirty Years' War by 1750.

The control which the Dukes of Württemberg exercised over their domain reduced the work available in such a densely populated region. The expenses of maintaining a court and hunt in the period following the Thirty Years' War, as well as the funding of lavish construction projects, more about which will be said later, led the Dukes to take short-sighted steps in the exacting of revenues as opposed to developing trade and commerce that would have accrued far greater sums over the long-term.[123] By collecting import/export taxes and selling trade and manufacturing privileges, the government of Württemberg curtailed its development of free trade and commerce. In the weaving business, for instance, companies favoured by the Duke dictated the prices of all finished goods, regardless of the raw material costs. When weavers protested by boy-cotting these monopolies and establishing their own viable businesses, several were imprisoned. A loss of free commerce did not just prevent the development of new markets, but total dependency on the monopoly of the privileged reduced weavers and knitters to mere labourers. As a result, they belonged to the poorest segment of Württemberg society.[124] Advisors who pointed out that a few thousand guilders in the treasury of

Duke Carl Eugen had accrued at the expense of millions in lost business were either dismissed or imprisoned.[125]

What happened to weavers happened to other tradespeople as well. Stocking-knitting also became an important home-based industry in which even children were expected to supplement the low earnings of marginal farms.[126] Both the weaving and stocking-knitting trades figured prominently in the occupations of Heinrich Stieff's ancestors and relations. The invention in 1589 of the stocking loom by the English clergyman William Lee enabled knitters, despite its difficult operation, to produce stockings five times faster than previously, threatening the livelihood of all hand-knitters. Possibly for this reason, Queen Elizabeth I refused Lee a patent for the machine, forcing him to take his invention across the Channel where he was welcomed by Henry IV of France. Knowledge of the loom was brought to Germany and Württemberg by French Protestant stocking-knitters who managed to flee France after the annulment of the Edict of Nantes in 1685. A centre of stocking production developed in Ebingen, about 40 km south-west of Münsingen. Stockings which only the wealthy could afford previously became an article much in demand, particularly since the stocking loom was versatile enough to take spun cotton, linen, fine sheep's wool, and even silk thread. The loom consisted of more than 3,500 parts, the metal alone weighing about 275 kg. Only the wealthy and/or those with a substantial land base could afford one. A few master weavers managed to acquire more and more of the looms, employing poor people who needed extra income but at the same time putting hand-knitters in equal poverty out of work. Münsingen's three stocking-knitters belonged to the lower 30% of society in terms of wealth, with an average property value of 153 guilders. This compares to seven innkeepers in the same community with possessions averaging at 1,938 guilders each and four merchants at 583 guilders each. Twenty-eight weavers also had low property values, ranging from no possessions at all to 596 guilders, or on average 198 guilders per household. This wide range in incomes distinguished "employees" from "employers" -- poor journeymen as opposed to wealthier masters who could afford set-up costs and equipment.[127]

A final example of proto-industrial developments is the *Ziegler*, or brick- and tile-maker, a trade in which Heinrich Stieff was seasonally employed. Münsingen's brickworks were situated one kilometre out of town at today's *Ziegelhäuser*, on the road southward to Buttenhausen and Hundersingen. The Münsingen *Ziegler* of 1733 was entitled to 10 wagon loads of wood, enough for 5 firings of 10,000 bricks each.[128] Manufacturing bricks and roof-tiles in such quantity was tedious work that a master would assign his journeymen. It was also seasonal employment according to an old custom, beginning on March 19th and ending on October 16th of each year. This business was not regulated as a guild; rather production sites were passed on as inherited "fiefs" (*Erblehen*).[129] A brick- and tile-maker of Urach, 15 km north-west of Münsingen, was one of the town's wealthier citizens.[130] The number of *Ziegler* who were wealthy farmers and *Schultheiße* in other parts of Württemberg underscores the wealth connected to this trade. These select few benefitted from their inherited wealth and privilege enough to exploit local clay deposits and, above all, to gain access to sufficient timber from nearby forests as 8-10 cords were required per firing. Four Münsingen *Ziegler* had property values ranging from 18 to 816 guilders. The wealthiest boasted the third highest property value in the town, being surpassed only by an innkeeper's 3,953 guilders and a merchant's 1,050 guilders. The poorest, with a property value of 18 guilders, was undoubtedly a journeyman. Following the innkeeper, merchant, and tile-maker in terms of wealth were the tanner and nailsmith, all of whom managed larger manufacturing establishments[131] and employed poor labourers.

In a tax assessment undertaken in 1733, the total property value of Münsingen's residents was estimated at 91,838 guilders. Only a small portion (12,226 guilders) was generated by trade activity. The larger part of the property (71,082 guilders) consisted of gardens, pastures, cultivated land, and other real estate, underscoring the primacy of wealth on the basis of land even in an urban centre such as this.[132] The importance of agriculture was also manifest in the town's number of farm animals: 100 horses,[133] 400 head of cattle, almost 300 milk cows, 500 sheep, 100 pigs, and 50 goats, in addition to many smaller animals. If one considers the town's population, animal husbandry continued to be an important aspect of farming in the Swabian Highlands, providing work to herders of sheep, cows, horses, pigs, and, the lowest of these, geese.

Land availability played an important role in proto-industrialization, both for those in possession of it and for those without. Medick[134] argues that proto-industry was the outcome neither of poverty or the initiator of an industrial proletariat. Scarcity of land, however, provided low-cost labour over an extended period of time, and cottage-based industries and agriculture in many regions co-existed successfully, fluctuating only in seasonal intensity. Even the tiniest plots of land raised their owners' financial stability above those with no land at all. This allowed people to marry and start families, combining what they could grow on their land with what they could earn as labourers. A direct relationship exists in the numbers who owned marginal farmland and those who found work simultaneously in trades requiring little investment, like spinning, weaving, shoe-making, and tailoring. An oversupply of workers in these trades suppressed personal earnings further.[135] It comes as no surprise that the largest percentage of emigrants[136] falls into this category. On the other hand, trades such as brick- and tile-making, stocking-knitting, and tanning required large investments to equip themselves for the proto-industrial era, capital that could only be raised by those whose land holdings exceeded "marginal". These people were not driven, but rather chose to be active in farming to generate additional revenues. This early stage of industrial development shows that land base determined one's status as employer and employee. Total dependence on land was gradually lessened and finally eliminated later in the 18th century, but lack of land drove thousands overseas, especially after long and severe winters, poor growing seasons, or floods as in the years 1708/1709, 1725, 1737,[137] 1741, and 1745/1746. Of the 4,050 Württembergers known to have left between 1747 and 1750, almost two-thirds made their way to North America,[138] including Heinrich Stieff and his family.

Exacerbating the effects of the Dukes' ill-conceived fiscal policies, overpopulation, and land scarcity were the results of French incursions into Württemberg during the Palatine War (1688-1697) and Spanish War of Succession (1701-1714). Although recovery from the Thirty Years' War had scarcely been achieved, French troops arrived and devastated large areas of Württemberg, many villages and towns including Pforzheim, Calw, and Vaihingen in 1693. High war contributions were forced from the inhabitants at that time. Münsingen was plundered by the French on July 4, 1703,[139] and another incursion into Württemberg occurred in 1707.

In spite of the hardships that befell his people, Duke Eberhard Ludwig embarked in 1704 on the construction of his magnificent palace, Schloß Ludwigsburg, the most splendid of all those built in competition with other absolutist princes in imitation of Louis XIV's building passion.[140] The palace included 18 buildings with more than 400 rooms and extensive grounds and is an impressive example today of the various stages of Baroque architectural development.[141] Eberhard Ludwig accepted eagerly the suggestions of his three architects during the palace's 29-year construction period. The costs so overstrained the financial capacity of his realm that the Duke witnessed completion only of the external structures in 1733, the year of his death. The inner furnishings, left to his successors, were not completed until the end of the 18th century. Duke Karl Eugen (1744-1793) built four more palaces including the Neue Schloß in Stuttgart. In fact, the Dukes of Württemberg pursued one of the most extravagant life styles of any dynasty.[142] Considering that there were only about half a million inhabitants, a courtly entourage of 2,000 which swallowed up millions of guilders and theatre and opera performances which cost 100,000 guilders each[143] placed a heavy burden on the subjects.

Of particular interest to the Münsingen area was another of the Dukes' passions, namely the hunt. When Emperor Maximilian invested Count Eberhard in 1495 with the Dukedom of Württemberg, he granted him sole hunting rights regardless of civic, ecclesiastic, or other jurisdictions, and above all private land ownership.[144] The Münsingen Highlands were renowned for their extensive oak forests where wild boars and stags could thrive on acorns in abundance. Over the centuries, the Dukes' subjects repeatedly complained about severe crop damages caused by stray game. One of the demands during the peasant revolt, it may be remembered, was freedom of the hunt for all, precisely to keep such damage under control. When subjects took matters into their own hands in 1517, orders were issued by Duke Ulrich, for example, to blind anyone caught in the woods with a gun. Despite the scarcity of land, thousands of acres remained uncultivated at times because damage by wild boars rendered planting uneconomical. Not even in the sorry aftermath of the Thirty Years' War did the Dukes desist from this destructive pursuit.

Around 1700, the nature of the hunt changed under French influence. Rather than entering the woods and fields with beaters and dogs, chasing the animals on horseback to exhaustion and then killing them with a lance, the "hunt" took place close to the palace at specially designed sites set out with Moorish pavilions, man-made lakes, and water-fountains. Each forest district had to deliver a certain quota of stags, wild boars, deer, foxes, badgers, and rabbits, which would then be released into these areas so that his Highness could shoot them at point-blank range and in large numbers from a safe location outside the barriers. In the Urach forest district around Münsingen, a count of 1,300 stags was recorded in 1717. In desperation, an official in Buttenhausen oversaw the erection of a fence around the village fields; however this was deemed to upset the stags and thus the enjoyment of his Princely Highness and ordered dismantled. In 1725, the citizens of Münsingen pleaded with Duke Eberhard Ludwig to release them from the duties of game care and hunting assistance, to no avail.[145] This socage, i.e. protecting and feeding the game, involved no fewer than 3,427 men, 2,181 horses, and 1,745 teams of oxen. In addition, farmers of the district had to maintain 97 hunting dogs and 163 other dogs specially reared for the wild boar hunt, called *Sau-Rüden*. Dukes Eberhard Ludwig (1693-1733) and Karl Alexander (1733-1737) surpassed all their predecessors in their predilection for the hunt, and herds of 30 to 50 sows were reported grazing the fields like cattle. After Karl Alexander's untimely death, a new administrative regent with rare insight ordered an end to this nuisance, and 1,600 stags and 600 boars were shot, to the relief of Münsingen farmers. But under Karl Eugen (1744-1793), courtly catch-release-and-shoot hunts were once more reinstated. The total catch at one of these on the occasion of his birthday was a staggering 330 boars, 151 stags, 150 deer, 2 chamois, 2 wolves, 2 lynxes, 270 foxes, 36 badgers, and 3,002 hares, not counting hundreds of pheasants, partridges, wild ducks, and pigeons. Only in the wake of the French Revolution, when

94

the Duke became less certain of his divine rights, when his subjects baulked at their obligations regarding the hunt and tending of game, when his foresters were being threatened, and when after one night in September 1790 all the feeding stations in the Urach district went up in flames, did the Duke permit his game to be chased off peasants' fields or, if necessary, to be shot by specially appointed wardens.

Although regrettably few emigration lists from Württemberg sources have survived,[146] it is clear that the Dukes were well informed at the time and did not ignore the departure of so many of their subjects. Official analyses of the 1740-1750's exodus were surprisingly candid when the Duke's councillors examined local reports of the *Schultheiße* and other officials. Subjects complained little about the standard feudal tithes but singled out the lack of protection from wild game as one of the main irritants. Whereas earlier officials denigrated emigrants as beggars and idle subjects, reports now acknowledged that "only a third were worthless, lazy people ...."[147] Later in the 18th century, church and town officials as well as the lower aristocracy dared to be more outspoken: "... the general evil of game damage has awakened the tendency and penchant in some subjects to emigrate and ... more will follow if this continues ...."[148] As a legacy of past hunting traditions, the staghorn was incorporated in the coats of arms of Württemberg and Münsingen (fig. 10).[149]

All of the above difficulties and abuses left people few choices. The Swabian work ethic became closely interrelated with "... the fervent though not fanatical Pietism of Württemberg."[150] Sources on one hand make it abundantly clear that "... [r]eligious reasons as such do not enter into the picture [as causes for emigration]"[151] since Württemberg was Lutheran and most emigrants were members of Protestant congregations; on the other hand, the economic and political conditions which drove these people to emigrate also shaped their religious outlook and deepened their spirituality. A Württemberg village pastor of the times wrote:

If a man beats his dog the whole day, it will run away and seek another master who will treat it better. Now everyone beats the common people. The duke beats them, the soldiers beat them,

Figure 10
The Münsingen town crest: black stag horns on a silver/white background.

Courtesy: Stadtarchiv Münsingen

96

the huntsmen beat them. This they will not endure, but run away and seek another master, namely, Christ; and he who seeks Christ is a pietist.[152]

Hans Medick concludes in his study of weaving in Laichingen, Württemberg: "What began as a search for the origins, dynamics, and peculiarities of a local and regional proto-industrial capitalism, ended with research into ... Württemberg pietism."[153] "Surviving through weaving" was not based solely on economic factors but also on the outlook of Lutheran pietists. Their Protestant ethic was founded on the understanding of a personal following of Christ along the narrow and difficult path of life, practising perseverance and acceptance in the face of toil, hardship, sickness, and even death -- as in the case of so many of their children. A belief in divine providence, endurance to the end, and the sanctification of perseverance itself were appropriate attitudes in the realities of Württemberg society. This Protestant work ethic of the struggling weaver, journeyman, or hired hand is clearly different and more appropriate under the circumstances than that of Calvin's entrepreneurial capitalism where worldly economic success is viewed as a sign of divine blessing and selection. Yoder also recognizes: "The many references to taking the Lord's Supper in common before leaving are proof of the strong hold the things of religion had on many [emigrants]."[154] Such religiosity guided emigrants from Württemberg in North America, including the Stieff family, who spread these qualities -- hard work, resilience, quiet self-reliance and suffering, acceptance, and faith -- along the Petitcodiac.

Emigration of such large numbers was not just viewed as a loss to Württemberg along mercantilist lines but as an embarrassment, and every effort was made by the Dukes' officials to deflect blame away from the ruler and onto the *Neuländer*. Recruiters were no less active in Württemberg than in the County of Wertheim, using similar methods and being rewarded with large numbers of "freights". As early as 1717, the Württemberg authorities spoke of the "emigration fever" and "emigration obsession", of "simplistic minds" who fell victim to "fanatical Missionarii".[155] Directives for the *Neuländers'* arrest and punishment were disseminated by the Duke's officials in 1749 and 1753, to little

97

avail. A clever operator who managed to remain at large was the stocking-weaver Johann Georg Landenberger from Ebingen. He and two accomplices escaped to Pennsylvania in 1743 after slandering a town official. Three years later he returned alone in typical *Neuländer* fashion, well-dressed and with money to show.[156] Twice he returned to North America, each time after convincing a considerable number of families to emigrate, but in the end he bought an inn in Ebingen and settled down as one of the town's wealthier citizens. Another *Neuländer* of the worst kind was Jacob Friedrich Heerbrand, who operated a network of about twenty recruiting agents throughout south-western Germany from his base in Heilbronn on the Neckar River. Because of Heilbronn's status as an Imperial City, hence a sovereign territory, it was a complicated matter to put a stop to Heerbrand's unsavoury business. Only when his reputation became a liability to the Rotterdam shipping agency Dunlop & Co. -- Heerbrand acquired the nickname *Höllebrand* ("Hellfire") -- did his activities come to an end. The shipping company Isaac & Zacharias Hope, mentioned above in connection with emigration from the County of Wertheim, listed Heilbronn as well as Reutlingen and Esslingen, both in the vicinity of Münsingen, as recruiting centres. Samuel von Waldo recruited in Württemberg and attracted a considerable number in the years 1742, 1744, and 1748.[157] Agents also appeared in early 1752 trying to interest subjects in the settlement of Nova Scotia. The government, however, waged a losing battle against the *Neuländer* who rarely operated openly on Württemberg soil.

The authorities also fought a petty, at times ugly, campaign against the spread of positive news concerning conditions abroad, trying to intercept and control former Württembergers back on visit, and even destroying emigrants' letters suspected of containing favourable reports about the New World.[158] Just as John Dick had recognized the impact of letters from relatives and friends in the case of the Lunenburg Germans, Württemberg authorities learned to fear such letters, which in Laufen/ Eyach in 1750 caused the exodus of 22 families from one small village.[159] On the other hand, if returning immigrants had encountered difficulties abroad, dissemination of such negative accounts was officially encouraged. By the Treaty of Tübingen, Dukes were no longer permitted to forbid emigration, yet they did everything in later years to intimidate their subjects by erecting psychological and administrative barriers. According to this agreement, subjects could move freely but not without paying their debts, alerting the authorities as to their intentions to move, and promising not to engage in hostilities against Württemberg for one year. As early as 1628, Duke Johann Friedrich instructed his officials to make prospective emigrants aware of their loss of citizenship rights, hence support from the homeland such as it was. This tactic was a significant deterrent because emigrants were then confronted with the prospect of having no place to go should the promises of better conditions in their destination prove false. Due to the high population losses of the Thirty Years' War and French incursions during the Palatine War, orders against emigration in the years 1709 and 1717 became more direct. Pointed instructions were disseminated to dissuade "these simplistic people from such destructive intentions" and to deal with their "insane lust"[160] to move away. Even the clergy were engaged to admonish their flock from the pulpit in this regard. If emigrants persisted and previous attempts to dissuade them proved unsuccessful, public hearings before the Duke were set up, at which time they had to ask permission and presumably give reasons for their plans. Their reluctance to confront the Duke with real causes for complaints is obvious. The Duke in his "fatherly" concern tried to change the subjects' minds "in order to protect them from harm". Such moral and public pressure was backed by directives against the liquidation of personal assets, forbidding the purchase of property from anyone intending to emigrate. If strictly enforced, this regulation would have made it difficult for anyone with means to leave, or conversely, only those without means could emigrate. That Württembergers became the second-largest group in Pennsylvania behind the Palatines, in spite of such deterrents to leave, underscores the strong desire to emigrate. Only toward the end of the 18th century, when the problem of overpopulation became better recognized, did the Duke relent and gradually abandon his active discouragement of emigration. By this change of policy he also "hoped to release dangerous social pressures to the outside of his realm,"[161] especially in the wake of the French Revolution. The Dukes and their councillors still viewed emigration as a manifestation of ill-disguised dissatisfaction, unrest, insubordination, and unruliness.

II.6 b Forefathers of Heinrich and Regina (Stahlecker) Stieff

Grandfather Johann *Heinrich* Stieff Sr.[162] is the first of this family who followed the Dukes' invitations to help stock up Württemberg's decimated population in Münsingen (fig.11). Around 1681 he married Anna Barbara Hess, born on January 24, 1657, the daughter of one of the town's bakers. This undoubtedly established Heinrich Sr. in the community since bakers belonged to one of the highest income trades.[163] He is listed as a stocking-knitter (*Strumpfstricker*), a trade well established in Münsingen along with weaving. This means, of course, that he did not belong to one of the wealthier trades, but had to work as a cottage crafter while carrying out some modest farming activity to feed his family. From the birth of his first son Augustin(us) on November 30, 1683, we can infer that Johann Heinrich Sr. was probably born around 1650 and made his way to Münsingen some time prior to 1680. Although he must have owned some property, there is no record of this since certain books such as the *Kaufbuch*, or "Land Registry", were begun only during the 1680's. Of Heinrich Sr.'s six known children, three died young, which was not inordinate, given Württtemberg's high infant mortality rate. Of interest here beside Augustin, father of the Petitcodiac German Johann *Heinrich*, is Augustin's younger brother Johann *Heinrich* Jr., born May 21, 1687, who married Anna Barbara Schwenk, daughter of the brick- and tile-maker (*Ziegler*) and associate justice (*Gerichtsverwandter*) Schwenk, in October 1711. Johann Heinrich Jr. became a knitter (*Stricker*) like his father and had ten children. In 1716 he bought a house with barn and land in Münsingen for 240 guilders, sold the house four years later to his brother Augustin, and purchased another of higher value for 400 guilders.[164]

Johann Heinrich Jr.'s property and situation in life contrast sharply to that of Augustin, a "shepherd and herder" (*Schäfer* and *Hirte*) who married Anna Barbara Worner of Ohnastetten, about 12 km west of Münsingen, and had eight children, one of whom was the Petitcodiac German Heinrich. Although Augustin bought this small, typical "poor people's"[165] house in 1720 (fig. 12), he lived and worked intermittently between 1710 and 1727 in Hundersingen, less than 10 km south of Münsingen. Although Hundersingen was an old village with a church

Figure 11

Early 19th-century lithography of the town of Münsingen. The church steeple was rebuilt in Gothic style later in that century.

Courtesy: Stadtarchiv Münsingen

101

Figure 12
Augustin Stieff's former house in Münsingen (on the right), demolished in
1997; in the background St. Martin's Church with the Gothic-style steeple.

Courtesy: Stadtarchiv Münsingen

102

dating back to 1287 (plate 4),[166] it was almost completely deserted for many years as a result of the Thirty Years' War.[167] The congregation had no minister between 1636 and the arrival of Pastor Johann Peter Denk in 1710,[168] who recorded the baptism of Augustin's first born, Katharina, on March 3rd of that year.[169] Hundersingen was a developing community then, no doubt offering opportunities not available in Münsingen or Ohnastetten. Five of Augustin's children were born in Hundersingen[170] although he possessed citizen's rights in Münsingen. Sometime after 1711, he may have left for Ohnastetten, but Heinrich's birth is not found in the village's baptismal records.[171] By 1720 Augustin had returned to Hundersingen with enough money to purchase a house in Münsingen. His brother, who had bought that house only four years previously, was able to purchase another of almost twice the value. In view of the earning capacities of herders and knitters, the sudden availability of such sums of money by both brothers at the same time strongly suggests an inheritance.

Some clues emerge as to why the younger Johann Heinrich Jr. fared better than Augustin. The contract by which Augustin purchased the house from his brother, as well as other documentation, reveals that he could not write despite the fact that universal schooling had been introduced in Württemberg in 1648. Rather than a lack of ability to acquire this skill, there may be other reasons. As the first-born, Augustin may have had to contribute more to the support of this young and struggling family. Especially at a time when child labour was an accepted practice, Augustin may have lacked the time, opportunity, parental support, and even insight as to the necessity of learning how to read and write.[172] Moreover, Johann Heinrich Sr. died on October 6, 1699, when Augustin was only 18 years old. As the oldest son, he would have been expected to help feed and look after his siblings and mother at a time when his own training as a stocking-knitter was not complete.[173] He would have begun this familial support at an even younger age should his father's death have occurred after a lingering illness and not suddenly and found it impossible to continue his training at a later date. Johann Heinrich Jr. was twelve at the time of his father's death and fourteen when his mother married Ludwig Genkinger of Münsingen on July 20, 1701, so that his apprenticeship occurred during more ordered times, and he completed his training as a knitter in the family tradition. All of

103

Johann Heinrich Jr.'s children remained in the family's knitting/weaving tradition. His son Konrad, born on August 9, 1712, even became a member of the town court, a position of status in the community comparable to that of his maternal grandfather, *Ziegler* Schwenk. It is clear that Heinrich Jr. married into a more affluent family, raising his and his children's fortunes and position in society. This upward mobility can also be observed in the case of Michael Lutz's uncle, Johann *Peter*, when he married into the En(t)z family.

The lower social status of Augustin Stieff repeated itself characteristically in the occupations of his children. Johann Heinrich,[174] the Petitcodiac German, became a brick- and tile-maker's helper. Michael followed his father's footsteps and became a shepherd, Johann Georg is listed as a tailor, an occupation with the lowest average value of possessions in Münsingen,[175] and Georg Friedrich, who joined his brother Heinrich in Philadelphia in 1753, was a shoemaker which, like the tailor's trade, was one of the most common occupations, ranging in the lower third of average incomes.[176] The downturn in the fortunes of this branch of the Stieff family must be one of the reasons why two of Augustin's sons sought their fortunes elsewhere. Another contributing factor may have been the tendency of descendants of post-war immigrants to Württemberg to see emigration as a viable option in times of adversity because of the precedent in their background.[177] As newcomers, they may not have become as deeply rooted in the region as families which had been living there since Alemannic times.

On February 25, 1745, Johann Heinrich Stieff married Regina Stahlecker,[178] a farmer's daughter from the small village of Honau, about 15 km west of Münsingen, belonging today to the town of Lichtenstein.[179] Regina came from a large,[180] old, and established family in the area. Her forefathers must have been attached as servants or serfs to the noblemen of Stahleck Castle, situated within 5 km of Honau. In 1583, a probable forbear named Gallus Stahlecker was recorded as living in Kleinengstingen, about 5 km above Honau on the plateau to the south.[181] Regina's grandfather, J. Michael Stahlecker (born c. 1640), was married three times.[182] The last of the children by his first wife, Eva, was David, who married Agnes Werner(in) on February 28, 1706, and the last of their six children was Regina Stahlecker, Heinrich Stieff's future wife, born on September 3, 1719. Three witnesses were recorded at her baptism: two relatives, Hans Martin Stahlecker (born 1696) and Anna Barbara Stahlecker (born 1699), and Sophia Regina Felner (born 1699), the first child of the first permanent pastor of Honau. Since the latter's is the only previous mention of the name Regina in the Honau records and since she stood as one of the witnesses at the baptism, it is presumed she was Regina Stahlecker's namesake.

On account of the gap in the Hundersingen records between 1711 and 1720,[183] Heinrich's exact date of birth is unknown; however Regina Stahlecker's birth in 1719 furnishes at least a clue[184] as most men were older than women on entering marriage.[185] If this holds true here, then Heinrich Stieff must have been born around 1715. Judging by Regina and Heinrich's ages at marriage, 26 and about 30, respectively, this couple was not young. Regina, thus, had her sons in North America when she was in her thirties. Although personal reasons may have delayed this marriage, lack of a secure income to start a family was a more common cause at that time. As the sixth child of David Stahlecker, who himself was the sixth child of Michael Stahlecker before the latter rose to the status of miller as the result of his second marriage, Regina could not have contributed much of an inheritance or dowry. Younger children of large families, especially daughters, tended to benefit less in matters of inheritance. There is a special note in the Münsingen church record that Heinrich had been Regina's *Beyschläffer*, i.e. her premarital partner, and the entry in the baptismal records that their daughter, Catharina Barbara (born July 28, 1745),[186] was "conceived out of wedlock,"(*expraemat[urus] concub[itus]*),[187] typifies the morally restrictive society in which guilds and the Church exercised an authoritative role. To limit competition and guarantee the morality of master tradesmen, guilds demanded that a prospective master's parents and even grandparents be of good standing in the community and irreproachable in their moral conduct. Church officials, who at the time of *Lex Alammanorum* of 720 A.D. had no say in matters of marriage and divorce, now saw fit to judge parishioners for the remainder of their lives with such entries, knowing full well that many couples were driven into premarital relationships for a lack of money and by the reluctance or refusal of authorities to grant them permission to marry.[188] Whereas in mercantilist terms it was in the interest of the Dukes to encourage marriages and large families, it was to the detriment of their realm if young and poor people produced children who might become a burden to the state. Chastisement and shunning by society, the Church, and rulers for failure to live up to expectations stand in stark contrast to the apparent acceptance of the licentious and immoral lives led with impunity by the Dukes and their many mistresses. Heinrich and Regina were fortunate to be allowed to marry, as couples with "premarital misdemeanours"[189] were often forbidden to do so, leaving emigration as the only alternative to an existence separate from their loved ones. Perhaps the couple decided to marry in Münsingen rather than Honau, the customary location being the bride's place of residence, because of Regina's condition and in view of her closeness to Pastor Felner's family; in any case, there can be no doubt that social pressures contributed to their move away from Münsingen and ultimate decision to emigrate.[190]

Heinrich's mother passed away on May 24, 1746, and within a year his father married Anna Barbara Haueisen. It is not clear how the only agricultural property, a half-acre plot located *Unter dem Hungerberg* ("Under the Hunger Hill") just outside of town, came into the family, but there appears to be a connection to the Haueisen family.[191] Heinrich owned it jointly with his brothers: Michael, Johann Georg, and Georg Friedrich. When the last entries in the registry book were made, both Johann Georg and Michael had passed away, and the land was in the possession of their respective widows; in the margin beside the other (former) owners' names is the entry: "Fridrich [sic] Stieff, Heinrich Stieff in America." This land, which was of poor quality,[192] could not have yielded much to support four Stieff families. Perhaps also for this reason, Heinrich and Regina sought better conditions in Seißen, about 20 km east of Münsingen, where two more of their children were born, Heinrich on July 5, 1747 and Christina on June 16, 1748, but after 2 or 3 years the parents chose to emigrate to Philadelphia.

Georg Friedrich Stieff, also listed as a co-owner of the Hungerberg property, settled in Schlaitdorf, about 30 km north-west of Münsingen. It is here that he married a shoemaker's widow, Maria Haubensack, on

February 4, 1744. Their first child, Regina, was born on October 7, 1744.[193] It is likely that Heinrich and Regina were an established couple at the time of baby Regina's birth, given that Friedrich's child appears to have been named after Heinrich's partner, Regina, who must have been a welcome addition to the Stieff family. Friedrich and Katharina had four more children in Schlaitdorf, only one of whom survived. Their daughters Regina and Maria Katharina (born August 22, 1751 and named after her mother) are entered in later Schlaitdorf church records as living in Pennsylvania with their parents. Indeed, sharing the hope of a better life in America, Friedrich's family followed Heinrich's to Philadelphia in 1753 -- further evidence of the closeness of the two families. They were part of the large exodus from Schlaitdorf alluded to earlier, which involved a total of twenty-two families and included even the mayor's.[194] One can only speculate as to the role Heinrich Stieff's letters to Friedrich may have played in their decision to emigrate.

It is a reflection on Augustin Stieff's situation in life that two of his sons emigrated. By leaving, Friedrich and Heinrich bettered the chances in life for their brothers Michael and Johann Georg, both of whom had marginal incomes, the one as a shepherd and the other as a tailor,[195] since they now became the sole owners of the Hungerberg garden plot. Their father Augustin retained his low social status to the end of his days, being variously described as a herder, shepherd, cowherd, and calfherd. His name is mentioned in two separate court cases in connection with this work.[196] In the first in 1750, he successfully appealed a fine by the Duke's forester for allowing cattle in his care to wander into the woods. Augustin convinced the court that excessive heat had caused the cattle to stampede and that he had done everything in his power, even alerting the forester, to minimize the damage. In the second court case in 1751, Augustin charged a horseherd for insulting and then physically assaulting him. That same year his financial situation was such that he decided to sell one half of his house. After the passing of his second wife, he remarried in 1757 at the age of 74. In the year before his death on October 9, 1761, Augustin sold the second half of his house. Judging by the many times he moved -- at least four times -- his was a life of searching for opportunities, of attempts to better his circumstances but ultimately of failure to achieve security for his children. His offspring were exposed to a variety of environments wherein his son Heinrich, at least, acquired skills and basic knowledge that distinguished him later on the Petitcodiac. Augustin's "mobility" was also passed on to his sons, Friedrich and Heinrich, the latter of whom especially followed suit, emigrating not only to Pennsylvania, but subsequently to the Petitcodiac -- first to "Monckton" and then to Hillsborough.

Heinrich and Regina Stieff emigrated in 1749 with the two children born in Seißen.[197] This shows that their first-born, Catharina Barbara, had died. The general reasons for their departure were similar to those of Michael and Walpurgis Lutz from the County of Wertheim: poverty, scarcity of land, and tales by *Neuländer*. In Württemberg, the excesses of the dukes were more pronounced, in particular their hunting pre-dilection which affected the herders in the Stieff family on account of the encroachment of game onto grazing land, as well the dukes' control of the weaving/knitting trades during the proto-industrialist period. In addition, bad harvests occurred during 1745 and 1746, and the Duke decided to raise a standing army for his protection against future incursions by the French; fear of being drafted was a motivation for some to leave.[198] Heinrich's personal reasons to emigrate probably included his unwillingness to bear the stigma of having committed premarital transgressions and his badly paid work as seasonal brick- and tile-maker. His employ at *Ziegler* Schwenk's, a relation by marriage to his uncle Heinrich Jr. and the latter's more prosperous family, may have caused him to leave Münsingen, as nothing is more odious than perceived exploitation and bad treatment by relatives. The permission by the Duke to emigrate is a statement about Heinrich and Regina since only the poor and those considered worthless, dispensable, and immoral were allowed, or even encouraged,[199] to leave. Their departure from the homeland would have been no less painful than that of Michael and Walpurgis Lutz, and there were probably similar plans that one or the other relative might join them if they were successful. Like the Lutz's, the Stieffs never returned home to see relatives or friends again. Other members of the Stieff family continued to live in Münsingen. Friedrich, a son of Johann Heinrich Stieff Jr., bought a house *am Bühl* ("at the Hill") in Münsingen. Next to Augustin's former house at *Pfarrgasse* 11 ("Pastor's Lane"), a Johannes Stieff owned and operated several steam-driven looms for woolens between 1847 and 1853, later relocating his successful business to Bad Cannstadt, today a suburb of Stuttgart, and proving that later on upward mobility was possible. No Stieffs are listed in Münsingen's current telephone directory.

ENDNOTES

[1] Hans Pahlow, *Deutsches Namenlexikon* (Frankfurt/Main: Suhrkamp, 1967), p. 423.

[2] Letter of March 30, 1990 by Prof. Dr. Rudolf Wolf, Fichtenstr. 3, 6274 Hünstetten, Germany.

[3] Hauptstaatsarchiv Stuttgart, Auswandererkarte Glatzle.

[4] Jacob Ricker Family, compiled by Raymond M. Short in 1978, Lutz Mountain Meeting House, Moncton, N.B.. This genealogy is incomplete in many places. Cf. also the 1770 Hillsborough Census.

[5] These are the "Articles of Agreement" between the land companies and the settlers which stipulated the conditions under which the new settlement was to be set up and what mutual obligations the land companies and settlers agreed to. This "Agreement" is a focus of discussion in Chapter V.

[6] Pahlow, *Deutsches Namenlexikon*, pp. 568 and 571.

[7] Letter of January 25, 1990 by Auguste Schulze Herding, Zetter Berg 59, 4420 Coesfeld-Lette, Germany.

[8] Letter of May 18, 1990 by Gunter Brandorff, Orionlaan 28, 7771 EK Hardenberg, The Netherlands.

[9] Kapp, *Geschichte ...*, pp. 14ff..

[10] Rupp, *Immigrants in Pennsylvania*, p. 341.

[11] Strassburger and Hinke, *Pennsylvania German Pioneers*, p. 648.

[12] An issue of the Tritz Family publication, *Lorraine Berceau des Tritz, Lorraine Cradle of the Tritz, Lothringen, Die Wiege der Tritz, Lorraine Cradle of the Tritz*, "Le nom 'Tritz' au fil des siècles" (December, 1986), pp. 20-22.

[13] *Loc. cit..*

[14] A Johann Jacob Treutz emigrated from Apfelstetten, near Münsingen in Württemberg, to Pennsylvania in 1749. He was accompanied by his wife, Magdalene, and six children; Datensatznummer: 10010019207, Auswandererkartei Glatzle, Hauptarchiv Stuttgart, Germany. Johann Jacob Treutz has been mentioned as being the same person as Jacob Treitz, but there are too many inconsistencies; Don Yoder, *Pennsylvania German Immigrants, 1709-1786* (Baltimore: Genealogical Publishing Co., 1980), p. 126.

[15] Ed. Howard Temperley, *Gubbins' New Brunswick Journals 1811 & 1813* (New Brunswick Heritage Publications, Fredericton, N.B., 1980), pp. 14, 19.

[16] *Ibid.*, p. viii.

[17] Dr. Louis Tritz, 3, bis Bd Charles Vaillant, F93290 Tremblay en France.

[18] The claim that the Tritz family originated in Lorraine is arbitrary since it is based on the village where Jost Tritz worked, in Bising, Lorraine, and not where he was born, in Niedaltdorf, Saarland. It is however unimportant because

110

it is only a question of a few kilometres, as long as one remembers that the inhabitants of the whole region spoke German, or rather a German dialect peculiar to the area, and that this region did not yet belong to France.

[19] *Lorraine-Berceau des Tritz,* "Nos pères et nos maires: 1600-1789." (A type-written Tritz history), April 1989, p. 7.

[20] *Loc. cit..*

[21] Many of the American Tritz are descendants of those who emigrated during the 19th century from Tünsdorf , about 15 km north of Niedaltdorf, Jost Tritz's birth place.

[22] *Ibid.,* p. 9.

[23] Cf. the projected Tritz coat of arms.

[24] Dr. Louis Tritz, "Wappen für die Familie Tritz", *Lorraine Berceau des Tritz ...,* Juin 1986, pp. 30f..

[25] Otto Langguth, "Auswanderer aus der Grafschaft Wertheim," Sonderdruck aus den *Familiengeschichtlichen Blättern,* 30. Jahrgang, Heft 3 (Leipzig: 1932), pp. 4ff..

[26] Peter Hofmann, *Die Ursiedlung "Werdheim" im Wandel der Zeit* (Wertheim: Rotadruck M. Weber, 1980), pp. 7ff.

[27] Hermann Ehmer, *Geschichte der Grafschaft Wertheim* (Wertheim: Verlag E. Buchheim, 1989) , pp. 27f.

[28] Ehmer, *Geschichte der Grafschaft Wertheim,* p. 29.

[29] Hofmann, *Die Ursiedlung "Werdheim"...,* p. 13. Much of the information about the name and the origins of Kreuzwertheim may be found in this book and also in an earlier version by the same author, *Heimatbuch der Marktgemeinde Wertheim* (Steinfeld: Verlag-Druckerei Karl W. Goldammer, 1967), pp. 14f..

[30] *Ibid.,* pp. 34f..

[31] Information about the Church of the Holy Cross in Kreuzwertheim was taken from an information sheet written by Peter Hofmann, the author of two books about Kreuzwertheim, *Die Ursiedlung "Werdheim" im Wandel der Zeit* and *Heimatbuch der Marktgemeinde Wertheim,* available at the church entrance.

[32] *Ibid.,* p. 9. Cf. also Ehmer, *Geschichte der Grafschaft Wertheim,* pp. 28ff..

[33] Ehmer, *Geschichte der Grafschaft Wertheim,* pp. 38f..

[34] Hofmann, *Die Ursiedlung "Werdheim" ...,* pp. 13f..

[35] Ehmer, *Geschichte der Grafschaft Wertheim,* p. 167.

[36] Hofmann, *Die Ursiedlung "Werdheim"...,* pp. 39 and 89ff..

[37] Cf. also Ehmers, *Geschichte der Grafschaft Wertheim,* p. 169.

[38] Hofmann, *Die Ursiedlung"Werdheim"...,* pp. 50f..

[39] Cf. E. Langguth, "Wertheims Geschichte ...," p. 26.

[40] Ehmer, *Geschichte der Grafschaft Wertheim,* pp. 184, 190.

[41] Hofmann, *Die Ursiedlung "Werdheim"* ..., p. 51.

[42] Ehmer, *Geschichte der Grafschaft Wertheim*, pp. 183 , 185.

[43] E. Langguth, "Wertheims Geschichte ...," p. 28.

[44] Cf. also O. Langguth, "Auswanderer aus der Grafschaft Wertheim ...," p. 1.

[45] This was particularly true for pastor Koppelmann of Kreuzwertheim; Ehmer, *Geschichte der Grafschaft Wertheim*, p. 203.

[46] Erich Langguth, "Häcker und Bauern -- Höhefelds Einwohner um 1600." Ein sozial- und familiengeschichtlicher Beitrag zur Orts- und Grafschaftsgeschichte, *Wertheimer Jahrbuch 1981/82* (Wertheim: Verlag des Historischen Vereins Kreuzwertheim e.V., 1983), p. 56.

[47] A *Schultheiß* is rather like a judge and official representing a community, often appointed by the ruler to act as an intermediary with his subjects. A more detailed account of the position and duties of the *gräfliche Schultheiß* is given by Erich Langguth in his contribution to the history of the Peter Herrschaft-Haus in Kreuzwertheim: "Peter Herrschaft, seine Ämter und seine Familie," *Historie in Kreuzwertheim, 400 Jahre Peter Herrschaft-Haus* (Kreuzwertheim: Geschichts- und Heimatverein Kreuzwertheim e. V.-Verlag, 1994), p. 17.

[48] The value of a cow was about 20 guilders.

[49] He was *leibhuhnpflichtig*, i.e. as a sign of his subservience to his lord, a serf had to "donate" a chicken. Very poor people only delivered the head and could keep the rest for their own use; E. Langguth, *Häcker...*, p. 108.

[50] *"Ist ein armer Hecker gewesen, hat auch etwa(n) deß Vihs gehüt, hat auch gar wenig zum Besten gehabt."* (E. Langguth, *Häcker* ..., p. 108.)

[51] One son was called Johannes *der Jüngere*, the "Younger", to differentiate him from his uncle, i.e. Michael's brother called Johannes, *der Ältere* ("the Older"); cf. Lutz Family genealogy.

[52] In German: *Höhefelder Lücke*; E. Langguth, *Häcker* ..., p. 56.

[53] 60 *Kreuzer* is the equivalent of one guilder.

[54] Town Archives Wertheim: Stadtarchiv Wertheim, LWGemA, Renter-Rechnung 1688/89, Folg. 43r..

[55] Creutzwertheim Lagerbuch (Liegenschaften) 1710, Stadtarchiv Wertheim, p. 119.

[56] This was 3 "Morgen", 1 quarter "Morgen" and 17 "Ruten". Some comparative measurements are: 1 Morgen = 2/3 acre, 1 Rute^2 = about 12m^2, 1 Hectare = 4 Morgen = about 2.5 acres.

[57] Gemeindearchiv Kreuzwertheim Nr. 81: Lager und Schatzungsbuch Kreuzwertheim 1710, 1765 angefertigte Abschrift, p. 69: LUTZ, Hans Georg: *20 R Hofraite außen bey dem untern Thor, bestehet an einem Wohnhauß und einem Kuchengärtl darneben; lieget zwischen Philipp Amenden Hofstatt und der*

gemeinen Haßlocher Gaßen; stößt vornen an die Schafgaßen, hinten an Leonhard Amenden Hofstatt.

[58] The letter "ß" in German is pronounced like a double "ss", so Anna Walpurgis' maiden name would be pronounced "veessler".

[59] Cf. the signature of Charles Jones in the "Articles of Agreement" is in the shape of a cross. This settler arrived with the Petitcodiac Germans on the same ship.

[60] The guild laws were only changed after 1871.

[61] The village of Kreuzwertheim is simply marked by the name *Creütz*. Ehmer, *Geschichte der Grafschaft Wertheim*, p. 177.

[62] *Die Ursiedlung "Werdheim"* ... , p. 20.

[63] Hofmann, *Die Ursiedlung "Werdheim"*..., pp. 17ff..

[64] Ehmer, *Geschichte der Grafschaft Wertheim*, p. 216.

[65] Manfred Schneider, "Weinbau in Kreuzwertheim", Eingefangener Sonnenschein, *Historie in Kreuzwertheim*, 400 Jahre Peter-Herrschaft-Haus (Kreuzwertheim: Geschichts- und Heimatverein Kreuzwertheim-Verlag, 1994), pp. 98-123. This article appeared in a publication of the Historical Society of Kreuzwertheim with contributions by Erich Langguth, Paul Schauber, and Manfred Schneider.

[66] Peter Hoffmann, *Heimatbuch der Marktgemeinde Kreuzwertheim* (Scheinfeld: Verlag-Druckerei Karl Goldhammer, 1967), p. 55.

[67] Schneider, "Weinbau ...," p. 104.

[68] *Ibid.*, pp. 99/121.

[69] Andrew Jefford and the German Information Service, London, *Wines of Germany*, (Mainz: Deutsches Weininstitut GmbH, 1993-1994), p. 40; my italics.

[70] Schneider, "Weinbau ...," p. 104.

[71] Curiously enough, John Lutz[2] had a set of twins although no others were uncovered in the early generations studied.

[72] The value of more than a day of hard work in the field.

[73] O. Langguth, "Auswanderer aus der Grafschaft Wertheim", p. 13. The guilder (*Gulden*) was the common currency at this time. It was abbreviated as "fl" (Florin). A *Kreuzer*, also written "Xer," was a coin with a double cross on it. A year-old pig or heifer cost 10fl, an old cow could be bought for 15fl, a young one for 18fl, and a mare for 30-52fl.

[74] Schneider, "Weinbau ...," pp. 106, 108.

[75] *Gubbins' Journals*, pp. 27, 36, and 56. In his book *Germany and the Emigration 1816-1885*, p. 10, Mack Walker quotes the eminent 19th-century economist Friedrich List: "The more the growth of rural population exceeds the proper proportion to the amount and productiveness of land, the more the land value increases while the value of labour and man declines; while in uncultivated

or thinly populated but fruitful countries the reverse relationship prevails, for there land has little or no value, and man and labour much."

[76] Otto Langguth, "Auswanderer aus der Grafschaft Wertheim," p. 2. This article is also my source for details about Höhefeld, County Wertheim, the *Neuländer* Buch, and Samuel von Waldo. Cf. also Don Yoder, "Pennsylvania German Pioneers from the County of Wertheim," *Pennsylvania German Immigrants*, pp. 153-189.

[77] Don Yoder, *Pennsylvania German Immigrants*, p. 191

[78] O. Langguth, "Auswanderer aus der Grafschaft Wertheim," p. 12. The *Neuländer* enticed many people, even those not initially inclined toward leaving. There are examples where economic difficulties were used merely as a pretext for more personal problems which the prospective emigrants wanted to leave behind. A case in point is the gunsmith Johann Christoph Breitenherd, who left Wertheim for Pennsylvania in 1753. He had married the daughter of the well-known gunsmith Graß, and although Breitenherd inherited the business, his mother-in-law shared the premises with the married couple. Breitenherd made guns of exquisite craftsmanship and quality, examples of which are on display in the Wertheimer Museum today. The fact that there were six residences of various sovereigns on location, all undoubtedly in need of fine rifles and guns, speaks for the assured income of a competent gunsmith. Yet, in Breitenherd's application for emigration he cited low income and economic hardship as reasons for his decision to seek his fortunes outside the fatherland. Unfortunately for him, the Catholic Prince and Lutheran Count of Wertheim were of one mind not to let such a craftsman go without charging him dearly for his departure. Breitenherd's reasons for leaving must have been serious enough to risk a journey with two young daughters, only six months and two years of age. His high release fee reflected the magnitude of the loss of such a skilled artisan to the County. Breitenherd came to own a shop in Lancaster County, Pennsylvania: "Doubtless he was one of the makers of the famous Lancaster or 'Kentucky' Rifles for which our Pennsylvania German gunsmiths were famous;" Don Yoder, *Pennsylvanian German Immigrants*, p. 197; Erich Langguth, "Büchsenmacher und Büchsenschifter- alte Handwerkskunst in Wertheim," Messebeilage der *Wertheimer Zeitung* (Wertheim, Sept. 29, 1995), pp. 4-5.

[79] *Ibid.*, p. 235.

[80] Stadtarchiv Wertheim, LWRosA, Lit.Br. 387b.

[81] *"Anna Catharina Müller, Tochter des Jacob Müller, ledig, mit leerer Hand von ihren Eltern, welche arm sind, gegangen."* O. Langguth, "Auswanderer aus der Grafschaft Wertheim," p. 15.

[82] *Auswanderungsfieber* and *Emigrationsunwesen;* another term used was *Leichtsinnige Pruritus Emigrandi* ("irresponsible lust to emigrate"). O. Langguth, "Auswanderer aus der Grafschaft Wertheim", p. 11.

114

[83] O. Langguth, *"Auswanderer aus der Grafschaft Wertheim"*, pp. 10 ff..

[84] Don Yoder, *Pennsylvania German Immigrants*, p. 226.

[85] *Ibid.*, p. 240.

[86] Hofmann, *Die Ursiedlung "Werdheim"* ..., p. 117.

[87] Sieveking, "Unsere Auswanderer aus dem Werretal ...," p. 12. Hans Knapp in his article, "Warum sie ihre Heimat verließen" (*Viernheimer Auswandererbuch,* p. 19), states on April 15, 1852 that the mayor of Viernheim submitted a proposal to town council that money be made available to transport 404 of its citizens to North America.

[88] The original sources in Münsingen, some entries in the Stieff Bible as well as property transactions in "Monckton" and Hillsborough spell Heinrich's last name with a double "f". Although numerous North American sources render it as "Stief", the original version will be used for descendants of the Münsingen Stieff family throughout this study. In terms of modern German orthography, the spelling of "Stief" as "Stieff" is an anomaly. The double consonant "ff" suggests a short preceding vowel, but the diphthong *"ie"* denotes a long vowel, like the English "ee". Major General Helmut Stieff belonged to the inner circle of resistance against Hitler. After the unsuccessful assassination attempt on Hitler's life in July 1944, Stieff was executed. Hans Royce, Erich Zimmermann, Hans-Adolf Jacobson, *20. Juli 1944* (Stuttgart: Bundeszentrale für Politische Bildung, 1964), pp. 11, 72f., 128ff., 138, 212, 224, 234, 352. On the basis of the spelling of his last name, he could be a descendant of the Münsingen Stieffs and therefore related to the Petitcodiac Germans.

[89] Pahlow, *Deutsches Namenlexikon*, p. 501.

[90] These villages include Oberkumbach, Alfalter, Altensittenbach, Kirchensittenbach, Ottensoos, Hohenstadt, Happurg, Vorra, Eschenbach, Hohenstadt, Pommelsbrunn, Hersbruck, and Velden.

[91] Karl-Ernst Stief.

[92] Günter Körner, "Ein Birkenauer 'Komplott' wegen des Hirtenlohns (1705)," *Birkenauer Geschichtsverein*, pp. 56-59, based on: Bestand 13/11 in the Freiherrlich Wamboltisches Archiv.

[93] *Ibid.*, p. 57.

[94] Several Heinrich, Christian, and Friedrich Stiefs are listed in Berlin in the 19th century. Prussia, Austria and Russia attracted considerable numbers of emigrants from Germany in the 18th century, but their descendants would become candidates for emigration to North America only in the latter part of the 19th and the first half of the 20th centuries, after political circumstances and living conditions had seriously deteriorated. It is, therefore, unlikely that "Johann Heinrich Stief," born in Seiffersdorf of County Hirschberg in Silesia and christened in Hirschberg in 1713, is the Petitcodiac German "Heinrich Stieff" or even a relative. Information supplied by Manfred Raupach, Conrad-von-Soest-Str.

30, 3509 Bad Wildungen, Germany.

[95] St. Anne's became Frederick's Town, or "Fredericton", named after King George III's second son, Frederick, who was the Bishop of "Osnaburg". The latter name was also briefly considered as a tribute to *Osnabrück*, Frederick's realm. It was perhaps at this point in time that the myth regarding Heinrich Stieff's place of origin began. Osnabrück originated as a bishopric, founded about 780 A.D. by Charlemagne, and is a city today of about 150,000 located approximately 100 km west of Hanover. As one of the curiosities that resulted from the Thirty Years' War on account of the town's mixed Protestant and Catholic population, Osnabrück was to be ruled alternately by a Protestant prince and a Catholic bishop, Frederick being one of the former.

[96] Esther Clark Wright, *The Petitcodiac,* A Study of the New Brunswick River and of the People who settled along it (Sackville, N.B.: The Tribune Press, 1945), p. 54.

[97] Evangelisch-Lutherischer Gesamtverband Osnabrück, Arndtstr. 19, 4500 Osnabrück Niedersächsisches Staatsarchiv, Schloßstr. 29, 4500 Osnabrück, Germany.

[98] This was originated by the Steeves family tradition, Clark Wright, *The Petitcodiac*, p. 54. Many have simply copied these assertions, e.g.: Sharon Fehr, *Steeves, Ruggles, Rippley, Passion, Gray Families, 1730-1984*, typescript, 16 pages, donated by Loraine St. Jean, Waterloo, Ontario, on microfilm by the Genealogical Society of Utah.

[99] Les Bowser informed me in December 1997 that he had discovered marriage records about a Heinrich and Regina Stieff in the archives of the Protestant church in Münsingen, Baden-Württemberg. By matching the names of Heinrich's wife, brother and spouse, which I had located previously in Pennsylvanian sources, I determined this Johann Heinrich was indeed the sought-after Petitcodiac settler.

[100] The oldest human remains were found in this region, such as the ones of the Homo Heidelbergensis (ca. 530,000 B.C.) and Homo Steinbergensis (ca. 200,000 B.C.). Forty caves and fifteen camps provide evidence of human habitation during the Palaeolithic age. Small figurines carved out of ivory between 35,000 and 50,000 years old belong to the earliest and best works of prehistoric art recovered on German soil. The hunters' and gatherers' mode of existence was eventually replaced by agriculture, facilitated by the loess soil of the region. For the more specific history around Münsingen during the Stone, Bronze, and Iron ages, consult Hartmann Reim, "Zur Besiedlung der Münsinger Alb in vor- und frühgeschichtlicher Zeit," *Münsingen: Geschichte, Landschaft, Kultur* (Sigmaringen: Stadt Münsingen, 1982), pp. 464-475.

[101] Southern Germany was the origin of the flourishing Celtic culture, which expanded via migration westward to France and from there to Spain and the

116

British Isles. This area, therefore, became a departure point for both Celtic and Germanic waves of emigration.

[102] Karl & Arnold Weller, *Württembergische Geschichte im südwestdeutschen Raum,* 10th Edition (Stuttgart: Theiss Verlag, 1989), pp. 16ff..

[103] H. Dödderer, H. Engelhart, V. Götz, M. Rosenauer, "Schafweiden und Wacholderweiden," *Münsingen: Geschichte, Landschaft, Kultur,* p. 558.

[104] Immo Eberl, "Münsingen im Mittelalter: Vom alemannischen Dorf zur altwürttembergischen Stadt," *Münsingen: Geschichte, Landschaft, Kultur,* p. 38; *Huntari* means "one hundred".

[105] Karl & Arnold Weller, *Württembergische Geschichte ...,* p. 29

[106] Immo Eberl, "Münsingen im Mittelalter ...," p. 39.

[107] Karl & Arnold Weller, *Württembergische Geschichte ...,* p. 29.

[108] *Ibid.,* pp. 43ff. ; Immo Eberl, "Münsingen im Mittelalter ...," p. 37.

[109] *Ibid.,* p. 38.

[110] Bernhard Bischoff, "Der Chor der Stadtkirche von Münsingen und andere Chorbauten von Meister Peter von Koblenz und seinem Umkreis," *Münsingen: Geschichte, Landschaft, Kultur,* pp. 117-133; cf. also Jürgen vom Grafen, *Begleiter durch die Martinskirche Münsingen,* a 12-page pamphlet for tourists with pictures (Münsingen: VG Public Relations, n.d.).

[111] Immo Eberl, "Münsingen im Mittelalter ...," p. 37.

[112] *Ibid.,*" p. 62.

[113] In recognition of the Count's many contributions, the emperor elevated Eberhard's domain to a dukedom toward the end of his life.

[114] Karl & Arnold Weller, *Württembergische Geschichte ...,* p. 101.

[115] *Ibid.,* p. 177.

[116] *Ibid.,* p. 354.

[117] In 1598 and 1624 there were 184 households in Münsingen; Wolfgang Zimmermann, "Geschichte-Münsingen," *Der Landkreis Reutlingen,* Bd. II (Sigmaringen: Landesarchivdirektion Baden-Württemberg, 1997), p.130. Hermann Wenzel's article, "Familie und Kindheit im 16. und 17. Jahrhundert," (*Münsingen: Geschichte, Landschaft, Kultur,* p. 279), claims that there were 300 houses, i.e. households or families, in the 16th century. Zimmermann calculates that Münsingen's population of 50 inhabitants in 1646 was "one-quarter" that of the pre-war figure. This must be incorrect since, according to his own sources, there were 184 households in 1598 and 1624 which could not have consisted of only 200 people. Under the title "Zeittafel" (*Münsingen: Geschichte, Landschaft, Kultur,* p. 354), the number of inhabitants of Münsingen in 1645 is given as only 40 residents.

[118] Between 1721 and 1773, the population of Münsingen grew rapidly, exceeding 1,000 for the first time in 1783; Zimmermann, "Geschichte-Münsingen," p. 130.

[119] Hans Medick, *Weben und Überleben* ..., pp. 340f..

[120] *Ibid.*, pp. 355ff..

[121] *Ibid.*, p. 372.

[122] It should be noted that all of Heinrich and Regina's American-born boys survived in the new environment, whereas their first child died in Germany and the next two on the boat trip over.

[123] Hans Medick, *Weben und Überleben*, pp. 49ff..

[124] *Ibid.*, pp. 97ff..

[125] *Ibid.*, pp. 53ff..

[126] Susanne Goebel, "Von den Anfängen der Strumpfwirkerei auf der Rauen Alb," *Schwäbische Heimat*, 40, 1989, p. 124.

[127] Zimmermann, "Geschichte-Münsingen," pp. 130ff.

[128] *Ibid.*, p. 132 and Osterloh-Gessat, *Von Erd bin ich gemacht*, p. 35.

[129] Elke Osterloh-Gessat, *Von Erd bin ich gemacht* (Karlsruhe: Info Verlagsgesellschaft Karlsruhe, 1996), p. 36.

[130] Medick, *Weben und Überleben* ..., p. 119.

[131] Zimmermann, "Geschichte-Münsingen," p. 134.

[132] *Loc. cit.*.

[133] The number of horses in itself is not sufficient proof for Münsingen's agricultural base since active trade would demand a large number of draught horses, but in connection with the number of other animals, it is evidence of the application of horses to agriculture.

[134] Medick, "Proto-industrielles Handwerk in einer ländlichen Gesellschaft," *Weben und Überleben*, pp. 142ff..

[135] Arnold Scheuerbrandt, "Die Auswanderung aus dem heutigen Baden-Württemberg ...," *Historischer Atlas von Baden-Württemberg*, XII, 5 (Stuttgart: Kommission für geschichtliche Landeskunde in Baden-Württemberg, 1983), p. 3.

[136] Hippel, *Auswanderung aus Südwestdeutschland*, p. 51.

[137] Hippel also comes to the conclusion that the emigration boom in 1738 was mainly the result of the bad harvest in 1737; *ibid.*, p. 60. Among those who left in 1738 was 15-year old Andreas Huber, and in 1741, Hans Nickolaus Eisenhauer, two of whose descendants became presidents Hoover and Eisenhower of the United States.

[138] Scheuerbrandt, "Die Auswanderung aus dem heutigen Baden-Württemberg," p. 5.

[139] "Zeittafel zur Geschichte der Stadt," *Münsingen: Geschichte, Landschaft, Kultur*, p. 354.

[140] Karl and Arnold Weller, *Württembergische Geschichte* ..., p. 201.

[141] *Knaurs Kulturführer Deutschland* (München: Droemersche Verlagsanstalt, 1985), pp. 465ff..

[142] Cf. also Karl and Arnold Weller, *Württembergische Geschichte ...*, p. 183.

[143] Kapp, *Geschichte der deutschen Einwanderung in Amerika*, pp. 72ff.

[144] Heinrich Pesch, "Waidwerk und Wild in herzoglicher und königlicher Zeit," *Münsingen: Geschichte, Landschaft, Kultur*, pp. 509-520.

[145] "Zeittafel zur Geschichte der Stadt," *Münsingen: Geschichte, Landschaft, Kultur*, p. 354.

[146] "By executive order, the early lists of emigrants kept by the Württemberg government, along with reports on the property of the emigrants, sent to the authorities by the local village-mayors, were destroyed;" Don Yoder, *Pennsylvania German Immigrants: 1709-1786* (Baltimore: Genealogical Publishing Co., 1980), p. 27. Cf. also von Hippel, *Auswanderung aus Südwestdeutschland*, p. 46.

[147] Yoder, *Pennsylvania German Immigrants*, p. 9.

[148] Hippel, *Auswanderung aus Südwestdeutschland*, pp. 61f..

[149] In heraldic tradition, the staghorn is also a symbol of strength. Hans Biedermann, *Knaurs Lexikon der Symbole* (München, 1989), p. 196: "... das Geweih ... in der Heraldik ... hat ... 'die Deutung der Stärcke.'"

[150] Don Yoder, *Pennsylvania German Immigrants*, p.23.

[151] *Ibid.*, p. 10. Cf. also Hippel, *Auswanderung aus Südwestdeutschland*, p. 56.

[152] Don Yoder, *Pennsylvania German Immigrants*, p. 10.

[153] Hans Medick, *Weben und Überleben*, p. 35.

[154] Don Yoder, *Pennsylvania German Immigrants*, p. 30.

[155] *Ibid.*, pp. 67, 73.

[156] *Ibid.*, pp. 75ff..

[157] Scheuerbrandt, "Die Auswanderung aus dem heutigen Baden-Württemberg," pp. 41-42.

[158] Hippel, *Auswanderung aus Südwestdeutschland*, pp. 67ff..

[159] Johann Jacob Landenberger brought back two favourable letters from emigrants who had left Laufen/Eyach in 1746; Don Yoder, *Pennsylvania German Immigrants*, p. 82.

[160] Hippel, *Auswanderung aus Südwestdeutschland*, p. 97.

[161] *Ibid.*, p. 108.

[162] For the identification of the four bearers of the name Johann Heinrich Stieff, refer to the Stieff Family genealogy.

[163] Fifteen persons are listed as bakers, whose lowest value of possession was 69 guilders, the highest 744 guilders, with an average of 342, making bakers the fifth wealthiest trade in Münsingen. Those with the lowest income were probably the journeymen in the employ of master bakers, whose income must have been relatively high; Zimmermann, "Geschichte-Münsingen," pp. 130ff..

[164] Stadtamt Münsingen B 100, fol. 492v-493r.

[165] Münsingen archivist Roland Deigendesch describes Augustin's house at Pfarrgasse 11 as a typical poor people's house, first mentioned in 1712 and probably built in the second half of the 17th century. It was originally only a two-storey structure with a third floor added after Augustin sold it. One year before his death on October 9,1761, Augustin sold the second half of this house to his son Johann Georg for 215 guilders, having previously sold him the first half in 1751. It remained the property of this son and his descendants until 1802, and parts of it -- many houses had multiple owners -- belonged to a Magdalena Stieff until 1859. In the end it fell into a bad state of repair and was demolished only in 1997; letter of February 6, 1998 from Roland Deigendesch to me.

[166] W. Holderle, *Gottes Wort bleibt ewig: 700 Jahre Kirchengemeinde Hundersingen* (Dettingen/Erms: Evang. Kirchengemeinde Hundersingen, 1987), p. 5.

[167] An account of the year 1654 reported that Hundersingen had been almost completely deserted for the last nineteen years. About twenty people were living in the village at that time, and the church and manse were in a bad state of repair; *Ibid.*, p. 39. The gristmill in Hundersingen was so badly damaged in the war that it collapsed in 1653 and was rebuilt only in 1750; *Ibid*, p. 9.

[168] *Ibid.*, p. 7.

[169] Kirchenbuch Hundersingen, Bd. 1, fol. 22v, Hundersingen, Baden-Württemberg, Germany.

[170] Pastor Johann Peter Denk took charge of the Hundersingen congregation from 1710 until 1715 when Georg Friedrich Gottschick succeeded him. Two of Augustin's children, Katharina and Benedikt, were born in 1710 and 1711, respectively, followed by three more: Anna Maria in 1720, Johann Georg in 1723, and Johannes in 1727. All were duly entered in the Hundersingen church records, but three of his sons -- Heinrich, Michael, and Georg Friedrich -- were not. Over sixty other entries between 1711 and 1720 show that other baptisms were recorded in the Hundersingen *Kirchenbuch*. Thus it cannot be said that these records are incomplete. Augustin must have lived somewhere else at the time when these three sons were born, and thus Heinrich's place and date of birth remain undetermined.

[171] Herbert B. Steves, *From Stief to Steves*, typed genealogy of the Stieff family, 1998 (Address: Herbert B. Steves, P.O. Box 2005, Angel Fire, NM 87710 U.S.A.) claims that Georg Friedrich, Heinrich, and Michael were born in Ohnastetten, but baptismal records show no evidence of Heinrich's birth there between 1710 and 1720.

[172] Passenger lists, such as that in which Michael Lutz signed his name, are ample proof that it was not uncommon for immigrants to be illiterate in spite of compulsory education in their country of origin.

[173] It took four years for the apprenticeship and a further three as a journeyman to complete the training as a stocking-knitter; Susanne Goebel, *Von den Anfängen der Strumpfstrickerei auf der Rauhen Alb*, p. 125.

[174] Johann Heinrich Jr.'s third child, born on July 13, 1717, was also called Johann Heinrich.

[175] Nine tailors plied their trade in Münsingen with an average property value of 118 guilders; Zimmermann, "Geschichte-Münsingen," p. 134.

[176] Eighteen shoemakers worked in Münsingen with an average property value of 179 guilders; *loc.cit.*. It is not surprising that farmers and farmhands, weavers of various sorts, tailors, and shoemakers made up more than half of all emigrants; Don Yoder, *Pennsylvania German Immigrants*, p. 28.

[177] Scheuerbrandt, "Die Auswanderung aus dem heutigen Baden-Württemberg," p. 1.

[178] The Dekanatsarchiv Münsingen marriage record spells Regina's maiden name "Stalegger"and in their daughter's baptismal entry "Stallegger". Reutlingen archival records render her family's name variously as Stahleckher, Stahleker, Stalecker, and Stahlneckher.

[179] "On February 25 [1745], Johann *Heinrich* Stieff, tile- and brick-maker by trade, legitimate, single son of the local calfherd Augustin Stieff, was married during the hour of prayer [sometime between 6 and 9 p.m.] as a previous bedmate to Regina Stalegger, farmer's daughter from Honau of the district Pfullingen"; Dekanatsarchiv Münsingen, 509, Münsingen, Germany, p. 82.

[180] There are over fifty entries of this name in the Honau Baptismal Records between the years 1667 and 1720.

[181] "Gallus Straße" near the market square in Honau may have been named in his honour since the first name was of greater importance then. His name "Gallus Stahlecker" was derived from "Gallus, the Stahleck inhabitant/servant".

[182] Honau church records were kept only from 1667 on. After Michael Stahlecker's marriage to his second wife, Margaretha Reiflin, in 1688, he proudly called himself a "miller" (*Müller*).

[183] Kirchenbuch Hundersingen, Bd. 1, Hundersingen, Baden-Württemberg, Germany.

[184] The dates for the brothers' marriages give no hint of their relative ages. Friedrich Georg was married in Schlaitdorf on February 4, 1744, Michael in Münsingen on January 11, 1745, and Heinrich in Münsingen a month later, on February 25, 1745.

[185] Whereas 22 was the average marital age for women in pre-industrial Europe, it was 33 for men since they were obliged to gain financial security first; Herwig, *Hammer or Anvil*, p. 10.

121

[186] Heinrich Stieff's aforementioned cousin Konrad, who became a knitter and member of the town court, was one of the witnesses at the baptism. The other witness was the wife of *Ziegler* Schwenk, Heinrich's employer and a relative of Konrad.

[187] Dekanatsarchiv Münsingen, 503, Tauf- und Totenregister (Registry of Baptisms and Deaths) 1736-1785, Münsingen, Germany, p. 54.

[188] Scheuerbrandt, "Die Auswanderung aus dem heutigen Baden-Württemberg," p. 5.

[189] *Loc. cit.*.

[190] The frequency of remarks about illegitimate children in emigrants' statistics suggests that emigration was an escape from societal chastisement and a hope for more tolerant attitudes in a new land; Don Yoder, *Pennsylvania German Immigrants*, pp. 32ff..

[191] The exact size was ¾ *Morgen* and 11½ *Ruten*. The land is sloped and stony. The original owners were Daniel Walter, followed by Christoph Freytag (crossed out in the registry), then a Georg Friedrich Haueisen (a sister of the Stieff brothers was married to a Haueisen, and Augustin's second wife was also called Haueisen.). Later entries were H[ans] Jerg Stieffen Wittib ["widow"] and Michael Stieff Schäffers ["shepherd"] W[itwe] ["widow"]; cf. Stadtarchiv Münsingen, B 128, Steuermessbuch [Registry Book for Taxable Properties] 1720-1772, Münsingen, Germany.

[192] The name of the hill where their land was located may have been a reflection of its bad quality and that only those driven by hunger cultivated it. It has reverted to grassland today.

[193] *Ehebuch* (Marriage Register) # 553, Schlaitdorf Church Records, Schlaitdorf, Baden-Württemberg, Germany.

[194] Don Yoder, *Pennsylvania German Immigrants,* p. 29.

[195] Michael Stieff later came to own a house on Münsingen's *Hauptstraße* (Main Street) which must be considered an accomplishment for a person of his occupation; letter of February 6, 1998 from archivist Roland Deigendesch to me.

[196] Stadtarchiv Münsingen, B 15-16 Stadtgerichtsprotokolle 1750-1758, Münsingen, Germany.

[197] Werner Hacker, *Eighteenth-Century Register of Emigrants from Southwest Germany* (Apollo, Pennsylvania: Closson Press, 1994), p. 445, records that only the two children born in Seißen accompanied their parents in 1749. The Stieffs brought a Bible published by Johann Andre Endters in Nürnberg, Germany in 1747, which they most likely acquired before they left. Since German Bibles were printed in Pennsylvania by the Sauer Press, it is improbable that the Stieff Bible was purchased in Pennsylvania. It was also customary for emigrants to bring Bibles with them from Germany. The birth of Christina on June 16, 1748

also suggests that they emigrated in 1749 before the birth of their second son, Johann Jacob, who was born in America on November 11, 1749.

[198] Hippel, *Auswanderung aus Südwestdeutschland,* p. 62.

[199] Scheuerbrandt, "Die Auswanderung aus dem heutigen Baden-Württemberg," p. 3.

CHAPTER III

The Journey Westward

With an average of twenty weeks in transit and a confirmed arrival date of November 22, 1752, Michael Lutz would have departed from Kreuzwertheim sometime in June. This would not leave much preparation time, considering that the date of final permission from Wertheim officials was April 21, 1752. A list of belongings of the Körner family from the village of Vockenrot, about 2 km from Kreuzwertheim, gives an indication of what immigrants considered essential for the journey to America. This family spent about 90 guilders on shirts, socks, buttons, thread, sheep skins for pants, shoes, hats, a trunk, prunes, and a quarter bucket of hard liquor. Like Heinrich and Regina Stieff, many emigrants also brought along a Bible.[1] Since Michael and Walpurgis Lutz's possessions amounted to 120 guilders, preparations for the journey must have swallowed up the lion's share of their resources, especially if no additional assistance from family or friends was provided. Even under the most favourable of circumstances, Michael had only money enough to reach Rotterdam. Such a departure was the first in a series of giant leaps of faith. Swayed by the promises of recruiters and letters of former emigrants, both Michael Lutz and Heinrich Stieff must have hoped to be able to sign on with a shipping company, allowing them to pay back the cost of the journey after arriving in America.

The trip to Rotterdam must have appeared simple enough because the Rhine is a direct connection with this busy port. Located on the Main, a tributary of the Rhine, Wertheim was an important point of transfer for passengers and freight. Convenient and speedy travel by ship was available but only to those who could afford it.[2] Less expensive means of travel from the Spessart area where Kreuzwertheim lies was the wooden raft, which even poorer emigrants could afford. For centuries German forests had been a source of lumber to Holland in the building of dykes and ships and to the Ruhr area in providing timber supports for coal-mining constructions. Logs were floated downriver in the form of rafts, which could at the same time transport people. The boat trip to Rotterdam cost about 8 guilders per passenger when the Lutz family emigrated.[3] Since the two children,

Catharina and Peter, were both under four years of age, they travelled free of charge. Heinrich and Regina Stieff did not enjoy the convenience of a larger river passing by their home town. They had to transport their possessions about 50 km by cart before reaching the Neckar River, their closest navigable body of water. The distance to Rotterdam from Kreuzwertheim and Seißen, which today may be covered on the *Autobahn* in a matter of hours, took travellers of the 18th century three to four weeks. It was not only the speed of the boats and currents which determined their travel time but also the presence of over thirty customs stations *en route*, exacting tolls for a host of independent princedoms, dukedoms, and city-states. Each one of these "mini-realms" insisted that travellers pay for the privilege of passage. Government officials then were no less astute than today in pulling money out of people's pockets, and for mere trifles passengers could be held up for days at a time, meanwhile having to spend additional money for food and moorage. Travellers were easy prey to the greed of individual rulers who stripped them of even their last meagre savings.

Upon the emigrants' arrival in Rotterdam, much, if not all, of their monies had been spent. *Neuländer* and ships' captains often delayed departures from Rotterdam further in a deliberate attempt to bankrupt travellers so that they could not afford a change of heart, even if they had regrets, and were compelled to sign anything demanded of them. The government of Holland put shipping companies under heavy bond that they actually transport the people overseas whom they had brought into the country.[4] Competition for "freights" to be shipped overseas came to a head near Emmerich, at the border between the Duchy of Cleves and The Netherlands. A goodly number signed on with specific agents at this point, for without signatures *Neuländer* could not exact their payment of about one ducat per adult.[5] As a rule, emigrants could not pay for their passage to North America.[6]

An exploitive business relationship existed between the recruitment of emigrants, their transportation from Holland to North America, and subsequent contracts which allowed captains and shipping companies to "sell" their passengers upon arrival to defray all costs of transportation. Reasons for the appalling abuses in this business were twofold: business partners in these ventures were numerous and not equal, and there was no repeat business. Unscrupulous merchants would normally have put themselves out of business by their unsavoury reputations, but since there was a seemingly endless supply of poor, naïve, and desperate customers, their abuse and exploitation continued for more than a century, until finally in 1819 a law was passed forbidding the practice.

Before departure from Holland, most emigrants of that time had to sign an "Accord"[7] drawn up in English, a language they were not familiar with. The *Neuländer*, as supposedly impartial friends, claimed to make certain that their countrymen were not disadvantaged. In reality, they added into the contract the cost of the journey from the Dutch border to Rotterdam, any cash advances to the emigrant, and the recruiting fee as part of the actual cost of the sea voyage.[8] The cost per "freight" was £10 in Philadelphian currency,[9] or 60 guilders, and the journey down the Rhine at least 40 guilders.[10] Using conservative figures, Mittelberger estimated the journey's cost at 200 guilders per person from the average German town to Philadelphia.[11] Winthrop P. Bell concludes that, at the rate of 1½ shillings per day, labourers could work off their ocean passage portion in 118 days.[12] At an exchange rate of 1 guilder for 2 shillings,[13] the 200 guilders in Mittelberger's more inclusive estimate could have been earned in 267 days at the same daily wage. Even if Walpurgis Lutz did not find employment, Michael should have been able to redeem himself and his wife in at most two years. No matter what calculations, daily wage rate, and cost estimates one uses for the journey, the length of time it took immigrants to pay off their debts was always much higher than it should have been. Depending on their age, ability to work, skills, and debt load, the average length of "bondage" per individual was between three and six years,[14] and much longer when dependents were involved.

The emigrants' eagerness to attain a better life in the New World played into the hands of those who stood to profit from the emigration business. Clearly, it was in the interest of the shipping companies to transport as many emigrants as possible in the smallest available space and at the least expense and risk. Although regulations existed regarding the "space allowance per freight",[15] the interpretations by captains varied greatly and with disastrous results. A berth 6' x 2' x 2'9" (183 x 61 x 84 cm) was considered adequate, but in many cases this rule was not adhered to, as recorded in the transportation of Lunenburg Germans. The space between decks was from 4'6" to 5'6" (137 cm - 166 cm) so that most adults could not stand upright. It was accepted practice to transport one passenger per ton of ship displacement, although there were cases where 450 were cramped into a 300-ton vessel and 400 into a 270-ton vessel. Some berths were in three tiers, 18" wide and 2' high: " ... one lot of emigrants were given only 7 square feet per person (86 of them, with their baggage, crowded together in a space 25' x 24'6")."[16] Air quality and sanitation were dreadful under these conditions. A lack of proper ventilation on the *Ann*'s 1750 voyage resulted in a high mortality rate among Lunenburg Germans, and conditions were doubtless no better for those emigrants destined for Philadelphia.

The food on board was generally inadequate, despite lists suggesting otherwise, because it was expected that emigrants would supplement their diets with their own supplies. However, constant delays usually meant that such foodstuffs were exhausted well before anchors were ever heaved. In a contract between the shipping firm Isaac & Zacharias Hope and twenty-three families, the latter were promised: "... good bread, meat, bacon, flour, rice, barley, peas, syrup, butter, cheese, beer and good fresh water."[17] The shipper also agreed "to clean the ship twice daily with vinegar and juniper berries, to cause fresh air." For each "freight", the weekly fare read as follows:

Sundays	-	one pound of beef boiled with rice
Mondays	-	barley and syrup
Tuesdays	-	one pound of white wheat flour
Wednesdays	-	one pound of bacon with peas
Thursdays	-	one pound of beef boiled with rice
Fridays	-	one pound of white wheat flour and a pound of butter
Saturdays	-	one pound of bacon, a pound of cheese, and six pounds of bread for the whole week.

In a postscript, the shipper wrote:

Because we as old merchants, who have transported people for twenty years and more, have recognized that bacon and meat are very strongly salted, from which salted provisions scurvy and other diseases arise, and the High Germans moreover are more used to fresh, rather than heavily salted provisions, we offer the passenger two or three fresh meals weekly ....[18]

The main problem was, notwithstanding all good intentions to feed passengers properly, that spoilage of provisions was high, e.g. beer, water, meat, and vegetables; anything not dried or salted did not keep. But intentions in the "Palatine trade"[19] were not always good, in spite of specific agreements:

[The most frequent complaint was the]... scantiness and poor quality of food served out to the passengers on the voyages. Revolting details of conditions often have to do with putrid and wormy food and incredibly foul water. Not infrequently contemporary mention of the emaciated and feeble state of immigrants upon landing in the New World is coupled with reference to the insufficient food on the voyage -- almost as though this were a familiar and well-understood circumstance. And notes of mortality at sea are often attributed partly to 'starvation'.[20]

There are many detailed accounts of conditions aboard emigrant ships.[21] One such contemporary report was left by Gottlieb Mittelberger, who departed from Germany via Cowes, England in 1750 and returned home in 1754.[22] He observed that during the two- to four-week crossing from Holland to Cowes, many immigrants consumed the provisions which had been intended for their voyage to Philadelphia, which could take another 8-12 weeks at sea. In the following abbreviated passage, Mittelberger's description of conditions on board explains why there was an average mortality rate of 10% on German emigrant ships.[23] This figure does not include the considerable casualties which occurred after disembarkment in North America:

... there arises in the ships a pitiful misery, stink ..., vomiting, all sorts of seasickness, fever ..., scurvy ..., mouth rot and the like, which are all caused by the old and very strongly salted food and meat, and by the very bad and putrid water by which many are pitifully ruined and die.

Added to this are the lack of food, the hunger, thirst ..., wetness ..., besides other hardships since lice often become such an awful plague, especially with sick people, that one can wipe them from the body. This misery comes to a high pitch when one has to endure a storm for two to three days and nights during which everyone believes the ship will go down with all its people. In such distress everyone prays and cries miserably ....

Among the healthy, there was at times [such] emotionality that they cursed one another or themselves and the hour in which they were born .... They blamed one another for the journey... and swore revenge but mostly on the people-thieves [i.e. the *Neuländer*].

Some sigh and cry out: Oh, if I were only at home again ..., [there are] those who feel guilty about having advised the journey. They are driven to despair, so that one cannot comfort such depressed people anymore. In a word, the sighing, crying and lamenting continues day and night, so that the heart of even the most hardened soul who hears this could bleed ....

A woman in our ship was in labour when we had a severe storm. She could not give birth under these circumstances. Because she was far back in the ship so that she could not be brought to the front, they pushed her through an opening in the side of the hull and dropped her into the sea.

Children between 1 and 7 years of age rarely survived the sea voyage. Parents sometimes have to watch their children languish miserably from want, hunger, thirst and other circumstances and see them die and be thrown into the water. I have unfortunately seen such pitiful and very sad events with 32 children of our ship who were committed to the sea. The parents were grieved even more because their children didn't have little beds in the earth but were

129

eaten by fish of prey .... [The meals] were almost unpalatable on account of the dirt, and the water which is distributed on board is often very black, thick and full of worms that one cannot drink it without aversion in spite of the greatest thirst .... The great hunger and thirst taught one to eat and drink everything but many an immigrant lost his life doing so.[24]

There are accounts in the files of the German Society of Philadelphia where ships were overladen by a factor of two or even three and almost half the emigrants, that is 400 out of 900, died *en route*.[25] Because of overloading, captains at times reduced the already meagre rations to half and even a quarter. Heinrich and Regina's two-year-old son Heinrich and one-year-old daughter Christina, who are known to have left with their parents,[26] are assumed to have shared the fate of many such children during the ocean voyage since no record of them has been found in Pennsylvania.

Many reports described the arrivals as walking skeletons and ghosts, like those previously mentioned who journeyed on the *Ann*. When yellow fever broke out in Philadelphia in 1749, it was the recent arrivals from Germany who, in their emaciated and weakened condition, succumbed to it *en masse*. As a result, Philadelphians referred to the disease from then on as "German distemper".[27] As was customary in those days, a doctor would examine the arrivals for communicable diseases. They were then marched, usually the same day, to the Court House in Philadelphia to pay homage to the King and then escorted back to their ship to await release on being "purchased" by an interested buyer.

When land was sighted, there was generally great rejoicing because an end to the suffering was in sight. It was like an elixir, in particular to the sick. Little did they know that they would have to remain on board, sometimes for weeks, until a buyer could be found to whom they could sell their services and who would, in return, pay their debts. The sick and weak, who needed to get off board first, were usually the last to disembark because no one was interested in buying them. Many an emigrant died in harbour in full view of the promised land. Strong, healthy men and women, in particular those with a trade, were excellent investments and did not have to wait long for a buyer. On the other hand, retired military officers and scholars were bad "merchandise" which nobody wanted. In an account of 1797,[28] von Bülow mentioned the case of a Russian army captain who could not be sold even at a discount of 50% of the "freight" owing.[29] Interested parties would often come from places several days' journey away when they heard that an immigrant ship had arrived or when they read immigrant "For Sale" notices in the Philadelphia papers.[30] If certain members of a family did not find a buyer, other members had to take over their share, sometimes indenturing themselves for ten years or more. In particular, children between five and ten years of age had to "serve" until they were twenty-one years old to pay off their "half-freight" of 30 guilders in cases where their parents could not. Should a family member have died during the voyage, the survivors were held responsible for their deceased brothers and sisters, mothers and fathers, husbands and wives. Not only children died in large numbers but also adults over the age of forty. Children ten and older who became orphaned *en route* were obliged to indenture themselves until twenty-one years of age[31] in order to pay off their deceased parents' full freights. Children could do little but watch their siblings being sold to different masters:

> As potential customers could not all gather at seaports when ships arrived, whereas the ships were anxious to get rid of their human cargoes quickly, a class of speculators grew up, who could buy redemptioners in batches, march them through the colonies in pathetic droves, bargaining with farmers and others along their routes, and selling their human merchandise at the best terms they could achieve. Families often irreparably sundered.[32]

If a servant of this kind wanted to get married, he or she had to pay £5 - £6 for each outstanding year of bondage.[33] Many, however, did not wait to pay their way out of intolerable or unjustly long periods of redemption as shown by the numerous notices about run-away servants in Philadelphia and Germantown newspapers.[34]

Of the Petitcodiac German families, it is known that Michael Lutz arrived in Philadelphia on board the *Phoenix* on Wednesday, November 22, 1752. The captain of the ship was Ruben Honor, who sailed to North America in the usual way from Rotterdam via Cowes on the Isle of Wight. Of the 150 heads of families who arrived alive, 13 remained on board

131

because they were too sick to walk to the Court House. Twenty-five signed with an "X", meaning they could not write; however Michael Lutz signed his name in good writing style as Jörg Michel Lutz. Walpurgis and both small children survived the voyage despite all hardships. The social and financial status of Michael Lutz and Heinrich Stieff in Germany show that they belonged to the overwhelming majority of immigrants of their day who had to indenture themselves for a period of several years to pay for the crossing. No information is available on the "purchase" of either Michael or Heinrich as indentured servants, nor is it known how many of their years in Pennsylvania were spent in this manner. Although "... there was abundant opportunity for abuse and exploitation, and there is evidence enough to show that these were widespread,"[35] the redemptioner principle in itself was a good one, enabling many thousands of German-speaking and other immigrants to come to North America. During the indenture period they could grow accustomed to the climate, to the different requirements in agriculture, and in general to their new lifestyle, notably the seemingly unlimited freedom which many Germans found confusing.[36] An inherent problem in this system was that they were more or less penniless at the end although certain "freedom dues" were to be issued to the person at that point, like clothing, a few implements, and seed grain.[37] Land prices by the middle of the 18th century, however, had risen beyond the means of the average immigrant. Long gone were the days of William Penn, who had stipulated that an indentured servant at the end of his service might take up fifty acres at a quit-rent of only half of what his master had paid for equal acreage.[38] Land, like so much else in North America, had become an object of speculation involving prominent Philadelphians and yet, in the absence of this activity, the Petitcodiac Germans might never have been enticed to come up to Nova Scotia.

ENDNOTES

[1] O. Langguth, "Auswanderer aus der Grafschaft Wertheim," p. 9. In this estimate of expenses, the cost of a rifle (11 guilders) was not included; a rifle was part of Körner's belongings, but most emigrants did not own one.

[2] Ehmer, *Geschichte der Grafschaft Wertheim*, p. 217.

[3] O. Langguth, "Auswanderer aus der Grafschaft Wertheim," p. 9.

[4] Bell, *Foreign Protestants*, p. 137.

[5] A ducat was a gold coin worth about 3 guilders or approximately 10 days of hard physical labour. Kapp, *Geschichte ...*, p. 289; O. Langguth, "Auswanderer aus der Grafschaft Wertheim," p. 5. One British £ was worth about 12 guilder/florins, and 1 guilder/florin was thus about 2 shillings. These equivalents are very approximate; Bell, *Foreign Protestants*, p. 261.

[6] Kapp, *Geschichte ...*, p. 290.

[7] *Ibid.*, p. 291.

[8] After 1729, a head tax of forty shillings was levied by the authorities of Philadelphia on Germans and Blacks. A similar but lower tax of 20 shillings on the Irish was revoked after nine months; Kapp, *Geschichte ...*, p. 291.

[9] £1.7 Pennsylvanian equalled £1.0 sterling in 1770; cf. Bell, *Foreign Protestants*, pp. 143f.. The English £ to florin ratio was about 1:10-12.

[10] This figure differs from that of 8 guilders suggested by O. Langguth. Mittelberger must have included all the incidental costs such as food, customs, passage fees, etc..

[11] Kapp, *Geschichte ...*, p. 286.

[12] Bell, *Foreign Protestants*, p. 143f.. Complicating factors in these calculations are the various currencies used. The British £, before its change to the decimal system, consisted of 20 shillings and each shilling of 12 pence.

[13] *Ibid.*, p. 260.

[14] Kapp, *Geschichte ...*, p. 294.

[15] Bell, *Foreign Protestants*, p. 232.

[16] *Ibid.*, p. 233. In the following I am drawing on information from pp. 153-155, 168-169, 241, and 256-257.

[17] O. Langguth, "Auswanderer aus der Grafschaft Wertheim," p. 14.

[18] *Loc. cit.*.

[19] Bell, *Foreign Protestants*, p. 241.

[20] *Ibid.*, pp. 240-241.

[21] *Ibid.*, p. 219; Kapp, *Geschichte ...*, pp. 278ff..

[22] *Ibid.*, p. 280. Many of Mittelberger's claims are substantiated by other accounts such as the records of the Harrisburg State Archives and the German Society of Pennsylvania, which, in later years, did much to assist the victimized Germans.

[23] Kapp, *Geschichte ...*, p. 280. See also the mortality rate in transit among the Lunenburg Germans arriving from 1750-1752; Bell, *Foreign Protestants*, p. 251.

[24] Kapp, *Geschichte ...*, pp. 283ff..

[25] *Ibid.*, p. 289.

[26] Werner Hacker, *Eighteenth-Century Register of Emigrants from Southwest Germany* (Apollo, Pennsylvania: Cosson Press, 1994), p. 445.

[27] *Ibid.*, p. 288. This same susceptibility to disease as the result of stressful voyages must have been the underlying reason why so many Irish succumbed to cholera on Grosse Île, Québec, during the last century.

[28] D. von Bülow, *Der Freistaat von Nord-Amerika in seinem neuesten Zustand*, 2 Theile, 12, II (Berlin: 1797), pp. 86-101.

[29] Kapp, *Geschichte ...*, p. 296.

[30] These advertisements are useful in tracing immigrants upon their arrival in Philadelphia. There is a room filled with uncatalogued newspapers in the Historical Society of Pennsylvania which might yield a great deal of information about the Petitcodiac Germans some day.

[31] Kapp, *Geschichte ...*, pp. 294ff.; cf. also Bell, *Foreign Protestants*, pp. 142 ff..

[32] *Ibid.*, p. 145.

[33] The use of the term "bondage" in this context is clearly different from the one used with serfs. If each year was valued at £5 to £6 and a freight cost £10, it follows that the voyage could have been payed off in two years or less.

[34] Edward W. Hocker, *Genealogical Data Relating to the German Settlers of Pennsylvania and Adjacent Territory from Advertisements in German Newspapers Published in Philadelphia and Germantown, 1743-1800* (Baltimore: Genealogical Publishing Co., Inc., 1981).

[35] Bell, *Foreign Protestants*, p. 146.

[36] Roeber, *Palatines, Liberty, and Property*, pp. 17ff..

[37] *Ibid.*, pp. 144f.. Mittelberger even mentioned that a man was to be given a horse and a woman a cow; cf. Kapp, *Geschichte ...*, p. 295.

[38] Frank Ried Diffenderffer, *German Immigration into Pennsylvania* and *The Redemptioners* [Originally Published as Part VII of *Pennsylvania: The German Influence in its Settlement and Development* (Lancaster, Pennsylvania: Pennsylvania-German Society, 1900] (Baltimore: Genealogical Publishing Co., 1977), pp. 267f..

CHAPTER IV

The Petitcodiac Germans in Pennsylvania

Since the latter part of the 17th century, Pennsylvania had been the preferred American destination for German-speaking immigrants. William Penn had visited Germany personally in August 1677 in the hope of recruiting settlers for his proposed colony. His expectations of support were well founded because German pietists had turned away from dogmatic institutions back to more mystical, spiritualistic, and Anabaptist traditions in reaction to the roles played by established churches during the Thirty Years' War. The hostile attitude of the Lutheran church toward pietistic sects, in contrast to Penn's invitation to share his ideals of religious freedom, radical pacifism, and friendship, precipitated the dream of a truly Christian life in the New World and affirms a direct link between pietism and German emigration to North America. Following William Penn's visit to Mennonites in Krefeld and Quakers in Frankfurt/Main, pietists there founded the *Frankfurter Companie*, which bought about 10,000 acres of land from Penn's agent in London for the settlement of fellow-believers. The founding of Philadelphia[1] by Dutch and German Quakers in 1682 was followed by the arrival of 13 Krefeld families on October 6, 1683, who subsequently founded Germantown on the eastern bank of Wissahickon Creek, about 11 km north of the Old Philadelphia centre, under the leadership of Franz Daniel Pastorius. This marked the beginning of large-scale German immigration to North America, and thousands followed these first pioneer families in the next decade alone. The promise of religious freedom initially caused many persecuted people to seek a new life in Philadelphia, but the town's reputation as a thriving community attracted others who, while never persecuted, had been living in economically depressed circumstances. Extensive areas of the proprietary colony[2] were settled by *Pennsylvanisch Deutsche* in such numbers that Anglophones living in their midst often became linguistically and culturally assimilated. The Germans soon over-flowed from Old Philadelphia and Germantown to adjacent areas such as Roxborough, just west of Germantown and between Wissahickon Creek and the Schuylkill River.[3] They also spread toward Frankford on the Delaware River, about 10 km north-east of Philadelphia, and toward Barren Hill, about

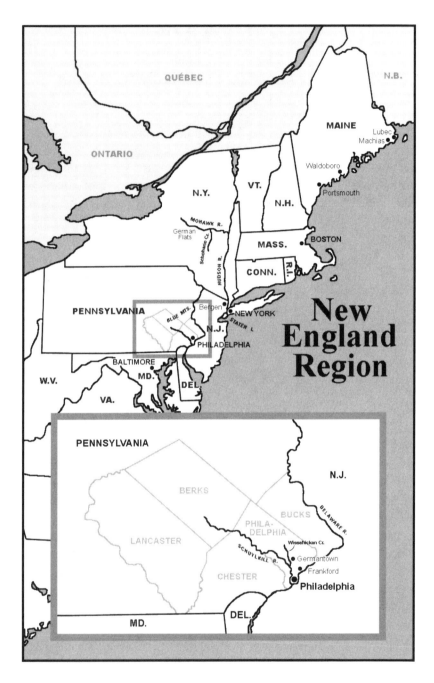

Map 2

10 km north of Germantown near Whitemarsh and beyond Chestnut Hill. Eventually they settled further north in Montgomery County and particularly in Lancaster County to the west. This area has remained a centre of Pennsylvania German culture, renowned for foods such as *Sauerkraut*, *Schnitz* (dried apple slices), *Speck* (smoked bacon), a variety of baked goods, sausages, and cheeses, as well as for characteristic farming, building, and heating techniques, paper-making and printing in the Germantown area,[4] styles of furniture, weaving, writing (*Fraktur*), drawing and embroidery (with characteristic heart, tulip, and bird motifs), and not least of all, for the Conestoga wagon and Pennsylvania rifle.

The influx of many new immigrants around 1750 exceeded the ability of these vibrant and prosperous German communities to provide all newcomers with employment and affordable land. The Petitcodiac Germans -- Copple (*Koppel*), Lutz, Ricker, Sommer, Stieff, Treitz, and Wortman(n) -- found themselves at this time caught up in the oversupply of labour which must have hindered their attempts to settle, enough that they once more felt inclined to seek new opportunities elsewhere.

Through numerous baptismal records of St. Michaelis and Zion Lutheran Churches in Philadelphia[5] and St. Michael's Evangelical Lutheran Church in Germantown, significant information can be gleaned for some of the Petitcodiac Germans, helping to fill out the picture of their beginnings in North America and to confirm that the Lutz, Stieff, and Sommer families had been living in the vicinity of Germantown, Pennsylvania since about 1750 and probably knew one another.[6] These entries furthermore establish that the religious background of these families was Lutheran and not Baptist.[7] Information obtained from the journals of two Pennsylvanian clergymen sheds additional light on the Petitcodiac Germans during this phase of their lives. These pastors made their congregations aware of other German-speaking settlements, including that of Lunenburg in Nova Scotia, and were better informed about them and the opportunities there than has hitherto been realized.

One entry in the baptismal records of St. Michael's Lutheran Church (fig. 13) in the heart of old Philadelphia is for Anna Margaretha Lutz, who was born March 4, 1755 and baptized March 10th. Her parents were Jürg

Figure 13

St. Michaelis Evangelical Lutheran Church in Philadelphia, built 1743, demolished 1870; picture drawn by Birch, 1799.

138

Michael Lutz[8] and Anna Wallpurge [sic], who lived *4 Meilen aus der Stadt* (four miles out of town).[9] The witnesses were David and Anna Margaretha Heim. Since it is recorded that Michael Lutz, along with Matthias Sommer and Heinrich Stieff, was naturalized several years later[10] in the Township of Roxborough, Michael's place of residence may have been near there. Georg Michael Lutz, Anna Walpurgis, and their two children had not only been fortunate enough to survive the sea voyage but also to enter the services of someone close to Philadelphia and not in some remote part of Pennsylvania. Since Roxborough was a rural area then, it is most likely that Michael worked as a labourer on a well-established farm, gaining valuable experience about larger-scale operations in North America. At St. Michael's Evangelical Lutheran Church in Germantown (fig.14), Georg Michael Lutz and Anna Walpurgis returned the favour on February 16, 1756 by standing as witnesses at the baptism of Anna Walpurger [sic], the daughter of David and Margaretha Heim.

Michael's older brother Thomas, his wife Barbara, and their son Friedrich arrived in Philadelphia in 1755.[11] Another son, Johannes, was born to this couple two years later and baptized in St. Michael's Lutheran Church. Thomas left Germany three years after his brother, lived fairly close to him upon arrival, and likely decided to come at Michael's recommendation (the special circumstance[12] that permitted his emigration). All this suggests that Michael and Walpurgis must have settled reasonably comfortably, enough at least to invite their kin to join them, especially after the birth of their son Thomas about 1753. Michael's brother Thomas remained permanently in Philadelphia, began a second branch of the Lutz family, and his descendants have recently been in contact with those of Michael Lutz in Moncton. The baptismal register for Germantown's St. Michael's Evangelical Lutheran Church includes an entry on August 13, 1758, for the infant Georg Michael, the son of Georg Michael Lutz and "Anna Marg.[sic]; his wife." Anna *Margaretha* was the name of Michael's daughter and Anna Walpurgis, his wife. Undoubtedly a mistake was made and the names of the mother and daughter inadvertently interchanged. This erroneous entry has been the source of misunderstanding by Lutz descendants in New Brunswick who believed that Michael Lutz' wife was called Anna Margaretha. Since this church and many others often relied on itinerants and guest preachers, mistakes undoubtedly occurred, especially if the baptism took place in the

139

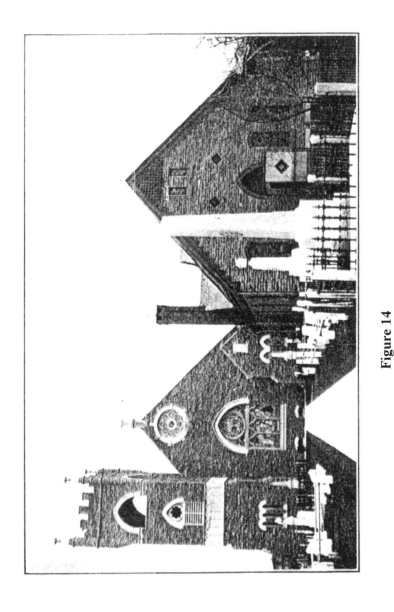

Figure 14

St. Michael's Lutheran Church of Germantown, first German Lutheran Congregation in Pennsylvania, organized in 1730; Picture by Moses King, *Philadelphia and Notable Philadelphians* (New York: Moses King, 1901), p. 116.

parents' home -- and if the particulars were entered into the church records only *after* the jovial, Old Country-style celebrations had come to an end.[13] There are records for the son Michael Lutz[14] in New Brunswick, as well as for John[15] and Henry.[16] The Lutz family may have left the Germantown area sometime before 1766, which might explain the absence of some of these birth records there.

Perhaps the most significant recent discovery in this context is an entry made on April 20, 1766,[17] at which time Jacob Stieff and Anna Catharina Lutzin (the suffix *"in"* denotes the feminine form of the name Lutz) stood as witnesses at the baptism of Anna Margaretha Pflanz in St. Michaelis Lutheran Church, Philadelphia. Written in a margin above is the German inscription: *"Leute die heute abreisen nach Nova Schottland"* ("People who depart for Nova Scotia today"). This confirms their date of departure from Philadelphia which was not previously known.[18] Jacob Stieff and Anna Catharina Lutz, at 17 years of age, were old enough to be sponsors since Catharina was born in Kreuzwertheim on January 11, 1749 and Jacob in Philadelphia on November 14, 1749.[19] That these two stood together at the altar on the very day they were supposed to leave may have been no mere coincidence, for Anna Catharina Lutz and Jacob Stieff, as the first-born children of the pioneer Lutz and Stieff families, were also the first Petit-codiac German couple to be married in their new homeland, on January 28, 1772.[20] Their birth dates indicate that the bride was 23 and the groom 22 at the time of their wedding.

On September 17, 1753, Heinrich Stieff's brother Friederich[21] arrived in Philadelphia on the ship *Richard and Mary*. This same "George Friederick Steif" [sic], or "Steiff" [sic],[22] and his wife, Maria Catharina [sic], were sponsors at Germantown church baptisms in 1755, 1756, and 1758, including that of Frederic Stieff,[23] the fourth son of Heinrich and Regina Stieff. As shown by the date of their first-born son Jacob, Heinrich and his wife had been in North America at least since November of 1749. According to tax records, "Henry Stiff" paid his taxes in Brecknock, Lancaster County, in 1751.[24] Both Stieff couples were raising their families at the same time. Birth records show that Heinrich and Regina's American-born second, third, and fourth sons were from the Germantown vicinity; no records have been located for the fifth, sixth, and seventh sons, suggesting that the family lived

141

either at Barren Hill or somewhere else. Like the Lutz's, the Stieffs were back in Philadelphia by 1766. The above entries prove, contrary to many sources,[25] that all of Heinrich and Regina's surviving seven sons were born in North America, beginning in 1749 with Johann Jacob.[26] They also show that in Philadelphian records Heinrich's wife was still known as *Regina,* and not as "Rachel", the name she came to use in Hillsborough. It is no surprise to see how Americans could have changed the Latin-German name *Regina* (German: "Raygeenah" with a "g" as in "give") to Rachel, since many an immigrant has had his or her name changed beyond recognition by the different phonetic rules of English.[27]

There is considerable archival evidence for the Sommer family in Philadelphia, Germantown, and Barren Hill, including some indication as to why they may have thought it best to leave Pennsylvania. The first mention of Matthias Sommer is the occasion of his marriage to Christina Nullin (again the feminine form "*in*" of the name "Null") at St. Michaelis Lutheran Church in Philadelphia on October 23, 1749. About a half year later, he and his wife Christina (Sommerin) stood in the same church as witnesses at another wedding.[28] Here in November 1750 they baptized their daughter Anna Catharina[29] and three years later, Eva Magdalena. No birth records were located for Sarah or Christianna, who were also likely daughters from Matthias's first marriage. There is no further record of Christina after she and Matthias were witnesses at a marriage on November 20, 1752, and sponsors at the baptism on October 7, 1753, of Margretha Sommer, whose father Hans Georg Sommer was perhaps a relative.[30] Christina must have died sometime in 1757, for on August 15, 1758, the widower Matthias Sommer from Frankford, south-east of Germantown along the Delaware River, married Magdalena Aldmann, a widow from the same community. A daughter, Elizabeth, was born to this couple on August 5, 1759. Clark Wright mentions that Matthias was the father of three other girls [31] -- besides Sarah, Deborah, and Rachel born in 1764.[32] Sarah was likely a daughter of Christina, given her 1771 marriage date, but Deborah was the eldest daughter of Andrew Sommer and thus Matthias' granddaughter. Andrew, born around 1765, was Matthias Sommer's only male heir by his second wife, Magdalena (Aldmann). It is assumed that she came up to Nova Scotia although her name appears nowhere in local documents. It is curious that Andrew did not name one of his eight daughters after his mother although several are named after his sisters. Sarah (Sommer) Allen and Rachel (Sommer) Stieff also never used the name Magdalena.

Sometime after Elizabeth's birth in 1759, Matthias and his wife moved from Frankford to the Germantown area. There they attended the Germantown church but soon became embroiled in what Rev. Heinrich Melchior Mühlenberg, a well-known pastor of this community, referred to disparagingly as "revolution and persecution"[33] within the Germantown congregation. According to Hocker: "A strong element in the Germantown congregation was antagonistic to the trend toward Pietism which in its milder form received the approbation of Muhlenberg .... Under the pastorate of a pronounced Pietist ... the disputes culminated in a split in St. Michael's congregation."[34] In spite of Mühlenberg's efforts, the minority sympathetic to Pietistic theology was ousted. Valentin Müller[35] (also spelled "Mueller" and "Miller"), who co-signed the agreement to settle either in "Monckton" or "Frankfort" in Nova Scotia but later renegued, was also involved in these disturbances which surfaced in 1753 and continued for about a decade. A number of German Lutheran and Reformed families founded the new St. Peter's Lutheran church in Barren Hill, about 11 km north of Germantown in Whitemarsh Township. In 1758, Valentin Müller was mentioned as one of the Lutheran trustees to acquire an acre of land to establish a graveyard and schoolhouse at the future Barren Hill Church site.[36] This stone church, for which Rev. Mühlenberg laid the cornerstone, was completed in 1763, but the costs of the building were such that members of the congregation had difficulty meeting their payments. Rev. Mühlenberg was one clergyman to preach to this Reformed Lutheran congregation at Barren Hill, which did not have a regular pastor until 1793. So, too, did Rev. Michael Schlatter,[37] a lifelong friend of Mühlenberg.

Both Revs. Mühlenberg and Schlatter contributed greatly to the spiritual lives of the parishioners in the Philadelphia, Germantown, and Barren Hill churches. Schlatter was an energetic, at times controversial, figure who returned to Europe twice and held many pastoral positions in Pennsylvania and New Jersey: "Between 1747 and his first return to Europe ... in 1751, he travelled more than 8,000 miles and preached 635 times."[38] In 1757, he became a chaplain in the Royal American Regiment on Foot and was present at the siege and capture of the French stronghold of Louisbourg in July 1758, where he must have met Samuel von Waldo. He preached to Germans in Halifax, Nova Scotia, and agreed to deliver a call to Mühlenberg from the Lutherans of Halifax and Lunenburg. Schlatter served as chaplain in the 2nd Battalion of the Royal American Regiment, composed of German, Dutch, and Swiss Protestants, during the Henry Bouquet expedition against First Nation tribes in 1764[39] and likely met the German Adam Hoops, future proprietor of Germantown, N. B. (cf. Chp. V.1), who also served under Bouquet and later invited him to become a shareholder in the Germantown land development scheme. After 1758, Rev. Schlatter made his permanent home in Chestnut Hill, slightly north of Roxborough and Germantown, Pennsylvania. Such proximity suggests that his knowledge of Nova Scotia and experiences there were communicated on numerous occasions to the Philadelphia, Germantown, and Barren Hill congregations. This shows that there were direct links throughout the 18th century between Lunenburg/Halifax and Germantown/Philadelphia and that the Germans of Nova Scotia were not as culturally isolated as once thought. The Schlatter-Hoops connection furthermore confirms that the proprietor of Germantown, N.B., namely Adam Hoops, was well-acquainted with the northern provinces before he became involved in settlement schemes along the Petitcodiac River.

The importance of Rev. Heinrich Melchior Mühlenberg to this story, in addition to his being the "Father of Lutheranism in America,"[40] rests in the publication of his *Journals* in three volumes, which contain a wealth of information about life in Pennsylvania and shed light specifically on the activities of the Petitcodiac Germans. On March 1, 1765, Rev. Mühlenberg entered in his *Journal*: "In the forenoon we had a wearisome conference with several trustees of the Barren Hill Church. Present ... from Barren Hill, Christoph Rabe, Matth. Sommer, Valentin Müller, Christoph Selig ...."[41] An entry two weeks later[42] recorded that an agreement had been reached between trustees of the Barren Hill and Philadelphia churches that Mühlenberg would assume the Barren Hill Church debt of £531 and try to collect this money in Europe for the church's benefit, as well as provide occasional pastoral visits to the Barren Hill Church. The accord was signed by trustees Christoph Rabe, Matthias Sommer, and Valentin Müller of the Barren Hill Church and trustees Wrangel, Keppele and Rev. Mühlenberg of the Philadelphia Church with Johann Michael Selig as witness.[43] Since "the reuniting of the Germantown congregation in 1764 deprived ... [the Barren

144

Hill Church] of some of its strongest members"[44] when the latter church property was deeded to the parent Philadelphia Lutheran congregation in 1766, one may conclude that two of the leaders, Matthias Sommer and Valentin Müller, probably thought it wiser to abandon the sinking ship and seek their fortunes elsewhere rather than stay and watch in humiliation how their "separatist" cause of the last few years evaporated. As late as April 1, 1766, their signatures as trustees of the Barren Hill Church appear in a letter to the Archbishop of Canterbury,[45] a full two months *after* they signed the "Articles of Agreement" to become settlers of "Monckton" along the Petitcodiac River (cf. Chp. V.2 concerning this "Agreement"). On the latter document, the signatures of Matthias Sommer and Valentin Miller [sic] immediately follow that of John Hughes, the businessman in charge of this settlement scheme (figs.1, 1a).

Whereas the documentary evidence suggests some personal reasons as to why the Sommer family left the Germantown/Philadelphia area, such reasons are absent for the Lutz and Stieff families. It is puzzling that Thomas Lutz and Frederick Stieff, both of whom followed their brothers to the New World, managed to settle successfully in Philadelphia while Michael Lutz and Heinrich Stieff, who presumably invited them to this land of opportunity, felt by 1766 that it was time to embark on yet another search for a better life. Catharina Müller of Kreuzwertheim, one of many who arrived with the large-scale immigration around 1750, also succeeded eventually, as a letter of 1780 sent to Wertheim attests, in which the author claimed, "the war has made many of our countrymen rich."[46] Realities of the day, however, must have fallen short of the expectations of many an immigrant. Perhaps it was simply a quest for that ultimate goal, i.e. a farm large enough to feed a growing family. A promise of free land was held out, and the distance seemed short, certainly for those who had already crossed the Atlantic.

It was not just through Rev. Schlatter that potential emigrants to the Petitcodiac heard about Nova Scotia but also through Rev. Mühlenberg, who wrote in his diary in late fall of 1764:

In the evening I was invited to the home of some English friends where there was a Colonel who is the king's agent for giving out the vacant land in Nova Scotia, ... I was asked whether I, too, would not like to take up several thousand acres for my three sons. A thousand acres cost between £2 and £3 Sterling for the surveying fee, and the land is free of ground rent for ten years; however, some building must be done upon the land within three years. It is in a cold climate, like that of the kingdom of Sweden, and it is very hard to cultivate anything in such a terrible wilderness, but in a very short time the said agent has already disposed of 300,000 acres to prominent Englishmen here in Philadelphia. The agent's name is M'Nutt.[47]

There can be little doubt that the availability of inexpensive land in the northern provinces was a topic widely discussed in the German congregations of the Philadelphia area. The invitation of this well-known pastor to an evening with Alexander McNutt was a masterstroke in public relations. Mühlenberg, whose influence was far-reaching, had no idea that this invitation had brought him in contact with an entrepreneur and schemer *par excellence*, whose claims that he had "... already disposed of 300,000 acres to prominent Englishmen ... in Philadelphia" were as inflated as his insatiable lust for land in later years when the actual grants were distributed. Despite his controversial character, Alexander McNutt must be recognized as one of the catalysts in the resettlement of Germans to "Neuschottland", part of which became New Brunswick. Since Mühlenberg was not just a man of God but also a man of practicality, he undoubtedly spoke of the golden opportunities in the northern provinces, especially to his parishioners in greatest need.

Knowledge of Nova Scotia which Rev. Mühlenberg, his trustees, and the greater Philadelphia congregations possessed came also through direct contacts with Lunenburg rather than solely *via* Rev. Schlatter and promoter Alexander McNutt. On May 21, 1765, Mühlenberg made a *Journal* entry regarding "a communication from Hallifax [sic] ... [i]n Nova Scotia, concerning congregational affairs."[48] A later entry on June 19th mentioned "a so-called preacher who came here [to Philadelphia] about twelve years ago from Nova Scotia, by way of New York, and has been serving several poor congregations in the Blue Mountains. His mother, a widow who lives in Hamburg, has been importuning me by letter for two years to send her news concerning her son."[49] This so-called preacher was Daniel Schumacher, a theology candidate, who sailed on the *Speedwell* to Halifax in 1751 at age 22 and married Catherine Haun in that city two years later, in July of 1753.[50] It is surprising that Schumacher left Halifax in the year of his marriage, never to take occupancy of the town lot to which he held title in Lunenburg. Instead, he decided to serve congregations in the Blue Mountains, despite the fact that there was such a desperate need for German-speaking Lutheran ministers in Lunenburg. Schumacher's later "unfavourable reputation in Pennsylvania"[51] had perhaps already begun in Nova Scotia, prompting his untimely departure from the region.

One further entry in the *Journals* as late as 1768, postdating the departure of the Petitcodiac Germans for "Monckton", confirms the extent of knowledge Rev. Mühlenberg and his congregations in Philadelphia had concerning the affairs and needs of Lunenburg, N.S.: "A letter from Lüneburg, in Nova Scotia, signed by several Germans, was read. We added what we had learned concerning Lüneburg from other *oral and written reports.*"[52] Similar information which W.P. Bell obtained much later as part of his research about Lunenburg[53] already surfaces in condensed form in the Mühlenberg's *Journals*, particularly regarding the struggles of the Lunenburgers to obtain a Lutheran minister who could preach to them in German. Somewhat amused, Mühlenberg added:

> Those Germans [of Lunenburg], however, who are strong-minded seem to have [a] congenital suspicion and empathy against every foreign language and prefer, if possible, to live and die faithful to their mother tongue. For they suppose that German was probably the language which Adam and Eve originally spoke in Paradise, all contrary opinions of the *critici* notwithstanding.[54]

As late as 1770, Mühlenberg was in contact with a Swedish-German colleague, Rev. Paul Daniel Bryzelius of "Lüneburg, Nova Scotia", who was finally sent by the British to fulfill the wishes of the German immigrants in that community. Documents reveal, moreover, that the knowledge which Petitcodiac settlers had of Lunenburg resulted in direct communications between the two German settlements, for Rev. Bryzelius visited the Petitcodiac Germans in 1768 and preached to them in their mother tongue.

ENDNOTES

[1] Philadelphia means "brotherly love" in Greek and was known as the "Quaker City".

[2] Pennsylvania remained in the possession of the Penn family until the American War of Independence.

[3] Insight into Pennsylvanian life during the colonial period can be gained through local-historical studies such as Philip E. Pendleton, *Oley Valley Heritage: The Colonial Years 1700-1775* (Birdboro, Pennsylvania: Pennsylvania German Society, 1994).

[4] Wilhelm Rettinghaus founded the first papermill on this side of the Atlantic in 1690, and Christoph Sauer printed the first German Bible on American soil in 1743.

[5] Two separate Lutheran Churches existed in Philadelphia in the 18th century, which were both demolished in the 19th century but whose records were later combined.

[6] Although several examples of the names Ricker, Tritz/Treitz, and Wortman were found in Pennsylvanian sources, those of Petitcodiac Germans were not among them.

[7] David G. Bell, ed., *Newlight Baptist Journals of James Manning and James Innis* (Hantsport: Lancelot Press, 1984), p. 57. Clark Wright claims in *Samphire Greens* (p. 4) that the Stieffs were Baptists in Pennsylvania.

[8] Because numerous emigrants with the surname Lutz are on record in both Philadelphia and Germany, it has been difficult at times to determine who is who. There are several by the name of Michael Lutz alone. One Michael Lutz is recorded in Periomen Township, Montgomery County in the 1770's, and another emigrated from Wertheim in 1752. The circumstances and general poverty of the latter were similar to the Kreuzwertheim emigrant. Both wanted to emigrate to Pennsylvania.

[9] Comment in the margin of Anna Margaretha's baptismal record.

[10] Their date of naturalization was September 22, 1765.

[11] He had only 21 "Gulden" worth of personal property; cf. O. Langguth, "Auswanderer aus der Grafschaft Wertheim", p. 22.

[12] *Ibid.*, p.11: "*Keinem leibeigenen Untertanen [wird] das Emigrieren, außer in ganz besonderen ... Fällen erlaubt.*"

[13] "In the colonial era, ... liquor flowed freely as part of family entertainment as well as those social events where the folk community gathered, e.g. baptisms, weddings, funerals .... After the temperance reform, drinking, like some of the older folk-cultural amusements and recreations, was made into a sin ... [and] temperance [became accepted] as normative for religion;" Don Yoder, *Discovering American Folklife: Studies in Ethnic, Religious, and Regional*

Culture (Ann Arbor, Michigan: UMI Research Press, 1989), p.133.

[14] Michael Lutz[2] or Michael Lutz[3] purchased property in Hillsborough in 1800 and is listed as a father of six in the 1803 Census of this township.

[15] Clark Wright, *The Petitcodiac*, p. 47; Clark Wright, *Planters and Pioneers*, rev. ed. (Hantsport, N. S.: Lancelot Press, 1982), p. 198.

[16] In the 1775/1783 Hillsborough census, Henry Lutz is listed as a "young man".

[17] St. Michaelis and Zion Lutheran Church, Philadelphia Baptisms: 1745-1771.

[18] I published my discovery in an earlier article, "Early German Settlements on the Petitcodiac River in New Brunswick," *German Canadian Yearbook*, XIII (Toronto: Historical Society of Mecklenburg, 1993), pp. 124-148.

[19] St. Michaelis and Zion Lutheran Church, Philadelphia: Johann Jacob Stieff, son of Heinrich and Regina, born November 14, 1749.

[20] Clark Wright, *Samphire Greens*, p. 33. The incorrect or missing data regarding the birth dates of Catharina and Jacob in the Appendix of Clark Wright's book, *Samphire Greens,* and other genealogies can now be filled in.

[21] This passenger is listed as "Geor. Fred. Stkief" in: Ralph B. Strassbourger and W. J. Hinke, *Pennsylvania German Pioneers* (Norristown: 1934/1966), List 201A. Don Yoder in his book, *Pennsylvania German Immigrants* (p. 122) lists him as "Georg Friedrich Stieff".

[22] *Georg, George, Jurg* and *Jürg* are all the same name, as can be seen with *Georg, Jurg,* and *Jürg* in the Lutz family, i.e. the grandfather of Michael Lutz. The different spellings of the name *Stieff* should also not confuse the reader into thinking that this is a different family. The entries in the back of the Stieff-Bible are spelled: "Stiff," "Stif," and "Stüff" -- three versions by the same person since the handwriting is identical. Standardization of orthography had not taken place, and people at the time were more concerned with the way a name sounded rather than the way it was written. The name *Treitz*/Trites is another example of this phenomenon.

[23] Frederick was born on August 8, 1755 and baptized on November 9, 1755.

[24] Gary T. Hawbaker and Clyde L. Groff, *A New Index: Lancaster County Pennsylvania before the Federal Census,* Vol. 3, Index to the 1750 Tax Records (Elizabethtown: Gary T. Hawbaker, n.d.).

[25] Clark Wright, *The Petitcodiac*, p. 54; many others use this author as a source.

[26] It also shows that the Hillsborough "Census" of 1770, discussed in the next chapter, was correct. The "Henry Steeve" family is listed as consisting of seven Americans and two Germans, which means that the boys were all born in America and their parents, Heinrich and Regina, in Germany.

[27] The name "Rachel," which was uncommon in Germany at that time, has given rise to much speculation, e.g. that Regina's maiden name was "De Cour"; cf. Sharon Fehr, *Steeves, Ruggles, Ripley, Passon, Gray Families, 1730-1984*, 16 pages typescript. Cf. also Frederick Walter Hilbig, *Americanization of German Surnames*; Diss. University of Utah (1958).

[28] St. Michaelis Lutheran Church, April 1, 1750.

[29] According to the records of St. Michaelis and Zion Lutheran Churches, Anna Catharina Sommer was baptized on November 18, 1750 and Eva Magdalena on March 11, 1753.

[30] Another entry appears in the burial records for a George Sommer, possibly the same Hans Georg, who died at the age of 29 in 1758.

[31] Clark Wright, *Planters and Pioneers*, p. 284; it is uncertain which girls she was referring to although they may have been the three for whom records were found.

[32] Rachel Sommer, born January 31, 1764, married Frederick Stieff on June 25, 1780, at age 16.

[33] Charles H. Glatfelder, *Pastors and People*, German Lutheran and Reformed Churches in the Pennsylvania Field, 1717-1793, Vol. I, Pastors & Congregations (Bremigsville, Pennsylvania: The Pennsylvania German Society, 1980), p. 370.

[34] Edward W. Hocker, *Germantown: 1683-1933* (Germantown, Philadelphia, Pa.: author, 1933), pp. 64f..

[35] Valentin Müller arrived on board the *Edinburgh* on September 5, 1748; Daniel Rupp, *A Collection of... Thirty Thousand Names of German, Swiss, Dutch, French Immigrants in Pennsylvania from 1727 to 1776* (Baltimore, Maryland: Genealogical Publishing Company, 1965), p. 181.

[36] Article on Barren Hill, Whitemarsh Township: Glatfelder, *Pastors & People*, p. 370. Unfortunately, numerous documents for this church have been lost, including baptismal records that might have helped this study.

[37] For more information on this pastor, consult Marthi Pritzker-Ehrlich's article, "Michael Schlatter (1716-1790): A Man-In-Between," *Yearbook of German-American Studies*, Vol. 20 (Lawrence, Ka.: Society for German-American Studies, 1985), pp. 83-95.

[38] *Ibid.*, p. 117.

[39] Marthi Pritzker-Ehrlich, "Michael Schlatter (1716-1790) ...," p. 90.

[40] Bell, *Foreign Protestants*, p. 156.

[41] *Journals of Henry Melchior Muhlenberg in Three Volumes*, translated by T. G. Tappert and J. W. Doberstein, Vol. II (Philadelphia: Evangelical Lutheran Ministerium and Muhlenberg Press, 1955), p. 206.

[42] The meeting took place on March 13, 1765.

[43] *Journals of ... Muhlenberg*, p. 209.

150

[44] Glatfelder, *Pastors & People*, p. 370.

[45] *Journals of... Muhlenberg*, p. 303.

[46] O. Langguth, "Auswanderer aus der Grafschaft Wertheim," p. 14.

[47] *Journals of... Muhlenberg*, p. 143.

[48] *Ibid.*, p. 235.

[49] *Ibid.*, p. 244.

[50] Clark Wright, *Planters and Pioneers*, p. 272.

[51] Bell, *Foreign Protestants*, p. 393.

[52] *Journals of... Muhlenberg*, p. 370; my italics.

[53] Bell, *Foreign Protestants*, pp. 580 ff..

[54] *Journals of... Muhlenberg*, p. 370.

CHAPTER V

Northbound to a Vacant[1] Land

The hopes for unlimited and inexpensive land in North America that had attracted thousands of impoverished Germans proved increasingly unattainable in the second half of the 18th century. The southern portion of the present United States was to a large extent taken up by plantations. New settlers were frustrated in their attempts to find land for themselves and also to secure gainful employment in the early years since most field labour was carried out by slaves.[2] In the northern states which accepted the bulk of the immigrants, good land for settlement was becoming evermore scarce, especially in Pennsylvania which was the destination of many German immigrants and whose population by 1770 had grown to a quarter million. Land further west belonged to indigenous peoples by treaty with the British Crown and was not available for settlement at this time.

For political, economic, and military reasons, Britain sought to settle its more northerly possessions, in particular Nova Scotia, which had been handed over to England by France in the Peace of Utrecht of 1713. When the Fortress of Louisbourg in Cape Breton returned to the French in 1748 under the Treaty of Aachen, the English responded quickly to counterbalance this presence by founding Halifax a year later.[3]

In a letter to the Lords' Commissioners for Trade and Plantations on July 14, 1749, Governor Cornwallis stated that the British immigrants who had arrived the previous month were totally unsuited as settlers. He suggested that German and Swiss Protestants be encouraged to settle instead because they had earned a good reputation and were credited with the successful development of Pennsylvania by Lord Halifax and Governor Shirley of Massachusetts. The recruitment of such settlers in central Europe, their arrival in Halifax, and the founding of Lunenburg took place over the next five to six years. Further settlement was interrupted by the Seven Years' War (1756-1763),[4] in which Prussia and Great Britain prevailed against Russia, Austria, and France. In addition, large tracts of heretofore cultivated land became vacant in 1755 when the English expelled the French-

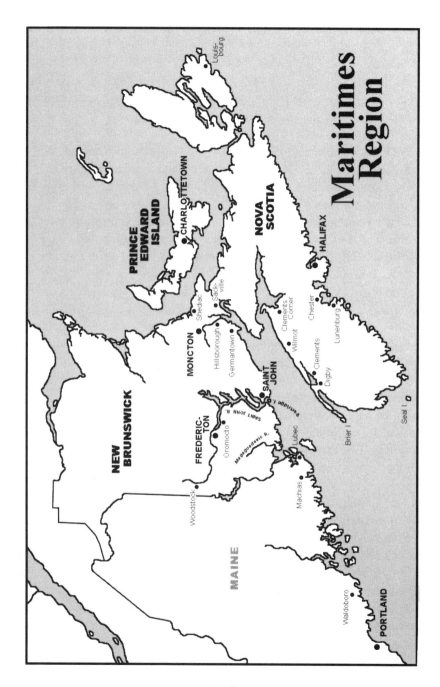

Map 3

153

speaking Acadians upon their refusal to swear allegiance to the British King.[5]

To resettle this area with trustworthy Protestant stock became all the more essential. Governor Lawrence of Nova Scotia issued his proclamation to this effect on October 12, 1758:

> Whereas by the late Success of His Majesty's Arms at the Reduction of Cape Breton, and its Dependencies, as also by the Demolition and entire Destruction of Gaspee, Meremichi, and other French Settlements, situated on the Gulf of St. Lawrence, and on St. John's River and the Bay of Fundy, the enemy, who have formerly disturbed and harassed the Province of Nova Scotia, and much obstructed its Progress, have now been compelled to retire and take Refuge in Canada, a favourable Opportunity now presents for peopling and cultivating, as well as the Lands vacated by the French, as every other Part of this valuable Province ....[6]

Another proclamation was issued shortly thereafter detailing the size of the individual townships and the grants to the settlers.[7] Rather than encouraging people to settle directly as in the case of Lunenburg, British government officials opted to grant land to private companies which would, in turn, be responsible for the settling.[8] It is not surprising that few were prepared to petition the government for land grants until the end of hostilities.[9] Even without the challenges of war, investment risk was high since the Crown had the right to escheat land if insufficient improvements were carried out and a certain quota of settlers not met. Lord Halifax and members of the Lords of Trade were understandably anxious about the vacuum created after the Acadians' evacuation.[10] These circumstances played into the hands of a very colourful and energetic entrepreneur, Colonel Alexander McNutt, whose reputation was highly regarded in some quarters but hotly disputed in others.[11] As soon as he heard about Lawrence's advertisements, McNutt approached the Germans and Quakers of Pennsylvania, including Rev. Mühlenberg and Benjamin Franklin.[12] His contacts with officials in Halifax appear to have impressed Governor Wilmot, who wrote to the Lords of Trade:

154

... [P]ersons are come in behalf of several Associations of Commercial people and others in good circumstances to view the country and examine what advantages the settlement and cultivation of it may produce. By their accounts the number of Germans annually imported in the older colonies of America has so overstocked the lands within convenient distance of navigation that many of them have lately been obliged to move into Carolina and Virginia .... nothing is wanting in Nova Scotia but a sufficiency of labouring people.

... [T]he proposed settlements are to be undertaken by people of very sufficient and able circumstances and that the establishment of so many German families will serve to divert the annual current of German immigration from the older colonies to Nova Scotia, which will be materially strengthened by the acquisition of these "frugal, laborious and industrious people," who will not only improve and enrich their property but, if need be, "pertinaciously defend it".[13]

Included in this letter was a list of companies and individuals who had submitted applications for grants of land, among them a "German Company" in Philadelphia which had requested 100,000 acres. Most of the eventual grantees of the Petitcodiac River settlement may be found on this list: Dr. Franklin & Co., Clarkson & Co., and William Smith & Co..[14] McNutt seems to have left such a deep impression in Halifax that, in all the grants mentioned by Governor Wilmot and including that for the Petitcodiac River,[15] McNutt's name appears as one of the principal shareholders: "The granting of land reached its frenzied climax during the last half of October 1765. Wilmot and his council made township grants during this short period that totalled more than two and a half million acres in addition to other smaller but still substantial ones."[16] Three land grants and their ensuing settlements are important in this context: Germantown, on the upper reaches of the Shepody River, settled in 1765; "Monckton" on the Petitcodiac River, settled in 1766; and Hillsborough, on the opposite side of this river, settled a year or two later (1767-1768) although its land was granted in 1765. The companies involved in these settlements acquired large portions of vacated Acadian farmland, in particular the fertile salt marshes adjacent to the Petitcodiac and Shepody Rivers.

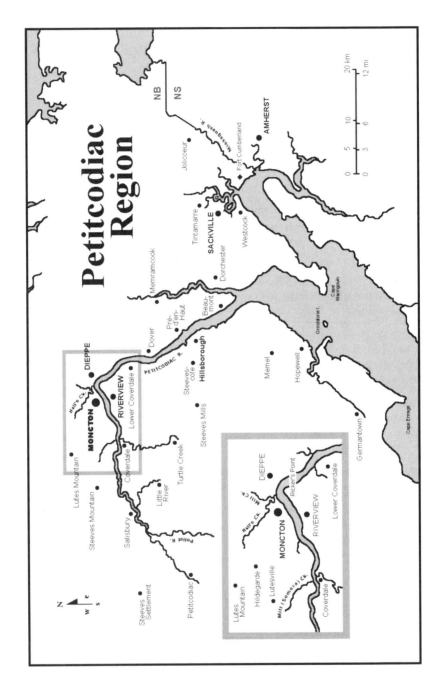

Map 4

156

V.1 Germantown, N. B.: the Story of an Unsuccessful Settlement[17]

Adam Hoops, a businessman of German background from Philadelphia, headed what for 18th-century Pennsylvania was a powerful group of entrepreneurs, all of whom became involved in the speculative land deal for "Germantown" (Shepody/Hopewell), N.B.. These included three Swiss in the service of the British[18] -- Major General Henry Bouquet, Col. Frederick Haldimand (the later Governor-in-Chief of Canada), and Col. Frederick DesBarres (the later Lieutenant-Governor of Cape Breton and Prince Edward Island) -- as well as another German by the name of Peter Hasenclever and an American, Hugh Wallace.[19] The document for their land grant bears the date September 24, 1765.[20] In a letter to the Lords of Trade a few weeks later, Governor Wilmot of Nova Scotia informed his superiors in London of the progress being made in the settlement of the territories (fig. 15):

> There has lately arrived here a Ship with Twenty German Families from Philadelphia for settling a Township on the North side of the Bay of Fundy. The Settlement of that part of the Province with Industrous people, who will defend and preserve their Property, I look on to be a Step necessary for keeping the Indians in Awe, and for the Tranquility of the more internal parts of the Province .... These Settlements are undertaken by persons of Sufficient Circumstances & Abilities, and I make no doubts of their being very Advantageous to the Publick.[21]

The two-week gap between September 24th as recorded on the land grant, and the October 9th arrival of the settlers on the northern shore of the Bay of Fundy suggests that their recruitment and departure from Pennsylvania preceded the actual legal granting of the land to Adam Hoops' group. It was a leap of faith, or "trust in a sure thing," given the shareholders' power base, and also the late time of year that caused the anxious settlers to depart before ink could be put to paper.

The proprietors of the Shepody, or "Hopewell Grant",[22] were well-acquainted with the recipe for successful settlement which had been followed in Pennsylvania and Lunenburg. They did not, however, carry out recruitment in Germany, only in Pennsylvania where a scarcity of

157

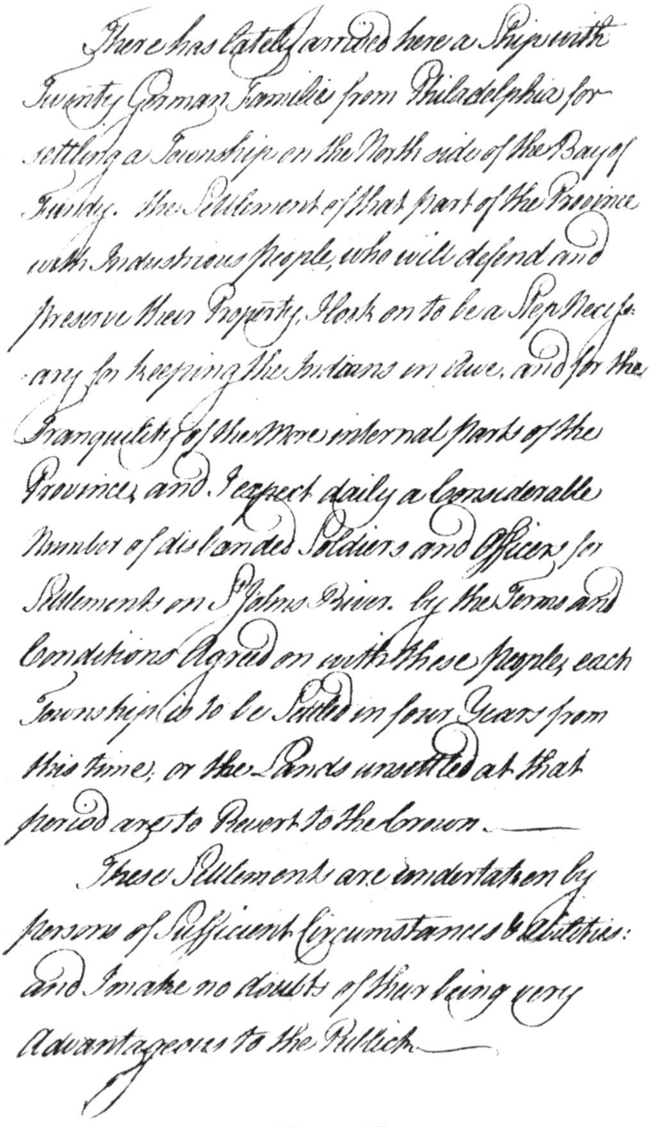

There has lately arrived here a Ship with Twenty German Families from Philadelphia, for settling a Township on the North side of the Bay of Fundy. the Settlement of that part of the Province with Industrious people, who will defend and preserve their Property, Stock on to be a Step Necessary for keeping the Indians in Awe, and for the Tranquility of the More internal parts of the Province, and I expect daily a Considerable Number of disbanded Soldiers and Officers for Settlements on St. Johns River. by the Terms and Conditions Agreed on with these people, each Township to to be Settled in four Years from this time, or the Lands unsettled at that period are to Revert to the Crown. ——

These Settlements are undertaken by persons of Sufficient Circumstances & abilities: and I make no doubt of their being very Advantageous to the Publick ——

Figure 15
Excerpt from a letter Governor Wilmot wrote on Oct. 9, 1765 informing the "Lords of Trade" about the arrival of German families at the Bay of Fundy.

Courtesy: National Archives of Canada

inexpensive land prompted twenty families to follow Adam Hoops' call to move north. Like the later settlers of Hillsborough and "Monckton", these families originated from German-speaking areas in Europe, and the shores and salt marshes of the Shepody River became, at least for a short while, their new home. They called their settlement "Germantown", perhaps in memory of their country of origin but more probably after their most recent place of residence, namely Germantown, Pennsylvania.

The names "Germantown", "Germantown Lake", and "German Creek" (plate 5) on the upper reaches of the Shepody were for a long time the only clues that Germans had lived in this part of Albert County.[23] An old newspaper article claimed: "It is said, Germantown, the site of the Calhoun grant, took its name from the fact that five German families resided in that part at the time the French were there. They are said to have been linen weavers of great skill."[24] A later account asserted: "Germantown near the western boundary of the Calhoun grant had been settled at an early date by a party of Germans from Pennsylvania, who were weavers of great skill. It is supposed they afterwards joined their fellow countrymen at Hillsborough."[25] French archival material and census registers do not substantiate the claims of these articles, namely that Germans were settled there at the time of French rule. A survey, evaluation, and inventory of settlements in Nova Scotia undertaken in the fall of 1763[26] by provincial surveyor Charles Morris revealed no German presence in this region either. J.B. Brebner asserted in his book *The Neutral Yankees of Nova Scotia* that there were no settlements between Sackville and the Saint John River,[27] for along the Bay of Fundy the rough highland came close to the coast without any large river valleys. The more northerly shoreline of the bay at the estuaries of the Shepody, Petitcodiac, and Memramcook Rivers was reported to be ideal for agriculture, but this land was reserved for settlement by disbanded soldiers. Morris' survey and inventory cannot be regarded as accurate in every detail, however, and neither can Brebner's comments, which were based on these earlier findings. Morris failed to notice any Acadians in the Memramcook Valley, who had taken refuge there and in the adjoining woods during their expulsion by the English. So, too, were Acadians living along the Shepody River in the same general area as the German settlement, for in the Hopewell Census of 1766, issued on January 1, 1767,[28] mention is made of Acadians who must have remained behind secretly after the destruction of their settlement. This is the probable origin of the claim that Germans and French lived side by side, but such co-existence must have occurred *after* the British takeover. Of the 159 settlers mentioned in the 1766 Census, 24 were Acadian, 2 English, 12 Irish, 62 American and 59 German. Many of the "Americans" were children of Germans born in Pennsylvania.[29] Included in this figure were 20 native people, and there were also 3 blacks, brought by the settlement's manager as domestics and farm hands. In the Ward Chipman Papers,[30] several people are mentioned in 1765 and later as debtors to the owners of the "Hopewell Grant", to which Germantown belonged. Names like Frederick Burksdorf, Matthias Gerhart, John Hand, Peter Mathias, Jacob Cross (*Gross*), and others attest to their German origin.

Adam Hoops and most of the other shareholders of the Shepody settlement never set foot on their lands, much to the chagrin of Thomas Calhoun, a 30-year-old bachelor whom they sent as administrator and organizer of the settlement. Thomas's brother, William, who was 10 years his junior, came up to Germantown from Baltimore for a visit in 1771 and described the settlement in his diary:

> Shepody contains a vast tract of fine marsh ... on each side of this marsh are seen beautiful rising grounds, mostly clear where the French houses formerly stood. A great part of the marsh has been dyked and drained .... Upon this River is Hopewell Township, owned by Adam Hoops, claimed at the first settling of it. They laid out Germantown upon a rising land, about two leagues up the River, and left the management of the Settlement to my brother.[31]

Almost from the very beginning the settlers complained that the land and provisions promised them had never materialized. In a letter written to Colonel Haldimand in French, Frederick DesBarres[32] detailed the complaints of two settlers from Germantown who actually made the journey to Halifax in the summer of 1766 to present to Provincial Council a petition from the tenants with a list of grievances. Among the most serious accusations were claims they had not been assigned their promised holdings and thus had suffered a year's setback in their efforts. They had been unable to plant anything other than a few potatoes around their houses. In addition, Calhoun

160

had refused to supply them with provisions unless they signed a bond. During the winter they were in such dire need of warm clothing that they had been forced to go to Fort Cumberland (formerly Fort Beauséjour) and barter away provisions in return for apparel to keep from freezing. Calhoun, they claimed, had also insisted that their land allotment be confined to wooded upland with no access to the marshes, a serious obstacle in the first critical months when the marshland was more or less ready for cultivation whereas the woods had to be cleared, stumps pulled, etc., an almost impossible task without proper equipment and draft animals.[33] The two settlers were sent back from Halifax with *"une bonne Exhortation"*,[34] but Calhoun was also admonished to accommodate the settlers' needs better.

Instead of following DesBarres' advice, Calhoun countered with a letter to the Honourable William Nesbit, blaming everything on the settlers:

> ... [T]he settlers here have gone to great lengths in plots against the proprietors being led on by a few villains .... [T]hey are generally Extremely Ignorant and most of them greatly Indebted to the proprietors .... [T]hey have done no business in the farming way for near these two months past, and constantly meet two or three times a week to consult upon their schemes, which they keep a secret from me but it appears plain by their behaviour and by all that I can learn that they design to move from here very soon as they have not provided any hay for their Cattle and have been all employed in building Battoes and Canoes, to accomplish which they have been at Cumberland and exchanged a great quantity of their provisions Tools &c. for Pitch nails and other Materials &c. They have collected a considerable quantity of boards for that purpose from different parts of the proprietors lands where they had been left by the french.[35]

Calhoun warned the settlers not to trespass on the land of the proprietors and thanked Mr. Francklin, an entrepreneur and friend of DesBarres in Halifax, for dissuading the Germantown settlers from presenting "a memorial to the commander in Chief and Council, whereby they made great complaints against the proprietors and me which are all groundless."[36] Calhoun also lamented as to the lack of instructions he had received from his superiors.

Regardless whether he attempted to sue the tenants or not, they would never be able to pay up. Moreover, it appeared plain to him that they were "determined to move away if they are not Stopt by Some means."[37]

In October of the same year, after the situation in Germantown saw no improvement, another three settlers made the journey to Halifax, this time presenting their list of grievances to the Governor and Council. Now that this case had become one of charge and counter-charge, the government found itself unable to make any immediate decision, advising rather that the matter be referred to a court of law. The Council instructed the Hon. Nesbit to write to proprietor Adam Hoops and manager Thomas Calhoun, suggesting that they "... give these people provisions for the winter [i.e. 1766/1767] and keep them together till he could hear from the proprietor who it was to be hoped would order Mr. Calhoun to Settle them on Such Lands as they might Support them on ...." Nesbit revealed his prior knowledge of the situation in that he had "... a certain account from other people who have been there that the lands that have been assigned to them and offered to them are not fit for Improvement and Col. Haldimand who Saw them last fall [i.e. 1765] told them on seeing the place they were Sett down on that place would not do and they must have other lands given them."[38] The settlers' impoverished appearance made an impression on Nesbit and he "... advanced these people that came Down Something to buy them Shoes and [illegible] and for provisions to carry them home to Hopewell and sent them away tolerably well pleased that I would Write to you."[39]

Adam Hoops failed to heed Hon. Nesbit's warning that the land allotted the settlers had been deemed unfit for cultivation by several persons, including Haldimand himself, who realized even before the first winter of 1765/1766 that the settlers' allotment was inadequate. It is difficult to understand why Hoops would have ignored the advice of his partner, Haldimand, whose observations held credibility since he had taken the trouble to visit the Germantown settlement in its earliest phase and had discussed the problems with the settlers in their own language.[40] Although Nesbit had likewise informed Calhoun in this regard, there is no evidence to suggest that the Germantown manager heeded his advice either.

162

It is of note that those who could communicate with the Germantown settlers in their mother tongue, namely Haldimand and DesBarres, and who took the trouble to understand their needs came away favourably impressed. Frederick DesBarres [41] referred to them as an expensive learning experience because of their lack of dyke-building expertise, but he found them infinitely preferable in all other respects. [42] At the root of Calhoun's difficulties with the settlers may have been his confrontational manner and reticence to communicate with people whom he as an Englishman likely considered socially inferior to himself. Perhaps the German-speakers, who were in the majority, left Calhoun feeling ill-at-ease and threatened due to linguistic alienation. A hint that Calhoun's manner was not solely to blame may be detected in his reference to "parts of the Land as you [Haldimand] Intend to reserve." [43] The Germantown shareholders obviously had other plans initially, namely to reserve the good land which had been cleared and cultivated by the Acadians for other higher-paying customers. Adam Hoops, for example, made an agreement with a certain William Daniels, [44] one such paying customer from Philadelphia, for a 200-acre farm in the Germantown region. [45]

All this undoubtedly irritated the Germantown settlers, so that they expressed their frustrations to Anthony Wayne, agent for the owners of the nearby "Monckton" settlement, when he came down in the fall of 1766 to establish contact with them. The Hon. Nesbit promptly informed Adam Hoops about this visit: "Mr. Wayne who was this year at Petitcodiac and Saw your people can Inform you farther about it [the settlement] for the people made heavy complaints to him about it and offered to come to his land but he would not Suffer them[.] I send this [letter] by him." [46] Despite listening to their pleas, Anthony Wayne chose to ignore the plight of the Germantown settlers and rejected their offer to join his new settlement. [47] Acceptance of Hoops's Germans would certainly have bolstered the numbers in Wayne's settlement, but perhaps he considered it unethical to take advantage of the difficulties in Germantown. As subsequent actions proved, not every agent had Anthony Wayne's scruples when it came to "robbing the cradle" of another land company. Whatever moved Wayne to make his decision, this denied the Germantown settlers an opportunity which his own people in "Monckton" later benefitted from, namely the opportunity to join a neighbouring settlement when conditions in their own had deteriorated. [48]

As a result of the settlers' two journeys to Halifax and Calhoun's rebuttal, the Germantown families succeeded only in further harming their reputation. The Hon. Nesbit, who had "appeared on behalf of the Proprietor and Exhibited Mr. Calhoun's charge" when the settlers' complaints were read before the government and council, sided against the foreigners, claiming them to be "a very bad sett whose Intentions ... [were dubious regarding] the money & provisions ...[Hoops] so Generously supplied them with."[49] As to what Adam Hoops knew of the affair, he was as judgemental of the settlers as of the managerial capabilities of his agent: "I find the people there does no work, am afraid Calhoun does not Execute his authority properly, it is my opinion that the Settlers there is encouraged to behave in the Tumultuous manner they have done."[50] Half a year later Hoops' opinion had not changed when he again corresponded with Haldimand: "I can say but very little of the Industry of the Settlers, to Diminish the Expence we have Dismiss'd the Most of the People that were on wages and have Employed the Settlers that are indebted to us [to] Bank in the Marshes ...."[51]

Calhoun's detailed letter to Haldimand in March 1768 shows that he continued to experience difficulties more than two years after the founding of Germantown. Over the second winter of 1767/1768 the tenants lost several of the previous years' calves, which they attributed to a lack of upland pasture the previous summer: "... for that reason they seem in general resolved upon moving to Haha & Shepodee hill on account of getting upland pasture for their Cattle. I have endeavoured to dissuade them from it as much as possible but don't expect I can prevent it without using force, which I don't care to do, as you [Haldimand] have allowed them some liberty of making use of the cleared land ...."[52] By his own admission, Calhoun proved the validity of the settlers' earlier complaints in Halifax, i.e. that he had not allowed them to cultivate the land of former Acadian settlements, forcing them instead to clear virgin forest in the first critical months of settlement. It is not surprising that Thomas Calhoun should describe the settlers as "... discouraged and discontented .... I think if I should oppose them they would do nothing but endeavour to get off as the rest did."[53] From this statement it is clear that some of the settlers had, as early as the fall of 1767,[54] already left the settlement in boats they had built with boards taken from abandoned Acadian barns and houses. No doubt the remaining settlers also wanted to leave this intolerable situation when the right moment presented itself. Calhoun observed:

> ... [T]hey have not endeavoured to do anything during the Winter but tend their Cattle and get firewood, several of them are almost naked & I have been obliged to give them several articles of clothing to keep them from perishing, some of them have near expended what provisions I allowed them till May and has waisted their potatoes by feeding their Cattle with them. I expect I shall be obliged to allow them some more Flour & Corn -- as to pork I cant spare them any more.[55]

In the preamble to his description of the settlers' plight, Thomas Calhoun noted with amazing detachment that "nothing very material happened in this settlement since I wrote you last ..." and concluded with the statement, "I have lived peaceably this Winter." On the one hand, he acknowledged that several settlers were "almost naked", on the other hand he criticized them for not doing anything during the cold winter months but gather wood and tend cattle. It evidently did not occur to him that concentrating on warmth and nourishment was vital under the circumstances. Had he not forced the settlers to clear trees and allowed them rather to make hay on the cleared Acadian lands, they might not have had to feed potatoes to their cattle to keep them alive.

William Calhoun's diary, written five years later and after Thomas Calhoun had stepped down as manager, echoes the sentiments of his brother and blames the failure of the settlement on the bad quality of the people: "The Settlement ... did not succeed according to their wishes, occasioned by their sending a number of worthless settlers, some of whom had been brought up in the army, others had lived in Philadelphia, and had never been used to farming, but thought they were coming to get land, which produce[d] ... every[thing] necessary spontaneously, without cultivation."[56] Their ability to construct seaworthy vessels does not agree with the picture of the settlers as impractical and lazy, disbanded soldiers, ill-disposed toward work, and it is unlikely that any of these men were "brought up" in the army since standing professional armies were rare. There were those during the unusually long Thirty Years' War, or the various guards,[57] but soldiers on

German soil around 1750 were generally recruited for limited periods of time or were merely serving militia duty for the four weeks between planting and haying,[58] hardly long enough to spoil them for civilian life. Soldiers' attitudes such as laziness, rootlessness, and lack of family values cannot be laid against the settlers of Germantown because these men were also heads of families and undisputedly wanted to make a fresh start. It is more likely that they were naïve and overly hopeful after hearing the exaggerated accounts of company recruiters. As the cold days passed into weeks and months, their tremendous disappointment must have turned to anger at being exploited to the point where their lives had been put at risk.

William Calhoun's diary also reiterates the settlers' complaints, namely the insufficient food supplies and allotment of unsuitable land. The frigid weather conditions encountered already in October of 1765 suggest that the first winter in New Brunswick must have been particularly hard and set in before preparations were complete:

> ... [B]eing landed there late in fall, and their allowance of provisions which Mr. Hoops ordered ... [for] them, they lived so extravagantly that by the 28th of December several of them ran out of provisions, and though my brother gave them all he possibly could spare (it being a time when he couldn't go to any place in order to get a supply) yet it wouldn't satisfy them, but they gathered in a company and demanded more, saying they would have it, or lose their lives .... Finding that they could get nothing by their threats, they set off for Cumberland in order to make a complaint, but it being very cold and deep snow in the ground they didn't go very far before they returned. One of their principal leaders had his feet badly frozen, and some of the others had theirs a little touched with frost. They afterwards quarrelled among themselves, and beat one another shamefully. [After the arrival of new supplies from Philadelphia], [t]hey ... unanimously signified their displeasure at their lands, the laying out of which by the proprietor's direction highly dissatisfied them. Some of them ran away, others, who would do nothing for themselves, were kept dyking by my brother and making aboiteaux for the proprietor's use. He gave them good wages, but ... most of them got off one way or another after

continuing in the proprietor's employment for about five years, and finding his endeavors to make a settlement for the proprietors to no purpose without a better set of men, he (my brother) requested them to send another to manage their affairs, and was (notwithstanding his efforts to promote their interests) obliged to sue for his salary. The proprietor's affairs were next managed by Mr. Cummins, but they still got along very poorly ....[59]

It must have added insult to injury for the settlers to have to improve the marshlands by building dykes and *abois d'eau* intended solely for the benefit of prospective, high-paying customers. In the end, Thomas Calhoun sued his former employers in Philadelphia for £509 when their indifference to his pleas for firm instructions and involvement went so far as to the withholding of his wages.

In spite of all the troubles in Germantown, several successes could be reported as well. In the summer of 1766, 39 cows, 39 calves, and 1 bull were sent to Germantown *via* Boston, all of which thrived so splendidly that the usually reserved Adam Hoops could inform Haldimand optimistically: "Our cattle seems to thrive very well; in a Little time I hope we shall have Plenty of Beef to maintain the People."[60] As the ships from Shepody often returned under ballast and good-quality stones could be quarried near the shores of the Shepody River, Hoops turned his thoughts by early 1767 to the business potential of this non-perishable product, both in Pennsylvania and England. He wrote: "We have sent a small Sloop to Shepody which returned some time ago Ballast with Plaister of Palace Stone, a Large Mine or Quarry of it is found on the Red Bank on Shepody River, sufficient to load all the shipping to this Part of the World. I have made no Tryal of it yet but believe it to be very good and shall send a Sample of it to England to see if a Market can be found there."[61] Hugh Wallace was understandably jubilant: "... you'll see our settlement is in a good way & that they have something to sell. The Grindstones will be an affair of consequence as there is none so good I am told on the Continent, & our Plaster of Paris is as good as any in Italy as those say who have tryed it here & at Philad."[62]

On December 14, 1767, Hoops wrote to Wallace that the sloop *Belleze* had arrived from the Bay of Fundy with a freight of "4 to 5 hundred weight of cheese", "Potatoes & spruce, & sixty Grindstones."[63] According to Clark Wright, this is the "... first reported export of New Brunswick potatoes, the principal agricultural export of the province at the present."[64] In a subsequent letter to Haldimand, Hoops proposed to send him some of the abovementioned cheese and potatoes, adding: "I think it [the Germantown settlement] will now begin to bring in some income every year, provided care be taken of it and should we let it Drop, we not only lose the Land but the sum we have expended."[65] Four months later, however, Hoops had to acknowledge loss of some of the promised goods because of shipping problems: "[Of the] 4 Grindstones and 3 Cheeses, the produce from our Plantation in Nova Scotia, the potatoes were all spoiled by the ... Frost in the Harbour ...."[66] Despite this setback, the letter confirms that after two short years exports were possible, a remarkable feat in view of the hardships and premature departure of some of the inhabitants. Certainly the cows and calves were a contented lot over 1766/1767, for their milk production was abundant and especially when one considers how much is required to produce cheese. Some land was cleared, providing lumber for export and fuel for their own use, and considerable time must have been spent at Grindstone Island hewing out sandstone slabs.

The 1766 Hopewell Census statistics corroborate both the successes in Germantown and the settlement's limitations. Eight bulls, 61 cows, and 55 calves were grazing the pastures, along with 8 horses which were no doubt mostly for Thomas Calhoun and his guests' use. In a settlement of 159 people, only 8 "swine" were kept, and there were practically no crops such as wheat, rye, peas, oats, beans, only 2 bushels of barley and small amounts of flax and hemp. As a consequence, there was no need for a gristmill. Unfortunately, the Census makes no mention of potatoes, which were grown extensively. For all other food and supplies the residents of Germantown had to rely heavily on the townships of Cumberland and Sackville. These boasted wheat harvests of 690 and 1,035 bushels, respectively, and kept three gristmills in operation. Germantown also lacked its own sawmill so that boards and other building materials had to be transported by boat across more than 32 km of open water, but it did have its own fishing vessel which undoubtedly saw frequent service in supplying the young settlement with an alternate source of protein to pork. Perhaps a reflection of the difficult early years, the deaths of one man and one woman and the departure of three men and two women were recorded for the year 1766, but this was only the beginning of the exodus which numbered close to 100 people in the years following. As later entries in William Calhoun's diary show, the Calhoun brothers also left Germantown. William liked the area further up the coast so much that he decided not to return to Baltimore and joined the nearby Hillsborough settlement. He and Thomas must have agreed with Adam Hoops and Hugh Wallace that there was potential in the grindstone business; however during the loading of stones at nearby Grindstone Island (plate 6) in 1772, the brothers' boat capsized and both were drowned. Thomas Calhoun's widow, a daughter of the tenant Abiel Peck, continued the court action initiated by her husband and a good portion of the Hopewell Grant eventually came into her possession.

Although the governor in Halifax was interested primarily in the resettlement of former Acadian lands, land company shareholders were motivated by profit. Members of the Provincial Council in Halifax made certain that the best parcels of land were granted to their circle of friends;[67] many had close connections to the owners,[68] whom the Hon. Nesbit saw no difficulty in representing before the Governor and Council when settlers filed complaints. A number of government officials also had private interests in the profit of land companies.[69] The indifference with which Adam Hoops dismissed those whom he had brought to the Shepody River and who were no longer indebted to him speaks for itself. With no recourse, the settlers were compelled to barter their provisions and utensils for warm clothing and other essentials, a move which inevitably hindered their progress later on. In such lamentable conditions, they vented their frustrations out on one another, a reaction no different from that recorded earlier by Gottlieb Mittelberger on immigrant ships under similarly deplorable circumstances. It is no wonder they rejected Thomas Calhoun as their externally appointed Justice of the Peace, the very man whom they held responsible for their distress. He in turn was vexed by the landowners' ill-conceived and imprecise directives. Unfortunately, he was not a man to recognize, as would others, that creative interpretation of impractical instructions from superiors was frequently the only way to ensure success.[70]

Germantown was not the only settlement whose inhabitants suffered in this fashion. Just a few years later (1767-1769), Petitcodiac Germans in the settlement of "Monckton" found themselves in similarly desperate circumstances when their plea for help to landowners in Philadelphia went unanswered. But, in contrast to the Petitcodiac Germans, most Germantown settlers -- with the exceptions of Joseph Brackman(n), Frederick Burkdorf/Burkstaff, Jacob Gross,[71] and Charles Myers (*Karl Meier*) -- abandoned their struggle for land and a future along the Petitcodiac River. The boats which the Germans of Shepody built must have carried their occupants safely back to Pennsylvania, for twenty years later John Frederick Burksdorf, first mentioned in the Ward Chipman Papers of 1765 as a debtor to the landowners of Germantown, returned to Canada as a United Empire Loyalist. He had served in the Royal Fencible Americans and was rewarded with a grant on the Magaquadavic River in New Brunswick.[72] Probably a relative of this John Frederick was the above-mentioned Frederick Burksdorf/Burkstaff, who must have continued dyking in Germantown because of outstanding debts with the owners, but by 1771 all had been let go, and Burksdorf/Burkstaff, Brackman, and Myers went upriver to join their fellow countrymen in Hillsborough, where they were listed as residents in 1775.[73]

V.2 The Petitcodiac Germans in "Monckton"[74]

During William Calhoun's stay with his brother Thomas in the summer of 1771, he made the following entry in his diary:

> On Sunday after divine service, performed by Mr. Eagleson, we proceeded up the river as far as the Great Bend, about twelve miles from Mr. Lesdernier's and twenty from the mouth of the river ....
> The Bend is about thirteen miles from Shediac at the Gulf of St. Lawrence. There are some Dutch families here, who are making out very well.[75]

"Monckton" was the settlement on the northern shore beyond the "Bend"[76] of the Petitcodiac River, and the "Dutch", or *Deutsche*, refer to several Pennsylvania German families living there since 1766. The grant for "Monckton Township" was first awarded in October of 1765 by Governor Wilmot and his Council to a conglomerate of four Philadelphia land companies[77] whose owners were mostly Pennsylvanian entrepreneurs and land speculators. The driving spirit behind this consortium was John

170

Hughes, a successful businessman. His friend and supporter was Benjamin Franklin, founder of one of the participant land companies, Franklin & Co., who invited John Hughes and later the young surveyor, Anthony Wayne, to be shareholders in his firm.

For many years little was known about the origins of these German families and the circumstances which caused them to move to the shores of the Petitcodiac River in New Brunswick,[78] a fact exemplified in the following newspaper article from the last century:

> A colony of Germans from the Rhine had settled in Pennsylvania. Though Pennsylvania was fair, the land fruitful, the climate and products similar to the fatherland, ferocious animals lurked in the recesses of the forest, and venomous serpents beset their paths. Some of the colony had fallen victim to the rage of the panther and the deadly fangs of rattlesnake, and they murmured, as did the Israelites of old, 'Hast thou taken us away to die in the wilderness.' They learned of a land to the northward which was represented to be more fair, more fruitful, with farms already under cultivation, with fruitful orchards, fertile meadows and broad fields, only awaiting the hands of the husbandman ....

> Early in May, 1765, Hendrick Steves, Hans Lutes, Jacob Trites, Jacob Ricker, Karl Jones, -- Somers, their women and children, set sail, as pioneers to spy out the land, and if their report was favourable, others were to follow in the spring. They took with them their lightest household goods, their stores of linen, so dear to the German housewife, their tools, books and one year's provisions. The sloop was to return in the following spring, bringing others, the goods left behind, their stock seeds and provisions for the second year.[79]

Although cougars and rattlesnakes occur in Pennsylvania, probably less commonly today than in the 18th century, they were unlikely the cause for the Germans' departure. The attributes of the land along the Petitcodiac were also exaggerated. Several of the first names were replaced by typically German ones, like "Hans" and "Karl", and some erroneous claims such as

171

the promised return of a ship in the following spring, discussed later in this chapter, have persisted to the present day.

A surprisingly accurate early account of the origins of the Petitcodiac Germans came from the pen of the Hon. Judge Bliss Botsford, who was born in 1813 and spent his adult years in Moncton where he became acquainted with many of the old inhabitants of the area. In the five years before his death in 1890, he delivered several addresses, one of which appeared in *The Daily Times* on January 19, 1885 under the title "The First Settlement on the Banks of the Petitcodiac: A Prolific Family: The Days when Moncton was an Alderswamp."[80] Botsford claims that the settlers "left the Rhine in the year 1749 and proceeded to Pennsylvania, then a British colony. They ascended the Delaware and purchased and improved lands on the Schuylkill, about 18 miles above Philadelphia."[81] Botsford names most of the settlers correctly and even the captain of the ship who brought them to the Petitcodiac, but in other details such as the year of their arrival and the number of families, he introduces inaccuracies which were accepted for nearly one hundred years. W.O. Raymond, who undertook valuable research at the beginning of this century, also contributed to the confusion as to how Heinrich Stieff came to Hillsborough.[82] The origins of these settlers have since been traced through the Public Record Office in London, local sources, and the Archives of the Historical Society of Pennsylvania.[83]

Documents in the Hughes Papers, which include extensive correspondence between Anthony Wayne and Alexander McNutt as well as copies of Hughes' replies, give insight into the actions of "Monckton's" landowners and the problems which confronted them in the creation of a successful settlement. From the very beginning the letters attest to the difficulties John Hughes faced in dealing with McNutt, the same recruiter whom Rev. Mühlenberg heard in Philadelphia in the fall of 1764 expounding upon the world of opportunities opening up in Nova Scotia. Although McNutt had initially aroused the interest of Hughes and other Pennsylvanian entrepreneurs and given his word to use his good offices to reserve land for settlers whom Hughes might recruit, no reservations transpired and Hughes became alarmed:

... Several persons of Merit and fortune Undertook at my Instance to Engage Settlers for the Colony of Nova Scotia, and have ... procured Great Numbers to put themselves in a posture for Removing this Spring and many are now and have been Some time past on Expenses to their Great Disappointment & Damage so that some of them are Determined to go Else where .... But all threaten to Arrest me and some I believe will ... Recover Considerable Damages, as many put themselves out of Business ... I Do without further Ceremony Insist that you Comply with your promises and have the Land Reserved or I must be obliged in my own Defense to use you as the people use me .... I should be very Sorry to be obliged to Sew [sue] you for breach of contract, ... for God sake Sir Do not procrastinate any Longer or our plan may Miscarry and we be put to Monstrous Expense, besides the Loss of Reputation, which as I am, not only a Merchant but a farmer, and Iron Master, will injure me Extremely in my Business in Each Branch.[84]

Although Hughes' next letter of a month later continues to threaten McNutt that any suit for further damages to Hughes and his associates would ultimately be recovered from McNutt, it deals primarily with the best methods of settling new townships. Both John Hughes and Benjamin Franklin wanted to avoid mistakes made earlier in the settlement of New York, Pennsylvania, and Virginia, where first-generation settlers had been allowed to pick and choose " ... the best Spots of the Land to themselves and by that means the Country is very Ill settled ...."[85] Hughes advised instead "... to have the Township divided into small Tracts ... and by that Means the proprietor of Each Township would be Interested in Getting Settlers and Dividing the Lands properly so that the whole face of the Country would soon be settled in the best manner."[86] Every attempt was made to ennoble these land speculation schemes, lending them an almost philanthropic air:

... [T]he Great Advantage the Crown would Reap by Granting the Lands in Townships is Striking. If it is Considered that by that means there is first a Great number of men Engaged by their Interest to Get their Lands Settled, and Secondly that these men must and will use all their Interest & Influence to remove poor people to the Colony that otherwise would never have it in their power to get

173

there, and by that means Thousands of the poor would be Rendered Usefull and happy. For it is an Undoubted truth that there is in the Interior parts of all the old Colonies Thousands of poor people that would be glad to meet with a Little Encouragement to Transport themselves by Adventagious to Britain by promoting trade ....[87]

These statements underscore the poor circumstances of the early settlers at the Petitcodiac, as well as the general feeling of dissatisfaction ever more frequently voiced by the impoverished classes concerning their hardships in the New World. As for Hughes, his patience would continue to be tested for some time before any of McNutt's promises ever bore fruit.

Almost a year lapsed between the above letter to McNutt and April of 1765 when Anthony Wayne, newly qualified as a surveyor,[88] was dispatched to Halifax to inspect and survey the lands McNutt was to secure for the four Philadelphia land companies. Wayne reported that he was well received by McNutt and would shortly be sailing with him "... all along the Coast ... and up the bay of Fundy & the River Petitcoodiack & meet Captain Caton [of Caton & Co.] & Mr. Jacobs [shareholder in William Smith & Co.] at the head of said River."[89] In Hughes' June 1st reply to Wayne, he wrote with satisfaction that he had just been " ... appointed the officer to put the Stamp Act into Execution ...,"[90] a measure that would speed up the granting of land[91] on the one hand but, as events unfolded, adversely affect the "Monckton" settlement on the other. Whereas Wayne was hopeful to obtain a "Number of Townships"[92] in his reply to Hughes, a month later he was forced to admit:

> ... [O]ur affairs has not met with the Desired Success in this place as we Expected .... I wrote ... Giving you an account of my proceedings & with an account of the lands, which I had made a pitch on. These very lands has in my Absence been reserved to Gentlemen of our Acquaintance, who knew that I had surveyed & chosen them. It surprises me the more as it was at Coln McNutts request I took that tour with a promise of having the refusal of any lands, along the Coast.[93]

174

Not only was it McNutt but also "Ministers ... some of [whom] acted in a Double Capacity."[94] The stakes in these land dealings were high, and any niceties of tactical manoeuvring had given way to blunt language, bluffs, and ruses.

This was most assuredly baptism by fire in colonial politics which the barely 20-year-old Anthony Wayne received in Halifax, remembered in American history as "Mad Anthony" for the reckless daring he demonstrated in the 1779 recapture of the British-held post at Stoney Point, New York.[95] As early as 1765, Wayne showed considerable maturity and insight in his dealings with the Provincial Council in Halifax. John Hughes and Benjamin Franklin must have recognized Wayne's potential when they entrusted him with the important role of negotiator, surveyor, and agent for such a vast land, and Wayne did not fail them. In his report to Hughes in Philadelphia two months later, he revealed his secret strategy: "... [T]hey want to Cull part of the best land on Petitcoodiack for Some of the favorite Gentlemen in Halifax" and in order to prevent this " we have made a faint as if we would leave the Province without taking up any Lands & have Set up our Names for that purpose."[96] Wayne was also learning how to assure himself of the support of government officials, such as the Hon. William Nesbit, Speaker of the Assembly in Halifax. In a document detailing among other expenses those of his 1765 stay in Halifax, Wayne requested reimbursement for "Cash paid for a wine present that was Delivered as a reward to Mr. Nesbett [sic] in Halifax for Obtaining a Grant for 6,000 Acres of Land on Petitcodiac ... as well as for services done for us last year."[97] Small "rewards" such as this make it clear why Nesbit found himself defending the land companies in their dispute with the settlers of Germantown.

Although there had been ample warnings before, Wayne was nevertheless taken aback at the machinations of both the Council and McNutt:

I had greatest reason to believe from the private sentiments of many of those Gentlemen, that we would Meet with no Difficulty in Obtaining them [more favourable settlement conditions], that we requested.

175

But to our [Mr. Jacobs' and Wayne's] great surprise when they met in Council, notwithstanding, the repeated assurances, of the Majority of them, that they would do all in their power, for us ... [t]hey very sively told us, it was not in their power to Grant any other terms than those they had before proposed.

... I have been Informed, by several Gentlemen of the Council, that Coln. McNutt had made Interest privately against us ... that we had Nothing to do with the terms, or anything Else, & was only Employed as Surveyors under him, that he was the person Applyed to by all the Company's concerned ....

This Dispicable & Unjust proceedings of McNutt, I did not find out till my return here the 18th of Sept ....[98]

In the end John Hughes and the companies he represented received only two grants out of at least four they had reserved, one on the Saint John River called "Frankfort,"[99] and the other on the Petitcodiac River called "Monckton" (fig. 16). They also had to accept McNutt's name as one of the grantees for both of these although his influence waned shortly thereafter (fig. 17). In a nine-page document called the "Articles of Agreement", dated January 24, 1766, twenty-three members of the four land companies headed by John Hughes agreed on how to divide up the two 100,000-acre townships and they drew lots for the various parcels of land.

There was agreement that "... the plot marked KK, in the said plan shall be given to the first Protestant Society that shall build a House for public Worship therein."[100] It was to be located within the designated site for the Township's "Village" at the centre of the grant in the vicinity of Mill Creek, between Lots 4 and 5, near present-day Allison. A Baptist church (Allison Baptist Church) and cemetery (Wilson Cemetery) were begun in the "Glebe and School Lot" within the first decade of the 19th century since the Town Clerk and Justice of the Peace James Watson Esq., to whom the land was deeded in 1810, reserved in 1813 "... one acre already given adjoining Christopher Horsman's Line for the Benefit of a Baptist Meeting House ...."[101] The establishment and location of the Free Meeting House had little to do with provisions outlined in the original agreement and was the outcome

176

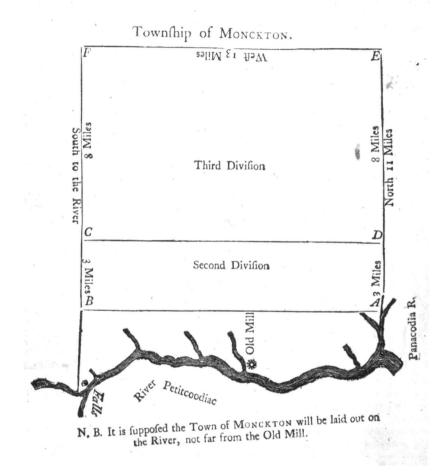

Township of MONCKTON.

West 13 Miles

F   E

South to the River   8 Miles

Third Divifion

8 Miles

North 11 Miles

C   D

Second Divifion

3 Miles

3 Miles

B   A

Panacodia R.

* Old Mill

Falls

River Petitcoodiac

N. B. It is fuppofed the Town of MONCKTON will be laid out on the River, not far from the Old Mill.

Figure 16
Map of "Monckton" township as attached to the "Articles of Agreement" of
William Smith & Co..

Courtesy: Historical Society of Pennsylvania, Philadelphia
Photo: Rainer L. Hempel

177

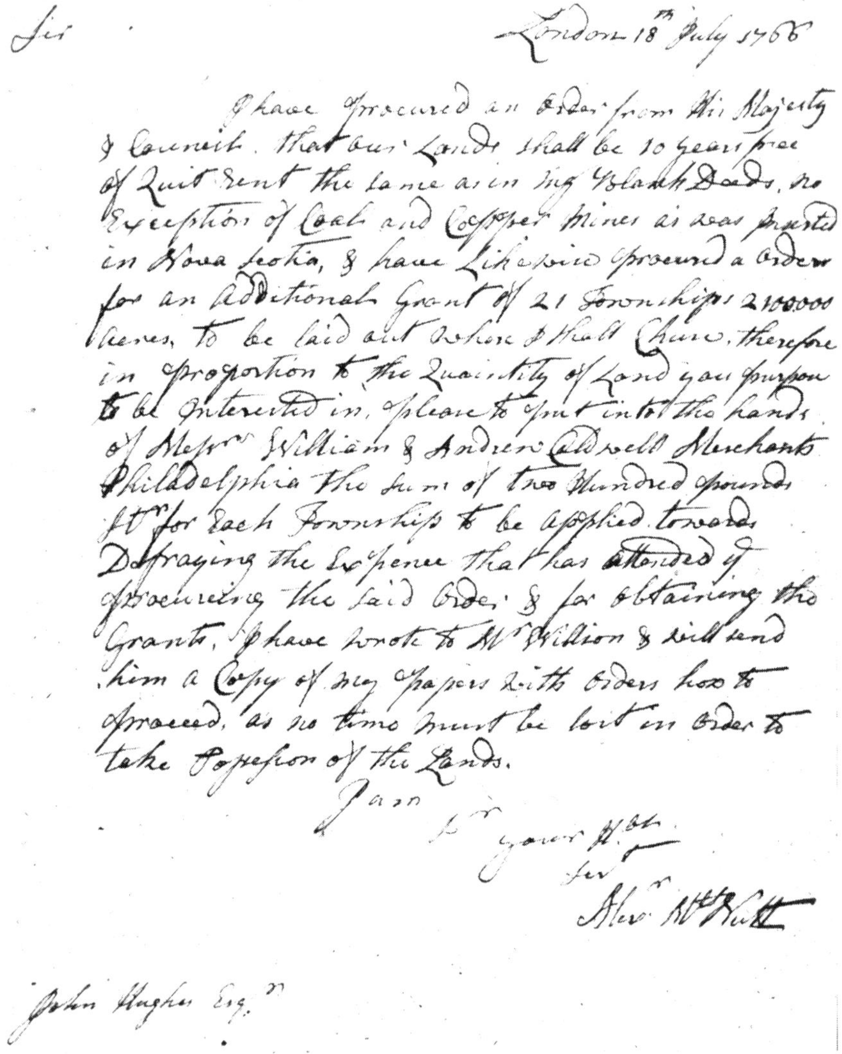

Sir London 18th July 1766

I have procured an Order from His Majesty & Council that our Lands shall be 10 years free of Quit Rent the same as in my Blank Deeds, no Exception of Coal and Copper Mines as was granted in Nova Scotia, & have Likewise procured a Order for an Additional Grant of 21 Townships 2100000 Acres, to be laid out when I shall Chuse, therefore in proportion to the Quantity of Land you purpose to be Interested in, please to put into the hands of Messrs William & Andrew Caldwell Merchants Philadelphia the sum of two Hundred pounds Str for each Townships to be applied towards Defraying the Expence that has attended y procuring the said Order & for obtaining the Grants. I have wrote to Mr Willison & will send him a Copy of my papers with Orders how to proceed, as no time must be lost in Order to take Possesion of the Lands.

I am Sr your Hbl. Servt
Alexr McNutt

John Hughes Esqr

Figure 17

Letter by Alexander McNutt from London on July 18, 1766 showing his continued interest in the settlers even after their landing on June 3, 1766.

Courtesy: Historical Society of Pennsylvania, Philadelphia
Photo: Rainer L. Hempel

of a later ecumenical effort undertaken on land purchased for this purpose in 1821. This second house of worship was needed when the location for the Township's village shifted eastward to Lot 9 (Jacob Treitz Sr.'s grant) and the land adjacent to Hall's Creek as the result of bringing an upgraded "King's Highway" down from Lewisville around 1811 to make a corner at today's King/Main Street intersection.[102] The "Articles of Agreement" also stipulated that "... the Streets of the said two Towns [Monckton and Frankfort] shall be laid out parallel or as nearly parallel as conveniently may be to the Boundary Lines of the respective Grants ...."[103] Agreement between these early plans and the layout of present-day streets in Moncton was decided by various provincial surveyors, in particular Ebenezer Cutler, who worked from the old grants and adapted these to the needs of the growing community.

On January 27, 1766, three days after the agreement for partitioning of the townships had been signed, nine prospective settlers committed their signatures/marks to another document, also known as "Articles of Agreement" (figs.1, 1a, 2).[104] This second document bound the settlers for a period of five years (i.e. to 1771) as tenants to Franklin & Co.[105] They agreed to begin "within the Month of April next ... their Journey or Voyage to the Colony of Nova Scotia ..." and were promised "one Lott of Forty feet in Breadth and Two Hundred and Twenty five feet or thereabouts in Depth or Length [in the town] to be drawn for by Lott in a fair and Candit Manner ...." After the settlers had fenced their land and erected a "House with a Stone or Brick Chimney in it," the land company agreed in turn to transfer the property to the settlers. As well, "Two Hundred Acres of Good Land for every Family of Five protestant persons ... " were laid out for them, on which they were to " ... clear, Fence & improve or Till Two Acres of Corn Land, and also clear, Fence and Mow one Acre of Meadow Ground and plant fifty Apple Trees ..., [whereupon] John Hughes or his Heirs will release the Tracts of Land so Improved to the person or persons so improving respectively ...." The arbitrary spellings of the settlers' names in the document (in quotation marks) as compared to their signatures (in italics) has caused confusion as to their real names. *Mathias Sommer* was recorded by the clerk as "Matthias Summer", *Heinrich Stieff* as "Henry Stief", and *Jacob Treitz* as "Jacob Trites"; only the name of Michael Lutz was spelled correctly. Four other persons whose signatures also appear on the document but who did not

179

join their cosignatories on the journey to this part of Nova Scotia[106] --
perhaps on account of the interminable delays caused by Alexander McNutt
are: "Andrew Criner" (*Andres Greiner*), "Jacob Cline" (*Jacob Klein*),[107]
"Matthias Lentz" (*Mathias Lenz*), and "Valentine Miller" (*Valentin Müller*),
i.e. the same Müller involved in the Barren Hill Church affair with Matthias
Sommer.

The settlers' date of departure from Philadelphia on April 20, 1766, and
date of arrival on June 3, 1766, as ascertained from a letter written by
Captain John Hall (cf. Appendix),[108] show that they spent a total of 44 days
on board, an inordinate length of time for such a short journey. Since this
was a chartered trip, they likely bypassed the regular ports-of-call, except
perhaps Digby,[109] but may have taken the opportunity to sail up the Saint
John River to stop over at the consortium's "Frankfort" settlement. Captain
Hall brought his passengers, including the German families in question and
a certain Rev. John Eagleson,[110] up the Petitcodiac River to the banks of
Panaccadie Creek,[111] a natural landing place on the easternmost border of the
land grant and today's boundary between the municipalities of Moncton and
Dieppe.[112]

Sailing up the Petitcodiac River, these newcomers would have passed by
the deserted Acadian settlements of Chipoudie, Anse-des-Larosette, Village-
des-Blanchard, and Village-des-Lacouline.[113] Solitary stone chimneys,
mounds around the foundations of burned farmhouses, and an occasional
barn or outbuilding that had escaped destruction gave them glimpses of an
earlier people and their ultimate fate. As the ship neared its destination at the
confluence of the Petitcodiac and Panaccadie Creek (Hall's Creek), the ruins
of Terre Rouge came into view. Less than a decade had passed since the
forced departure of its inhabitants. A graveyard and the charred remains of
a chapel near the river bank, old fences, and further up the river off "Mill
Creek" (today's Somers Creek), the rotting timbers of a grist mill stood in
contrast to orchards about to bloom, all silent reminders that others had
toiled here. More enduring than wooden structures were the earthen dykes
which Acadians had built to reclaim marshland from the salty tidal waters
of the Bay of Fundy (plate 7). Repairs to sluice gates (*abois d'eau*) would
assure the newcomers an abundance of fertile land for immediate cultivation,

but alder saplings reclaiming the upland were evidence that the rest of this once flourishing region had begun to revert to its primordial state.

According to Capt. Hall, the future looked promising: "We Landed Safe at Petitcoodiac the third Day of June and Our people was well pleased with the Land but most tired out with a Long pasage .... I ... got a hoghead[114] of petators for them to plant ... and I believe they are all planted by this time."[115] Hall and the settlers found the grass so rich and green that they would have been unable to plow it under even if they had had " ... the Best plowes & horses Pencilvania can aforde, for it is so tuff." The "... Land is strong anough Even for hemp for the Inglish grass is a bove our neese & is pasture anough for to fatten a 1000 head of Cattle." Captain Hall also bought a yoke of oxen and "... What Young Cows ... [he] Could: for tha [they] said the[y] should not go Idle, but Work as Well ... & give milk two."[116] In a letter to a fellow clergyman, Rev. John Eagleson confirmed that Captain Hall tried his best to look after the settlers at this critical time:

Mr. Hall I believe saw every difficulty that might arise to them & did every thing in his power to remedy it by empowring Mr Wethered to supply them with whatever necessaries they might want which he was at some considerable pains to do in the best & most convenient manner he possibly could; which I am sensible he did by borrowing supplies for them out of the King's Stores when they were disappointed of the Provisions purchased for them by Mr Wayne at Halifax; this he did by hiring a Vessel & procuring hands when ye Season was far advanced that it was very difficult to procure persons who wou'd undertake it & ye men who went one lost his Life & ye other was so much frost bit in his feet that he is not able of doing any thing to procure himself a subsistance.[117]

An expense account set up by Anthony Wayne, mentioned earlier in connection with a "Reward" for the Hon. Mr. Nesbitt, also lists an expenditure of almost £2 "for fish hooks and Lines, for Settlers."[118] Wayne charged Hughes £33:5:5[119] for "time and Expenses from the 8th of June till the 19th of Nov'r in Nova Scotia in Services done ... & purchasing Provisions for Settlers etc." and £3:18:0 "for Seed Grain".[120] A second list, entitled "Nova Scotia Lands", details debits *and* credits during 1766 (fig. 18)

181

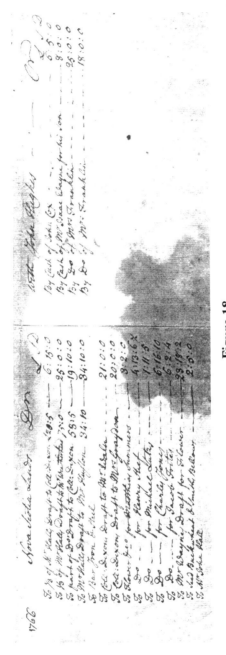

Figure 18

Anthony Wayne's list of expenses charged to John Hughes's account which proves that settlers' supplies were obtained locally.

Courtesy: Historical Society of Pennsylvania

182

and records "Flower &c for Matthias Summers ... Henry Stief ... Michael Lutz ... Charles Jones ... Jacob Trites ... Mr. Wayne ...,"[121] for a total of £48:9:3, a considerable sum in those days. In addition, an order for buckwheat seed was included, clearly intended as an early harvest supplement. The mention of flour and seed grain contradicts Stieff family oral tradition that the settlers were without flour during the first winter, had to save what grain they had for seed, and were forced to eat turnip mush instead of cereals.[122]

Each of the above-mentioned documents sheds light on the issue of supplies and living circumstances shortly after landing. Eagleson's letter states that the settlers had three sources for provisions: Mr. Wethered, who lived close to Fort Cumberland and whom Hall authorized to provide the settlers with the necessities of life; the "King's Stores", presumably those of the garrison at Fort Cumberland; and Mr. Wayne, who sent provisions from Halifax but whose choices may not all have been appropriate in the settlers' eyes. Several sums of money owed for these supplies are listed in the "Nova Scotia Lands" document. There are two drafts totalling £78:10 payable to "Coll. Dixon" -- the same amount mentioned in Hall's letter to William Smith -- which were payment requests to company manager John Hughes for supplies from the garrison. A sum of £75 was to go to "Mr. Weatherhead" for livestock he supplied, and £23:18:2 were owed Wayne for flour shipped out from Halifax. Only the Sommer, Stieff, Lutz, Jones, and Treitz families are listed as having received flour since they were sponsored by Benjamin Franklin & Co.. Requests for payments from the other sponsoring companies are not available although it is assumed that the Rickers, Copples, and Wortmans also received their fair share of supplies. These expenditures show that considerable efforts were made on behalf of the settlers immediately upon arrival.

A closer look at the amount of flour supplied each family is revealing. Michael Lutz[123] had to get by on about £1's worth of flour. Matthias Sommer and Heinrich Stieff, both with large families, were supplied with slightly more than £3 and £4's worth, respectively, yet the smaller families of Charles Jones and Jacob Treitz were given more than £6's worth each. Directives for the distribution of these uneven amounts surely came from John Hughes.

There has been repeated speculation that Charles Jones was related to Hughes since this promoter's wife was a Jones: "Hughes was a relative, almost certainly a brother-in-law of Charles, as there is indication that Hughes was married to Charles' sister."[124] If this familial connection holds true, Charles, as a man unable to sign his name,[125] may have been enticed to leave by his aspiring brother-in-law, who was grooming his reputation in Philadelphian society. On the other hand, perhaps Hughes -- himself a merchant, farmer, and iron-master -- believed this to be a chance for a man to excel whose talents were practical by nature. That there were special circumstances is supported by the fact that Charles Jones, an Anglophone, took part in a settlement scheme that consisted of Germans only.

If Charles Jones received extra supplies as John Hughes' brother-in-law, the special treatment accorded Jacob Treitz probably lay in the esteem Hughes held for this settler. Again, the "Nova Scotia Lands" document may contain some clues. The inclusion of such items as "Bar Iron & Steel" and "Smiths Bellows" shows that at least one of these settlers -- probably Jacob Treitz -- was a blacksmith, a trade vital to a young settlement. No specific reference could be found to confirm Jacob Treitz's blacksmithing capabilities although large, hand-wrought nails used in the Treitz Haus (dated about 1775 and built on Treitz property) may be the best evidence yet.[126] It was not a unique occurrence to provide incentives for a valued tradesman. Thomas Calhoun must have encouraged Abiel Peck to move over to Germantown from Sackville in 1766 to practise this trade. In the "Articles of Agreement", Jacob Treitz' name was added on at the end of a list of settlers' names, in handwriting differing from that of the original scribe, suggesting that he was important enough to be recruited after the date of signing of the other heads of families. Conceivably, Treitz was provided special incentives and continued to be favoured later as evinced by the large quantity of flour. It may be no coincidence either that Jacob Treitz drew Lot No. 9 and situated his farm near several convenient old landing sites (on Hall's Creek, Fisher's Creek, off the Petitcodiac River, etc.), which was ideal for blacksmithing and farming. The success of his farm was evident to William Calhoun in 1771 when he first set eyes on "Monckton".

Both the "Nova Scotia Lands" document and Capt. Hall's letter also hold clues concerning the question as to whether the settlers all arrived at the same time.[127] Although Hall did not refer to them by name, he wrote to his associate William Smith: "Our people was well pleased with the Land ...." These were the two Jacob Rickers, Sr.(widower) and Jr. accompanied by his wife and children Mary, Rosanna, Christina, and Michael, who were sponsored by this company.[128] Hall also refers to the carrying out of Hughes' order to "Buy a cow and calf for Each of his [Hughes'] setlers," which means that the Jones, Lutz, Sommer, Stieff, and Treitz families were also on board and received livestock. John Copple and Georg Wortman, who came with Clarkson & Co., must have arrived at this time, too, because the cost of supplies obtained from Col. Dixon and Mr. Wethered on behalf of the settlers was divided by three, suggesting that three companies sent settlers and that each company was responsible for one-third of all expenses incurred. For example, only £25 of the £75 payable to Mr. Wethered were charged to John Hughes' company. Since it is known that Caton & Co. did not recruit anyone for the "Monckton" settlement, this confirms that the Copples and Wortmans were present at the landing.

The families must have made immediate preparations for the coming winter near the location where Capt. Hall set them ashore. Five short months and a multitude of tasks necessitated the use of land previously cleared and dyked by Acadians. Within two weeks of landing the settlers had planted about 200 lbs. of potatoes, and since the foundations of some Acadian houses were still in place, it is likely that they made use of them or at least reutilized some of the stones for the foundations of a few small pioneer "cabins" that were to be their shelter during the first winter or two. Three such structures may have been what Loyalists Reuben Mills and Ichabod Lewis saw when they arrived in the area by boat from Sackville/Westcock.[129] The settlers did not proceed to their individual grants immediately, but appear to have built a communal shelter for their livestock which, by census time in December of 1766, consisted of 2 horses, 5 oxen, 12 cows, 3 calves, and 6 pigs, underscoring again that they were not without the necessities of life. Remnants of fences[130] and the presence of at least one "old barn" suggest that the south-easternmost part of the grant served as a community pasture initially. A stand of trees left in one corner had been spared the axe to provide shade for grazing animals and was still used for this purpose 50 years later. Mutual assistance in barn- and house-raising, a common practice among Pennsylvania Germans and continued by Mennonites to this day,[131] must have enabled the settlers to complete shelters for man and beast before the onset of winter. It is likely that some of the families shared accommodations during these first critical months, in particular those who did not have the extra manpower provided by older male children, such as the Copple, Ricker, and Wortman families.

After the first group of settlers had come ashore, notices in American newspapers addressed to prospective new settlers continued to be published. On March 8, 1768, the *Pennsylvania Chronicle* ran an announcement that industrious families could apply to Anthony Wayne in Chester County, John Hughes of Upper Merion, south-west of Old Philadelphia, and Benjamin Jacobs in New Providence, Philadelphia County, for land in either of the company's two townships of "Monckton" or "Frankfort".[132] In view of later hardship suffered by the "Monckton" settlers, the land companies' claim is of particular interest, that "...[in] the first mentioned Township a considerable number of Families from this Province have been Settled for Two Years past and ... have expressed the highest Approbation of the Lands in Letters to their Friends." The need for this advertisement suggests that some of the business partners must have been anxious to recruit more settlers while the settlement was still faring reasonably well, at least in its first two years of existence (fig. 19). There is mention in the Jacobs Papers that other ships arrived with settlers and provisions but that these people did not adhere to their agreements. Benjamin Jacobs Jr. remembered his father saying that

> ... in accordance with the scheme inferred to ... [i.e. the settlements of "Monckton" and "Frankfort"] the Company sent to Nova Scotia two vessels loaded with colonists equipped with spades, shovels, axes and implements of husbandry -- when the immigrants arrived there however they found land enough beyond the limits of the towns which had been laid out for them and scattered about wherever they chose taking with them the tools and provisions. -- The result was an entire failure.[133]

There is no other supportive evidence that two vessels with colonists came to "Monckton Township".[134] In the Census of 1766, 49 Germans, 7 Americans and 4 Irish were listed as residing there, for a total of 60 persons.[135] Almost all adults and approximately 18 German boys and 17

186

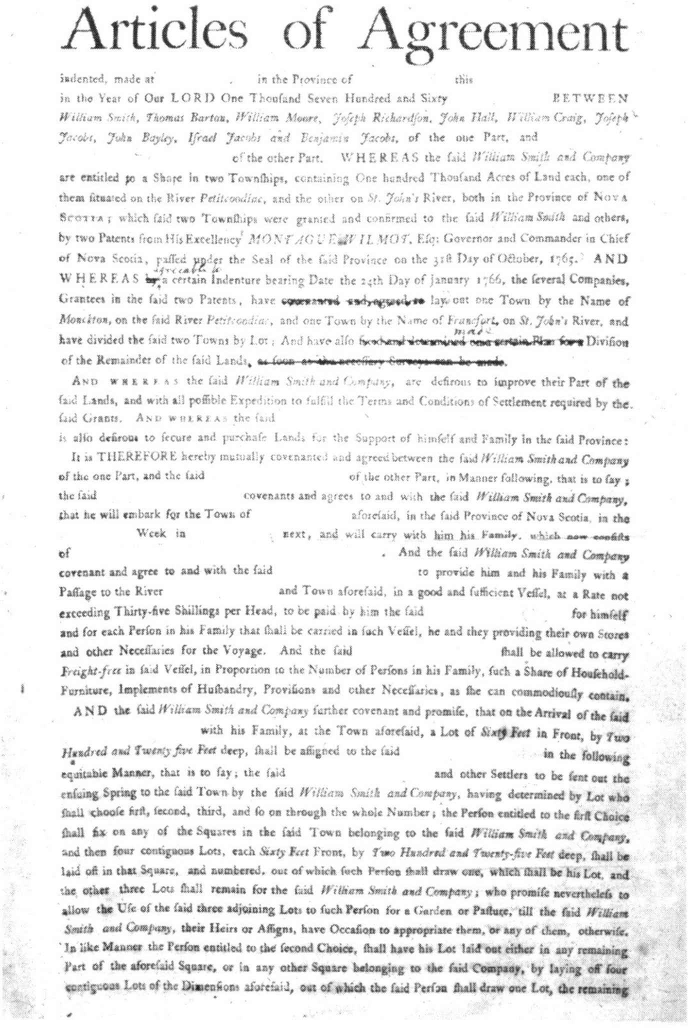

Articles of Agreement

indented, made at in the Province of this in the Year of Our LORD One Thouſand Seven Hundred and Sixty BETWEEN *William Smith, Thomas Barton, William Moore, Joſeph Richardſon, John Hall, William Craig, Joſeph Jacobs, John Bayley, Iſrael Jacobs* and *Benjamin Jacobs*, of the one Part, and of the other Part. WHEREAS the ſaid *William Smith and Company* are entitled to a Share in two Townſhips, containing One hundred Thouſand Acres of Land each, one of them ſituated on the River *Petitcoodiac*, and the other on *St. John's* River, both in the Province of NOVA SCOTIA; which ſaid two Townſhips were granted and confirmed to the ſaid *William Smith* and others, by two Patents from His Excellency MONTAGUE WILMOT, Eſq; Governor and Commander in Chief of Nova Scotia, paſſed under the Seal of the ſaid Province on the 31ſt Day of October, 1765. AND WHEREAS ~~by~~ agreeable to a certain Indenture bearing Date the 24th Day of January 1766, the ſeveral Companies, Grantees in the ſaid two Patents, have ~~covenanted and agreed to~~ lay out one Town by the Name of *Monckton*, on the ſaid River *Petitcoodiac*, and one Town by the Name of *Francfort*, on *St. John's* River, and have divided the ſaid two Towns by Lot; And have alſo ~~fixed and determined one certain Plan for a~~ made Diviſion of the Remainder of the ſaid Lands, ~~as ſoon as the neceſſary Surveys can be made~~.

AND WHEREAS the ſaid *William Smith and Company*, are deſirous to improve their Part of the ſaid Lands, and with all poſſible Expedition to fulfill the Terms and Conditions of Settlement required by the ſaid Grants. AND WHEREAS the ſaid is alſo deſirous to ſecure and purchaſe Lands for the Support of himſelf and Family in the ſaid Province:

It is THEREFORE hereby mutually covenanted and agreed between the ſaid *William Smith and Company* of the one Part, and the ſaid of the other Part, in Manner following, that is to ſay; the ſaid covenants and agrees to and with the ſaid *William Smith and Company*, that he will embark for the Town of aforeſaid, in the ſaid Province of Nova Scotia, in the Week in next, and will carry with him his Family, which ~~now conſiſts of~~ . And the ſaid *William Smith and Company* covenant and agree to and with the ſaid to provide him and his Family with a Paſſage to the River and Town aforeſaid, in a good and ſufficient Veſſel, at a Rate not exceeding Thirty-five Shillings per Head, to be paid by him the ſaid for himſelf and for each Perſon in his Family that ſhall be carried in ſuch Veſſel, he and they providing their own Stores and other Neceſſaries for the Voyage. And the ſaid ſhall be allowed to carry *Freight-free* in ſaid Veſſel, in Proportion to the Number of Perſons in his Family, ſuch a Share of Houſehold-Furniture, Implements of Huſbandry, Proviſions and other Neceſſaries, as ſhe can commodiouſly contain.

AND the ſaid *William Smith and Company* further covenant and promiſe, that on the Arrival of the ſaid with his Family, at the Town aforeſaid, a Lot of *Sixty Feet* in Front, by *Two Hundred and Twenty five Feet* deep, ſhall be aſſigned to the ſaid in the following equitable Manner, that is to ſay; the ſaid and other Settlers to be ſent out the enſuing Spring to the ſaid Town by the ſaid *William Smith and Company*, having determined by Lot who ſhall chooſe firſt, ſecond, third, and ſo on through the whole Number; the Perſon entitled to the firſt Choice ſhall fix on any of the Squares in the ſaid Town belonging to the ſaid *William Smith and Company*, and then four contiguous Lots, each *Sixty Feet* Front, by *Two Hundred and Twenty-five Feet* deep, ſhall be laid off in that Square, and numbered, out of which ſuch Perſon ſhall draw one, which ſhall be his Lot, and the other three Lots ſhall remain for the ſaid *William Smith and Company*; who promiſe nevertheleſs to allow the Uſe of the ſaid three adjoining Lots to ſuch Perſon for a Garden or Paſture, till the ſaid *William Smith and Company*, their Heirs or Aſſigns, have Occaſion to appropriate them, or any of them, otherwiſe. In like Manner the Perſon entitled to the ſecond Choice, ſhall have his Lot laid out either in any remaining Part of the aforeſaid Square, or in any other Square belonging to the ſaid Company, by laying off four contiguous Lots of the Dimenſions aforeſaid, out of which the ſaid Perſon ſhall draw one Lot, the remaining

Figure 19
Printed "Articles of Agreement" for prospective settlers for William Smith & Co.. Jacob Ricker Sr. and Jr. must have signed these forms.

Courtesy: Historical Society of Pennsylvania, Philadelphia
Photo: Rainer L. Hempel

German girls are accounted for through later census records. Although there were casualties in the difficult early years (cf. Genealogical Reference), no one was reported to have died by the end of 1766. Since no records are available for 1767 to 1770, little is known about births, marriages, or deaths during this period. It is believed that the Wortmans had at least one son, Anna Catharina Sommer married Liffe Chappel (c. 1768) and bore a son in 1769, Mrs. Ricker Jr. and Rosanna Treitz each had one daughter, and Matthias Sommer, Mrs. Ricker Jr., and perhaps Mrs. Copple died.[136]

Because of Benjamin Jacobs Jr.'s claim of *two* ships chartered by William Smith and Co., one wonders whether the second vessel was not to take settlers to "Frankfort" Township, perhaps in cooperation with another company in the consortium. Both Jacobs of William Smith & Co.[137] and Capt. Caton of Caton & Co.[138] had personally inspected the lands along the St. John River and found them to be excellent for a township anywhere below St. Anne (Fredericton). Since Caton & Co. sent no settlers to "Monckton", perhaps they concentrated on "Frankfort". The length of time it took Capt. Hall to reach the Petitcodiac settlement suggests that he may have sailed up the St. John River first and for more than just a glimpse of the grant at the head of the tide, about 150 km upriver, althought it is claimed that the settlers did not like the "Frankfort" grant for one reason or another.[139] In fact, four of the nine signatories of the Articles of Agreement never arrived in "Monckton". It has been supposed they " ... changed their minds between January and April [1766]"[140] while still in Philadelphia, but it is curious that almost one half would decide not to honour a formal contract with a land company wherein they legally bound themselves to a five-year period as tenants. Perhaps Valentin Müller,[141] Andres Greiner, Jacob Klein,[142] and Matthias Lentz did disembark at "Frankfort" after all, but for reasons given in the Jacobs Papers or due to difficulties which later afflicted "Monckton" too, the settlement did not thrive. It is certain that considerable activity on the part of the land companies occurred along the Petitcodiac in the years immediately following the settlers' landing, and it would be a mistake to blame the period of hardship,[143] so often alluded to, on the companies' failure to send a second ship with supplies and seed.[144] Difficulties did arise about two years after their arrival when financial support from Philadelphia ceased and local supplies were no longer available, compelling several of the families to move to the Hillsborough settlement, on the south-western shore of the Petitcodiac River about 15 km downstream from "Monckton".

There is contemporary evidence of the plight of the settlers by the year 1769 as recorded in a letter by American businessman and surveyor, Charles Baker, who wrote to John Hughes on behalf of the settlers and Samuel Wethered of Cumberland after visiting the "Monckton" settlement in early June of that year (figs. 20, 20a):

> About four Weeks ago I arrived in this Province from Nova Scotia and thought to have Call'd on you in Philada but as my Busyness Call'd me out of Town Sooner than I expect'd I had not Time –

> My Busyness with you was On Acct your Setlers in Nova Scotia they all of them when I was Coming away Begg'd that I would take the Trouble to Call on you and See what you had a mind to do as they must move of your Land unless you Assist them Very Soon, it being Imposable for them to live any longer without assistance. They beg that you would let them have some Working Cattle and some Cloaths and Provisions untill they will be able to Raise it to themselves which they think will not be long. I think it is a Very Great Pitty that they Should be lett Suffer So much as they have done ever since they Went there as they are a Set of the Best Setlers in them Parts it has Surprised every one that knew them to see how they have lived since they went there Mostly on Herbs which they Gathered in the Marsh in the Spring &c.[145]

> Mr Wethred also begged the favour of me to Speak to you and See whether you would Answer his Acct or not as it has been a Very Great Hurt to Him he has Attach'd all the Cattle on Acct of the debt but does not Care to Sell them untill he knows whether you w'd do any thing or no. I am Sinseable that he has done nothing which he as your Agent or indeed as a Christian could well Avoid, and that he has a Great deal more Trouble Ab't it than all the Profits were Worth even if you had Setled his Acc't at first ....

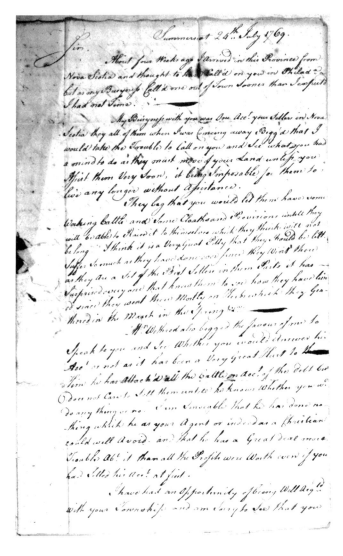

Figures 20/20a

Charles Baker's letter to John Hughes of July 24, 1769 which underscores
the settlers' suffering.

Courtesy: Historical Society of Pennsylvania, Philadelphia

Photo: Rainer L. Hempel

are so backward in doing anything on it as you have a great
deal of Very fine Marsh Land and the Upland Which has
been Cultivated Yeelds Grain Very Well I am Perswaided
it is only for Want of being thoroughly Acquainted with the
Value of it that makes you so Backward in Setling it
I am Sensible that so long as you keep it laying Wast
you loose Annually Some thousands of Pounds which
you might very Easyly Gain by Setling it in a Proper
Manner.

This at the Request of Mr Wethred and your Setlers I have made free to Write you and should be Glad if you
think proper that you Would Write me An Answer
as Soon as Convenient as I intend to go Back to them parts
very Soon again. I am Sir

Your most Obedt Humble

Charles Baker

191

This at the Request of Mr. Wethred and your Setlers I have made free to Write you and should be Glad if you think proper that you Would write me An Answer as Soon as Conveniant as I intend to go Back to them parts Very Soon again.[146]

Charles Baker had been hired as a surveyor by the "Monckton" land companies, but on his trip late in the spring of 1768 he may have dropped in at Martyn's tavern, the only such establishment in Cumberland, where ships usually stopped off before sailing up the Petitcodiac. No doubt Mr. Wethered, who took over this establishment in later years, was there to inform Baker that Hughes had not paid him, leaving the surveyor concerned he might not receive his wages from Clarkson and Co. either. This fear may have been reinforced after talking to the settlers about their suffering as a result of Hughes' apparent insolvency. Wethered's name was mentioned several times -- in the earlier-quoted letter by Rev. Eagleson, in the list of expenses for the "Nova Scotia Lands", and in the above correspondence by Charles Baker -- as some sort of supplier/agent for the "Monckton" settlement. No agent was living on site, as in Germantown and Hillsborough; there was only John Hughes in far-off Philadelphia, trying to coordinate the activities and divergent wishes of twenty-two associates.[147] The situation became critical when Wethered not only refused to support the settlers any longer but threatened to repossess his cattle after waiting over two years in vain for Hughes to settle his account. Although life could not have been easy initially and especially over the first winter, real hardship probably set in by the third winter (1768-1769).

Whether or not Charles Baker's letter was ever delivered into Hughes' hands,[148] one must conclude that the latter was unable to assist the settlers further. Hughes' appointment as officer for the implementation of the Stamp Act, which he accepted in 1765 as a favour from his business partner Benjamin Franklin, had become a liability a year later after Americans interpreted it as a form of taxation and fund-raising by the Crown. The wrath of the people came down squarely on the shoulders of John Hughes, the perpetrator of this evil and main obstacle to their demand "No Taxation without Representation", ruined his business, and put an end to his involvement in the Nova Scotia land speculation scheme. Even when the Act was repealed in 1766, Hughes was forced to leave Philadelphia and retire to his farm in Upper Merion, eventually moving to Charleston, South Carolina, where he died in 1772.

It was certainly no coincidence that Baker's letter to Hughes was written in Summersett, Pennsylvania, the hometown of the competing land company owner Adam Hoops. Charles Baker's concern over the welfare of "Monckton" may not have been as innocent as he wished to portray it in his letter. Well before writing on July 24, 1769, Baker knew that the settlers were poised to move, and he certainly must have discussed the matter with Robert Cummings, the manager of the Hillsborough settlement, who likely urged him to consult with his uncle as well. Hoops, in turn, may have prompted Baker to write the letter to Hughes in order to clear his own name of the taint of a seemingly underhanded business manoeuvre. All three men -- Charles Baker, Robert Cummings, and Adam Hoops -- must have been fully cognizant of the difficulties that plagued Hughes. One can only surmise as to the extent of the machinations, interrelationships, and competitiveness which existed between the land companies. The proof that Baker's letter was a ruse lies in the 1770 Hillsborough Census which recorded the yields and livestock of the previous year. The harvests of wheat, rye, peas, barley, hemp, and flax in 1769 confirm that Jacob Ricker Jr., Michael Lutz, and Heinrich Stieff had moved to Hillsborough even *before* Baker wrote his letter to Hughes. In order to prepare for such a harvest, these settlers crossed over to Hillsborough at least by the middle of May 1769,[149] if not earlier, depending on when the women and children were relocated. Whether Baker and Cummings were genuinely trying to help the settlers out or simply exploiting a situation in a troubled township is perhaps unimportant, the fact remains that there was no expectation Hughes would ever respond to Baker's pleas or pay his debt to Mr. Wethered. Cummings did not wait long to reward Baker for his good services in bringing more settlers to Hillsborough. In 1770, Thomas Calhoun left the employ of Adam Hoops as manager of Germantown, Cummings moved down to his uncle's settlement soon after to fill the vacant position and appointed Charles Baker the manager of Hillsborough in 1771.[150] Upon the death of his uncle Hoops that same year, Cummings felt obliged to leave Germantown in the hands of another agent and return to Baltimore.[151]

For a while it appeared as if "Monckton Township" were headed for the same fate as Germantown. According to the 1770 Hillsborough Census, three families crossed the Petitcodiac River in order to become part of this settlement -- the Lutz's, Rickers, and Stieffs -- apparently leaving the Copples, Jones's, Treitz's, and Wortmans in "Monckton".[152] These families stayed behind, not because there had been feuding or they were less in need but, in two cases at least, for apparent personal reasons. Charles Jones, as a possible relation by marriage to John Hughes, must have refused to support the settlement of a competitor, and Jacob Treitz must have been angry with Cummings for having led his daughter astray. Another reason why the Jones and Treitz families chose to remain in "Monckton" must have had to do with their choice lots, one with "Mill Creek" (Lot No. 4) and the other on Hall's Creek, strategically accessible by water (Lot No. 9), where they could farm and ply their trades probably as miller and blacksmith, respectively. The seemingly unfair distribution of flour to these two families may have been an attempt to allow them the time to establish a gristmill and smithy, whereas the other settlers were expected to prepare the fields and plant the first harvests, such as buckwheat and potatoes. It is not surprising therefore, that Jones and Treitz preferred not to abandon their properties. John Hughes' difficulties and the premature death of Charles Jones interrupted the development in "Monckton", but Jones's sons, Henry and John, returned in 1780 to farm and put the gristmill back in operation. It seems like a well-thought-out plan that Charles Baker, who had no intention to settle in "Monckton" but was entitled to a grant, was allowed to bid for land near the original Jones farmstead where Margaret Jones and her new husband, Abraham Treitz, may have settled around 1775, a year after Charles Jones's death. In this way, Abraham Treitz, who was not entitled to bid for land in 1778, could "buy back" his property from Charles Baker in 1780 after Baker's title was cleared.

Past researchers[153] have assumed that whole families either moved or stayed, but the 1775 and 1783 Hillsborough censuses and Millidge Report of 1788 reveal a stratagem of the Petitcodiac Germans by which they sought to ensure land grants in two different townships. Most families never left completely or at least not without the intention of returning and laying claim to their land in "Monckton". Three members of the Lutz family may have stayed behind, as well as Jacob Ricker Sr.. Christian Stieff returned in 1775,

194

followed by his brother Frederick in 1781, to take possession of the Stieff grant. Those families thought to have stayed in "Monckton" did not do so in their entirety either. Sometime after 1775 and before 1780, Jacob Ricker Sr. may have married Charles Jones's widow and moved with her family to Hillsborough, "retiring" in or near the homestead of his son, Jacob Ricker Jr.. Three Jones children likely accompanied them: Henry, John, and an unidentified daughter of age in 1783. The Ricker farm on the "Monckton" side (Lot No. 8) was taken over by Rosanna Ricker and her husband Jacob Treitz Jr..[154] While living in Hillsborough, Henry and John Jones became acquainted with their future spouses, Christinah (Ricker/Sommer/Wortman?) and Dinnis Daniels, respectively, but returned to "Monckton" sometime around 1780 to settle land awarded them as "the heirs of Charles Jones" -- possibly looked after for them in 1778 by Ricker Sr.. Andrew Sommer also came back to "Monckton" in the early eighties, more likely after reaching adulthood about 1783. He built a house on the property west of Jacob Treitz Jr., close to where Michael Lutz had resided until 1769.[155] Georg Wortman, who could not divide his young family to lay claim to land in both "Monckton" and Hillsborough, tried to assure himself of possibilities on both sides of the river as well. He did not leave for Hillsborough until after 1770 (but before 1773) and still appeared there in the 1783 census, at the same time claiming in the Millidge Report to have lived on his "Monckton" grant since 1780. The only families not to take advantage of these "double grant" possibilities were the Copples, who may not have been in a position to do so,[156] and the Treitz's, who, as a result of their purchase of the Charles Baker grant and Jacob Treitz Jr.'s inheritance/purchase of Ricker Jr's grant, obtained two additional tracts in "Monckton".

That the difficulties in the "Monckton" settlement which caused so many to leave were real is supported by other evidence such as a contemporary account in the journals of Lieutenant Colonel Joseph Gubbins, inspector of Troops in New Brunswick from 1810-1816, who recorded:

> I was this night accommodated in a good brick house (the first I had seen in the Province) [built about 1800] belonging to a German farmer named Tritz. This man informed me that he and his relations were the first white inhabitants that had settled in this part of the country and the difficulties they had to contend with, what appeared

to me almost incredible. His mother, he said, had lost the use of one of her arms, and not being able to protect herself from the flies, she was actually killed by them, they not being acquainted at that time of the method now practised of keeping off insects by smoak. They had been brought to the country by some speculators in land, whose means perhaps had failed and they were left to perish with hunger, which was very near being the case. When I saw them about twenty-five years afterwards, they were in possession of a most flourishing farm surrounded by others which they had established for their sons and daughters, who are married and settled in the neighbourhood.[157]

Christian Trites, in whose house Colonel Gubbins spent the night, must have had some inkling as to the difficulties which beset John Hughes. Ironically, it was Benjamin Franklin who, by appointing Hughes to oversee the implementation of the Stamp Act, inadvertently ruined Hughes' as well as his own investment in Franklin & Co. and imposed suffering and hardship on the Petitcodiac Germans during their first few years in "Monckton".

V.3 The Hillsborough Settlement

On October 31, 1765, Hillsborough Township was granted to Nova Scotia Council members John Collier, Joseph Gerrish, and Henry Newton, as well as to Robert Cummings (Adam Hoops' nephew) and James Boutineau, son-in-law of Michael Francklin, a prominent Halifax merchant, who later became Nova Scotia's Lieutenant Governor.[158] The Township itself was named after Lord Hillsborough, Secretary of State, who was also one of the Lords' Commissioners.[159] Shortly after his arrival in 1771, William Calhoun wrote in his diary:

Friday the 26th [of July] I went with my brother to Germantown, where I was kindly received to the country by Mr. Cummins. I returned home that evening. ... I concluded to stay some time in the country .... Sunday the 27th of July being a clear, pleasant day, ... I set out with Mr. Cummins, Mr. Eagleson and my brother to see the land and settlements in the Petitcodiac River, at the estuary of which I sat filled with amazement at the beauty of the River and the surrounding country. We landed at Moses [De]Lesdernier's Esq., Proprietary agent for the Township of Hillsboro'. From him I learned the terms of settling the aforesaid township, and as I liked the terms of the settlement very well ... I took a walk with my brother through the woodland and lots adjacent to it, and both being well pleased with the appearances of the land, we agreed to make application for five lots each. Each of these lots contained, facing the river, fifty acres of upland and ten acres of marsh. Continuing our walk we crossed over some land which was of excellent quality, and went to some neighboring farms, where they told us that everything put into the ground seemed to flourish.[160]

In spite of the beauty and quality of the land, Cummings had not been able to attract the numbers of settlers necessary under the terms of the grant, which stipulated that there be 500 Protestants in the Township by 1770. In the Census of this year, the new settlement of Hillsborough appeared for the first time, and only 100 persons were listed. Of these residents, almost one-third were recent arrivals from "Monckton", i.e. the Stieff, Ricker Jr./Sommer, Lutz, and Smith families.[161] Escheat of the Hillsborough grant was a real possibility. This perhaps more than anything else explains why Robert Cummings did not reject "robbing the cradle" of a competing land company, something Anthony Wayne had dismissed three years earlier. A breakdown of the 1770 Census reveals which Petitcodiac German families were living in Hillsborough by that date: "Henry Steeve" (4 men, 4 boys, 1 woman, of whom 7 are American and 2 German), Jacob Ricker Jr. (1 man, 2 boys, 1 woman, 6 girls, of whom 8 are American and 2 German), Michael "Lootz" (2 men, 1 boy, 2 women, 1 girl, of whom 2 are Americas and 4 Germans) and two "Swiss", Peter "Joannah"[162] and Moses Delesdernier,[163] besides several Anglophone and Acadian families. The members listed as "men" and "women" in each family are the husbands, wives and grown children. In Michael "Lootz's" case, for example, one of the men was Michael and the other, his son Peter, who was 18 in 1770; the two women were Anna Walpurgis (mother) and Anna Catharina (daughter), who was 20 as of December 31, 1769, when the 1770 Census was completed. Margaret and one of Thomas, Michael Jr., John, or Henry were the "girl" and "boy" and, since they were born in Philadelphia, were listed as Americans whereas the other four were German, having been born in Germany.[164]

197

The Petitcodiac Germans were successful in Hillsborough as the result of able management and fair treatment by their agents.[165] By the latter part of 1769, Heinrich Stieff owned 2 bulls, 4 cows, 5 "Young meat Cattle", and 8 sheep, these being the only sheep in Hillsborough. Jacob Ricker Jr. and Michael Lutz owned 2 cows each, and 3 and 2 calves, respectively. Few other residents possessed any livestock. Most of the Acadians harvested much higher quantities of wheat: John Babbinno [sic], Paul Babbinno, John Dubboy [sic], and Supoiyan Dupey[sic], all over 60 bushels. This compares with 16 bushels for Stieff, 2 for Ricker, and 6 for Lutz, no doubt on account of their recent arrival. On the other hand, the German families harvested the only rye crop within the community. Heinrich Stieff was also the only one to grow hemp, but truly impressive figures were achieved in the harvest of flax, over 3,000 pounds[166] for each of the German families, which together with the sheep's wool must reflect on their homespun and weaving activities to supply their own needs and perhaps to produce articles of trade, e.g. blankets, that might bring needed cash.

The 1770 returns show that Hillsborough was a very young settlement. With the exception of Heinrich Stieff, no one owned any working cattle, and there were no horses, mills, or boats of any large size. Hillsborough clearly depended on the outside assistance and services of such established towns as Cumberland and Sackville, which by 1770 had both grist- and sawmills, several fishing vessels, as well as sloops or schooners and large harvests in a variety of crops. The 1770 Census for Hillsborough, however, reveals the successes which the Stieffs, Rickers, and Lutz's were able to achieve after a single growing season.

Robert Cummings must have felt confident enough to leave Hillsborough in Baker's hands when he moved down to Germantown, and then to Baltimore two years later. In a letter to Charles Baker dated July 19, 1773, Cummings wrote: "... I expected to have had the pleasure of seeing you at Hillsborough before this time but my friends were much bent against my return to Nova Scotia to settle since which I have purchased a Small Estate in Maryland within Twenty Miles from Baltimore .... I have still a liking to Nova Scotia and hope to see you at Hillsborough next spring when I shall come and make out and give those people who are setled on my Land their Deeds ...."[167] Strained relations between the tenants and their absentee landlords developed in later years, but in 1775 it was the American War of Independence that imposed an arbitrary silence between the two. This probably prevented Cummings from ever setting foot in Nova Scotia again to hand over the deeds, despite his intent to do so, and he died in Baltimore two years later at the age of 48. In 1785, Jacob Ricker Jr., his son Michael, Peter Lutz, and three members of the Stiles family applied for grants as former tenants of "Mr. Robert Cummins [sic] and Mr. Adam Hoops."[168] The necessity to apply and give reasons in their applications that they were indeed the owners confirms that the former landlord never did hand over the deeds as promised. These men were advised to reapply the following year, together with numerous others including five of Heinrich Stieff's sons -- John, Matthias, Henry, Jacob, and Ludovic.[169]

Jacob Treitz and John Copple were the only German heads of families who never accepted the invitation by Robert Cummings and Charles Baker, in 1769 or later.[170] Just as Thomas Calhoun had befriended the daughter of his tenant, Abiel Peck, and made her his wife, so did Robert Cummings court Rosanna, Jacob Treitz's daughter. It is curious that both agents' fancy fell on blacksmiths' daughters, however Cummings never married Rosanna although he acknowledged the child out of their relationship, a daughter named Elizabeth, making provision for her before leaving for Baltimore in a will dated September 21, 1772.[171] Cummings appears to have deserted Rosanna[172] and young Elizabeth when he moved from Hillsborough to Germantown in 1770, despite the secretive care and interest he showed in them in his letter of July 17, 1773 to Charles Baker.

Researchers have *assumed* that Robert Cummings and Rosanna Treitz never formally married since Cummings presumably would have taken Rosanna and their child to Hillsborough, Germantown, and finally back to Baltimore with him. An important inconsistency between a more recent *Trites Genealogy* and the earlier one by Clark Wright[173] sheds light on this subject. Clark Wright states that Christian and Rosanna Stieff's first child was Henry, born in 1779, whereas the *Trites Genealogy* places a daughter, Rachel (named after Christian's mother), born in 1776, as their first child. Assuming the latter, more recent information to be correct, Rosanna could not have married Cummings when the daughter fathered by Christian was born a year before Cummings' death. Clearly, Rosanna must have given up on her former partner and married Christian Stieff around 1775, before news of Cummings' death ever reached her. An earlier suggestion that Cummings might have had a wife in Baltimore[174] is substantiated in the Will he left in the hands of Rev. Eagleson in 1772, to be opened only in the event of an accident. In it, Cummings makes reference to "Madam", who would be returning shortly to Baltimore and from whom the existence of his daughter by Rosanna Treitz was to be kept secret.[175] Elizabeth (Cummings) Stiles apparently thought well of both her parents and named a child after each.

By marrying Christian Stieff, Rosanna Treitz followed the example set by most of the other Petitcodiac German children who chose partners from their midst, yet her marriage to Christian was not usual in terms of 18th-century European morality. Rosanna was, after all, an unwed mother and since there was no scarcity of eligible women in these frontier communities (e.g. in the Ricker/Sommer family) the question arises as to why the Stieff family condoned, or possibly even encouraged, such a liaison. The most obvious and immediate reason was the love shared between the two, of which there is evidence in Christian Stieff's final Will and Testament made out shortly before his death in 1820. Partial reasons might be the closeness of the pioneering families at this time, their reluctance to create dissension, their respect for Christian's choice, wide acceptance of living common law in the absence of clergy, and the belief that Robert Cummings had taken advantage of a young woman's innocence. However, a more immediate reason may have been Regina and Heinrich Stieff's perception of Rosanna's predicament in view of their own premarital transgressions within the rigid, moralistic environment of small-town Germany. Rosanna and Christian's marriage may be viewed as an example of adaptation to the circumstances of frontier living, where societal *mores* gave way to the truly important matters of life.

The first Hillsborough marriage of two Petitcodiac Germans is thought to be that of Catharina Lutz and Jacob Stieff, on January 28, 1772.[176] According to Stieff family tradition, Jacob was "pretty young",[177] but in fact he was 22, now that his birth date has been established as November 14, 1749. He built a "big house about 30 rods"[178] from Heinrich Stieff's farmhouse. The wedding was a social event for people from miles around. William Calhoun recorded his journey and attendance:

Abraham Trites came from Petitcodiac, and gave us an invitation to go to Jacob Steeves' wedding, which was to take place on the following Tuesday; ... My brother and I set out to go as far as Petitcodiac, and we suffered very much from the intense cold, and had our snowshoes failed in the middle of the marsh between Shepody Hill and Cape Demozel [Cap Demoiselle], we would most certainly have perished before we could have reached a place where we could have struck up a fire. We travelled as far as Michael Lutes (a distance of about eighteen miles) when it became so cold that we dare not go further that night; ... [the following day we] proceeded to the house where the wedding was to take place, about a mile distant, where were gathered all the people of Hillsborough; and after the ceremony was over, we fell to dancing and frolicking until next morning .... [179]

Other Stieff sons married into the family of Martin Beck,[180] the "King's baker" at Fort Cumberland (fig. 21), who is listed in the 1770 Cumberland Census as comprising two Germans and five Americans, although he had been living in the area for a longer time. Beck's name appears on a petition in 1763 along with 67 others, all of whom applied to the Province of Nova Scotia for cleared land in Cumberland.[181]

According to the 1775 Hillsborough Census,[182] Beck is listed as living there in the company of his countrymen. His two daughters became the wives of two of Heinrich Stieff's sons; Mary married Henry Stieff (c. 1781) and had five surviving children while Sophia married Matthias Stieff (c. 1785), by whom she had 13 children. Thus, Heinrich Stieff became an in-law of the very man who had helped him out at Fort Cumberland during his first visit there more than a decade earlier.

Life in Hillsborough had been good. By 1775 the first-wed couple, Jacob and Catharina Stieff, had "... two children [John born 1773 and Leonard 1775], as well as 2 oxen, 3 yearlings, 2 heifers, 2 bull calves, a mare, a colt, 2 ewes, a lamb, 2 hogs, and 18 pigs. In addition, Jacob managed that year to raise 50 bushels of wheat, 18 of rye [for German bread], 13 of barley [and] 24 of peas [for soups], 4 of oats [for cereals], 60 of turnips [for the (in)famous " turnip mush"!], 50 of potatoes, and 1,000

Figure 21
Discovery of a badge of the "King's German Legion" in Point-de-Bute, N.B.
is evidence that Germans were stationed at Fort Cumberland.

Courtesy: Fort Beauséjour Museum, Aulac, N.B.
Photo: Rainer L. Hempel

202

pounds of flax [for weaving cloth]."[183] This certainly looked different from a few short years earlier.

"Henry Steeve Sen." is reported as having nine in his family in 1775, which is puzzling since Jacob was on his own by this time.[184] Stieff Sr.'s household was one of the largest and wealthiest in Hillsborough, not only on account of its manpower but also of his and Regina's farming expertise. They owned 12 oxen, 14 cows, 1 bull, 10 yearlings, and 12 calves as well as 3 horses, 42 sheep, and 30 pigs. Their harvest was equally impressive: 150 bushels of wheat (the highest in Hillsborough), 18 of rye, 16 of barley, 50 of peas, 100 of oats, 150 of turnips (again the largest in the settlement), 100 of potatoes, and 3,000 pounds of flax.

Jacob Ricker Jr. (born c. 1730) is listed in the 1775 Hillsborough "Census", the first conclusive evidence that two Jacob Rickers landed in 1766. The widower, Jacob Ricker Sr. (born c. 1705), came to "Monckton" as an older man and adjunct to the family of his son which has been common among immigrants who wish to look after their parents and not leave them behind. Jacob Ricker Sr. stayed in "Monckton" at least until 1775. Jacob Ricker Jr. had a very large household in 1775, nine in all, which included Michael Ricker, Andrew Sommer, and the unmarried Sommer and Ricker girls. The record of a 16-year-old "daughter of age" in Peter and Mary (*née* Ricker) Lutz's Hillsborough household in 1783 may shed light on the way these two families came to terms with the death of Jacob Ricker Jr.'s wife shortly after their arrival at The Bend. Michael Ricker was born in 1764/1765 and this "daughter" around 1767, near the time when Jacob Ricker Jr. lost his wife. When Ricker Jr. married Matthias Sommer's widow, his eldest daughter Mary must have helped out in looking after the infant and, after Mary's marriage to Peter Lutz, this "daughter" (sister) may have stayed with her. This couple settled at "Ricker's Point",[185] the present Point Park in Riverview, south of Jacob Ricker Jr., who had been established there since 1773 and had prospered by the time of the 1775 Census to judge by his livestock and harvest figures. Jacob Ricker Jr. reported some of the highest yields in the settlement for wheat, 140 bushels (second only to Heinrich Stieff at 150 bushels), peas at 47, oats at 98, and turnips at 130. Ricker Jr. had the largest flax harvest at 3,200 pounds, which may at first glance be a reflection of the large number of girls/women in his household engaged in weaving. Most Petitcodiac Germans grew flax in sufficient quantities for their weaving activities, but Jacob Ricker Jr. was the only one who claimed to support his family in later years, at least partially, by weaving. In a land transaction to Peter Lutz in 1796, the deed records Ricker's trade as "weaver".[186] Considering the ages of Ricker Jr.'s sons -- still "under age" in 1783 -- and the fact that there were 6 women/girls[187] in his household, these agricultural yields are remarkable for one man. One explanation may be Ricker's good fortune in being allowed to take over Robert Cummings' own well-established farm.

In the 1775 Census, Michael Lutz is listed as having 7 in his family. Since several of his children were married by this time, this appears to conflict with the earlier total of 6 in the 1770 Census. In view of information contained in the 1775/1783 "Census", however, the number of children in the Lutz family has been revised. This later "Census" reveals that there were at least 7, including "four sons of age ... three of these ... [on the] other side of the River [presumably in "Monckton"]." The names of Michael Lutz's five sons are now known: Peter (born 1751), Thomas (born c. 1753), Michael Jr. (born 1758), Johannes/John, (born c. 1761), and Heinrich/Henry (born c. 1763).[188] On his Hillsborough farm in 1775, Michael Lutz Sr. owned: 4 oxen, 4 cows, 1 yearling, 4 calves, 3 horses, 4 sheep, and 20 pigs. The family harvested 40 bushels of wheat, 6 of rye, 15 of barley, 22 of peas, 55 of oats, 110 of turnips (one of the highest in Hillsborough), 130 of potatoes (the second highest), and 1,500 pounds of flax.

The Georg Wortman household consisted of 7 members in the 1775 return. Since the census in his case was taken in 1773, it suggests that 3 children were born in Pennsylvania and 2 in "Monckton". In 1783, his family appears not to have increased and his children were still listed as "under age". One might conclude that the Wortmans "lost" at least three children, including the two eldest, who would have been of age then and already left home (cf. Wortman Family genealogy). In 1773, Wortman had only recently moved to Hillsborough, which explains his limited livestock: 2 oxen, 2 cows, 5 calves/yearlings, 4 sheep, and 1 pig, with no harvests at all. Frederick Burgsdorf (Burkstaff), Joseph Brackman(n), and Charles Myers[189] -- former Germantown settlers -- had also settled in Hillsborough by 1775.

It is noteworthy that most Germans cultivated rye, unlike English and French Hillsborough residents, showing the German preference for rye bread. The crop diversity shows that they did not want to rely on any one harvest alone. If one considers farm technology of the 18th century and the few years they had to develop their farms, the yields in Hillsborough are impressive, particularly in view of the multitude of pests and maggots that frustrate gardeners in this region.[190] The labour involved in producing a bushel of peas, as just one example, is enormous: cultivating, planting, weeding, harvesting, shelling, and drying. All were crops which could be easily dried and/or stored. In spite of the work-intensive nature of their endeavours, the Petitcodiac Germans succeeded in achieving a level of comfort in life unequalled to any they had known, in Pennsylvania and especially in Germany.

Although challenging, life was not without its rewards in these settlements, but all this was endangered by developments further south. The desire of the American colonies for freedom and independence from Britain, which, as previously stated, drove John Hughes from Philadelphia in 1767 and prevented the Petitcodiac Germans from obtaining their land grants, began in 1775 to affect them in yet another way. The personal safety and self-sufficient livelihoods for which these people had worked so hard became threatened at the onset of the Revolution by rebel vessels which began to ply the waters of the Bay of Fundy and Petitcodiac. Newspaper articles, such as the following from 1893 which mentions Jacob and Catharina Stieff specifically, relate countless episodes from this fractious period in history:

> The residents of the Lower Settlement (as Hillsborough was then most often called) were often raided by a group of robbers. The people had in their possession a bull, which was kept in a secluded place. These pirates managed to find out from some person belonging to another settlement where the animal was kept. It was soon captured and converted into food for the band .... After this they got together all the bedding there was at the house, made themselves a bed on the floor and went to sleep, leaving one of their members on guard. Jacob [Stieff] and his wife [Catharina] were left with nothing to sleep on but the bedstead. Katy ... said she gathered about her what clothes she wore and tried to get some sleep. Jacob

205

did not try to sleep, and some time during the night he discovered the guard had gone to sleep. He made up his mind to get his axe and dispatch them before they could wake up. Only the earnest entreaties of his wife prevented this resolution being carried out. How many tragedies have been averted by the gentle persuasions of a woman![191]

This is quite a compliment to Catharina (Lutz). The Hillsborough settlers held Abiel Peck as that "person belonging to another settlement", namely Germantown, responsible for disclosing the secret location of the bull to the pirates, and for generations there were no marriages between these families even though the distance separating them was small. That there was no love lost between the Pecks and the Petitcodiac Germans undoubtedly went back further than the bull incident since Peck, of English-American background, had taken the side of Calhoun against the German-speaking settlers in Germantown. Rachel Peck, Thomas Calhoun's widow, eventually secured a large portion of Germantown which went to her second husband Robert Dickson.[192] Many reports corroborate the suspicions of the Hillsborough Germans, who supported the British Crown, that Abiel Peck was an American sympathizer whose untoward political activities at "Shepperdy"[193] encouraged pirates from Machias and areas further south on the New England coast to make his farm their meeting place. An episode described by the young preacher William Black of Amherst, Nova Scotia, whose many visits to the Petitcodiac River are discussed in the following chapter, is valuable reading in this context:

In the night a number of plunderers came to Mrs. Stieves' [Heinrich Stieff's widow in Hillsborough] and demanded something to eat, and remained till morning. They were from Machias, and are a set of wretches who cloak their villany by the agitations of the times; ....

They detained us from going up the river [to "Monckton"] for about two hours and a half, when the tide was so far spent that we could not go. This they did with the design to prevent us from informing the people of their coming.

206

...We left the Point [Ricker's Point] in the morning about one a.m. intending to get before the plunderers, but being in a whale boat and we having only a canoe, they had the advantage and easily passed us in the river. At the village [near Allison and Abraham Treitz' farm] we fell in with them again. I now spoke my mind to them more fully showing them that they could not escape the damnation of hell unless a speedy repentance should prevent ....

They killed an ox and a sheep, plundered the mill [the Jones brothers' gristmill on Mill Creek] of all the flour they could find, and left some families almost destitute of clothes and bedding. Yet they attempted to take neither my clothes, nor watch, nor anything belonging to me.[194]

Although the events described in Black's diary entries of November 22 and 24, 1782 show the menace of privateers until the end of the American War of Independence, such raids became less frequent after the failure of the Eddy Rebellion in 1776, which was an attempt by rebel sympathizers to take Fort Cumberland. Slowly those residents of Germantown[195] and Hillsborough[196] who had sought refuge at the fort were able to return to their homes. By 1783, a number of Acadian and Yorkshire families lived in Hillsborough alongside the German families of: Peter Lutz, the widow Regina Stieff "with a large quantity of stock", Jacob Ricker Sr. "with 2 sons and 1 Daughter of age," Jacob Ricker Jr. "with 2 nearly full grown sons", Georg Wortman, Martin Beck with 11 children, Jacob Stieff with 5, John Stieff with 4, Henry Stieff with 1, "a Dutch woman with three Children",[197] as well as "Lutwick" and Matthew Stieff, and Henry Lutz, all three listed as single men ready to start households within one year. Jacob Ricker Jr.'s step-daughters, as well as his own daughters Mary, Rosanna, and possibly Christina were all married by 1783. Andrew Sommer, Michael Lutz Sr. (with his son John), Frederick and Christian Stieff, and Georg Wortman had returned to "Monckton" to take possession of their grants. Moses Delesdernier, the "Proprietary agent for the Township of Hillsboro"[198] and cosignatory of an agreement with landowners Michael Francklin and Joseph Gerrish,[199] was by this time living part-time at Cumberland.

When escheat of the grant was being considered by the government, i.e. that the Francklin/Gerrish land investment revert to the Crown for non-fulfilment of conditions, Gerrish's son-in-law, Joseph Gray, appealed to Halifax that his "... Father in Law [Gerrish] being possessed of two-fifths of the Township of Hillsborough Carried on the settlement of it at a great Expense and in 1765 or 1766 sent men of Abilities to Philadelphia, Germany and Other parts for the purpose of Inviting Settlers to their Lands and which was the means of Encouraging great numbers of Industrious families resorting to the Province ...."[200] Gray also mentioned the hindrance and impact the American War of Independence had had on the settlement of the Township:

> In 1776 when His Majesty Garrison at Fort Cumberland was attackd and the besiegers in their retreat fell upon our settlement which they plundered of the Cattle Grain and the Tennants wearing apparell and other matters and the settlers many of them were driven away to the Fort at Cumberland for safety and there in order to support themselves and families were obliged to Enlist themselves as soldiers whereby they were lost to me as Tennants.

> During the continuance of the War the Enemy in Armd vessels frequently Committed depredations and put a stop to the progress in settling our Lands and reduced us to the Necessity of being one night in bed and the next under Arms besides the Charge of maintaining an armd vessel in the Bay of Fundy for our Defence.[201]

In a margin opposite the names of the 1783 portion of the Gray petition, a telling comment sums up the landowners' dilemma: "The late Troubles in America has prevented a Return of the Produce in Grain or Increase of Stock of any of these Inhabitants."[202] In a separate letter attached to Gray's petition and dated October 23, 1783, officials in Halifax and London corroborate Gray's claims and attest to his status in Nova Scotia:

> ... Joseph Gray Esquire has resided in the Province Thirty Three Years, ... he ... has conducted himself with Credit & Reputation and manifested a Steady Attachment to the British Constitution & Government, ... and exerted himself for many Years in settling the

208

Township of Hillsborough in this Province to which he is one of the Heirs at Law. ... [T]he Troubles in America not only check'd the Increase of the Inhabitants, but effectively prevented a further Fulfilment of the Conditions of Patent, as American Privateers frequently visited that settlement and committed great Depredations among the Inhabitants, in so much that many Families were obliged to remove themselves for Protection into other Parts to the great Detriment of the Proprietors.

Joseph Goreham, commander of Fort Cumberland during the Eddy Rebellion and later resident of London, added in the margin of this document that he, too, was able to "... confirm the foregoing and also [to] declare ... that during ... [his] Command at Fort Cumberland ... the Enemy's Privateers and Armed Vessels frequently went into the River Petitcodiack and landed in the Township of Hillsborough plundering the Inhabitants & drove many of them from that Settlement who were obliged to retire for Protection to the Fort ...."[203] The attestations to Joseph Gray's good moral character and other corroborative evidence regarding the American pirate raids support the information provided in his submission as being reasonably accurate. Gray was awarded some recognition for the work and money his father-in-law had expended when a large section of land was granted to him, including "Gray's Island", a piece of elevated land which later became Hillsborough's burying ground. Michael Francklin eventually divested himself of his interests in Hillsborough to Joshua Mauger, who was able to obtain 3,464 acres above Weldon's Creek.[204] By and large, the Township became divided among settlers who cleared and cultivated the land -- some Acadian families, the Petitcodiac Germans, immigrants from Yorkshire, and United Empire Loyalists. In spite of the 1778 land grants in "Monckton Township" which drew some people back, Hillsborough remained a predominantly German community well into the 19th century, variously referred to as the "Steeves colony"[205] or "Dutch Village", and this was the case for good portions of Albert County at least up until the 1851 Census.

ENDNOTES

[1] The British authorities considered the land vacant despite the presence of the aboriginals and were unaware of Acadians in hiding.

[2] Christopher Moore, *The Loyalists* (Toronto: MacMillan of Canada, 1982), p. 15.

[3] For a detailed account of the early history of Nova Scotia and the reasons for certain British settlement schemes, refer to Chapter II of Winthrop P. Bell's book, *The "Foreign Protestants" and the Settlement of Nova Scotia*. The story of the settlement of Lunenburg is the main subject of Bell's book, which had long been out-of-print and was reissued by the Centre for Canadian Studies at Mount Allison University in 1990, ed. L.D. McCann, "... to emphasize the seminal importance of the pioneering study" (Quote on front cover of reprint).

[4] North American sources often refer to this conflict as the French and Indian Wars on account of the French army's use of "Indian" allies in the fighting.

[5] W.O. Raymond, "Colonel Alexander McNutt and the Pre-Loyalist Settlements of Nova Scotia," *Transaction of the Royal Society of Canada*, Section 11, 1911, pp. 25ff..

[6] PANS, Halifax, Call Number: MG100 Vol. 47, No. 58.

[7] This declaration, also known as the "Charter of Nova Scotia" and dated January 11, 1759, contains assurances regarding civil and religious liberties and a constitution. Thomas Chandler Haliburton, *An Historical and Statistical Account of Nova Scotia*, Vol. 1 (Halifax: Joseph Howe, 1829), p. 220.

[8] The settlement of Lunenburg was only the second instance in which colonization was undertaken by the British government itself, the first being the settlement of the Palatines after the exodus of 1708-1709. In all other cases the land was granted to "chartered companies", or proprietors, with certain conditions attached. The company was usually responsible for recruiting settlers, providing transportation, start-up tools, and seeds. The settlers agreed to pay a nominal "quit-rent" to the proprietors and were therefore often referred to as "tenants." The land company hoped to reap its profits from the sale of certain restricted lands, the value of which had increased since the colony's establishment. Examination of proprietors' correspondence for the Moncton-Hillsborough settlement illustrates the nature of this business practice; cf. Winthrop P. Bell, *The Foreign Protestants*, pp. 9ff..

[9] Although sizeable grants were awarded under Governor Lawrence until 1760, they paled in comparison to those under his successors, Lieut. Governor Belcher and Governor Wilmot. Cf. W.O. Raymond, "Pre-Loyalist Settlements ...," pp. 84-85.

[10] Letter dated July 18, 1756 by the Lords of Trade to Governor Lawrence, reproduced in Raymond, "Pre-Loyalist Settlements ...," pp. 34-35.

Plate 1

Hoffenthal in Labrador (Hopedale in Labrador about 1782), "lies 55 degrees 40 minutes northern latitude; the house is 54 feet long and 24 feet wide; watercolour by Peter Ferber after an original drawing by Jens Haven."

Courtesy: Unitätsarchiv Herrnhut

Plate 2

Kreuzwertheim town crest: Black Celtic cross on a white/silver background in the top half of the crest, three white roses with yellow centres on a light blue background in the lower half.

Courtesy: Michael Lutz (1766) Descendants

Plate 3

Baptismal font in the Church of the Cross at which Michael Lutz and his two German-born children were christened.

Photo: Rainer L. Hempel

Plate 4
Hundersingen church, a familiar sight for Heinrich Stieff as a young boy.

Photo: Adèle Hempel

Plate 5
German Brook and German Creek near Germantown, Albert County.

Courtesy: Albert County Museum
Photo: Rainer L. Hempel

Plate 6

Grindstone Island (on the left) and Shepody Mountain, near Germantown.

Photo: Rainer L. Hempel

Plate 7

View from Beaumont on the Petitcodiac toward Moncton; the high grass on the fertile marshes with remnants of Acadian dykes on the right.

Photo: Rainer L. Hempel

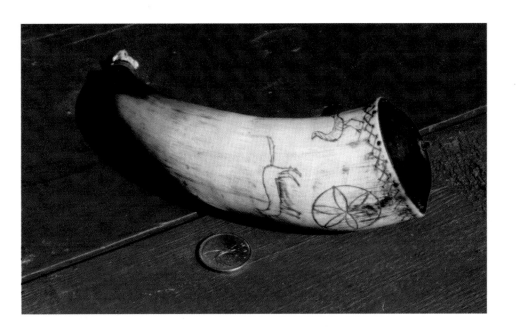

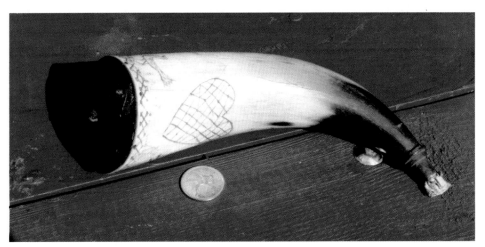

Plate 8/8a

The richly-decorated powder horn found in the Germantown region of New Brunswick shows many Pennsylvania German motifs such as the bird, the heart, the "Hex", and pattern which fills out the heart and adorns the lower, thicker end of the horn. The 25-cent coin serves as a comparison of size.

Photos: Rainer L. Hempel

Plate 9
A *Meerschaumpipe* found in the Germantown area is testimony to the German predilection for smoking.

Courtesy: Albert County Museum, N.B.
Photo: Rainer L. Hempel

Plate 10
Quilts of the Petitcodiac region with traditional and adapted Pennsylvania
German "Hex", flower, and sun motifs.

Courtesy: Lutz Mountain Meeting House, Moncton, N.B.
and Albert County Museum, N.B.
Photos: Rainer L. Hempel

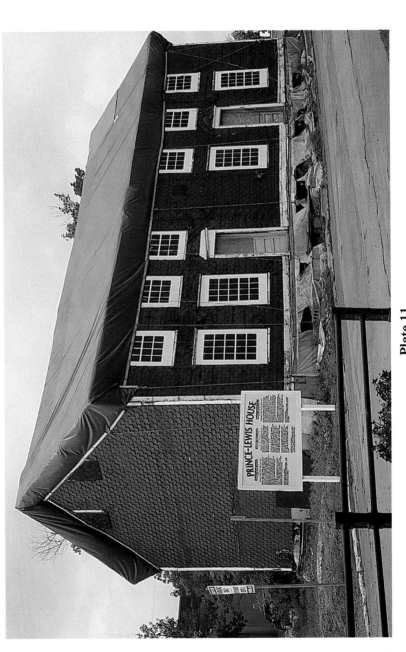

Plate 11

Treitz Haus, the former Treitz-Prince-Lewis House, in 1999 before proposed restoration (for close-up of panel see fig. 44).

Photo: Rainer L. Hempel

Plate 12

Home of "King" John Steeves, first son of Johann Jacob Stieff[2] and Anna Catharina Lutz[2], in Edgett's Landing, N.B.. This house is thought to be the oldest remaining Steeves house, erected c. 1795 at the time of John Steeves' marriage to Jane Beatty, but on the verge of collapse in 1999 when this photo was taken. The south-eastern portion of the house on the left, a 4.5 by 7.2 metre (about 16 x 24 foot) structure, was the original homestead, not unusual for the times when large families had to share basically one room.

Photo: Rainer L. Hempel

Plate 13

William Henry Steeves House in Hillsborough, in which this Father of Confederation was born in 1814. Built originally as a one-room cottage in 1812, it was expanded in 1814 to accommodate Joseph Steeves' growing family. The inset shows a "Lunenburg Bump", the German *Erker*, over the main entrance of this house (photo taken in 1951, William Steeves House, ref. no.: 984.11.2), a characteristic of Lunenburg German architecture, not uncommon in areas settled by Petitcodiac Germans.

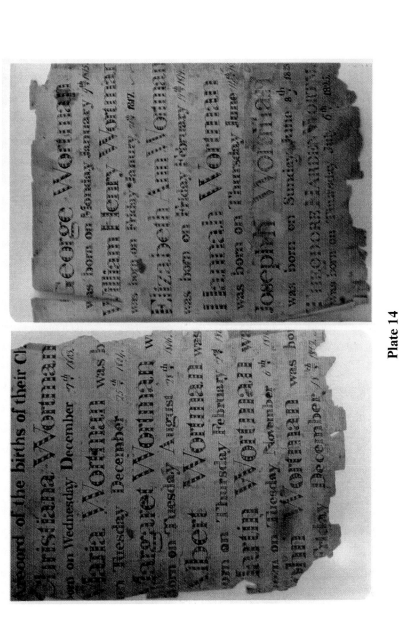

Plate 14
Martin Wortman Bible.

Photos: Joyce Wortman

Plate 15

Moncton's first mayor descended from one of the German pioneer families. "Squire" Jacob Wortman on the far left about two years before his death in 1897; others in the photo from left to right: F.W. Sumner, Fred Givan, Charles McLaren, and Charles Foster.

Courtesy: Moncton Museum
Photo: Rainer L. Hempel

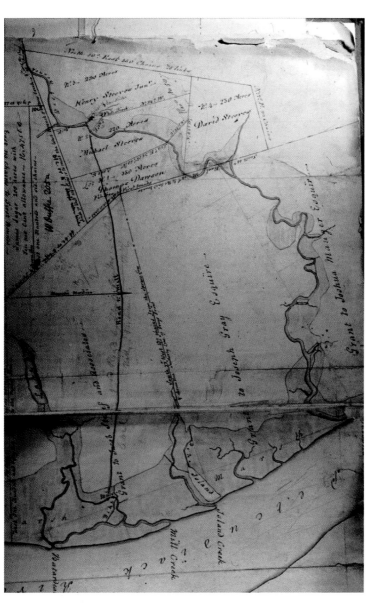

Plate 16

Detail of Hillsborough grant map showing the "Road to Mill", connecting the Stieffs' saw and grist mills on the lower Mill Creek to those on the faster currents of upper Weldon Creek, called Frederick Brook.

Courtesy: Provincial Archives of New Brunswick

Plate 17

Granite marker on even ground (on the right in top photo and detail) in English, French, and German at Settlers' Landing in Moncton near the confluence of the Petitcodiac River and Hall's Creek. Followed by the settlers' names, the English text reads:

JUNE 3, 2000

THIS SETTLERS' LANDING SITE IS DEDICATED DURING THIS MILLENNIUM YEAR TO HONOUR THE CONTRIBUTION OF MONCKTON TOWNSHIP'S FIRST PERMANENT SETTLERS. THESE EIGHT FAMILIES ARRIVED ON JUNE 3, 1766, AT HALL'S CREEK. ORIGINALLY FROM GERMANY & WALES, THEY SAILED FROM PENNSYLVANIA, UP THE BAY OF FUNDY, TO RECEIVE PROMISED LAND GRANTS AND SETTLE THE GREATER MONCTON AREA.

Photos: Rainer L. Hempel

[11] HuP, letter from Halifax by Anthony Wayne to John Hughes, dated Oct. 7, 1765, which describes McNutt's backroom dealings as "Dispicable & Unjust". Cf. also W.O. Raymond, "Pre-Loyalist Settlements ...," p. 85; McNutt seems to have antagonized several officials not just in government circles in Halifax (pp. 60, 74ff.) but also in London, England (p. 78).

[12] *Papers of Benjamin Franklin*, XII, Jan. 1765 - Dec. 1765 (Cambridge, Mass.: Yale University Press, 1961), pp. 345-350.

[13] W.O. Raymond, "Pre-Loyalist Settlements ... ," pp. 85-86; C. Alexander Pincombe and Edward W. Larracey, *Resurgo*, Vol. I (Moncton: The City of Moncton, 1990), p. 53.

[14] W.O. Raymond, "The Pre-Loyalist Settlements ...," p. 86; also HuP, the "Articles of Agreement" between the land companies and settlers (i.e. John Hughes and Mathias Sommer, Charles Jones, Heinrich Stieff, Michael Lutz, and Jacob Treitz) which lists all the businessmen involved in this land speculation scheme.

[15] According to Raymond (*Ibid.*, p. 91), McNutt had no merit in the establishment of the townships on the Petitcodiac River, but a letter to John Hughes from Alexander McNutt in London and dated July 18, 1766 (HuP), attests to his involvement in the enterprise even after the settlers had arrived.

[16] *Papers of Benjamin Franklin*, p. 347.

[17] I published an account of this settlement under the title, "Germantown -- die Geschichte einer deutschen Siedlung in Neubraunschweig," *German-Canadian Yearbook,* eds. Gerhard Friesen and Karin Gürttler, IX (Toronto, Ont.: Historical Society of Mecklenburg Upper Canada, 1986), pp. 49-62.

[18] Bouquet, Haldimand, and DesBarres were born in Switzerland within four years of one another, were all of Huguenot descent, and ended their careers as high-ranking officers in the service of Great Britain in North America. Bouquet and Haldimand had been childhood friends and served together for a time as Swiss mercenaries under the King of Sardinia. In the expedition against Fort Duquesne, Adam Hoops had been Bouquet's officer in charge of supplies. Bouquet was one of the most successful officers on the British side in the Seven Years' War and died in 1765, at about the time that the grant for Germantown was passed. DesBarres and Haldimand were comrades in arms at Ticonderoga in 1757. DesBarres saw active duty in 1758 during the second capture of Louisbourg and at Quebec City in 1759, and Haldimand was the first to march into Montreal, taking formal possession of the city in 1760. Hugh Wallace was Haldimand's business agent, and Peter Hasenclever was an ironmaster from Germany.

[19] NBM, Albert County Envelope V.1, Land Company 1765, extracts from a letter by Geo. M. Wells of New York regarding an early land company.

[20] Clark Wright, *The Petitcodiac*, p. 26.

[21] PANS, Governor Wilmot's letter of October 9, 1765, C.O. 217, Vol. 21, pp. 179-181.

[22] Clark Wright, *The Petitcodiac*, pp. 26f..

[23] In 1846 this County was named after Queen Victoria's consort, Albert, second son of Duke Ernst I of Sachsen-Coburg-Gotha.

[24] NBM, Miscellaneous Scrapbook, Shelf 42, "Albert County History" in the *St. John Sun*, (n.d.). This article was written when Thomas Calhoun's nephew, George Calhoun, was "Registrar of Deeds" in Albert County, circa 1820-1840.

[25] NBM, Miscellaneous Scrapbook, Shelf 42, "Historical Sketches of Albert County" in the *Daily Times*, May 17, 1929. Several families seem to have moved up to Hillsborough over a period of years after about 1768.

[26] John Bartlet Brebner, *The Neutral Yankees of Nova Scotia* (New York: Columbia University Press, 1937), p. 50.

[27] *Ibid.,* p. 61.

[28] The Census for 1766, which lists many townships in Nova Scotia, can be found under PANS, RG 1, No. 443. Whereas no nominal census for the townships of "Monckton", Cumberland, Sackville, and Hopewell in this year exists, the one for Hillsborough in 1770 in the same repository records the names of heads of households and their harvests, livestock, etc.. No official census was filed in 1775 and 1783, instead an unofficial "General Return" for the owners of the township. The 1775/1783 "Census" should for this reason be called Joseph Gray's Petition. More information in this context will be furnished later in this chapter.

[29] The Hillsborough Census of 1770 lists the children of Germans born in Pennsylvania as "Americans". This is contrary to the Moncton Census of 1766 where they were counted as German.

[30] Clark Wright (*The Petitcodiac*, pp. 26f.) refers to these archives as the "Dominion Archives".

[31] William Calhoun, *Diary*, NBM, Ganong Papers, Box 32, Packet 7, pp. 1-2. Only excerpts were found in the Ganong Papers. The diary almost in its entirety, from Calhoun's departure in Baltimore on June 13, 1771 and up until January 31, 1772, was published in the *Chignecto Post*, Sackville (October 26, 1876 - February 8, 1877).

[32] Letter by DesBarres to Haldimand, August 21, 1766, PANS, R.G. Vol. 366, No. 10.

[33] Colonel Gubbins provides a vivid description of the years of backbreaking effort taken to accomplish this task: *Gubbins' Journals*, pp. 19f..

[34] PANS, R.G. Vol. 366, No. 10.

[35] Letter by Thomas Calhoun to William Nesbit, September 3, 1766, HaP, A-665.

[36] *Loc. cit..*

[37] *Loc. cit..*

[38] William Nesbit to Adam Hoops, November 2, 1766, HaP.

[39] *Loc. cit..*

[40] Frederick Haldimand had fought in the Prussian army under King Frederick the Great before joining the Army of the Electoral Prince of Hanover and British King, George II, in 1754. The Haldimand Papers also contain letters in German addressed to the General.

[41] Frederick DesBarres received his education in Basel, a city in the German-speaking region of Switzerland.

[42] J.J.W. DesBarres to Haldimand, February 7, 1767, (HaP): *"Les Familles Almandes, quoique d'aillieurs en tout autre point de Vue, infiniment preferables, vous couterons cher dans l'Apprentissage de la Culture - des terres basses d'un Païs ou l'Experience leur manque* [sic]."

[43] Thomas Calhoun to Haldimand, "German Town," March 4, 1768, HaP.

[44] Mr. Daniels and his family settled near Shepody Hill, where William Calhoun and Robert Cummings met him while out bear hunting; William Calhoun's Diary, "Early Chignecto Records," No. 10, *Chignecto Post*, Sackville, N.B.. Cf. Jones Family genealogy for Daniels' family connection to Moncton settler John Jones.

[45] Clark Wright, *The Petitcodiac*, p. 32.

[46] William Nesbit to Adam Hoops, "Halifax, 2 November 1766," HaP.

[47] Alan Rayburn in his book, *Geographical Names of New Brunswick* (Ottawa: Surveys and Mapping Branch, Department of Energy, Mines and Resources, 1975), wrote under the *"Germantown"* heading: "Settled in 1765 by Germans from Pennsylvania who later moved to Hillsborough." The rejection of these settlers by Anthony Wayne confirms the "Monckton" Census figures obtained by the end of 1766, namely that they did not move upriver that fall.

[48] The settlement of Lunenburg, N.S., was accompanied by similar accusations and sentiments of neglect, which resulted in threats of desertion and even an armed rebellion in December 1753; Bell, *The "Foreign Protestants"*, pp. 457ff.. Governor Lawrence in a letter to the Lords of Trade on August 1, 1754 suggested measures which "might have a good Effect ... on the German Settlers, many of whom had formerly deserted to the French;" Thomas B. Akins, *Acadia and Nova Scotia: Documents Relating to the Acadian French and the First British Colonization of the Province, 1714-1758,* Reprint (Cottonport, Louisiana: Polyanthos, Inc., 1972), p. 228. The French, sensing the mood in the settlement, were suspected to have made efforts in the person of "Le Loutre to entice away the Germans;" Letter from Mr. Cotterel to Col. Sutherland, March 18, 1754, Atkins, *Acadia and Nova Scotia*, p. 208.

[49] Nesbit to Hoops, Nov. 2, 1766, HaP.

[50] Hoops to Haldimand, December 9, 1766, HaP.

[51] Hoops to Haldimand, August 23, 1767, HaP.

[52] Calhoun to Haldimand, March 4, 1768, HaP. It must be assumed that the Acadians had cleared and settled considerable upland at Haha and Shepody "hill" (Shepody Mountain).

[53] Loc. cit..

[54] These settlers were not the first to leave the settlement as the 1766 Hopewell Census recorded the departure of five during the previous year.

[55] Calhoun to Haldimand, March 4, 1768, HaP.

[56] William Calhoun, Diary, p. 2.

[57] One such guard was the Swiss Guard, under the King of Sardinia, in which Henry Bouquet served as a lieutenant-colonel.

[58] For a good account regarding military service in Germany at that time and the so-called "mercenary Hessians", consult Terrence M. Punch, "Hessian Auxiliary Troops in North America: Auxiliaries, Not Mercenaries," German-Canadian Yearbook, Vol. XIII (Toronto: Historical Society of Mecklenburg Upper Canada, 1994), pp. 235ff..

[59] William Calhoun, Diary, pp. 2-3.

[60] Hoops to Haldimand, Sommersett, August 23, 1767, HaP.

[61] Hoops to Haldimand, August 23, 1767, HaP.

[62] Clark Wright, The Petitcodiac, p. 31.

[63] Loc. cit.; cf. Hoops to Haldimand, February 11, 1768, HaP.

[64] Clark Wright, The Petitcodiac, pp. 31f..

[65] Hoops to Haldimand, February 11, 1768, HaP.

[66] Hoops to Haldimand, June 10, 1768, HaP.

[67] Anthony Wayne to John Hughes, Halifax, October 7, 1765, HuP.

[68] Several councillors were landowners themselves, e.g. Burbidge and Best, who reserved 3,000 acres of the best land on the Shepody River; cf. Clark Wright, Planters and Pioneers, p. 24.

[69] DesBarres to Haldimand, May 30, 1768, HaP; DesBarres detailed the agreement regarding the settlement of Hillsborough with the signatures of Michael Francklin, Moses Delesdernier (both personal friends of DesBarres) and Joseph Gerrish.

[70] J. S. McLennan, Louisbourg: From its Foundation to Fall, 1713-1758 (Halifax: The Book Room Ltd., 1979), p. 6.

[71] J. Gross received land in the Germantown area. Richard Gross, a son of Jacob, is mentioned in the Harper Ledgers (cf. Chp. VII.2) and was settled in Hillsborough by 1797. Possibly he or his father had been involved in blacksmithing as R. Gross paid for supplies with a smith's anvil (£8:13:0) on May 6, 1809. Richard Gross became a shipwright for many years.

214

[72] Clark Wright, *Planters and Pioneers,* p. 70.

[73] Clark Wright, *Samphire Greens,* p. 26. Their names are listed in Joseph Gray's petition of Hillsborough in 1775; PANS, CO 217, Vol. 59, Microfilm 13,861.

[74] Because of a clerical error in 1786, the "k" in Monckton was dropped in later documents; Pincombe and Larracey, *Resurgo,* p. 96. For the present purposes, the "k" has been retained when referring to the 18th-century settlement.

[75] William Calhoun, *Diary,* pp. 3-4. This comment suggests that there was more than one German family living there, also that Calhoun may have considered the Jones family German.

[76] Clark Wright, *The Petitcodiac,* pp. 22, 38, 68; "The Bend" is referred to as a topographical sighting for Moncton. Going up the Petitcodiac River, Moncton extends westward from the location where the river makes a 90° angle, or bend, to the left.

[77] The names of the four companies were: Clarkson & Co. (Matthew Clarkson, Gerardus Clarkson, Edward Duffield, and John Naglee), Franklin & Co. (John Cox Jr., Benjamin Franklin, John Hughes, and Anthony Wayne), Caton & Co. (Isaac Caton, James Caton, and John Relfe), and William Smith & Co. (Thomas Barton, John Bayley, William Craig, John Hall, Joseph Jacobs, Israel Jacobs, Benjamin Jacobs, William Moore, Hugh Neil, Joseph Richardson, and William Smith).

[78] At the time when these settlers arrived in 1766, this area was part of Nova Scotia, becoming the separate province of New Brunswick only in 1784 after the arrival of the United Empire Loyalists.

[79] NBM, Albert County Scrapbook, Shelf 31, Name of Paper not given, March 27, 1883. The article gives a detailed, in some places rather imaginative, account of the experiences of the early German settlers on the shores of the Petitcodiac River. Of note here is the absence of the Copple and Wortman family names.

[80] Pertinent excerpts from Botsford's paper can be found in Pincombe and Larracey, *Resurgo,* Vol. 1, pp. 383-399. One must note, however, that by the time Botsford's interest in Moncton's history was kindled in the 1830's, only a handful of second-generation Petitcodiac Germans were still alive.

[81] *Ibid.,* p. 387.

[82] Raymond erroneously claimed that the early settlers came to "Monckton, now known as Hillsborough" in the year "1765"; Raymond, "The Pre-Loyalist Settlements...", p. 90.

[83] Clark Wright was the first to examine archival material from Philadelphia for her books *The Petitcodiac, Samphire Greens,* and *Planters and Pioneers.*

[84] Letter, Hughes to McNutt, May 29, 1764, HuP. There are other letters in the Hughes Papers, one dated January 1, 1765, in which McNutt agreed to assist John Hughes, Benjamin Franklin and others and to use his "Best Endeavour, to have four Townships allotted in the Province of Nova Scotia, for them and their Associates." Another document, dated March 1765 and signed by John Hughes and Anthony Wayne, specifies the kind and location of land they desired.

[85] B. Franklin, J. Foxcraft, and John Hughes to McNutt, July 10, 1764, HuP.

[86] *Loc. cit..*

[87] *Loc. cit..*

[88] *Papers of Benjamin Franklin*, p. 346.

[89] Wayne to Hughes, Halifax, April 10, 1765, HuP.

[90] Hughes to Wayne, June 1, 1765, HuP.

[91] The Stamp Act was passed by the British Parliament in March 1765 and went into effect on November 1, 1765. This was a form of taxation applied to official documents before they could be processed, an expense that grantees hoped to avoid by having their transactions concluded before that date; *Papers of Benjamin Franklin*, p. 347. Due to strong opposition, targeted at Hughes as officer in charge, the Act was repealed in 1766, practically at the same time the "Monckton" settlers set sail.

[92] Wayne to Hughes, Halifax, July 9, 1765, HuP.

[93] Wayne to Hughes, Halifax, August 5, 1765, HuP.

[94] *Loc. cit..*

[95] After his successes in the Revolutionary War, Wayne ended his career in 1794 as commander-in-chief in the war against native tribes in Ohio. His negotiations with native peoples for large tracts of land were evidence of his tenacity, courage, and bargaining skills honed as a member of the Colonial Assembly in Pennsylvania before 1775 and as a Congressman for Georgia in 1791.

[96] Wayne to Hughes, Halifax, October 7, 1765, HuP.

[97] Document entitled: "John Hughes Esq' ... in Acc't Current with ... Anthony Wayne ...," HuP.

[98] *Loc. cit..*

[99] Document of land grant to "Alexr McNutt, Mathew Clarkson and Associates, Novr 1. 1765," HuP.

[100] "Articles of Agreement" between the four land companies and McNutt, HuP.

[101] WRO, Libro D-1, 122; registered June 15, 1814. The earliest person to be buried in the cemetery was Abraham Treitz' first wife, Margaret, who died on April 12, 1806.

[102] Cf. A. Hempel, "Updated Chronology of Events relating to the Prince-Lewis House: Road Development between 1799-1816, as revealed in early land

transactions at The Bend," unpublished (Sackville, N.B., October 17, 1999), MAUL, Bell Collection, p. 11.

[103] "Articles of Agreement" between the four land companies and McNutt, HuP.

[104] "Articles of Agreement" between Hughes and the settlers, signed on January 27, 1766, HuP. Any future references to the "Articles of Agreement," including the following four excerpts, pertain to this second one.

[105] The Rickers were sent by William Smith & Co., and John Copple and Georg Wortman by Clarkson & Co., for whom no "Articles of Agreement" exist. Although Capt. Caton accompanied Wayne, McNutt, and Jacobs in their search for suitable land along the Bay of Fundy in August 1765, Caton & Co. does not appear to have sent any settlers to the Petitcodiac.

[106] Cf. Clark Wright, *The Petitcodiac*, p. 45.

[107] Jacob Klein also attended St. Michaelis Lutheran Church in Philadelphia.

[108] The letter by Capt. John Hall was discovered by Mrs. Muriel Lutes-Sikorski in 1983 in the William Smith Papers regarding Nova Scotia, HSP. Capt. Hall was the master of the vessel that transported the settlers to "Monckton". He was an associate of William Smith & Co., and his letter dated June 13, 1766, informed his employer William Smith about the successful landing and circumstances of the settlers.

[109] Pincombe and Larracey, *Resurgo*, Vol. 1, p. 387.

[110] Clark Wright, *The Petitcodiac,* pp. 44f.. The minutes of the Second Presbytery of Philadelphia recorded on April 14, 1766, that Rev. John Eagleson, a passenger on the ship which brought the settlers to Nova Scotia, "proposes shortly to set sail from this Part for Nova Scotia."

[111] This creek was later renamed Hall's Creek in honour of Captain Hall.

[112] Although Hall's Creek is normally accepted as the boundary, there is a small strip of land on the east side of it which never belonged to the Parish of Dorchester and as a consequence is not part of today's Dieppe.

[113] Paul Surette, *Petcoudiac: Colonisation et Destruction (1731-1755)* (Moncton, N.B.: Les Editions d'Acadie, 1988), p. 35.

[114] A hogshead is about 235 litres or the contents of a large barrel.

[115] Since Capt. Hall was able to procure seed potatoes in such quantity, they could not have been uncommon and may have been considered a staple already, especially in Philadelphia. These potatoes flourished in "Monckton" and must have constituted a principal component of their diet over the winters of 1767 and 1768.

[116] Capt. John Hall's letter and a transcript are reproduced in their entirety in the Appendix.

[117] Letter by Rev. John Eagleson to Rev. Dr. Allison, dated October 1767, quoted from Clark Wright, *The Petitcodiac*, p. 44.

[118] Document "John Hughes Esq' ... in Acc't Current with ... Anthony Wayne ...," HuP.

[119] Such amounts are read as pounds, shillings, and pence.

[120] Document "John Hughes Esq'... in Acc't Current with ... Anthony Wayne ...."

[121] List of Debits and Credits, entitled "1766 Nova Scotia Lands," HuP. This balance sheet is a valuable source of information concerning the settlement's needs and supplies.

[122] Clark Wright, *The Petitcodiac*, p. 45. Despite a debit for seed grain to settlers made on one account sheet, the 1767 "Monckton" Census lists no harvest, of grains or anything else, but Cumberland (population 334), where supplier Wethered lived, and neighbouring Sackville (population 349), recorded a combined wheat harvest in excess of 1,700 bushels, proving that there was abundant food available within walking, and certainly riding, distance. Also, because the Petitcodiac River and Bay of Fundy never freeze over entirely on account of their strong currents, these waters could have served as supply routes for desperate people, even in winter.

[123] Information contained in the 1766 "Monckton" Census and especially Hillsborough censuses of 1770, 1775, and 1783 reveal that the Michael Lutz family numbered 9 and not 6 as previously assumed; Clark Wright, *The Petitcodiac*, p. 47.

[124] Geneva Jones Emberley, *Descendants of Charles Jones of New Brunswick from 1766* (no location, publisher or date), p. 2; cf. Clark Wright, *The Petitcodiac*, p. 45.

[125] In the "Articles of Agreement" Charles Jones marked his name with an "X".

[126] A long-established blacksmith shop that existed late into the 19th century was situated on the Treitz grant which Christian, Jacob's third son, inherited from his father in 1790, on the south side of the Post Road (present-day Main Street), where the King's Highway intersected. In the first decade of the 19th century, this operation was in the midst of some modest commercial activity which involved the shipping of lumber, a tavern run by William Steadman in 1805, and a "shop" run by James Watson Esq. in 1808. The area attracted William Steadman, who married Christian Treitz's eldest daughter, Hannah, and who claimed to be a blacksmith from early on; WRO, Libro C-1, 488: registered April 3, 1812.

[127] Cf. Pincombe and Larracey, *Resurgo*, I, p. 63.

[128] A great deal of confusion has surrounded the Jacob Ricker name. Many researchers, including Clark Wright, did not realize that two heads of

218

families were concealed behind the one name. The 1766 "Monckton" and 1770 Hillsborough censuses give few clues, however Joseph Gray's Petition (the 1775 and 1783 Hillsborough censuses) lists Jacob Ricker "Jr." in 1775 as having a family of 9, and Jacob Ricker "Sr." in 1783 as the head of a household of 5.

[129] Judge Botsford's Speech of Jan. 19, 1885: "When ... [Reuben Mills and Ichabod Lewis] located themselves at the Bend (as it was then designated) [c. 1784] there were but three log cabins in the place;" Pincombe and Larracey, *Resurgo*, I, p. 392. This reference, however, is most likely to three wooden farmhouses on Lot 9 belonging to Jacob Treitz Jr., Jacob Treitz Sr., and Christian Treitz (listed from east to west), who were well established and successful by 1784. The "three" is most significant -- Abraham Treitz was settled on Lot 5 from 1775 on and was the only Treitz head of a household who never settled on Lot 9. The first house may already have been vacated by Jacob Treitz Jr., who claimed to be on Lot 8 from 1780 on. That the houses were "log *cabins*" is questionable as they were more likely second-generation structures, i.e. either log or timber-frame houses; cf. John I. Rempel (*Building with Wood* [Toronto: University of Toronto Press, 1980], pp. 31-33) for a distinction of these building types. Three structures and their related barns just west of the landing place at The Bend on a military map of 1799 may represent the three Treitz houses; National Map Collection, Ottawa, Ontario, Overland Route between Halifax, N.S. and Fredericton, N.B., 1799, commissioned by His Highness the Duke of Kent, Commander in Chief in North America, No. 34201.

[130] WRO, Libro C-1, 487: Christian Stieff (grantor) to John Bentley (grantee), dated March 12, 1812.

[131] John I. Rempel, *Building with Wood*, pp. 217ff..

[132] Clark Wright, *The Petitcodiac*, p. 39.

[133] JP, Book 1684-1769.

[134] Clark Wright supported Benjamin Jacobs Sr.'s claim of additional ships on the basis of her calculation that an additional 15 Germans were unaccounted for. This argument, however, is weakened in view of her failure to include in her tally: Jacob Ricker Sr., 3 additional children in the Lutz family, the young Wortman family, and a possible second Treitz daughter; Clark Wright, *The Petitcodiac*, p. 48. Paul Surette seems to have accepted Clark Wright's mistaken notion that German settlers left the "Monckton" Township within the first year of their arrival: "En 1766, trois des quatre compagnies y amènent des colons qui comprennent encore beaucoup d'Allemands de la Pennsylvanie. Mais, l'année même de leur arrivée, bon nombre de ces familles quittent la Petcoudiac; elles vont ailleurs en Acadie où les terres ne sont pas encore concédées;" Paul Surette, *Histoire des Trois-Rivières*, p. 30.

[135] Collections of the Nova Scotia Historical Society, Report on Raymond's "Pre-Loyalist Settlements of Nova Scotia," X. The Census was

actually signed by Lieut.-Gov. Michael Francklin on December 16, 1766. The list of names for the "Monckton" Census is no longer available, which has created among other difficulties the confusion that there was only one Jacob Ricker.

[136] In order that Ricker Jr. could marry Sommer's widow, Ricker's wife must have died; cf. Pincombe and Larracey, *Resurgo*, I, p. 90. The 1775 and 1783 Hillsborough censuses provide more accurate information about the Ricker Sr. and Jr., Lutz, and Wortman families which necessitated a re-evaluation of earlier assumptions about the composition of the Petitcodiac German families upon arrival in 1766. Two German males are unaccounted for but may have been Charles Myers and his brother from Germantown, who turned up in Hillsborough before 1775.

[137] Wayne's letter to Hughes, July 9, 1765, HuP.

[138] Letter by Isaac Caton to Mr. Jacobs and Mr. Wayne, August 15, 1765, WP, Vol. 1, p. 5.

[139] Clark Wright, *Samphire Greens*, p. 11.

[140] Clark Wright, *The Petitcodiac*, p. 45.

[141] Valentin Müller had a son confirmed in Philadelphia in 1772, which suggests that he may have left the "Frankfort", N.B., settlement and returned to Pennsylvania by this date.

[142] George Cline (Klein), a possible relation settled at Passamaquoddy and married about 1800; Martha Ford Barts, *Passamaquoddy-Genealogies of West Isles Families* (St. John, N.B.: Lingley Printing Co. Ltd., 1975), p. 42.

[143] *St. John Sun,* March 8, 1893, Albert County Scrapbook, Shelf 31, Provincial Museum, St. John, N.B. and Clark Wright, *Samphire Greens*, p. 92.

[144] The handwritten account, *Pioneer History* by Howard Steeves (1832-1916), a schoolmaster in Albert County, claims that "... Cpt. Hall sailed away promising to return with supplies," a promise he did not keep; Maimie (Wilbur) Steeves, *Fundy Folklore* (N.p.: Albert County Historical Society, Inc., 1970), p. 52. There are many details in Hall's letter of June 3, 1766, about provisions he procured for the settlers but no mention of any intention to return.

[145] Both Charles Baker's letter and Clark Wright's family tradition emphasize marsh greens as an early food in this context, but there were other sources of "fresh vegetables" such as young dandelions which are still eaten in Germany and Pennsylvania; Nancy Roan, "Nineteenth and Twentieth Century Pennsylvania-Mennonite Foodways," *From Pennsylvania to Waterloo: Pennsylvania-German Folk Culture in Transition*, eds. Susan M. Burke and Mathew H. Hill (Kitchener, Ont.: Joseph Schneider Haus, 1991), p. 103.

[146] Letter from Charles Baker to John Hughes, "Summerseat", July 24, 1769, HuP.

[147] There were a total of 23, but McNutt was not an active participant.

[148] Pincombe appears to doubt whether the letter was ever delivered; *Resurgo*, I, p. 69.

[149] Since flax has a growing season of 95-120 days, wheat about 100, and barley 95, the seeds had to be in the ground sometime in May. This does not take into consideration the time required to cultivate the fields before seeding and planting. The frost-free period in this part of the Province is between 120-130 days.

[150] Charles Baker took over Robert Cummings' position in Hillsborough and, only after 1777, that of Moses Delesdernier, who had been retained as an agent by Joseph Garrish and Michael Franklin for their portions of the Hillsborough grant; John C. Hatt, *A Historical Study of the Delesdernier Family: Early Inhabitants of Nova Scotia and New Brunswick* (Fredericton, N.B.: 1983), type-written manuscript, p. 24 (one copy deposited with the Southeastern Branch N.B. Genealogical Society, Moncton Public Library, Moncton, N.B.).

[151] Clark Wright, *The Petitcodiac*, pp. 35, 51ff..

[152] Michael Lutz did not remain on the "Monckton" side "at the Bend", as Dan Soucoup asserts in his recently published book, *Historic New Brunswick* (p. 54), rather he returned to "Monckton" in the fall of 1783. The Irish family of Robert Smith also moved over to Cummings' property at this time.

[153] Clark Wright, *The Petitcodiac*, p. 47; Pincombe and Larracey, *Resurgo*, I, pp. 70ff..

[154] The Millidge Report states that Jacob Treitz Jr., Andrew Sommer, and John and Henry Jones settled on their land in "Monckton" in 1780 when titles to their lots had been cleared; Millidge Report, MAUL, Webster Manuscript Collection. This may have been an exaggeration in each of their cases, since it was to their advantage to show the new Provincial Government how long they had been "improving" their lands.

[155] The Lutz's and Copples did not receive grants where they had originally settled. This must have been particularly trying for John Copple, who was allotted new land much further west after he had lived on the Sommer grant for twelve years.

[156] According to the Millidge Report, John Copple died around November 1780 and may not have been well for some time before this (see Chapter VI).

[157] Sunday, July 14, 1811, *Gubbin's Journals*, pp. 14f.. The Treitz Haus, the former Prince-Lewis House on Bendview Court, Moncton may be one of the Treitz's residences referred to. Three of Christian's children were settled on their own in 1811 but only two in Moncton, Hannah and Lewis. Although Jacob Jr. and Abraham Treitz were deceased, some of their children were also settled in the new "village" on Treitz's Lot No. 9.

[158] In later years, Michael Francklin bought out John Collier and James Beautineau, and Joseph Garrish took over Henry Newton's share, so that only three owners remained: Robert Cummings, Michael Franklin, and Joseph Garrish. Cf. John C. Hatt, *A Historical Study of the Delesdernier Family: Early Inhabitants of Nova Scotia and New Brunswick.*

[159] Clark Wright, *The Petitcodiac*, p. 24. A letter by DesBarres from "Tatmagushe" on May 30, 1768 informed Haldimand of a settlement scheme for Hillsborough which had been signed by Michael Francklin, Josef Gerrish and Moses Delesdernier on March 26, 1768; HaP.

[160] William Calhoun, *Diary*, p. 3.

[161] Although Martyn Hatt and his wife are listed as "Irish" with 2 American children in the 1770 Hillsborough Census, several by the name "Hatt" came over from Switzerland in 1751 and 1752 to settle in Lunenburg, in particular Jacob Hatt, who had a son called "Martin".

[162] Peter Jonah came to Halifax on the *Speedwell* in 1752. During the journeys from his home in the tiny Württemberg possession of Mömpelgard/Montbéliard, first to Halifax, then to Lunenburg in 1753, and finally to Hillsborough in 1768, he has been variously recorded under such names as: Pierre Jeaune, Jonet, Jeaunaie, Joinet, Joney, Jeauney, Jonais, Josnet, Joannah, and Jonia.

[163] Hillsborough Census of 1770, Provincial Archives, Fredericton, N.B.; Moses Delesdernier came to Halifax on the *Alderney* in 1750. He settled at Pisiquid, N.S., in the vicinity of Fort Edward, took an active part in the expulsion of the Acadians while "on special service" for the British (John C. Hatt, *A Historical Study of the Delesdernier Family ...*), and lived for a while on Block C in Halifax's Dutch (*Deutsch*) Town before settling in Hillsborough; cf. Terrence M. Punch, "Dutch (Deutsch) Town," *Neuschottländer Bote,* ed. Eva Huber, Vol. II, No. 3 (Halifax: The Little Dutch Church Restoration Society, Fall 1997), p. 5. Many of his descendants moved over to Dover, N.B., where they changed their names to "Dernier". In his old age, Delesdernier must have returned to Halifax, for he died there on September 8, 1811, and is buried in St. Paul's Cemetery at Barrington and Prince Streets.

[164] The 1766 "Monckton" Census does not appear to have used the method of calling children of German settlers born in North America "American". It is not clear why three Lutz boys, probably aged 17, 12, and 9 would not have gone over to Hillsborough with their parents; three boys were also on the "other side of the River for this year [June 1, 1783]" thirteen years later.

[165] An example of far-sighted settlement practices can be seen in comments on the last page of the 1783 Hillsborough Census (Cf. Appendix): "This settlement has cost upwards of ten thousand Pounds Sterling, including Interest of money ... because the Produce of Grain and Increase of Stock has not

been received by the Proprietors, but left on the Premises from year to year for this ten years past as a Trust, or ready Supply for such Tenants as Annually engage to Settle, and by this Mode, we are never at a loss of Stock and Grain to furnish new Tenants that may offer, and the Heirs of the late Joseph Gerrish Esq. [have] ... now a very great Quantity of Stock on the Premises for that purpose, and indeed the last will and Testament forbids taking it off the Premises."

[166] The unit in the Census indicates "Hundreds". The Rickers, for example, harvested 30 "Hundreds" of flax, or about 1½ tons.

[167] Clark Wright, *The Petitcodiac*, p. 52.

[168] PANB, New Brunswick Land Grants, Microfilm F 1029. Christian returned to "Monckton" about 1775 to look after the interests of the Stieffs on that side of the river while Rosanna and her daughter Elizabeth had remained in the Treitz home in "Monckton" until she and Christian married c. 1775.

[169] *Ibid.*, Microfilm F 1032.

[170] Cf. Clark Wright, *The Petitcodiac*, pp. 49ff..

[171] PANB, New Brunswick Land Grants, Microfilm F 6648, Clark Wright, *The Petitcodiac*, pp. 53ff..

[172] This *Trites Genealogy* lists 1753 as Rosanna's year of birth, which would have made her -- at age 14 in 1767 -- a rather youthful bride of a 38-year-old man, giving birth to a son, Benjamin, erroneously attributed to her. A letter by John Eagleson in 1787 suggests that Elizabeth was of age, i.e about 16 years in that year, meaning that she was born about 1770/1771; Petition by Rev. John Eagleson and Charles Baker on behalf of Rosanna Treits [sic] for land belonging to the late Robert Cummins [sic], PANB, New Brunswick Land Grants, Microfilm F 6648.

[173] This Trites Genealogy lists a daughter Rachel (b. 1776) and Clark Wright has Henry (b. 1779) as the first-born; Clark Wright, *Samphire Greens*, Appendix B, p. 2.

[174] E. Larracey, *Chocolate River*, p. 50.

[175] Petition by Rev. John Eagleson and Charles Baker on behalf of Elizabeth Cummings for land from Robert Cummings' former grant in Hillsborough; PANB, New Brunswick Land Grants, Microfilm F 6648.

[176] The first Petitcodiac German to be married after her arrival in 1766 was Anna Catharina Sommer, to (Eliphalet) Liffe Chappell in 1767. Although the 1783 Hillsborough "Census" clearly states that Peter Lutz had a "Daughter of age" (i.e. 16 years, born circa 1767), this does not mean he and Mary Ricker were married then. It is impossible that Mary Ricker brought this girl into the marriage from a previous relationship since she was only eleven in 1767. It is also unlikely that Peter, at age 17, was the father. Mary and Peter's first child was born around 1774. Cf. Jacob Ricker Jr. Family genealogy for a possible explanation of this "daughter".

[177] E. Larracey, *Chocolate River*, p. 33.

[178] *Loc. cit..*

[179] William Calhoun's Diary, "Early Records of Chignecto," No. 12, *Chignecto Post,* Sackville, N.B..

[180] Martin Beck's name is variously spelled with a "B" or "P", which is confusing since Abiel Peck, an American from Boston of no relation to him, lived in Germantown.

[181] Howard Trueman, *The Chignecto Isthmus and Its First Settlers* (Toronto: William Briggs, 1902), pp. 31-32.

[182] It is not quite accurate to call this list of names, livestock, and produce a "Census" since no original "Census" for 1775 (and 1783) has been discovered. Proof that it existed is shown in an "Abstract of the number of Families settled in Nova Scotia ... August 1775," which counted "about 45 families two thirds of which are Acadians" in the townships of Hopewell, Hillsborough, and "Monckton"; Bruce G. Wilson, *Records of our History: Colonial Identity, Canada from 1760-1815* (Ottawa: National Archives of Canada, 1988), p. 43. Two separate lists have survived. One appears to be a copy of the 1775 Hillsborough Census plus names of those who left and arrived between 1775 and 1783. It is prefaced by the statement: "A General Return of the Number of Families that have been settled in the Township of Hillsborough in the County of Cumberland and General Return of Stock, etc., etc., ..." The other list is a "Return of Inhabitants in the Township of Hillsborough in the County of Cumberland, June 1, 1783." Both these lists were included in a petition in 1783 by Joseph Gray, son-in-law of Joseph Gerrish who was one of the original co-owners of Hillsborough. This petition was written when escheat of the Township appeared imminent and the owners had to prove that the settlement was thriving and a great deal of effort and money had been expended. The "Joseph Gray Petition" has become synonymous with the 1775/1783 "Census", PANS, CO. 217, Vol. 59, Microfilm 13,861.

[183] *Loc. cit.*; cf. also Joseph Gray Petition.

[184] The 1783 Hillsborough "Census" provides a separate column for "Relations ... residing with their Friends," suggesting an accepted practice that "Friends" were staying with families in this settlement. It is conceivable that the numbers of several Hillsborough families in 1775, including the Stieffs, reflected additions from "Monckton" families who decided to stay but allowed, or encouraged, some of their members to move to Hillsborough.

[185] It was "Rickarspoint" (Ricker's Point) where Rev. William Black visited during his missionary trip to The Bend on January 16, 1782. This became later known as Lutz Point (after Peter Lutz) and later still as Outhouse Point (after Simon Outhouse), as the owners changed. Peter and Mary Lutz may have married around 1773, but Peter must have continued working on his father-in-law's farm

as there were no farming statistics available for him in 1783. Rev. Eagleson claimed in the previously cited petition concerning Elizabeth Cummings that "... Mr. Ricker's Sons [Peter Lutz and Michael Ricker] are also settled on said lands without any agreement with anyone impowered;" PANB, Microfilm F 6648. Jacob Ricker Jr., his son Michael, and Peter Lutz received title to their lands in 1788, a year after the above letter was written.

[186] WRO, Libro B-1, 154.

[187] The 1775 "Census" counts 9 members in the Ricker Jr. family, one fewer than in 1770; Anna Catharina and Sarah Sommer had since married and left the household.

[188] In the 1783 Hillsborough "Census", Henry Lutz is listed as a "young man", old enough to start his own family.

[189] Several German families by the name of "Meyer" also settled in Lunenburg in 1751/1752. Although none of their children were called "Charles", it is possible that Charles Myers did not come via Germantown, N.B. but may have originated in Lunenburg like the Jonah family.

[190] Col. Gubbins perceptively refers to this: "The gardens in this part of America often suffer materially from a variety of destructive insects of species happily not common in England, and that have baffled every remedy...:" *Gubbins Journals*, pp. 70f.. The inspector continues that in Captain Powell's garden hardly anything was left standing, except potatoes and gooseberry and currant bushes.

[191] "Hendrick Steeves and his Wife and Seven Stalwart Sons," NBM, Scrapbook Albert County, Shelf 31.

[192] Title to this land went to Rachel's second husband, lawyer Robert Dickson from Sackville, probable son of Charles Dickson Esq.. Calhoun's widow did not live long to enjoy her court success as she predeceased her father, who died in 1802.

[193] Clark Wright, *The Petitcodiac*, p. 62. For the Stieff family tradition on Peck's betrayal and pirate raids, cf. pp. 56, 61ff..

[194] Mathew Richey, *A Memoir of the late Rev. William Black* (Halifax, N.S.: William Cunnabell, 1839), pp. 91f. (November 22-24, 1782). Sources for William Black's *Journals* are scattered. Black's *Journal*, The *Arminian Methodist Magazine*, Vol. 14, is difficult to obtain. Another source for Black's *Journal* entries is Arthur Betts, *Bishop Black and his Preachers*, 2nd. enlarged ed. (Sackville Tribune Press, 1976).

[195] Clark Wright, *The Petitcodiac*, p. 27.

[196] Clark Wright, *Samphire Greens*, p. 27.

[197] No name is attached to this 1783 entry. By elimination, this "Dutch woman" is most likely widow Brackman now with three children (she had 2 in 1775).

[198] William Calhoun, *Diary*, p. 3.

[199] DesBarres to Haldimand, May 30, 1768, HaP.

[200] Letter of June 1, 1783, quoted from Clark Wright, *The Petitcodiac*, p. 50.

[201] *Ibid.*, pp. 50-51.

[202] *Loc. cit.*.

[203] Joseph Gray Petition.

[204] Clark Wright, *The Petitcodiac*, p. 50.

[205] *Ibid.*, p. 58.

CHAPTER VI

History and Stories of the Petitcodiac

VI.1 Land Deeds for "Monckton" and Hillsborough

Despite temporary setbacks for the settlers during the American Revolution, these did not thwart their long-term achievement of security and financial stability; however, one problem still confronted them, namely, they did not own the land on which they had toiled so hard and which was the culmination of all their efforts over the last decade and a half. Although the Revolution to the south had managed to come knocking at their doors, threatening their personal safety and property, its outbreak also laid open an avenue by which they could better their status from that of tenant to landowner. The general suffering at the hands of American marauders fuelled older resentments[1] which the settlers had harboured for years against their American landlords, whose profit-driven motives and insincere promises undoubtedly stirred up deeper memories of the behaviour of princes and lords in their homeland. The example set by Thomas Calhoun and his wife Rachel, who sued Adam Hoops's company for back-wages and won, showed the Petitcodiac Germans a way of obtaining title to their land; they were the catalyst for a host of legal challenges launched against delinquent landowners, which proved that the individual could stand up to those of the privileged New World aristocracy. Insisting on their right to be landowners was the ultimate proof that the Petitcodiac Germans had finally shaken themselves free of the shackles and confines of a restrictive web of Old Country customs and privileges, something they would also pursue on the religious front.

Since all communications with Philadelphia ceased as a result of the war, the settlers found themselves entitled to take legal action against their absentee landowners for neglect and breach of contract. When the decisions by the Cumberland County Court of Common Pleas[2] came down in their favour, the Township's real estate was seized and portions of it auctioned off.[3] Settlers could bid for the various parcels of land to redeem their costs and losses which had accrued over the years. When news of the judgements

227

reached the proprietors in Philadelphia, there was consternation on their part, and they were convinced that biased judges had cheated them out of years of work and large sums of money.

The documents issued at the courthouse in Cumberland by Deputy Provost Marshal J. Thomas Watson give details regarding the size, location, price in "Halifax Currency", and former owners of each parcel of land, thereby revealing which land company had sponsored the various settlers.[4] Every "Grantee" received two "Deeds", one in 1778 and another in 1780, which at first glance seems peculiar. The later deeds provide the reasons why two were necessary as, for example, John "Cople's", which stated that "... the Property of Mess'rs Mathew Clarkson & Company Merchts of Philadelphia ... was taken by Execution and the time of Redemption Allowed by law of this Province ... [has] Elapsed."[5] The land companies were evidently not able to take advantage of a two-year grace period to pay their debts to the settlers. On November 11, 1780, several of those who had arrived on June 3, 1766, gathered at the Cumberland court house near present-day Point de Bute to receive title to their land. It was a long-awaited day, fourteen years after their arrival. However, not all of the original settlers lived to experience this moment of triumph, namely Matthias Sommer, Charles Jones, and Heinrich Stieff. Matthias Sommer, as mentioned earlier, passed away between 1767 and 1768.[6] His widow married Jacob Ricker Jr., who applied on behalf of the Sommer family. The deeds for Lot No. 7[7] were issued in the name of the "Heirs of Mathew Sommers."[8]

Charles Jones died in 1774, and his 2,263 acres (Lot No. 4) were awarded to heirs, Henry and John.[9] It is unclear who applied for the heirs of Charles Jones, as both boys were still underage in 1778, unless possibly Jacob Ricker Sr.. There is circumstantial evidence that Jacob Ricker Sr. may have married Charles Jones's widow. Although Charles Jones stayed in "Monckton", his sons may have been living in Hillsborough before 1780 as suggested in the Millidge Report. Henry Jones actually married Christina (Ricker/Sommer/Wortman ?) from this settlement and John Jones's wife came from this coast, too. In the 1783 Hillsborough Census, Jacob Ricker Sr.'s household recorded two grown sons and one grown daughter, who might have been Henry, John, and a sister. Georg Wortman's listing in the

1783 Hillsborough Census, for example, includes three sons who, according to the Millidge Report, had already moved back to "Monckton" but who had been residents of Hillsborough until recently. The existence of a "Margaret Ricker" in Hillsborough who made purchases on William Harper's trading ship *Weasel* in 1797[10] opens the possibility that she was the widow of Jacob Ricker Sr. since the other Rickers at this time had spouses with different names.[11] Margaret was also the name of Charles Jones's eldest daughter (Abraham Treitz's wife),[12] possibly named after her mother, and the name was carried through later generations as well. If it can be shown that Charles Jones's wife was called Margaret, then it is likely that the Jones family moved to Hillsborough after Charles's death as part of the Ricker Sr. family and that this new head of the combined family applied for land on behalf of Jones's two heirs.

In the case of the Stieff land grant (Lot. No. 3), the first deed in 1778 was made out to "Henry Steef",[13] the second in 1780 to the "Heirs of Henery Steef",[14] indicating that Heinrich Stieff died between 1778 and 1780. Another reference to his death is the entry in the right-hand margin of Joseph Gray's Hillsborough petition of June 1, 1783 that "Henry Steeve Sen. ... lately died, left a widow."[15] It is assumed that he passed away in 1779 (figs. 22, 23), shortly before the birth of Christian and Rosanna (*née* Treitz) Stieff's first son, named Henry in memory of Heinrich. The couple's second son was named after Rosanna's father, Jacob. It was supposed that Heinrich Stieff was barely 50 years of age when he died.[16] The discovery of Heinrich Stieff's Münsingen origins suggests, however, that he was closer to age 65.

Of the seven German families, Jacob Treitz Sr., Michael Lutz, Jacob Ricker (Sr. and Jr.), Georg Wortman, and John Copple were alive fourteen years after their arrival, by which time many of their sons and daughters had made homes in "Monckton" and Hillsborough. John Copple, unfortunately, barely survived receipt of his land title. His wife had died about six months after the sheriff's sale of 1778, leaving a three-year-old daughter, Judith. As was the "practice with the aged Germans of this country to make an agreement with someone of their children, (if they have any), or some other person in whom they can confide, to enjoy the property with which they are possessed at the time of such agreement, and maintain them during their lives," John Copple leased his grant to William Wilson in exchange for

Figures 22/23

Commemorative stones for Heinrich and Regina Stieff in the Hillsborough Baptist Cemetery with incorrect spelling of their names and date of arrival.

Photos: Rainer L. Hempel

support for himself and Judith, "as long as he should live ... and until she should arrive at the age of 18 years."[17] In late 1780, fifteen months after such an agreement with Wilson was signed, Copple died and Judith was placed in the care of the administrator of the estate, Justice Charles Dickson Esq. of Sackville, where she died in 1787 at little more than 10 years of age. It was perhaps the realization of his impending death which caused Copple to transfer his 1,718 acres of marsh and woodland to Judith when his grant (Lot. No. 2) was confirmed on November 11, 1780.[18] The Copples are the only Petitcodiac German family in the "Monckton" settlement to have left no descendants and, as a result, are often omitted in historical accounts of the region.

For £55 in damages and £7:17:3 in costs, Jacob Treitz Sr. received over 2,000 acres (i.e. 8 km²) of property (Lot. No. 9) in present-day Moncton, stretching from Hall's Creek to Jonathan Creek.[19] For this reason he has been called the "Father of the City of Moncton".[20] All nine properties, as they were granted in 1778, had frontage along the Petitcodiac and extended back in a rectangle, containing both marsh and upland and between 1,620 and 2,190 acres. Next to Treitz and proceeding upriver came Jacob Ricker (Jr.),[21] who was awarded 1,900 acres (Lot. No. 8), and bordering him were the descendants of Matthias Sommer, now related to the Rickers by marriage, with 2,100 acres. Sommer's neighbour was Michael Lutz,[22] who sued for £50 in damages and £7: 17: 3 in costs and received 1,977 acres (Lot. No. 6). To his west was Charles Baker, the American businessman who had visited the Petitcodiac in June of 1769 and remained active in these settlements afterwards. As indicated earlier, he promptly sold his property (Lot. No. 5) to Abraham Treitz, to whom it was deeded in November 1780.[23] Charles Baker's suit against the Philadelphia grantees was for lack of payment for services rendered in the surveying of the various land grants. This case is intriguing because a note in the *Jacobs Papers* appears to contradict Baker's claim, stating that 25 shillings were paid by Benjamin Jacobs, one of the owners, "... for 1/10 of Charles Baker's Acct: for Surveying Monckton Township in Nova Scotia for Doctor Smith & Com: Share the whole of which is twelve pounds ten shilling and Six pence ...."[24] Somewhere along the line, monies may have been misappropriated or otherwise withheld from their intended recipient. Thus, Charles Baker qualified to receive land in the township even though he did not belong to the eight original pioneer families and may never have had any intention of settling there.

Situated at the most westerly end of "Monckton" Township lay Georg Wortman's property of 1,166 acres (Lot No. 1),[25] this being the difference between his original grant of 1,750 acres[26] and that portion he sold Joshua Geldart around 1778.[27] In these 1780 grants Wortman is recorded as a resident of Hillsborough, like Michael Lutz, the "Heirs of Mathew Sommers", and Jacob Ricker Jr., while Abraham and Jacob Treitz Sr. were from "Monckton". Michael Lutz, Jacob Treitz Sr., and Jacob Ricker Jr. were listed as "farmers", which must have been the fulfilment of their dreams. The gathering of so many of the original settlers in Cumberland on this auspicious November 11, 1780, must have been an occasion of much celebration and merriment. Given their distances away from home, some area inn likely enjoyed a brisk business that evening.

The Hillsborough claims were settled a short while after the successful conclusion of those in "Monckton" Township. In a deed signed in the same court house on March 4, 1781, the heirs of Heinrich Stieff took possession of "Fifty Acres of Marshland, and Six hundred Acres of cleared upland and Wood land, with One Dwelling House and Out Housing ... Bounded ... on the South on the Lands belonging to the above mentioned Heirs of Henry Steef .... [T]he said land ... [was] formerly the Property of Robert Cummins [sic]... and was taken in Execution and the time of Redemption allow'd by law of this Province being Elapsed."[28] From the wording of the deed, Stieff had previously owned land adjoining the new property which Cummings (now deceased) and his heirs had lost in like manner as the "Monckton" proprietors. A deed in 1782 recorded one such grant by agent Moses Delesdernier Esq., on behalf of proprietor Joseph Gerrish Esq., to John "Steeve".[29] The signing of this agreement, which gave John Stieff 50 acres of upland, 10 acres of marsh, and 140 acres of "Wilderness Lott", was witnessed by Charles Baker and Michael Lutz Sr.. Other Hillsborough tenants acquired land grants from their former landlords too. On December 12, 1780, Peter Lutz, "husbandman", sold three parcels of land in Hillsborough totalling 200 acres to Charles Baker for £15. The fact that the property was still "... subject to a Yearly Rent of One Penny farthing p. Acre, p. Annum, to be paid to ... Michael Francklin or his Assigns ..."[30]

confirms that Peter Lutz had been a tenant of Michael Francklin and that the Lutz family benefitted from grants both in Hillsborough and "Monckton". The heirs of Heinrich Stieff filed an "Agreement" at the Cumberland courthouse in 1784, [31] in which the seven sons stipulated jointly the division of their father's property in Hillsborough *and* "Monckton", the latter going to Christian and Frederick and the former to the other five. Much of this had, of course, been decided and carried out within the family years earlier but only recorded in a formal document when New Brunswick became a province.

One consequence of creating a separate administrative entity from Nova Scotia was that applications for grants had to be addressed to officials in Fredericton. On January 24, 1785, Jacob Ricker Jr. petitioned for land in Hillsborough for himself and on behalf of his 20-year-old son Michael, his brother-in-law Peter Lutz, and several members of the Stiles family, stating to Thomas Carlton Esq. that " ... about 12 years ago [in 1773] ... [they] were put upon a tract of land as tenants in the Township of Hillsborough, consisting of 20,000 acres, taken up by Mr. Robert Cummins and Mr. Adam Hoops ...."[32] In a group petition with 25 others in 1786, Peter Lutz, Michael Ricker, and five of the Stieff sons -- Jacob, John, Matthias, Henry, and "Lodwick"-- eventually received 200 acres each. Jacob Ricker Jr. was granted 300 acres because he had been settled there for 13 years and had 10 children.[33] Land grant maps show transactions in subsequent years and the spread of Petitcodiac Germans throughout Hillsborough and "Monckton" (figs. 24-28). By the time the Millidge Report was submitted in March of 1788, sixteen heads or potential heads of families[34] lived in Moncton: Jacob Treitz Sr., his sons Abraham, Jacob Jr., and Christian, Heinrich Stieff's sons Frederick and Christian, Wortman brothers Jacob, Martin, and John, Andrew Sommer, Henry and John Jones, Michael (and John) Lutz, Christopher Horseman, and William Wilson. Collectively, they owned 224 acres of cleared upland, 582 acres of dyked marsh -- and 16,156 acres of wilderness! Among the livestock were 130 cows, 56 oxen, 200 sheep, but only 19 horses.

233

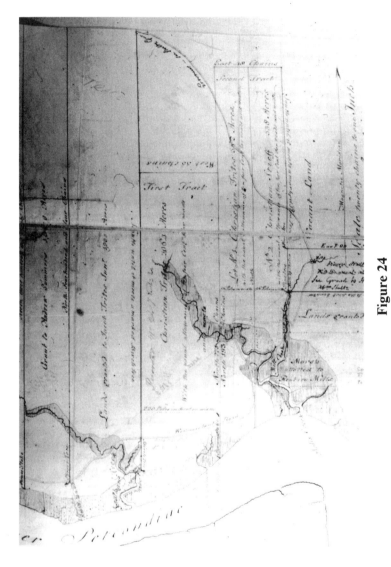

Figure 24
Contemporary grant map for Moncton at "The Bend".

Courtesy: Provincial Archives of New Brunswick

234

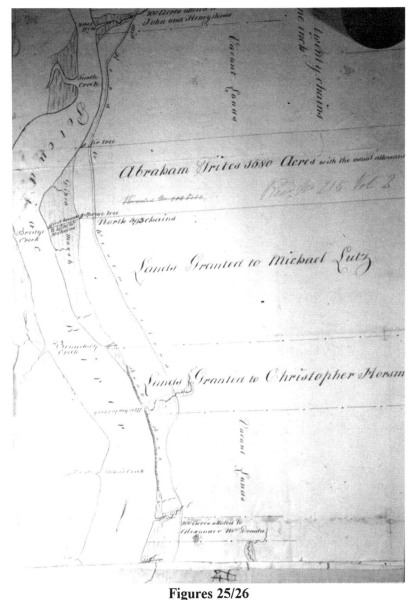

Figures 25/26
Contemporary grand maps for the western parts of "Monckton Township".

Courtesy: Provincial Archives of New Brunswick

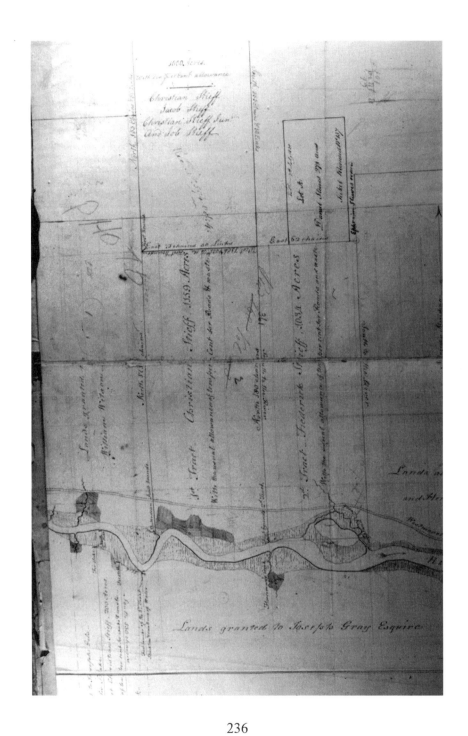

236

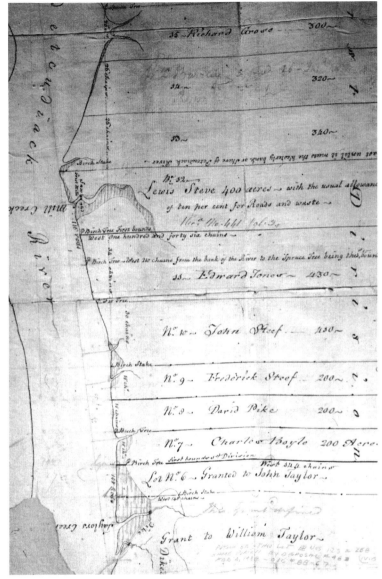

Figure 27

Contemporary grant map for Hillsborough.

Courtesy: Provincial Archives of New Brunswick

237

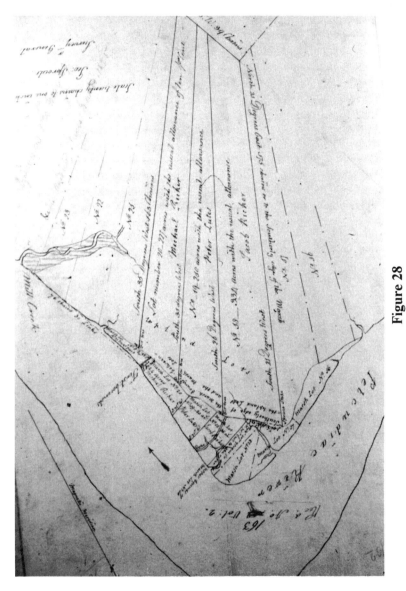

Figure 28

Contemporary grant map for Coverdale, the opposite side of "The Bend".

Courtesy: Provincial Archives of New Brunswick

238

VI.2 Matters of the Spirit

The challenges faced in land ownership were accompanied by those of a spiritual kind as the Petitcodiac Germans felt deserted and in need of pastoral care. Lieutenant Governor Francklin, former co-owner of the Hillsborough settlement, must have sensed his obligation to these people, as well as to the Acadians,[35] and attempted to answer their needs. He intended to grant them the same privilege just accorded the Germans of Lunenburg -- albeit reluctantly and after a great deal of complaining and lobbying -- namely their own minister who could preach to them in their mother tongue.[36] In 1767 German-speaking Rev. Paulus Bryzelius was selected to minister to the Lunenburg Germans. A Swede by birth, Bryzelius had come to North America as a missionary of the Moravian Church, or *Herrnhuter Brüdergemeine*, but was ordained by the Anglican Bishop of London to fill the bilingual post in Lunenburg. Bryzelius's close friend Rev. Heinrich Mühlenberg, the previously mentioned dean of Lutheran churches in the New England states, kept in close contact with Bryzelius until the latter's death in 1773. Mühlenberg exerted a moderating influence on the Lutherans in Lunenburg when they claimed that Bryzelius was an Anglican masquerading in a Lutheran garb. Bryzelius's many letters to the Society for the Propagation of the Gospel attest to his initial struggles in obtaining German texts, but also to his successes in ministering to his flock. In a letter to Dr. Daniel Burton, "Secretary to the Society for the Propagation of the Gospel in Foreign Parts," dated January 9, 1769, Bryzelius made mention of his ministry to the Petitcodiac Germans in the summer of 1768:

> His Honour the Lieut' Governor Franklin, who is very desirous & vigilant to see every thing prosper & go well both in Church & Government Affairs, was pleased to desire me to visit some of the New setled Countys on the other Side of the Bay of Fundy who are destitute of Public Worship. Also I took a Tour last Sumer of several hundred miles which I performed in Six Weeks, & during that Time I officiated both in English & German in the Counties of Hilsborough, Moncton & Shepardy [Germantown]. Some of their Children which I baptized were Four or Five Years old. The poor People in those Places were exeeding glad after So long fasting to hear the Word of God; for there has been no Minister up that Way

since their Settlements began. Several desired of me to administer the Lords Supper to them, but alas! there was in all these Places not a drop of Wine to be had. They begged me for Gods Sake not to leave them, but that I shou'd come again next year to officiate among them if possible.[37]

This letter furnishes evidence that the Germans of Lunenburg and the Petitcodiac were, at least through the person of Bryzelius, aware of one another's existence and that a German-speaking minister attended to the spiritual needs of the Petitcodiac Germans after two years' subsistence in Nova Scotia's wilderness. There is no evidence that Bryzelius or any other German-speaking minister ever visited the Petitcodiac Germans again.

The general view held by British authorities was that German-speaking pastors would retard the settlers' acquisition of English and "prevent the thorough union and harmony with the rest of his Majesty's Subjects."[38] They hoped that, by the appointment of an Anglophone pastor, German as a language would fall into disuse. In his letters to the Lunenburg Germans, Rev. Heinrich Mühlenberg recommended Anglicans, whom he regarded as "... our closest and best friends and well-wishers .... [T]he doctrine of the English established church is the most similar and closely related of any in the world to our evangelical one .... They have admitted the Swedish minister [Bryzelius] as a senior Lutheran and myself, to preach in their churches, and we have had them preach in ours."[39] It is not surprising that the British authorities, when they encouraged ministers at all, dispatched only Anglicans to represent the Church of England.

One such minister was Rev. John Eagleson, who had sailed up the Petitcodiac together with the German families in 1766. Eagleson was a Presbyterian minister, originally from Ireland, who had requested to go to Nova Scotia sometime after April 14, 1766.[40] In two letters, both dated October 22, 1767, Lieutenant Governor Francklin and Provincial Secretary Richard Bulkley recommended that Rev. Eagleson be re-ordained by the Church of England in order to minister to the greater Parish of Cumberland, N.S..[41] After his ordination by the Bishop of London in 1768, Eagleson returned to Nova Scotia under the auspices of the Society for the Propagation of the Gospel and held Divine Worship in Hillsborough on July

28, 1771, shortly after William Calhoun's arrival from Baltimore. Over the next two years, Eagleson undoubtedly made contact with Rev. Paulus Bryzelius, a fellow minister in the Society. Like his Lunenburg counterpart, Eagleson was encouraged to range further afield. In one letter,[42] he reported to the Society that he had had to preach the anniversary sermon "in lieu of Mr. Bryzelius, lately deceased," also that he was the first Protestant clergyman to tour St. John's Island (Prince Edward Island)[43] since the establishment of its own separate government. Eagleson also preached in Sackville and "Tantramarre" and, undoubtedly at the request of Lt. Gov. Francklin, visited the Petitcodiac Germans in 1774, reporting to the Society later: "I last Summer visited the Townships of Hillsborough & Monckton on the River Peticodiac, in which Visit I had the Honor of being Accompanied by his Excellency Lieut Govr Francklin, where I read prayers & preached two Sundays to a Considerable Audience of English & Dutch [German] Settlers & Baptized 14 Children ...,"[44] among whom must have been Jacob and Catharina Stieff's' first-born son John. In 1775 he married 4 couples, buried 1 child, and had 16 communicants. Eagleson was not able to minister to the Petitcodiac Germans again for, during the Eddy Rebellion in 1776, he suffered the misfortune of being captured by rebels and taken to Boston, where he was incarcerated for more than a year.[45] Upon his return to Cumberland, he found his property destroyed and library ransacked. Eagleson maintained that he had been "victimized" for his pro-British views and waited out the remainder of the war in the relative safety of Halifax, loudly denouncing his parish as "a bed of sedition"[46] on account of certain individuals' sympathies toward the rebel cause. When news of Eagleson's "dissolute life style ... reached the Bishop's notice, ... he was defrocked in 1790 on the grounds of drunkenness and incompetence."[47] Eagleson had always been fond of drinking and, although popular with his parishioners, was ruthless when it concerned competition from other ministers who appeared to intrude into his territory. He sued a fellow clergyman who dared to establish himself in Cumberland and had another arrested, along with his worshippers, while preaching at Fort Cumberland.[48]

The diaries of these "Dissenting Fanaticks",[49] as Eagleson called them in his letter of January 16, 1775 to the Society, shed light on the role the Petitcodiac Germans played during this lively, at times heated, period of Maritime religious history. These diaries were kept by Henry Alline and

William Black, both itinerant preachers who ministered occasionally to the settlers. In *Bishop Black and His Preachers*, Arthur Betts claims that "... Black was the first minister to work among them [the Petitcodiac Germans] ...."[50] This assertion fails to acknowledge Bryzelius's and Eagleson's visits, as well as information in Alline's and Black's own journals.

Henry Alline's[51] "charismatic and uniquely spiritual" personality, mystical theology, creative powers, and " ... unusual ability to communicate to others his profound sense of Christian ecstasy ..."[52] turned the religious map of the Maritimes upside down. His belief in the "rapture of the New Birth" and the "ravishing of the Spirit" challenged the established religious order, if there was one, between the year of his spiritual awakening in 1775 at 27 years of age and his premature death in 1784. Early in 1781, Alline paid Cumberland County a visit that was to last seven or eight weeks. While there he met William Black, who described Alline in his *Journal* as "a young man from Falmouth, who was very zealous in the cause ... [and initially] a great blessing to many."[53] Before taking his leave, Alline proposed to his listeners that they give up their Methodist discipline. Some time afterwards, Alline sent another preacher who, according to Black, "sowed dissention, and poured out a flood of the rankest Antinomianism, which afterward produced dismal fruits."[54] Alline's journal entry of July 27, 1781 recording his first visit to the Petitcodiac reads:

> I rose by break of day on account of the tide; we sang and prayed and refreshed our bodies, and set out to go lower down the river, and stopt at the lowest village [Hillsborough or Steeve's Village], where I had promised to stop as I returned. The people were chiefly Germans, but they universally attended, and many were taken hold of by the word. Most of them could understand English and would not take a denial, but I must visit them again if I lived: which I promised I would, if I ever came to the country again.[55]

The "powerful impact on the Germans of Hillsborough"[56] was temporary. On the occasion of Alline's second visit one year later, he encountered opposition, and his disappointment is expressed in his journal entry of May 6, 1782:

We came to a village of Dutch people [near today's Allison] about twelve at night, where I intended to stop and preach. The next day I preached two sermons and the people gave attention, but were so chained down to the form of religion or godliness without the power, ... and were so strict in their forms, that it was almost impossible to convince them that they were no christians; or that they needed anything else. But there was *a young man among them*, who was brought to the knowledge of Christ, and enjoyed great liberty in his mind, who laboured much with this people, but they looked on him as one under a delusion because he told them, that their being baptized and going to the Lord's supper, with all the other forms they practised, would not save them, and that they would be as certainly lost as if they had never practised any of them; telling them, that they must know what it was to be born again and feel it in their own souls, exclusive of all their externals. O the blindness of the poor wretched race of Adam, while in an unregenerate state.[57]

These remarks concerning the Petitcodiac Germans seem rather judgmental; however, as will become evident later, there were good reasons for Alline's cooler second reception. If he had been able to visit more often, this opposition might have been overcome but, as it was, Alline appears not to have returned and this last impression became an enduring one. The young man "who was brought to the knowledge of Christ" and "had laboured much with his people" was likely Christian Stieff.[58] He was converted by William Black of Cumberland, was a devoted Christian, and frequently held devotional meetings. It was Christian Stieff's wife, Rosanna, who "... was converted under Henry Alline; she was the first person converted on the Petitcodiac River -- and at the time was considered *insane*."[59] Thus, the schism which occurred in the Maritime religious landscape may also have divided Christian and Rosanna's family although he surely forgave Rosanna her youthful slip, and both must have rejoiced in each other's spiritual renewal. In his *Journal*, William Black made many references to the dreadful, destructive force of "antinomianism", a doctrine which held that the faith and dispensation of grace frees a Christian from the obligation of adhering to moral law. By making reference to King David's relationship with Bathsheba, Black wrote that "... under pretence of honouring free grace ... [the Allinites] taught publicly, that no believer should make shipwreck of his faith; that his soul never sinned, though he should lie or get drunk; that David himself, or his soul, never sinned, while in Uriah's bed, -- it was his body only."[60] It can be no coincidence that Rosanna, with a record of serious transgression in 18th-century morality as the mother of an illegitimate child, eagerly accepted Alline's teachings that "... a believer is like a nut thrown in the mud, which may dirty the shell, but not the kernel."[61] Rosanna may have been considered "insane" initially, but the numbers of people who flocked to hear Alline steadily grew so that she found herself eventually in more accepted company.

William Black, a young, self-appointed preacher from the Amherst area of Nova Scotia, also decided to come and minister to the Petitcodiac Germans, just after Alline's first visit. Black was not even of legal age[62] in the early summer of 1781 when he made his initial address to the settlers of Hillsborough and "Monckton". Over several years he braved the cold, loneliness, mosquitoes, bad accommodations, smoky cabins, not to mention the "Petitcodiac ... one of the most dangerous and formidable rivers in Nova Scotia."[63] Black summarized his first trip: "I took a tour up the river Petitcodiac, and spoke to the people of the goodness of God, and the way of salvation through faith, but they remained in general *hard and stupid*. However, the word did not wholly fall to the ground, *one being awakened*, and the next time I visited the river, set at liberty ...."[64] Mathew Richey, author of *A Memoir of the late Rev. William Black*, identified this person as "... Christian Steeves, a German, who was deeply awakened."[65] Richey actually preached at Christian Stieff's' home in Salisbury almost forty years after this event, finding "... the good old man steadfast in the covenant of his God, and full of hope, blooming with immortality. He [Christian Stieff] alluded with thrilling emotion to the period when Mr. Black first visited them, bringing the glad tidings of great joy ...."[66] On Black's second trip, just after his twenty-first birthday, he preached to the "poor, hardened people of Petitcodiac River."[67] This time he took a whole week to minister to the settlers of "Dutch Village",[68] or Hillsborough, preaching to them about sixteen times. Black also made his way up to the other settlement on the north shore and past the bend in the river which he simply called the "Village", near today's Allison and close to where Abraham Treitz, the Jones brothers, and Christian and Frederick Stieff farmed.[69] Black set out from Amherst a third time on November 10, 1781, delivered a sermon at

Tantramar on the 13th, and arrived "[on the]14th at Hillsborough, where ... [he] preached to the Germans, and early next morning set off in a log canoe for French Village ...,"[70] probably Près d'en Haut, across the Petitcodiac River to the north, a crossing that almost cost him his life. Undaunted, he returned to the area again early in the New Year. The *Journal* entry for January 23, 1782 reads: "After preaching at the Village, I left the people in tears, and set forth home. I spent the night at Mr. A[braham] Trite's, where I preached."[71] In August of this year, he again touched the life of one of the Petitcodiac Germans:

About nine in the morning [on the 24th], I preached at the Village, and afterward met the society. Truly this was a powerful season. Old Mrs. Stieves,[72] who had been in deep distress, was brought into glorious liberty. The Sun of Righteousness arose with healings in his wings, and her mourning was turned into raptures of joy! She spoke of the goodness of God till all in the room were melted into tears. Mrs. Stieves was a person of excellent moral character, and had strictly attended to some of the outward duties of religion; but she now saw the necessity of inward holiness. When some of her sons were (previously) awakened, she opposed them, supposing they were lead away by a deceiver.

When ... Baker, Esq. J.P., was up the river, she wrung her hands in great distress, and cried, O that Black! that Black! he has ruined my sons! He has ruined my sons! But the last time I was here, the Lord opened her understanding, and she saw her need of a deeper work. Sore distress, arising from conviction, seized upon her soul; and she had no rest until today. -- Leaving many in tears, we left off with the tide about one o'clock, and arrived at Hillsborough in time for preaching ....[73]

This entry suggests that widow Regina Stieff was visiting with her sons Christian and Frederick in proximity to the "Village" settlement and that she was a troubled mother over 1781-1782 as she watched her sons come under Black's powerful influence. Frederick was also "set ... at liberty"[74] during one of Black's prayers, several days after his mother. The account of Regina's conversion also shows that even she, at 62 years of age, seems to have become conversant in English. There is no question that her children and grandchildren could speak it. "Mrs. Stieves" difficulties did not appear to end here because Black reported three months later having been in Hillsborough on November 22, 1782, the day she was taken hostage by raiding American privateers, who surely had been informed she was widowed and living alone.

A chronology of Alline's and Black's visits helps to explain the differences in welcome each was accorded during his initial contact with the Petitcodiac Germans. Henry Alline's July 1781 visit was probably the first ministry they had had since Rev. Eagleson's tour in the summer of 1775.[75] The thrill of having a charismatic 33-year old preacher in their midst resulted in a very positive reception. Therefore, when William Black arrived to minister to them only a few weeks later, he found the people cool and reserved, leading him to believe that they were "hard and stupid" in spiritual matters. After years of no spiritual guidance whatsoever, suddenly here were two eager preachers in one summer. Black's youthful age was undoubtedly a factor. In their view, he was too young -- perhaps not even 21 years of age -- to be a minister,[76] and his emotional and forceful delivery must have put the settlers on guard. Accustomed to a more restrained, Lutheran style of worship from the Old Country and Pennsylvania, the Petitcodiac Germans must have required some time to adjust to the outward displays of belief and inner conflict which William Black appears to have expected from his flock. He never tired mentioning examples of visible emotion and conversion. One man "could do little else the whole night but praise the Lord, being too happy to sleep;"[77] another was found "kneeling on the snow, crying and praying in the bitterness of his soul."[78] Black left "many in tears" on August 23, 1782; three days later "there was weeping and rejoicing on every side", "heaving breasts", and those who "were pricked to the heart"[79] or "trembled exceedingly under the word."[80] Given her austere upbringing, it is little wonder that Regina Stieff feared her two sons had been led astray by Black, "ruined" in her words under the spell of "enthusiasts and fanatics."[81] Black sensed the initial reservations of the Petitcodiac Germans towards him, entering in his *Journal* on May 19, 1782: "I received a very pressing letter from Petitcodiac, requesting me to return there ... immediately, and informing me that my last visit had been made a great blessing; that now the *prejudices* of the people began to banish, and several were under deep

246

concern."[82] By the time Alline returned for a second visit to the Petitcodiac a year later, Black had already made significant inroads in his ministry on at least four separate occasions and over longer periods of time. He had earned the settlers' trust and friendship, and no doubt seized the opportunity to caution them well against the dangerous teachings of "antinomianism". This explains Alline's cooler second reception which he, in turn, lamented in his *Journal*. The division, contention, and controversy which Alline's return caused everywhere, even in Black's hometown of Amherst, was less pronounced amongst the German settlers.

The way in which the Petitcodiac Germans implored Rev. Bryzelius from Lunenburg to stay with them more than ten years earlier attests to the fact that they were not as "hard and stupid" in spiritual matters as William Black had supposed them to be on his first visit. That the Heinrich Stieff family brought a large Bible (fig. 29) to North America further confirms their reverence for the word of God. At a time when the family's total earthly possessions could be contained in a trunk or two, the inclusion of this Bible stands in contradiction to Richey's interpretation of Black's early comments, that the Petitcodiac Germans "were lamentably ignorant of the things of God and with a few exceptions apparently unsusceptible of any serious interest in the subject."[83] So, too, was the hand-written, personalized religious inscription (fig. 30) in the Stieff Bible, given here in translation:

> Heinrich Stiff [sic], joy and love to one thing
> Makes all toil and work appear small.
> Everything depends on God's blessings, [for] those who believe.
>
> God so loved this world, that He gave his only begotten Son,
> So that all who believe in Him shall not perish,
> But have eternal life.
> For God alone [be] the honour (glory).
>
> Heinrich Stiff, Jacob Stif, Johannes Stiff, Christian Stüff[84]

By July 1783, when William Black discontinued regular visitations to the Petitcodiac, he had grown to appreciate the residents there as "a simple, loving people indeed, happy in God."[85] The actual number of trips he made

Figure 29

The German Bible which Heinrich Stieff brought with him. The ten-cent coin on the right serves as a comparison of size.

Courtesy: Provincial Archives of New Brunswick
Photo: Rainer L. Hempel

248

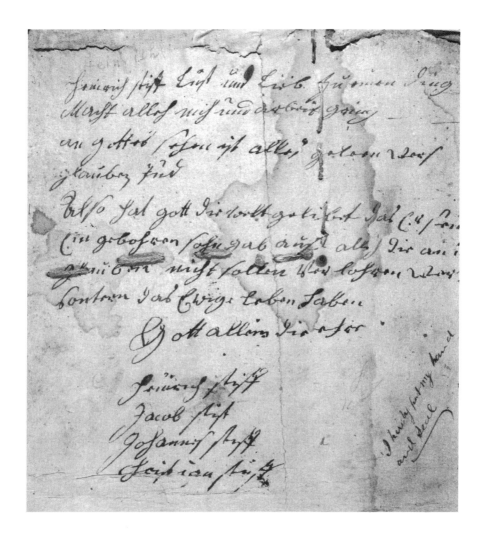

Figure 30

Entry in German script on the inside cover of the Stieff Bible. Note the difference in spelling of Heinrich, Jacob, Johannes, and Christian's last names, evidently written by the same hand.

Photo: Rainer L. Hempel

249

to their communities, of which at least ten are documented in his *Journals*, shows the special concern and regard Black held for these people.[86]

The Petitcodiac Germans took an active part in the spiritual life and development of their adopted land. Heinrich Stieff's third son, Christian, was called "preacher",[87] likewise his fifth son Henry (fig. 31), known as "Henry the preacher".[88] Henry Jr.'s eldest son, John, was said to have been an "Allinite Preacher".[89] The stigma attached to Rosanna (Treitz) Stieff for having been converted by Henry Alline seems to have been overcome a generation later: "Some of Alline's followers became Methodists, but for the most part they gradually coalesced to form the powerful Baptist Church of Nova Scotia."[90] In his later years, "Henry the preacher" became a Baptist, which stunned his fellow parishioners, in particular since the revelation of his change of heart was made at a meeting when the question of hiring a Methodist preacher headed the agenda. He is largely credited with the organization of the Baptist church in Hillsborough.[91]

The conversion of the majority of the Petitcodiac Germans first to Methodism under William Black and later itinerants such as James Mann[92] and William P. Early, and then to Baptism requires examination as these settlers appear to have been at the forefront of radical evangelicalism in New Brunswick, at the same time belonging to a larger movement away from the established order and churches. The "obsession with religious ecstasy and dramatic conversionism," combined with "exaggerated emphasis both on the emotions and on all sensory perceptions"[93] which had alarmed Regina Stieff initially, began to sweep through the Maritimes at the height of the American Revolution and did not abate until the early years of the 19th century. It was the continuation of an older Protestant piety,[94] but "a piety infused by a remarkable degree of anarchistic ecstasy and intense spirituality."[95] It appeared to be more important for Nova Scotians and New Brunswickers to attain liberty in matters of the spirit than in the secular arena of politics. Many theories have been proposed to explain why Atlantic Canada, while rejecting the American Revolution and what it represented, was in the religious realm "more radical, more anarchistic, more democratic, and more populist than its American counterpart."[96] Having decided in favour of the King and a more centralized form of government with limited input and influence meant that no local power emerged to maintain religious cohesion.

250

Figure 31
Gravestone of Henry Steves (Stieff) in the Hillsborough Baptist Cemetery,
fifth son of Heinrich Stieff and grandfather of William Henry Steeves, Father
of Confederation.

Photo: Rainer L. Hempel

This resulted in depoliticized religion with greater individual rights where communal pressure, as manifested in the new United States,[97] was less dominant. The religious revival in the Maritimes has been viewed as an escape from the confusion and threat of a world at war to the comfort and security of revival meetings and the promise of rewards of a different kind.[98] It has also been regarded as a revolt of common people in remote areas against the capital city, Halifax, the Anglican Church, and the governing *élite* -- all symbols of authority and tradition. Radical evangelicalism in the Maritimes challenged the British order of society, its hierarchy, inequality, and patronage, putting forth new concepts concerning the individual, family, and true equality in the sight of God, in particular that of women.[99] The British establishment viewed these developments with alarm. Anglican leaders such as Charles Inglis feared that Congregational, Methodist, and proto-Baptist New Lights were "engaged in a ... plan of a total revolution in religious and civil government."[100] These words echo closely the sentiments which led to the repression and eventual extermination of Anabaptists in Germany almost three hundred years previously. Although the time for such punishing action was past and the Anglican establishment found itself unable to mount an effective counterthrust, except in its stronghold Halifax,[101] repercussions were felt from another quarter, affecting the religious picture further. American Methodists stopped sending their itinerant preachers because too many had returned later, infected with the "New Light cancer".[102] The vacuum created by the absence of Methodist preachers was quickly filled by Henry Alline's Baptist disciples, resulting in a Baptist Reformation -- or "revolution".[103]

The above is one explanation why the majority of Petitcodiac Germans became Baptists, but there are other reasons to take into account: "[R]eligious passion was for the ... pioneers and planters, the essential, throbbing, thrusting stream of reality. For them, ... pecuniary desires, and entrepreneurialism were worldly temptations provided by the devil and were to be assiduously avoided at all cost."[104] It is not coincidental that this excerpt could have come from a page in the book of Württemberg Pietism.[105] Matthias Sommer, one will recall, found himself involved in -- and eventually excluded from -- the upheavals of Germantown's St. Michaelis congregation because of his sympathetic stance toward Pietistic theology.

252

The Sauer press in Philadelphia must be viewed as a major contributing factor in the religious development of the Petitcodiac Germans. The title of an article, "The Sauer Family: An American Printing Dynasty,"[106] gives an indication of this family's importance, not just in the United States but in New Brunswick as well because the grandson of the founder of the Sauer press came to this province as a Loyalist. Christopher Sauer Sr. was born in Germany in 1695 and began printing in 1739, first an almanac and later in the same year a newspaper entitled *Die Germantowner Zeitung* ("The Germantown Paper"). "Radical Pietists like Sauer were intensely religious and keenly moral but at the same time fiercely critical of the lapses of institutional life in church and state."[107] Sauer Sr. was a staunch member and supporter of the Church of Brethren, or Dunkers, a sect of Christian believers which originated in the Pietist movement in Germany and whose adherents believed in baptism by triple immersion.[108] They advocated peace, brotherhood, temperance, the fellowship of all Christians, simple living, and alternative service in place of military conscription. Like the Baptists, they had been persecuted in Germany, but in the atmosphere of tolerance that welcomed them in Pennsylvania, they concentrated in Germantown and reorganized their church in 1719.

In 1743 Sauer published the first Bible in the American colonies.[109] His printing activity afforded him a large audience and his outspokenness on moral issues, a wide and faithful following. On several occasions he also played a pivotal role in Pennsylvanian politics. Sauer's " ... publicity on problems within struggling colonial Lutheran and Reformed congregations made him unpopular with their clergy" and his strong, pacifistic views did not endear him to certain military officers or politicians either. His son Christopher Jr. continued in the spirit of his father.[110] When the profits from the second edition of the Bible were greater than anticipated, representing undue profit from the Word of God, Sauer Jr. founded a new Christian periodical, the first religious magazine in America available free of charge to subscribers of his Germantown paper. This supplement contained religious essays, sermons, hymns, original poetry and contributions by the well-known schoolmaster Christopher Dock, "including his two hundred rules of conduct for children."[111] Sauer's impact on his readership regarding true Christian devotion and freedom from sectarianism is incalculable.[112] Through the numerous Sauer publications and enlightened teachings of Rev.

Mühlenberg, the Petitcodiac Germans were able to distance themselves from certain unpopular attitudes of Old Country Lutheranism. Suspicions with which mainstream churches viewed lesser-established denominations were allayed, enabling these settlers to embrace new religious persuasions like Methodism and Baptism in their second adopted homeland.

Past histories appear to have been unaware of the presence, background, and possible influence of the Petitcodiac Germans on early New Brunswick society. Even George Rawlyk claimed that in this province " ... most of the population was of Loyalist background, a rough cross-section of American colonial society before the revolution,"[113] implying that those who arrived before the Loyalists were insignificant in number and influence. No explanation has been offered why "... the first Baptist itinerant to arrive in New Brunswick in the first decade of the nineteenth century was greeted by large numbers, ... who needed little if any convincing to be immersed."[114] The Petitcodiac Germans before anyone else, based on their German and Pennsylvanian backgrounds, were predisposed to carry the banner of Baptist Christianity as a portion of unfinished reformation from their country of origin and as an expression of self-determination on the religious level. The high number who accepted the Baptist persuasion underscores this claim.[115]

The active involvement of the German settlers in spiritual matters stands in contrast to Col. Joseph Gubbins' remarks in 1811 on the state of religion in much of the province, obviously from the vantage point of a Church of England adherent:

> In remote situations, such as poor new settlers have to begin upon, they degenerate very rapidly to a state of barbarism. For want of clergymen the magistrates are empowered to perform the marriage ceremony, and frequently had recourse to, but the mutual consent of the parties is often the only contract, and christening or any other religious ceremonies are hardly thought of. The inhabitants of New Brunswick are mostly egregious fanatics or without any idea of religion.[116]

Gubbins failed to mention that, at this time and as was the case until 1835, neither Baptists nor Methodists were permitted to perform marriages although they had the largest number of adherents in the more isolated areas of New Brunswick.[117] His privileged view of pioneer life could not appreciate what David Bell recognized, that the "... frontier needed the social organization religion could provide ...."[118] Contrary to Col. Gubbins's impressions, later assessments of the German settlers' spirituality were more favourable: "[I]n eighteenth- and early nineteenth-century New Brunswick the Christians in Hillsborough and neighbouring Hopewell townships were one of the most consistently fertile preaching grounds, [and] the Germanic [sic] Protestants of Hillsborough were to exert an influence on New Brunswick religious development out of all proportion to their number."[119] The development toward religious freedom, begun by Luther but stopped short by repression of the Anabaptists and others, continued first in Pennsylvania and later along the Petitcodiac. Exposure to different religious persuasions in Philadelphia, including those supported by the press of the German Sauer family, prepared the Petitcodiac settlers to be open-minded in the face of new developments after their arrival in "Monckton" and Hillsborough. This should be compared to the static nature of the Lunenburg Germans' religious life. Having come directly from Germany and never having experienced the "crucible" effect of Philadelphia or the religious upheavals of later New Brunswick, they insisted on Lutheran ministers for generations. This closed-mindedness, made light of by Rev. Mühlenberg, was a reflection of the evangelical church in Germany which closed itself off from "the stimulus and competition of the sects"[120] and continued to be suspicious of all other denominations.

VI.3   The Spirit of Enterprise

The ability to work quietly and tenaciously in the face of setbacks and obstacles was not just an outgrowth of the Petitcodiac Germans' "pietistic" background, as mentioned in connection with the Stieff family in Württemberg, but also the result of having lived under absolutist princes. It was better to keep a low profile and go unnoticed even when there were good reasons for complaint.[121] Based on past experience, they harboured deep-rooted suspicions against the attention of authorities that might lead to negative consequences.[122] This has resulted in a dearth of entries about the settlers in government records, making secondary sources indispensable to the portrayal of life then. Moreover, pioneering and the struggle for survival

Figure 32
Margareth (Lutz) Stieff buried beside her husband John Steves (Stieff) in the
Hillsborough Baptist Cemetery.

Photo: Rainer L. Hempel

256

allowed little time for the contemplation of heritage or the passing on of written accounts of their individual and collective life experiences. What is said, therefore, of the Stieffs can be said of most of the Petitcodiac Germans: "... [They] were very circumspect people who kept out of trouble and out of official records to an amazing degree."[123]

There is an abundance of oral and anecdotal history, however, which illustrates the settlers' spirit of enterprise and how they strove for a better life in the New World. Various newspaper articles and Clark Wright's numerous stories belonging to Stieff family tradition give an indication of the wealth of material available. Whereas Clark Wright tempered the often unbridled imaginations of certain storytellers with the facts that she was able to glean from various archival documents, others have given too loose a rein in matters of dates and historical accuracy. One account or other relates that Heinrich Stieff made the cuckoo clock on exhibit in the Albert County Museum (fig. 33),[124] or that he was alive in 1811, trading in plaster with a ship he built himself; there is no end to the telling and retelling of his exploits. Confusion often arises due to the simple failure to identify repeated names with designations such as "Jr." or "Sr.". To embellish the difficulties during the early period, one story even claims that the food shortage was so severe that a soup bone was passed from house to house.[125] Some of these stories must be dismissed for reason of improbability or in the face of established chronological information, but others should not be dismissed as they may well have a historical basis.

The settlers accredited an Acadian named Pierre Belliveau with their survival. He had apparently been away hunting and missed the English attack on the French settlements during the expulsion. After hiding in the woods for about eight years, he observed Cpt. Hall's ship sailing up the Petitcodiac River. Many versions of the experiences of these first years exist. The following abbreviated account gives an impression of how events were viewed about one hundred years later:

> He [Belliveau] had observed the approach of the sloop. He had watched their [John Hall's and the settlers'] landing and building, during the nights he had lurked about their cabins with the keen eye, ear and stealthy tread of the hunter. He recognized the tongue of the

257

Figure 33
The clock which Heinrich Stieff brought with him to North America.

Courtesy: Albert County Museum, N.B.
Photo: Rainer L. Hempel

258

foe of his race. He recognized that others spoke an unknown tongue. After the sloop sailed he no longer heard the hated language of the English and ventured to approach.

He was accorded a hearty welcome. The colonists shared with him their supplies. He in turn supplied them with game, the victims of his prowess in hunting. He taught them his skill in trapping and tracking game. Guns he had, but his ammunition had been long expended. The colonists were able to supply him with this. In return he stocked their larders with moose, deer and bear meat. ... The cold was more intense and the days shorter than they had ever experienced. Slowly the days dragged on and the spring seemed long in coming ... In April under his instructions they made maple sugar. This was a unexpected treasure, and, with the fruit from the old orchards, added much to their comfort.

All summer they claim to have waited in vain for the promised supply ship and subsisted on marsh greens and berries, preserving the fruit from the old Acadian orchards with maple sugar.[126] Their provisions had been exhausted by the beginning of the next winter. They had even run out of gunpowder, but they persevered and made salt from sea water for preserving their fish and meats:

... In this manner they lived for six long years, and never saw the face of man other than themselves.... They had not even the consolation of a whiff of tobacco, so dear to the German heart. At intervals during their exile they had heard at sundown the distant boom of a cannon, but they knew not where or what it was. By some it was thought to be thunder; others attributed it to [a] supernatural agency. Belleveau alone knew, but his dread and hatred of the English was such that he was careful to conceal his knowledge, and rather encouraged the idea that it was supernatural .... Steves determined to build a boat and coast the shore, till he found whether others lived in the world than themselves. He did so, and rounding Cape Meringuin heard the sunset gun at Fort Lawrence .... Next morning, despite the protestations of old Belleveau, who dreaded nothing so much as falling into the hands of the English, he turned the prow northward, and in a few hours sighted Fort Lawrence, surmounted by the English flag. Concealing boat and crew, Steves advanced alone. On reaching the Fort he was questioned, but having entirely forgotten the little English he knew he was unable to make himself understood. Luckily, a German named Jacob Beck was attached to the Fort.... By means of this interpreter, Steves was able to tell his tale of suffering. He was hospitably received and his companions welcomed with him. Food they had long been strangers to was set before them. Never was morsel more delicious than the bread of "Beck, der King's paker." The boat was loaded with provisions; ammunition and guns were supplied ....

Steves went again and again to Fort Lawrence. His ingenuity made him valuable and he was given a cow for his services. The great trouble was to get her home. Nothing daunted, he built a larger boat and took her home, and another luxury was added to the community. At last there was grain enough for seed and to spare. Barley soup was made. "Tat vas good -- der svetest and besht dinner as ever vas," in the language of the narrator descendant of the old stock.

Prosperity began to dawn. Their sons and daughters intermarried, the chaplain at Fort Lawrance officiating. Their dependants are now scattered all over the eastern section of the province principally in Albert, Westmorland, and King's counties ....[127]

Some of the above details have already been discounted, such as the claim that they did not have cows and that Heinrich Stieff needed to transport one from Fort Cumberland in a homemade boat, as the letter by Capt. Hall specifically mentioned that Hughes ordered him to buy a cow and calf for each of his settlers and the 1766 "Monckton" Census listed 12 cows in their possession. It was also Martin Beck (not Jacob) who was stationed at Fort Cumberland (not Fort Lawrence). The claim that the days were shorter than they had ever experienced is also not true. All Petitcodiac Germans came from an area in Germany between the 48th and 52nd parallels latitude whereas in New Brunswick they settled between the 45th and 46th, making the days longer rather than shorter in their new home. This does not dispute, however, that the winters in "Monckton" were colder than in Germany and Pennsylvania. Although the general tenor of their suffering is accurate and supported by contemporary accounts, the claim that the enormous challenges and hardships lasted six years is exaggerated. As William Calhoun noted in his diary, prosperity of the German settlers at "The Bend" had arrived by July 1771. Indeed, the evidence presented earlier suggests that three years at most -- from 1766 to 1769 -- was the duration of the difficult period.

The stories of assistance from Belliveau abound, as do those of friendly native people who offered help at the critical time when starvation appeared imminent. Considering the circumstances of the settlers, it would have been difficult for them to survive without help from those who inhabited the area before and possessed the knowledge to live "off the land." Although the settlers were resourceful, frugal, and practical people, accustomed to life in rural Germany, they were also steeped in the accumulated knowledge and traditions of their forefathers from the Old Country. There, too, they had to make do with what the land offered them, and they knew the herbs which would heal a bruise and those which would cure a cough. They could foretell the weather by signs in the sky and had a built-in calendar for the agricultural year, when seeds had to be sown for best yields and when harvesting ought to be complete. Anyone who has come from another continent knows how different the vegetation and wildlife can be in North America. When the Petitcodiac Germans came to the New World, certain aspects of their previous knowledge were rendered useless, or possibly even hazardous. Life in Pennsylvania had not prepared them for the different flora, fauna, and climate of such a northern maritime location. Should they have tried a berry or mushroom, for example, which resembled edible ones from home and yet were poisonous, the results could have been lethal. As well, the extremely variable weather patterns that meet at the head of the Fundy -- cold Labrador winds, strong Westerlies, and gales from the tail-ends of tropical storms -- compounded by early fall frosts, often heavy snowfalls and late springs must have been unsettling to newcomers familiar with milder climates in Germany and Pennsylvania.

Friendly "Miigmags"[128] and Acadians provided the German settlers with information, drawn from the traditions of their own respective forefathers. During the winter, for example, "... [t]he boys [of the settlers] occupied themselves making hand sleds and hauling wood for the fire which was kept burning all night and day. The Indians[129] taught them to make snowshoes with which they were all well fitted out."[130] Heinrich Stieff's boys are said to have copied Belliveau's canoe, dug out from a massive pine log.[131] As well, " some friendly Indians ... came around occasionally and taught them to trap and hunt,"[132] a skill which the Germans had never acquired in their homeland as it was forbidden to all but the nobility on pain of severe punishment. Not just the meat was important to their survival in the early years but also the furs, to guard against frigid weather and cold winds.

In this domain of cultural interplay and exchange of ideas, it is not clear in what language the Germans, Acadians, and Miigmag communicated. The theory that the name "Rachel", which is uncommon in German, might be a clue that Heinrich Stieff's wife was of French Huguenot descent and thus able to speak French with the Acadians and perhaps Miigmags, must be rejected since it is now known that her original name was "Regina" Stahlecker from Honau, in the district of Reutlingen, Württemberg. Belliveau, who is said to have hated and feared the English, probably could not speak the language of his foes. In all likelihood, the spoken word was not a central issue. Somewhat later, Moses Delesdernier[133] and perhaps Pierre Joannah helped interpret between the French and Germans. The Miigmag, Acadians, and Germans most probably intercommunicated on a non-verbal level,[134] where acceptance and appreciation of one another's cultural backgrounds resulted in a greater ability to cope with the elements, enhanced comfort levels, and improved chances for survival. Such mutual coexistence is undoubtedly a lesson for those who dwell on the differences and conflicting claims of neighbouring cultural groups.[135]

Charles Baker had seen the settlers collect "Herbs ... in the Marsh in the Spring &c...," which Clark Wright called "samphire and goose tongue greens and the cow cabbage."[136] Although Baker's letter implies that marsh greens were eaten only in desperation, they continue to be enjoyed many generations later.[137] The Pennsylvania German tradition of "hot salad of dandelion or other spring greens with a sweet-sour bacon dressing"[138] shows that gathering spring greens was a time-honoured activity that bridged the gap between the last rotten apples and shrivelled turnips in the root cellar[139] and the first fresh vegetables in the garden. It is not certain whether the Miigmag imparted the knowledge about these edible plants directly or *via* the Acadians, in the person of Pierre Belliveau and no doubt others too, when the Germans were taught about the currents of the river and the tides, how to hunt and snare game, make weirs and fish for seafood, how to extract salt from sea-water for preserving meat and fish, and how to boil the sap of sugar maples to produce syrup and sugar for the preservation of fruit. Directly or indirectly, the Miigmag must have been involved since they were presumably the ones who taught the Acadians a century and a half earlier.

The collection and boiling of sugar maple sap, which remains a spring ritual in New Brunswick today, was adopted early by the German settlers, proof of which is found in William Harper's ledgers. By further refining the syrup, pure sugar could also be obtained. A sugar mould in the shape of a heart (fig. 34) [140] -- a traditional Pennsylvania German motif -- with a letter "T" (for Treitz ?!) in German "Fraktur" carved in the bottom, was undoubtedly made and used by one of the early settlers. William Calhoun praised the gooseberries and "larger quantities of raspberries than ... [he] had ever seen before."[141] One time he found his men so busy gathering raspberries that they failed to pay attention to their canoe, allowing it to run aground with the falling tide. There are several references in Calhoun's diary to apple and wild cherry trees which had been broken apart by bears trying to get at the fruit. As part of the "Articles of Agreement," each settler had agreed to plant fifty apple trees, but by the year 1771 when Calhoun made his entries, it was too early for these to have reached the fruit-bearing stage. These must have been former Acadian orchards which Calhoun alluded to more than once. Apples were an important ingredient in Pennsylvania German cuisine, particularly sliced and dried as *Schnitz*. They could be used in pies and such unusual dishes as *Schnitz un Gnepp*, together with ham and dumplings. These dried apple slices were also a source of vitamins over the long winter months.

Venison was an important contribution to the table of the settlers. An old powder horn of Pennsylvania German origin, with characteristic motifs such as the heart, bird, and "Hex" sign (plate 8, 8a), was discovered in the early 20th century near Germantown, N.B. and probably carried by a German hunter from the early settlement. William Calhoun mentioned duck-hunting[142] and also described his adventures on a bear hunt in the company

Figure 34
This sugar mould in the shape of a heart may well have belonged to a
member of the Treitz family.

Courtesy: University Press of New Brunswick Ltd.

of Robert Cummings.[143] Bears were not just hunted for pleasure but their meat and fur.[144] On his inspection tour of New Brunswick militia some forty years later, Col. Gubbins also remarked upon the local abundance of moose, deer, caribou,[145] as well as smaller game such as hare and partridge.[146]

The sea, rivers, and lakes also yielded abundant food. Calhoun perceived "a great number of salmon jumping up some distance from the mouth of the [Shepody] River,"[147] of which his party caught about thirty in nets. "Salmon holes" made catching them particularly easy. He similarly reported "large quantities of flounders and eels,"[148] and at one time, when his men were unsuccessful in making a catch for the next meal, he was "compelled" to dine on clams! Col. Gubbins had no such aversion to oysters, found in immense banks near Shediac, N.B..[149] On January 22, 1772, Calhoun entered in his diary that he went to Shepody Lake (also called "German Lake")[150] in the company of his brother Thomas "to catch a mess of trout."[151] Col. Gubbins also made repeated references to the abundance of fish all over the Province's coastal waters, such as salmon, codfish, haddock, pollock, and especially herring which, near the island of Grand Manan, were at one time so numerous that they "splashed the water in such a manner as to resemble a heavy rain storm."[152] These examples make it clear that fresh sea food was available year round. Perhaps to show that nature also provided the ingredients for a good refreshment and that no one had to sail the 8 or 9 leagues (approx. 40 km) to Cumberland's tavern to have "a fine time",[153] Calhoun recounted a visit to some neighbouring Acadians who "entertained ... [him] very kindly, and gave ...[him] spruce beer to drink ...."[154]

The information flow was not one-sided. There was cultural exchange from the Petitcodiac Germans to the Acadians in the form of various food preparations, e.g. *Sauerkraut* and *Kartoffelklöße*,[155] the more familiar Acadian version being known as *poutine râpée*. Father Clément Cormier, founder of the Université de Moncton, acknowledged their German origin according to oral tradition among the Acadians and his own investigations into this traditional "Acadian" dish. When he was served *Kartoffelklöße* in southern Germany, he called them "Bavarian knôdel [*Knödel*]".[156] Whereas Acadians put various kinds of meat in the centre of these dumplings, Germans use homemade bread *croûtons* instead. However, if flour for bread was scarce in the first few years, the Germans may well have added small pieces of carefully rationed salt-beef, making this a kind of "poor man's" meat-and-potato dinner. Potato-growing was well established in 18th-century Pennsylvania, and the potato was a key staple made available to the settlers of all three Petitcodiac settlements. It was also much more versatile than turnip in way of preparation.

The potato as a staple in the settlers' diet is a subject of interest. Michael and Walpurgis Lutz came from an area in Germany which did not know the potato until about the year 1770, approximately twenty years after their departure. Protestant Waldenser refugees from the valleys of Piemont in France first brought the potato to Württemberg in 1699,[157] where the Stieffs lived, although there is some doubt that such culinary delights as *Kartoffelklöße* were developed at such an early date since the potato was first accepted as animal fodder.[158] Prussian King Frederic II introduced the potato to Kolberg in 1744 in the wake of a severe famine following the first Silesian War, but in contravention to his strict orders, many Germans only accepted it years later as fit for human consumption.[159]

Some Petitcodiac Germans likely only learned to appreciate potatoes and make *Kartoffelklöße*[160] in Pennsylvania, which was a veritable melting pot of German-speaking peoples from many regions of Central Europe as evidenced by the emergence of a distinct dialect *Pennsilfaanisch Deitsch*.[161] If knowledge of these dishes had not been passed on to Acadians earlier, then Jacob and Catharina Stieff's marriage, which all residents of Hillsborough and area were invited to attend, was a good occasion for serving up cultural delicacies. Without doubt, every effort was made by the Stieff family to tempt guests with their best traditional fare; perhaps the Acadians invited to the festivities flattered their hostess by asking for her recipes.

Plentiful harvests, as documented in the 1775 Hillsborough Census, enabled the Petitcodiac Germans to continue their Old-Country culinary traditions alongside those learned in Pennsylvania. "A great many noodle and dumpling dishes which link Pennsylvania German with the *Mehlspeisen* [flour-based] cuisine of South Germany ..."[162] were likely prepared up and down the Petitcodiac from their grain harvests, such as a pauper's dish from Bavaria, the *Dampfknödl* ("steamed dumpling") which the Petitcodiac

Germans may have eaten sweetened with maple sugar. *Spätzle*, a hand-pressed noodle specialty from Württemberg made from such simple ingredients as flour, eggs, and water, was possibly prepared by the Stieff family. The famous German tradition of sausage-making flourished in Pennsylvania, giving North America such delicacies as "bratwurst", "liverwurst", "frankfurters", and "wieners". Soups were another favourite in Pennsylvania, mostly of the flour and potato variety, which put to use the potato slurry left behind in the making of *Kartoffelklöße*. The variety of *Kuchen* ("pies") in Pennsylvania German country continued with such prevalence that this region has been called the "center of the American pie belt."[163] The Petitcodiac Germans brought these and other traditions north with them, such as the making of cheese, which became one of the first exports from Germantown and the Petitcodiac, as well as their favourite, shredded cabbage preserved for winter as *Sauerkraut*.

In both Hillsborough and Moncton, the Petitcodiac Germans practised their gardening and horticultural traditions, mostly the domain of women. The day before her marriage to Frederick Stieff and move up river,[164] Rosanna (*née* Ricker), the widow of Jacob Treitz Jr., assigned dower rights of her property (fronting today's Petitcodiac Lake in Moncton) to her son Jacob and daughters Catherine, Margaret, and Hannah. Although the premises were given to Jacob, Rosanna at the same time reserved "one half of the dwelling house to ... [her daughters] with one half of the garden in front thereof .... It ... [is] further understood now that the daughters ... are to have ... the privilege of the kitchen and one third part of the cellar."[165] The German tradition of planting vegetable and herb gardens by their houses, observed elsewhere in Canada,[166] was evidently alive in Moncton too. Her garden must have been of considerable size and of such importance to the family that she would bequeath it jointly to three daughters residing nearby, granting them kitchen facilities and root cellar access for cleaning and storing their vegetables. At least two of the daughters had their own families, Catherine and Margaret, who were married to John Bennett[167] and shoemaker William Maugher, respectively. In doing so, Rosanna ensured that her daughters and new daughter-in-law, Rebecca Wilbur, would be well provided for.

Another German tradition was family cohesion, especially when it became a question of looking after the aged. Stephen Millidge referred to this tradition in his report on John Copple's agreement with William Wilson, and Col. Gubbins made the same observation when he wrote: "Nothing is more objectionable in the American character than the want of attachment to parents. This is certainly more observable in the families of English origin than in either the descendants of the Germans or French, who mostly constitute communities of their own connections."[168] This could be observed with Jacob Stieff, who built his farm within 30 rods from his father's house, as well as with many other Stieffs who remained in Hillsborough. The desire to be close to his son in old age must have been part of the reason for Jacob Ricker Sr.'s move from the family farmstead in "Monckton" to Hillsborough. The proximity of Christian Treitz' residence to that of his father[169] made the youngest son a good choice to look after Jacob Sr., just as Job Steeves cared for his mother Rosanna (*née* Treitz) when she became old. Examples of this are numerous, as shown in the 1851 Moncton Census: Mary Lutz (aged 95) was living in her son's household, likewise Christinah Jones (aged 89) with her son.

The assertion that the Germans were excellent weavers[170] has been made of the Germantown settlers in many different accounts: "They are said to have been linen weavers of great skill."[171] This claim was also applied to the German pioneers further up the Petitcodiac River. An article in the *St. John Sun* recounts this aspect of Albert County history:

> One morning, the last of June, 1776,[172] they were surprised to see a small schooner coming around the cape. They watched her until they came to anchorage. She proved to be a trading vessel. Hendrick and his boys proceeded to her with a bundle for furs to trade for goods. The traders, think[ing] to get furs for a mere nothing, made an offer; but Mr. Steeves, finding he could not make a fair trade, threw his bundle of furs over his shoulder, told his boys to follow, adding: "We'll go home and eat our turnip mush awhile longer." The traders coming to the conclusion that he was the wrong man to get a big "sift" out of, let him make his own terms. With the *thread* they procured from the traders the family went to work making linen out of the flax they had raised every season. They made a loom, and in a short time they had all the linen they needed.[173]

268

Since Heinrich and Regina Stieff, as well as Jacob Ricker Jr., were steeped in weaving and knitting traditions, a knowledge of the mechanics of weaving has to be presumed for all the Petitcodiac Germans, particularly in view of the close contacts they maintained with one another. It is of note that they were spinning and weaving flax for linen and sackcloth and not just wool, which required less skill. Given their backgrounds, it was entirely possible for them to produce the necessary tools, spinning wheels, and looms from local wood sources. Peter Lutz and his son, Michael, were known wood-workers, as revealed by William Harper, as well as Frederick Stieff and others. Clark Wright makes reference to her ancestors' improvisational skills and knowledge of weaving:

> When Heinrich Stief and his sons needed any tool or implement, they had to make it. They had and passed on through the generations a variety of technical skills and a desire to make and do. The granddaughters and great-granddaughters were often noted weavers. (I am still using blankets one great-granddaughter made one hundred years ago.) They wove carpets and blankets, and *homespun* for clothing.[174]

The harvest in 1775 of ten "pounds" of flax in Hillsborough by Jacob and Catharina (Lutz) Stieff, as well as the large amounts by "weaver" Jacob Ricker Jr. and other Germans listed in Joseph Gray's return, is further evidence of these people's weaving activities.[175] The cultivation of flax was a tradition in the Swabian Highlands,[176] and knowledge of it must have been brought over by the Stieff and Ricker families. Weaving was carried on in other centres, too, as William Penn learned in Krefeld where he spoke to dissenters caught up in proto-industrial activities related to this trade. Many German immigrants were actually displaced weavers, who continued planting flax and plying their trade in the New World. In fact, Germantown, Pennsylvania became known as an important weaving centre in early American history.[177]

The use of bricks in fireplaces, chimneys, and later as a building material for houses was also introduced to the Petitcodiac region by Germans, as well as by certain English "Planters". Although few of these early bricks have been unearthed since the exact location of the original homesteads is unknown, later evidence shows that the firing of bricks, even in large quantities, was common practice among these settlers. The disaster which befell Michael Lutz's son, John,[178] shows that fires were an all too frequent occurrence in wooden houses, started by candle accidents, open fireplaces, and creosote build-up in chimneys. The frame-house which Christian Treitz probably built around 1782 was another such home destroyed by fire.[179] As a result of this, Christian opted for a brick house, which was more enduring than wood, preferred by Germans in the homeland, and a "luxury" he could finally afford. This house, built c. 1800 on a hewn stone foundation, served its various inhabitants until February 18, 1972 when, ironically, fire gutted out the interior, and the decision was made to tear down the walls of the remaining shell. Some of the reddish-brown bricks, rather unstable and crumbly today, were salvaged from the ruins and are on permanent exhibit at the Moncton Museum. While the house was still standing, these were described as "almost uniform in size, approximately 7¾ by two inches, ... roughly finished, giving the wall an irregular pattern."[180] Clay of similar colour can be found on the banks of the nearby Petitcodiac River. Recent tests confirm that the clay was most probably taken from the mudflats of the Petitcodiac River at "Bald Marsh" and that the bricks for Christian's house were moulded and fired on location.[181] An ordinary open hearth or bonfire was sufficient for the primitive potter. Even kilns were relatively easy to construct, consisting of a fire-pit under an enclosed structure with a vent above to allow combustion gases to escape.[182] This brick house in which Lieutenant Colonel Gubbins spent a night in 1811 was the first he had seen in the Province, but such quality construction -- Gubbins called it "a good brick house" -- which withstood a salty Maritime environment for almost two hundred years did not come about without previous knowledge and experience. Heinrich Stieff, a *Ziegler* (brick- and tile-maker), must have been the source of this expertise although he died over a decade before the construction of Christian's house. In a closely-knit community, sharing information was as important as sharing supplies. With his trade, Heinrich Stieff must have assisted all along in the identification of fire-clays for special bricks required in the construction of chimneys stipulated in the "Articles of Agreement" of 1766. Heinrich's expertise in fabricating ordinary bricks must also have become common knowledge, just as weaving and knitting. Brick houses in the Dorchester and Coverdale areas may have been the legacy of Heinrich Stieff.[183] The easy accessibility of good-quality clay (in some areas clay of potter-quality is just below the surface) made brick a choice of the more affluent in the post-pioneer stage. The remnants of a kiln on the Chapman farm in Coverdale confirm that the bricks for this house, built in 1824, were made on location.[184] This can be assumed for the other brick houses around 1800, especially in view of the unnecessary transportation of some 40,000 bricks required to build the average 19th-century house.

The settlers' improvisational skills, mentioned in connection with weaving, were applied in every aspect of pioneer life. The circumstances in this unsettled land were such that most everyday household items, like chairs, tables, beds, chests, cupboards, kitchen utensils, and even more specialized implements, had to be fashioned of wood or other locally available materials. Whereas tables and chairs are prone to be discarded after intensive use over a short period of time, less bulky items used only intermittently, e.g. small chests, cribs, sugar and butter moulds, spoons, and specialized kitchen utensils, have survived to the present day. Pennsylvania Germans continued ethnic customs from their homeland by adorning utensils and pieces of furniture with motifs, such as stylized flora and fauna (especially tulips, peacocks, partridges, and mythical birds), rhomboidal[185] and scroll-shaped patterns, a myriad of different hex-signs,[186] and above all the heart.[187] Furniture and utensils embellished with these ethnic signatures have been discovered in or near former German settlements along the Petitcodiac River, confirming that their inhabitants did bring traditional customs north with them (plates 9 and 10, figs. 35-43) and underscoring claims about the settlers' creativity within the whole region.[188]

Of particular interest in this context is the Treitz Haus (plate 11, fig. 44),[189] once known as the Prince-Lewis House, situated on the west side of Bore Park in Moncton. Research to date suggests that this building was possibly erected c. 1775 as a home for Jacob Treitz Jr. and his new wife, Rosanna Ricker, with the help of their fathers, Jacob Treitz Sr. and Jacob Ricker Sr., making it the oldest known building in Moncton today and one of the oldest in New Brunswick. After the log-cabin phase of 1766 - c. 1770, this two-storey, timber-frame structure may have been the fourth or fifth of its kind in Monckton Township, after others of the Treitz Sr., Ricker Sr., and Jones families. Jacob and Rosanna Treitz Jr. were one of two

Figure 35
The pattern at the top, the scrolls of the holding rack, and above all the heart shape grooved in the board, as well as the inverted heart which gives shape to the lower part of the holding board, are characteristic Pennsylvania German motifs.

Courtesy: University Press of New Brunswick Ltd.

Figure 36
The pattern near the top and the "Hex" motifs below point toward a Pennsylvania German origin of this chest from the Moncton region.

Courtesy: University Press of New Brunswick Ltd.

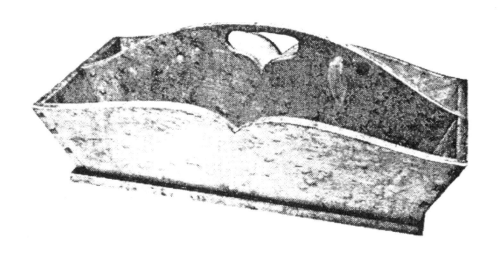

Figures 37/38
The cutlery box and sheath for this hand-made knife from the Port Elgin region of New Brunswick show the ethnic signatures of Pennsylvania Germans.

Courtesy: University Press of New Brunswick Ltd.

Figures 39/40 and 41/42 on the next page
The butter moulds show Pennsylvania German motifs and patters such as
plants and flowers (tulips), adaptations of the "Hex" or sun motif, and the
heart.

Courtesy: Albert County Museum, N.B.
Photos: Rainer L. Hempel

274

275

Figure 43
Carved wooden spoon, typical of Pennsylvania Germans;   note the
characteristic heart motif in the handle of the spoon (Spoon in possession of
the Arsenault family of Minudie, N.S., descendants of Hilaire Arsenault,
builder of many churches in the 1840's).

Photos: Bernard LeBlanc

Figure 44

Information panel during the restoration phase of the Treitz Haus, the former Prince-Lewis House (see Plate 10).

Photo: Rainer L. Hempel

277

second-generation, Petitcodiac German couples to marry in "Monckton" at this time, the other being Abraham Treitz and Margaret Jones, who likely moved into or near the Jones homestead located near "Mill Creek" (Allison); however Jacob Treitz Jr. and Rosanna Ricker are distinguished as the only "Monckton" couple involving two Pennsylvanian-born Germans.

Numerous features point to an early date for the house: its Georgian style,[190] hand-wrought iron nails with unusually wide heads, hand-hewn beams, hand-made bricks between one exterior wall, large boards (some measure over 60 cm in width), accordion-split laths, and the original black paint of the wainscotting, but it is the heart motif carved out of a panel above a doorway (fig. 45), suggestive evidence of the use of a double-sided stove between the so-called "backroom" and "sitting room", and vestiges of a *Flurküchenhaus*[191] floor plan which show a decided Pennsylvania German connection and suggest a pre-19th century date when most of the first-generation Pennsylvania German pioneers were still alive.

Through a detailed analysis of early land transactions at "The Bend", there is reason to believe that a dwelling house, barn, and other outbuildings likely stood on a cleared tract of upland on the east side of and near a bend in the old Westmorland Road, or "Great Road", looking out toward the Petitcodiac River,[192] with cleared land for a garden and pasture in the immediate vicinity. It seems reasonably certain that the house had a root cellar, and this as well as some of the foundation stones could have had an Acadian origin. After the first occupants decided to move into the former Ricker Sr. farmstead c. 1780-1783, the farm with the present house was presumably leased to new arrivals to "The Bend," such as Ebenezer Cutler and William Steadman.[193] Thomas Prince, who possibly rented initially, may have purchased the house from William Steadman, Christian Treitz or Christian Stieff, depending on the date and exact location. When the Westmorland Road was straightened, the house was in the way and moved in early 1811 to its "Main Street" location. Around 1835 Ichabod Lewis took it over and renovated it in order to operate an inn out of the older right-hand side and to provide living-quarters for his family in the newer left-hand addition. The historical legacy of this house is, therefore, as multifaceted as that of the Petitcodiac region, uniting Acadian, German, and Loyalist cultures under a single roof.

278

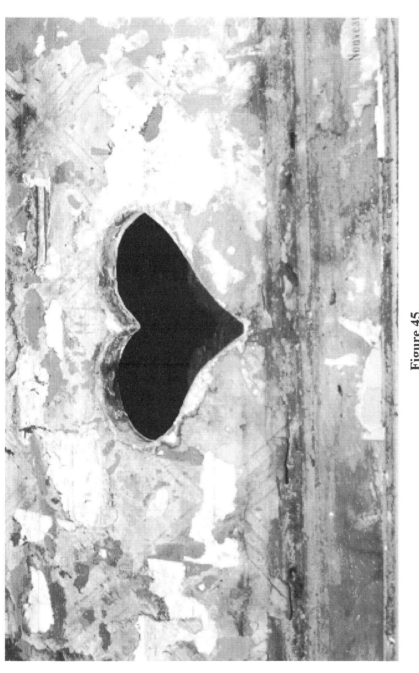

Figure 45

The carved-out heart in a wooden panel of the Treitz Haus in Moncton shows the influence and participation of Pennsylvania Germans during its construction.

Photo: Rainer L. Hempel

279

Until the turn of the century, the Petitcodiac Germans of Moncton depended on traders like John Bentley (Dec. 11, 1754 - June 21, 1837), who plied the Bay of Fundy with his floating trading post and warehouse, supplying the settlers with goods they could not fashion themselves and that would make their lives a little easier. Likewise, William Harper (1764 - 1834), whose first wife Sarah Hamm[194] was a German Loyalist whom he met on their voyage up to Saint John, used his schooner *Weasel* in a similar fashion along the Petitcodiac before opening up stores at "The Bend" and later North Joggins (Rockport, N.B.). Harper's business and transaction ledgers provide evidence of the lively trading which took place at that time, also as to the lack of hard currency still troubling the Petitcodiac Germans.

In Hillsborough, one of their own, Jacob Stieff, operated a retail outlet for which an application was filed on May 12, 1795, and guarantors William Botsford, Esq. and John Stieff pledged their support on July 2nd of the same year. The wide-ranging business interests of the Stieffs also included keeping a tavern, and licences were obtained three years in succession under the name of Matthias Stieff, beginning in 1800. Five years later a John Stieff also paid for such a licence and paid the customary £20 registration fee on December 17, 1808; on this occasion John Keillor, Esq., and William Smith let their names stand as guarantors.[195] With the opening of the American ports to "British"[196] ships after 1814, the sons and grandsons of the Petitcodiac pioneers expanded their trading activities and branched out into other areas of expertise, especially shipbuilding according to Stieff family tradition[197] and recurring newspaper accounts of the last century:

The first vessel was built in 1816 by Jacob Steeves' [and Catharina Lutz's] three sons, Jacob, John and Leonard. She was called the Three Brothers, and would carry about sixty tons .... In 1818 the Steeves brothers built three miles of tram road, for the purpose of hauling plaster. Probably this was the first three miles of railway built in the province. It was built simply by grading where the land was hard; where it was soft or marshy the track was built up with timber and covered with poles. The rails, which were made of wood, were fastened to the sleepers with wooden pins. The cars would carry from two to three tons; they were drawn by two or three oxen or horses. The plaster at that time was worth from three to four dollars a ton on the shore.[198]

Another report in a different paper continues to describe the ship built by Jacob and Catharina's sons:

[The vessel]... was employed chiefly in carrying plaster to Lubec, Maine, (the only seaport for this then) where it was sold and such commodities as the colonists needed brought back. She was re-topped about thirty years after and employed in carrying plaster from the quarries on the south shore of Shepody Bay .... This vessel carried about eighty tons which was in those days considered a large cargo. At Joe's Creek another vessel was built by Joseph and Isaac Steeves and was employed in trading between Hillsboro and St. John, taking lumber and bringing back cash and supplies. She was named the "Martha Ann" after Martha the wife of Joseph, and Ann the wife of Isaac. Joseph Steeves also built another vessel of smaller size in the same place called the "Mary" after his daughter Mary, about 1830. There was another vessel built by the Steeves brothers at Gray's Island called the "Independence".[199]

These activities lessened the dependence on Saint John and outside traders and brought welcome cash into the hands of the settlers' grandchildren.

The event of an explosion which occurred during this shipbuilding and trading era is repeated in several accounts and can be traced back to a real occurrence though impossible to verify in every detail:

Hendrick Steeves [Heinrich's 5th son] built himself a vessel and became a trader. One day after his return from a voyage bringing his usual supplies, he had brought a novelty in the shape of a jackknife. None of the younger people had ever seen a knife that would open and shut. Their quality was tested by striking fire with gunflints. The children found this proceeding very entertaining and on the following Sunday, when the older people had gone to meeting, they tried the same experiment with the knives but with different results. A spark struck by a careless hand dropped into a keg of powder, the explosion blew off the roof of the house and burned a girl by the name of Mary very badly about the face. She was blind for life. A sieve that had been hanging on the wall in the kitchen was afterward found intact on the marsh near the river.[200]

A similar version of this event claimed that the "explosion blew the house to pieces, killing a girl named Kathrina Stieff,[201] blinding and maiming a number of others. This was the first death in the community, in 1795."[202] In the Lutz Family genealogy, the sixth child of Johann Jacob Stieff and Catharina Lutz, a daughter born in 1777[203] named Nancy, is listed as "blinded by gunpowder",[204] suggesting that there was a real basis to these accounts of an explosion. It is also entirely probable that Henry Stieff had a daughter called Mary; in fact, several children – probably girls – may be unaccounted for (cf. Henry Stieff – Stieff Family genealogy).

The entry of July 16, 1811 by the inspector of troops in New Brunswick, Col. Joseph Gubbins, recounts an example of an unacceptable spirit of enterprise by one of the grandsons of Heinrich Stieff:

I inspected the 1st Battalion of the Westmorland County militia commanded by Major Gay, an active and intelligent person. Rubern Steves [sic][205] of this corps was ordered to be fined by his captain according to law, on the 11th of last month, for gross misbehaviour in the ranks. This he resisted, and he endeavoured to stab several individuals who helped to take him into custody. In the presence of Justice of the Peace Sinton,[206] he vowed he would revenge himself with the lives of those who assisted with his apprehension. For these crimes, as specified in the commitment, he was sent to goal, but Justice Sinton (a New Light preacher) a few days afterward wrote to Justice Keiler [sic] (whose residence is close to the goal) a paper purporting to be a copy of Steves's commitment, but in fact representing the man's crime to be only a trifling misdemeanor, and adding a strong recommendation that he should be set at liberty, which accordingly took place upon his giving security for his good conduct in a trifling sum. I mention this as a sample of the manner that the laws are enforced in these out of the way parts .... [207]

Col. Gubbins must not have known that William Sinton Esq.'s daughter, Ann (Nancy), was married to Reuben Steeves' cousin, Henry Steeves, the eldest son of Christian and Rosanna. Undoubtedly, it was less the fact that Sinton was a New Light preacher, about whom Gubbins made other oblique comments in his *Journals*, but that family pressure was brought to bear on the Justice of the Peace to see that the sentence be reduced.

Many of these stories seem to centre around the Stieff/Steeves family, and with good reason. Heinrich Stieff had seven sons, whose surnames were used by their wives and descendants. Since all the Stieff boys initially married German girls, the Stieff name eventually included every other Petitcodiac German name as well as the Becks. The Treitz, Wortman, Lutz, Ricker, and Sommer families together produced only 15 males, which explains why Steeves have dominated. Two-sevenths of the original Lutz family became Stieff descendants since both Catharina and Margaret married sons of Heinrich Stieff. Rosanna Treitz became a Stieff, likewise Rachel Sommer and two of Martin Beck's daughters. Heinrich Stieff's 72 grandchildren were, in turn, extremely prolific, many of whom settled in the immediate area (plate 12). The grant map of Hillsborough (fig. 27) and their business activities as reflected in the Harper Ledgers give an impression of the Stieff presence there.[208] Perhaps due to sheer numbers, the Stieffs were able to nurture a sense of family tradition which predated that of the other families. Beginning with a "Steeves picnic" on July 1, 1867,[209] when no agreement could even be reached concerning the first names of their ancestors, continuous efforts have been made by this family to obtain genealogical information, culminating in the work of the dedicated researcher and Stieff descendant, Esther Clark Wright. Because of the countless intermarriages, the story of the Stieffs is, to some extent, the story of the other Petitcodiac Germans, for whom less verbal and written history has been passed down.

Georg Michael and Anna Walpurgis Lutz had at least 43 identified grandchildren. Their German-born son, Peter, remained on the Hillsborough side of the Petitcodiac with his wife Mary Ricker and 12 children. John, born during Michael and Walpurgis' years in Pennsylvania, eventually inherited 1,400 acres of the original 1,900 the family had obtained on the "Monckton" side and resided there with his wife Elizabeth Charters and 12 children. Michael Lutz must have died about 1793[210] (i.e. prior to September 22, 1794) and left a will although it appears to have been lost. All children inherited property which was know by a plan made by Deputy Surveyor Ebenezer Cutler.[211]

John and Elizabeth's seventh child was John Jr., who apparently disappeared without a trace. In 1995, a descendant[212] of John Jr. provided evidence that his forbear had emigrated to the United States. In a letter of recommendation, "Robert Scott Justice of the Peace and Minister of the Col.[onial] Parliament" recognized "... that the Bearer, Mr. John Lutes, is a Native of Monckton, in the County of Westmorland and Province of New Brunswick, of a well Reputed Family, and having been Acquainted with him from His Cradle Can Certify that he is a Sober Honest Young Man, and as he is Desirous to Emigrate to the United States beg to Recommend him to All Honest Men ...." John Lutes Jr. applied for and accepted United States citizenship in 1843, promising that "on solemn oath ... he will support the Constitution of the United States, and that now he doth absolutely and entirely renounce and abjure all allegiance and fidelity to any foreign Prince, Potentate, State of Sovereignty whatever, particularly Victoria Queen of the United Kingdom of Great Britain and Ireland." Luckily, neither Michael nor Walpurgis Lutz lived long enough to know about this desertion from the fold, especially after their encounters with American renegades during the War of Independence.

A recurring story from the Lutz family history tells of young William Lutz of Hillsborough who had fallen in love with Mary Brown,[213] of whom his parents perhaps did not approve. Rather than submit to familial pressures, he decided to leave the narrow confines of Hillsborough, took his beloved and made his way by night in a flimsy craft across the uncertain tidal waters of the Petitcodiac toward Dorchester. Everyone assumed they had drowned in the attempt, like so many others,[214] for they were never heard from again. Several generations afterward, an entire Lutz clan emerged from the woods of Annapolis Valley, Nova Scotia, descendants of this couple. As in the case of other Lutz's who left New Brunswick during the last century, this family retained the original spelling of their surname "Lutz" and never changed over to the Anglicized version "Lutes".

Jacob Treitz and his family had prospered in the "Monckton" settlement as well. Revenues from their lands and possible blacksmithing, facilitated by John Hughes' support soon after the 1766 arrival, must have provided enough of a boost to enable his son, Abraham, to purchase Charles Baker's 1,630-acre grant in 1780, once litigation against the land companies had been concluded. As well, all 1,900 acres of the Ricker Jr. grant were sold shortly after 1780[215] to Jacob Treitz Jr., who had married Rosanna Ricker a few years earlier.[216] Christian had inherited the western part of Jacob Treitz Sr.'s grant, measuring 1,064 acres by 1790, and in this year, Jacob Treitz Sr. divided the remaining eastern half of his grant between his son-in-law Christian Stieff and son Christian into two supposedly equal portions.[217] Of the three sons, it was most likely Christian who plied his father's trade, living closest to him above "Bald Marsh" on the Petitcodiac River, east of today's Gunningsville Bridge. The most easterly 532 acres came into the possession of Christian Stieff as Rosanna's husband, which included the location where the settlers probably spent their first winter and which was beginning to be viewed as prime real estate by the late 18th century.[218]

Jacob and Elisina Treitz had about 44 known grandchildren. The oldest son, Abraham, took Margaret Jones as his wife, and they had 13 children by the time she died in 1806 at age 46. His second wife, Experience Ward/ Gore/Forster, who had been married several times before, survived him after not quite two years of marriage. The second oldest Treitz son, Jacob Jr., married Rosanna Ricker, who bore him up to 13 children, while Christian, the youngest son, married Catherine Jones and had 9 children. Treitz's only daughter, Rosanna, had a child by Robert Cummings around 1770[219] and 8 more in her marriage to Christian Stieff. The issue of her relationship with Cummings was Elizabeth, who remained with Rosanna in the Treitz Sr. and later Christian Stieff households until her marriage to Reuben Stiles of Hillsborough.[220]

It is not coincidental that two of the Treitz boys married daughters of Charles Jones, who also remained in "Monckton" presumably on his "Mill Creek" property although he died only a few short years later, in 1774. Henry and John Jones spent several years away from "Monckton" township, perhaps in Hillsborough in Jacob Ricker Sr.'s household, before obtaining their grant as heirs of Charles Jones (Lot No. 4), to the west of the farm where their sister Margaret and Abraham Treitz resided. The brothers divided their lot in half, the older, Henry, settling on the western half and younger, John, on the eastern half, commonly know as the "Mill lot" by 1811.[221] Henry moved back to "Monckton" with his German wife, Christinah (Ricker ?/Sommer ?/Wortman ?),[222] where they had a family of at least 10 children. John seems to have remained single for a few years in "Monckton" until marrying "Dimas" Daniels[223] from Hopewell, with whom he also had about 10 children.

Of those children included in the 1851 Moncton Census, all claimed to have "German" background, suggesting that the pioneer Jones family had German connections, possibly from Philadelphia. William Calhoun's July 1771 diary entry regarding the prosperity of the German families at "The Bend" includes the Jones among the "Dutch" even at this early date. Maintaining the German language was an issue in the household of Margaret Jones and Abraham Treitz to judge by the stipulation in his will that his youngest daughter (probably Rachel) be instructed "to read and write intelligibly in the mother tongue."[224] Johannes/John Lutz, Michael Sr.'s son, also had a background in this language judging by his signature in 1822 (fig. 46). The claim in a 19th-century newspaper account, quoted earlier, that Jones's first name was "Karl" and last name "Johannes"[225] is evidence of the continued belief that this family was German. Charles Jones and his wife must have learned at least some German in the early years of isolation, as often happened to Anglophones in German-speaking regions of Pennsylvania, if they were not fluent in German before their arrival, as many Jones families were members of German congregations in Philadelphia.[226] On the other hand, they may also have served as interpreters for the German colonists, linking them to the Anglophone world which surrounded them. In spite of Jones's illiteracy and early death, he and his descendants acquitted themselves well. It is believed that the Jones occupied a portion of their original grant of land until the 20th century,[227] a claim only a few other Petitcodiac German families could make.

Many of the descendants of the Petitcodiac Germans remained close to the soil and chose related professions. The piety of the settlers[228] is reflected in the large number who became ministers, missionaries, teachers, nurses, doctors, and social workers -- all professions with high ideals of service to people. Heinrich Stieff's practicality and business sense was passed on to the numbers who started businesses of their own or chose the banking

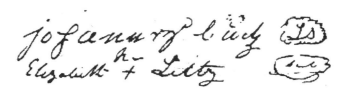

Figure 46

The signature of Johannes/John Lutz[2], above that of his wife Elizabeth (Charters), in 1822 in German ("Gothic") script, the only such example in documents of the 19th century in connection with the early settlers, showing that German was still in use at least until this time. His wife, being of Anglophone extraction, used the customary Latin script.

Figure 47

William Henry Steeves, Father of Confederation, great-grandson of pioneer Heinrich Stieff.

Courtesy: National Archives of Canada

profession. His genius of improvisation and technical "know-how" was carried forward by those who became contractors, factory-owners, garage-operators, well-drillers, etc.. Their interests lay more in the practical aspects of life than in the arts:[229] "The Steeves might take steering wheel in hand, or hammer or saw, or scalpel or hoe, but they seldom took a pen in hand .... It was the Steeves way, to do the job in hand and to suffer, without making a song about it."[230]

One who inherited the traits of his forefather, Heinrich Stieff, was great-grandson William Henry Steeves, born in Hillsborough in 1814. He became a merchant, lumber-dealer, and ship broker. In 1846 he was elected to the New Brunswick Legislative Assembly, five years later to the Legislative Council, and eventually selected as one of the delegates to the conferences in Charlottetown and Quebec City which resulted in the foundation of the Dominion of Canada (plate 13, figs. 47, 48). With one of their own as a Father of Confederation, it is no wonder that the Stieffs held a picnic on July 1, 1867 to honour their illustrious relative and family. Although practical and "down-to-earth" Heinrich would probably have disapproved, the only granddaughter of William Henry Steeves[231] became the Duchess of Somerset. Another great-grandson of Heinrich was Manoah Steeves, who after living for a while in Chatham, Ontario, made his way to the Pacific Coast and settled on Lulu Island in the Fraser River Delta. He wrote his surname "Steves", which is the way all his descendants spelled their names, and the town they founded on Lulu Island was called Steveston. Another Steeves briefly became governor of Idaho and, as a medical officer, founded a medical clinic in Salem, Oregon, where he also served a term as mayor.

Whether the descendants of the Petitcodiac Germans ventured afar or stayed at home, they made their mark. The business and entertainment development of Magnetic Hill at the foot of Lutz Mountain found its origins in the enterprising spirit of Muriel Lutes, who started selling ice-cream in 1933 on the driveway at the foot of her father's farm. This ice-cream was not the variety of the 2000's, but made in the traditional way whereby natural ice from the shed -- one of the winter chores -- was chipped and mixed with salt. The natural ingredients for the ice-cream were churned in a tin bucket which rested in the super-cooled mixture of icy brine in a wooden tub. Muriel Lutes's younger brother was paid ten cents a load to crank the freezer to arrive at this delicacy. The fudge and fruit drinks, and eventually a gas

288

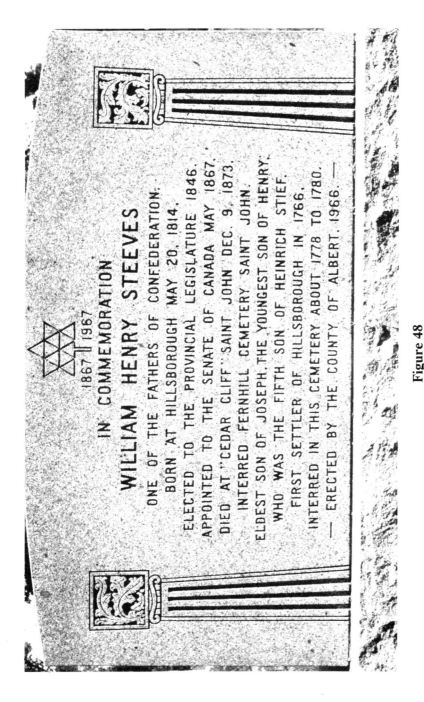

1867 1967

IN COMMEMORATION
WILLIAM HENRY STEEVES
ONE OF THE FATHERS OF CONFEDERATION.
BORN AT HILLSBOROUGH MAY 20, 1814,
ELECTED TO THE PROVINCIAL LEGISLATURE 1846.
APPOINTED TO THE SENATE OF CANADA MAY 1867.
DIED AT "CEDAR CLIFF" SAINT JOHN DEC. 9, 1873.
INTERRED FERNHILL CEMETERY SAINT JOHN.
ELDEST SON OF JOSEPH, THE YOUNGEST SON OF HENRY,
WHO WAS THE FIFTH SON OF HEINRICH STIEF,
FIRST SETTLER OF HILLSBOROUGH IN 1766.
INTERRED IN THIS CEMETERY ABOUT 1778 TO 1780.
—— ERECTED BY THE COUNTY OF ALBERT 1966. ——

Figure 48

Tombstone of William Henry Steeves in the Hillsborough Baptist Cemetery.

Photo: Rainer L. Hempel

pump complete with tall glass cylinder, made this "canteen" a success. It soon became the first non-government post-office with its own stamp marked "Magnetic Hill" and expanded even further to become the largest quality china shop in Eastern Canada. Although the buildings have all disappeared, Magnetic Hill at the foot of Lutz Mountain continues to be a Maritime destination, having been developed into a major tourist attraction in conjunction with the Magnetic Hill Zoo and Waterslide Park. Muriel Sikorski (*née* Lutes) spent a good portion of the proceeds from her business to finance the establishment of the Lutz Mountain Heritage Foundation and Meeting House (fig. 49) in 1975 and to research the Lutz family history.[232]

The other families -- Rickers,[233] Sommers,[234] and Wortmans[235]-- are also beginning to organize and computerize their genealogies, especially the Wortmans, who have made great strides in their research over the last decade and a half. Jacob Ricker Jr.'s daughter, Mary, became a Lutz as the wife of Peter, while their daughter Rosanna became a Treitz as the wife of Jacob Jr.. Less was known about Michael Ricker and his wife Catherine (*née* Stiles?) of Hillsborough, as well as Sommer's son, Andrew, who moved back to "Monckton" in 1780, however sources such as the William Harper Ledgers, the Land Registry Office for Westmorland County, the Registry of Land Grants in Fredericton, etc. shed some light on their later activities (cf. next chapter). Michael and Catherine Ricker had six sur-viving children, all of whom remained in Coverdale/Hillsborough for many years. Their son Jacob remained a farmer while William learned the shoemaker's trade, in all likelihood from Peter Lutz Sr.. Andrew Sommer, with his wife "Amy/ Emily", also remained a farmer but had to accept a certain Donald MacDonald as neighbour after the latter petitioned on November 15, 1788 to settle on the half of the Sommer grant escheated from Anna Catharina Sommer's mariner husband, Eliphalet ("Liffe") Chappell, of Baie Verte.[236] Like his father's household, Andrew's was dominated by women. Eight of his 10 children were female so that, like the Rickers, only two males continued the Sommer surname. In the post-pioneer period, Sommer had dealings with such well-known Moncton businessmen as James Kelly and Thomas Prince, and he was the owner of a mill site, which Prince rented from him. Another creek has since been renamed "Somers Creek" in memory of Andrew Sommer's grandson by the same name.

Figure 49
Lutz Mountain Meeting House, Moncton, home of the Lutz/Lutes
genealogical archives.

Photo: Rainer L. Hempel

More information exists on settlers Georg Wortman(n) and his wife, Maria/"Moriah" (*née* ?), who was alive in June of 1797 when she made purchases from William Harper's trading vessel.[237] In *Planters and Pioneers*,[238] Clark Wright lists three sons: Jacob, Martin, and John although there were at least that many more -- David, James, and Albert.[239] After a stay of about seven years in Hillsborough, Georg Wortman returned with his family to his grant on the westernmost portion of "Monckton" Township sometime after November 1780, likely around 1782.[240] When Georg Wortman died around December of 1787,[241] both his widow and sons should have inherited the family grant, excluding the portion sold to Joshua Geldart circa 1777. However, there are two disturbing documents from around 1792 in which Georg Wortman's widow appealed to Governor Thomas Carleton Esq. for a grant in her own name. She wrote that she was settled in Westmorland County "upwards of twenty years ..., has some small children which she is labouring for to maintain and bring up in the fear of God .... [Her] other children which is married and other[s] grown up to the years of maturity is usurping over her with the ideas that they will get a grant of land from your Excellency. Petitioner [Moriah Wortman] humbly requests that your Excellency will be graciously Pleased to give her a grant in her own name."[242] When she received no response to her petition, she wrote a letter in which she appealed as a "poor woman" to his Honour to have "piety [sic] upon [her] distress." She had "allowed the [grown-up] boys to get a grant in their name provided they would endeavor to support [her] and the young children which they promised to Perform but they soon forgot their promise ...."[243] Jacob, Martin, and John Wortman were granted 700 acres of the original grant on June 14, 1797, with no mention that Maria's application was successful although she lived beyond this date.[244] In 1801 Martin decided to supplement his farm income by opening a retail business[245] with Alanson Lewis as "guarantor", and in 1805 Jacob, a farmer, sold his share of the homestead to his brothers, Martin and John (fig. 50).[246]

Jacob Wortman and Sarah (*née* Clinton) had eight children and, although they did well in the Moncton area, eventually decided to leave with their children excepting Lavenia, who was married to John Price. An extant Bible from the Martin Wortman family contains genealogical information beginning in 1812 (plate 14).[247] According to an entry, Jacob, aged 58, left with his family for Ohio on August 27, 1827, that is three years before the

292

Figure 50
Tombstone of John, son of Georg and Mariah Wortman, in the Salisbury
Cemetery.

Photo: Karon Wortman Scott

293

aforementioned John Lutz Jr., Michael Lutz Sr.'s grandson, turned up in the same State. He might have been following the older couple's trail, or, more likely, one of their daughters. Records show that Jacob and Sarah Wortman became landowners in Ohio later in 1827, and this is also where they were buried. Some of their descendants moved further west, leaving records in Iowa and Montana, reaching Oregon by wagon train along the Oregon Trail. The Wortman Bank, founded by this branch of the family in McMinnville, Oregon, was the last privately owned bank in the United States. In 1903, brothers Frank and Ralph Wortman were the first to drive a steam-powered car over the Rockies to reach the Pacific. This vehicle was restored in 1960 and is now on display in the above-mentioned Key's (former Wortman) Bank.

Back in Salisbury, Martin Wortman and his wife, Mary Jane Hopper, raised a family of 12 children while John Wortman, who married Hannah Stieff (Frederick and Rachel Stieff's daughter), had at least seven. A fourth-generation Jacob Wortman, a son of David, became a member of Moncton's first town council in 1855 and three years later defeated his opponent by a wide margin in a mayoralty race, becoming the first descendant of the original settlers to be elected to the highest civic office of the town which his forefathers had helped found. In later years he became the town's Stipendiary Magistrate,[248] the only "judge" on location, who held court in his hotel/grocery store and continued to do so until another Petitcodiac German descendant, Judge C.A. Steeves, succeeded him.[249] Jacob Wortman's term of office fell into the period when the Canada Temperance Act was passed in 1878.[250] Temperance supporters had suggested for some time that Magistrate Wortman was somehow responsible for the lax enforcement of the Act, which saw the number of liquor vendors in Moncton actually increase. Wortman interpreted the attacks not just as personal criticism but as a denigration of his pioneer family. On February 23, 1784, he summarily dismissed the marshal and his constables from office, whom he blamed for their lax enforcement of the law, despite the fact that they had been appointed by Town Council. Such was the authority of "Squire Wortman" that the town found itself without police protection until the officers were "reinstated" by Council. Magistrate Wortman weathered the storm resulting from this dismissal, especially from the anti-temperance camp, and continued in office (plate 15). He died in Moncton in 1897 at the age of 82.

Although the name Wortman(n) has several variants in Germany, the New Brunswick versions "Wortman" and "Wartman" apparently trace their different spellings to occurrences during the last century. The original Wortman land grant was furthest west, at today's Boundary Creek and therefore most distant from Moncton's town core. According to family oral history, several Wortmans established themselves in successful and respectable enterprises in Moncton only to have their good names sullied by certain country cousins who came into Moncton on weekends and repeatedly behaved in a most despicable and uncouth manner. Since the Monctonian Wortmans were not prepared to tangle with these "backwoods" ruffians and no longer wanted to be identified with their namesakes in these unwholesome events, they simply changed their names to "Wartman".[251]

Significant contributions of the Petitcodiac descendants undoubtedly rest in the religious realm, but also in their ever-present spirit of enterprise, diligence, and practicality. This must also be applied to the homemaking front (so often ignored in the larger scheme of historical events) where the "neatness and love of good cooking of the good German *hausfrau*"[252] was amply reflected, likewise in their weaving and other handiwork -- all of which distinguished these women throughout the region. The large parcels of land which came into the possession of the Petitcodiac Germans may have been sufficient in the first and second generations, but as time went on, many descendants sought land and employment elsewhere. History began repeating itself in New Brunswick just as in the German homeland a century earlier, where subdivided lots were eventually deemed too small to sustain a family. This created a new type of emigrant from the Petitcodiac and adjacent regions, whose wanderings can be traced to every corner of North America and beyond, shown by the number of entries in the telephone books of large centres such as New York, Chicago, Los Angeles, Vancouver, and Toronto. In Boston, for example, there are over one hundred Steeves listings alone, many of whom trace their ancestry back to New Brunswick. Not only did the Petitcodiac Germans profoundly affect the history of New Brunswick, they also contributed, by sheer virtue of their numbers, to the population figures of both Canada and the United States.

Despite the increasing importance of trade and commerce during Rosanna Treitz's earlier years, agriculture, land ownership, and real estate

295

transactions remained the basis of entrepreneurial activity. After his departure for Baltimore, Robert Cummings wrote Charles Baker instructing him to transfer his belongings in Germantown over to Rosanna, that she was to sell them, buy furs with the proceeds, and invest the profits in cattle as a long-term capital venture for her and her child.[253] Even the urbanite Cummings considered the raising of cattle the best investment at this time for a woman, rather than engaging in some trade or business activity. This is certainly the way the original settlers and many of their children viewed the future. Along the Petitcodiac they had been able to realize their old dreams of being simple folk, tilling their fields and maintaining a self-sufficient lifestyle. In "Monckton" this pristine state was disturbed by the arrival of Loyalists, many of whom were less interested in farming than starting businesses such as lumbering, stores, shipbuilding, and inns. These later arrivals had been more established in the former British provinces, and many came with sufficient funds not to have to regress to the pioneering level. As a consequence, land values appreciated in areas of business activity, tempting the original settlers and their children to sell their by now more subdivided parcels of original grant land in order to purchase larger, more cohesive, and less expensive farmland elsewhere, leaving the impression that they were abandoning the fruits of their toil and that of their parents to others more enterprising and astute. Christian Stieff's eventual sale of lots near an early landing on Hall's Creek to finance the purchase in 1811 of 2,000 acres on Steeves Mountain, is evidence of this "post-pioneer" trend.[254] Just as the Germans had built on and benefitted from the toil of the Acadian farmers before them, so too did the Loyalists reap the rewards of the Germans' pioneering efforts.

The purchase and resale of land, including lot subdivisions from their initial grants, was an activity engaged in by most Petitcodiac Germans to a greater or lesser degree and also stemmed from the recognition that land possession in itself meant little. Their early habit of amassing as much land as possible was gradually replaced by a more realistic concept of what could actually be done with such large tracts, of which only small portions could be cultivated with the manpower at their disposal. After trapping, logging, and agriculture, land sales to generate cash for business ventures became an accepted practice of the Petitcodiac Germans. This change in activity was in keeping with developments taking place in the first decade of the 19th century. Their grandchildren and great-grandchildren, who eventually abandoned the dreams of their forefathers and ceased yearning for the simple country life, joined the Loyalist children in the business world or became lumberjacks and shipyard workers. Their daughters became the wives of later arrivals at "The Bend", such as Yorkshire descendant John Bowser,[255] William Steadman,[256] Thomas Prince,[257] and Alexander Wright,[258] and if ambitious and financially secure enough in later years, encouraged their sons to become doctors and lawyers.[259] Many of the later descendants of the original settlers also saw their future further west and left New Brunswick, as illustrated by the earlier examples.

ENDNOTES

[1] Most inhabitants of Nova Scotia were originally from the New England provinces, i.e. they were "Yankees". Along with everyone else in Nova Scotia, they became victims of American sea marauders from Machias, Maine, and Salem, Massachusetts, where piracy had become a sport and business. No single factor during the American War of Independence appears to have played more into British hands than the raids by privateers, for they alienated many pro-American sympathizers; Thomas H. Raddall, *His Majesty's Yankees* (Halifax, N.S.: Nimbus Publishing Ltd., 1942), pp. 301, 315f, 328f, 356ff.

[2] Today's Westmorland County, New Brunswick was part of Cumberland County, Nova Scotia before 1784.

[3] Pincombe and Larracey, *Resurgo*, I, p.71; Clark Wright, *Samphire Greens*, p. 28; Clark Wright, *The Petitcodiac*, pp. 47f..

[4] The Millidge Report of 1788 also lists the names of the various land companies which sponsored the individual settlers; MAUA, Webster Manuscript Collection, 7001.

[5] PANS, Nova Scotia Deeds, Microfilm 17540/1, Book C. p. 134. Pincombe suggests a legal clause in an Act passed in 1758 which made it necessary to rerecord these deeds in 1780; Pincombe and Larracey, *Resurgo*, I, p. 73.

[6] Jacob Ricker Jr., the head of the Ricker/Sommer household, paid the expenses of the lawsuit against the land companies in 1778 and settled the division of the estate; Millidge Report, p. 4.

[7] The lots were numbered from west to east: No. 1 (Georg Wortman's) to No. 9. (Jacob Treitz Sr.'s).

[8] PANS, Nova Scotia Land Deeds, Microfilm 17540/1, Book C, pp. 49, 96.

[9] *Ibid.*, pp. 56, 136. Cf. also Pincombe and Larracey, *Resurgo*, pp. 72, 88.

[10] Harper Ledger (1797-1799): MAUA, June 9,1797, Webster Manuscript Collection.

[11] Jacob Ricker Jr.'s spouse was called Maria Magdalena, and Michael Ricker's was Catherine. No document had been located in New Brunswick that mentions Maria Magdalena Ricker by name.

[12] Clark Wright does not offer any suggestions for the name of Charles Jones' wife whereas some later genealogies mention the name "Catherine" -- also the name of the second daughter -- as her name. No record has been found which confirms either "Margaret" or "Catherine" as the name of Charles Jones' spouse.

[13] PANS, Nova Scotia Land Deeds, Microfilm 17540/1, Book C, p. 55.

[14] *Ibid.*, p. 94.

[15] *Loc. cit..* This entry in the column headed "Remarks" pertained to the year 1783 when the report was made. Each name is accompanied by separate statements in two columns; one specifies the number in the family, livestock, etc. "as per Return in 1775" (some were returns for the years 1773, 1774, or 1776 instead) and the other of each family as per 1783, with such laconic comments as "Since dead", "Died with the Small Pox in 1776", or "Since dead, his Widow married". The entry for "Henry Steeve Sen." belongs to this category. Those who had left the settlement by 1783 were marked with entries such as "Since removed out of Township", or "Since removed to Memramcook". Most names, however, were accompanied by the words, "Now residing on the Premises". In a separate section below the families of the 1775 entries were twenty-seven additional names. Many of these new arrivals in Hillsborough were the children of the Petitcodiac Germans who had become of statistical age (adults) between 1775 and 1783.

[16] Clark Wright, *Samphire Greens.*, p. 30.

[17] Millidge Report, p. 7.

[18] PANS, Nova Scotia Land Deeds, Microfilm 17540/1, Book C, p. 134.

[19] Clark Wright, *Samphire Greens*, pp. 50, 98. The Treitz property was large enough to rival that of many Old-Country noblemen.

[20] Pincombe and Larracey, *Resurgo,* pp. 71f..

[21] PANS, Nova Scotia Land Deeds, Microfilm 17540/1, Book C, pp. 52, 99. The absence of any distinction between Jr. and Sr. in the deeds in "Monckton" suggests that Jacob Ricker Sr. did not apply for land there. Since Jacob Ricker Sr. was an older man and his children and those in the Sommer family were provided for, it explains the absence of applications for land in Hillsborough as well where he probably died soon after 1783. His death must have obviated distinguishing between Jacob Ricker Sr. and Jr. afterwards.

[22] PANS, Nova Scotia Land Deeds, Microfilm 17540/1, Book C, pp. 51, 97.

[23] *Ibid.,* p. 95.

[24] The date on the receipt is September 25, 1771, JP.

[25] PANS, Nova Scotia Land Deeds, Microfilm 17540/1, Book C, p. 135.

[26] *Ibid.,* p. 62.

[27] *Ibid.,* p. 63.

[28] *Ibid.,* p. 144.

[29] *Ibid.,* p. 150: deed dated March 4, 1782.

[30] *Ibid.,* p. 133.

[31] *Ibid.,* p. 294. The date of the agreement was April 6, 1784.

[32] PANB, New Brunswick Land Grants, Microfilm F 1029.

[33] *Ibid.,* Microfilm F 1032. The 10 children represent the total number in Ricker Jr.'s household -- 8 Sommer (7 daughters and Andrew) and 2 Ricker Jr. children (Michael and daughter "Sarah") -- although they were all married and

settled on their own by 1786.

[34] Most of these men were married with the exception of Martin and John Wortman, who were 16 and 11/12 years of age, respectively, and still living at home with their recently widowed mother, Maria.

[35] Paul Surette et la Société historique de la vallée de Memramcook, *Histoire des Trois-Rivières* (N.p., la Société historique de la vallée de Memramcook, 1981), pp. 33ff..

[36] Bell, *Foreign Protestants*, pp. 580-607.

[37] PANS, Microfilm 14847.

[38] Bell, *Foreign Protestants*, pp. 583, 601.

[39] *Ibid.*, p. 595.

[40] Clark Wright, *The Petitcodiac*, p. 44.

[41] PANS, Microfilm 14847.

[42] *Loc.cit.*, letter dated December 27, 1773.

[43] To Native people the island was *Abegweit*, "the one cradled by water". When the French came, they gave it the name "Ile St. Jean" hence the English "St. John's Island". In 1799, the island was renamed Prince Edward Island in honour of Edward, the Duke of Kent and father of Queen Victoria.

[44] Letter of January 16, 1775 to S. P. G., PANS, Microfilm 14847.

[45] Cf. John Eagleson's letter to the S.P.G., dated January 30, 1779, PANS, Microfilm 14848; also John Clarence Webster, *The Forts of Chignecto* (Shediac, N.B.: published by author, 1930). Joseph Goreham, commander of Fort Lawrence, reported that Rev. Mr. Eagleson, acting as Chaplain, was taken with many others during the seizure of a provision sloop on November 7, 1776.

[46] Gladys Trenholm, Miep Norden, Josephine Trenholm, *A History of Fort Lawrence, Times, Tides and Towns* (Edmonton: Sherwood Printing Ltd., 1985), p. 186.

[47] Barbara M. Schmeisser, Information Sheet on John Eagleson, Parks Service Atlantic Region, Halifax, N. S., 1996.

[48] Trenholm, Norden, Trenholm, *A History of Fort Lawrence* ... , pp. 85-86, 198.

[49] PANS, Microfilm 14847.

[50] A. Betts, *Bishop Black and his Preachers*, p. 10; Betts did not mention the Petitcodiac Germans by name, rather as residents of the area where Black preached.

[51] Henry Alline (1748-1784) was a clergyman and religious poet originally from Rhode Island.

[52] George Rawlyk, ed., *New Light Letters and Spiritual Songs: 1778-1793* (Hantsport, N. S.: Lancelot Press, 1983), p. 4.

[53] Thomas Jackson, ed., *The Lives of Early Methodist Preachers*, I-VI, Vol. V (London: Wesleyan Conference Office, 1873), p. 259.

[54] Loc. cit..

[55] James Beverley and Barry Moody, eds., *Journal of Henry Alline* (Hantsport, N. S.: Lancelot Press, 1982), pp. 174-175.

[56] David G. Bell, ed., *Newlight Baptist Journals of James Manning and James Innis* (Hantsport, N. S.: Lancelot Press, 1984), p. 65.

[57] *Journal of Henry Alline*, pp. 179f.; my italics.

[58] *Newlight Baptist Journals*, p. 65.

[59] *Religious Intelligencer*, November 16, 1855, as quoted in *Newlight Baptist Journals*, p. 136.

[60] Jackson, *The Lives ... of Methodist Preachers*, p. 251.

[61] *Ibid.*, p. 271.

[62] Black was born in 1760 and on his first visit in early summer of 1781 was barely 21 years of age.

[63] Betts, *Bishop Black ...*, p. 10.

[64] Black's *Journal, The Arminian Methodist Magazine*, Vol. 14, p. 179; my italics. Black used the same words, "hard and stupid" when he described his own frame of mind before he found deliverance. He meant one's inability to react emotionally, to "shed a tear"; Jackson, *The Lives of ... Methodist Preachers*, p. 247.

[65] Richey, *A Memoir of the late William Black* (Halifax: William Cunnabell, 1839), p. 46.

[66] *Ibid.*, p. 47.

[67] Black's *Journal*, p. 179; cf. also Betts, *Bishop Black ...* , pp. 10-11.

[68] Black also refers to a "Dutch Settlement" as the site of his sermon on March 9, 1783.

[69] Refer to the map in Shirley A. Dobson, *The Word and the Music, The Story of Moncton's Central United Church and its Methodist Roots* (Moncton, N.B.: Central United Church, 1994), p. 13.

[70] Richey, *A Memoir ... of William Black*, p. 48.

[71] Abraham Trites' home was located near where the Kenneth E. Spence Memorial Home now stands (35 Atlantic Baptist Ave.), i.e. on the north shore of the Petitcodiac River, a short distance east of Mill Creek; cf. Dobson, *The Word and Music*, pp. 7, 13.

[72] The progressive change to the English spelling of the name *Stieff* is visible here. Black still used the German diphthon "ie", but changed the German "f" to "v". In the later spelling, the English "ee" has replaced the German "ie", which represents the same sound.

[73] Richey, *A Memoir... of William Black*, p. 80.

[74] Black's *Journal*, Sunday, August 26, 1782.

[75] It is unknown who married Frederick Stieff and Rachel Sommer on June 25, 1780, a date gleaned from a family Bible inscription. Henry Jones and

Christinah (Ricker/Sommer/Wortman ?) likely married around the same time. Both couples may have had to travel over to Fort Cumberland to complete marriage registrations (their marriages do not appear in the Cumberland or Sackville Townbooks). No other Petitcodiac German couples seem to have married after 1775 and before 1780.

[76] Cf. also Dobson, *The Word and the Music* ..., p. 7.

[77] Black's *Journal*, January 13, 1782.

[78] *Ibid.*, January 23, 1782.

[79] Betts, *Bishop Black* ... , p.11.

[80] Dobson, *The Word and the Music* ..., p. 14.

[81] Betts, *Bishop Black* ..., p. 11.

[82] My italics.

[83] Richey, *Memoir*..., p. 46

[84] The Stieff Bible belongs to the permanent collection of the N.B. Archives, Fredericton, N.B..

[85] Dobson, *The Word and the Music,* p. 15.

[86] It is uncertain who married two Petitcodiac German couples, Henry Stieff and Maria Beck from Hillsborough and "Moncktonians" Christian Treitz and Catherine Jones c. 1781-1782; Revs. Alline and Black could not perform this ceremony because they did not belong to the established church.

[87] Clark Wright, *The Steeves Descendants* (Author, 1965), p. 292.

[88] Clark Wright, *Samphire Greens*, p. 55.

[89] *Newlight Baptist Journals* ..., p. 292.

[90] Pincombe and Larracey, *Resurgo*, p. 82; cf. also Brebner, *The Neutral Yankees* ..., p. 186.

[91] Clark Wright, *Samphire Greens*, pp. 54f..

[92] James Mann visited the Petitcodiac circuit in the fall of 1792. The general acceptance of Methodism by the Stieffs is shown by their financial contributions. Donors mentioned include Jacob, John, Christian, Frederick, and Henry Stieff, as well as their mother Rachel (Regina). Rev. Early visited the Petitcodiac Germans in the winter of 1792; Shirley A. Dobson, *The Word and the Music: The Story of Moncton's Central United Church and its Methodist Roots* (Moncton, N.B.: Central United Church, 1994), p. 18.

[93] George A. Rawlyk, *The Canada Fire: Radical Evangelism in British North America, 1775-1812* (Kingston & Montreal: McGill-Queen's University Press, 1994), pp.3f.. In Germany, mid-18th-century *Empfindsamkeit* (the "Age of Sensibility") with its roots in Pietism, signalled a change in attitude toward the acknowledgement and display of emotions. The developments leading toward the Romantic period, i.e. its increased subjectivity and emphasis on feelings, was a phenomenon observed world-wide.

[94] The view that the "Evangelical-Revivalist-Reform movement ... [was] partially derivative from continental Pietism" was also expressed by Don Yoder in his study, *Discovering American Folklife*, p. 132.

[95] *Ibid*, p. 4.

[96] *Ibid*, xvi.

[97] *Ibid*, pp. 135 ff..

[98] Cf. M. W. Armstrong, "Neutrality and Religion in Revolutionary Nova Scotia," *New England Quarterly*, IX (March 1946), pp. 50-62. The deep religiosity of Germans affected by the Thirty Years' War illustrates this human attempt to find security in another realm.

[99] Cf. G. Wood, *Radicalism of the American Revolution* (New York: Knopf, 1992), p. 96. Not just were these times crying out for liberty in North America, but on the European continent as well where sacred heads of royalty would roll beneath the guillotine.

[100] I.E. Bill, *Fifty Years with the Baptist Ministers and Churches of the Maritime Provinces of Canada* (Saint John, N.B.: Barnes & Co., 1880), p. 191.

[101] Rawlyk, *The Canada Fire*, p. 138.

[102] *Ibid.*, p. 133.

[103] *Ibid.*, p. 174.

[104] *Ibid.*, p. 140.

[105] Pietism was a movement of Protestant Germany during the 17th and 18th centuries which rejected the emphasis on ritual and formal worship of established Lutheranism in favour of a more personal relationship with God and renewal of the Church. Its undercurrents are similar to those which gave rise to the Anabaptists (Mennonites and Hutterites), Zinzendorf's Moravian Bretheren, the Dunkers and, more indirectly, the Quakers. They all emphasize central aspects of Pietism and can be considered dissenting sects which tried to follow Christ's teachings of the Sermon on the Mount, advocating simple, righteous living, avoidance of violence and service to people in need. It is not surprising that many immigrants became adherents of one or the other of these churches in Pennsylvania. Mühlenberg and other clergymen in Pennsylvania, who received their training in Halle, Germany, were also sympathetic toward Pietism. The Wesley Brothers followed the lead of earlier dissenters in the latter part of the 18th century when Methodists separated from the Anglican Church. So great was the interrelationship and esteem that existed between these various dissenting churches that John Wesley paid Count von Zinsendorf the compliment of translating some of his prayers as poetry, thereby acknowledging the Count's influence on the Evangelical revival; Robert Van de Weyer, ed., *Book of Prayers* (New Jersey: Castle Books Edison, 1997), p. 395ff.. It appears that Methodism was for most Petitcodiac Germans a "stepping stone" over to Baptism.

[106] Donald F. Durnbaugh, "The Sauer Family: An American Printing Dynasty," *Yearbook of German-American Studies*, 23 (Lawrence: University of Kansas Printing Service, 1988), pp. 31-40.

[107] *Ibid.*, p. 33.

[108] The Church of the Brethren was organized in Germany in 1708 and is one of several such congregations. Count von Zinzendorf's *Herrnhuter Brüdergemeine* (or Moravians), mentioned earlier, is another branch that developed from German Pietism and spread to North America. The name "Dunkers" was derived from the German word, *tunken* ("to immerse").

[109] Durnbaugh, "The Sauer Family: An American Printing Dynasty," p. 32.

[110] He continued using paper manufactured by the German-operated Rittenhouse Paper Mill (est. 1690), the first New World paper producer, located just outside Germantown, Pennsylvania.

[111] Durnbaugh, "The Sauer Family: An American Printing Dynasty," p. 35.

[112] The wide distribution of Sauer's papers and impact on his readership are also emphasized by A.G. Roeber's *Palatines, Liberty, and Property*, pp. 175ff..

[113] Rawlyk, *The Canada Fire*, p. 174.

[114] *Loc.cit.*.

[115] The "rage for dipping", as it was coined pejoratively by Anglican clergy at the time, wrongly suggests an element of compulsion and fashion in this practice. The appeal of a public demonstration of one's commitment in this cleansing ritual cannot be dismissed, as well the "powerful democratic and egalitarian impulse"; Rawlyk, *The Canada Fire*, p. 173.

[116] *Gubbins' Journals*, p. 23. Gubbins did not refer to the Petitcodiac Germans by name, but the implication is clear. Also, Rosanna Treitz's relationship to Robert Cummings, her subsequent marriage to Christian Stieff, and her religious persuasion would have met with Gubbins' profound disapproval.

[117] *Ibid.;* cf. editor's footnote.

[118] David Bell, *Newlight Baptist Journals ...*, p. 85.

[119] *Ibid.*, p. 57. "Germanic" should read "German" since the former refers to a branch of Indo-European languages, such as English, Danish, Dutch, and German.

[120] Bainton, *The Reformation ...*, p. 107.

[121] The saying: "*Gehe nicht zu deinem Fürst, wenn du nicht gerufen wirst!*" ("Don't go to your prince unless you are called!") reflects this experience and attitude, counsel which Germans in Canada tend to keep to this day, accounting to some extent for the low profile of this ethnic group.

[122] Jacob Treitz's attitude to "authorities" is revealed in connection to the repeated reregistrations of his "Monckton" tract of land. The property was first

granted by Nova Scotia in 1778, then again in 1780. When the New Brunswick government insisted that all properties be reregistered in 1784-1785, Treitz seems at first to have ignored this requirement, which almost resulted in escheat of the property. It is unlikely that he was not aware of this requirement, but his procrastination may have been a form of protest against the take-over by New Brunswick, suggesting an entirely different attitude toward "government". As it was, the New Brunswick authorities granted Treitz Sr. his "crown land" in 1790. After his death in 1791, his son and son-in-law had to wait for registration of their inheritances.

[123] Clark Wright, *Samphire Greens*, p. 73.

[124] Albert County Museum, Riverside Albert, N.B.. A newspaper account of March 27, 1883 claims: "Hendrick Steves, the smith of the colony, was a very ingenious mechanic. A cuckoo clock, made by him during their exile, still exists ...." (NBM, Albert County Scrapbook, shelf 31). I had detailed pictures of the clock examined by experts at the Deutsches Uhrenmuseum (German Clockmuseum) in Furtwangen in the Black Forest, and the clock was found to date in the 18th century. On account of the simple design of the clock face and the fact that it is without paint, it was suggested that the face, together with the opening for the cuckoo, may have been replaced at one time; Letter by Beatrice Techen, March 8, 1990, Deutsches Uhrenmuseum, Gerwisstr. 11, 7743 Furtwangen, Germany. This is an example of an early cuckoo clock, invented around 1720 in the Black Forest where the clock industry originated; Karl and Arnold Weller, *Württembergische Geschichte im südwestdeutschen Raum* (Stuttgart: Theiss Verlag, 1989), p. 199. Frederick Stieff's will lists, among other items pertaining to the "homestead", a clock which may well be the family's brought from Germany; WRO, Libro L-1, 181.

[125] Howard Steeves' *Pioneer History* as related in Maimie (Wilbur) Steeves' book *Fundy Folklore* (N.p.: Albert County Historical Society, Inc., 1970), p. 52.

[126] Although not mentioned here, a method of preservation undoubtedly used along the Petitcodiac was that of drying berries and fruit, in particular apples called *Schnitz*, which was very popular among the Pennsylvania Germans. Special drying sheds were constructed for this purpose in Pennsylvania, which may also have been built on the homesteads in the Petitcodiac region; Nancy Roan, "Nineteenth-and Twentieth-Century Pennsylvania-Mennonite Foodways," *From Pennsylvania to Waterloo: Pennsylvania-German Folk Culture in Transition*, p. 106.

[127] The Early History of Albert County, Newspaper of March 27, 1883, NBM, Albert Co. Scrapbook, Shelf 31. Clark Wright attempted to accommodate accounts like this alongside historically proven facts in her book *Samphire Greens*, pp. 17 ff..

[128] Mildred Milliea, a teacher of the Miigmag language, suggested that the more accurate name for her people is "Miigmag" in the dialect of the New Brunswick area. Since the Mi'kmaq of Nova Scotia are part of Abraham Gesner's story in the chapter about Loyalists, the different dialects in New Brunswick and Nova Scotia will be reflected in the different spellings: "Miigmag" for New Brunswick and "Mi'kmaq" for Nova Scotia.

[129] The term "Indian", antiquated and offensive to many native people, is used here solely for purposes of accurate quoting.

[130] Jordan Steeves, *Saint John's Times*, March 8, 1893, NBM, Albert County Scrap Book, Shelf 31.

[131] Edward Larracey, *Chocolate River* (Hantsport, N.S.: Lancelot Press Ltd., 1985), p. 48.

[132] *Loc. cit..* Milner, in his *History of Albert Co.* (Vol. I, p. 13), mentioned the assistance of friendly native people as well; NBM, Milner Papers B 1, PK 5, Shelf 12.

[133] Moses Delesdernier was known for "his ability to converse in all the languages used by the settlers" in Hillsborough; John C. Hatt, *A Historical Study of the Delesdernier Family: Early Inhabitants of Nova Scotia and New Brunswick*, p. 26.

[134] Having come from a region close to France, the Treitz family may have been exposed to French and was perhaps able to communicate in that language. All of the settlers must have had some English because of their contacts with Pennsylvanian officials, most of whom were Anglophone.

[135] In a moving ceremony at the Lutz Mountain Meeting House on July 21, 1995 on the occasion of the 25th Anniversary of the founding of the Lutz Family organization, the Lutz/Lutes descendants formally thanked the Miigmag and Acadians for the assistance rendered to their forefathers more than two centuries ago.

[136] Clark Wright, *Samphire Greens*, p. 23.

[137] *Loc. cit..*

[138] Yoder, *Discovering American Folk Life*, p. 119.

[139] The importance of root cellars at that time is underlined by the fact that Rosanna Treitz (*née* Ricker) "bequeathed" space in her root cellar to her daughters Catherine, Margaret, and Hannah; WRO, Libro D-1, #2399, 477.

[140] Robert Cunningham and John Prince, *Tamped Clay and Saltmarsh Hay (Artifacts of New Brunswick)* (Fredericton, N.B.: University Press of New Brunswick Ltd, 1976), p. 145.

[141] William Calhoun's Diary, No. 8, *Chignecto Post*.

[142] *Loc. cit..*

[143] *Ibid.*, No. 10.

[144] *Gubbins' Journals*, p. 29.

[145] *Ibid.*, p. 12.

[146] *Ibid.*, p. 24.

[147] William Calhoun's Diary, No. 8, *Chignecto Post.*

[148] *Loc. cit..*

[149] *Gubbins' Journals,* p. 66.

[150] This lake was drained around the turn of the 20th century.

[151] William Calhoun's Diary, No. 12, *Chignecto Post.*

[152] *Gubbins' Journals,* p. 55.

[153] William Calhoun's Diary, No. 12, *Chignecto Post.*

[154] *Ibid.*, No. 8.

[155] I have sampled Acadian *poutine râpée (fraîche),* and they are without doubt a variation of German *Kartoffelklöße.* The recently introduced "fast-food" dish, also called *poutines,* consisting of French-fries smothered in gravy and melted cheese curds, should not be confused in this context, although this was undoubtedly another dish the Germans prepared with *Bratkartoffeln,* or home-fried potatoes, as cheese curds were a protein staple when meat was rare.

[156] Clément Cormier, "Les cahiers," *Société historique acadienne,* 1er cahier, 1961, p. 31.

[157] Karl and Arnold Weller, *Württembergische Geschichte ...,* pp. 180f.

[158] In the Reutlingen District, the potato was in general use in 1771; *Der Landkreis Reutlingen,* Vol. I (Sigmaringen: Landesarchivdirektion Baden-Württemberg, 1997), p. 170. The potato was also known in the Swabian Highlands around Münsingen about 1745-1750; Memminger, *Beschreibung des Oberamts Münsingen* (Stuttgart: 1825), p. 71. The main food for human consumption, however, was *Dinkel* ("spelt" grain) which was consumed both in the form of bread and as a porridge; letter of January 18, 1998 to me by Münsingen archivist Roland Deigendesch.

[159] Herwig, *Hammer or Anvil,* p. 9.

[160] *Kartoffelklöße* is a vegetarian adaptation of the *Hackfleischkloß* (ground pork meat dumpling), which was more expensive. While Germans in Germany may have been unable to afford meat, the records confirm that the Petitcodiac Germans had sufficient meat supplies after their move to Hillsborough, if not before.

[161] The Pennsylvania German dialect reflects the different origins of the immigrants. The Pennsylvania German Society has recently published the first *Pennsylvania German Dictionary,* that includes both English to Pennsylvania German and Pennsylvania German to English, by Eugene E. Stine, introd. by Rev. Willard W. Wetzel, Editor, and Dr. Glenys Waldman, Librarian and Curator, Grand Lodge of Pennsylvania (Birdboro, PA: The Pennsylvania German Society, 1996).

[162] Don Yoder, *Discovering American Folk Life,* p. 129.

[163] *Ibid.*, p. 121.

[164] The marriage between Rosanna Treitz (*née* Ricker) and Frederick Stieff took place on January 16, 1816.

[165] WRO, Libro D-1, #2399: 477.

[166] The Canadian Government Committee for Agriculture in Ottawa made the following observations in its report of 1924: "The City of Regina can be divided into two sections. The western portion is inhabited mostly by the English, and the eastern section, called Germantown, mostly by Germans ... [who] have gardens which the women and children cultivate in the evenings so that they can save money in this way." Hartmut Froeschle, *Auf dem Ahornbaum* (Toronto: German-Canadian Historical Association, 1997), p. 67.

[167] John Bennett's profession may have been that of a medical doctor. A "Dr. Benet" attended to Christian Stieff in his later years, as recorded in William Harper's third ledger (March 6, 1815 and March 8, 1816 entries), to be distinguished from "George Bennett" of Salisbury.

[168] *Gubbins' Journals*, p. 22.

[169] Cf. A. Hempel, "Updated Chronology of Events relating to the Prince-Lewis House ..." (Sackville, N.B.: October 17, 1999), pp. 1f.. A 1799 Military Map shows the general location of the three Treitz farmsteads, with Jacob Treitz Sr.'s in the middle of Lot 9 on property only granted to Christian in 1790 and 1792 (WRO, Libro A-1, 299). Christian lived approximately 350 metres away from his father.

[170] Any influence in weaving technique and patterns, as manifested in extant artifacts, must be left to future research although at least one sample of Pennsylvania German craftsmanship is on exhibit in the Albert County Museum, Hopewell Cape, N.B. and one in the Lutz Mountain Meeting House in Moncton.

[171] *Daily Times*, Historical Sketches, May 20, 1924, NBM, Miscellaneous Scrapbook, Shelf 42.

[172] The size of ship indicates that this trader could not have come from a distant port, perhaps Saint John, although well-known trader John Bentley from that city, whose wide-ranging business interests included the lending of money in the form of mortgages, must be ruled out since he only arrived with other Loyalists c. 1783; cf. *Loyalist All*, compiled and edited by Gart Bonsall Pipes (N.B. Branch, U.E.L. Association of Canada, 1985), p. 165.

[173] *St. John Sun*, March 8, 1893, NBM, Scrapbook Albert County, N.B.: my italics. Cotton thread was often used for the warp while the weft was of linen.

[174] Clark Wright, *Samphire Greens*, p. 92; my italics. The term "homespun" can refer to woven yardage for hand sewing and to yarn for hand-knitted clothing items.

[175] Huia Ryder's article "History of Handicrafts" shows no awareness of the weaving/ knitting expertise of the Petitcodiac German women. Ryder makes

308

only vague reference to weaving having been "brought to New Brunswick by New England settlers;" *Arts in New Brunswick*, eds. R.A.Tweedie, Fred Cogswell, W. Steward MacNutt (Fredericton, N.B.: The University of New Brunswick Press Ltd., 1967), p. 233.

[176] Hans Medick, *Weben und Überleben ...*, pp. 210f..

[177] Peter Etter Sr. opened up a stocking (weaving) factory in the New World.

[178] On April 20, 1815, *The Royal Gazette* of Saint John reported a serious fire in John Lutz's house: "On the 30th ... the house of Mr. John Lutz at Monkton [sic], County of Westmorland, was burned to the ground and a grandchild of Mr. Lutz perished in the flames -- Mrs. Lutz and all the small children except the youngest are severely burnt -- the flames raged with unabated fury, which rendered all assistance to save the property, of no avail -- his wheat, provisions, wearing apparel, etc., etc., were totally destroyed. Mr. L. and his eldest sons were at home during this melancholy catastrophe -- we have not heard how the fire originated." Another notable fire destroyed all the Stieff records which were kept at John Stieff's former homestead. The Stieff Bible escaped the flames because it had been lent to another member of the family; Clark Wright, *Samphire Greens*, p. 82.

[179] Pincombe and Larracey, *Resurgo: The History of Moncton*, Vol. I , pp. 97ff.. The fire likely took place c. 1800.

[180] *Ibid.*, p. 98.

[181] New Brunswick artist Claude Roussel found samples taken near the confluence of the Petitcodiac River and Hall's Creek to be of a modelling plasticity not suitable for his purposes of controlling shapes. When baked at 983°C, the result was sandy in texture and not very hard. Ceramics specialist Marie Ulmer from the Université de Moncton stated that satisfactory bricks shaped of Moncton and Dieppe clay could be produced if fired at 1000°C since some sand in bricks is apparently acceptable. Another source confirms: "Bricks and tiles are normally made of unmodified clays maturing at the same temperature as earthenware [between 1000°C and 1200°C]...;" Henry Hodges, *Artifacts: An Introduction to Early Materials and Technology* (London: John Baker Publishers Ltd., 1976), p. 24.

[182] *Ibid.*, pp. 35ff..

[183] Acadians used field stones for their chimneys and fireplaces. Robert Cunningham and John B. Prince are not convincing in their suppositions that the Acadians fired their own bricks; Cunningham and Prince, *Tamped Clay and Saltmarsh Hay* (Fredericton, N.B.: University Press of New Brunswick Ltd., 1976), pp. 161ff..

[184] This information was conveyed to me in 1998 by Jim Flemming, owner of the Chapman farm in Coverdale, N.B..

[185] Most of these symbols and patterns were common in different regions of Germany and can still be seen today, such as the rhomboidal pattern in the Bavarian coat of arms.

[186] Don Yoder and Thomas E. Graves, *Hex Signs: Pennsylvania Dutch Barn Symbols and their Meaning* (New York: E.P. Dutton, 1989), pp. 20, 56.

[187] Cf. J. Russel Harper, *A People's Art: Primitive, Naïve, Provincial and Folk Painting in Canada* (Toronto: University of Toronto Press, 1974); Rolf Wilhelm Brednich, *Mennonite Folklife and Folklore: A Preliminary Report*, National Museum of Man Mercury Series (Ottawa: National Museums of Canada, 1977); Nancy Lou Gellermann Patterson, *Swiss-German and Dutch-German Mennonite Traditional Art in the Waterloo Region, Ontario*, National Museum of Man Mercury Series (Ottawa: National Museums of Canada, 1979). Susan M. Burke and Matthew H. Hill, *From Pennsylvania to Waterloo: Pennsylvania-German Fork Culture in Transition* (Kitchener, Ont.: Joseph Schneider Haus, 1991); research in this area is only in its infancy. Many more examples of Pennsylvania German art and decorations probably still lie hidden in the attics of southern New Brunswick homes.

[188] Bob Cunningham and John Prince, "Foreword", *Tamped Clay and Saltmarsh Hay (Artifacts of New Brunswick)* (Fredericton, N.B.: University of New Brunswick Press, 1976). The authors spoke of artifacts which were found along with others in "a most creative part of that history-rich Province, New Brunswick." The spoon of Pennsylvania German origin discovered in Minudie, N.S. on the south side of the Bay of Fundy illustrates the spread of these artifacts to adjacent areas.

[189] Bernard LeBlanc, Curator of the Musée Acadien, Université de Moncton, called me in June 1998 to inform me about his discovery of the heart motif in what he called the Prince-Lewis House (civic address: 4 Bend View Court, Moncton). It is called the "Old Lewis Inn on Bend View Court" in Pincombe and Larracey, *Resurgo*, I, p. 132. Research by Adèle Hempel and Bernard Leblanc into the origin of the Treitz Haus has lead to a better understanding of the exact location of the settlers' landing and the early development of the lands that formerly belonged to Jacob Treitz Sr., Christian Treitz, and Christian Stieff.

[190] Cf. Marion Macrae & Anthony Adamson, *The Ancestral Roof: Domestic Architecture in Upper Canada* (Toronto, Vancouver: Clarke, Irwin & Company Ltd., 1963), pp. 3-32; Henry Glassie, Pattern in the Material Folk Culture of the Eastern United States (Philadelphia: University of Pennsylvania Press, 1968), pp. 56ff. As is known from Pennsylvania, Germans adopted the Georgian house as their own.

[191] Edward A. Chappell, "Acculturation in the Shenandoah Valley: Rhenish Houses of the Massanutten Settlement," *Common Places: Readings in*

American Vernacular Architecture, eds. Dell Upton and John Michael Vlach (Athens and London: The University of Georgia Press, 1986), pp. 27-57; Mary Mix Foley, *The American House* (New York: Harper and Row Publishers, 1980), pp. 59ff.; Cynthia G. Falk, "Symbols of Assimilation or Status? The Meanings of Eighteenth-Century Houses in Coventry Township, Chester County, Pennsylvania," *Winterthur Portfolio: A Journal of American Material Culture*, Vol. 33 (Chicago: University of Chicago Press, Summer/Autumn 1998), pp. 107-134.

[192] A search of the earliest recorded land transactions on Jacob Treitz Sr.'s original Lot 9 has been carried out for the area around Harper's Lane since Prince family tradition claims that the Treitz Haus was located at the corner of this lane. However, research suggests that the house predates the existence of Harper's Lane and that it was only "near" the junction of the King's Road and Harper's Lane. One property under consideration is that sold to William Steadman by Christian Treitz on April 11, 1812 (WRO, Libro C-1, 502). Another property under consideration, minus a house, was sold by Christian and Rosanna Stieff to James M. Kelly and his wife Jerusha on March 2, 1816 (WRO, D-1, 347: registered March 5, 1816). A much later description of Kelly's property and "Monkton Inn", which he built and ran, mentions a "wood shed or house said barn [not built by Kelly]", implying that this may have been an earlier barn left standing behind where a farmhouse had stood (*Ibid.*, 0-1, 293: registered May 19, 1836). A garden east of either proposed house location is suggested in a property deeded to John Bentley on March 12, 1812 abutting to the south-east of the house location, which makes reference to "a hole in the ground where formerly stood the corner post of a garden fence" and "... the first above described cedar posted garden fence" (*Ibid.*, C-1, 487: registered March 31, 1812). For further information on this subject, cf. Adèle Hempel's two unpublished reports, the first: "Updated Chronology of Events relating to the Prince-Lewis House , Moncton, N.B. (c. 1775), focused on the years c. 1769 - 1816" (July 26, 1999) and a more recent one with the same title but for the years c. 1799-1816 (October 19, 1999), MAUL, Bell Collection. Cf. also unpublished drawings of properties at "The Bend" rendered by Bernard LeBlanc, Curator, Musée Acadien, Moncton (1998/1999).

[193] Ichabod Lewis reserved to purchase through a mortgage the eastern half of Jacob Treitz Sr.'s Lot 9 on October 15, 1785 (*Ibid.*, A-1, 39: registered November 10, 1785), which would have included the house in question, however he annulled this agreement in 1789 (*Ibid.*, A-1, 228: registered July 8, 1789). Surveyor Ebenzer Cutler seems to have arrived at "The Bend" c. 1792 and was appointed "Town Clerk" and "Assessor" for Moncton for the year 1793. In the following year he served as a "Commissioner of Highways" and as one of the "Overseers of the Poor"; however, in 1795 Cutler became the "Surveyor of

Lumber" for Dorchester, suggesting that his residency in Moncton was never permanent (Sackville, N.B., Local Records, 1748-1883: MAUL, Westmorland County, N.B., Records of Proceedings at the General Session of the Peace, 1785-1809, M.G. 9, A 12-11, III, Public Archives of Canada, Microfilm 5331.

[194] The couple was married on November 12, 1791, but Sarah died in Saint John in 1808.

[195] Sackville, N.B., Local Records, 1748-1883: MAUL, Westmorland County, N.B., Records of Proceedings at the General Session of the Peace, 1785-1809, M.G. 9, A 12-11, III, Public Archives of Canada, Microfilm 5331.

[196] From the American War of Independence until after the War of 1812, Britain and the United States mutually forbade entry of "enemy" ships into their harbours. This did not prevent the illegal trade of such commodities as grindstones and plaster, which both Bentley and Harper engaged in by transferring their cargoes onto ships registered in the United States near the border in Passamaquoddy Bay.

[197] Maimie (Wilbur) Steeves, *Fundy Forklore*, pp. 47-55.

[198] *St. John Sun*, March 8, 1893: NBM, Albert County History. St. John, N.B..

[199] NBM, Albert Co. History, Cb. File.

[200] From a type-written version of a *History of the Steeves,* author unknown, given to me by Esther Clark Wright, p. 16.

[201] Katharina Stieff (1790-1827) was the 9th child of John Stieff and Margaret Lutz and 5 years old at the time.

[202] NBM, Albert Co. Scrapbook, Shelf 31, newspaper article, no author cited, March 27, 1883. It is not true that this was the first death to occur in Hillsborough settlement. Heinrich Stieff died between 1778 and 1780 as well as numerous children in infancy. The Stieff Family genealogy records no deaths of children around 1795 althought such deaths are difficult to uncover.

[203] In one Stieff Family genealogy, Nancy is listed as the sixth child of Jacob Stieff and Catharina Lutz, born in 1787. It makes more sense that she was 8 years old playing with flints rather than 18.

[204] Lutz Family geneology, Lutz Mountain Meeting House, Moncton, N.B.

[205] Reuben Steeves was the fifth child of Frederick Stieff and Rachel Sommer when the couple already lived near Allison.

[206] William Sinton, Esq. was Justice of the Peace in the Coverdale area at that time. There were others, such as James Watson, who were also good friends of Justice Keillor.

[207] *Gubbins' Journals*, pp. 17-18.

[208] Cf. grant map of Hillsborough.

[209] Clark Wright, *Samphire Greens*, pp. 82ff.

[210] Michael Lutz Sr. was still alive on March 13, 1792, for on this date he sold 500 acres of land to Christopher Horseman; WRO, Libro A-1, 358 (registered June 28, 1792).

[211] Several references are made to Michael Lutz Sr.'s will, including when John Lutz and his wife later sold a portion of their farm to William Chapman (WRO, Libro F-1, 94: registered January 22, 1822). In September 1794, two of John's siblings in Hillsborough sold their "Monckton" inheritances to him (Peter Lutz, grantor: WRO, Libro B-1, 64: registered October 15, 1794 and John Stieff, grantor on behalf of his wife Margaret Lutz: *loc. cit.*).

[212] Roy Lutes of Leewood, Kansas, included copies of a letter of recommendation from Moncton and a certificate of naturalization in the United States, Lutz Mountain Meeting House, Moncton, N.B.. The letter was signed by several others on September 3, 1830, and the date of United States citizenship was documented in the State of Ohio on March 28, 1843.

[213] Mary may have been a great grand-daughter of John Brown, who according to the 1783 Hillsborough Census "Died with the Small Pox in 1776."

[214] One of these was Abiel Peck, born in 1729, "a native of Boston and one of the first settlers of this place [Germantown] who on the 16th of December 1802, unfortunately Perished in a boat, in the 73rd year of his age; leaving upwards of three-score descendants to lament his melancholy fate;" Clark Wright, *The Petitcodiac*, p. 65. Peck's estate was valued at £1,996 as of December 28, 1802; WPR.

[215] WRO, Libro A-1, 145: registered Nov. 9, 1780.

[216] Clark Wright, *Samphire Greens*, p.44. A great deal of confusion surrounds the ages of the Treitz children, an issue that cannot be settled until the birth records from Pennsylvania become available. It seems reasonable to assume that Jacob Treitz Sr. looked after his first-born, Abraham, when he purchased the Charles Baker grant for him and provided for Jacob Jr. when he purchased Ricker Jr.'s grant for an unknown amount (unrecorded deed); cf. PANB, Microfilm F 1042, January 31, 1801. Christian, the youngest, inherited a good portion of Jacob Treitz Sr.'s grant when the latter became too old to farm it himself.

[217] WRO, Libro A-1, 298f.: registered April 16, 1791. As it later turned out, Christian Treitz's land measured 562 acres and Christian Stieff's only 532.

[218] As a result of the many land sales and transfers, it is difficult to establish the exact locations of the pioneers' homes, particulary in view of vague descriptions and a limited number of maps. The locations of Jacob Treitz's houses have been determined approximately; cf. A. Hempel's unpublished "Summary of Treitz House #3 Chronology ("Treitz-Prince-Lewis House") as based on her "Early History of Treitz Family's Lot 9, Monckton Township" (May 23, 2000).

[219] The claim in a Treitz genealogy, *The Descendants of Jacob and Elisina Treitz (1731-1791) (17?-?)* (Lutz Meeting House, Moncton, N.B.), that

313

Rosanna had two children by Cummings, Elizabeth *and* a boy named Benjamin, born in 1767, is incorrect. In his Will, Cummings states that his "natural son, Benjamin" should receive one-quarter of his Hillsborough share, and that an equal portion go to Elizabeth, his "natural daughter, by Rosanna Treits [sic]." It is clear from the context of the Will that Benjamin was the issue of his relationship with "Madam" in Baltimore as he makes special mention that only the existence of Elizabeth be kept secret; petition on behalf of Rosanna Treitz and Elizabeth Cummings, PANB, Land Petitions, Surveyor General, George Sproule, 1787, Microfilm F 6648.

[220] Clark Wright, *Samphire Greens*, pp. 45ff.

[221] John Jones exchanged 200 acres ("... commonly called the Mill lot originally granted unto the said John and Henry Jones with all appurtenances thereunto belonging ....") with farmer James Charters Jr. on April 15, 1811 for £5; cf. WRO, Libro C-1,464, registered June 13, 1811.

[222] Henry Jones is buried in the Pioneer Cemetery on the Salisbury Back Road in Salisbury. He died on January 20, 1840 at age 82. His wife, "Christinah" was the executor of his will; *New Brunswick Probate Records,* 1833-1839, Mount Allison University Library, Sackville, N.B..

[223] Geneva Jones Emberly, *Descendants of Charles Jones of New Brunswick form 1766*, p. 7; this author claims that John married Barbara "Trites", "probably the daughter of Jacob Trites Jr.," which is incorrect since Dimas Jones' identity was discovered in several land transactions alongside her husband John (WRO, Libro C-1, 464; Libro T-1, 109) and the connection to William Daniels' family made through his probate record (WRO, Libro C-1, 413 and Clark Wright, *Planters and Pioneers*, p. 97).

[224] WRO, Libro C-1, 428. There is the possibility of interpreting Abraham Treitz' use of the term "mother tongue" as "native language" or literally as tongue of the mother if she was Anglophone. Either way, the presence of another language is acknowledged. For Abraham Treitz, however, as a German speaker, the term "mother tongue" would have meant *"Muttersprache"*, i.e. German.

[225] Pincombe and Larracey, *Resurgo*, Vol. 1, p. 67.

[226] Pennsylvania German Society Proceedings and Addresses, *Pennsylvania German Church Records of Births, Marriages, Burials*, Etc.. 3 Vols. (Baltimore: Genealogical Publishing Co., Inc., 1983).

[227] Emberley, *Descendants ...*, p. 5. Henry Jones sold his farmstead when he was ready to retire from farming (WRO, Libro T-1, 358, sale in 1829 to Ephraim and Daniel Steeves), but John Jones' sons continued on a smaller portion of their father's farm after his retirement (WRO, Libro T-1, 109, registered 1841).

[228] Upon landing, the settlers are said to have knelt down and prayed; cf. Clark Wright, *Samphire Greens*, p. 88.

[229] *Ibid.,* pp. 90ff.. There are exceptions such as Dan Steeves of Mount Allison University in Sackville, N.B., an artist with a growing reputation.

[230] *Ibid.,* p. 73; subsequent information about the Steeves was taken from same source, pp. 75-80.

[231] By that time the spelling of the name "Stieff" had almost consistently been changed to "Steeves".

[232] Information about Muriel Sikorski *(née* Lutes) and the Magnetic Hill development was provided by Dawn Lutes, Muriel Sikorski's niece and Executive Director of the Muriel Lutz-Sikorski Fund.

[233] Raymond M. Short made a good attempt in 1978 with his type-written geneology, *The Ricker Family,* a copy of which may be found in the Lutz Mountain Meeting House, Moncton, N. B.. It is, however, like all genealogies, in need of continual updating.

[234] John Alexander Somers' interesting biographical account, *85 Years a Nova Sotian,* is an example of uncollected genealogical information. The author was born in 1911 and is a descendant of a John A. Somers, who was born in the 1820's, died in 1918, and is buried in Baie Verte; Cumberland County Museum, Amherst, N.S., Archival no. 9810.

[235] Dorothy Gunness of McMinnville, Oregon, has compiled a Wortman Genealogy and account of considerable length and detail, type-written copies of which are in the possession of Karon Wortman Scott, 141 Connell St., Woodstock, N.B., E7M 1K7; Joyce Wortman, RR #1 (Salisbury Road), Moncton, N.B.; and V. "Bing" Geldart, P.O. Box 494, Salisbury, N.B. E4A 3E0. Much of the following information about the Wortman family was contributed by Dorothy Gunness' manuscript, *We are Wortmans* (McMinnville, Oregon: Gunness Enterprise, 1989). Since 1995, the *Wortman Quarterly* is published in Winnipeg by D. Wayne Wortman, 61011 RPO. Grant's Park, Winnipeg, Man., R3M 3X8.

[236] PANB, Land Petitions, Surveyor General George Sproule, 1789, Microfilm F 1034. MacDonald effectively appealed to the New Brunswick Government and obtained the property *(Ibid.,* Microfilm F 1035 [1788] and F 1038 [1791]). It was Stephen Millidge, in effect, who reported Chappell's neglect of property and brought about its escheat. By November 15, 1788, MacDonald had already been "sometime a resident in Monkton" (Microfilm F 1035) and, therefore, knew that Chappell's property remained vacant. He came recommended to the government by Robert Scott and William Sinton. Where MacDonald first lived in "Monckton Township" or with whom is undetermined.

[237] MAUA, Harper Ledger (1797-1799), purchases during a trip up the Petitcodiac River on June 9, 1797.

[238] Clark Wright, *Planters and Pioneers,* p. 330.

[239] In Joseph Gray's petition, Georg Wortman is listed in 1773 as having a family of seven, i.e. five children, and was still residing in Hillsborough in 1783,

315

which appears to contradict the Millidge Report claims. Only Jacob and Martin were born by 1773, suggesting that the Wortmans lost three children during their first decade in "Monckton" and Hillsborough.

[240] Millidge Report, March 18, 1788.

[241] This date is at variance with claims elsewhere that Georg Wortman died in 1788; Stephen Millidge reported that Georg Wortman had died four months previously, i.e. to the date of the report of March 18, 1788.

[242] PANB, Provincial Land Registry, Microfilm F 1038 (1792).

[243] Department of Lands and Mines, N.B., # 126, quoted from Dorothy Gunness, *We are Wortmans*, pp. 9f.. It is not known how many daughters Georg and Maria Wortman had; *Ibid*,. p. 12.

[244] Dorothy Gunness, *We are Wortmans*, pp.14ff..

[245] Westmorland County, N.B., Records of Proceedings at the General Session of the Peace, 1785-1809. Alanson was the father of Moncton businessman Ichabod Lewis.

[246] *Ibid.*, p. 9.

[247] This Bible is in the possession of Mr. Evan O'Blenis of Salisbury, N.B..

[248] Pincombe and Larracey, *Resurgo,* Vol. I, p. 161; Larracey, *Resurgo,* Vol. II, p. 65.

[249] *Ibid.*. p. 274.

[250] Pincombe and Larracey, *Resurgo*, Vol I, pp. 331ff.

[251] This account was contributed by Mrs. Joyce Wortman, RR #1, Moncton, N.B.. By changing their names, the "Wartmans" will confuse future genealogists since this alters the meaning of the name, from "dwellers on elevated ground" to "watchmen". It may also have been embarrassment or misunderstanding of the origins of the name "Wortman" which led the family to encourage the pronunciation "Workman" as is prevalent today.

[252] Clark Wright, *The Petitcodiac*, p. 55.

[253] Robert Cummings' letter to Charles Baker, July 19, 1773, " Petition on behalf of Rosanna Treits [sic] for land belonging to the late Robert Cummins [sic]", PANB, Land Petitions, Surveyor General, George Sproule, 1787, Microfilm F 6648.

[254] Registration of Deeds for Christian Stieff and Christian Stieff Jr. of two 1,000-acre tracts of land on Steeves Mountain, Moncton Township, July 15, 1811, *Province of New Brunswick Crown and Grant Index.*

[255] John Bowser, tailor and marshland farmer, married Abraham Treitz's daughter, Margaret, and bought a two-acre property from William Harper in 1814.

[256] William Steadman, blacksmith and entrepreneur, married Hannah Treitz, eldest daughter of Christian Treitz.

[257] Miriam Stieff, daughter of Ludovic Stieff, became the wife of Thomas Prince.

[258] Pamela Treitz, daughter of Lewis Treitz, Esq. and granddaughter of Christian Treitz, married shipbuilder Alexander Wright (1811-1888) of Moncton.

[259] Dr. E.O. Steeves, Dr. John Bennett, and Magistrate Steeves are examples around the turn of the 20th century.

CHAPTER VII

Homesteading and Beyond

VII.1 New Names in a New Province

The American War of Independence affected the Petitcodiac Germans in other ways than just harassment by raiders in the Bay of Fundy and the severing of communication between landowners and tenants. Their lives were profoundly altered by the arrival of thousands of residents fleeing the British colonies which rejected continued allegiance to Britain. These new arrivals had remained loyal to the British cause either by refusing to support the rebels or by actively fighting them. Although the Germans of the Petitcodiac did, in fact, become beneficiaries of this conflict by obtaining their land deeds at a time when anti-American sentiment ran high, their loyalty to Britain was not contingent upon any ultimate guarantee of reward. On the contrary, many "Loyalists" lost everything in their move northward and were never adequately reimbursed. This was also the case for many German immigrants from these same colonies who likewise chose to remain faithful to the Crown.

New Brunswickers reflect proudly on their Loyalist heritage each year in festivals, such as Saint John Loyalist Days, however surveys of the general public have revealed that many in this province and elsewhere know little about the ethnocultural origins of these ancestors:

> [Canadians and Americans] at all levels of education have been taught far too long that the Loyalists of the American Revolution were English .... [T]he myth that these political and war refugees were English 'blue-blood' still persists after 200 years. Almost the exact opposite is true, of course. Losers in a bitter civil war, these exiled Americans were as diverse ethnoculturally as they were in their faith, their livelihood and their economic status. To understand and accept these facts is a basic step toward grasping the elusive Canadian identity.[1]

318

Fewer than 50 percent of the three million people living in the British colonies in 1775 were of British descent: "[T]here can be no question that the English or British element was in the minority"[2] among the Loyalists if the latter can be regarded to have represented a cross-section of the society which they abandoned. About one-third of Pennsylvania and one-quarter of New York were inhabited by German-speaking settlers.[3] Moreover, special reasons emerge as to why settlers of German descent opted to remain "loyal". These taken into account, it comes as no surprise that the United Empire Loyalists comprised an even higher proportion of German descendants as compared to their former demographic distribution throughout the New England states:

> What is today generally called the Delaware Valley or the mid-Atlantic states, namely, New Jersey, eastern Pennsylvania, Delaware and Maryland, had been settled by a very large German mosaic prior to the outbreak of the American Revolution. Until the revolutionaries, or the rebels, became disgruntled with their King, George III, and British Parliament, this large area ... was dotted with villages, towns and cities named after similar communities of Continental Europe, principally of the Rhine River area of central Europe. These Alsatians, Lorraines, Swiss, Flemish, French Huguenots and Palatines in general had maintained their cultural identity for nearly 100 years, many speaking only their native German language in 1775, the year signalling the outbreak of the American Revolution. When this fratricidal war came to an end at Yorktown on 17 October 1781, many of these third generation German-speaking settlers fled to British North America as refugee Loyalists. Such names as Eisenhower, Pennypacker, Hoover, Wan[n]amaker, Hershey, Goodyear and Rittenhouse reflect today the powerful influence these German-Americans have had in North America.[4]

One of these U.E.L. groups stands out in particular, namely that settled by the Crown in the valleys of the Hudson, Mohawk and Schoharie Rivers in the early years of the 18th century. These were the descendants of those aforementioned starving Palatines who had come down the Rhine at Queen Anne's invitation in the years 1708-1709 and whom the British authorities had resettled in this area at considerable expense,[5] a scheme, which in the short, term proved to be advantageous to no one, neither to the settlers nor the Crown. Some had settled in the American colonies taking a rather circuitous route *via* Ireland, for example the Dulmage/*Dolmetsch* family which was settled by the British first in Ireland in order to establish a Protestant presence there. The bulk of the families, however, came over to North America directly from England in the years following 1709. In time, descendants of these Palatines would repay the English for this kindness by remaining loyal to the British cause.[6] A contributing element to their loyalty was the influence of such men as Sir John Johnson, the son of an Irish father[7] and German mother, who succeeded in winning over both Mohawks and Germans in the Mohawk Valley to the British cause. Before Johnson fled to Canada in 1776, he formed the famous 84th Royal New York Regiment, the so-called "Royal Greens", comprised mostly of his German neighbours.[8] Whereas the bulk of the "Royal Greens" including Johnson settled in Ontario, many other Loyalists from New York and the other colonies came to Nova Scotia, which at that time included the territory later to become New Brunswick.

Another contributing factor to the disproportionately large number of Germans among the Loyalists were the activities of Christopher Sauer who is listed as "Christopher Sowers (Sauer), printer" from Pennsylvania, served as a translator in the War of Independence, arrived in Saint John, N.B. in 1785, and subsequently obtained a land grant along the Hammond River.[9] His father was "... an elder among the Brethren (Dunkers), [who]... attempted a neutral position in the conflict; like them he was not persuaded that rebellion against the monarchy that had granted them religious toleration and economic independence was legitimate."[10] Christopher Sauer openly resisted rebellion and began using the press, that he had inherited from his father, as an anti-revolutionary mouthpiece. He was forced to abandon Germantown but continued his attacks in British-held Philadelphia, where he published the Loyalist newspaper, *Der Pennsylvanische Staats-Courir, oder einlaufende Wöchentliche Nachrichten* ("The Pennsylvanian States Courier, or Incoming Weekly News"), from 1777 to 1778.[11] After the withdrawal of British troops in June 1778, Sauer left Philadelphia to set up a book and stationary store in New York, still held by the British. This business, however, was short-lived since most of Sauer's time was spent supporting the British war effort, a significant departure from his early Dunker and Quaker upbringing. In his own words, he "... served as a Guide, a German Printer, and Translator, and from Time to Time procured Intelligence for three successive Commander-in-Chiefs, Sir William Howe, Sir H. Clinton, and some for Sir Guy Carleton."[12] There is much documented evidence that Sauer worked as an undercover agent in the German-speaking neighbourhoods of Philadelphia, setting up fifth column-type sabotage of American troops. In the years 1782-1783, Sauer published another pro-Loyalist newspaper, *The New-York Evening Post*, which appealed "to Germans in Pennsylvania and neighboring provinces ... [with his] *Zuschrift* [("Letter to the Editor") and which] was one of the hardest-hitting polemics of the bitter war."[13] There can be no doubt that his extensive journalistic activities and covert efforts convinced many German-Americans to side with the British cause as his papers received wide distribution throughout Pennsylvania, New York, and also in bordering New Jersey and Maryland, from where large numbers of German Loyalists also departed.

Toward the end of hostilities, many of those who had supported the British or who wished to remain neutral left their homes in the rebellious states and fled to the more northern provinces still under British control. "[T]he largest ethnic group of Loyalists to settle in upper Canada was the German."[14] In order to make a similar claim for New Brunswick, considerably more research into the Loyalist genealogies of this province would be required. It is safe to say, however, that many more of New Brunswick's Loyalists were of German descent than have hitherto been recognized.

There were several main sources for these Germans: troops known collectively as Hessians, "provincials" ("colonials") in the service of the British, and private citizens forced to flee because they were deemed not to have supported the Revolution. It was in the interest of the German princes -- and the British as well[15]-- that the number of returning German auxiliaries be reduced in view of the head money promised by Britain, either for the loss of a subject in fighting or for the cost of a subject's return voyage home. In addition, "German princes and margraves had ordered that officers and men with bad records were to be left behind in America."[16] In his article "Case History of a Settlement", Maxwell Sutherland traces the development of the

Township of Clements near Digby, N.S., founded by such disbanded officers and men from regiments of Anhalt-Zerbst, Brunswick, Hesse, Waldeck, and Ansbach-Bayreuth. About one hundred Germans had been allotted land, but crop failure and the termination of government provisions in 1788 reduced their number in subsequent years; nevertheless, Clements started out as a purely German settlement not unlike "Monckton Township".

Men who had fought for the British cause in provincial regiments also came north as Loyalists. It had been a long tradition to use provincials in the various conflicts that arose throughout North America. The attack on Fort Beauséjour, for instance, was carried out with troops recruited in the New England states. The previously-mentioned Germans and Swiss from Maryland and Pennsylvania who had served with quartermaster Adam Hoops in the Régiment Bouquet, which saw action during the second capture of Louisbourg in 1758 and the decisive battle of Quebec in the following year,[17] are another example of colonial troops. In the American War of Independence, the British also used provincial regiments alongside regular troops and German auxiliaries and after the hostilities had subsided, these soldiers and their families also headed north.

There were other possible areas where Loyalists or Tories could have gone to find refuge from American harassment and persecution. The West Indies was one such destination, but this was considered too dangerous on account of climatic differences and the risk of tropical diseases. Another was Canada, but this was thought too far and its inhabitants, the French, too different in their language and customs. Moreover, the French were of a different religious persuasion than the predominantly Protestant stock of Tory New Englanders,[18] and perhaps even worse was the fact that France, the parent country of Canadians, had lent its support to the rebellious colonies.[19] Nova Scotia to the north-east was the province of choice, a place where Loyalists could feel welcome yet still remain close enough to their American homes to harbour the dream of an eventual return south.

In several waves between mid-May and mid-November 1783, about fifteen thousand Loyalists, including their family members, disembarked in Nova Scotia.[20] Clark Wright identified some of these families in her book, *The Loyalists of New Brunswick*: "The German names, about 40, are mostly

322

from the Pennsylvania 'Dutch' families, although a few members of the so-called Hessian mercenaries drifted into New Brunswick."[21] This, however, is a gross miscalculation of the German presence within the United Empire Loyalist fold. In his study *The German Canadians 1750-1937*, Heinz Lehmann suggests that "... [a]mong the mass of Loyalists who settled on the St. John River at that time, we have to assume a large number of German-American refugees and probably most of the twelve hundred Brunswick mercenaries. The latter were discharged in 1783 and settled in New Brunswick, then still part of Nova Scotia."[22] The extent of the German component is also reflected in the large number of those who declared their German ancestry in the City of Saint John, Kings Co., and Queens Co. as late as 1871, when awareness of their heritage became increasingly blurred.[23] In Clark Wright's incomplete list, at least 40, in addition to those from David Bell's list[24] (marked "*") stated that their origin was Germany or that they had served in Hessian, Brunswick, and Waldeck regiments, or in the Regiment Specht. Their names were: Althouse (*Althaus*), Barnard, Bodtner, Boehn (Behn[25]), Borrell*, Brill, DeDollwick*, D'Ehrenstein, Duphnack, Effa or Effee, Folkins, Foss (*Voss*), Grimmer, Grothe*, (Dr.) Gunter,[26] Hauser*, Hecht, Hennigar (Adam, Christopher, and Michael), Hildebrandt, Humbert*, Kern,[27] Reading*, Rhein, Ritter (first names: Frederick and Hyronemus),[28] Sagerburgh/ Segerberg, Sarvenier/Shampier (*Schomber*, *Schanparr*), Schoenewolf (*Schönewolf*),[29] Slip(p) (*Schlipp*), Sowers (*Sauer*), Stannick or Stennick, Straeder (*Sträder*), Young* (*Jung*), Warner*, Wintzer, Woodland, and Woodly. The latter two, as well as Henry Reading and George Young, must have Anglicized their names radically.

In a cursory look through Clark Wright's list of Loyalist names, one can easily identify more than triple the number of German names than what she recognized.[30] Although Clark Wright was a descendant of Petitcodiac Germans, she was unfamiliar with the German language and the different phonetic laws that govern it as opposed to English, hence unable to identify Anglicized names, nevertheless, she did acknowledge that: "New Brunswick Loyalists represented a cross-section of the older communities from which they came."[31] Two well-known Anglicized names from the United States serve to illustrate this point: Rockefeller, a descendant of the simple immigrant *Roggenfelder*, who made it from rags to riches, and *Kreisler*, whose automotive talents led to the Chrysler car. An example from Nova

Scotia's Lunenburg community is the surname *Weihnacht*, the German word for "Christmas", spelled variously today: Weihnot, Whynacht, Whynot,[32] etc.. Other common Lunenburg examples are the names Crouse (*Kraus* or *Krause*) and Creaser (*Grieser*). The names Dobblestyne (*Doppelstein*) and Engleheart (*Engelhart*) in New Brunswick fit into this same category.

Straight translations of names were fairly common, e.g. *Braun* became Brown, *Schwartz/Schwarz* changed to Black, *Müller* to Miller, *Schmidt* to Smith, *Eisenhauer* to Ironcutter, *Fuchs* to Fox, *Kratz* to Scratch,[33] etc.. The well-known aviation pioneer, *Weisskopf*, called himself "Whitehead" in America. Perhaps this explains the case of the Loyalist in New Brunswick by the unusual name of "Youngshusband". Many Americans named Young are descendants of the German *Jung* family.[34] Was Youngshusband's original name *Jungmann* or *Junghans*? It is unwise, however, to make assumptions in all cases, especially with New Brunswick Loyalist names like: Albert, Frost, Hand, Harris, Horn, Martin, Richard, Ring, Winter, Ferdinand, Frank(s), Phil(l)ip(ps), and Sebastian. All of these are common in German but would require further genealogical research to verify their exact country of origin.

The following examples are names of United Empire Loyalists who came to New Brunswick but whose names are not easily recognizable as German: Brewster/Bruster was *Armbruster*,[35] Coon -- *Kuhn*, Dusenberry -- *Düsenberg/Düsenburg*, Keithline/Keithland/Cathline -- *Küchlein*,[36] Rednor/Ridnar/Ridnor -- *Redner*, Riger/Rigar -- *Rieger*, Rikeman/Ryckman -- *Reichmann*, Rainkellor -- *Reinkeller/Rheinkeller*, Shonnard -- *Schönert*, Snider -- *Schneider*, Schriver -- *Schreiber*, Summers/Somers -- *Sommer*, Switzer/Sevitzer -- *Schwei(t)zer*, Wanamaker/Wonemaker -- *Wanne(n)-macher*, Warner/Verner -- *Werner*, Weatherhold -- *Wiederholt*, and Weedeman -- *Wiedemann*. Still other immigrants of German descent who arrived at approximately the same time and were not included in Clark Wright's list moved to New Brunswick from elsewhere in the Maritimes, for example from Halifax or Lunenburg, such as Willem Ricker, who "removed from Boblick now called Argyle in Nova Scotia to Indian Island and lived there some time."[37] The Westmorland Marriage Register[38] from 1790 to 1835 lists the German names: Kusse, Riehse/Riefse, and Rolb.

324

The Index of New Brunswick Land Petitions[39] lists names of those who petitioned for land in the province from 1783 to 1857, including those selected by Clark Wright and hundreds more, enabling these people to be traced as to where they took up land, how many children they might have had, and what changes their names underwent.[40] Some of these names have many entries, such as Stymiest (*Steinmetz*), listed about twenty times under various spellings: Steimeist and Stymest (1785), Stymitson (1793), Stymist (1799), Stymiest (1810), Stymeist (1812), Stymeest (1847), and so on. Interspersed among these new arrivals are hundreds of land requests from the Petitcodiac Germans and their descendants in all variety of spelling: Lutz/Lutes, Ricker/Riecker, Somers/Sommers/Summers, Stief/Steef(s)/ Steeve(s)/Steves, Treits/Treitz/Trites, and Wortman/Workman/Waterman.

VII.2 A Blending of Old and New

All these Germans or descendants of Germans mixed in with pre-Loyalist families, including the Petitcodiac Germans, together with the bulk of other United Empire Loyalists and later arrivals. It has been said that the Loyalists replaced the pre-Loyalists. The earlier example of Christian Stieff, who sold smaller parcels of his land near the settlers' landing in order to purchase about 8 km² on Steeves Mountain, supports Clark Wright's contention that, despite some displacement, both groups benefitted and enhanced one another. The derogatory statement of one Loyalist claims commissioner that pre-Loyalists, among them the Petitcodiac Germans, were "a despicable race, ready to sell their improvements, as the Loyalists are enabled to purchase from them,"[41] need not be taken seriously since the Petitcodiac Germans and other pre-Loyalists had merely shown their ability to adapt and take advantage of opportunities as they presented themselves. Loyalists, on the other hand, had already progressed beyond rough frontier conditions in the southern colonies prior to their arrival in New Brunswick and, in many instances, had acquired the necessary cash not to have to revert to primitive land-clearing and settlers' work. Often they opted to buy established farms: "The Pre-Loyalists were in fact taking part in a shrewd, sensible, and useful transaction. They could buy land elsewhere in the province for a trifling sum, and, with the additional funds at their disposal from the sale of their former holdings, they could in a short time be more comfortable than before."[42] This explains why so many of the Petitcodiac

Germans no longer farmed along the river where they first settled but began to disperse throughout the province, as later land transactions indicate. Settlements such as Steeves Mountain, Lutes Mountain, Pollett River, and Petitcodiac (Steeves Settlement), among others, were part of the move away from the original land grants and more populated "village" areas to rural New Brunswick, pushing the frontier inland.

Such scattering into outlying areas no doubt hastened the loss of German as a language of communication. Germans from eastern Pennsylvania, Maryland, New Jersey, and the Hudson, Mohawk and Schoharie river valleys in New York State still spoke their language because these were regions where Germans had been living in high concentrations.[43] Such a claim, however, cannot be made with certainty for Loyalists of German ancestry from other American locations. In New Brunswick, dispersion resulted in a loss of "critical mass" and sense of ethnic cohesion, both of which are important factors in language maintenance. Furthermore, the Petitcodiac Germans were no longer isolated from their Anglophone neighbours as was the case in some remote areas around Lunenburg where spoken German survived well into the 20th century.[44] This increased contact caused the German language to disappear altogether, and even within the Petitcodiac German communities[45] this linguistic changeover may have been complete by 1850. Although Germans continued to immigrate to New Brunswick in the 19th and 20th centuries, these later arrivals were few by comparison to the total population and could never have turned around the trend to abandon German as a language of communication.

The annals of the Maritime provinces and Canada give testimony to the mark left by the German Loyalist families Fisher (fig. 51),[46] Tupper (fig. 52),[47] Schurman,[48] Wohlhaupter,[49] and Etter (fig. 53).[50] Recent research into early Moncton history[51] shows the interaction between descendants of the Petitcodiac Germans and the Loyalists, some of whom were also of German origin such as the Gesner[52] and Stultz[53] families. Originally from New Jersey, Henry Stultz was granted land at Dorchester Cape and the Memramcook River in 1786 before settling just outside of "Monckton" to start up grist- and sawmills on his 300-acre grant at "Mill Creek". Stultz petitioned to the province in 1801 for the land (registered in 1813) where he claimed to have begun his operation and "... erected a Dwelling House,

Figure 51
Charles Fisher, Father of Confederation and Premier of New Brunswick.

Courtesy: National Archives of Canada

327

Figure 52

William Henry Steeves and Charles Fisher, two Fathers of Confederation of German descent from New Brunswick, standing side by side on the far left; Sir Charles Tupper, the only other of German origin, in speaker's pose in front of the table on the right.

Courtesy: National Archives of Canada

328

Figure 53

Etter House on Etter Ridge, N.B., built in 1832 by Peter Etter III, descendant of Peter Etter, German Loyalist.

Photo: Rainer L. Hempel

329

Sawmill and Gristmill on the Mill Creek so called ... upon ungranted lands above and next to Reuben Mills Grant ... , having resided thereon with his family more than 6 years [i.e. at least since 1795] ...."[54] He entered into business with others in the area, such as brother-in-law Ichabod Lewis, who resided nearby and received his 200-acre grant 1817.[55] Henry Stultz Sr. died around 1822, but his family stayed in the Parish of Dorchester area for years.[56] Lewisville might have been called Stultzville if Henry Stultz Jr. had not concentrated his efforts after 1833 on his 220-acre Salisbury grant and left "Creek Village" to the Lewis family, which received an additional 300-acre grant there in 1829.[57]

The marriages of Ichabod Lewis' younger brother Felix to Elizabeth Trites (daughter of Jacob and Rosanna Treitz Jr.) and Reuben Mills' eldest son David to Jane Trites (Abraham and Margaret Treitz's daughter) show the blending of pioneer descendants with Loyalists. Another important example is the 1811 marriage of Loyalist Thomas Prince, prominent Moncton entrepreneur and Justice of the Peace in later years, to Miriam Stieff (daughter of Ludovic Stieff of Hillsborough), for whose father Prince may have worked before settling at "The Bend" in early 1813. Descendants of the German Loyalist Gesner family also intermarried with the Petitcodiac Germans. The first cousin Jacob Gesner of the renowned geologist and researcher Abraham Gesner married Elizabeth Trites of Moncton (Christian Treitz's fourth daughter) in 1816 and through her inherited a small section of "Bald Marsh". Jacob's mother was Elizabeth Steadman, whose younger brother William had settled there in 1801 and married Christian and Catherine Treitz's eldest daughter, Hannah, two years later.[58] William Steadman continued a growing tradition of blacksmith shops at "The Bend",[59] which later serviced the stagecoach and burgeoning shipbuilding industries.

Intermingling with Loyalists was merely the continuation of a process begun shortly after arrival when, for example, Anna Catharina and Sarah Sommer married "Planter" sons Eliphalet Chappell and Benjamin Allan of Cumberland as early as 1767 and 1771, respectively. The same process with Yorkshire settlers is exemplified by the marriages of Margareth Wortman to Alexander Donkin (Duncan) of Amherst in 1795,[60] Rachel Steeves (daughter of Johann and Catharina Stieff) to Robert Colpitts Jr. of Hillsborough in

330

1795,[61] and Margaret Trites (Abraham Treitz's daughter) to John Bowser in 1808.

The Genealogical Reference provides evidence of the increasing frequency of marriages between Petitcodiac Germans, pre-Loyalists, and Loyalists. Moncton's first house of worship, the Free Meeting House, is an illustration of the admirable cooperation which existed between the pioneer settlers and later arrivals. One of the earliest "registered" sales of land by William Steadman, who profited considerably over the years by parcelling off his 50-acre tract of land from Christian Treitz, allowed Ichabod Lewis and Solomon Trites, "Trustees for taking charge of and building a house of Worship,"[62] to proceed with plans for the construction of an ecumenical house of worship in a prominent location within the "Village", at the junction of the King's Highway and the main road leading to the "Mountain Settlement", a stone's throw away from the "business district".

Whereas many remained on their land and bartered agricultural products for supplies they could not fashion or raise themselves,[63] others began, often as an activity during the winter months, to develop expertise in "manufacturing" certain items which became articles of trade. A reflection of these transactions can be found in the three extant Harper Ledgers[64] mentioned earlier, rescued from a blaze in 1834 which destroyed Harper's store. These contain detailed records of his customers and the merchandise they "bought" and "sold", first from his trading vessel, the *Weasel*, and later from his permanent store location in Moncton. By comparing customers' "purchases" and "barter payments", a picture begins to emerge as to their respective occupations, incomes, lifestyles, and to a certain extent, status in society. Although later intermarriages between the Petitcodiac Germans and New England Planters, Loyalists, and Yorkshire settlers blurred the distinctions between these ethnic groups, many of the Petitcodiac German families, at least in the years around the turn of the century, did not have the liquid capital to share fully in the opportunities introduced by financially more secure Loyalists. On a sales trip up to "Petticoatiyak" in June of 1797, under separate accounts, Margaret Ricker, Jacob Ricker Jr., and Michael Ricker each bought rum,[65] for which cash may not have been immediately available. Listed in a year-end inventory of "Amounts brought forward" as of February 1, 1800, Peter Lutz owed £11:14:2, Michael Ricker £7:3:6, and

Michael Lutz[66] £3:13:8 (all from Lower Coverdale); payments in cash or "kind" were made later, such as "2 bushels of oats" bartered by Peter Lutz, (maple) sugar by Michael Ricker, and "cash and victuals" by Jacob Ricker Jr. (possibly for Margaret's purchase).

The second Ledger is testimony to the increased business activities of the Petitcodiac Germans. On November 4, 1808, Michael Steeves [67] (John and Margaretha Stieff's son) made sundry purchases such as a sugar dish, plates, pepper, brimstone (sulphur), iron, muslin, and calico, for which he delivered (maple) sugar on April 20, 1809, perhaps the product of an early sugaring-off season. Harking back to pioneer days were payments by fur, such as fox, made by James Stieff,[68] and "Beer" and rabbit skins by Andrew Sommer.[69] John Stieff "Seigr"[70] bought 6 teaspoons, 2 "pains" of glass, 13 quarts of rum, among other items, and paid for them with 15 lbs. of sugar, onions, apples, and cash.[71] John Steeves, identified as a "boat keeper",[72] was another of Harper's customers. A Jacob Steeves [73] exchanged sugar for his purchase of 6 knives and forks, 4 yards of calico and another yard of cloth. Another Jacob Steeves Jr.[74] paid for his supplies with two ploughs. William Steeves "Seign." (Jacob and Catharina Stieff's son) paid for his purchases with sugar, in addition to 5½ cords of "lathwood", which were valued at £11:5:3,[75] and David Steeves (John and Margaretha Stieff's son) used staves for barrel-making as barter for knives, forks, window glass, buttons, and extravagances such as tea, a looking glass, a silk handkerchief, tobacco and "spirits".[76] This lumber undoubtedly came from the sawmills operated by the Stieff brothers in Hillsborough (plate 16), one of which was built and owned by Ludovic Stieff on "Mill Creek".[77] Henry Steeves (Christian and Rosanna Stieff's son) lavished a rather expensive (11-shilling) shawl[78] on his wife Ann/Nancy (née Sinton) and a gallon of spirits, presumably for himself, for a little more than 7 shillings.[79] About three months apart in 1808, both John Lutz[80] and Andrew Sommer[81] embarked on building projects as evidenced by their purchases of glass, hinges, screws, planes, and large quantities of nails. John was able to pay for his acquisitions a short time later with butter and oats. Andrew still had a balance owing in July 1810; however this did not seem to have disturbed Harper unduly for Andrew was a respected Monctonian and one of the community's original settlers to survive to 1840.[82] In 1837, Andrew's estate was estimated at £900, but his Last Will and Testament bespeaks his humbleness and Old-Country frugality in the face of death, instructing that he wished to be "decently buried in the Church yard of Moncton beside ... [his] spouse without any funeral pomp and with ... little expense ...."[83] During his lifetime though, as befitted his social position, Andrew indulged in the purchase of a fashionable "Beaver Hatt" at the time of his building project. John Bowser, Moncton's first professional tailor, bought one of these hats earlier in the year,[84] in time for his June 12th wedding to Margaret Trites; and, not to be outdone, other established Petitcodiac Germans or their spouses followed suit, such as Abraham Steeves (John and Margaretha Stieff's son) and blacksmith William Steadman.

Not always fashion but availability dictated the purchase of certain items. On Harper's July 1808 run up the Petitcodiac, a large number of scythes was sold. One customer was "Henery Steives Signr.", Heinrich Stieff's fifth son, whose other acquisitions reflect his business and leisure activities: 1 pair of compasses, 1¼ (lbs?) shot, 1 log chain, and 1 gallon of rum. Another of the original settlers to buy a scythe was Peter Lutz. Beside the customary one or two gallons of rum/spirits, the Ledger makes mention of indigo, paper, several knives, ribbon, a "Mackral line",[85] and tacks and nails, which Peter paid for in the winter with 2 barrels of apples, 6 chairs, "1 Lot Cart Spokes",[86] and cash, indicating that he spent his slow months as a carpenter and wheelwright. John Lutz, his brother (or son) Michael, a John Stieff, and particularly Michael Ricker were major suppliers of butter, delivered in firkins, an English hollow measure of a quarter barrel.[87] The large sales of butter by the Lutz's should not come as a surprise since pioneer Michael already owned 51 cows in 1788, the highest number in "Monckton".[88] Such were the quantities of butter produced along the Petitcodiac that Harper was able to ship 66 firkins of it to Halifax in December of 1808. Income from this and other products allowed for such post-pioneer purchases as "shaving soap"[89] for Michael Ricker and "2 Spelling Books" for "Lewis Steves",[90] suggesting that education had become a consideration.[91] Christian Treitz [92] was one of the exceptions with regard to solvency as he was usually able to pay in cash.

Although trading activities and incomes were on the rise, insolvencies were not uncommon for those involved in risky business ventures. In 1812, Michael Ricker "indentured" (i.e. sold) for £500 all the Hillsborough property inherited from his father to brothers Solomon and Charles Trites. The Rickers moved to Hampton, King's Co., for a number of years,[93] but it must have been their desire to return "home" when circumstances permitted. In a petition to the Crown prepared July 14, 1815 by a Sackville lawyer, Michael Ricker appealed his case and that of his unmarried, 22-year-old son Jacob, that at fifty years of age "his Family consists of his wife and 6 children, ... that ... [he] had a grant of 200 acres of land[94] on the south side of the Petitcodiac River nearly opposite the Bend, about 25 years since [c. 1790], which he greatly improved by dyking about 24 acres of marsh, and by clearing 30 acres of upland, upon which he built a dwelling house and barn. That owing to *pecuniary embarrassments* ... [he] was obliged to sell the same."[95] He was now requesting a grant of three vacant lots south of "Mill Creek" (Lower Coverdale), not far from Stoney Creek and about one mile from "The Bend" on which he and his son, both "farmers by occupation, ... will immediately settle ...."[96] Michael and son Jacob were granted two of the three lots, but Andrew Steeves (Frederick Stieff's son) succeeded in getting the other, where "Mill Creek" flows into the Petitcodiac. This Jacob Ricker (＊ 1792/1793; cf. Ricker Family genealogy), who farmed successfully with his father Michael in later years, was the third "Jacob Ricker", being the great-grandson of Jacob Ricker Sr. and grandson of Jacob Ricker Jr..[97]

Also about 1812, trader and investor John Bentley foreclosed on Ludovic Stieff, resulting in his loss of one-fifth of his father Heinrich's Hillsborough grant plus land he had purchased from Martin Beck Jr. at "Mill Creek" (in Hillsborough). But Ludovic, too, was successful in his petition in 1813 for new land in the Turtle Creek area (fig. 54).[98] The proximity of these two financial insolvencies suggests some joint venture which may have gone awry, such as the sinking of a shipment of limestone or lumber, or a war-related misfortune. The bulk of trade and commerce at this time was in agricultural products, primarily butter, cheese, and (maple) sugar, all of which were highly work intensive. As a consequence, land continued to be considered an important investment, exemplified by the group application for additional grants as late as 1809 [99] by four members of the extended Treitz family, none of whom experienced any loss of land like Michael Ricker or Ludovic Stieff. Christian Treitz, with his sons William and Lewis (Lodwick) Trites, and nephew Solomon Trites (Abraham's son) applied for and received

Figure 54
Tombstone of Lewis Steves (Ludovic Stieff[2]) and Elizabeth Porter in the
Turtle Creek Cemetery.

Photo: Rainer L. Hempel

lots in Hillsborough and "Monckton", respectively, knowing that these two particular locations were temporarily vacant but would not remain so for long. An aspect of brothers Solomon and Charles Trites's later business partnership seems to have been land speculation and mortgage/loan grants, whereas Lewis Trites (Christian's son) eventually formed a partnership with family members from his wife's side and used the title "trader".[100] Lewis Trites became an influential person in Moncton and later Salisbury, earning the title "Esq."[101] and serving for a time as Justice of the Peace, but Christian's younger son, William, appears to have been less successful, at least in his early years. Although he obtained a 500-acre tract of land on "Bald Marsh" from his father in 1820, directly west of the family homestead, only four years later he had indentured the property for £499: 9: 6,[102] which E.B. Chandler Esq. called a year later.[103]

As the growing selection in goods traded by Harper indicates, availability and affordability resulted in more comfortable circumstances for the settlers in spite of occasional cash shortages. Col. Gubbins observed this firsthand in 1811 when he wrote:

> Although bullion does not abound yet the general course of the trade which gives employment to the lumberers and plaster men and encouragement to agriculture and the fisheries is evidently adding to the intrinsic wealth to the country. Within the last few years ... the general improvement in the appearance of the peasantry, as well as in the comfort of their dwellings and in the number and value of their stock, is very observable.[104]

Barter was still the preferred method of payment in Harper's third ledger (1816-1820). As Gubbins also observed, lumbering the virgin stands and quarrying plaster and grindstones had gained in importance.[105] Increased affluence also raised the level of alcohol consumption, of note in the accounts of William Steadman,[106] John Bowser,[107] and Christian Treitz,[108] who bought gin, bitters, toddy, brandy, wine, and large quantities of rum. William Steadman also smoked, a habit he shared with Henry Stultz, Christian Treitz, and John Lutz. Bowser received credits to his accounts by making clothes for Harper's family and customers, such as "trowsers" and coats for £0:7:6 each and "surtout pantaloon" overpants for £1:13:9, but also offered veal, lamb, and beef from his farm[109] in addition to cash. Steadman made nails and paid with a "note", a form of cashless transfer of funds, which came to be used with increasing frequency. Lumberman Henry Stultz exchanged thousands of feet of boards, floor planks, clapboard siding, and large quantities of shingles for sundries such as silk, onions, raisins, molasses, shoes, a teapot, and tobacco.[110]

Whereas the Stultz's business reflects an unchanging production of lumber over the twelve years covered by the last two Harper Ledgers, Peter Lutz Sr.'s activities are an example of versatility and adaptation to changing demands along the Petitcodiac. By 1818, payments of beef, butter, apples, oats, potatoes, and, for the first time, cheese and hay (by the ton) were augmented by the sale of home-made buskins and "stone" (grindstones). Whereas shoes, shoe repairs, and the previously mentioned carpentry work may have been a steady form of employment,[111] substantial sums were also involved in the quarrying of stone. One delivery alone fetched £10:15:0.[112] Payments with stone by several members of the Lutz and Stieff families, like Peter Lutz Sr.'s sons Peter Jr. and William and Henry Stieff Sr., but above all by Michael Ricker and his son Jacob, clearly show that the Petitcodiac Germans became part of this industry which "constantly employ[ed] upwards of 5,000 tons of shipping."[113] Production from the Stieffs' two sawmills in Hillsborough, to judge by the entries in the Harper Ledgers, surpassed the output of the Stultz operation on Mill ("Stultz") Creek. In addition, the Stieffs as a family offered considerable diversity of product line, as earlier examples illustrate. Even Reuben Steeves, the "troublesome recruit" of 1811, settled down with a family and paid for household necessities with hay, stone, wood, and barrels of flour. Peter Lutz Sr.'s oldest son, Michael, followed the example of other Petitcodiac Germans and built and operated a sawmill in the 1820's after he crossed the river from Hillsborough to establish himself near Fox Creek.[114]

The Harper Ledgers also reveal certain trade relationships, such as those between Michael Ricker and the business partners Thomas Prince, Ichabod Lewis, and William Steadman,[115] and they provide information on the status of a number of Petitcodiac Germans as employers and employees. Solomon Trites, for example, was a successful farmer, who paid William Harper with mutton, beef, pork, veal, tallow, and buckwheat. On several occasions, he also paid cash for purchases on John Broom's account with Harper, suggesting that Trites paid for Broom's bills in lieu of wages.[116] Michael Ricker did the same for a David Dickey from Amherst. On the other hand, a local hand like William Trites received £1:15: 0 from Harper for general labour, including repairs to the schooner *Weasel*.[117] John Lutz Jr. paid for merchandise by hauling goods, Andrew Sommer by ploughing, and Matthias Sommer by "1 day's teaming."[118] Michael Lutz earned £4:10:0 by building "stere [stair] frames", possibly for Harper's new store, and £9:0:0 from James Kelly, innkeeper and partner in business with Israel Powell, for a "store [?] frame".[119]

Certain exotic imports, such as coffee,[120] "Madeira Wine", silk, and "Marocca[n] slippers",[121] which some Petitcodiac Germans could afford, illustrate their passage beyond the hard and modest "pioneer" lifestyle of the early years. This process was hastened by events in Europe, where Napoleon cut the British off from the continent, causing them temporarily to rely more on supplies from their North American colonies. Better access to American markets after the War of 1812 partially filled the gap left at the conclusion of these hostilities. A unique example of this transition can be found in the provisions of Abraham Treitz's will,[122] made out on November 26, 1810.[123] His second wife, Experience,[124] whom he had married less than two years previously, received an annuity of £74, which assured her a comfortable standard of living. Abraham also looked after his children. The executors were instructed "... to teach, or cause to be taught ... [his son] Abraham ... to qualify him to be bound an apprentice to a merchant at age sixteen and give him two suits of clothes."[125] The second of his under-aged sons, John, was to receive "schooling fit for a Farmer."[126] Although Abraham Trites Jr. never lived to become a merchant -- he died at age 15 less than a year after his father -- the provision shows Abraham Sr.'s recognition that employment in trade and commerce had become an accepted alternate "profession" for Petitcodiac Germans. An inventory carried out in June of 1811 by Moncton assessors Ichabod Lewis and Malcolm Wilmot estimated the value of Abraham Treitz's assets at £3,772. This represented remarkable wealth at a time when a labourer earned £0:4:0 a day, a supper and bed at an inn cost £0:2:0, a cow about £6, a gallon of rum £0:5:0 - £ 0:10:0, an iron shovel £0:7:6, and a beaver hat £1:10:0.[127] Both Abraham Treitz Sr. (fig. 55) and Jr. are buried in the Wilson Cemetery, Moncton, beside the family

Figure 55

Abraham and Margaret (Jones) Treitz' tombstones (alongside those of their children) in the "Wilson Cemetery" in Allison.

Photo: Rainer L. Hempel

339

farm. When Christian Treitz welcomed Joseph Gubbins in 1811 into his brick house overlooking Bald Marsh, he had already lost both parents, his brother Jacob and, very recently, his brother Abraham. His sister Rosanna lived more than a decade longer, but Christian survived all his siblings, to the dawn of the stagecoach era; he died in 1836 and was buried in the Free Meeting House Cemetery.

None of these farming and trading activities would have been possible without access to land and raw materials. The freedom for which their forebears had fought in vain in the Peasant Wars made the attainment of a higher standard of living possible. Peter Fisher, author of *Sketches of New Brunswick*, published in Saint John in 1825, in which he attempted to take stock of and report on the Province's contemporary state of affairs, recognized the impact of finally becoming "yeomen" along the shores of the Petitcodiac River. Fisher writes of the settlers' spirit of freedom, their reliance on their resourcefulness with their axes and a few other simple tools to provide themselves with houses and most implements of husbandry.[128] It was precisely this material, wood, and access to it, which led to personal independence, something that had been altogether denied the peasants of Germany.[129] Princes jealously guarded their "divine" right to forests and all that they yielded, i.e. lumber and game, because they knew all too well that wood represented wealth and power. By denying access to it, princes were able to perpetuate serfdom.[130] By emigrating, the Petitcodiac Germans and Loyalists each in their own way broke loose from this artificial, "slavish" dependency on the upper classes in an attempt to gain personal "freedom" -- or at least the chance to attain a self-reliant way of life -- where freedom, land, and wood stood side by side in the equation for success.

It was, however, the recognition of the settlers that attainment of this freedom was not enough if they were to continue to prosper. The acceptance of trade and commerce as alternatives to farming and hunting brought them into the business world and its practices such as litigation. Whereas payment for goods sold by William Harper was expected only when barter items became available, court records[131] of the day indicate that businessmen and others frequently resorted to litigation to ensure payment. Unfortunately, extant court minutes do not reveal any of the details regarding these disagreements, only the verdict in general terms. Probably during Michael

Ricker's time of insolvency in 1808,[132] William Harper sued for £12:1:4 "for damages which the said William Harper has sustained by reason of the non-performance of the promises and undertakings made by the said defendant Michael Ricker." The frequency of court appearances made by William Harper and James Watson Esq. suggest less than cordial relations with other Petitcodiac German customers too, such as William Harper versus Peter Lutz Jr. in 1818 and Charles and William Lutz in 1823, and James Watson versus Solomon Trites in 1810.

Trust in the justice system, such as it was then, is not surprising among Anglophones, and a large number of cases were brought before the Westmorland Court of Common Pleas, including suits against Petitcodiac Germans and Loyalists of German descent. For example, in June 1804 John Steadman Beckwith successfully sued "Lewis Steves" for £54:12:3 in damages and £3:14:1 in legal fees. At the same court session, Joseph Coffin was able to convince the judge that "Mathew Steve" owed him £100:11:0 for damages. These were substantial sums; however most suits involved smaller amounts, such as the one between Moncton businessman James Kelly and Christian Stieff in 1818 for the usual "damages sustained by reason of non-performance of promises." In this instance, Christian Stieff had to pay £7:12:1 and the customary legal fees, which usually amounted to between £2 and £4.

The German settlers also sought justice in matters against their English debtors. A particularly frequent plaintiff in 1808 was businessman Jacob Steeve,[133] who successfully sued Hugh Gallagher, Joseph Woodworth, William Barker, and Lewis Smith together for well over £100. Whereas John O'Neil's "endebtedness" to Mathew Steeve amounted to a little over £5 in 1805, a single Susannah "Luts" took bachelor Alexander Smith[134] to court for a sizable amount in 1813 and won. The award of an even £100 suggests that a non-monetary matter had been contested for which the defendant had to pay such large compensation, well over a year's wages for a labourer. German Loyalists also took legal action against Anglophones. The most active and successful was Titus Knapp, who was involved in no fewer than a dozen court cases between 1791 and 1823. Other names in this context are Henry Stultz, who sued Samuel Cornwell in 1788, and jeweller Peter Etter of Cumberland, who sued John Lockhart in 1790 and Gilbert Forsyth in 1791.[135]

Court actions in which both plaintiff and defendant were Petitcodiac Germans or German Loyalists may on one hand shatter the myth of blissful coexistence, on the other hand illustrate the growing trust in the laws and legal processes of their adopted country. It will be remembered that the settlers of Germantown, N.B., had rejected Thomas Calhoun as Justice of the Peace in the difficult years before 1770 and appointed one from amongst their own midst. Such suspicion and distrust had been allayed at least by 1785, from which date court records are available. The earliest date of a German settler suing another is November 19, 1788, when Jacob Treitz Sr. was awarded £7:2:11 in a decision against Martin Beck.[136] The only other example is that of an Elizabeth "Somers"[137] who, on September 8, 1818, successfully sued Christian Stieff of Moncton for £16:9:7. There are several instances in which German Loyalist descendants were involved, such as Titus Knapp in 1791 versus Martin Beck and Eldad Tupper, forbearer of Sir Charles Tupper.

A number of these trials in civil matters were conducted by judge and jury, and in the 1780's names of Petitcodiac Germans begin to appear in the court abstracts as "Petit Jurors", such as Abraham and Solomon "Trites" and Michael Lutz.[138] These "Jurors" were "summond at General Sessions of the Peace Holden at Westmorland in the County of Westmorland in the Province of New Brunswick."[139] The minutes of these sessions are available for the years 1785 to 1809, providing new insight into the roles these people played in the administration of their municipalities, as "Petit Jurors" by the end of the 18th century and eventually as members of the County's "Grand Jury" judicial system at the turn of the 19th century. The Grand Jury was called upon to deliberate on more serious, criminal matters, such as "riot", "Assault & Battery,"[140] "retailing Liquor without being licenced," or more commonly, "indebted[ness] to our Sovereign Lord the King"[141] (i.e. non-payment of taxes). In the first copy of Peace Session minutes available, Henry Stultz was listed as a "Grand Jury" member and Titus Knapp a "Petit Juror", suggesting that these German Loyalist descendants received immediate recognition in their communities, only one or two years after arrival, undoubtedly also on account of their better financial circumstances;

all other Grand Jurors were of British or American origin. The situation was reversed at the local level. The list of "Town Officers" for the year 1785 provides names of residents for four townships: Westmorland, Sackville, Hopewell, and "Petcudiack" ("Monckton" and "Hillsborough" combined). In 1786, "Monkton" is listed as a separate community, where the early German settlers filled nine out of thirteen available positions. Christian Treitz was the "Commissioner of Highways", William Wilson and Christopher Horseman "Surveyors of Roads", and Christian Stieff and Jacob Treitz Jr. the "Constables". "Overseers of [the] Poor" were Christian Treitz and "Lodwick" Stieff, and Abraham Treitz became "Town Clerk", a position he held for several years, as well as "Fence Viewer". William Wilson, Jacob Treitz Jr., and Henry Jones were "Assessors", and Jacob Treitz Jr. also "Collector of Taxes". In Hillsborough, four of thirteen positions were held by Heinrich Stieff's sons,[142] but there were peak years when the number of Germans reached ten of eighteen, as in 1790.[143] The ratio in Moncton was not to change a great deal over the next twenty years, except for the office holders' names, as the younger men such as John Lutz, Andrew Sommer, and Jacob Wortman attained maturity. In Hillsborough, Peter Lutz and Michael Ricker[144] assumed positions alongside those held by the Stieffs, and in Salisbury where Jacob Wortman lived from the late nineties on, he showed his versatility beginning in 1800 as "Commissioner of Highways", "Surveyor of Highways", "Collector of Taxes", and "Overseer of the Poor". Other town positions were added over time and as the need arose, such as "Pound Keepers", "Hogreaves", "Surveyors of Lumber", "Surveyors of Hay", and "Inspectors of Butter". When thistles became a problem in 1797, Jacob Stieff and Abraham Treitz were appointed "Inspectors of Thistles" for Hillsborough and Moncton, respectively, and when the decision was made in 1801 to build a new "Court House and Gaol" in Dorchester and to distribute the building costs over all seven County parishes, Michael Ricker became the collector for Hillsborough, Solomon Trites for Moncton, and Jacob Wortman for Salisbury.

The responsibilities of these office holders were clearly defined, as the example of the "Hogreave" illustrates. In a lengthy ordinance at the General Session of the Peace in 1802, regulations were drawn up that no bulls, stallions, boars, or rams were allowed to roam freely at certain times of the year. Particular attention was paid to pigs in that "no owner of any swine living within one mile of any neighbour or other Inhabitant shall suffer any swine to go at large out of his own pen, inclosure or pasture from the first day of April to the first day of December, unless such swine is sufficiently ringed on penalty of two shillings each swine for every offence ....."[145] It was the duty of the "Hogreave" upon complaint "to yoke such Hog for which he shall be entitled to receive two shillings .... And in case any Hogreave shall neglect to do his duty, for each neglect or offence he shall incur the penalty of the Law of the Province for Neglect of Duty."[146] The nature of these penalties is not elaborated upon, but all farmers must have been cognizant of the fines which accompanied such offences. Andrew Sommer, in 1794, was the first Petitcodiac German to be appointed hogreave.

Whereas in 1785 no Petitcodiac Germans were listed as "Petit Jurors" for Westmorland County, seven of a total of twenty-five were appointed in 1791, signifying their rise in stature: five Stieffs, John Lutz, Christian Treitz, in addition to Martin Beck (probably Jr.) and Henry Stultz. Their inclusion within the judicial system undoubtedly boosted the Petitcodiac Germans' confidence overall, enabling them to refer matters of contention to the courts, as seen in earlier examples. It was a rare occurrence when a Petitcodiac German was summoned before the Grand Jury, as on June 16, 1795 in the case of "The King vs. Jacob Tritz [Jr.]." "The Grand Jury present[ed] Jacob Tritz in feloniously stealing one hoe the property of Donald McDonald."[147] The Grand Jury, no doubt sensing the frivolous nature of McDonald's accusation, returned a "Not Guilty" verdict. Beginning in 1802, some Petitcodiac Germans even advanced to the rank of "Grand Juror". Christian Stieff was the first, to be followed by Christian Treitz, Frederick Stieff, Abraham Treitz, "Johannes" and Peter Lutz, and John and Matthias Stieff. The largest number in any given year was three out of a total of thirteen in the County appointed in 1804.

So strong was the German presence in Moncton and Hillsborough that many Anglophone families were drawn into their sphere of influence and ethnicity, just as had happened earlier in Pennsylvania where such surnames as MacDonald and Jones were encountered among members of German-speaking congregations. The 1851 censuses for Hillsborough, Coverdale, and Moncton reveal that all descendants of Charles Jones and Christopher Horsman considered themselves of German origin; Peter Jonah's descendants in Moncton called themselves German although those in Hillsborough preferred to be known as "Swedes". Others who claimed German origins include: Abraham Mitton, Charles McLean, John Crossman, all the Wilburs, and six of seven Wilson families of Moncton.[148] The Jones brothers had, of course, been living amongst the Germans since 1766, if not earlier, and, according to the Millidge Report, William Wilson since about 1779 and Christopher Horsman 1785. As all of these individuals' genealogies reveal, they and their descendants were married to Petitcodiac Germans many times over. It is not surprising that 19th-century historians believed Charles Jones's "real" name to be *Karl Johannes*!

The examples cited from the Harper Ledgers, Court Proceedings, and Sessions of the Peace for Westmorland underscore the high level of Petitcodiac German activity and their emergence from the "pioneer" stage. Their ethnic background did not benefit them initially, as they were no doubt strapped by financial and linguistic limitations, however the increasing frequency of appointments to public office and successes in farming and business were the result of Old Country values, such as Pietistic perseverance, hard work, and the ability to improvise and seek out new opportunities for their children, including those presented by "Planters" and Loyalists. Such documented evidence contradicts the notion that the Petitcodiac Germans were a simple folk who squandered the toil of the first generation by selling out to more energetic, enterprising Loyalists since the latters' successes were also contingent upon the Germans' spirit of cooperation and integration. It shows that they were leaving behind what Roeber claimed to be the German "obsession with household, family, property, and liberty of conscience"[149] to assert themselves in the affairs of the wider community.

This step into the Anglophone business and political realm, combined with geographic dispersion, mentioned above, hastened the loss of German as a language of communication. Abraham Treitz's stipulation that his daughter be taught to read and write in her mother tongue and John Lutz's signature in German script are evidence of continued use of their forefathers' language and efforts to maintain it in the years after 1800. The number of descendants claiming German background in the 1851, 1861, and 1871

345

Moncton Censuses show at least an awareness of their heritage until that time.

German as a spoken language appears to have survived a little longer in areas of southern New Brunswick where German-speaking Loyalists settled, as their numbers and better financial situation permitted a more conscious maintenance of linguistic and cultural pursuits. In keeping with the German penchant to spend their leisure time in clubs and societies, German Loyalists in Saint John founded the *Steinhammer* ("Stonehammer") *Club* for the study of local geological formations. As George Frederic Matthew[150] remembered it, the first members had gone to school in Philadelphia's Schuylkill River region (i.e. Germantown) and brought their collections with them to Saint John. Dr. Abraham Gesner was a member during his residence in Saint John. In the years when minutes of this club are available, i.e. 1861-1863, 1877-1878, and 1907-1908, the language of record had become English. The beginnings and purpose of the *Donnerstag ("Thursday") Club*, [151] whose programme for 1894 has survived, are less certain but, to judge by such societies in Germany named after days of the week, it was most likely a literary circle.

An "unflattering" example of German language and leisure activity is revealed in the following glimpse of early Saint John, found in the "confession of Peter Ackerman,"[152] one of four German Loyalists by this surname from New Jersey. Ackerman admitted to having "a bowl of grog" at Joseph Cutler's tavern in the company of Loyalist John "Rickets"[153] and fellow German Michael Knull. There they met up with the threesome Kemper, Rosman, and Nowland, who had a disagreement about staying at the inn. Rosman addressed Kemper in German first, then apparently physically assaulted him, at which point Ackerman entered into the fray: "... [he] thinks or does not know but that he also struck Kemper two or three times -- Ackerman says he himself was in liquor ...."[154]

The arrival of the German Loyalist Christopher Sauer in Saint John in 1785 with his wife and three children, a printing press, fonts of the best type, intent on launching a newspaper appeared to augur well for the publication of German reading material considering the tradition which he had continued from his father and grandfather in Pennsylvania. Although known for his

346

bold and energetic initiatives in the newspaper business, in provincial politics, and as a postmaster, it seems peculiar that he does not appear to have printed anything in German in Saint John despite the sizable German Loyalists population.

It is possible that Sauer considered the market too small, or he realized that little could be gained by competing against the well-established German printer Anthon Heinrich from Halifax, which had benefitted from a more continuous flow of German-speaking immigrants. A sizeable number of Germans destined for the settlement of Lunenburg chose to remain in Halifax, where they occupied at least two whole streets,[155] as the name "Dutch Village" implies. Moses Delesdernier, the later Hillsborough resident, was one of these early inhabitants, and Henry (Heinrich) Uthoff, whom Clark Wright listed as a New Brunswick Loyalist,[156] was on the executive of the *German Society* or *Hochteutsche Gesellschaft* founded on February 28, 1785, showing the continued interconnection and improved mobility between Nova Scotia and New Brunswick.

Since the German-speaking population of Nova Scotia numbered between 2,000 and 3,000 and, as Anthon Heinrich argued, "... a great number of almanacs ... is brought annually from the State of Pennsylvania into the Province and bought by the inhabitants of this land,"[157] he decided to produce an almanac in German. He prefaced the *Hochdeutsche Neu-Schottländische Calender* with the following entry:

> ... And so, it is through this printing shop that I want to expend my utmost effort to keep our native language in a current usage of which no old, upright German will be ashamed, not only in this land, but also in the United States of America -- although many of our youths in their presumption manifest an aversion to that.[158]

If Pennsylvanian almanacs were sold in Halifax and Lunenburg, they and those from the Haligonian press were probably also available in New Brunswick until the middle of the 19th century when the demand for such German language publications ceased with the passing of the second generation Petitcodiac Germans.

ENDNOTES

[1] Charles J. Humber, U.E., National President, The United Empire Loyalists' Association of Canada (1982-1984), foreword to Joan Magee, *Loyalist Mosaic, A* Multi-Ethnic Heritage (Toronto: Dundurn Press Ltd., 1984), p.13.

[2] *Ibid.,* p. 16.

[3] Magee, *Loyalist Mosaic,* pp. 19-22.

[4] *Ibid.,* p. 14.

[5] Cf. Knittle, *Early ... Palatine Emigration,* pp. 188-220.

[6] Magee, "John Dulmage (c. 1740 - c. 1814): A Loyalist of Palatine German Origin," *Loyalist Mosaic,* p. 180.

[7] *Ibid.,* p.15; Humber claims Johnson was of Scottish descent. Hartmut Fröschle, in *Die Deutschen in Kanada* (Eckart-Schriften, Heft 101 [Wien: Österreichische Landsmannschaft, 1987], p. 17), considers him to be of Irish origin.

[8] Hartmut Fröschle, *Die Deutschen in Kanada,* pp. 16ff..

[9] Clark Wright, *The Loyalists of New Brunswick,* p. 330.

[10] *Loc. cit..* The question of a religious origin of the Loyalist stance has so far been neglected: J. M. Bumsted, *Understanding the Loyalists* (Mount Allison University, Sackville, N.B.: Centre for Canadian Studies, 1986).

[11] Durnbaugh, "The Sauer Family: An American Printing Dynasty," p. 36.

[12] *Loc. cit..*

[13] Durnbaugh,"The Sauer Family: An American Printing Dynasty," p. 36.

[14] Magee, *Loyalist Mosaic,* p. 25.

[15] Fröschle, *Die Deutschen in Kanada,* p. 15.

[16] Maxwell Sutherland, "Case History of a Settlement", *Dalhousie Review,* Vol. 41, 1961-1962, pp. 65-74.

[17] Fröschle, *Die Deutschen in Kanada,* p. 14.

[18] Cameron Nish, "The 1760's", *Colonists and Canadians 1760-1867,* J. M. S. Careless, ed. (Toronto: Macmillan of Canada, 1971), p. 9.

[19] Clark Wright, *The Loyalists of New Brunswick* (Wolfville, N.S.: Lancelot Press, 1955), pp. 27ff..

[20] David Bell suggests that about 10,000 Loyalists spread out along the St. John Valley; David Graham Bell, *Early Loyalist Saint John* (Fredericton, N.B.: New Ireland Press, 1983), p. 17.

[21] Clark Wright, *The Loyalists of New Brunswick,* p. 159.

[22] Heinz Lehmann, *The German-Canadians 1750-1937: Immigration, Settlement and Culture,* transl., ed., and intr. Gerhard P. Bassler (St. John's, Nfld.: Jesperson Press, 1986), p. 43.

[23] Although the real number of descendants must have been much larger, the 1871 Census reveals that 2,006 New Brunswickers of the lower St. John River and 563 from York and Carleton Counties, the main Loyalist settlement areas, were aware of their German origin. By comparison, only 1,536 from the Petitcodiac River area declared their German ancestry in this census, underscoring again the relatively large German component among the Loyalists.

[24] D. Bell, *Early Loyalist Saint John*, pp. 175-255.

[25] John Behn of Hillsborough claimed to be a refugee from Augustine, U.S.A; PANB, Microfilm no. F 1032 (1786).

[26] Colonel Gubbins mentioned Dr. Gunter as having a practice in Fredericton in 1811. (*Gubbins' Journals*, p. 26). Dr. Charles Gunter (1762-1835) came from Prussia and had served as a surgeon in the Revolution.

[27] Michael Kern was a German Reformed (Calvinist) minister who appealed in August 1785 to His Excellency Thomas Carleton, Esq., of New Brunswick for support because he had been unable to find a congregation and could not "keep his family any longer from the utmost distress"; PANB, Memorial of Michael Kern.

[28] German Loyalists must have had continued contact with one another years after their arrival in New Brunswick, as can be traced in New Brunswick probate records. Christian Stroeder/Straeder, for example, made out a will (proved March 1800) which was witnessed by fellow German Loyalists James Sarvenier and Christopher Sauer; James Sarvanier, in turn, had his will witnessed by John Wolhaupter in 1803.

[29] Charles Schoenewolff, a member of the "Hessian Regiment du Corps" received a land grant on the "West side of the Meppech River" in New Brunswick in 1786; PANB, New Brunswick Land Grants, Microfilm F 1032.

[30] Obvious German names not identified as such include (those from D. Bell's list are marked "*"): Acker, Ackerman(n), Bancker, Bauch, Bayer, Beck, Betner, Blauvelt (*Blaufeld*), Blume, Bohle, Brett, Brinkerhoff, Burkestaff (*Burksdorf*), Dann*, Ludwig DeBeck, Decker, Duer, Dickerman(n), Diemar, Dier, Dif(f)endorf, Drost, Egbert, Erbe, Etter, Fass*, Ferdinand, Feudal*, Fick, Fis(c)her, Frink, Frit(s)ch, Gabel*, Ganter, Gesner, Geyer, Grass, Griff, Grim(m)*, Hagerman, Hallibach, Hamm, Hammel(l), Hanse*, Hanselpacker, Harbel*, Harkels*, Hauzman(n), Heister, Heller, Helm, Hoffman(n), Horner, Houzer (*Hauser*), Hutz, Hydecker (*Heidecker*), Kaiser/Kaizer/Keyser/Keezer, Kauzman(n), Kelberbrack, Knapp, Knepelner, Kniffen, Lantz, Leibig*, Lodwick*, Mann, Manzer, Marks, Maul, Myer (*Meier/Mayer*), Nase, Ol(t)z, Ott*, Ostermann, Puntzius, Quark*, Reisner*, Rheinwald, Ruland*, Sanger, Scheck, Schiek*, Schierman(n)/Sherman, Schurman(n), Shafner* (*Schaffner*), Sprick, Springer, Staal, Steenberrich, Stelle, Stern(e), Stultz, Tell*, Tupper, Uhthoff, Utt*, Ull, Waltman (*Waldmann*), Wanser*, Wicke, Wolf, Wolhaupter, and Wort/Wert.

[31] *Loc.cit.*. The point that "the settlers of New Brunswick were not too far from being a cross-section of the population of the old colonies" is also made by Howard Temperley, the editor of *Gubbins' New Brunswick Journals*, p. xviii. Unfamiliarity with the German language has led to peculiar statements, for example: "Matthias Somers was probably English or Welsh, as Somers is basically a British name ...;" Geneva Jones Emberley, *Descendants of Charles Jones of New Brunswick from 1766* (No place: no publisher, no date), p. 5.

[32] The name "Whicknact" occurs in the list of those who petitioned for land in New Brunswick in 1841; PANB, New Brunswick Land Grants, Microfilm, F 6637.

[33] An interesting life story relates to the Hessian soldier, *Kratz*, who was taken prisoner in the Burgoyne debacle with General von Riedesel's men, deserted, rejoined his regiment, was shipped back to Germany against his will, came back to his American wife, settled on the shores of Lake Erie, had a large family, and changed his name in 1791 to "Scratch"; Johannes Helmut Merz, "Johann Leonard Kratz, 1756-1829: A Hessian Soldier's Story of Hardship and Love", *German-Canadian Yearbook,* VIII (Toronto: Historical Society of Mecklenburg, 1994), pp. 245-262.

[34] George Young, a Loyalist, who settled in Saint John, came from Germany; D. Bell, *Early Loyalist Saint John*, p. 255.

[35] *Armbrust* is the German word for "crossbow", so that *Armbruster* means "crossbowman".

[36] This name was left off the list in the fourth edition of Clark Wright's book, *The Loyalists of New Brunswick*, 1981, but a descendant, Ralph B. Cathline, carried out detailed research and found that the father of U.E.L. Philip Keithline was the son of Johann Peter Küchlein, who emigrated from Kirchheimbolanden, Rhineland-Palatinate, to Pennsylvania in 1742.

[37] PANB, New Brunswick Land Grants, Microfilm F 1044, April 30, 1805.

[38] V. "Bing" Geldart and Ken Kanner, *Marriage Register Westmorland County, N.B.: 1790-1856* (No place: V. "Bing" Geldart and Ken Kanner, 1985).

[39] PANB, Index of New Brunswick Land Petitions, Microfilm F 6632 to F 6637.

[40] A few such names are: Asche, Benn, Bergen, Berger, Bettel, Biers, Blaau, Blaicher, Eckerman(n), Brenner, Buber, Buche, Eber, Eisler/Esler (variously spelled Isler, Estler, Esler, Ester, or Easler), Erwin (Ervin, Irvin), Faltz, Faus, Hagemeister, Hubbel, Hultz, Korner (*Körner*), Leister, Leizer, Lemke, Loden, Manser, Mesler, Messer, Mosher (Moser), Priester, Pulke, Rauzman(n), Remphoff, Rheim, Rolf, Ruckel, Schank, Schaules, Speer, Steinberg, Steinburg, Strech, Tann, Tempelman(n), Toback, Wagner, Wenn, Wetzel, Wirt, Witter, and Witzell.

[41] Clark Wright, *The Loyalists of New Brunswick*, p. 228.

[42] *Loc. cit.*.

[43] Cf. Kapp, *Geschichte* ..., Chapter 5: "Die erste Pfälzer Niederlassung in Neuburg am Hudson", Chapter 6: "Die pfälzisch-schwäbische Zwangs=Kolonie am obern Hudson," Chapter 7: "Flucht der Deutschen nach und Ansiedlung in Schoharie," Chapter 8: "Die Deutschen am Mohawk."

[44] David Artiss, "German Cultural Heritage Studies in Atlantic Canada," *Proceedings of the Atlantic University Teachers of German Conference 1979*, Rainer L. Hempel, ed. (Sackville, N. B.: Mount Allison University Press, 1979), p. 76. In 1979 there was a 96-year-old Lunenburger who could still speak German and some years previously, 94-year-old John Hirtle, who "was completely fluent in speech and song". Even today, there are reports from isolated areas about Lunenburgers with some command of German.

[45] The change of spelling from Lutz to Lutes only became established after the turn of the 20th century.

[46] A German Loyalist family is the "Fis(c)hers", of whom there are eight entries in Clark Wright's book, *The Loyalists of New Brunswick*. Two of these were brothers Ludwig and Peter Sr., who were among the last to arrive in New Brunswick before the onset of winter in late 1783. These brothers are of particular interest because of a rare account which a Fisher granddaughter collected from various conversations with Ludwig's wife, Mary, of the family's hardship and struggles during their first winter in New Brunswick. This family is also important because Ludwig and Mary's third child, Peter Fisher Jr., authored the first book on life in New Brunswick (Peter Fisher, *The First History of New Brunswick*, 1825, reprinted Woodstock, N.B.: Non-Entity Press, 1983). Many of Peter Fisher's seven sons and five daughters, as well as their descendants, became prominent and successful citizens of this Province such as Charles Fisher, premier of New Brunswick from 1854-1856 and 1857-1861 and Father of Confederation.

[47] Eldad Tupper is a forefather of Sir Charles Tupper, one of the "Fathers of Confederation" and Prime Minister of Canada. The Tuppers migrated from Kassel, Germany, to the New England States and came as Loyalists to Nova Scotia: Georg Weissenborn, "The Germans in Canada: A chronological survey of Canada's third European ethnic group from 1644 to 1977," *German-Canadian Yearbook*, IV (Toronto: Historical Society of Mecklenburg Upper Canada Inc., 1978), p. 42. Cf. also Clark Wright, *The Loyalists of New Brunswick*, p. 336. The Tupper family settled for several years in Westmorland, N.B., where Eldad served as officer in various capacities before relocating to Amherst, N.S..

[48] The American ambassador to Berlin for many years, J.B. Shurman, was descended from a respected German family from Bedeque, P.E.I.; Lehmann, *Zur Geschichte des Deutschtums in Kanada*, pp. 36f.. Schurman is a common name on Prince Edward Island today.

[49] Born in New York in 1771, John Wolhaupter was the son of Gottfried (later Geoffrey) Wolhaupter, a native of Saxony, Germany, who was in New York in 1759. John Wolhaupter arrived in Saint John well after the first wave of Loyalists had settled in New Brunswick, advertising himself in 1799 as a silversmith and watchmaker. He decided to move to Fredericton, where he advertised in 1819 that he intended to carry on the gold and silver business in Camperdown Street. Several pieces of John Wolhaupter's silver (marked with his initials "J.W.") are still found in New Brunswick. His son, Benjamin, was born in 1800 and, like his father, became a silversmith. He succeeded Edward Winslow as Sheriff of York County and remained in office for ten years until his death in 1857. Benjamin's son, Charles, became a silversmith, too, setting up shop in Chatham, N.B. in the 1830's, and another son, George, became a watchmaker. Young George Wolhaupter was an apprentice in his father's shop alongside Benjamin Tibbets, the later inventor of the compound steam engine, who became a trained watchmaker under Wolhaupter's tutelage.

[50] Peter Etter Jr. was a loyal Swiss-German jeweller after whose descendants "Etter Ridge" is named, which overlooks Fort Beauséjour and the Tatramar Marshes outside Sackville, N.B.. He was the son of Peter Etter Sr., who had emigrated from Switzerland in 1737 and whose stocking factory in Braintree had prospered, especially after his appointment as supplier to the British army. When the revolution came, his friendship and business connections with the Franklin brothers Benjamin and John and John Adams, later President of the United States, were of little benefit. The Etters had become Moravians, or members of the *Herrnhuter Brüdergemeine*, whose pacifism brought them into conflict with the revolutionary councils. (Their example and that of the Sauer family underscore the religious component of the Loyalist stance which has been ignored in past studies.) They had to flee to Boston in January of 1775, where Etter Sr. was appointed by the British authorities as official interpreter of French and German. Three months later they arrived in Halifax. Since the Etters had to leave all their looms and materials from the family business behind, Peter Etter Jr. became a sergeant in Colonel Joseph Gorham's Royal Fencible Americans, raised in 1775 for the defence of the Province of Nova Scotia and consisting mainly of Loyalist Americans. He was one of the defenders of Fort Cumberland in November 1776 when Jonathan Eddy and his band of American sympathizers launched their attack, and he returned to the area after the war, married, and became a jeweller. On the return voyage from Boston, his ship struck Briar Island December 26, 1797, and all the crew and passengers were drowned or frozen to death on the island.

[51] Adèle Hempel, *Chronology of Events Relating to the Prince-Lewis House*, type-written preliminary chronology of the Prince-Lewis House from 1770 to the present (1998), MAUL, Bell Collection.

352

[52] Listed in Clark Wright's *The Loyalists of New Brunswick,* are the names of two German Loyalists, the twin brothers Henry and Abraham Gesner (Sr.), both of whom served in the King's Orange Regiment. The Gesners are descendants of a renowned Swiss-German family. Konrad Gesner (1516-1565) earned his reputation as a gifted naturalist, scholar, and precursor of modern botany, and the later Solomon Geßner (1730-1788) became a well-known painter and poet. Henry and Abraham Gesner's grandfather was a learned man who emigrated from the Palatinate to America around the same time as the Petitcodiac Germans. The invaluable contribution which Henry Gesner's son, Abraham, made in the publication of his first book on geology, *Remarks on the Geology and Mineralogy of Nova Scotia* (pub. 1836), earned him a commission in 1838 to undertake a geological survey of New Brunswick and the distinction of being Canada's first geology consultant as well as the first provincial geologist in the British Empire. In recognition of his hydrocarbon research, he has been given the title "Father of the Petroleum Industry".

[53] Henry Stultz (Stults), a sawyer, arrived on the ship *Thetis* in 1783 with other Westchester Loyalists, such the Lewis family and Reuben Mills. His wife, Elizabeth (*née* Lewis), bore him at least nine children: Mary (* c. 1784), Sarah (* c. 1786), Henry Jr. (* c. 1787/1788), Elizabeth (* c. 1788), Gilbert (* 1790/1791), Abraham (* July 1793 † Jan. 3, 1875), Ann (* 1795/1796 † 1888), John (* c. 1804 † 1899), and Lewis (* c. 1806); cf. Stultz Family Genealogy by P.A. Fillmore, 1348 Robie St., Halifax, N.S..

[54] PANB, Province of New Brunswick Land Registry, Microfilm F 1042, February 7, 1801.

[55] *Province of New Brunswick Crown Land Grant Index* (Fredericton, N.B.: Natural Resources and Energy, 1988), I, 935: June 19, 1817.

[56] There are 19 entries of the name Stultz in the 1999/2000 Moncton telephone book and 4 in Sackville.

[57] *Province of New Brunswick Crown Land Grant Index,* II, 2479: Sept. 2, 1829.

[58] Pincombe and Larracey, *Resurgo,* I, pp. 103f.. The Steadman and Gesner families met in Cornwallis, N.S.. Jacob Gesner likely became acquainted with his wife-to-be during visits to Uncle Steadman in Moncton. It is unknown what trade Jacob pursued at "The Bend" in addition to farming or whether he had any business associations with his uncle. Years later, however, William Steadman's son, John, entered a mining agreement with Abraham Gesner, "... of the City of Halifax, geologist"; cf. WRO, Libro DD, 302, registered March 19, 1852. This may have involved Albertite deposits in Albert County which Gesner was not permitted to mine.

[59] It is significant to note that the Jacob Treitz Sr. property supported a long line of blacksmiths until the late 19th century: Jacob Treitz Sr., Christian

353

Treitz, James Watson (∗ c. 1760), Wm. Steadman Sr. (∗ 1776/1777), Solomon Powell (∗ c. 1750), Wm. Steadman Jr. (∗ 1809), John Beatty Jr., James Beatty II (∗ 1809), James E. Beatty (∗ 1830), and David Chapman.

[60] Marriage Application made out by Col. Robert Dixon in Cumberland, MAUA, Webster Collection (7001/134).

[61] *Loc. cit..* For the name Colpitts, cf. Esther Clark Wright, *Planters and Pioneers,* p. 87; *The Petitcodiac,* p. 57.

[62] WRO, Libro M-1, 13. Many of Steadman's earliest land sales went unrecorded, especially along the "Queen's Road" (Main Street), Moncton.

[63] Col. Gubbins observed the versatility of the people at the time: "The farmers, except those who contract for lumber, have almost everything made at home that is required for the use of their families. They are their own weavers, dyers, taylors, shoemakers and carpenters;" *Gubbins' Journals,* p. 23. Frederick Stieff's Last Will and Testament provides evidence of this versatility in the list of carpenter's tools of every description which were in his possession; Libro L-1, 181, Westmorland County Land Registry, Moncton. When payments had to be made for services such as a doctor's, they were often "in kind", such as those to Dr. Charles Gunther, whose fees were collected in the form of hay, salt fish, or pork; *Gubbins' Journals,* p. 26.

[64] Two of these ledgers, for the periods 1797-1799 and 1814-1820, are located in the Webster Collection at Mount Allison University and the third, for 1808-1810, at the Centre d'études acadiennes of the Université de Moncton. Occasional transactions which occurred outside these periods, especially long-term debts, are also contained in these ledgers.

[65] William Harper's first Ledger, MAUL, Webster Collection.

[66] This Michael Lutz may have been either Peter Lutz' s brother or son -- Harper does not specify.

[67] In the Harper Ledgers the name "Stieff" is variously spelled "Steves", "Steives", and "Steeves".

[68] Harper Ledger (1808-1810): December 12, 1808.

[69] Harper Ledgers (1797-1799): June 9, 1797; (1816-1820): Oct 17, 1817.

[70] The term "Seigr." behind the name in the second Harper Ledger means "Sr." and not "Esq.". Since Harper dealt primarily with Acadian customers from the Memramcook area in this ledger, it was likely a carryover from the French word "Seigneur" without conveying its meaning. The application of the term "Seign"/"Sr." to William Steeves illustrates this point, for he was no squire at 28 years of age! Harper was distinguishing this William from Matthias Stieff's William, born in 1775. In the first and third Ledgers, the terms "Jr.", "Sr.", and "Esq." were correctly used, the latter being an epithet of distinction that the bearer had ascended to the level of colonial gentry.

[71] Harper Ledger (1808-1810): August 8,1808.

[72] *Ibid.*, April 17,1808. This may have been "King" John Steeves, Jacob and Catharina Stieff's first son, who lived just up from Edgett's Landing.

[73] This is likely Christian Stieff's son, born in 1784, who referred in his Last Will and Testament on May 7, 1830 to his sugar camp up Coverdale River; WRO, Libro L-1, 516.

[74] This was probably Matthias and Sophia Stieff's second son, born May 3, 1788, who may have distinguished himself from Harper as "Jr." to avoid confusion.

[75] Harper Ledger (1808-1810): October 14, 1808.

[76] *Ibid.*, July 4, 1809.

[77] "... Lewis Steves and others in Hillsborough ... at the place called Mill Creek ... has built a Saw and Grist Mills...;" land sale by Joseph Woodsworth to James Watson, Esq., WRO, Libro C-1, 210: registered September 30, 1806.

[78] Harper Ledger, July 11, 1808.

[79] *Ibid.*, November 29, 1808.

[80] *Ibid.*, July 15, 1808; none of John's children were ready for their own homes at this early date, rather John may have wanted to expand his farmhouse for his large family -- his eleventh child was born in 1809!

[81] *Ibid.*, September 23, 1808.

[82] Matthias Stieff was another, who died on May 21, 1848. The longest surviving original settler was Mary Lutz, *née* Ricker, who was alive at 95 years of age in Coverdale when the 1851 Census was taken.

[83] Andrew Sommer's Last Will and Testament was made out on January 24, 1839 and executed on July 17, 1840; WPR, 1839-1842. Unfortunately, Andrew and Emily Sommer's burial sites are unknown although one would expect from Andrew's directions that they were buried at the Free Meeting House Cemetery, where son Mathias was buried five years after his father's decease.

[84] Harper Ledger (1808-1810): March 24, 1808.

[85] *Ibid.*, October 12, 1808.

[86] *Ibid.*, December 13, 1809.

[87] Harper weighed each butter quantity since the firkins delivered were of unequal size. Some customers paid with empty firkins which Harper could resell.

[88] Millidge Report.

[89] Harper Ledger (1808-1810): July 3, 1808.

[90] *Ibid.*, November 30, 1808.

[91] As of 1802, a school had been set up in "Monckton" and three in the Parish of Dorchester (one at Lewisville run by Mr. Lewis). £4 were set aside for a schoolmaster in "Steevesville" (Hillsborough). A Mr. Gleeson taught at the "Monckton" school; Sackville, N.B., Local Records, 1748-1883: Westmorland

355

County, N.B., Records of Proceedings at the General Session of the Peace, 1785-1809.

[92] Harper Ledger (1808-1810): November 26, 1808.

[93] On June 14, 1812, Michael Ricker ("yeoman") sold Jacob Ricker Jr.'s grant in Hillsborough; WRO, Libro C-1, 522: registered January 10, 1813.

[94] This is the grant for which he petitioned on January 28, 1786 with many others; PANB, New Brunswick Land Grants, Microfilm F 1032.

[95] *Ibid.*, Microfilm F 4178; my italics.

[96] *Loc.cit.*.

[97] Other Rickers, some of them perhaps related to those along the Petitcodiac, settled in New Brunswick, such as the previously mentioned Willem Ricker, who in 1805 claimed to have moved to Indian Island and Moose Island 30 years previously; PANB, New Brunswick Land Grants, Microfilm F 1044. A Joseph , John, and Jacob "Riecker" (Ricker) lived in King's County and applied for grants between 1810 and 1818. In 1824, Martin Rieker/Ricker Sr., "a native of Germany ... [and] old revolutionary & Soldier" applied for land. He had "encountered all the privations & Hardships of a new Settler, & ... [with his] numerous family (he having had 13 children, & 11 now living) is ... [poised] at the advanced age of 68 years to again proceed into an uncultivated wilderness;" *Ibid.*, Microfilm F 4198.

[98] In 1818, Matthias Stieff bought back from John Bentley for £150 the land taken from Ludovic by sheriff's execution and conveyed to Bentley about 1812; WRO, Libro E-1, 208.

[99] PANB, New Brunswick Land Grants, Microfilm F 4173: October 7, 1809.

[100] Cf. Treitz Family genealogy.

[101] Several of the Petitcodiac German descendants achieved the rank of "Esq.", to be distinguished from ordinary farmers and shopkeepers who owned property but were not considered wealthy. The lowest rung of society constituted the poor people, comprised of unskilled labourers, indentured servants, and slaves.

[102] WRO, Libro H-1, 478, registered October, 22, 1824.

[103] On November 18, 1825, William Trites' property was seized by the Sheriff and a year later (October 10, 1826), creditor John Trites (Abraham Treitz's youngest son) sued his older cousin William for £1,000 plus £5:12: 6 in legal fees; Libro H-1, 478, Westmorland County Land Registry. The Trites families must have been quick to forgive any bad feelings related to this episode, for a year later, on November 25, 1827, John Trites married Christian's daughter (William's sister), Jane. It is thought that John Trites was involved in ship-building, for six years later he went through similar litigations again, this time for two lesser amounts brought against James Kelly, Moncton innkeeper, entrepreneur, and ship-builder, who went into bankruptcy as the result of a major ship-related fiasco;

WRO, Libro M-1, 445: registered October 24, 1833 and Libro N-1, 14: registered March 27, 1834.

[104] *Gubbins' Journals*, p. 28.

[105] *Loc. cit..*

[106] Harper Ledger (1816-1820): January 4, 1815, October 11, 1815, May 9, 1816, July 15, 1816.

[107] *Ibid.*, January 14, 1815, November 6,1815, January 1817, June 2, 1817.

[108] *Ibid.*, February 1814 and 1816, November 1817.

[109] Veal was usually available in the spring, lamb in the summer, and beef in the fall. Sales of salt tended to increase in the fall, presumably for salting meats for winter storage, likewise the sale of vinegar for pickling.

[110] Harper Ledger (1816-1820): April to October, 1815. No purchases of alcoholic beverages were listed in Henry Stultz' account; Andrew Sommer may also have abstained as only one purchase was made, on behalf of one of his sons.

[111] *Ibid.*; on March 24, 1816, Peter Lutz was paid three shillings six pence for "Mending George Shoes", i.e. Harper's son's shoes. Harper distinguished Peter Lutz Jr. from his father, "Peter Lutze Sr.", by entering on May 11, 1819 "Peter Lutze shoemaker", confirming shoemaking as an established trade in the Lutz family. Son Michael also mended shoes, and Peter's relative and neighbour, William Ricker (Michael Ricker's son), may have trained under him and was listed as a shoemaker in the 1851 Hillsborough Census; likewise William Dalegant, husband of Peter's youngest daughter, Nancy Ann.

[112] *Ibid.*, July 1, 1819.

[113] *Gubbins' Journals*, p. 28. The grindstone industry came to be virtually monopolized by Amos Seamans (Simmons in the 1770 Census), also known as "King Seaman", who may have been of German extraction to judge by the ending "s" in the spelling of his name and the German name of his sister *Huldah*. A Württemberg farmer who arrived in Lunenburg, N.S. in 1752 had his name spelled "Seeman", which can be traced back to the German names *Siemons*, *Sähmann*, and *Seemann*.

[114] WRO, Libro P-1, 74 (Dec. 17, 1836).

[115] Harper Ledger (1816-1820): October 7, 1818.

[116] Solomon Trites may have lost his wife early in their marriage as only one son, Solomon Jr., has been attributed to him, so that hired farm help in 1816 may have been a necessity.

[117] Harper Ledgers (1816-1820): February/July, 1816.

[118] *Ibid.*, December 15, 1815.

[119] *Ibid.*, April 20, 1816 for Harper and May 12, 1816 for Kelly.

[120] *Ibid.*, February 23, 1815. Michael Ricker was the first Petitcodiac German to buy coffee at Harper's.

[121] *Ibid.*, February 1816 and January 1818.

[122] R. Wallace Hale, *Early New Brunswick Probate Records, 1785-1835* (Bowie, M.d.: Heritage Books, 1989), p. 460.

[123] Abraham Treitz died November 29th, and his will was proved on December 17, 1810.

[124] Experience Ward/Gore/Forster married Abraham Treitz on January 14, 1807 after three previous marriages. Her third husband was David Forster (1754/1755 - June 7, 1808), a schoolteacher at Cumberland. The tombstone inscription and probate record for Forster -- proved September 2, 1808 -- confirm that Abraham's marriage to Experience occurred in 1809 rather than 1807, as stated in a current Treitz family genealogy.

[125] *N.B. Probate Records*, p. 460. Another example of the recognition that education had become important can be found in Ludovic/Lewis Stieff's Will of January 4, 1827, in which he instructed his son Elisha (* 1802) to procure for his younger son David (* 1809), besides some farm animals and clothing, "... six months of schooling"; *ibid.*, p. 437.

[126] *Ibid.*, p. 437; John Frances Trites (* Dec. 1, 1798 † Oct. 17, 1884). John F. Trites' dealings with William Trites and James Kelly show that he became involved in far more than farming.

[127] William Harper paid James Kelly a relatively high £0:7:6/day's wages for cabinet work in his store; cf. Harper Ledger (1816-1820): June 10, 1816. Four shillings per day was the average rate of pay for general labour. For a summary of prices at this time, consult Helen Harper Steeves, *The Story of Moncton's First Store and Innkeeper* (St. John, N.B.: J. & A. MacMillan Ltd., 1924), pp. 57f.. Ms. Steeves was the great-granddaughter of William Harper.

[128] *Ibid.,* p. 21. Although a contemporary to Peter Fisher, Col. Gubbins had called this difference a degeneration into barbarism, Temberley, ed., *Gubbins' Journals,* pp. xixff..

[129] The highly skilled woodcarvers of the Ore Mountains (*Erzgebirge*) and Black Forest (*Schwarzwald*) of Germany underscore the scarcity of wood as they created small works of art often from waste pieces of this precious material.

[130] German history and literature are filled with stories in which those who helped themselves to the riches of the forests were criminalized. One example is the well-known *Novella* by Annette von Droste-Hülshoff, *Die Judenbuche* (1840), which depicts the tragic life of a young man, Friedrich (1738-1788), who became involved with members of a lumber-ring that plundered the nobility's forests in the Paderborn area near Braunschweig (Brunswick!).

[131] NAC, Westmorland County, N.B., Record of Proceedings in the Court of Common Pleas, 1785-1830.

[132] *Ibid.*, June 14, 1808.

[133] The frequency of litigations entered into by Jacob Stieff confirms his involvement in some form of retail operation.

[134] Alexander Smith married Ann Woodworth the following year, on August 4, 1814, and three months later on November 2nd, Susannah Lutz married David Steeves.

[135] The Westmorland Court Records also list German names which have not come to light in other documents, such as a Christian Muller who sued James Fitzgerald for as little as £2:2:4 on July 24, 1800. The name "Müller" occurs several times amongst the Lunenburg Germans.

[136] The court records do not indicate whether Martin Beck Sr. or Jr. was involved in these litigations. Martin Beck Sr. lived at least until 1803.

[137] Elizabeth (*née* Jones) "Somers" was the wife of Mathias Sommer, Andrew Sommer's eldest son; cf. Sommer Family genealogy.

[138] The name of Marius Myers, whose possible brother Charles ("Carl") Meiers was listed in the 1775 Hillsborough Census, appears as Petit Juror as early as July 1786, followed by John Myers in July 1787.

[139] General Sessions of the Peace, 1785-1809.

[140] *Ibid.*, "... first Tuesday of July in the Twenty fifth year of His Majesty's Reign A.D. 1785."

[141] General Session of the Peace, January 1798.

[142] Since Clark Wright's research centred on the Stieff family and Hillsborough, the even greater presence of Germans in Moncton escaped her notice.

[143] In 1790, seven of eighteen positions were held by Petitcodiac Germans, not counting three from the Beck family.

[144] In view of the positive role the Rickers played in Coverdale/ Hillsborough and Moncton, and their intermarriages with the Stieffs, Treitz, etc., Clark Wright's repeated pejorative remarks concerning the Ricker family are puzzling and must be based on personal bias; Clark Wright, *Samphire Greens,* pp. 48, 60.

[145] General Session of the Peace, June 1802.

[146] *Loc. cit.*.

[147] Jacob Ricker Jr. and son-in-law Jacob Treitz Jr. both felt considerable irritation toward "squatter" Donald McDonald, who convinced the Crown to grant him Liffe Chappell's Moncton property to the west of Andrew Sommer (1788, 1791). Jacob Ricker Jr. tried unsuccessfully in 1801 to have the land returned to him, but the Crown overturned his request (PANB, Microfilm F 1042: January 9, 1801). Relations between McDonald and Andrew Sommer must also have been strained, however this did not prevent the plaintiff's lawyer from calling upon Andrew and his wife "Amy" to testify as witnesses in the case.

[148] Most of these individuals had mothers with partial or complete German ancestry.

[149] A.G. Roeber, *Palatines, Liberty, and Property,* p. 23

[150] The Matthew Family Papers include an account of the formation of the *Steinhammer Club* and names of its members; NBM, Location /1 S 157- 1, F 10 - F 12.

[151] Travis Family, CB Doc., NBM. Continued progress in computer indexing of archival records should lead to more discoveries about the early activities of German Loyalists in New Brunswick.

[152] Contributed by David G. Bell of Fredericton; PANB, Supreme Court Records, 1784. Peter Ackerman is listed as a Loyalist in Clark Wright's book *The Loyalists of New Brunswick,* p. 225.

[153] *Ibid.,* p. 323; he is listed as John Ricket.

[154] PANB, Supreme Court Records, 1784; Knull, Rosman, and Kemper are not listed in Clark Wright's *The Loyalists of New Brunswick.*

[155] David Artiss, "German Cultural ... Studies," p. 76.

[156] Clark Wright, *The Loyalists of New Brunswick,* p. 337.

[157] *Ibid.,* p. 73.

[158] *Ibid.,* p. 74.

Epilogue

True to a German proverb, *Der ersten der Tod,/ Der zweiten die Not,/ Der dritten das Brot,* which predicted "death" for first generation immigrants, "need" and "misery" for the second, and "bread", the staff of life, for the third, most first-generation Petitcodiac Germans and many Loyalists of New Brunswick faced repeated life-threatening experiences, and some even untimely death. However, subsequent generations fared much better than the proverb concedes, to the extent that the progeny of the large, successful families had to seek their fortunes in new regions when accessible land and employment opportunities became scarcer at home. Examples cited previously have shown that these descendants provided significant manpower for other regions of the continent. Although in the 19th century the bulk of immigrants from German-speaking countries settled in Ontario, the Prairie provinces and British Columbia, swelling their numbers to the extent of becoming the third-largest ethnic group in Canada,[1] a small trickle still continued to come to New Brunswick. One example is the community named "Germany," a small settlement about 24 km north-west of Welsford, named in honour of the German settlers Knorr, Byers, Fromm, and Schenk who founded it in the 1800's.[2] Another example is the arrival in 1855 of the Schäfer and Jack families to Saint John. Wilhelm Friedrich Schäfer from Weinsberg, Baden-Württemberg, settled with his wife and four children in March while Johann Christian Jack from nearby Kirchheim, Baden-Württemberg, disembarked with his wife and six children that September.[3] Descendants of all these immigrants continue to live in New Brunswick although the name *Schäfer* has undergone a great deal of change, e.g. Shafer, Sheffar, and Sheffer.

By and large, further settlements comprising Germans in 19th-century New Brunswick were the result of expansion from existing locations like Hillsborough, Moncton, and Salisbury,[4] such as Coverdale,[5] Turtle Creek, Little River, Steeves Mountain, Lutz Mountain,[6] and Petitcodiac,[7] as well as the small community of Memel as Shepody (Germantown) expanded around 1830.[8] In the 1871 Census, a total of 4,478 New Brunswickers still declared themselves to be of German descent, a figure which actually peaked in the 1881 Census when 6,310 made this claim. As a reflection of the large number of Loyalists of German descent, the majority of these, i.e. 2,569, resided in Kings,[9] Queens, York, and Carleton Counties as well as the City of Saint John, whereas only a third, i.e. 1,536, were descendants of the Petitcodiac Germans. This lesser number may simply reflect a lack of awareness of their background because their forbears were confronted initially by problems of survival and less preoccupied with the preservation of language and culture, something Loyalists of German descent could better foster due to their healthier financial circumstances. In the post-World War I Census of 1921, the German component for all of New Brunswick had shrunk to a mere 1,698, reflecting at least to some degree a denial of heritage in response to anti-German sentiment. Reviewing these statistics in 1931, Heinz Lehmann wrote rather wistfully: "... [O]ne cannot escape the conclusion that ... [in New Brunswick] the German element, which dates back to the eighteenth century, is extinct today. After a few more decades perhaps not even a memory will survive of the quiet, stubborn pioneer effort and active participation in the opening up of ... New Brunswick to which thousands of Germans devoted themselves over the course of time."[10]

This gradual assimilation is part of cultural exchange, an ongoing process of contributions by immigrants and influence by society on the newcomers, which began with the immigrants' arrival in Philadelphia. Many later Loyalists adapted early and became part of the establishment as successful farmers and entrepreneurs, reluctant to abandon their position attained in British colonial society when the revolution broke out. The Petitcodiac Germans, however, were unable to settle successfully, so they decided to accept invitations from several land companies to realize their dreams of becoming landowners and farmers some day. The two decades spent in America before their departure north were important, not only as a period of debt repayment, but also as a time of adjustment to a new society, to see themselves and their religious persuasion in relation to others. The wilderness existence along the Petitcodiac River confronted them with entirely new challenges, the most elemental of which was sheer survival. By their own ingenuity, toil, persistence, and courage, this small group of families adapted to its new environment. Such self-sufficiency prevailed later, too, in matters of land ownership. The American War of Independence opened up, rather unexpectedly, a legal avenue for confronting proprietor neglect and exploitation, furnishing these settlers with the grounds to win

362

possession of the land they had cultivated for more than a decade. Their sense of self-worth in this new society had changed fundamentally from that of Old Country subservience to confidence in challenging their superiors, i.e. the New Country "lords" who had brought them to these shores as tenants. The right to own land and acquire wealth brought with it new career opportunities in farming, trading, shipbuilding, and related entrepreneurial activities.

These settlers also made new religious choices, a freedom not available in their country-of-origin, where princes had determined the "persuasion" of their subjects. Emigrants had learned to distrust the established order, in particular as it manifested itself in the excesses of the princes, guilds, and Church, and they learned to reject Old Country notions regarding the existence of smaller religious sects. In the free atmosphere of Pennsylvania, where William Penn had helped establish a haven for religious dissenters alongside mainstream churches, openness and tolerance toward other denominations was his express aim. Contact with people of differing faiths, the new ideas of the Brethren as expounded by Christopher Sauer through the medium of his press, as well as the enlightened views of Rev. Melchior Mühlenberg, mellowed the Petitcodiac Germans to the point of no longer insisting on a German-speaking Lutheran minister or church in their "Monckton" and Hillsborough settlements. On the other hand, they were not yet "free" enough initially to select or appoint preachers from within their own midst until the arrival of Revs. Henry Alline and William Black. Some of the first-generation settlers became "Allinite", or "Newlight", converts, but the majority accepted Methodism initially as a result of the devoted ministry of William Black. As a sign of their new faith, several of their own became preachers, extending this new-found freedom and self-reliance onto the religious level. The Stieffs' roots in Württemberg Pietism and Matthias Sommer's Pietist leanings directed their search for a style of worship in keeping with fundamental sects, such as the Baptists, with whom they shared a distrust of mainline churches and the established order. The sense of brotherhood and belonging in Baptist congregations appealed to the Petitcodiac Germans who, like most immigrants, were keenly aware of their isolation, rootlessness, and vulnerability in a new country. Acceptance of these new forms of worship in the English language also furthered the loss of German as the principal language of communication. Fluency in English, in turn, allowed them a role in shaping the religious landscape of the Maritimes and opened up opportunities in politics on the municipal, provincial, and federal levels, including active participation in Canada's very foundation.

The legacy of the Petitcodiac settlers extends beyond a small number of museum artifacts of German origin, such as the Stieff cuckoo clock and Bible, a powder horn, sugar and butter moulds, as well as the Treitz Haus with its heart motif and Christian Treitz's brick house. Their weaving expertise and culinary specialties such as *Kartoffelklöße* and *Sauerkraut* have been adapted and live on. Although they intermarried with Yorkshire settlers, fellow New Englanders, and Acadians, descendants of the various Petitcodiac German families at times claim to recognize certain physical and character traits which they attribute to their forbears. The copious entries of their Anglicized names in telephone directories across North America is the most tangible proof of their continued presence. In Moncton, the Steeves name is second only to the ubiquitous LeBlanc family.

Beginning with the Petitcodiac Germans and continuing with those who followed, one can trace the speed of cultural and linguistic integration of this ethnographically distinct group of people, who, except for their surnames, became virtually indistinguishable from their Anglo-Saxon[11] and Celtic neighbours in the third or fourth generation.[12] British settlers on the other hand also fully accepted Germans as equal partners and members within their communities,[13] a fact attested to by the many mixed marriages which occurred. Newcomers who bestir themselves and find success in a different ethno-linguistic area by necessity make contact with the ambient language more frequently, learn it more readily, and assimilate with greater ease. The "extinction" of the German element which Lehmann lamented was, therefore, an outcome predicated by one of these peoples' greatest attributes. Traditionally, German-speaking immigrants have found it easy to blend in because English[14] and German are closely related linguistically. Moreover, as a central people in Europe, Germans have been unusually receptive to outside influences and movements. This has enabled them to adapt readily to new conditions and surroundings, "adopting" a foreign land by becoming a part of it.[15]

Most of the early German immigrants to New Brunswick mixed in with the other residents of the province so completely that knowledge of their German roots simply became forgotten over the years. Where this was not the case, two World Wars and the resultant suspicions, even outright hostility, to things "German" led many to de-emphasize, or even deny, their German origins. Earlier widespread insistence that the term "Pennsylvanian Dutch" denoted "Dutch" rather than "Deutsch" was typical of this trend.[16] Canadian census statistics abound with examples where German descendants denied their ancestry, often by Anglicizing their names to conceal their origin. There are stories about Petitcodiac Germans who, in the general patriotic fervour to fight the *Kaiser*, or Hitler, felt obliged to "prove" their allegiance to Canada by volunteering for the armed forces or by investing their life-savings in war bonds. Such hesitancy to acknowledge their German heritage is not just a reaction of Germans and their descendants living beyond the borders of their country-of-origin. A similar phenomenon exists within Germany to this day, manifested by the popular concept of a "united" Europe wherein Germans might "submerge" themselves, also by a certain reluctance to acknowledge or take pride in the successes of Germany's post-World War II period.

The anti-German sentiments which arose in Canada as a result of the First and Second World Wars naturally impacted adversely on the recognition of contributions made by German-speaking pioneers to their adopted homeland. As the memories of these unfortunate conflicts fade and Germany regains acceptance as a positive and constructive force in the family of nations, a greater readiness, even eagerness, to learn more about the role of these immigrants and their descendants has emerged in New Brunswick and throughout Canada. The many articles in such publications as the *German-Canadian Yearbook, Canadiana Germanica* of the German-Canadian Historical Association, the *Mennonite Historian,* and others underscore the extent of this rekindled interest. They also reveal the wide-ranging contributions German immigrants have made within the larger framework of this country's past.

As part of the ongoing effort to record Canada's rich cultural heritage and to ensure that knowledge of New Brunswick's German-speaking pioneers be recognized and survive, this study set out to explore the background of these immigrants in their European homelands to comprehend more completely the political, religious, cultural, and social forces which impacted on the lives of their forefathers and to probe the personal circumstances that led them to seek their fortunes in the New World. Since these settlers and their descendants have become part of Canada's historical fabric, study of their European and Pennsylvanian backgrounds furthers not just knowledge of one piece of the Canadian mosaic but of Canada as a whole. Awareness of their own roots will also provide the descendants with a clearer image of their own identity. If one were to replace the word "American" with "Canadian", and the names "Wanamaker" and "Rockefeller" with those of "Steeves", "Fisher", "Lutes", or "Trites", the following quote could apply equally to Canadian society:

> ... [M]ost of the old [German speech] and culture ... [have] been thoroughly merged in what we call American culture. Where could one find more typical American careers than those by the names of Wanamaker and Rockefeller?
>
> Instead of this being a reason for neglecting the peculiarly German elements in our colonial life, it is a reason for studying them with increasing thoroughness. If the culture which they represented has lost its clear identity, if it is hidden in the general mass, its contribution has been more essential. If the Germans have become somewhat English in social habits, then the English have become somewhat German.[17] All this is a factor in making the American temper what it is.[18]

Heinz Lehmann need not have worried that the German element had become extinct on account of the loss of language, as a "central feature ... [of] German identity."[19] It lives on in new forms, perhaps less easy to discern since in the process of changing others, it has also changed itself.

While New Brunswick continues to be the destination of immigrants from German-speaking countries, seemingly perpetuating cultural exchange, integration, and assimilation, a cairn (fig. 56, 56a) and a granite marker (plate 17) have been erected at a location on the muddy riverbank of the Petitcodiac, close to where the first Germans landed on June 3, 1766.

366

Figure 56

Cairn at the confluence of the Petitcodiac River and Hall's Creek, designated as Settlers' Landing, near the place where the Germans landed on June 3, 1766.

Photo: Rainer L. Hempel

SETTLERS LANDING

In honour of the first permanent settlers of Moncton Township, the Steeves, Lutes, Trites, Jones, Somers, Ricker and Wortman families who came up the Petitcodiac from Pennsylvania and landed on the bank of this creek June 3, 1766, this memorial is erected by Heritage Moncton, in cooperation with their descendants.

En l'honneur des premiers colons qui se sont établis de façon permanente dans la municipalité de Moncton, notamment les Steeves, les Lutes, les Trites, les Jones, les Somers, les Ricker et les Wortman, des familles venues de la Pennsylvanie qui ont remonté la rivière Petitcodiac pour débarquer sur la rive de ce ruisseau le 3 juin 1766, ce monument est érigé par la société Heritage Moncton avec la collaboration de leurs descendants.

– 1983 –

Figure 56a

Close-up of plaque on the cairn to commemorate the arrival of the Petitcodiac Germans at Settlers' Landing.

Photo: Rainer L. Hempel

368

Standing as they do at the confluence of Hall's Creek, in full view of the river's "Bend" and overlooking modern-day developments at the boundary dividing Moncton and Dieppe, these memorials underscore the elements of promise, hope, and courage in the landing of a mere seven German families and one American in their midst,[20] together founders of the townships of "Monckton" and "Hillsborough". One might ponder whether or not these or any of the German-speaking Loyalist settlers ever felt themselves beckoned back to "Germany's yellow wheat fields" and "fruitful vineyards" while "striding through the woods of foreign lands," as Freiligrath's romanticized view of emigrants in his poem suggests. Whatever "events of days gone by drifted past their inner eye," they "dreamed these gleaming images" on their *own* land and in their *own* forests, which have long since given way to the City of Moncton, the Town of Riverview, and the Village of Hillsborough.

ENDNOTES

[1] Fröschle, *Die Deutschen in Kanada*, p. 8.

[2] Allan Rayburn, *Geographical Names of New Brunswick:* Canadian Permanent Committee on Geographical Names (Ottawa: 1975). The name "Germany" also occurs on a map by the Department of Lands and Mines as "Block 48 North of Germany Settlement," PANB, RS 656/1K/74/1.

[3] Mrs. E. A. Jack (Elgin, N.B. E0A 1P0) and Mrs. Eleanor Goggin (Box 492, Salisbury, N.B., E0A 3E0) kindly provided the archival evidence about these families. Mrs. Jack is the granddaughter of Johannes (John) Jack, who was born in Kirchheim in 1841 and died in 1913. He was 14 when his parents emigrated.

[4] *Ibid.*, p. 170.

[5] William F. Ganong, "Origins of Settlement in New Brunswick," *Transactions of the Royal Society of Canada*, Sec. II, p. 126.

[6] *Ibid.*, p. 146; Lutz Mountain was founded before 1811.

[7] *Ibid.*, p. 159.

[8] *Ibid.*, p. 149.

[9] A number of the Petitcodiac Germans also spread into King's County.

[10] Heinz Lehmann, *The German Canadians*, p. 45.

[11] Unlike the Scottish and French, the English were less known for their eagerness to mix with other races, in particular with the indigenous peoples of their conquered lands.

[12] Cf. Arthur Grenke, "German Land Settlement in Eastern Canada and Its Influence on Community Development and Assimilation," *German-Canadian Yearbook*, XV (Toronto: Historical Society of Mecklenburg, 1998), pp. 55f..

[13] The Petitcodiac Germans also intermarried with French settlers of the region, e.g. Brian Lutes of Moncton, who is Acadian and whose mother tongue is French.

[14] The word "English" is derived from the name of the Germanic tribe, the Angles, who settled the south-eastern part of Britain along with the Saxons and Jutes following the departure of the Romans.

[15] Fröschle, *Die Deutschen in Kanada*, p. 114.

[16] D. Artiss, "German ... Heritage," p. 75-76.

[17] Col. Joseph Gubbins, a man of good breeding and British manners, noted with disgust the change in his countrymen in New Brunswick: "It is remarkable that amongst the immediate descendants of the English, little of British manners or customs are to be found, either as to religion, neatness, frugality, husbandry, or even cooking;" *Gubbins' Journals*, p. 22.

[18] Dixon Ryan Fox, introd., Knittle, *Early ... Palatine Emigration*, p. vi.

[19] Arthur Grenke, "German Land Settlement in Eastern Canada and Its Influence on Community Development and Assimilation," *German-Canadian*

Yearbook, p. 55.

[20] Although Charles Jones's ancestors may have come from Wales, he was considered "American", not "Welsh", in the 1767 Census.

Genealogical Reference

These genealogies were compiled and/or re-examined by Adèle Hempel, who consulted birth, marriage, cemetery and probate records, as well as censuses, land transactions, Crown grant applications, family Bibles, and personal letters, as listed in the Bibliography. Where information was not available, possibilities and probabilities were entered on the basis of dates, related marriages, first names associated with certain families, and available partners. Since this is a first attempt to compile all genealogical information on the earliest generations of the German settlers into one, errors and omissions are bound to exist; documentation is fragmentary for these early years. Certain entries will also conflict with earlier work, as is inevitable with any genealogical update.

The following symbols denote: " ∞ " -- "married", " ∗ " -- "born", and "†" -- "died". In order to facilitate comparisons between generations and to coordinate these genealogies with those previously established for North American descendants of Petitcodiac Germans, the first pioneers (including their generation in Germany and Pennsylvania) have been assigned the superscript "[1]", their sons and daughters "[2]", their grandchildren "[3]", and so on. Counting back, the first pioneers' European parents are designated with capital letters "[A]", their grandparents "[B]", etc.. Actual birth and death dates have been entered whenever available. Split years (e.g. 1798/1799) were derived from information on tombstones and censuses when the deceased died in his/her 64th year, for example, with no mention of the actual birth date. Circa dates ("c.") are best approximations from available sources within about five years. To avoid confusion with superscripts that designate generations, footnotes are marked as "note" plus superscript number. The order of children in each family is established by Arabic numerals. The same order is retained in Roman numerals when these children become parents (except for the first entry in each genealogy which is assigned number "I"). Entries in bold print signify Petitcodiac Germans, their forbears and descendants, as well as a few German families which became closely associated with them such as the Beck family. Question marks (?) are used whenever an element of conjecture exists.

The German spelling of the names Lutz, Sommer, Treitz, and Stieff has been retained intentionally for the first two generations. In the third generation the Anglicized forms have been used since they were generally accepted by then. The first provincial census of the 19th century was compiled for 1803 and a second, more detailed one over the summer of 1851, both of which are used as points of orientation. The distinction in spelling between the Township of "Monckton" and town of Moncton after 1786 was not maintained in these genealogies since the lives of many settlers straddled the date when the "k" was dropped from the name.

A note of appreciation is extended to all those who helped in this effort especially to: V "Bing" Geldart of Salisbury, N.B., noted Yorkshire settler genealogist; Kay Milton of Hillsborough and archivist Roland Deigendesch of Münsingen, Germany, for the Stieff/Steeves family; Dawn Lutes of Moncton, Executive Director of the Muriel Lutz-Sikorski Fund, and archivist Erich Langguth of Kreuzwertheim, Germany, for the Lutz family; Norman Jones of Moncton for the Jones family; Joyce Wortman of Moncton, Karon Wortman Scott of Woodstock, N.B., and D. Wayne Wortman of Winnipeg, Man., publisher of the *Wortman Quarterly,* for the Wortman family;

BECK FAMILY

First Generation ("¹")

I **Martin Beck**¹ Sr. ($*$ c. 1735 in Germany † after 1803 in Hillsborough), baker at Fort Cumberland/Fort Beauséjour (Aulac, N.B.), resident of Hillsborough, Moncton, then Hillsborough permanently
∞ c. 1760 Maria or Johanna ("Hannah") (*née ?*) ($*$ c. 1740 in Germany † after 1803 in Hillsborough); note¹

---

¹ There is considerable difficulty in examining the Beck family because of its size and the frequent spelling of "Beck" as "Peck". This attempt to trace the family must be viewed as preliminary. According to the 1803 Hillsborough Census, this couple had one child still living at home (Joseph ?). In the 1770 Cumberland Census , the Beck family counted five children plus one man and

Second Generation ("²")

I   **Martin Beck**[1] **Sr.**
with Maria or Johanna ("Hannah")

  1 **Maria/Mary Beck**[2] (* 1759/1760 † June 3, 1826 in Hillsborough)
    ∞ c. 1783 **Henry Stieff**[2] (* 1757/1758 in Philadelphia † May 1, 1826
    in Hillsborough), son of **Heinrich Stieff**[1]

  2 **Martin Beck**[2] **Jr.** (* c. 1761 † before 1851), "Fence Viewer" for
    Hillsborough for 1790, appears to have moved away
    ∞ wife from Hillsborough ?; cf. note[2]

  3 **James Beck**[2] (* c. 1763 † before Sept. 27, 1848 -- died intestate),
    "Gauger" for Hillsborough in 1790, moved to Salisbury c. 1795
    ∞ c. 1795 Johanna (*née* Sherman ?) (* 1778/1779 † after 1851),
    "German"; cf. note[3]

---

wife; in 1775 only six family members were recorded, suggesting that not all family members were included in this count. The 1783 Hillsborough Census lists Martin Beck and wife, with "11 children, mostly grown up," and three Beck sons (of age or nearly so) are listed as potential heads of households: Martin Beck Jr., James Beck, and Jacob Beck. Four additional sons have been identified: Georg, Leonard, Michael, and possibly Joseph. This would suggest the existence of two daughters, perhaps called Hannah and Christianna.

[2] It is unclear why the Beck boys appear to have married so late unless this related perhaps to Martin Beck Sr.'s financial difficulties around 1790. Most Beck descendants seem to have settled in Salisbury eventually.

[3] Johanna claimed to be German in the 1851 Salisbury Census. Her parents were likely Young and Anna (*née* ?, German descendant) Sherman. Two American men of age are recorded for the household of "Young Sherman" in the Township of Cumberland Census of 1770, brothers Young and Ring. The latter's wife, Mary (*née* ?) (* 1761/1762 ∞ before 1788 † Oct. 23, 1823), is buried in the Salisbury Pioneer Cemetery, Salisbury Back Road. Both men had purchased land in Salisbury by late 1787.

4   **Jacob Beck**[2] (∗ c. 1765 † after March 1830 and before 1851), first
    appointment as "Constable" for Hillsborough in 1790, moved to
    Salisbury c. 1799 or earlier
    ∞ c. 1794 wife unknown (∗ c. 1775 † c. 1805); cf. note[4]
    ∞ Dec. 24, 1806 Ann Horsman (∗ c. 1788 † before 1851) from
    Moncton, daughter of Christopher and Mary (Wilbur) Horsman;
    cf. note[5]

5   **Sophia Beck**[2] (∗ 1767/1768 † Aug. 25, 1844 in Hillsborough)
    ∞ c. 1785 **Matthias Stieff**[2] (∗ 1760/1761 in Pennsylvania † May 21,
    1848 in Hillsborough), son of **Heinrich Stieff**[1]

6   Daughter **Beck**[2] ? ("Hannah" ?) (∗ c. 1770 † after 1797 ?)
    ∞ c. 1788 John Behn ? (∗ c. 1760 † early 1804 in Hampton Parish,
    King's Co. ?) (cf. **"Hannah" Treitz**[2] entry and footnote[65], p. 464)

7   **Georg(e) Beck**[2] (∗ c. 1772 † after 1803), of Hillsborough, later moved
    to Salisbury
    ∞ after 1803, wife unknown

8   **Leonard Beck**[2] (∗ c. 1774 † after 1810 and before 1833), in Salisbury
    before 1810

9   Daughter **Beck**[2] ? ("Christianna" ?) (∗ c. 1776 † after 1851 ?);
    cf. note[40]
    ∞ c. 1795 Jeremiah Crossman (∗ c. 1770 † after 1824 and before 1851),
    son of Robert and Suzanne (Govang) Crossman

10 **Michael Beck**[2] (∗ c. 1778 † after 1810 in Salisbury before 1810)

11 **Joseph Beck**[2] (∗ c. 1780 † after 1844), moved to Hopewell

---

[4] Two children were reported in the 1803 Salisbury Census for this couple.

[5] In early references this name is frequently spelled "Horseman". Mary
Wilbur was the daughter of Benjamin Wilbur Sr. of Sackville, whose will was
proved on July 10, 1789; her siblings were David Wilbur of Hopewell, and
Benjamin Jr. and Samuel of Hillsborough (WRO, Libro A-1, 248).

Third Generation ("³")

I **Maria/Mary Beck²**, Martin Beck¹
with **Henry Stieff²**
Couple's children listed in **Stieff Family** genealogy under **Henry
Stieff²**, **Johann** Heinrich¹, **Augustinus**ᴬ, **Johann Heinrich**ᴮ

III **James Beck²**, Martin Beck¹ Sr.
with Johanna (Sherman ?); cf. note⁶

  1 **Martin Beck³** (* 1798/1799 [tombstone], 1800/1801 [1851 Salisbury
     Census] † July 1, 1877 in Salisbury) from Salisbury
     ∞ May 29, 1828 Tryphena Vaughan (* 1806/1807 † Nov. 18, 1873 in
     Salisbury) from Salisbury

  2 **Christianna Beck³** (* Nov. 2, 1802 † Nov. 18, 1881) from Salisbury
     ∞ Jan. 24, 1830 **Daniel Steeves⁴** (* May 6, 1804 † March 31, 1881)
     from Hillsborough, son of **Henry Steeves³**, grandson of **Johannes
     Stieff²**, couple farmed near Salem, N.B.

  3 **Young Beck³** (* 1804/1805 † after 1851), farmer, single in 1851
     Salisbury Census

  4 **Hannah Beck³** (* c. 1806 † before 1844 ?) from Salisbury, sons
     Jacob and **William** in area in 1844
     ∞ April 1, 1824 Enoch Horsman (* c. 1800 † before 1844 ?), son of
     Christopher and Mary (Wilbur) Horsman; cf. note⁷

  5 **James Beck³** (* 1807/1808 † March 26, 1847) from Salisbury
     ∞ Feb. 3, 1842 **Nancy Steadman** (* c. 1812 † May 7, 1847),
     daughter of William Steadman and **Hannah Treitz³**

---

⁶ James Beck and his wife claimed two children in the 1803 Salisbury
Census.

⁷ William Horsman remembered Enoch Horsman's two sons, Jacob and
William, in his will, dated November 16, 1844, suggesting that their parents (not
mentioned) were no longer alive.

6 **Martha Beck**[3] (* c. 1812 † ?) from Salisbury
   ∞ Sept. 13, 1830 Henry Colpitts, son of Ralph and Maria (Jones)[3]
   Colpitts, couple seems to have left area

7 **John Beck**[3] (* 1815/1816 † after 1851) from Salisbury
   ∞ c. 1850 Ann/Nancy (*née* ?) (* 1828/1829 † Jan. 26, 1856), "Irish"
   in 1851 Salisbury Census

IV **Jacob Beck**[2], **Martin Beck**[1] Sr.
    with unknown first wife; cf. note[8]

1 **Ruth Beck**[3] (* 1795/1796 † Nov. 2, 1861) from Salisbury
   ∞ Nov. 26, 1818 **Jeremiah Lutz**[3] (* July 26, 1797 † after 1851), son
   of **Johannes Lutz**[2]

2 **Mary Beck**[3] (* 1797/1798 † after 1851) from Salisbury
   ∞ Oct. 19, 1826 **Robert Colpitts Jr.** (* c. 1797 † before 1851), son of
   Robert and **Rachel (Steeves)** Colpitts and grandson of **Christian
   Stieff**[2] and **Rosanna (Treitz)**[2], couple purchased Henry Jones'[2]
   farm in 1829

Jacob Beck[2]
with Ann Horsman

3 **Allen Beck**[3] (* c. 1807 † after 1871), blacksmith, appraiser of estates
   in Parish of Elgin (1851, 1871)
   ∞ Aug. 26, 1830 Jane Cane (* c. 1810 † ?), daughter of Charles and
   Jane Cane

4 **Lydia Beck**[3] (* 1808/1809 † Nov. 26, 1866) from Salisbury
   ∞ May 2, 1831 Samuel S. Wilmot (* 1803/1804 † Jan. 28, 1884), road
   surveyor, remarried Margaret A. (*née* ?) (* 1820/1821 † Nov. 28,
   1880)

5 **Hannah Beck**[3] (* c. 1811 † ?) from Salisbury
   ∞ July 9, 1828 **James Wortman**[3] (* May 6, 1796 † July 27, 1862),
   son of **Jacob** and Sarah **Wortman**[2]

---

[8] According to the 1803 Salisbury Census, this couple had two children.

378

6 **Lois Beck**[3] (* c. 1813 † ?) from Salisbury
   ∞ Dec. 13, 1832 Edward Dowling from Salisbury, appraiser in
   Hopewell in 1862

7 **Caleb A. Beck**[3] (* 1818 [gravestone], 1819/1820 [1851 Salisbury
   Census] † 1899) from Salisbury, carpenter
   ∞ Nov. 5, 1850 **Amanda ("Amelia" ?) Sherman** (* 1826/1827 [1851
   Salisbury Census], 1829 [gravestone] † 1912), daughter of Ring
   Sherman Jr. and **Rachel (Jacques)**, great-granddaughter of
   Christian Stieff[2] and **Rosanna (Treitz)**[2]

8 **Jacob Beck**[3] Jr. (* 1819/1820 † after 1877), farmer in Salisbury,
   appraiser of estates
   ∞ Aug. 1, 1851 **Mary Sherman** (* c. 1828 † ?), daughter of Ring
   Sherman Jr. and **Rachel (Jacques)**, great-granddaughter of
   Christian Stieff[2] and **Rosanna (Treitz)**[2]

V **Sophia Beck**[2], **Martin Beck**[1] Sr.
   with **Matthias Stieff**[2]
   Couple's children listed in **Stieff Family** genealogy under **Matthias
   Stieff**[2], **Johann** Heinrich[1], **Augustinus**[A], **Johann Heinrich**[B]

Other third generation Beck descendants with untraced lineages include:

1 **George (P.) Beck**[3] (* c. 1798 ? † ?) of Salisbury
   ∞ July 2, 1820 Mary Doyle of Moncton

2 **Joseph Beck**[3] (* c. 1800 † ?) of Hopewell
   ∞ Sept. 30, 1824 Melissa Akerley of Hopewell

3 **Eliza Beck**[3] (* c. 1812 † before 1851) from Hillsborough
   ∞ March 17, 1831 **Peter Jonah** (* 1810/1811 † after 1851), son of
   Marten Jonah and **Sophia Lutz**[3], grandson of **Peter Lutz**[2]

4 **Mariah Beck**[3] (* c. 1815 † after 1870) from Hillsborough
   ∞ May 28, 1841 Hiram Dickson (* ? † before 1870) from Hopewell,
   labourer, purchased home in Moncton in 1854

COPPLE (KOPPEL) FAMILY

First "Pioneer" Generation ("¹")

I   **John Copple**[1] (* c. 1740 in Germany ? † shortly after Nov. 11, 1780)
     ∞ c. 1765 wife unknown (* c. 1748 † after 1767 and possibly before 1770
     in Moncton), **Copple** resided near **Michael Lutz** family on Lot 7 until
     latter moved to Hillsborough in 1769, then may have lived independently
     until c. 1777 when William Wilson arrived, possibly from Londonderry,
     N.S.
     ∞ c. 1775 ? wife unknown, possibly Anglophone (* c. 1758 † May 1779);
     cf. note[9]

Second Generation ("²")

I   **John Copple**[1]
    with second wife

    1   **Judith Copple**[2] (* 1776/1777 † Sept. 1786 in Sackville), placed under
       guardianship of Charles Dixon Esq. and Mary Chandler, both of Sack-
       ville, after becoming orphaned

---

[9] A second marriage is speculative but based on the fact that John Copple left no other heirs and because his daughter's name is more probably English than German. Dates were arrived at from references made by Stephen Millidge in a transcript of his survey return, dated March 18, 1788 (MAUA, Webster Manuscript Collection, 7001/34).

JONES FAMILY

First "Pioneer" Generation ("[1]")

I   Charles Jones[1] (∗ c. 1725 † c. 1774 ?), Welsh ?; cf. note [10]
∞ c. 1750 ? Catharine[1] ? (Margaret ?) (*née* ?) (∗ c. 1730 † possibly after
1797 [cf. note[11]] and before 1803), possibly married c. 1775 **Jacob
Ricker Sr.**[1]?; cf. **Ricker Family** genealogy

Second "Pioneer" Generation ("[2]")

Charles Jones[1]
with Catharine[1] ? (Margaret ?)

1   Henry Jones[2] (∗ 1756/1757 in Philadelphia area † Jan. 20, 1840 in
    Moncton), farmer, gristmill operator with brother John[2]
    ∞ c. 1780 **Christina(h)** (**Ricker**[3] ?) (**Sommer**[2] ?) (**Wortman**[2] ?)
    (∗ 1761/1762 † after 1851 in Moncton); cf. note[12]

2   John Jones[2] (∗ c. 1758 in Philadelphia area † after 1836 in Moncton),
    husbandman, gristmill operator

---

[10] The Jones family, comprising five children, was likely the one family
classified as "American" in the 1767 "Monckton Township" Census. Charles
Jones' date of death is indicated in the Millidge Report (March 18, 1788): "...
about 14 years since [meaning 'ago']," i.e. fourteen years prior to 1788. No
document has been located confirming Charles Jones' wife's name as Catharine.
The fifth child is presumed to have been female since Charles Jones left only two
male heirs. No other daughters have been located.

[11] This date is correct only if the "Margaret Ricker" who made purchases
from William Harper's trading vessel in 1797 was Charles Jones'[1] widow; cf. W.
Harper, *Ledger*, I (MAUA, Webster Manuscript Collection), c. 1797-1799.

[12] Consult entries on Christina(h) Jones in the Ricker, Sommer, and
Wortman Family genealogies.

∞ c. 1786 "Dimmis" Daniels (∗ c. 1765 † after 1836), daughter of William Daniels Sr. and Martha (*née* ?) of Hopewell; cf. note[13]

3   Margaret Jones[2] (∗ 1760/1761) † April 12, 1806 in Moncton)
    ∞ c. 1775 **Abraham Treitz**[2] (∗ 1751/1752 † Nov. 26, 1810 in Moncton [in the 59th year of his age]), son of **Jacob** and **Elisina Treitz**[1] Sr.

4   Catherine Jones[2] (∗ 1762/1763 † April 1, 1851)
    ∞ c. 1781/1782 **Christian Treitz**[2] (∗ June 12, 1759 † June 22, 1836), son of **Jacob Treitz**[1] Sr.

5   "Daughter" Jones[2] ? (∗ c. 1764 † c. 1787 in Moncton ?), believed to be represented in 1767 "Monckton" Census
    ∞ c. 1785 possibly **Ludovic Stieff**[2] (∗ 1759 † March 15, 1827 in Turtle Creek, N.B.), son of **Heinrich** and **Regina Stieff**[1]

Third Generation ("3")

I   Henry Jones[2], Charles Jones[1]
    with **Christina(h)** (**Ricker**[3] ?) (**Sommer**[2] ?) (**Wortman**[2] ?)

1   **Charles Jones**[3] (∗ 1780/1781 † Oct. 23, 1850), husbandman

---

[13] "Dimmis" Jones' identity was discovered in several sources although the spelling of her name varies considerably ("Dimas"/"Demis"/ "Dinnis"/"Dimmis"). Clark Wright (*Planters and Pioneers*, p. 97) gives one of William Daniel Sr.'s children's names as "Dennis", based on a reading of it in Daniel's will, dated August 10 and October 25, 1800 (WCP, Libro 1, p. 76), leaving the impression this child was male. John Jones and wife "Dimmis" ("Demis") made out an indenture to sons Aaron and Asa Jones on October 27, 1836, (WRO, Libro T-1, 109: registered September 10, 1841). William and Lydia Jones named a daughter "Dimmis", after her grandmother (cf. Salisbury 1851 Census).

        Stephen Millidge consistently referred to John Jones first and then to Henry, yet no children for John have been identified between c. 1780-1787, a period of time in which Henry had four. Millidge's probable reason for naming John first was that his survey of "Monckton Township" was undertaken from east to west, arriving at John's farm first before Henry's. The location of their farms is verifiable in land grant documents.

∞ Nov. 19, 1805 **Deborah Sommer**[3] (* 1786/1787 † c. 1851),
eldest daughter of **Andrew Sommer**[2]

2 **Jacob Jones**[3] (* 1783/1784 † May 10, 1868), farmer
∞ Dec. 7, 1804 **Hannah Trites**[3] (* 1785/1786 † after 1851),
daughter of **Abraham Treitz**[2]

3 **Mariah (Miriam) Jones**[3] (* March 15, 1786 † Dec. 11, 1823)
∞ Jan. 16, 1806 Ralph Colpitts (* Jan. 1, 1778 † Jan. 21, 1856),
son of Robert and Margaret (Wade) Colpitts, Hillsborough

4 **Elizabeth Jones**[3] (* 1787 † 1869)
∞ c. 1815 **Mathias Sommer**[3] (* 1791/1792 † March 23, 1845), eldest
son of **Andrew Sommer**[2]

5 **Ann Jones**[3] (* c. 1790 † before 1851) of Moncton
∞ May 3, 1843 **Lewis (Lodowick) Trites**[3] Esq. (* Nov. 12, 1785
† Feb. 25, 1863), widower, son of **Christian Treitz**[2]

6 **Catherine Jones**[3] (* c. 1793 † after 1840 and before 1851)
∞ Feb. 29, 1816 **Job Steeves**[3] (* 1787/1788 † July 17, 1840), son of
Christian Stieff[2]

7 **Lydia Jones**[3] (* 1795 † 1840)
∞ June 3, 1819 **John ("4") Steeves**[3] (* March 18, 1788 † July 30,
1865), son of **John Stieff**[2]

8 **Henry Jones Jr**[3] (* 1800/1801 † Feb. 26, 1863)
∞ Oct. 31, 1822 **Mary Ann ("Polly") Steeves**[4] (* 1803/1804 † Aug.
19, 1875)

9 **Solomon Jones**[3] (* Jan. 27, 1804 † March 25, 1875)
∞ Dec. 8, 1825 **Margaret Ann Lutz**[3] (* March 23, 1803 † Dec. 23,
1886), daughter of **John Lutz**[2]

10 **Moses Jones**[3] (* 1805/1806 † Aug. 4, 1887), farmer
∞ Feb. 19, 1831 **Barbara Mitton** (* 1810/1811 † Jan. 28, 1872),
daughter of **Catherine Trites**[3] and Ralph Mitton of Coverdale

II   Margaret Jones[2], Charles Jones[1]
with **Abraham Treitz**[2]
Couple's children listed in **Treitz Family** genealogy under **Abraham Treitz**[2], **Jacob Treitz**[1] Sr.

III John Jones[2], Charles Jones[1]
with "Dimmis" ("Demis"/"Dinnis"/"Dimas") Daniels; note[14]

1 Nancy ("Mary Ann" ?) Jones[3] (* 1787/1788 † May 1880)
   ∞ c. 1812 **Samuel Steeves**[3] (* 1790/1791 † Dec. 25, 1868), eldest son
   of **Ludovic** and Elizabeth (Porter) **Stieff**[2]

2 Child Jones[3] ("Elizabeth" ?) (* c. 1789 † after 1803), possible
   daughter; cf. note[15]

3 Child Jones[3] (* c. 1791 † after 1803), possible daughter

4 Margaret Jones[3] (* c. 1793 † 1850) from Parish of Moncton
   ∞ Dec. 30, 1812 Samuel Mills (* c. 1788 † ?) from South Hampton
   Parish, N.S.

5 John Jones[3] Jr. (* 1795/1796 † after 1851), farmer
   ∞ Oct. 28, 1824 **Barbara Trites**[3] (* c. 1796 † before 1851), daughter
   of **Christian Treitz**[2]

---

[14] According to the 1803 Moncton Census, this couple had eight children. That these children have "disappeared" suggests they may have been young children who died or daughters who lost their maiden names through marriage. The eldest Ann/Nancy may have been "Mary Ann"/Nancy, to distinguish her from the later Anne (cf. Christian Treitz[2] family for similar example), otherwise the name repetition in one family is difficult to explain.

[15] A William Jones (* c. 1765 † c. 1855) of Cumberland, who married Mary Dobson (* March 14, 1767 † March 27, 1856), was not likely related to the "Monckton" Township Jones family. Sarah Jones, a widow, and two sons are listed in the Cumberland 1770 Census as "English". Elizabeth Jones[3] (* c. 1790 † ?), who married David Dobson Jr. of Cumberland on August 29, 1808, may have belonged to the Cumberland Jones family.

384

6 Martha Jones[3] (∗ 1797/1798 † after 1851), unmarried in 1851; cf. note[16]

7 Ann Jones[3] (∗ 1799/1800 † after 1851), unmarried in 1851

8 William Jones[3] (∗ 1801/1802 † Aug. 5, 1854, Lutz Mountain) ∞ Sept. 22, 1825 Lydia McLeod (∗ 1806/1807 † May 3, 1855, Lutz Mountain), daughter of A.W. McLeod

9 Asa Jones[3] (∗ 1803/1804 † after 1851), husbandman, unmarried in 1851

10 Aaron Jones[3] (∗ 1806/1807 † July 7, 1895), husbandman ∞ c. 1835 **Caroline Bennett** (∗ 1817/1818 † Dec. 5, 1860), daughter of John Bennett and **Catherine Treitz**[3], daughter of **Jacob Treitz**[2]

IV Catherine Jones[2], Charles Jones[1]
with **Christian Treitz**[2]
Couple's children listed in **Treitz Family** genealogy under **Christian Treitz**[2], **Jacob Treitz**[1] Sr.

V "Daughter" Jones[2] ?, Charles Jones[1]
with **Ludovic Stieff**[2]
Possible issue of this couple listed in **Stieff Family** genealogy under **Ludovic Stieff**[2], **Heinrich Stieff**[1] Sr.

---

[16] Siblings Martha, Ann, and Asa are all listed as "German" and living together in the 1851 Moncton Census.

LUTZ FAMILY
in Höhefeld

I Christoph Lutz^F (* ? in Höhefeld † c. 1611 in Höhefeld), day labourer in vineyards and herdsman
∞ **Anna**^{F} (*née?*) (* ? † c. 1612)

   1 **Michael Lutz**^{E} (* ? in Höhefeld † ?)
     ∞ after 1605

   2 Johannes Lutz^E Sr. (* c. 1573 † 1654), mentioned as herdsman in 1622, married three times, most children died young

   3 Veit Lutz^E

   4 Anna Lutz^E

   5 Eva Lutz^E

I **Michael Lutz**^{E}, **Christoph**^{F}

   1 **Nicolaus Lutz**^{D} (* c. 1614 † Dec. 2, 1669, killed transporting lumber)
     ∞ June 17, 1639 **Christina Hofmann**^{D} (* c. 1607 † June 14, 1672), widow

   2 Johannes Lutz^D Jr. (* c. 1618 † Oct. 8, 1685)
     ∞ June 17, 1639 Barbara^D Baumann (* c. 1612 † April 11, 1642), widow
     ∞ Aug. 26, 1642 Anna Schorger^D (* c. 1624 † Nov. 2, 1674), all children died in infancy

I **Nicolaus Lutz**^{D}, **Michael**^{E}, **Christoph**^{F}
   with **Christina Hofmann**^{D}

   1 Barbara Lutz^C (* Feb. 21, 1642 † ?)

   2 **Martin Lutz**^{C} (* July 9, 1643 † Dec. 8, 1677)

∞ Aug. 26, 1662 **Eva Schmid(t)**^{C}, who on Feb. 15, 1681 married Hans Wilhelm Adelmann^C

3   Eva Lutz^C (∗ May 22, 1646 † ?)

4   Wilhelm Lutz^C (∗ April 28, 1649 † April 6, 1694)
∞ June 8,1669 Christina Wehner^C

Lutz Family
in Kreuzwertheim, Pennsylvania, Moncton, and Hillsborough

II   **Martin Lutz^C, Nicolaus^D, Michael^E, Christoph^F**
with **Eva Schmid(t)^C**

1   **Johann <u>Georg</u>** ("Jörg") **Lutz^B** (∗ 1665/1666 in Höhefeld † Oct. 20, 1737 in Kreuzwertheim), dragoon in 1699
∞ Feb. 14, 1688 **Regina Schöner(t)^B** (∗ Nov. 5, 1657 † Feb. 3, 1730), daughter of Hanß Schönhard, Kreuzwertheim; cf. note[17]
∞ Jan. 23, 1731 Agnes Schöning, widow of Philipp Amend

I   **Johann <u>Georg</u>** ("Jörg") **Lutz^B, Martin^C, Nicolaus^D, Michael^E, Christoph^F**
with **Regina Schönert^B**

1   Anna Regina Lutz^A (∗ April 25, 1688 † Dec. 23, 1689)

2   **Johann <u>Wilhelm</u> Lutz^A** (∗ Dec. 22, 1690 † Jan. 19, 1775)
∞ Nov. 6, 1714 **Maria Barbara Müller^A** (∗ Oct. 21, 1696 † Nov. 29, 1780), daughter of **Michael Müller^B** of Kreuzwertheim

3   Johann <u>Peter</u> Lutz^A (∗ Nov. 27, 1692 † Sept. 21, 1762), "field judge"/inspector
∞ Oct. 20, 1716 Anna <u>Catharina</u> Enz^A (∗ Aug. 3, 1686 † Dec. 14, 1764), couple had 5 children, only 2 survived and/or are listed

4   Lorenz Lutz^A (∗ Dec. 14, 1699 † Nov. 19, 1719)

---

[17] As the spouse of Regina Schönert, Johann <u>Georg</u> Lutz was granted residence status in Kreuzwertheim on March 8, 1688.

Johann <u>Georg</u>
with Agnes Schöning

5   Johann Georg Lutz[A] (* July 11, 1732 † Jan. 30, 1814), never
    married

First "Pioneer" Generation ([1])
including German and Pennsylvanian siblings

II   **Johann <u>Wilhelm</u> Lutz[A], Georg[B] ("Jörg"), Martin[C], Nicolaus[D],
Michael[E], Christoph[F]**
with **Maria Barbara Müller[A]**

    1   Dorothea Elisabeth Lutz[1] (* Jan. 23, 1717 in Kreuzwertheim
        † ?)

    2   Johann Thomas Lutz[1] (* July 6, 1718 in Kreuzwertheim
        † [buried] Feb. 6, 1719)

    3   Johann <u>Thomas</u> Lutz[1] (* March 8, 1720 in Kreuzwertheim
        † in Pennsylvania), emigrated to Pennsylvania in 1755
        ∞ Feb. 16, 1751 Barbara Schreiner[1] (* April 7, 1717 in
        Sachsenhausen † ? in Pennsylvania)

    4   **Georg <u>Michael</u> Lutz[1]** (* April 7, 1723 in Kreuzwertheim
        † 1793/1794 in Moncton, N.B.), emigrated to Pennsylvania
        aboard *Phoenix,* arrived in Philadelphia on Nov. 22, 1752,
        farmer with large dairy herd
        ∞ Nov. 14, 1747 **Anna <u>Walpurgis</u> Wießler**[1] (* c. 1730
        † after 1792 and before 1803 in Moncton, N.B.); cf. note[18]

    5   Maria Eva Lutz[1] (* July 10, 1726 in Kreuzwertheim † buried
        Feb. 4, 1746)

    6   Anna Clara Lutz[1] (* June 5, 1730 in Kreuzwertheim † ?)
        ∞ Sept. 5, 1752 Peter Müller

---

[18] Michael Lutz's wife was called "Anna" ("Nancy") in later years; cf.
WRO, Libro A-1, 71: Jan. 30, 1786.

7   Johann Michael Lutz[1] (* Jan. 19, 1734 in Kreuzwertheim
      † Nov. 4, 1804 in Kreuzwertheim)
      ∞ Oct. 24, 1758 Anna Margaretha Dinkel [1] (* March 9, 1724
      † April 9, 1798)

III   Johann Peter Lutz[A], **Georg**[B] ("Jörg"), **Martin**[C], **Nicolaus**[D],
      Michael[E], **Christoph**[F]

  1   Johann Nicolaus Lutz[1] (* May 4, 1727 † Sept. 27, 1792),
      village and field judge
      ∞ Nov. 7, 1758 Ursula Maria Wießler[1] (* June 9, 1733
      † Jan. 9, 1799)

Second "Pioneer" Generation ("[2]")
including their German and Pennsylvanian cousins

III   Johann Thomas Lutz[1], **Wilhelm**[A], **Georg**[B] ("Jörg"), **Martin**[C],
      Nicolaus[D], **Michael**[E], **Christoph**[F]

  1   Friedrich Lutz[2] (* Oct. 6, 1751 in Kreuzwertheim † ?)

  2   Peter Lutz[2] (* June 12, 1753 in Kreuzwertheim † July 8,
      1754 in Kreuzwertheim)

  3   Johannes Lutz[2] (* July 30, 1757, bapt. Aug. 7, 1757 in
      Philadephia † ?)

IV   **Georg Michael Lutz**[1], **Wilhelm**[A], **Georg**[B]("Jörg"), **Martin**[C],
     Nicolaus[D], **Michael**[E], **Christoph**[F]
     with **Anna Walpurgis Wießler**[1]

  1   **Anna Catharina Lutz**[2] (* Jan. 11, 1749 in
      Kreuzwertheim † 1827 in Hillsborough)
      ∞ Jan. 27, 1772 **Jacob Stieff**[2] (* Nov. 14, 1749 † Oct. 9,
      1803), eldest son of **Heinrich** and **Regina Stieff**[1]

  2   **Peter Lutz**[2] (* March 12, 1751 in Kreuzwertheim † after
      March 10th and before April 1, 1825 in Lower Cover-

389

dale, N.B.), farmer, shoemaker, woodworker, trader (selling grindstones, etc.)

∞ c. 1773 **Mary Ricker**[3] (∗ 1755/1756 † after 1851 in Lower Coverdale), daughter of **Jacob Ricker**[2] Jr.; cf. note [19]

3 **Thomas Lutz**[2] (∗ c. 1753 in Pennsylvania † after June 20, 1797), moved to "other side of the River" Petit-codiac from Hillsborough around 1782; had dealings with Bedford Boultenhouse, Loyalist from Sackville (cf. note[20]); possibly left New Brunswick after 1797
   ∞ wife unknown

4 **Anna Margaretha Lutz**[2] (∗ March 4, 1755 in Philadelphia † Jan. 2, 1828 in Hillsborough)
   ∞ April 30, 1774 **John Stieff**[2] (bapt. Feb. 7, 1752 † Feb. 1, 1821), son of **Heinrich** and **Regina Stieff**[1]

5 **Georg Michael Lutz**[2] Jr. (∗ July 12, 1758 in Philadelphia † after 1803 in Hillsborough ?), moved to "other side of the River" Petitcodiac from Hillsborough around 1782 for a year; possibly left New Brunswick
   ∞ wife unknown

6 **Johannes/John Lutz**[2] (∗ c. 1761 in Philadelphia area † after 1826 and before 1851 in Moncton), farmer and cheese producer; cf. note[21]

---

[19] Mary Lutz (*née* Ricker), aged 95, lived in Coverdale with her son John and daughter-in-law "Lidia" when the 1851 Albert County Census was taken.

[20] Bedford Boultenhouse, the father of Sackville shipbuilder and captain Christopher Boultenhouse, was awarded £11:13:0 in a judgement against Thomas "Loots" on June 20, 1797; MAUL, Westmorland County, N.B. Record of Proceedings in the Court of Common Pleas, 1785-1830, Microfilm 5331.

[21] In land transactions with William Chapman in 1822 and with son-in-law Christian Steeves in 1826, John Lutz signed his name in German script as "Johannes Lutz". His wife signed her name "Elizabeth" Lutz although in her oath the name "Rebeccah" is entered; Westmorland ... Registry, Libri F-1, 95 and H-1,

∞ c. 1788 Elizabeth Charters (∗ c. 1770 † after 1845 and
before 1851 in Moncton), daughter of James and Alice
(Winsmore) Charters Sr., who moved from Hillsborough to Moncton shortly after 1783

7   **Heinrich/Henry Lutz**[2] (∗ c. 1763 in Philadelphia area
† ?), "young man" (i.e. about 20 years of age) in 1783
Hillsborough Census; no further information available,
therefore either left area shortly afterwards or died;
cf. note[22]

VII   Johann Michael Lutz[1], **Wilhelm**[A], **Georg**[B] ("Jörg"), **Martin**[C],
Nicolaus[D], **Michael**[E], **Christoph**[F]

1   Conrad Christoph Lutz[2] (∗ March 3, 1765 in
Kreuzwertheim † March 29, 1840 in County Wert-
heim)
∞ Aug. 7, 1792 Dorothea Fertig[2]

Third Generation ("³")

I   **Anna Catharina Lutz**[2], **Michael**[1], **Wilhelm**[A], **Georg**[B], **Martin**[C],
Nicolaus[D], **Michael**[E], **Christoph**[F]
with **Jacob Stieff**[2]
Couple's children listed in **Stieff Family** genealogy under **Jacob
Stieff**[2], **Heinrich**[1], **Augustinus**[A], **Heinrich**[B]

---

543. Elizabeth's identity was discovered when her full name ("Elizabeth Lutz")
was mentioned in her brother James Charters' last will, dated August 3, 1842
(WCP, Libro IV, p. 53). James mentions other siblings: brothers Samuel, William,
John, Timothy and sisters Mary Ann Outhouse, Nancy Turner, and Mary Brown.

[22] Henry Lutz was listed previously as a child of John Lutz, but this is
disproved in a letter of descendant James Brown[4], son of Martha Lutz[3] (addressed
to cousin Elizabeth Lutz[4], daughter of John Lutz[3] Jr.), dated April 2, 1872 and on
file in the Lutz Mountain Meeting House, Moncton, N.B.. The fates of Thomas,
Michael Jr., and Henry Lutz are unknown.

II   **Peter Lutz[2], Michael[1], Wilhelm[A], Georg[B], Martin[C], Nicolaus[D], Michael[E], Christoph[F]**
with **Mary Ricker[3]**; cf. note[23]

      "Sarah Ricker[3]" ? (* 1767 † ?), "adopted" daughter (of age by June 1, 1783), possible younger sister of **Mary Ricker[3]**; cf. **Ricker Family** genealogy

1   **Michael Lutz[3]** (* 1774 [40 years of age on Jan. 8, 1815] † after 1851), farmer, carpenter, sawmill operator, family moved from Hillsborough to Moncton area c. 1808, settled near Fox Creek (Parish of Dorchester) sometime before 1815; cf. note[24]
    ∞ c. 1795 wife unknown (* c. 1778 † c. 1828)
    ∞ Jan. 15, 1829 Elizabeth (*née* ?) Gallagher (* 1777/1778 † March 6, 1863 in Dover), widow of Hugh Gallagher

2   **Sophia Lutz[3]** (* c. 1776 † before 1848)
    ∞ c. 1793 Marten Jonah (* c. 1769 † after 1842 and before April 1848), son of Pierre and Elizabeth Jonah

3   **Mary Pauline ("Polly") Lutz[3]** (* c. 1778 † before 1842)
    ∞ c. 1797 Henry Jonah Sr. (* 1771 † 1842), son of Pierre and Elizabeth Jonah

4   **Rose Anna ("Rosina"?) Lutz[3]** (* 1780 † 1811)
    ∞ c. 1798 Robert MacFarlane (* 1766/1767 in Aberdeen, Scotland † Feb. 23, 1851 in Dover, N.B.), mariner; remarried Margaret

---

[23] According to the 1803 Hillsborough Census, this couple had four children, which appears to represent those children 10 years of age and under.

[24] According to the 1803 Hillsborough Census, this couple had six children, although this seems high (cf. note[28]). Michael Lutz was appointed Surveyor of Lumber in Moncton for 1809 (ST). In 1815, he had seven children and had never had any crown land granted to him before. According to Alexander Brown and David Mills (Dec. 17, 1836), Michael Lutz[3] built and operated a sawmill "... to the north of the Road from the Bend to Shediac, in the Parish of Dorchester" near Fox Creek, on land granted originally to Pierre Bourque; cf. WRO, Libro P-1, 74.

Beatty (* 1788/1789 † before 1847 ?) on June 23, 1812, daughter of John Sr. and Jane Beatty; cf. note[25]

5   **Elizabeth Mary Lutz**[3] (* 1782/1783 † after 1851)
    ∞ c. 1799 John Geldart Jr. (* c. 1778 † May 28, 1854 in Elgin, N.B.), son of John Sr. and Martha Geldart

6   **Peter Lutz**[3] **Jr.** (* 1784/1785 † after 1851); cf. note[26]
    ∞ May 7, 1816 Eunice Jonah (* c. 1798 † before 1822), daughter of Henry Jonah Sr. and Mary Pauline **Lutz**[3]
    ∞ March 28, 1822 Elizabeth Leeman (* 1791/1792 † after 1851), daughter of Robert and Ann Leeman, Coverdale

7   **John Lutz**[3] (* 1788 † 1867)
    ∞ Jan. 12, 1815 **Rosanna Steeves**[3] (* March 18, 1796 † c. 1826), **Frederick Stieff's**[2] daughter
    ∞ Dec. 6, 1827 Lydia Wilbur (* 1804/1805 † after 1851), daughter of Benjamin Jr. and Rachel Wilbur of Hillsborough

8   **Susanna Lutz**[3] (* 1790/1791 † 1876)
    ∞ Nov. 2, 1814 **David Steeves**[3] (* March 2, 1782 † 1847), **John Stieff's**[2] son; **Susanna Lutz**[3] was **David Steeves**'[3] second wife

9   **Charles Lutz**[3](* March 19, 1794 † Dec. 8, 1870), farmer at Mud Creek, Hillsborough, later at Boundary Creek, Moncton
    ∞ Nov. 6, 1817 **Margaret Steeves**[3] (* April 17, 1800 † Jan. 27, 1868), **Frederick Stieff's**[2] daughter

10   **Margaret Lutz**[3] (* 1795 † 1874)

---

[25] In the marriage register, Margaret Beatty's age was given as "23", which would make her a twin of Esther Beatty. If the "23" was mistakenly read for "28", her birthdate would have been 1783/1784, which seems more likely in view of the Beatty Family genealogy.

[26] Peter Lutz Jr. and wife Elizabeth sold a parcel of land to a Thomas Greeno on January 20, 1825; WRO, Libro H-1, 42. A link with the Greeno family was already established when Barbara Lutz married Moses Greeno.

∞ Oct. 26, 1820 Daniel McLean (* 1779 in Scotland † 1872), **Margaret**[3] and **Nancy Ann Lutz**[3] appear to have married in a double ceremony

11 **Barbara Lutz**[3] (* c. 1798 † ?); cf. note[27]
∞ Nov. 6, 1823 Moses Green(o) (* c. 1798 † after 1842) from Coverdale, possible son of Thomas Greeno and grandson of Moses Greenough, Township of Conway, N.S. (1770)

12 **Nancy Ann Lutz**[3] (* 1800/1801 † after 1851)
∞ Oct. 26, 1820 William Dalegant (Daligan) (* 1796/1797 † after 1851) from Hillsborough, shoemaker

IV **Anna <u>Margaretha</u> Lutz**[2], **Michael**[1], **Wilhelm**[A], **Georg**[B], **Martin**[C], **Nicolaus**[D], **Michael**[E], **Christoph**[F]
with **John Stieff**[2]
Couple's children listed in **Stieff Family** genealogy under **John Stieff**[2], **Heinrich**[1], **Augustinus**[A], **Heinrich**[B]

V **Georg Michael Lutz**[2], **Michael**[1], **Wilhelm**[A], **Georg**[B], **Martin**[C], **Nicolaus**[D], **Michael**[E], **Christoph**[F]
with unknown wife; cf. note[28]

---

[27] In a suit against Alexander Smith, Susanna Lutz was awarded £100 on June 14, 1814. The witness for the defence was Jacob Steeves and those for the plaintiff were Susanna's parents, Peter and Mary Lutz, and her likely sister, Barbara; Westmorland County, N.B. Record of Proceedings in the Court of Common Pleas, 1785-1830.

[28] According to the 1803 Hillsborough Census, a Michael Lutz household had six children. It seems unlikely that Michael Lutz[3] had six children by 1803. Another early reference to a Michael Lutz was his purchase on May 2, 1800 of two parcels of land in Lower Coverdale from Enoch Groom (known as "Lot 3", located half way between Mill Creek and Stoney Creek; WRO, Libro C-1, 47: registered June 8, 1807), witnessed by Delia Cornwall and James Watson. The possibility does exist that Michael Lutz[3] bought this property due to its proximity to father Peter Lutz' farm and his relatively recent marriage. Once only, in 1801, was a Michael Lutz[3] referred to as "Jr." when he served his first term of office as a

394

VI   **Johannes/John Lutz², Michael¹, Wilhelm^A, Georg^B, Martin^C, Nicolaus^D, Michael^E, Christoph^F**
with wife Elizabeth Charters; cf. note[29]

1   **William J. Lutz³** (∗ Nov. 8, 1789 † June 11, 1861)
∞ c. 1812 **Susannah Trites³** (∗ c. 1794 † after 1851), **Jacob Treitz²** Jr.'s daughter

2   **Lydia Lutz³** (∗ April 23, 1791 † before 1872)
∞ Aug. 5, 1814 Oliver McGarvie

3   **Olive Lutz³** (∗ Jan. 30, 1793 † 1872)
∞ Feb. 13, 1813 **Christian Steeves³** Jr. (∗ c. 1790 † Feb. 25, 1829), **Christian Stieff²** Sr.'s son

4   **Zachariah Lutz³** (∗ May 27, 1795 † March 10, 1864)
∞ c. 1817 Mary Jonah (∗ 1799/1800 † Oct. 3, 1881), daughter of John James Jonah, granddaughter of Peter Jonah; cf. note[30]

5   **Jeremiah Lutz³** (∗ July 26, 1797 † after 1851)
∞ Nov. 26, 1818 **Ruth Beck** from Salisbury, N.B. (∗ 1795/1796 † Nov. 2, 1861), possible daughter of **Jacob Beck²**, Salisbury

6   **Catherine Lutz³** (∗ June 18, 1799 † before 1872)
∞ Jan. 14, 1819 Martin Wilson (∗ 1792/1793 † Dec. 27, 1870), son of William and "Catherine" (*née* **Wortman** ?)² Wilson of Moncton

---

Constable for Hillsborough, implying the presence of a Michael Lutz² (S.T.). It is uncertain where Michael Lutz's² family lived c. 1785-1803, nor does he appear to have sold a Moncton inheritance from his father to John Lutz² as did his two Hillsborough siblings in 1794.

[29] According to the 1803 Moncton Census, this couple had seven children.

[30] Another Mary Jonah married James Cusack on March 28, 1823. James Cusack stood as a witness when Peter Lutz made his last will and testament on March 10, 1825.

7   **John Lutz**[3] Jr. (∗ April 23, 1801 † after 1872), emigrated to
     United States c. 1830, possibly with **Christian** and **Olive
     (Lutz**[3]**) Steeves**[3] **Jr.**
     ∞ June 3, 1832 Mary Malin (∗ 1809 in Jefferson Co., Virginia
     † 1891 in Nebraska)

8   **Martha Lutz**[3] (∗ March 23, 1803 † March 30, 1874), twin
     ∞ Jan. 3, 1821 John Brown (∗ 1799/1800 † May 27, 1863), of
     Moncton, possible son of John and Mary (Charters) Brown of
     Moncton, grandson of John Brown, bricklayer from Cumberland

9   **Margaret Ann Lutz**[3] (∗ March 23, 1803 † Dec. 23, 1886), twin
     ∞ Dec. 8, 1825 **Solomon Jones**[3] (∗ Jan. 27, 1802 † March 25,
     1875), son of Henry Jones[2] and **Christina(h) (Ricker**[3]**/
     Sommer**[2]**/Wortman**[2] **?)**

10   **Ruth Lutz**[3] (∗ Oct. 16, 1805 † before 1860)
     ∞ Jan. 21, 1830 John Crossman (∗ June 4, 1806 † June 5, 1890),
     son of Robert Crossman Jr. and Mary Ellen Geldart

11   **Elizabeth Lutz**[3] (∗ Sept. 13, 1809 † May 11, 1890)
     ∞ Oct. 13, 1831 Thomas Wheaton (∗ 1806 † 1887) of Salisbury,
     probable son of Daniel and Ann (Wilson) Wheaton

12   **Eunice Lutz**[3] (∗ Jan. 7, 1812 † after 1872) of Salisbury
     ∞ Jan. 22, 1836 John Kay (∗ c. 1810 † ?), son of William
     Kay Jr. ? of Salisbury

RICKER FAMILY

First "Pioneer" Generation ("¹")

I   **Jacob Ricker**¹ Sr.(* c. 1705 in Germany, possibly Bodelshausen, Baden-Württemberg † c. 1785 in Lower Coverdale, N.B.); cf. note³¹
   ∞ c. 1730 name unknown (possibly "Anna Maria") (* c. 1710 † c. after 1751 in Pennsylvania)
   ∞ c. 1775 ?, possibly "Margaret" (Jones ?), widow of Charles Jones¹ ? ; cf. **Jones Family** genealogy; note³²

Second "Pioneer" Generation ("²")

Jacob Ricker¹ Sr.
with name unknown (possibly "Anna Maria")

1   **Jacob Ricker**² Jr. (* c. 1730 † after Jan. 31, 1801 and before end of 1802, presumably in Lower Coverdale), farmer, weaver
   ∞ c. 1754 "Rosanna" ? (*née* ?, German) (* c. 1735 † c. 1767 in Moncton)
   ∞ c. 1769 **Maria Magdalena (Aldmann) Sommer**¹ (* c. 1730

---

³¹ Pioneer Jacob Ricker¹ Sr. is possibly Johann Jacob Riecker, miller from Bodelshausen, Baden-Württemberg, Germany, who arrived in Philadelphia on the "Phoenix", September 25, 1751. If so, Jacob Ricker² Jr. had a younger brother: Georg Ricker (bapt. July 17, 1745 in Bodelshausen, Germany † ? in Pennsylvania ?). Possible relations of the Ricker¹ family were: (1) Martin "Riecker" (* c. 1756 in Germany † after 1824), married about 1785, who applied for land in 1802 in Bouctouche, Kent Co. and in Hampstead, Queen's Co. in 1824; and (2) John "Ricker" (* c. 1762 presumed in Germany † c. 1819), who married c. 1790 Christyane (*née* ?) and applied with Martin Ricker in 1802 for land in Bouctouche but moved to Springfield, King's Co. around 1818.

³² In 1783 Jacob Ricker Sr. had a wife, two sons, and one daughter (all of age). It is unknown whether these children were Rickers or children brought into the household by marriage. It seems unlikely that "Margaret Ricker" was this daughter "of age", unmarried 14 years later. The possibility also exists that "Margaret Ricker" was a third wife of Jacob Ricker Jr. (cf. note³³).

† after 1780 and probably 1783, but before 1803), widow of
Matthias Sommer[1]; cf. note[33]

2   Son **Michael** ? (**Ricker**[2] ?) (∗ ? [of age in 1783] † ?); cf. note[34]

3   Son (**Ricker**[2] ?) (∗ ? [of age in 1783] † ?)

4   Daughter (**Ricker**[2] ?) (∗ c. 1765 [of age in 1783] † ?)

Third Generation ("3")

I   **Jacob Ricker**[2] **Jr., Jacob Ricker**[1] **Sr.**
     with first wife; cf. note[35]

---

[33] Jacob Ricker Jr.'s wife's name is never mentioned in local documents
so that it is only assumed she was "Maria Magdalena" and not an unrecorded third
wife of Matthias Sommer. One cannot dismiss the possibility that Sommer's
widow died sometime after 1780 and that Jacob Ricker Jr. took "Margaret" (*née?*)
for his third wife.

[34] If Jacob Ricker Sr. married Charles Jones[1]' widow (cf. Jones Family
genealogy), the children listed under Jacob Ricker Sr.'s name in the 1783
Hillsborough Census might represent Jones' two sons, Henry and John, and a
"daughter" although one would expect Henry Jones to have been listed as the head
of a new household unless he had already moved back to Moncton. Twice the
name Michael Ricker[3] was referred to as Michael Ricker "Jr.", suggesting the
presence of a Michael Ricker "Sr.":   Michael Ricker Jr. as Constable in
Hillsborough (1789) and Michael Ricker Jr. as Surveyor of Highways in
Hillsborough (1801) (Sackville Townbook). All other entries were simply for
"Michael Ricker", who, as Jacob Ricker Jr.'s son, would have been old enough to
receive all these appointments.

[35] Jacob Ricker[2] Jr.'s number of children was reported differently in the
various censuses, reflecting when daughters had married and left home:

1770 Hillsborough Census: 6 girls, 2 boys
    Rickers: Mary, Rosanna, (Christinah or Sarah ?), Michael
    Sommers: Sarah ?, Christianna, Elizabeth, Rachel, Andrew
                   Catharina married)

1   **Mary Ricker**[3] (∗ 1755/1756 † after 1851 in Lower Coverdale)
     ∞ c. 1773 **Peter Lutz**[2] (∗ March 12, 1751 † after March 10th and
     before April 1, 1825 in Lower Coverdale), eldest son of **Michael**
     and **Walpurgis Lutz**[1]

2   **Rosanna Ricker**[3] (∗ c. 1758 in Pennsylvania † after 1823 and
     before 1830 in Moncton)
     ∞ c. 1775 **Jacob Treitz**[2] Jr. (∗ c. 1752 † Oct. 1802 -- died intes-
     tate), son of **Jacob Sr.** and **Elisina Treitz**[1],
     ∞ Jan. 16, 1816 **Frederick Stieff**[2] (∗ Aug. 8, 1755 † c. 1830),
     widower, son of **Heinrich** and **Regina Stieff**[1]

3   **Christina(h) (Ricker**[3]**/Sommer**[2]**/Wortman**[2] **?)** (∗ 1761/1762
     † after 1851); cf. note[36]

1775 Hillsborough Census: 7 children
     Rickers: Rosanna (Christinah or Sarah ?), Michael (Mary married)
     Sommers: Christianna, Elizabeth, Rachel, Andrew (Anna
                Catharina and Sarah married)

June 1, 1783 Hillsborough Census: 2 nearly full-grown sons, all daugh-
                -ters married
     Rickers: Michael ("Sarah Ricker" possibly living with Peter and
                Mary Lutz)
     Sommers: Andrew

March 16, 1788 Millidge Report refers to 1 son and 5 daughters as heirs
                of Matthias Sommer

In a group petition to Fredericton, alongside Jacob Ricker's name is the
entry "10 children been settled 13 years" (Microfilm F 1032, PANB), which must
refer to the total number of children in the combined Ricker/Sommer household:

     Rickers: Mary, Rosanna, (Christinah or Sarah ?), Michael
     Sommers: Anna Catharina, Sarah, Christianna, Elizabeth, Rachel,
                Andrew.

[36] "Christinah" may have been a Ricker or Wortman (cf. Wortman Family
genealogy) since the name duplication "Christinah"/"Christianna" in Matthias
Sommer[1]'s family seems unlikely. Andrew Sommer also never called any of his

∞ c. 1780 Henry Jones[2] (∗ 1756/1757 † Jan. 20, 1840, buried in Pioneer Cemetery, Salisbury), son of Charles Jones[1]

4   **Michael Ricker[3]** (∗ 1764/1765 † after 1820 in Lower Coverdale), dairy farmer, entrepreneur, maple sugar producer
    ∞ c. 1785 "Catharine" (*née* Stiles ?) (c. 1767 † after 1820 in Lower Coverdale), possible daughter of Nathaniel and Keziah (Kilborn) Stiles; cf. note[37]

5   **"Sarah Ricker[3]"** ? (∗ c. 1767 ? † ?); cf. note[38]
    ∞ Dec. 8, 1784 James Wilson ? of Londonderry, N. S. (possible relation of William Wilson of Moncton)

I   **Jacob Ricker[2] Jr., Jacob Ricker[1] Sr.**
    with second wife **Maria Magdalena (Aldmann) Sommer[1]**, widow of **Matthias Sommer[1]**

---

eight daughters "Christinah" although Elizabeth, Rachel, Sarah, and Catherine appear to have been named after his siblings. In the 1851 Moncton Census, Christinah Jones was listed as an 89-year-old "Dutch" widow living in the household of Moses and Barbara Jones.

[37] According to the 1783 Hillsborough Census, Nathaniel Stiles had one daughter of age, i.e. born c. 1767, name unknown. Jacob Ricker seems to have been a friend of Nathaniel Stiles as they petitioned together along with their sons and sons-in-law for title to adjacent Hillsborough properties on January 24, 1785 (PANB, Microfilm F 1029), around the time Michael Ricker may have married. More research is still needed on "Catharine's" line. (The name "Ruth" was used by both Stiles sons, Oliver and Reuben, as well as by Michael Ricker.)

[38] Jean M. Holder, *Nova Scotia Marriage Bond Index 1763-1864* (Publ. No. 14 of the Genealogical Association of Nova Scotia, 1997), Microfilm 15926. James Wilson may have been related to the Moncton Wilson family. A later James Wilson signed as a witness in a land transaction between Aaron and Caroline Jones and John Bennett (WRO, Libro Q-1, 468: reg. July 8, 1839). "Sarah Ricker" may have been raised by Mary Ricker[3] in Jacob Ricker[2] Jr.'s household and then in Peter Lutz's[2], after Mary Ricker[3] and Peter Lutz[2] married c. 1773. This couple resided next door to Jacob Ricker[2] Jr.'s household from the time of their marriage on.

Couple produced no known children; cf. **Sommer Family** genealogy for children brought into **Jacob Ricker**[2] Jr.'s household

Fourth Generation ("4")

I   **Mary Ricker**[3], **Jacob Ricker**[2] Jr., **Jacob Ricker**[1] Sr.
    with **Peter Lutz**[2]
    Couple's children listed in **Lutz Family** genealogy under **Peter Lutz**[2], **Michael**[1], **Wilhelm**[A], **Georg**[B], **Martin**[C], **Nicolaus**[D], **Michael**[E], **Christoph**[F]

II **Rosanna Ricker**[3], **Jacob Ricker**[2] Jr., **Jacob Ricker**[1] Sr.
    with **Jacob Treitz**[2] Jr.
    Couple's children listed in **Treitz Family** genealogy under **Jacob Treitz**[2] Jr., **Jacob Treitz**[1] Sr.

III **Christina(h)** (**Ricker**[3]/**Sommer**[2]/**Wortman**[2] ?), **Jacob Ricker**[2] Jr., **Jacob Ricker**[1] Sr.
    with Henry Jones
    Couple's children listed in Jones Family genealogy under Henry Jones[2], Charles Jones[1]

IV **Michael Ricker**[3], **Jacob Ricker**[2] Jr., **Jacob Ricker**[1] Sr.
    with wife "Catharine"; cf. note[39]

    1   **Rosanna Ricker**[4] (* 1785/1786 † after 1851)
        ∞ Dec. 22, 1808 John Wilson (* c. 1782 † c. Sept. 1845) of Hillsborough and later Moncton, possible son of William and Catherine (*née* **Wortman** ?)[2] Wilson of Moncton

    2   **Sarah Ricker**[4] (* c. 1788 † after 1832 and before 1851)

---

[39] According to the 1803 Hillsborough Census, this couple had six children, therefore two (or more ?) children may be unaccounted for and/or died as infants. In a petition to Fredericton dated July 14, 1815, Michael Ricker claimed to have a wife, six children, and to be 50 years of age (PANB, Microfilm F 4178).

∞ Nov. 27, 1806 **Jacob Steeves**[3] (∗ 1784 † 1832), son of **Christian Stieff**[2]

3 **Jacob Ricker**[4] (∗ 1792/1793 † before 1851), farmer
∞ July 10, 1823 Olive Ward (∗ 1799/1800 † after 1851),
possible daughter of Nehemiah Ward Jr. of Sackville

4 **Ruth Ricker**[4] (∗ c. 1800 † before 1851)
∞ Jan. 10, 1819 Thomas Leeman (∗ c. 1795 † before 1851),
son of Robert and Ann Leeman of Coverdale

5 **Ann Ricker**[4] (∗ 1805/1806 † after 1851)
∞ March 6, 1828 **Robert Crossman** (∗ 1805/1806 † before
1851), whose German mother was "Christiana" (*née* Beck ?
Brackman ?) (∗ 1775/1776 † after 1851); cf. note[40]

6 **William Ricker**[4] (∗ 1806/1807 † after 1851), shoemaker in
Hillsborough
∞ Nov. 24, 1831 **Abigail Steeves**[3] (∗ 1810/1811 † after
1851), daughter of **Ludovic Stieff**[2]

---

[40] "Christiana" (∗ 1775/1776 † after 1851) married Jeremiah Crossman
(∗ c. 1774 † after 1822), Robert's father, about 1796. At least two possibilities as
to Christiana's identity exist. She may have been a daughter of Martin Sr. and
Johanna Beck as the name surfaces in the third generation. It could also have been
that she was a daughter of Joseph Brackman (∗ ? † after 1775 and before 1783),
who may have been a German to come up from Germantown to Hillsborough c.
1771-1774. His name appears in the 1783 Hillsborough Census "as per return in
1775, since dead," indicating that his wife and three children survived him.
Possibly, Brackman married a German woman from Hillsborough and "Christiana"
was their second child. No male Brackman descendants have been traced and
widow Brackman's whereabouts are unknown after 1783.

SOMMER FAMILY

First "Pioneer" Generation ("¹")

I   **Matthias Sommer**¹ (∗ 1720 † 1767/1768 in Moncton)

∞ Oct. 23, 1749 **Christina Null**¹ (∗ c. 1730 † c. 1757 in Philadelphia)

∞ Aug. 15, 1758 **Maria Magdalena Aldmann**¹ (∗ c. 1730 † after 1780 and probably 1783 but before 1803, presumably in Lower Coverdale), widow; cf. note[41]

Second "Pioneer" Generation ("²")

I   **Matthias Sommer**¹
with **Christina Null**¹

1   **Anna Catharina Sommer**² (bapt. Nov. 8, 1750 in Philadelphia † after 1803), resided near Baie Verte, N.B.
∞ 1767 Eliphalet Chappell (∗ c. 1747 † after 1800), son of Jabez and Zipporah Chappell of Cumberland

2   **Eva Magdalena Sommer**² (bapt. Feb. 6, 1753 in Philadelphia † died as infant ?), doubtful she came with Sommer family to N.B.

3   **Sarah Sommer**² (∗ c. 1755 † after 1823 in Parish of Botsford), resided near Baie Verte, N.B.
∞ Jan. 1, 1771 Benjamin Allan (∗ 1734/1735 † April 14, 1823), son of William Esq. and Sarah Allan of Cumberland, N.S.

4   **Anna Christianna Sommer**² (∗ c. 1757 † after 1809), resided in Cumberland
∞ c. 1775 Nathaniel Fails (Fales) (∗ c. 1750 † c. 1779), son of Atwood Fails of Amherst, N.S.
∞ March 27, 1780 George Dobson Jr. (∗ June 21, 1751 † Jan. 13, 1809), son of George Sr. and Mary (Baker) Dobson of Fort Cumberland

---

[41] Maria Magdalena Aldmann does not appear to have brought any children from her first marriage into the second.

403

I   **Matthias Sommer**[1]
      with **Maria Magdalena Aldmann**[1]

5   **Elizabeth Sommer**[2] (∗ Feb. 13, 1759 † after 1788), believed to have
        come with Sommer family to N.B. but difficult to trace due to fre-
        quency of name
        ∞ c. 1780 ? husband unknown

6   **Christina(h) (Sommer**[2]**/Ricker**[3]**/Wortman**[2] **?)** (∗ 1761/1762 † after
        1851); cf. note[42]
        ∞ c. 1778 Henry Jones[2] (∗ 1756/1757 † Jan. 20, 1840), son of Charles
        Jones[1]

7   **Rachel Sommer**[2] (∗ Jan. 31, 1764 prob. in Barren Hill, Pennsylvania
        † 1814 in Moncton)
        ∞ June 25, 1780 **Frederick Stieff**[2] (∗ Aug. 8, 1755 † c. 1830 in Monc-
        ton), son of **Heinrich** and **Regina Stieff**[1]

8   **Andrew ("Andreas") Sommer**[2] (∗ c. 1765 prob. in Barren Hill,
        Pennsylvania † June 1840 in Moncton), farmer; cf. note[43]
        ∞ c. 1787 "Amy"/"Emily" (*née* Beck ? Lewis ? Smith ?) (∗ c. 1770
        † before 1839)

Third Generation ("3")

VIII   **Andrew ("Andreas") Sommer**[2], **Matthias Sommer**[1]

---

[42] Cf. "Christina(h)" also in the Ricker and Wortman Family genealogies.

[43] No local documents refer to Andrew by his German name. The probate
record of Andrew Sommer's last will and testament was filed on Jan. 24, 1839 and
proved July 17, 1840 (WPR, p. 20). Land transactions and certain names show a
link between Alanson Lewis and Andrew Sommer, but the name "Martin" does not
run in the Lewis family as it does in the Beck family. The Sommer family claims
that Andrew's wife was Elizabeth Smith although no documentation could be
found to confirm this. "Amy/ Emily's" family background requires further
research.

with "Amy"/"Emily"; cf. note[44]

1   **Deborah Sommer**[3] (* c. 1788 † after March 7, 1849 and before 1851)
    ∞ Nov. 19, 1805 **Charles Jones**[3] (* 1780/1781 † Oct. 23, 1850), eldest son of Henry and **Christina(h)** (**Ricker**[3]/**Sommer**[2]/**Wortman**[2] ?) Jones[2]

2   **Elizabeth Sommer**[3] (* 1790/1791 † Oct. 13, 1856 in Wilson Cemetery, Allison), twin ?
    ∞ c. 1821 **Charles Trites**[3] (* 1783/1784 † June 3, 1856), son of **Abraham** and Margaret **Treitz**[2]

3   **Rachel Sommer**[3] (* 1790/1991 † after 1851), twin ?
    ∞ March 14, 1815 Timothy Horsman (* 1787 † 1847), son of Christopher and Mary (Wilbur) Horsman

4   **Mathias Sommer**[3] (* 1791/1792 † March 23, 1845)
    ∞ c. 1815 **Elizabeth Jones**[3] (* 1786/1787 † after 1851), daughter of Henry and **Christina(h)** (**Ricker**[3]/**Sommer**[2]/**Wortman**[2] ?) Jones[2]

5   **Martin Sommer**[3] (* c. 1793 † before 1851 ?)
    ∞ Feb. 27, 1817 **Sarah ("Sally") Trites**[3] (* c. 1800 † after 1843 and before 1851?), possible daughter of **Jacob** and Rosanna (Ricker) **Treitz**[2] Jr.

6   **Sarah Sommer**[3] (* c. 1796 [1800/1801, according to 1851 Census] † after 1851), likely not a twin of Susanna
    ∞ Jan. 6, 1820 James Anderson (* 1795/1796 † after 1851) from Moncton, son of James Anderson Jr. of Hopewell ?

7   **Lucy Sommer**[3] (* c. 1798 † after 1839)
    ∞ date ? husband unknown; couple may have left Moncton area

---

[44] In the 1803 Moncton Census, Andrew Sommer has eight children, which agrees with the above entries.

8　Susanna Sommer[3] (∗ 1800/1801 † after 1851); cf. note[45]
∞ March 29, 1821 Anthony Simpson (∗ c. 1800/1801 in England
† after 1851), resided in Shediac

9　Catherine Sommer[3] (∗ 1804/1805 [tombstone], 1809/1810
[1851 Census], † Sept. 30, 1877), resided in Shediac
∞ Sept. 4, 1828 Stephen Nickerson (∗ 1802/1803 † after 1851),
farmer, possible son of Jeremiah Nickerson Jr., originally from
Liverpool, N.S.

10　Rebecca Sommer[3] (∗ 1810/1811 † after 1851)
∞ Oct. 8, 1829 Jacob Trites[4] (∗ 1802/1803 † after 1851), son of
Abraham Trites[3] and grandson of Jacob Treitz[2] Jr.

REGINA (STIEFF) STAHLECKER FAMILY
in Honau vicinity, District Reutlingen, Baden-Württemberg

I　Gallus Stahlecker[D] (∗ c. 1580 † ?), Regina's possible great-great-grand-
father in Kleinengstingen, on the "Alb" above Honau

　I　Gall Stahlecker[C] (∗ c 1610 † ?), Regina's possible great-grandfather
in Kleinengstingen

　　I　Michael Stahlecker[B] (∗ c. 1640 † ?), Regina's grandfather,
miller in Honau 1675
∞ c. 1667 Eva[B] (née ?)
∞ c. 1687 Margareta Reifl(in)[B] (five more children between 1688
and 1694)
∞ after 1694 Anna Barbara Tröster [B]

---

[45] Andrew Sommer left the same amount of money in his will to daughters
Lucy and Susanna. If Lucy had been single in 1839, he likely would have wanted
to provide her with extra support. There are problems with the birthdates of
daughters Lucy, Susanna, and Catherine, but they are listed in this order according
to Andrew's will.

I   **Michael Stahlecker**[B], **Gall(us)**[C], **Gallus**[D]
      with **Eva**[B]

     1   Hans Jacob Stahlecker[A] (∗ March 22, 1668   † ?)

     2   Hans Friedrich Stahlecker[A] (∗ Feb. 14, 1670   † ?)

     3   Margaretha Stahlecker[A] (∗ Jun. 29, 1673   † ?)

     4   Catharina Stahlecker[A] (∗ Feb. 25, 1675   † ?)

     5   Veronica Stahlecker[A] (∗ April 22, 1678   † ?)

     6   **David Stahlecker**[A] (∗ Aug. 27, 1680   † ?), farmer in Honau
        1706
        ∞ Feb. 28, 1706 **Agnes Werner(in)**[A] (∗ April 12, 1682   † ?),
        daughter of Jacob and Anna Maria Werner[B] in Honau

First "Pioneer" Generation ("1")
and their German siblings

VI   **David Stahlecker**[A], **Michael**[B], **Gall**[C], **Gallus**[D]
      with **Agnes Werner(in)**[A]

     1   David Stahlecker[1] (∗ April 8, 1707   † as infant)

     2   Anna Maria Stahlecker[1] (∗ Aug. 15, 1708   † ?)

     3   Michael Stahlecker[1] (∗ Feb. 13, 1711   † ?)

     4   Johann Jacob Stahlecker[1] (∗ Feb. 16, 1714 † young)

     5   Ludwig Stahlecker[1] (∗ May 23, 1717   † ?)

     6   Anna Barbara Stahlecker[1] (∗ April 24, 1718   † ?)

7   **Regina Stahlecker**[1] (* Sept. 3, 1719 in Honau † after
     1783 and before 1803 in Hillsborough, N.B.); note[46]
     ∞ Feb. 25, 1745 **Johann Heinrich Stieff**[1] (III) (* c. 1715
     in vicinity of Münsingen, Baden-Württemberg
     † c. 1779 in Hillsborough)
     Couple's children listed in **Stieff Family** genealogy
     under **Johann Heinrich Stieff**[1], **Augustinus**[A], **Johann
     Heinrich**[B]

     Witnesses at **Regina's**[1] baptism:
       Martin Stahlecker (* May 27, 1696 † ?)
       Anna Barbara Stahlecker(in) (* May 2, 1699 † ?)
       Sophia Regina Felner(in) (* Aug. 15, 1696 † ?),
         daughter of first pastor in Honau, Johann Friedrich
         Felner, likely namesake of **Regina (Stahlecker)
         Stieff**[1]

STIEFF FAMILY

Johann Heinrich Stieff[B] (Sr.) (* c. 1650 † Oct. 6, 1699 in Münsingen, Württemberg)
∞ c. 1681 **Anna Barbara Hess**[B], Münsingen baker's daughter (* Jan. 24, 1657
† April 22, 1726), remarried July 25, 1701 Ludwig Genkinger of Münsingen

1   **Augustinus Stieff**[A] (* Nov. 30, 1683 † Oct. 9, 1761 Münsingen), herds-
     man
     ∞ Oct. 3, 1707 **Anna Barbara Worner**[A] (* April 8, 1683 in Ohnastetten
     † May 24, 1746 in Münsingen)
     ∞ Jan. 23, 1747 Anna Barbara Haueisen[A] (* ? † before 1757)
     ∞ Jan. 25, 1757 Christina Hauptmann[A] (* ? † July 1, 1761)

2   Johann Heinrich Stieff[A] (* Jan. 4, 1685 † as infant)

3   Johann Heinrich Stieff[A] (Jr.) (* May 21, 1687 † ?), knitter in Münsingen

---

[46] It is possible that Regina Stieff died around 1797 when Ludovic Stieff[2]
named his daughter "Rachel"; cf. Ludovic Stieff's family.

∞ Oct. 13, 1711 Anna Barbara Schwenk[A], daughter of Conrad Schwenk[B], Münsingen tilemaker and associate justice

4   Georg Friedrich Stieff[A] (* Jan. 31, 1690 † ?)

5   Ferdinand Stieff[A] (* Nov. 16, 1692 † ?)

6   Susanna Barbara Stieff[A] (* ? † June 1699)

First "Pioneer" Generation ("[1]")
including Württemberg and Pennsylvania siblings

I   **Augustinus Stieff [A], Johann Heinrich[B]**
    with **Anna Barbara**[A]

1   Katharina Stieff[1] (* March 11, 1710 in Hundersingen, Württemberg † Sept. 29, 1774 in Münsingen)

2   Benedikt Stieff[1] (* April 20, 1711 in Hundersingen, bapt. April 23, 1711 in Münsingen † ?)

3   Georg Friedrich Stieff[1] (* c. 1712 in Ohnastetten † Nov. 15, 1795 in Reading, Berks Co., Pennsylvania), shoemaker, arrived in Philadelphia on *Richard and Mary* Sept. 17, 1753
    ∞ Feb. 4, 1744 Maria Katarina Haubensack,[1] shoemaker's widow, in Schlaitdorf, Württemberg

4   **Johann <u>Heinrich</u> Stieff**[1] (III) (* c. 1715 † c. 1779 in Hillsborough, N.B.), brick- and tilemaker, emigrated from Seißen, Württemberg, to Pennsylvania in 1749
    ∞ Feb. 25, 1745 **Regina Stahlecker**[1] ("Stahlegger") (* Sept. 3, 1719 in Honau † after 1783 and before 1803 in Hillsborough), farmer's daughter from Honau, Württemberg

5   Michael Stieff[1] (* c. 1717 † ? in Münsingen), shepherd
    ∞ Jan. 11, 1745 Anna Barbara Walter

6   Anna Maria Stieff[1] (* April 24, 1720 in Hundersingen † ?)
    ∞ May 22, 1756 Johannes Haueisen[1] in Münsingen with illeg. child, Catharina Barbara[2] (* April 7, 1749 † April 19, 1749)

7   Johann Georg Stieff[1] (* March 31, 1723 in Hundersingen † ?), tailor

8   Johannes Stieff[1] (* May 14, 1727 in Hundersingen † ?)

III   Johann Heinrich Stieff[A], **Johann Heinrich**[B]
     with Anna Barbara Schwenk[A]

1   Konrad Stieff[1] (* Aug. 9, 1712 in Münsingen † ?), knitter in Münsingen, member of town court in 1761
∞ Sept. 1, 1739 Katharina Thein (* ? † 1761)

2   Johann Friedrich Stieff[1] (* Oct. 29, 1713 in Münsingen † ?), knitter
∞ Feb. 11, 1738 Christina Lock, hatmaker's daughter

3   Johann Heinrich Stieff[1] (IV) (* July 13, 1717 in Münsingen † ?), weaver
∞ Dec. 24, 1741 Anna Maria Hess[1], weaver's daughter

4   Anna Katharina Stieff[1] (* May 1716 in Münsingen † ?)

5   Maria Barbara Stieff[1] (* April 1, 1720 in Münsingen † 1743 in Stuttgart/Bad Cannstadt, Württemberg)

6   Johannes Stieff[1] (* c. 1720 † ?)
∞ April 18, 1747 Rosina Barbara Freitag[1]

7   Augustin Stieff[1] (Jan. 1725 † as infant)

8   Laurentius Stieff[1] (* Oct. 31, 1726 † ?)

9   Augustin Stieff[1] (* c. 1727 † ?)
∞ June 30, 1750 wife unknown

10   Johann Jacob Stieff[1] (* July 21, 1729 † Jan. 27, 1732)

Second "Pioneer" Generation ("²")
and Pennsylvania cousins

III   Friedrich Stieff[1], **Augustinus**[A], **Johann Heinrich**[B]
with Maria Katarina Haubensack,[1]

     1   Regina Stieff[2] (∗ Oct. 7, 1744 in Schlaitdorf, Württemberg † ? in Pennsylvania)

     2   Georg Friedrich Stieff[2] (∗ Jan. 23, 1746 † Nov. 3, 1746)

     3   Anna Maria Stieff[2] (∗ Dec. 9, 1747 † April 15, 1748)

     4   Jacob Friedrich Stieff[2] (∗ May 5, 1749 † Feb. 26, 1751)

     5   Maria Katarina Stieff[2] (∗ Aug. 22, 1751 in Schlaitdorf, Württemberg † ? in Pennsylvania)

IV   **Johann Heinrich Stieff**[1], **Augustinus**[A], **Johann Heinrich**[B]
with **Regina Stahlecker**[1] ("Stahlegger")

     1   **Katharina Barbara Stieff**[2] (∗ July 28, 1745 (*ex praemat. concub.*) in Münsingen † c. 1746 Münsingen)

     2   **Heinrich Stieff**[2] (∗ July 5, 1747 in Seißen † c. 1749 at sea during trans-Atlantic crossing ?)

     3   **Christina Stieff**[2] (∗ June 16, 1748 in Seißen † c. 1749 at sea during trans-Atlantic crossing ?)

     4   **Johann Jacob Stieff**[2] (∗ Nov. 14, 1749, bapt. Nov. 16, 1749 in Philadelphia † Oct. 9, 1803 in Hillsborough), farmer, trader
∞ Jan 28, 1772 **Anna Catharina ("Kitty") Lutz**[2] (∗ Jan. 11, 1749 in Kreuzwertheim † 1827 in Hillsborough), daughter of **Michael** and **Walpurgis Lutz**[1]

     5   **Johannes/John Stieff**[2] (∗ June 25, 1751, bapt. Nov. 24, 1751 in Philadelphia † Feb. 1, 1821 in Hillsborough), lived on farm-

stead north of Gray's Island, farmer, grist- and sawmill operator ?, tavernkeeper ?; cf. note [47]

∞ April 30, 1774 **Anna <u>Margaretha</u> ("Peggy") Lutz**[2] (* March 4, 1755 in Philadelphia, Penn. † Jan. 2, 1828 in Hillsborough), daughter of **Michael** and **Walpurgis Lutz**[1]

6   **Christian Stieff**[2] (* Feb. 23, 1753, bapt. April 29, 1753 in Germantown † Oct. 5, 1820 in Moncton), farmer, "preacher"
∞ c. 1775 **Rosanna Treitz**[2] (* c. 1755 † c. 1825), daughter of **Jacob Treitz**[1] Sr.

7   **Frederick Stieff**[2] (* Aug. 8, 1755, bapt. Nov. 9, 1755 in Germantown, Penn. † c. 1830 in Moncton), farmer; cf. note[48]
∞ June 25, 1780 **Rachel Sommer**[2] (* Jan. 31, 1764 † 1814), daughter of **Matthias Sommer**[1]
∞ Jan. 16, 1816 **Rosanna (*née* Ricker**[3]**) Treitz** (* c. 1760 † before 1830), widow of **Jacob Treitz**[2] Jr.

8   **Henry Stieff**[2] (* 1757/1758 in Pennsylvania † May 1, 1826 of fever in Hillsborough), farmer, grist- and sawmill operator ?, preacher
∞ c. 1781 **Mary Beck**[2] (* 1759/1760 † June 3, 1826), daughter of **Martin Beck**[1] Sr., Hillsborough

9   **Ludovic/Lewis Stieff**[2] (* late 1759 in Pennsylvania † March 15, 1827 in Turtle Creek, N.B.), entrepreneur, grist- and sawmill owner/operator in Hillsborough, farmer at Turtle Creek
∞ c. 1785 " ? " Jones[2] ? (* c. 1764 † c. 1787), possible daughter of Charles Jones[1]; note[49]

---

[47] John Stieff signed his name "Johannus Stives" in his will.

[48] Frederick Stieff made out his will on May 7, 1830 and had passed away by May 5, 1832; WRO, Libro L-1, 181: reg. April 5, 1831.

[49] Ludovic Stieff was a resident of Moncton from c. 1785 to c. 1787, after which time he moved back to Hillsborough (S.T.). His first daughter appears to have been born during these years, but he may have lost his wife in childbirth.

∞ c. 1788 ? Elizabeth Porter (∗ 1769/1770 † Jan. 17, 1850), possible daughter of Elisha and Miriam (Russ) Porter from Cornwallis, N.S.

10   **Matthias Stieff**[2] (∗ 1760/1761 in Pennsylvania † May 21, 1848 in Hillsborough), grist- and sawmill operator ?, tavernkeeper
∞ c. 1785 **Sophia Beck**[2] (∗ 1767/1768 † Aug. 25, 1844), daughter of **Martin** and **Johanna Beck**[1], Hillsborough

Third Generation ("[3]")

IV   **Johann Jacob Stieff** [2], **Johann Heinrich**[1], **Augustinus**[A], **Johann Heinrich**[B]
with **Anna Catharina ("Kitty") Lutz**[2]

1   **"King" John Steeves**[3] (∗ 1772/1773 † Dec. 12, 1858 in Hillsborough), lived at Edgett's Landing, farmer, said to have apprenticed to blacksmith John Beatty Sr. (Clark Wright), boatkeeper
∞ c. 1795 Jane ("Jennie") Beatty (∗ 1772/1773 † Sept. 22, 1848 in Hillsborough), daughter of John Sr. and Jane Beatty of Hillsborough, farmer and probable blacksmith, born in Ireland

2   **Leonard Steeves**[3] (∗ 1774/1775 † Aug. 6, 1833 in Hillsborough -- died intestate)
∞ c. 1800 Rebecca Beatty (∗ c. 1780 † after 1833), daughter of John Sr. and Jane Beatty of Hillsborough

3   **Nancy Steeves**[3] (∗ 1776/1777 [84 years in 1861] † before 1871 ?), single, blinded in gunpowder accident; note[50]

---

[50] This Nancy Steeves may be confused with Nancy (Sinton) Steeves, Henry Steeves'[3] wife , who was 73 in 1851 and blind.

4   **Rachel Steeves**[3] (* c. 1779 † after 1783 and before 1803),
     single; cf. note[51]

5   **William Steeves**[3] (* 1780/1781 † Nov. 8, 1848)
     ∞ Dec. 1, 1807 Esther Beatty (* 1788/1789 † Nov. 15, 1864),
     daughter of John Sr. and Jane Beatty of Hillsborough

6   **George Steeves**[3] (* Dec. 1, 1785 † May 15, 1870), "Esq." by
     1844
     ∞ c. 1812 Martha Smith (* June 18, 1788 † Nov. 30, 1839),
     daughter of Charles and Suzanne (Govang) Smith, Hills-
     borough
     ∞ June 6, 1844 Elizabeth Smith (* July 24, 1796 † May 16,
     1871) from Salisbury, possible daughter of Robert and
     Hannah Smith of Salisbury

V   **Johannes/John Stieff**[2], **Johann Heinrich**[1], **Augustinus**[A], **Johann
     Heinrich**[B]
     with **Anna Margaretha ("Peggy") Lutz**[2] ; cf. note[52]

1   **Michael Steeves**[3] (* Dec. 13, 1774 at "Gray's Landing", N.B.
     † Jan. 3, 1840), farmer, quarried plaster of Paris c. 1805
     ∞ Oct. 3, 1801 Mary Smith, daughter of Caleb Smith of Wind-
     sor, N.S., born in Kilkenny, Ireland of English parents; no
     children reported in 1803 Hillsborough Census

2   **Rachel Steeves**[3] (* Dec. 13, 1776 † as infant)

3   **Rachel Steeves**[3] (* June 18, 1778 at "Gray's Landing"
     † 1847 in "Upper Canada")
     ∞ c. 1798 Thomas Dawson (* 1775/1776 † Aug. 11, 1834 at
     Wolverton, Ont.) of Hillsborough, quarried plaster of Paris
     c. 1805

---

[51] The 1803 Hillsborough Census reports five children in this family,
suggesting that Rachel Steeves died as a young child before this date.

[52] The 1803 Hillsborough Census reported seven children in this family,
believed to be those living at home as of the end of 1802, i.e. numbers 6 and 8 - 13.

4   **Henry Steeves**[3] (* April 30, 1780 † Oct. 28, 1852), quarried
    plaster of Paris c. 1805
    ∞ c. 1800 Ann Hopper (* Nov. 3, 1777 † 1856), daughter of
    John and Margaret Hopper, Hillsborough

5   **David Steeves**[3] (* March 2, 1782 at "Gray's Landing"
    † 1847), quarried plaster of Paris c. 1805
    ∞ Feb. 13, 1807 Jane Boyd (* 1784/1785 † April 20, 1814)
    "late of Hopewell", daughter of Adam and Mary Ann Boyd
    of Hopewell
    ∞ Nov. 2, 1814 **Susanna(h) Lutz**[3] (* 1790/1791 † 1876),
    daughter of **Peter** and **Mary (Ricker) Lutz**[2]

6   **Abraham Steeves**[3] (* Jan. 29, 1784 at "Gray's Landing"
    † Sept. 16, 1869)
    ∞ Nov. 22, 1808 Elizabeth Brown (* c. 1790 † 1834) of
    Hillsborough, granddaughter of John Brown of Hills-
    borough, who died of smallpox in 1776
    ∞ c. 1835 Sarah (*née* Steeves ?)
    ∞ ? Elizabeth Ann (*née* ?) Rogers/Wortman (* c. 1800 † after
    1865), widow of **John Wortman**[2]

7   **Peter Steeves**[3] (* Dec. 17, 1785 at "Gray's Landing" † died
    before 1803 Census), not mentioned in father's will, dated
    April 13, 1819

8   **John "4 " Steeves**[3] ("John-under-the-hill") (* March 17, 1788
    at "Gray's Landing" † July 30, 1865)
    ∞ Dec. 8, 1814 Rebecca Woodworth (* c. 1795 † c. 1818),
    daughter of Joseph and Elizabeth (Beatty) Woodworth of
    Hillsborough
    ∞ June 3, 1819 **Lydia Jones**[3] (* 1795 † 1840), daughter of
    Henry and **Christina(h) (Ricker**[3]**/Sommer**[2]**/Wortman**[2] **?)**
    Jones[2]
    ∞ Oct. 30, 1842 Mary (Osborne) Taylor (* c. 1790 † ?) of
    Hillsborough, widow of William Taylor

9   **Catharina Steeves**[3] (* March 3, 1790 at "Gray's Landing"
    † Nov. 13, 1827 in Hillsborough)
    ∞ May 11, 1810 William Duffy (* 1778 Donegal, Ireland

† 1845 [tombstone partially obliterated] in Hillsborough),
married Sept. 13, 1828 widow Elizabeth Gunning
(* 1790/1791 † Aug. 20, 1868)

10   **Isaac Steeves**[3] (* Sept. 22, 1792 at "Gray's Landing"
     † Oct. 11, 1887)
     ∞ Nov. 23, 1815 Ann Smith (* c. 1795 † ?) of Hillsborough,
     possible daughter of James Jr. and Mary Ann Smith,
     Hillsborough (or Lewis and Elizabeth [Colpitts] Smith
     [Clark Wright])

11   **Thomas Steeves**[3] (* Feb. 17, 1795 at "Gray's Landing"
     † Oct. 11, 1869)
     ∞ Oct. 5, 1827 Judith Wilson (* c. 1808 † ?), daughter of
     Richard and Margaret (Hopper) Wilson, Moncton

12   **Joel Steeves**[3] (* April 11, 1798 at "Gray's Landing"
     † March 6, 1871)
     ∞ Jan. 4, 1821 Mary Smith (* 1801/1802 † July 19, 1836) of
     Hillsborough, possible daughter of James Jr. and Mary Ann
     Smith, Hillsborough (or Lewis and Elizabeth [Colpitts]
     Smith [Clark Wright])
     ∞ c. 1838 Rebecca Smith (* 1806/1807 † Oct. 23, 1869),
     cousin of **Joel Steeves'**[3] first wife, i.e. possible daughter of
     Charles and Margaret Smith, Hillsborough

13   **Stephen Steeves**[3] (* Jan. 23, 1800 at "Gray's Landing"
     † July 3, 1871)
     ∞ March 4, 1830 Jane Garland (* March 5, 1802 † 1901),
     possible daughter of Patrick Garland

VI   **Christian Stieff** [2], **Johann Heinrich**[1], **Augustinus**[A], **Johann
     Heinrich**[B]
     with **Rosanna Treitz**[2]; cf. note[53]

---

[53] The 1803 Moncton Census reported five children in this family,
believed to include only unmarried children at this time, i.e. numbers 4 - 8.

1 **Rachel Steeves**[3] (* 1775/1776 † March 24, 1859 at Dickie
  Mountain, Kennebecasis, N.B.)
  ∞ Nov. 28, 1795 Robert Colpitts Jr. (* Nov. 25, 1769 in
  Sellaly, England † Nov. 8, 1855), son of Robert J. and
  Margaret (Wade) Colpitts Sr.

2 **Henry Steeves**[3] (* 1779 ? † 1830 ?)
  ∞ Sept. 22, 1800 Nancy Ann Sinton (* 1778/1779 † after
  1851), blind in 1851, daughter of William and Eleanor
  (Geldart) Sinton Esq., miller

3 **Mary Steeves**[3] (* 1780/1781 † after 1851)
  ∞ c. 1796 John Jacques (* 1775 † 1827), son of Joseph and
  Eleanor (Geldart) Jacques, couple ran inn at "Moncton
  Bottom" (Salisbury) c. 1820

4 **Susanna Steeves**[3] (* 1781/1782 † Oct. 26, 1842)
  ∞ c. 1803 **Abraham Trites**[3] (* 1779/1780 † Jan. 20, 1836),
  son of **Jacob Treitz**[2] Jr.

5 **Jacob Steeves**[3] (* 1784 † 1832), farmer and maple sugar
  producer
  ∞ Nov. 27, 1806 **Sarah Ricker**[4] (* c. 1788 † after 1832 and
  before 1851), daughter of **Michael** and Catharine **Ricker**[3]

6 **Job Steeves**[3] (* 1787/1788 † July 17, 1840)
  ∞ Feb. 29, 1816 **Catherine Jones**[3] (* c. 1799 † after 1840),
  daughter of Henry and **Christina(h) (Ricker**[3]/**Sommer**[2]/
  Wortman[2] ?) Jones[2]

7 **Christian Steeves**[3] (Jr.) (* 1789/1790 † Feb. 25, 1829),
  emigrated to Harrison Co., Ohio in 1829, possibly with
  John and Mary (Malin) **Lutz**[3] Jr., **Olive's** brother and
  sister-in-law
  ∞ Dec. 13, 1813 **Olive Lutz**[3] (* Jan. 30, 1793 † 1872),
  daughter of **John** and Elizabeth **Lutz**[2]

8 **Ann Steeves**[3] (* c. 1793 † Nov. 11, 1838)
  ∞ c. 1810 James Carlisle (* c. 1785 † ?), son of Robert
  Carlisle, innkeeper on Salmon River, couple farmed in
  Parish of Sussex

VII   Frederick Stieff², Johann <u>Heinrich</u>¹, Augustinus^A, Johann
       Heinrich^B
       with **Rachel Sommer**²; cf. note⁵⁴

    1   **Andrew Steeves**³ (∗ March 24, 1782 † Aug. 28, 1846 in
         Hillsborough), farmer in Coverdale
         ∞ Dec. 16, 1806 Elizabeth Smith (∗ c. 1787 † ?) of Salisbury,
         possible daughter of Robert and Hannah Smith (or Charles
         and Margaret [Wallace] Smith [Clark Wright])

    2   **Hannah Steeves**³ (∗ Nov. 10, 1783 † c. 1838)
         ∞ Nov. 5, 1805 **John Wortman**² (∗ 1776/1777 † Aug. 5,
         1847 in Salisbury), son of **Georg** and **Mariah Wortman**¹

    3   **Lewis Steeves**³ (∗ Feb. 26, 1785 † Oct. 16, 1859)
         ∞ Oct. 17, 1809 **Elizabeth Helen Trites**³ (∗ 1788/1789
         † Oct. 10, 1855), daughter of **Abraham** and Margaret
         (Jones) **Treitz**²

    4   **Moses Steeves**³ (∗ Jan. 30, 1787 † after 1808 ?); cf. note⁵⁵
         ∞ wife unknown

    5   **Reuben Steeves**³ (∗ Feb. 20, 1789 [∗ 1786/1787 according to
         1851 Census] † after 1851), farmer
         ∞ Dec. 23, 1813 **Lydia Trites**³ (∗ 1793/1794 † after 1851),
         daughter of **Jacob** and **Rosanna (Ricker) Treitz**²

---

⁵⁴ The 1803 Moncton Census reported eight children, believed to include
numbers 2 - 9; Andrew Steeves may no longer have been living at home.

⁵⁵ A Moses Steeves is mentioned in William Harper's *Ledger* II (Aug. 6,
1808) in relation to William Wilson of Moncton as well as residents of Sackville,
N.B., suggesting that they had business interests in common. He is not mentioned
in Frederick's last will and testament, thus may have left the area since no heirs are
named either. This person should not be confused with Moses Steeves⁴ (∗
1807/1808 † Oct. 21, 1890) buried in the Steeves Settlement United Baptist
Cemetery or with Moses Steeves⁴ (∗ 1812/1813 † May 3, 1846), who resided near
McLatchy's Bridge, Turtle Creek.

6   **Charles Steeves**[3] (* March 31, 1791 † 1846), farmer in Moncton
∞ Nov. 19, 1813 **Ruth Stiles** (* 1794/1795 † after 1851), daughter of Reuben Stiles and **Elizabeth** Cummings/**Treitz**[2]

7   **Joshua Steeves**[3] (* Feb. 22, 1793 † June 23, 1870), resided at Pollett River
∞ Oct. 30, 1817 **Rosanna Jacques** (* 1797 † 1884), daughter of John Jacques Sr. and **Mary Steeves**[3] and grandson of **Christian** and **Rosanna (Treitz**[2]**) Stieff**[2]

8   **Rosanna Steeves**[3] (* March 18, 1796 † c. 1826)
∞ Jan. 12, 1815 **John Lutz**[3] (* 1788 † 1867), son of **Peter** and **Mary (Ricker**[3]**) Lutz**[2]

9   **Margaret Steeves**[3] (* April 17, 1800 † Jan. 27, 1868)
∞ Nov. 6, 1817 **Charles Lutz**[3] (* March 19, 1793 † Dec. 9, 1870), son of **Peter** and **Mary (Ricker**[3]**) Lutz**[2]

10   **Ann (Nancy) Steeves**[3] (* Jan. 11, 1803 † 1858 ?)
∞ June 29, 1826 **John Jacques** Jr. (* 1803 † 1870), son of John Jacques Sr. and **Mary Steeves**[3] and grandson of **Christian** and **Rosanna (Treitz**[2]**) Stieff**[2]

11   **Ephraim Steeves**[3] (* Nov. 27, 1805 † Oct. 25, 1883)
∞ Jan. 8, 1829 **Jane Mitton** (* 1807/1808 † Aug. 25, 1890), daughter of Ralph Mitton and **Catherine Trites**[3]; double wedding with Elizabeth Mitton and **John Steeves**[4]

12   **Daniel Steeves**[3] (* July 17, 1807 † Feb. 7, 1865)
∞ Jan. 20, 1828 **Margaret Mitton** (* 1806/1807 † March 24, 1889), daughter of Ralph Mitton and **Catherine Trites**[3], granddaughter of **Christian Treitz**[2]

VIII   **Henry Stieff**[2]**, Johann** <u>**Heinrich**</u>[1]**, Augustinus**[A]**, Johann Heinrich**[B] with **Mary Beck**[2]; cf. note[56]

1 **John Steeves**[3] ($*$ Feb. 29, 1782 † Sept. 29, 1857), preacher
   ∞ Feb. 11, 1806 **Mary Ann Trites**[3] ($*$ May 12, 1787 † 1848),
   daughter of **Christian Treitz**[2]

2 **Martin Steeves**[3] ($*$ Fall 1784 † 1868)
   ∞ c. 1808 Susan Hayward ($*$ c. 1790 † c. 1814), daughter of
   Henry and Isabella (Griffith) Hayward, Mountville, Albert
   Co.
   ∞ Aug. 13, 1815 Oranda Milton ($*$ c. 1790 † 1819), daughter
   of Henry and Rhoda (Wickwire) Milton
   ∞ c. 1820 Mary Smith ($*$ 1795 † 1869), probable daughter of
   James and Mary Ann Smith, Hillsborough

3 **Hannah Steeves**[3] ($*$ c. 1786 † after 1871)
   ∞ c. 1805 William Burton ($*$ c. 1780 † c. 1820)
   ∞ Dec. 16, 1823 Branch Milton ($*$ c. 1785 † c. 1838),
   widower, son of Henry and Rhoda (Wickwire) Milton,
   Hopewell
   ∞ Sept. 30, 1840 Samuel Copp Jr. ($*$ c. 1780 † ?), widower
   from Hopewell

4 **James Steeves**[3] ($*$ May 3, 1788 † July 24, 1831)
   ∞ Nov. 22, 1811 Mary Ann Cameron ($*$ c. 1793 † ?),
   daughter of John and Ann (Smith) Cameron, Hillsborough;
   remarried in 1837

5 **Joseph Steeves**[3] ($*$ 1789/1790 † March 30, 1842)
   ∞ c. 1813 **Martha Gross**[3] ($*$ Nov. 24, 1793 † Jan. 16, 1883),
   second daughter of **Richard** Sr. and Mary (Taylor) **Gross**[2];
   cf. note[57]

---

[56] Eight children are reported in Henry Stieff's family in the 1803
Hillsborough Census, suggesting that three may have been lost in early childhood.

[57] Richard Gross Sr. ($*$ 1761/1762 in Philadelphia † March 17, 1841 in
Hillsborough) may have come up to Germantown as a young boy with his father
Jacob, settling in Hillsborough as a ship's carpenter/shipwright around 1792. His
wife was Mary Taylor ($*$ 1767/1768 † April 17, 1837), daughter of William

IX   **Ludovic/Lewis Stieff[2], Johann <u>Heinrich</u>[1], Augustinus[A], Johann Heinrich[B]**
with possible first wife; cf. note[58]

    1   **Margaret Steeves[3]** (* 1786/1787 possibly in Moncton
       † July 29, 1827)
       ∞ July 5, 1808 John Milton (* 1782/1783 † Jan. 8, 1860),
       son of Henry and Rhoda (Wickwire) Milton

IX   **Ludovic/Lewis Stieff[2], Johann <u>Heinrich</u>[1], Augustinus[A], Johann Heinrich[B]**
with Elizabeth Porter

    2   **Miriam Steeves[3]** (* 1789/1790 in Hillsborough † May 16,
       1815, buried in Hillsborough)
       ∞ July 4, 1811 Thomas Prince (* 1783/1784 † Nov. 20, 1851
       in Lewisville, buried in Free Meeting House Cemetery,
       Moncton), son of Thomas and Hannah Prince of North Yar-
       mouth and Belfast, Maine, married on Dec. 15, 1815 Sarah
       Lewis (* 1788/1789 † after 1851), daughter of Ichabod and
       Rebekah (Read) Lewis

    3   **Samuel Steeves[3]** (* 1790/1791 † Dec. 25, 1868)
       ∞ c. 1812 Nancy ("Mary Ann") Jones[3] (* 1787/1788 † May
       1880), daughter of John Jones[2] of Moncton

    4   **Rhoda Steeves[3]** (* 1791/1792 † May 8, 1867)
       ∞ Dec. 20, 1808 John Woodworth (* c. 1787 † c. April
       1834), son of Joseph and Elizabeth (Beatty) Woodworth

    5   **Frederick Steeves[3]** (* 1792/1793 † Nov. 15, 1859 at Turtle
       Creek)

Taylor from Memramcook.

[58] The 1803 Hillsborough Census reported seven children in Lewis Stieff's household, likely representing numbers 3 - 9. The eldest two daughters may have been living or working elsewhere.

∞ Jan. 6, 1818 Ann Smith (* 1796/1797 † June 7, 1867) of Salisbury, probable daughter of Robert and Hannah Smith of Salisbury

6   **Susannah Steeves³** (* 1795/1796 † Oct. 5, 1821)
∞ c. 1818 Branch Milton (* 1792 † c. 1838), son of Henry and Rhoda (Wickwire) Milton

7   **Rachel Steeves³** (* 1797/1798 † c. 1865 ?)
∞ March 15, 1821 **Isaac Dawson** (* Aug. 6, 1800 † March 18, 1888), son of Thomas Dawson and **Rachel Steeves³**, grandson of **John Stieff²**

8   **Lewis Steeves³** (* 1798/1799 † ?)
∞ Oct. 18, 1825 Jane Kay (* c. 1805 † ?) from Salisbury, daughter of William and Eleanor (Sinton) Kay of Salisbury

9   **Elisha Steeves³** (* 1801/1802 † Nov. 21, 1872/3 at Turtle Creek), lived at Baltimore, N.B.
∞ Feb. 8, 1828 Adelia ("Delia") Smith (* 1807/1808 † Feb. 2, 1877 at Turtle Creek), daughter of Robert and Hannah Smith of Salisbury

10   **Enoch Steeves³** (* 1803/1804 † Oct. 18, 1826 at Turtle Creek)

11   **Elizabeth Steeves³** (* 1805/1806 † Nov. 14, 1826 at Turtle Creek)

12   **David Steeves³** (* 1808/1809 † Feb. 18, 1851 at Dawson)
∞ Feb. 10, 1831 **Jane Steeves⁴** (* Sept. 8, 1812 † ?), daughter of **John Stieff's²** son, **Abraham Steeves³**

13   **Abigail Steeves³** (* 1810/1811 † after 1851)
∞ Nov. 24, 1831 **William Ricker⁴** (* 1806/1807 † after 1851), shoemaker, son of **Michael** and Catharine **Ricker³**, likely resided near Turtle Creek -- two sons buried there

14   **Henry Steeves³** (* Oct. 12, 1812 † March 28, 1890)

∞ Aug. 9, 1836 **Rosanna N. Steeves**[4] (* March 9, 1829 † ?),
daughter of **Christian Stieff's**[2] son, **Jacob Steeves**[3], and
Rosanna Ricker[4]

15 **Arizena Steeves**[3] (* Jan. 1815 † March 10, 1888)
∞ Aug. 1, 1833 **Solomon Steeves**[4] (* c. 1813 † ?), brother of
Rosanna N. Steeves[4] (cf. previous entry)

X **Matthias Stieff**[2], **Johann Heinrich**[1], **Augustinus**[A], **Johann
Heinrich**[B]
with **Sophia Beck**[2]; cf. note[59]

1 **Aaron Steeves**[3] (* Oct. 18, 1786 † May 7, 1845)
∞ c. 1812 Freelove Lewis (* 1789/1790 † Dec. 8, 1841),
daughter of Ichabod and Rebekah (Read) Lewis, Parish of
Dorchester (Lewisville)

2 **Jacob Steeves**[3] (* May 3, 1788 † after 1846 and before
1851)
∞ Nov. 12, 1818 Eleanor Bleakney (* 1805/1806 † Nov. 5,
1856), daughter of William and Barbara (Jacques) Bleakney

3 **Alexander Steeves**[3] (* June 9, 1790 † 1874)
∞ Feb. 8, 1816 Sarah Horsman (* 1786/1787 † Sept. 22,
1852), daughter of Christopher and Mary (Wilbur) Horsman
∞ Feb. 25, 1864 Martha (*née* ?) Parker (* c. 1808 † ?), widow

4 **Elizabeth Steeves**[3] (* Sept. 14, 1792 [1790/1791 tombstone]
† Aug. 20, 1868 in Hillsborough)
∞ Oct. 12, 1815 John Gunning (* c. 1790 † drowned Sept. 6,
1828)
∞ Sept. 13, 1828 William Duffy (* 1778 Donegal, Ireland
† 1845 in Hillsborough [tombstone partially obliterated]),
widower, son of Patrick Duffy

---

[59] The 1803 Hillsborough Census reported six children in Matthias Stieff's
household, suggesting that this represents those 10 years of age and under, i. e.
numbers 4 - 9.

5   **William Steeves**[3] (* Feb. 14, 1794 † drowned Sept. 6, 1828)
    ∞ March 1, 1820 Ruth Randall (* May 7, 1800 † ?), daughter
    of Samuel and Sarah Randall of Hillsborough, remarried in
    1848

6   **Ann Steeves**[3] (* May 1796 † April 15, 1888)
    ∞ May 13, 1824 James Dawson (* c. 1795 † drowned Sept.
    6, 1828)
    ∞ c. 1855 John Taylor (* 1782 † ?), widower

7   **Allen Steeves**[3] (* 1797/1798 † Dec. 20, 1877)
    ∞ Jan. 22, 1830 Elizabeth A. Calkin (* c. 1811 † Feb. 10,
    1870), possible daughter of James Calkin, Hopewell

8   **Charles Steeves**[3] (* 1799/1800 † Sept. 11, 1862), twin ?
    ∞ July 19, 1832 Martha Carlisle (* 1814/1815 † April 23,
    1889) from Hillsborough, daughter of William and Eliza-
    beth Carlisle of Hillsborough

9   **Hannah Steeves**[3] (* 1801/1802 † Jan. 1885), twin ?
    ∞ Nov. 7, 1827 George Henry McDonald (* c. 1800 † before
    July 15, 1830), school teacher from Sackville, possible
    relation of Donald and Ann (Smith) McDonald
    ∞ Feb. 27, 1835 Edwin Mollins (* 1809 in England † ?)

10 **Simon Steeves**[3] (* 1804 † 1879)
    ∞ Jan. 1, 1838 **Mariah Sommer**[4] (* 1812/1813 † March 1,
    1863), daughter of **Matthias Sommer**[3], son of **Andrew
    Sommer**[2]
    ∞ c. 1865 Eliza Ann (**Wortman**[3]) Steeves (* 1818/1819
    † after 1865), widow of **Abrahm Steeves**[4]

11 **Mansfield Steeves**[3] (* 1808/1809 † Oct. 22, 1887)
    ∞ Dec. 31, 1835 Ann Mollins (* 1809/1810 † July 18, 1877),
    sister of Edwin Mollins (cf. above entry)

12 **Mary Steeves**[3] (* 1810/1811 † Feb. 7, 1884)
    ∞ July 23, 1829 **Richard Gross**[3] Jr. (* Dec. 26, 1806 † Feb.
    25, 1876), son of **Richard** Sr. and Mary (Taylor) **Gross**[2]

13   Matthias Steeves[3] (* 1812/1813 † as infant); cf. note[60]

TREITZ FAMILY

First "Pioneer" Generation ("1")

I   **JacobTreitz**[1] **Sr.** (* c. 1720 † c. 1791), farmer, blacksmith ?
∞ c. 1749 **Elisina**[1] (*née* ?) (* c. 1730 † c. summer 1786 ?), died from blackfly bite infection; cf. note[61]
∞ c. 1787 **"Christina"**[1] (Brum ["Broom"]?) (* ? † before 1803 in Moncton ?), possible widow from Lunenburg, N.S.; cf. note[62]

Second "Pioneer" Generation ("2")

JacobTreitz[1] **Sr.**
with **Elisina**[1] (*née* ?)

---

[60] A "Modest Steves" who payed up a balance for purchases in 1808/1809 from William Harper (W. Harper, *Ledger,* II, p. 185,) possibly at Memramcook, N.B., may have been Henry Stieff's daughter-in-law because he bought an ox chain from Harper on her behalf. Since "Modest" is a French name, perhaps she married into the Stieff family although no marriage registration has been located.

[61] Christian Treitz claims to Col. Gubbins in 1811 that his mother was killed by flies. From the context, the wording could suggest a date of about 25 years ago, or c. 1786. Although a massive attack of blackflies could be fatal, it is more likely she died from a resultant infection; Gubbins, *Journals,* p. 14.

[62] Documents before 1785 list the first name of Jacob Treitz Sr.'s wife as "Elisina" (WRO, Libro A-1, 37, 39, 41), but later her name was recorded as "Christina" or "Christiane" (*Ibid.*, 298, 299). Several Treitz genealogies attribute these first names to Jacob Sr.'s wife although they never occur together, which ignores the possibility that they may have belonged to two different women, Elisina being the mother of the Treitz children and Christina/Christiane, Jacob's spouse in the last few years of his life. Solomon Trites had help on his farm c. 1816 from a "John Broom" (W. Harper, *Ledger,* III), who may have been John Christian Brum from Lunenburg, N.S., whose mother was Christianah Brum. Later "Brooms" in Moncton (1851) claimed to be German.

1   **Abraham Treitz**[2] (* 1750/1751 † Nov. 26, 1810 [in the 59th year of
     his age], in Wilson Cemetery, Allison, N.B.), farmer
     ∞ c. 1775 Margaret Jones[2] (* 1760/1761 † April 12, 1806 [in the 46th
     year of her age], in Wilson Cemetery, Allison), daughter of Charles
     Jones[1]
     ∞ Sept. 21, 1810 Experience (*née* ?) Ward/Gore/Forster (* 1757/1758
     † Jan. 6, 1841), died as wife of Ralph Siddall Esq. of Cumberland

2   **Jacob Treitz**[2] Jr. (* c. 1752 † Oct. 1802 -- died intestate), farmer,
     entrepreneur ?
     ∞ c. 1775 **Rosanna Ricker**[3] (* c. 1758 † after 1823 and before 1830),
     daughter of **Jacob Ricker**[2] Jr.; cf. note[63]

3   **Rosanna Treitz**[2] (* c. 1755 † c. 1825)
     partner: c. 1769/70 Robert Cummings (* 1729 † 1777), Adam
     Hoops' nephew and land agent
     ∞ c. 1775 **Christian Stieff**[2] (* Feb. 23, 1753 in Germantown, Penn.
     † Oct. 5, 1820 in Moncton), son of **Heinrich** and **Regina Stieff**[1]

4   **Christian Treitz**[2] (* June 12, 1759 † June 22, 1836 in Free Meeting
     House Cemetery, Moncton), farmer
     ∞ 1781/1782 Catherine Jones[2] (* 1762/1763 † April 1, 1851 in Free
     Meeting House Cemetery, Moncton), possible daughter of Charles
     Jones[1]

5   **"Hannah" Treitz**[2] ? (* c. 1763 † after 1797), possible daughter;
     cf. note [64]

---

[63] Rosanna Treitz (*née* Ricker) married Frederick Stieff on Jan. 16, 1816.
In his will (c. 1830), Frederick made no provisions for Rosanna, suggesting that she
had already passed away.

[64] The small number of children in Jacob and Elisina Treitz' family
suggests that several may have died and/or are unaccounted for, one possibly being
a "Hannah" Treitz[2]. All three of Jacob and Elisina Treitz' sons named one of their
daughters Hannah, perhaps after a sister although Hannah was also a popular
Anglophone name. No extant documentation has been found to confirm this. It is
also uncertain which Treitz son -- Abraham or Jacob Jr. -- was the older of the two.

∞ c. 1785 John Behn (∗ c. 1760 † early 1804 in Hampton Parish, King's Co. ?); cf. note[65]

Third Generation ("³")

I   **Abraham Treitz²**, Jacob Treitz¹ Sr.
with Margaret Jones²; cf. note[66]

1   **Solomon Trites³** (∗ 1776/1777 † May 13, 1851 at Free Meeting House Cemetery), farmer, entrepreneur
∞ c. 1801 wife unknown, no children recorded in 1803 Moncton Census
∞ May 27, 1845 Delia (*née* Cornwall ?) Watson (∗ 1781/1782 † after 1861), possible daughter of Samuel Sr. and Sarah Cornwall, widow of James Watson Esq. of Moncton, merchant and Justice of the Peace from 1800-1813

2   **Margaret Trites³** (∗ 1779/1780 † Jan. 9, 1827 in Wilson Cemetery, Allison, N.B.), possibly not included in 1803 Moncton Census

---

[65] John Behn/Boehm/Beam, a Hessian soldier, who claimed to be a "refugee from Augustine" (1786) (PANB, Microfilm F 1032: "John Baynes"), applied for and obtained land in Hillsborough Township near the bend in the Petitcodiac River (Lot 23), south of Jacob Ricker² Jr.'s lot. Sometime after 1786, Behn moved over to Moncton where he was appointed "Constable" in 1791, "Commissioner of Highways" in 1792, and "Fence Viewer" in 1794. He claimed to be from the "Township of Monkton" when he sold his Hillsborough property to Abraham Treitz in 1797 (WRO, Libro B-1, 218: reg. Dec. 17, 1797) before he moved away, possibly to Hampton Parish, King's Co.. Stephen "Behn", perhaps a relation, resided in Dorchester c. 1805-1820.

[66] The 1803 Moncton Census reported six children over 10 years of age, i.e. numbers 3 - 8, and four children under 10, i.e. numbers 9 - 12 in Abraham Treitz' family. Solomon was reported separately, Margaret may have worked outside the home, and Jerusha is only attributed to be a Treitz.

∞ June 12, 1808 John Bowser (∗ c. 1775 † after 1832), tailor, possible son of Richard Bowser (∗ 1731/1732 † ?) of Annapolis, N.S.; cf. note[67]

3 **Jacob Trites**[3] (∗ 1780/1781 † May 27, 1867), moved from Moncton to Hillsborough, settled c. 1815 in Coverdale
∞ Dec. 14, 1805 Ann Taylor (∗ 1788/1789 † Jan. 1840), daughter of George and Mary Taylor, Dorchester

4 **Charles Trites**[3] (∗ 1882/1783 [1851 Census], 1783/1784 [tombstone], 1788/1789 [PANB, F 4180] † June 3, 1856 in Wilson Cemetery, Allison); cf. note[68]
∞ c. 1821 **Elizabeth Sommer**[3] (∗ 1790/1791 † Oct. 13, 1856 in Wilson Cemetery, Allison), daughter of **Andrew Sommer**[2]

5 **Hannah Trites**[3] (∗ 1785/1786 † after 1851)
∞ Dec. 7, 1804 **Jacob Jones**[3] (∗ 1783/1784 † May 10, 1868 in Pioneer Cemetery, Salisbury), son of Henry and **Christinah (Ricker**[3]**/Sommer**[2]**/Wortman**[2] **?) Jones**[2]

6 **Catherine Trites**[3] (∗ c. 1788 † possibly before 1836)
∞ Feb. 3, 1807 Ralph Mitton (∗ c. 1785 † before 1844) from Hillsborough, son of John and Elizabeth Mitton, remarried Margaret Scott (∗ ? † 1844) from Salisbury

---

[67] Margaret Trites'[3] marriage to John Bowser seems late. No parishes of origin were entered in the marriage register so that John Bowser's background remains uncertain. He does not appear to have been a son of Thomas Bowser of Sackville, who had a younger son John, although this family was also involved in the tailoring trade. John Bowser's name first appeared in Hillsborough in 1808, where he witnessed a land transaction between Michael Ricker and Peter Lutz (WRO, Libro C-1, 275: reg. February 29, 1808).

[68] Charles Trites claimed to be 28 years of age and single in a land petition dated July 8, 1817 (PANB, Microfilm F 4180); this age conflicts with that entered on his tombstone. In either case, no reason is known why this couple "married" so late (no marriage registration located). It is unclear why Elizabeth is not called "wife" in Charles' will and why her maiden name is used; "wife of" appears on her tombstone, though virtually obliterated.

428

7   **Jerusha (Trites ?)**[3] (* 1790/1791 † April 20, 1836 in Wilson
     Cemetery, Allison), died when she "unfortunately fell into a
     subterraneous channel made by the freshet near the mill dam
     and was drowned" (tombstone inscription); cf. note[69]
     ∞ c. 1812 James M. Kelly (* 1787/1788 † before 1851 ?), native
     of Ireland, arrived in N.B. in 1810, woodworker, house joiner,
     proprietor of "Monkton Hotel" (c. 1816-c. 1833), shipbuilder
     and entrepreneur with Israel Powell (mariner), remarried in
     Nov. 23, 1838 Mary E. Chapman of Dorchester, innkeeper's
     widow

8   **Jane Trites**[3] (* c. 1793 † after July 1840 and before 1842)
     ∞ Nov. 2, 1809 David Mills (* c. 1785 † after Feb. 1842 and
     before 1851), eldest son of Reuben and Deborah (Lewis) Mills
     of Dorchester, farmer, grist- and sawmill owner/operator in part-
     nership with Alexander Brown and Jesse Mills in Dorchester, re-
     sided at different times in Parishes of Dorchester and Moncton

9   **Elizabeth Helen Trites**[3] (* 1794/1795 † Oct. 10, 1855)
     ∞ Oct. 17, 1809 **Lewis Steeves**[3] (* Feb. 26, 1785 † Oct. 16,
     1859), son of **Frederick** and **Rachel (Sommer) Stieff**[2]

10   **Abraham Trites**[3] (Jr.) (* 1795/1796 † Sept. 7, 1811 in Wilson
     Cemetery, Allison)

11   **Barbara Trites**[3] (* c. 1797 † after 1844 and before 1851)
     ∞ July 16, 1815 Nicholas Pearson III (* c. 1792 † 1844), son of
     Nicholas Jr. and Hester Pearson of Hopewell (second son called
     Solomon, daughter Margaret)

12   **John (Francis) Trites**[3] (* Dec. 1, 1798 † Oct. 17, 1884)
     ∞ Nov. 15, 1827 **Mary Jane Trites**[3] (* 1808/1809 † June 8,
     1884), daughter of **Christian** and Catherine (Jones) **Treitz**[2]

---

[69] This tombstone inscription may be making reference to a mill dam on
James Charter Jr.'s property on "Mill Creek" (today's Somers Creek) or to a mill
dam in the Parish of Dorchester owned by David Mills, Jerusha's possible brother-
in-law, and Jesse Mills. Jerusha's burial in a row amid Abraham Treitz's
immediate family members suggests she belonged to this family although no
documentary proof could be found to confirm this.

13   **Rachel Trites**[3] (* 1802/1803 † June 9, 1812 in Wilson Cemetery, Allison); cf. note[70]

I   **Abraham Treitz**[2], **Jacob Treitz**[1] **Sr.**
with wife Experience Ward/Gore/Forster
No children from this marriage, but three step-children (two probably already married)

1   Abel S. Gore[3] Esq. (* c. 1785 † after 1847 and before 1851); cf. note[71]
∞ c. 1805 wife unknown

2   Policene Gore (* 1787/1788 † Nov. 26, 1853)
∞ c. 1806 and before 1808 Thomas Trueman (* 1785/1786 † Sept. 19, 1858), son of William and Ann Trueman of Westmorland

3   Deborah Gore[3] (* April 30, 1791 † May 12, 1832)
∞ Jan. 24, 1811 **Lodowick (Lewis) Trites**[3] (* Nov. 12, 1785 † Feb. 25, 1863), son of **Christian** and Catherine **Treitz**[2]

II   **Jacob Treitz**[2] **Jr.**, **Jacob Treitz**[1] **Sr.**
with **Rosanna Ricker**[2]; cf. note[72]

---

[70] Rachel Trites[3] may be Abraham and Margaret's youngest child. Abraham referred to his "unmarried daughters" in his will (1810), these possibly being Jerusha, Barbara, and Rachel. Rachel is buried alongside Abraham Trites[3] Jr., who died a year earlier, and both lie next to Abraham Treitz[2]. The possibility cannot be ruled out altogether that Rachel was the youngest child of Jacob Treitz[2] Jr. although no other members of this family appear to have been buried in the Wilson Cemetery.

[71] Abel Gore returned from Halifax to purchase an "Old Landing" in 1831 and joined the trading business of Lewis Trites & Co..

[72] When Jacob Treitz Jr.'s estate was settled, Rosanna was given the statutory one third and the remainder divided into ninths, suggesting that there were nine surviving children (or sons/daughters of these children if any of his own

1 **Isaac Trites**[3] ? (∗ c. 1776/1777 † possibly c. end 1802 [like
   father] or before "Widow Treitz' ninths" determined ?),
   constable in Moncton in 1802; cf. note[73]
   ∞ wife unknown

2 **Abraham Trites**[3] (∗ 1779/1780 [tombstone] † Jan. 20, 1836 at
   Free Meeting House Cemetery, Moncton), twin ?; cf. note[74]
   ∞ c. 1803 **Susanna Steeves**[3] (∗ 1781/1782 † Oct. 26, 1842 at Free
   Meeting House Cemetery, Moncton), daughter of **Christian
   Stieff**[2]

3 **Elizabeth Trites**[3] (∗ 1779/1780 [1851 Census] † after 1851 in
   Salisbury), twin ?; cf. note[75]
   ∞ c. 1797 Felix Lewis (∗ 1774/1775 † after 1851 in Salisbury),
   farmer, youngest son of Alanson and Mary Lewis

4 **Reuben Trites**[3] ? (∗ c. 1785 † after 1815 and before "Widow
   Treitz' ninths" determined ?), witness at signing of **Abraham**

---

children had predeceased him) when the estate was divided. Eight of Jacob Treitz Jr.'s children have been positively identified and five are attributed to him on the basis of the 1803 Moncton Census, which specifies four presumably unmarried children over 10 years of age (i.e. numbers 2, 4, 5, 6) and seven under 10 (i.e. numbers 7 - 13).

[73] An Isaac Trites witnessed the signing of Christian Trites'[3] will in September 1835 (WPR, Vol. II, 57). No information could be found on this Isaac Trites, therefore it is uncertain whether he was Christian's nephew or grandchild.

[74] Rosanna Trites[4] (spinster) provided for the erection of her parents' tombstones in 1848, at which time a chronological error may have occurred making Abraham and Elizabeth appear as twins.

[75] Elizabeth and Felix Lewis called their third son Isaac (∗ c. 1802), suggesting that the name was in her family, possibly in memory of Isaac Trites deceased. Ichabod was their oldest child, born in 1798/1799 (PANB, Microfilm 4181: Oct. 8, 1818).

Treitz'[2] will on Nov. 26, 1810; cf. note[76]

∞ ? wife unknown

5   **Catherine Trites**[3] (* c. 1787 † c. 1847); cf. note[77]
    ∞ c. 1805 John Bennett (* c. 1780 † before 1838), son of Caleb
    and Anna Bennett of Hopewell, possible doctor in Moncton

6   **Margaret Trites**[3] (* 1790/1791 † after 1851), twin ?
    ∞ c. 1810 William Maugher (* c. 1785 † after 1830 and before
    1851), shoemaker in Dorchester

7   **Hannah Trites**[3] (* 1790/1791 † after 1851 in Moncton), twin or
    perhaps younger
    ∞ Jan. 14, 1819 William Horsman (* 1776/1777 † Dec. 1844),
    son of Christopher and Mary (Wilbur) Horsman, Moncton

8   **Lydia Trites**[3] (* 1793/1794 † after 1851)
    ∞ Dec. 23, 1813 **Reuben Steeves**[3] (* Feb. 20, 1789 † after 1851),
    son of **Frederick** and **Rachel (Sommer) Stieff**[2]

9   **Jacob W. Trites**[3] (III) (* 1794/1795 † Jan. 4, 1879)
    ∞ Feb. 9, 1815 Rebecca Wilbur (* 1798 † c. 1860) of Hopewell,
    possible daughter of Frederick Wilbur Jr. of Hopewell
    ∞ May 7, 1863 **Jane Steeves**[4] (* Sept. 8, 1812 † ?), daughter of
    John Stieff's[2] son **Abraham Steeves**[3]

---

[76] A Reuben Trites (* 1829/1830 † after 1865), son of Jacob Trites[3] and grandson of Jacob Treitz[2] Jr., obtained a 100-acre land grant identified as 83 Block 1 Moncton West (Crown Grand Index, reg. Dec. 28, 1865). The relative infrequency of the name suggests that this Reuben[4] may have been named after his father's brother Reuben[3].

[77] This Catherine, as well as Christian Treitz'[2] daughter by the same name, have been confused with Catherine Trites[4] (* July 12, 1816 † November 31, 1844, buried in the Wilson Cemetery, Allison), whom James Dunlap married on January 19, 1841, the daughter of Charles Trites[3] and Elizabeth Sommer[3] (e.g. Pincombe and Larracey, *Resurgo,* I, p. 104).

10   **Susannah Trites**[3] (* 1795/1796 † after 1851 at Lutes Mountain)
∞ c. 1813 **William J. Lutz**[3] (* Nov. 8, 1789 † June 11, 1861 at
Lutes Mountain)), son of **John** and Elizabeth (Charters) **Lutz**[2]

11   **Amos Trites**[3] ? (* c. 1798 † after 1815 but before "Widow Treitz'
ninths" determined ?); cf. note[78]

12   **Sarah ("Sally") Trites**[3] (* c. 1800 † after 1843 and before
1851 ?); cf. note[79]
∞ Feb. 27, 1817 **Martin Sommer**[3] (* c. 1795 † before 1851),
son of **Andrew** and Emily **Sommer**[2]

13   Child **Trites**[3] ? (* c. 1802 † died as infant ?), possibly child
"Rachel" in Wilson Cemetery, Allison (cf. also **Abraham
Treitz's**[2] youngest child)

III   **Rosanna Treitz**[2], **Jacob Treitz**[1] **Sr.**
with partner Robert Cummings

1   **Elizabeth Cummings**[3] (* c. 1770 † c. 1840)
∞ c. 1787 Reuben Stiles (* c. 1764 † c. June 1798), son of
Nathaniel and Keziah Stiles, farmer in Hillsborough
∞ Oct. 23, 1832 William Colpitts (* June 1775 † before April 18,
1843), farmer, son of Robert and Margaret (Wade) Colpitts,
Hillsborough; remarried Olivit (*née* ?)

III   **Rosanna Treitz**[2], **Jacob Treitz**[1] **Sr.**[1]
with husband **Christian Stieff**[2]

---

[78] An Amos Trites is mentioned in connection with Solomon Trites in a
suit versus Joshua Wethered dated December 19, 1815 (Westmorland County, N.B.
Record of Proceedings in the Court of Common Pleas, 1785-1830). No other
references have been found, making Amos' lineage uncertain.

[79] Sarah Trites is the only daughter of Jacob Treitz Jr. whose one-ninth
inheritance does not appear to be recorded in the Westmorland County Registry
Office, however, her husband, Martin Sommer, sold a house in this area with all
the household furniture to Catherine Bennett in an unrecorded transaction which
may have been part of Sarah's ninth (WRO, Libro P-1, 528: reg. June 21, 1838).

Couple's children listed in **Stieff Family** genealogy under **Christian Stieff**[2], **Johann Heinrich**[1], **Augustinus**[A], **Johann Heinrich**[B]

IV   **Christian Treitz**[2], **Jacob Treitz**[1] **Sr.**
      with Catherine (Jones); cf. note[80]

1   **Hannah Trites**[3] ($*$ 1782/1783 † July 15, 1863 at Free Meeting House Cemetery, Moncton)
     ∞ Nov. 17, 1803 William Steadman ($*$ 1776/1777 in Cornwallis, N.S. [1851 Moncton Census] or 1777/1778 [tombstone] † Nov. 18, 1854 at Free Meeting House Cemetery, Moncton), son of John and Frances Steadman of Cornwallis, N.S., arrived in Moncton area c. 1800, blacksmith before 1805 and farmer, tavernkeeper from 1805-1807

2   **Lodowick/Lewis Trites**[3] Esq. ($*$ Nov. 12, 1785 † Feb. 25, 1863), farmer, entrepreneur; cf. note[81]
     ∞ Jan. 24, 1811 Deborah Gore[3] ($*$ April 30, 1791 † May 12, 1832), **Abraham Treitz's**[2] step-daughter
     ∞ May 3, 1843 **Ann Jones**[3] ($*$ c. 1790 † before 1851), daughter of Henry and **Christinah (Ricker**[3]**/Sommer**[2]**/Wortman**[2] ?) Jones[2]

3   **Mary Ann ("Nancy") Trites**[3] ($*$ May 12, 1787 † 1848)
     ∞ Dec. 11, 1806 **John Steeves**[3], eldest son of **Henry** and **Mary (Beck) Stieff**[2]

4   **Maria/Mary Trites**[3] ($*$ 1789/1790 † after 1851)
     ∞ Jan. 2, 1813 James Robertson Esq. ($*$ 1785/1786 † before 1851 in Moncton -- died intestate), native of Great Britain; cf. note[82]

---

[80] The 1803 Moncton Census reported six children for this couple, suggesting that one child may have been living or working elsewhere.

[81] The firm of Lewis Trites & Co. (1830) consisted of partners Lewis Trites, Abel S. Gore, Edward D. Gore, and Abel G. Trueman († March 17, 1832), grandson of Experience Ward/Gore/Forster/Treitz/Siddall.

[82] WPR, Libro IV, p. 268: court date Dec. 22, 1851.

434

5   **William Trites**[3] (* c. 1792 † ?), carpenter, husbandman, went
    bankrupt in Nov. 1825, appears to have moved away after 1831
    and before 1835, or died
    ∞ c. 1815 ? wife unknown

6   **Elizabeth ("Betsy") Trites**[3] (* c. 1796 † after 1835 and before
    1851?)
    ∞ May 16, 1816 Jacob Gesner (* c. 1793 † before 1851?), son of
    Abraham Gesner (I), German U.E.L., and Elizabeth Steadman
    (sister of William Steadman, Moncton blacksmith)

7   **Alice (Elsy) Trites**[3] (* c. 1798 † after 1835 and before 1851?)
    ∞ Aug. 2, 1816 Edward Grant (* c. 1792 † after 1840 and before
    1851 ?)

8   **Barbara Trites**[3] (* c. 1803 † after 1835 and before 1851)
    ∞ Oct. 28, 1824 John Jones[3] (Jr.) (* 1795/1796 † after 1851), son
    of John and Dimmis (Daniels) Jones[2] Sr.

9   **Mary Jane Trites**[3] (* 1808/1809 † June 8, 1884)
    ∞ Nov. 15, 1827 **John Francis Trites**[3] (* Dec. 1, 1798 † Oct. 17,
    1884), son of **Abraham Treitz**[2]

435

WORTMAN(N) FAMILY

First "Pioneer" Generation ("1")

I   **Georg Wortman**[1] (* c. 1735 † c. Dec. 1787 in Moncton, N.B.)
∞ c. 1758 **Mariah**[1] **("Moriah")** (*née* ?) (* c. 1740 † after 1797 and before 1803 in Moncton ?); cf. note[83]

Second "Pioneer" Generation ("2")

I   **Georg Wortman**[1]
with wife **Mariah**[1] **("Moriah")**

1   Child (**Wortman**[2]/**Ricker**[3]/**Sommer**[2] ?) ("Christina" ?) (* 1761/1762 in Pennsylvania † after 1851 ?); cf. note[84]
∞ c. 1780 Henry Jones[2] ? (* 1756/1757 in Pennsylvania area † Jan. 20, 1840 in Moncton)

2   Child **Wortman**[2] ? ("Catherine" ?) (* c. 1763 in Pennsylvania † after 1810 ?)
∞ c. 1781 William Wilson Sr. ? (* 1756 † before March 1810), possibly from Londonderry, N.S.; cf. note[85]

---

[83] The Wortman family configuration on arrival in 1766 is uncertain, but calculations from the 1767 "Monckton" Census suggest the Wortmans might have had two girls and one boy, i.e. numbers 1 - 3. Five children were reported in 1773 and five again by June 1, 1783. The 1803 Moncton Census reported only the household of Martin Wortman[2], who had just recently married. It is unclear why Jacob's name was not included in the 1803 Salisbury Census. Nothing is known about Widow Wortman or her unmarried children at this date.

[84] According to the 1775 Hillsborough Census, the Wortmans had five children by 1773. It is possible that the unknown children were daughters (i.e. numbers 1 and 2). Both could have married and left Hillsborough before 1783.

[85] Almost all Wilsons in the 1851 Moncton/Salisbury Census claimed to be "Dutch". Third generation Wilson/Wortman name correspondences are compelling: e.g. George, Martin, Jacob, and John.

3 Child **Wortman**[2]? ("David" ?) (∗ c. 1764 in Pennsylvania † ?),
  possible son who left Hillsborough before 1783; cf. note[86]

4 **Jacob Wortman**[2] (∗ Nov. 1768 in Moncton † Sept. 8, 1843 in Scio
  [New Market], Ohio), farmer, moved from Moncton to Salisbury
  c. 1799, according to Bible entry departed for Ohio Aug. 27, 1827;
  cf. note[87]
  ∞ c. 1788 Sarah (*née* Clinton ?) (∗ Jan. 1770 † Dec. 15, 1836),
  possible daughter of Alexander Clinton, resident of Salisbury by
  1796 or earlier; cf. note[88]

5 **Martin Wortman**[2] (∗ Dec. 1771 in Moncton † Jan. 28, 1828),
  farmer, shoemaker (1797), cordwainer (1800), retailer (1801),
  "Commissioner of Highways" and "Assessor" for Moncton first in
  1803
  ∞ June 28, 1803 Mary Jane Hopper (∗ Aug. 1781 † after 1826 ?),
  daughter of John and Margaret Hopper, Hillsborough

6 **Margaret ("Margrot") Wortman**[2] (∗ c. 1774 in Hillsborough † after
  1805); cf. note[89]
  ∞ Nov. 28, 1795 Alexander Duncan ("Donkin") (∗ 1765/1766 † after
  1851) of Westmorland Co., "Scotch"

7 **John Wortman**[2] (∗ 1776/1777 in Hillsborough † Aug. 5, 1847 in
  Boundary Creek, N.B.)

---

[86] An unidentified Wortman is mentioned in connection with Francis
Drake in a land petition in Sunbury Co. in 1800 (PANB, Microfilm F 1041),
possibly David.

[87] A "J. Wortman" was appointed "Fence Viewer" in Moncton for the
year 1790. Jacob Wortman was "Overseer of the Poor" in 1792, "Constable" in
1794, etc..

[88] Alexander Clinton is mentioned in a group petition by Charles Cane,
filed January 10, 1797 (PANB, Microfilm F 1040).

[89] There is record of only one Wortman daughter although it is believed
there were others. This couple's marriage registration is located in the MAUA,
Webster Collection (7001/134).

∞ Nov. 5, 1805 **Hannah Steeves**[3] (∗ Nov. 10, 1783 † c. 1838), daughter of **Frederick Stieff**[2]

∞ Feb. 1, 1840 Elizabeth Ann Rogers (∗ c. 1800 † after 1865) of Hopewell

8   **James Wortman**[2] (∗ c. 1780 in Moncton † after 1823), farmer, purchased land from Martin on March 17, 1823; cf. note[90]
     ∞ ? wife unknown

9   **Albert Wortman**[2] (∗ c. 1783 in Moncton † after 1820); cf. note[91]
     ∞ c. 1812 ? wife unknown

Third Generation ("3")

III   **Child ("David" ?) Wortman**[2], **Georg Wortman**[1]

1   **James M. Wortman**[3] (∗ c. 1800 † ?) of Sunbury Co.
     ∞ c. 1826 Rachel Harned , daughter of Alward Harned

2   **David Wortman**[3] (∗ June 8, 1823 † 1887) of Kingsclear
     ∞ Aug. 11, 1826 Francis Everitt of Kingsclear

IV   **Jacob Wortman**[2], **Georg Wortman**[1]
      with "Sarah" (*née* Clinton ?)

1   **David Wortman**[3] (∗ 1789/1790 † March 20, 1872) of Salisbury, farmer
     ∞ October 22, 1812 Mary Churchal
     ∞ date ? Elizabeth Reddin

---

[90] James Wortman's name is mentioned in the Parish of Moncton in 1803; Gunness, *We are Wortman*, p. 11.

[91] In 1805 Albert and Martin owned land jointly; *Loc. cit..* Margaret, James, and Albert may be the children whom "Moriah" Wortman alluded to in her appeal for land in 1792, and it was Albert, who was possibly living in Moncton "above" John Phinney c. 1820 (PANB, Microfilm F 4186).

2 **Martin Wortman**[3] (* 1792/1793 in Moncton † June 21, 1866 in Carroll Co., Ohio) of Salisbury, farmer, settled in Carroll Co. in 1832
∞ May 18, 1815 Nancy Anne Cane (* 1791 † 1868), daughter of Charles and Jane Cane, Salisbury

3 **James Wortman**[3] (* May 6, 1796 in Moncton † July 27, 1862) of Salisbury, farmer
∞ July 9, 1828 **Hannah Beck**[3] (* c. 1811 † ?), daughter of **Jacob Beck**[2], Salisbury
∞ date ? Elizabeth Rawlings

4 **Jerusha Wortman**[3] (* Oct. 25, 1797 in Westmorland Co. † Sept. 11, 1836) of Salisbury
∞ June 24, 1818 George Foster (* c. 1790 † ?) of Salisbury

5 **John Wortman**[3] (* 1799/1800 in Westmorland Co. † 1846 in Salisbury)
∞ Dec. 19, 1822 Rebecca Cane (* c. 1802 † ?), daughter of Charles and Jane Cane, Salisbury
∞ date ? Martha Dillon Larkins

6 **Ruth Wortman**[3] (* c.1802 † ?) of Salisbury
∞ Dec. 16, 1818 William Morrison (* c. 1790 † ?) of Salisbury

7 **Lavenia Wortman**[3] (* 1804/1805 in Westmorland Co. † March 27, 1847) of Salisbury
∞ October 24, 1822 James A.C. Price (* 1802/1803 † after 1851) of Salisbury

8 **Moses George Wortman**[3] (* 1809/1810 in Westmorland Co. † 1848/1850)
∞ 1831 Melinda Campbell (* c. 1815 † ?), Sackville ?

V **Martin Wortman**[2], **Georg Wortman**[1]
with Mary Jane Hopper

1 **Christina Wortman**[3] (* Dec. 27, 1803 † died as infant)

2 **Mariah Wortman**[3] (* Dec. 24, 1804 † March 2, 1862)

of Moncton

∞ Nov. 4, 1830 Allen Wilmot (* 1802/1803 † Jan. 6, 1889),
son of Malcolm Wilmot, Moncton entrepreneur and Justice
of the Peace from 1814-1834, later in Boundary Creek

3   **Margaret Wortman**[3] (* Aug. 28, 1806 † ?) of Moncton
∞ July 7, 1824 Joseph A. Sherman, son of Young and Anna
Sherman, Salisbury

4   **Albert Wortman**[3] (* Feb. 2, 1809 † Dec. 29, 1830)
∞ ? Mary D. ? (* 1817/1818 † after 1851)

5   **Martin Wortman**[3] (* Nov. 7, 1810 in Salisbury † Oct. 10, 1881
in Cambridge, N.B.)
∞ Sept. 23, 1834 Anne Freeze, Point de Bute, N.B.
∞ date ? Slipp (*Schlipp*)

6   **John Wortman**[3] (* Dec. 18, 1812 † after 1851)
∞ c. 1847 **Margaret Lutz**[4] (* 1827/1828 † after 1851)

7   **George Wortman**[3] (* Jan. 9, 1815 † after 1891)
∞ ?

8   **William Henry Wortman**[3] (* Jan. 20, 1817 † after 1891)
of Moncton
∞ July 13, 1849 Mary E. Wilmot (* 1830/1831 † April 2, 1860),
daughter of Malcolm and Elizabeth (Bentley) Wilmot Esq.,
Boundary Creek
∞ c. 1862 Arabella Lavenia Beckwith (* 1814/1815 † Sept. 7,
1891) of Parish of Harvey, N.B.

9   **Elizabeth Ann Wortman**[3] (* Feb. 19, 1819 † ?) of Moncton
∞ Nov. 8, 1849 **Abraham Steeves**[4]
∞ c. 1865 **Simon Steeves**[3] (* 1804 † 1879)

10   **Hannah Wortman**[3] (* June 14, 1821 † Feb. 6, 1889)
∞ May 8, 1841 James Lewis Wilmot (* 1808/1809 † Jan. 31,
1858), watchmaker, eldest son of Malcolm and Elizabeth
(Bentley) Wilmot Esq.
∞ c. 1860 Thomas Jardine (* June 14, 1821 † Feb. 26, 1889),
widower

440

11 **Joseph Crandall Wortman**[3] (* June 8, 1823 † 1887) of Moncton
   ∞ Nov. 5, 1850 Elizabeth Parkin (* 1832 † 1921 in Salisbury),
   daughter of John and Elizabeth (McLean) Parkin of Salisbury

12 **Theodore Harding Wortman**[3] (* July 6, 1826 † after 1891)
   of Moncton
   ∞ Jan. 3, 1850 Mary Jane Smith (* c. 1830 † ?) of Salisbury
   ∞ date ? Elizabeth Jane Mitton, widow of Charles Ayles,
   Coverdale

VII **John Wortman**[2],**Georg Wortman**[1]
   with **Hannah Steeves**[3]

   1 **Jacob Wortman**[3] (* Oct. 5, 1807 in Moncton † Aug. 25, 1870),
      farmer of Moncton
      ∞ Dec. 25, 1834 Martha Smith (* 1808/1809 † Sept. 26, 1851)
      of Coverdale, "Dutch" in 1851 Moncton Census
      ∞ c. 1853 **Amy Horsman** (* c. 1820 † ?), daughter of Timothy
      and **Rachel (Sommer**[3]**)** Horsman

   2 **Frederick Wortman**[3] (* 1809/1810 in Moncton † April 15, 1877
      in Boundary Creek), farmer
      ∞ c. 1835 Mercy Woodworth (* 1810/1811 † March 28, 1869
      in Boundary Creek), daughter of Joseph and Elizabeth (Beatty)
      Woodworth, "Dutch" in 1851 Moncton Census

   3 **Isaiah (Isaac ?) Wortman**[3] (* 1814 in Boundary Creek † 1892
      in Coverdale); cf. note[92]
      ∞ c. 1840 Jane Chapman (* c. 1820 † ?), Lower Coverdale,
      daughter of Nelson and Jane Chapman of Coverdale

   4 **Pamela Wortman**[3] (* 1815 [1825 according to 1851 Moncton
      Census] † Jan. 7, 1854 in St. Martins, N.B.)
      ∞ Jan. 20, 1837 Alexander Follet Fownes (Founds) (* 1813/1814
      † after 1851)

---

[92] A brother "Isaac" and not "Isaiah" is mentioned (WPR Libro IV, p.
401).

5   **John Dimock Wortman**[3] (* 1816/1817 in Salisbury, N.B.
     † October 21, 1847 in Salisbury) of Moncton
     ∞ May 2, 1846 Mary Emily Chapman (* c. 1825 † ?) of Lower
     Coverdale, daughter of Nelson and Jane Chapman of Coverdale

6   **Alexander Wortman**[3] (* 1818/1819 † June 25, 1857
     in Boundary Creek)
     ∞ ?; had a natural child by Ruth McFeters, child residing at
     Benjamin Jonah's in Coverdale

7   **Ludwick Wortman**[3] (* c. 1820 † after 1847), mentioned in
     J. D. Wortman's will, dated Oct. 17, 1847, as his brother

VIII   **James Wortman**[2]**, Georg Wortman**[1]
        ∞ ? no known wife or children

IX   **Albert Wortman**[2]**, Georg Wortman**[1]
      ∞ ? no known wife or children

I   **David Wortman**[3]**, Jacob**[2]**, Georg Wortman**[1]
     ∞ Mary Churchal

     1   **Jacob Wortman**[4](* 1815 † July 22, 1897) of Dorchester
          Parish, innkeeper, merchant, first Petitcodiac German
          Mayor and Stipendiary Magistrate of Moncton, claimed
          to be "English" in 1851 Moncton Census
          ∞ May 14, 1835 Mary Hicks (* c. 1820 † ?) of Sackville

Sources

Archival and Unpublished

"Articles of Agreement" for the Township of Monckton. HSPA. *Hughes Papers*. Historical Society of Pennsylvania

"Albert County History." NBM. *St. John Sun*, no date. Scrapbook, Shelf 42. New Brunswick Museum.

Albert County History. NBM. Cb. File. *St. John Sun*, March 8, 1893.

Auswandererkartei Glatzle. Hauptstaatsarchiv Stuttgart. Stuttgart, Germany.

Calhoun, William. NBM. *Diary*. Ganong Papers, Box 32, Packet 7.

Cemetery Inscriptions, Westmorland County, N.B. Vols. I-X. MAUL. Transcribed by Douglas Ayer.

Census Records: New Brunswick 1851, 1861. Transcriptions for Albert and Westmorland Counties: 1851. Microfilm 5655. MAUL.

Cumberland Town Book. MAUL. Fort Lawrence, Nova Scotia: 1766-1841, Microfilm 5334.

Dekanatsarchiv Münsingen, Germany: No.: 509, p. 82. No.: 503, *Tauf- und Totenregister* (Registry of baptisms and deaths) 1736-1785, p. 54.. B 128, *Steuermessbuch (*registry book for taxable properties) 1720-1772. B 15-16, Stadtgerichtsprotokolle (Court proceedings) 1750-1758.

Department of Lands and Mines. PANB. "Block 48 North of Germany Settlement." Id. no.: RS 656/1K/74/1.

DesBarres, Frederick. PANB. Correspondence. R.G. Vol. 366, No. 10.

Deutsches Uhrenmuseum, Gerwisstraße 11, 7743 Furtwangen, Germany

Early History of Albert County, 1924. NBM. Scrapbook Albert County.

"Early History of Albert County." NBM. Albert County Scrapbook, Shelf 31. Name of newspaper not given. March 27, 1883.

Etter, David Lorne. *The Etter Family History*, 1998. Type-written copy, available from the author at 62 Royal Masts Way, Bedford, N.S., B4A 4B7.

Etter Family History, Peter Etter, United Loyalist. Type-written family tree.

The Etter Family of Westmorland and Cumberland Counties. Type-written seven-page additional information and details about the descendants of Peter Etter subsequent to their arrival in Halifax in 1776. Linda Fury (*née* Etter), Murray Corner, N. B..

Evangelisch-Lutherischer Gesamtverband Osnabrück, Arndtstr. 19, 4500 Osnabrück and Niedersächsisches Staatsarchiv, Schloßstr. 29, 4500 Osnabrück, Germany.

Fehr, Sharon. *Steeves, Ruggles, Rippley, Passion, Gray Families, 1730-1984.* Genealogical Society of Utah. Typescript, 16 pages.

Gray, Joseph. Petition. PANS. COR 217, Vol. 59 (Microfilm reel no. 13,861).

Gunness, Dorothy. [Pacific City, Oregon] *Wortman Geneology* 323 pp. type-written, in possession of Mrs. Joyce Wortman, RR# 1 (Salisbury Road), Moncton, N.B..

Haldimand Papers, NAC. A-665.

Harper Ledgers, for two periods: 1797-1799 and 1814-1820. MAUA. Webster Collection, for period 1808-1810, Library of the Université de Moncton, Moncton, N.B..

Hatt, John C.. *A Historical Study of the Delesdernier Family: Early Inhabitants of Nova Scotia and New Brunswick* (Fredericton, N.B.: 1983), type-written manuscript, Southeastern Branch N.B. Genealogical Society, Moncton Public Library, Moncton, N.B.).

Hempel, Adèle. *Chronology of Events Relating to the Prince-Lewis House* (Sackville, N.B.: Nov. 9, 1998; July 26, 1999; Oct. 17, 1999), type-written preliminary chronologies of the Prince-Lewis House, Bell Collection, Marjory Young Bell Library, Mount Allison University, Sackville, N.B..

------. *Summary of Treitz House #3 Chronology* ("Tretiz-Prince-Lewis House"). Early History of Treitz Family's Lot 9, Monckton Township. Prince-Lewis House Committee, City Hall, Moncton, N.B. May 23, 2000. Unpublished.

Hilbig, Frederick Walter. *Americanization of German Surnames.* University of Utah: Dissertation, 1958.

"Historical Sketches of Albert County." NBM. *Daily Times,* May 17, 1929. Scrapbook, Shelf 42.

"Historical Sketches." NBM. *Daily Times,* May 20, 1924. Scrapbook, Shelf 42.

"Hendrick Steeves and his Wife and Seven Stalwart Sons." NBM. Scrapbook Albert County, Shelf 31.

Honau *Kirchenbuch* (Church Records). Honau, Baden-Württemberg, Germany.

444

Hughes Papers, HSPA.

Hundersingen *Kirchenbuch* (Church Records). Hundersingen, Baden-Württemberg, Germany.

Jacobs Papers. HSPA. Book 1684-1769.

Lawrence, Governor of Nova Scotia. Proclamation. PANS. MG100, Vol. 47, No. 58.

Lutz Genealogy. Lutz Mountain Meeting House, Moncton, N. B..

Lutes, Roy. Leewood, Kansas. Correspondence. Lutz Mountain Meeting House, Moncton, N.B..

Matthew Family Papers. NBM.

Milner, John. NBM. *History of Albert Co. Milner Papers* B 1, PK 5, Shelf 12.

Millidge Report of 1788. MAUA. Webster Manuscript Collection, 7001.

Moravian Mission Stations in Labrador. Archiv der Brüder-Unität, Hernhut, Saxony, Germany.

National Map Collection, Overland route between Halifax, N.S. and Fredericton, N.B., 1799, Map commissioned by His Highness the Duke of Kent, Commander in Chief in North America, No. 34201, Ottawa, Ontario.

New Brunswick Land Petitions on Microfilm. PANB. Indexes, 1783-1857.

New Brunswick Vital Statistics from Newspapers, Vol. I, 1784 to Vol. V, 1832-1834. Compiled by Vital Statistics Committee, New Brunswick Genealogical Society. Fredericton, N.B.: The Society, 1982-1984.

Nova Scotia Miscellaneous Censuses, 1767-1838. MAUL. Microfilm 5656.

Nova Scotia Vital Statistics from Newspapers, 1769-1812 . Compiled by Terrence M. Punch. Halifax, N.S.: Genealogical Committee of the Royal Nova Scotia Historical Society, 1981.

Paulsen, Kenneth Stewart. *Settlement and Ethnicity in Lunenburg, Nova Scotia, 1753-1800: A History of the Foreign-Protestant Community.* University of Main: Thesis, 1996.

Records of Proceedings at the General Session of the Peace, 1785-1809. Sackville, N.B. MAUL. Local Records, 1748-1883: Westmorland County, N.B., M.G. 9, A 12-11, III, Public Archives of Canada, Microfilm 5331.

Ross, Eric DeWitt. *The Government of Charles Fisher of New Brunswick, 1854-1861.* University of New Brunswick: Thesis, 1954.

Short, Raymond M.. *The Jacob Ricker Family*, 1978. Lutz Mountain Meeting House, Moncton, N. B..

Schlaitdorf *Ehebuch* (Marriage Register) #553. Schlaitdorf, Baden-Württemberg, Germany.

Society for the Propagation of the Gospel in Foreign Parts. PANS. Microfilm 14847.

Somers, John Alexander. Cumberland Museum, Amherst, N.S. *85 Years a Nova Scotian*. N.p.: N. publ., no date (archival no. 9810).

St. Michael's & Zion Lutheran Church, Philadelphia, Penn.. Baptisms 1745-1771, Marriages 1745-1764, Burials 1745-1771.

St. Michael Evangelical Lutheran Church, Germantown [Philadelphia], Penn. [Abstracts].

Stadtarchiv Wertheim, Baden-Württemberg, Germany. LWGemA, Renter-Rechnung 1688/89, Folg. 43r.. LWRosA, Lit.Br. 387b.

Stadtarchiv Wertheim. Creutzwertheim Lagerbuch (Liegenschaften) 1710. Lager und Schatzungsbuch Kreuzwertheim 1710, 1765 angefertigte Abschrift. Gemeindearchiv Kreuzwertheim Nr. 81.

Steeves, Jordan. NBM. *Saint John's Times*, March 8, 1893. Albert County Scrap Book, Shelf 31.

Steves, Herbert B. . *From Stief to Steves*, typed genealogy of the Stieff family . Address: Herbert B. Steves , P.O. Box 2005, Angel Fire, NM 87710 U.S.A..

Stief Clock. Albert County Museum, Riverside Albert, N.B..

Stief Bible. PANB.

Travis Family, NBM. CB Doc..

Trites Geneology, Lutz Mountain Meeting House, Moncton, N.B..

Wells, Geo. M. NBM. Letter about a 'Land Company 1765.' Albert County Envelope V. 1.

Westmorland/Albert County Land Deeds. WRO.

Westmorland County Census Record, 1803. *Generations: Genealogical Newsletter*. Compiled by Elizabeth Sewell. June 1979.

Westmorland County Probate Records, 1785-1885. MAUL. Microfilm 5355.

Westmorland County, N.B., Records of Proceedings at the General Session of the Peace, 1785-1809. MAUL. Sackville, N.B., Local Records, 1748-1883, Microfilm 5331; NAC. M.G. 9, A 12-11, III.

William Smith Papers. HSPA. Letter by Captain John Hall to William
  Smith of William Smith & Co..
Wilmot, Governor of Nova Scotia. PANS. Correspondence. COR, Series
  217, Vol. 21, pp. 179-181.
Wortman Bible. Owner: Mr. Evan O'Blenis of Salisbury, N.B..
Wortman, Jacob. Moncton Museum Archives, Moncton, N.B. (Photo) File
  No.: AP 973.91.1.

Published

Abbott, Edith. *Historical Aspects of the Immigration Problem.* Chicago,
  Illinois: University of Chicago Press, 1926.
Akins, Thomas B.. *Acadia and Nova Scotia: Documents Relating to the
  Acadian French and the First British Colonization of the Province,
  1714-1758,* Reprint. Cottonport, Louisiana: Polyanthos, Inc., 1972.
Akenson, Donald Harman. *The Irish in Ontario: A Study in Rural History.*
  Kingston and Montreal: McGill-Queen's University Press, 1985.
Arndt, Karl J.R.. "The Peter Rindisbacher Family on the Red River in
  Rupert's Land: Their Hardships and Call for Help from Rapp's
  Harmony Society." *German-Canadian Yearbook,* I. Toronto: Histor-
  ical Society of Mecklenburg Upper Canada, 1973, 95-106.
------. "Halifax and Lunenburg in 1782, or Halle and London as Sources for
  German-Canadian Research. (With Pastor Schmeisser's Report of 1782
  from Nova Scotia)." German-Canadian Yearbook, IV. Toronto:
  Historical Society of Mecklenburg Upper Canada, 1978, 114-121.
Artiss, David. "German Cultural Heritage Studies in Atlantic Canada."
  *Proceedings of the Atlantic University Teachers of German Conference
  1979.* Ed. Rainer L. Hempel. Sackville, N. B.: Mount Allison
  University Press, 1979, 71-82.
------. "The 'Waldo Scheme': General Samuel Waldo and his 'Longshot'
  Claim to the Territories of Nova Scotia and New Brunswick."
  *Annalen/Annals/Annales, 8: German-Canadian Studies in the Nineties,
  Results and Projects.* Ed.. Lothar Zimmermann Toronto: German-
  Canadian Historical Association, 1993, 58-65.
Auerbach, Inge and Otto Fröhlich, eds.. *Hessische Truppen im
  Amerikanischen Unabhängigkeitskrieg* [HETRINA], Vols. I-VI. Mar-

burg, Germany: Archivschule Marburg-Institut für Archivwissenschaft, 1976-1984.

Auerbach, Inge, ed.. *Hessische Auswanderer* [HESAUS], Vol. I. Marburg, Germany: Archivschule Marburg-Institut für Archivwissenschaft, 1987.

Bagnell, Kenneth. *Canadese: A Portrait of the Italian Canadians*. Toronto: Kenbar Productions Ltd., 1989.

Bainton, Roland H.. *The Reformation of the Sixteenth Century*. Boston: The Beacon Press, 1952.

Bassler, Gerhard P.. "German Overseas Migration to North America in the Nineteenth and Twentieth Centuries: Recent German Research from a Canadian Perspective." *German-Canadian Yearbook*, VII. Toronto: Historical Society of Mecklenburg Upper Canada, 1983, 8-21.

Barkhouse, Joyce. "Abraham Gesner, M.D.." *The Loyalists in Nova Scotia*. Eds. D. Wetmore and L. Sellick. Hantsport, N. S.: Lancelot Press, 1983, 102-110.

Bartl, Cornelia. "The Loss of the German-Canadian Image." *German-Canadian Yearbook*, XIII. Toronto: Historical Society of Mecklenburg Upper Canada, 1994, 307-323.

Barts, Martha Ford. *Passamquoddy-Genealogies of West Isles Families*. St. John, N.B.: Lingley Printing Co. Ltd., 1975.

Bates, Walter. *Kingston and the Loyalists of the "Spring Fleet"*. Ed. W.O. Raymond. Saint John, N.B.: Barnes & Company, 1889. Reprint. Frederiction, N.B.: Non-Entity Press, 1980.

Bausenhart, Werner. *German Immigration and Assimilation in Ontario*. Ottawa, Toronto, New York: Legas, 1989.

Beavan, Frances. *Sketches and Tales illustrative of the Life in the Backwoods of New Brunswick, North America*. London: George Routledge, 1845.

Bell, David Graham., ed.. *Newlight Baptist Journals of James Manning and James Innis*. Hantsport, N. S.: Lancelot Press, 1984.

------. *Early Loyalist Saint John*. Fredericton, N.B.: New Ireland Press, 1983.

Bell, Winthrop P.. *The "Foreign Protestants" and the Settlement of Nova Scotia*, 2nd ed.. Sackville, N.B.: Centre for Canadian Studies, Mount Allison University, 1990.

Belliveau, John Edward. *The Monctonians: Citizens, Saints, and Scoundrels*. Hantsport, N.S.: Lancelot Press, 1981.

448

Beringer, Walter. "A Leader of his People: Scenes from the Life of Albrecht Ulrich Moll alias William Berczy (1744-1823)." *German-Canadian Yearbook*, VIII. Toronto: Historical Society of Mecklenburg Upper Canada, 1984, 95-114.

Betts, Arthur. *Bishop Black and his Preachers*, 2nd. enlarged ed.. Sackville, N. B.: Tribune Press, 1976.

Beverley, James and Barry Moody, eds.. *Journal of Henry Alline*. Hantsport, N. S.: Lancelot Press, 1982.

Bischoff, Bernhard. "Der Chor der Stadtkirche von Münsingen und andere Chorbauten von Meister Peter von Koblenz und seinem Umkreis." *Münsingen: Geschichte, Landschaft, Kultur*. Eds. R. Bütterlin and V. Götz,. Sigmaringen: Stadt Münsingen, 1982, 117-133.

Bowser, Reginald B. *Dorchester Island and Related Areas*. N.p.: N. publ., 1986.

Brebner, John Bartlet. *The Neutral Yankees of Nova Scotia*. New York: Columbia University Press, 1937.

Brednich, Rolf Wilhelm. *Mennonite Folklife and Folklore: A Preliminary Report*, National Museum of Man Mercury Series. Ottawa: National Museums of Canada, 1977.

Buchloh, Paul G.. *Die Vergessenen Deutschen*. Kiel: Englisches Seminar der Universität Kiel, 1983.

Bülow, D. von. *Der Freistaat von Nord-Amerika in seinem neuesten Zustand*, 2 Theile, 12, II. Berlin: 1797.

Bumsted, J. M.. *Understanding the Loyalists*. Mount Allison University, Sackville, N.B.: Centre for Canadian Studies, 1986.

Burke, Susan M. and Mathiew H. Hill. *From Pennsylvania to Waterloo: Pennsylvania-German Folk Culture in Transition*. Kitchener, Ontario: Joseph Schneider Haus, 1991.

------. *The Peoples of Canada: A Pre-Confederation History*. Toronto: Oxford University Press, 1992.

Calhoun, Robert M.. *The Loyalists in Revolutionary America, 1760-1781*. New York: Harcourt Brace Jovanovich, 1973.

Canadiana Germanica: A Journal for Geman-Canadian Studies and News Bulletin of the German-Canadian Historical Association and the Historical Society of Mecklenburg Upper Canada. Quarterly Publication. Toronto: 1982-1994.

449

Careless, J. M. S., ed.. *Colonists and Canadians 1760-1867.* Toronto: Macmillan of Canada, 1971.

Carroll, Emmerson and A. Joyce Tingley. *Years of Pilgrimage and History of the First United Baptist Church, Moncton.* Hantsport, Nova Scotia: Lancelot Press, 1978.

Chadwick, Owen. *The Reformation.* Baltimore: Penguin Books, 1964.

Chappall, Edward A. "Acculturation in the Shenandoah Valley: Rhenish Houses of the Massanutten Settlement." *Readings in Vernacular American Architecture.* Eds. Dell Upton and John Michael Vlach. Athens and London: The University of Georgia Press, 1986, 27-57.

Clarke, Ernest. *The Siege of Fort Cumberland, 1776: An Episode in the American Revolution.* Montreal: McGill-Queen's University Press, 1995.

Clark Wright, Ester. *The Loyalists of New Brunswick.* Wolfville, N.S.: Lancelot Press, 1955.

Colley, Linda. *Britain: Forging the Nation, 1707-1837.* New Haven: Yale University Press, 1992.

Conrad, Margaret, ed.. *They Planted Well: New England Planters in Maritime Canada.* Fredericton, N.B.: Acadiensis Press, 1988.

Craig, Gordon A. *Deutsche Geschichte: 1866-1945.* München: Verlag C. H. Beck, 1985.

Crowly, Terry. *Clio's Craft: A Primer of Historical Methods.* Toronto: Copp Clark Pittman Ltd., 1988.

Cumming, L.M.. "Abraham Gesner, Author, Inventor, and Pioneer Canadian Geologist (1797-1864)." *The Geological Association of Canada, Proceedings,* XXIII. Ottawa: 1971, 1-5.

Cunningham, Robert and John Prince. *Tamped Clay and Saltmarsh Hay (Artifacts of New Brunswick).* Fredericton, N.B.: University Press of New Brunswick Ltd., 1976.

Debor, Herbert Wilhelm. "Early German Immigration in Nova Scotia." *German-Canadian Yearbook,* I. Toronto: Historical Society of Mecklenburg Upper Canada, 1973, 67-70.

------. "German Soldiers in the American War of Independence as Settlers in Canada." *German-Canadian Yearbook, III.* Toronto: Historical Society of Mecklenburg Upper Canada, 1976, 71-93.

Der Landkreis Reutlingen, Vol. I. Sigmaringen: Landesarchivdirektion Baden-Württemberg, 1997.

Der Reggeboge. Willard Wetzel, ed.. The Pennsylvania German Society (P.O. Box 244, Kutztown, PA 19530-0244).

Dhillon, Mahinder Singh. *The Sikhs in Canada and California.* Vanncouver: Shromani Akali Dal Association of Canada, 1981.

Diffenderffer, Frank Reid. *The German Immigration into Pennsylvania and Redemptioners.* Part VII of *Pennsylvania: The German Influence in its Settlement and Development; A Narrative and Critical History.* The Pennsylvania-German Society *Proceedings and Addresses,* Vol. X, 1900; rpt.: Baltimore, Maryland: Genealogical Publishing Company, Inc., 1977.

Dobson, Shirley A.. *The Word and Music.* Moncton, N.B.: Central United Church, Moncton, N.B., 1994.

Dödderer, H., H. Engelhart, V. Götz, M. Rosenauer. "Schafweiden und Wachholderweiden." *Münsingen: Geschichte, Landschaft und Kultur.* Eds. R. Bütterlin and V. Götz. Sigmaringen: Stadt Münsingen, 1982, 557-567.

Duden: Das Neue Lexikon. 10 Bde.. Mannheim, Leipzig, Wien, Zürich: Dudenverlag, 1996.

Durnbaugh, Donald F.. "The Sauer Family: An American Printing Dynasty." *Yearbook of German-American Studies,* 23. Lawrence: University of Kansas Printing Service, 1988, 31-40.

du Roy, Anton Adolf. *Tagebuch der Seereise von Stade nach Quebec in Amerika, 1776.* Ed. & transl. Gerhard Teuscher. Deutschkanadische Schriften, No. B3. Toronto: German-Canadian Historical Association, 1983.

Durstling, Hans. "Romanticism and Real Estate: The Germans of Port Elgin [N.B.]." *Atlantic Insight,* October 1986, 33-34, 36-38.

Early Families. Prepared by New Brunswick Genealogical Society South Eastern Branch, 1987. [Xerox copy of 196-page computer print-out with name index.]

Eberl, Immo. "Münsingen im Mittelalter: Vom alemannischen Dorf zur altwürttembergischen Stadt." *Münsingen: Geschichte, Landschaft und Kultur.* Eds. R. Bütterlin & V. Götz. Sigmaringen: Stadt Münsingen, 1982, 37-94.

Ehmer, Hermann. *Geschichte der Grafschaft Wertheim.* Wertheim: Verlag E. Buchheim, 1989.

Elliott, Bruce S.. *Irish Migrants in the Canadas: A New Approach.* Kingston and Montreal: McGill-Queen's University Press, 1988.

Emberley, Geneva Jones. *Descendants of Charles Jones of New Brunswick from 1766.* N.pl.: n.pub., n.d..

Encyclopedia Canadiana. 10 vols. Toronto, Ottawa, Montreal: The Grolier Society of Canada, 1966.

Ennals, Peter and Deryck Holdsworth. "Vernacular Architecture and the Cultural Landscape of the Maritime Provinces -- A Reconnaisance." *Acadiensis,* Spring 1981, Vol. X, No. 2, 86-106.

------. *Home: The Making of the Canandian Dwelling Over Three Centuries.* Toronto: University of Toronto Press, 1998.

Epp, Frank H.. *Mennonites in Canada, 1786-1920 : The History of a Separate People.* Toronto: Macmillan of Canada, 1974.

Esselborn, Karl, trans.. *Emanuel Crespels Reisen in Kanada und Schiffbruch bei der Rückkehr nach Frankreich.* Hessische Volksbücher. Ed. Wilhelm Diel. Friedberg: Selbstverlag, 1915.

Fairweather, Lillian C.. "Interiors of Pioneer Houses in New Brunswick." *Canadian Geographical Journal,* May 1944, 238-243.

Falk, Cynthia G.. "Symbols of Assimilation or Status? The Meanings of Eighteenth-Century Houses in Coventry Township, Chester County, Pennsylvania." *Winterthur Portfolio: A Journal of American Material Culture,* Vol. 33, Sommer/Autumn 1998, 107-134.

Faust, Albert Bernhardt. *The German Element in the United States,* 2 vols.. Boston and New York: Houghton Mifflin Co., 1909.

Feldes, A., S. Goebel, M. Maul, R. Neukamm-Baumeister, I. Pfaff. *Menschen, Maschen und Maschinen: Eine Ausstellung zur Geschichte der Maschenindustrie in Albstadt-Elbingen.* N. pl.: Arbeitskreis Heimatpflege im Regierungsbezirk Tübingen, 1987.

Fellows, Robert F.. *The New Brunswick Census of 1851 Albert County N.B., Canada.* Fredericton, N.B.: Genealogical Section, Provincial Archives of New Brunswick, 1980.

Field, Richard. "The Soloman House: Residence of Leslie J. Langille, Lunenburg, Nova Scotia." *The Canadian Antiques and Art Review,* September 1980, Vol. II, No. 11, 35-38.

Filby, P. William and Mary K. Meyer, eds.. *Passenger and Immigration Lists Index: A Guide to Published Arrival Records of about 500,000 Passengers who came to the United States and Canada in the*

Seventeenth, Eighteenth, and Nineteenth Centuries, 3 vols. with supplements. Detroit: Gale Research Co., 1981.

Fisher, Peter. *The First History of New Brunswick* (1825). Rpt. Woodstock, N.B.: Non-Entity Press, 1983.

Fogleman, Aaron Spencer. *Hopeful Journeys: German Immigration, Settlement, and Political Culture in Colonial America, 1717-1775.* Philadelphia: University of Pennsylvania Press, 1996.

Foley, Mary Mix. *The American House.* New York: Harper and Row Publishers, 1980.

Francis, Douglas and Donald Smith, eds.. *Reading in Canadian History.* Toronto: Holt, Rinehart and Winston of Canada, 1990.

Fröschle, Hartmut. *Die Deutschen in Kanada,* Eckart-Schriften, Heft 101. Wien: Österreichische Landsmannschaft, 1987.

------. *Adler auf dem Ahornbaum: Studien zur Einwanderung, Siedlung, Kultur- und Literaturgeschichte der Deutschen in Kanada.* Ed. Lothar Zimmermann. Toronto: German-Canadian Historical Association, 1997.

------. "The German-Canadians: A Concise History." Trans. Georg K. Weissenborn. German-Canadian Yearbook, XII. Toronto: Historical Society of Mecklenburg Upper Canada, 1992.

------ and Lothar Zimmermann, eds.. "German Canadiana: A Bibliography." *German-Canadian Yearbook,* Special Issue, XI. Toronto: Historical Society of Mecklenburg Upper Canada, 1990.

Ganong, William F.. " A Monograph of the Origins of Settlements in New Brunswick." *Proceedings and Transactions of the Royal Society of Canada,* Sec. II (1904), 1-185.

Gay, Larry. *The Complete Book of Heating with Wood.* Charlotte, Vermont: Garden Way Publishing, 1974.

Geldart, V. "Bing" and Ken Kanner. *Marriage Register 1846-1887, Albert County New Brunswick.* N. pl.: V. "Bing" Gelddart and Ken Kenner, 1984.

------. *Marriage Register, Westmorland County, N.B.: 1790-1856.* N. pl.: V. "Bing" Geldart and Ken Kanner, 1985.

Gellermann Patterson, Nancy Lou. *Swiss-German and Dutch-German Mennonite Traditional Art in the Waterloo Region, Ontario,* National Museum of Man Mercury Series. Ottawa: National Museums of Canada, 1979.

Germantown and the Germans. 120-page book with an introduction by Edwin Wolf 2nd for "An Exhibition of Books, Manuscripts, Prints and Photographs for the Collections of The Library Company of Philadelphia and The Historial Society of Pennsylvania." Philadelphia, 1983.

Gillcash, Edith. *Taylor Village* [N.B.]. College Bridge, N.B.: Edith Gillcash, 1984.

Gillcash, Wayne, ed.. *The New Brunswick Census of 1851: Westmorland County.* Fredericton, N.B.: Public Archives of New Brunswick, 1981.

Gilroy, Marion. *Loyalists and Land Settlement in Nova Scotia.* Halifax, N.S.: Public Archives of Nova Scotia, 1980.

Glassie, Henry. *Pattern in the Material Folk Culture of the Eastern United States.* Philadelphia: University of Pennsylvania Press, 1968.

Glatfelder, Charles H.. *Pastors and People: German Lutheran and Reformed Churches in the Pennsylvania Field, 1717-1793*, I, Pastors & Congregations. Bremigsville, Pennsylvania: The Pennsylvania German Society, 1980.

Glover, Michael. *General Burgoyne in Canada and America.* Chatham, Engl.: Gordon & Cremonesi, 1976.

Goebel, Susanne. "Von den Anfängen der Strumpfwirkerei auf der Rauen Alb." *Schwäbische Heimat*, 40, 1989, 122-128.

Grenke, Arthur. "German Land Settlement in Eastern Canada and Its Influence on Community Development and Assimilation." *German-Canadian Yearbook*, XV. Toronto: Historical Society of Mecklenburg, Upper Canada, 1998, 31-56.

Grünewald, Georg. *Die deutschen Auswanderungen: Eine politisch-nationalökonomische Abhandlung.* Frankfurt am Main: Keßler Verlag, 1847.

Hacker, Werner. *Auswanderungen aus dem früheren Hochstift Speyer nach Südosteuropa und Übersee im 18. Jahrhundert.* Kaiserslautern: Heimatstelle Pfalz, 1969.

------. *Auswanderung aus Baden und dem Breisgau: Obere und mittlere rechtsseitige Oberrheinlande im 18. Jahrhundert.* Stuttgart: Theiss Verlag, 1980.

------. *Eighteenth Century Register of Emigrants from Southwest Germany* (to America and other countries). Apollo, Pennsylvania: Closson Press, 1994.

------. *Kurpfälzische Auswanderer vom Unteren Neckar: Rechtsrheinische Gebiete der Kurpfalz.* Stuttgart: Theiss Verlag, 1983.

------. *Auswanderung aus Rheinpfalz und Saarland im 18. Jahrhundert.* Stuttgart: Theiss Verlag, 1987.

Hale, R. Wallace. *Early New Brunswick Probate Records, 1785-1835.* Bowie, M.d.: Heritage Books, 1989.

Haliburtin, Thomas Chandler. *An Historical and Statistical Account of Nova Scotia,* I. Halifax: Joseph Howe, 1829.

Hamilton, William B.. *Place Names of Atlantic Canada.* Toronto: University of Toronto Press, 1996.

Hansen, Marcus Lee. *Atlantic Migration, 1607-1860.* New York: Harper and Brothers, 1940.

Harper, J. Russell. "Christopher Sower, King's Printer and Loyalist." *New Brunswick Historical Society Collections,"* 14, 1955, 67-109.

------. *A People's Art: Primitive, Naïve, Provincial and Folk Painting in Canada.* Toronto: University of Toronto Press, 1974.

------. *Painting in Canadian History,* 2nd Edition. Toronto: University of Toronto Press, 1977.

Hawbaker, Gary T. and Clyde L. Groff. *A New Index: Lancaster County Pennsylvania Before the Federal Census,* 3, Index to the 1750 Tax Records. Elizabethtown: Gary T. Hawbaker, n. d..

Hay, Eldon. *The Chignecto Covenanters.* Montreal and Kingston: McGill-Queens University Press, 1996.

Hempel, Rainer L.. "Recent German Immigration to New Brunswick." *Yearbook of German-American Studies,* XXIV. Lawrence, KS.: University of Kansas Printing Service, 1989, 89-96.

------. "Germantown: die Geschichte einer deutschen Siedlung in Neubraunschweig." *German-Canadian Yearbook,* IX. Toronto, Ont.: Historical Society of Mecklenburg, Upper Canada, 1986, 49-62.

------. "Early German Settlements on the Petitcodiac River in New Brunswick." *German Canadian Yearbook,* XIII. Toronto: Historical Society of Mecklenburg, Upper Canada, 1993, 124-148.

Herwig, Holger. *Hammer or Anvil?: Modern Germany 1648-Present.* Toronto: D. C. Heath and Company, 1994.

Heyse, Paul. "Die Pfälzer in Irland." *Gesammelte Werke,* Bd. IX. Berlin: Hertz, 1872-1901, 333-406.

Hippel, Wolfgang von. *Auswanderung aus Südwestdeutschland:* Studien zur Württembergischen Auswanderung und Politik im 18. und 19. Jahrhundert. Stuttgart: Klett-Cotta Verlag, 1984.

Hoar, William S.. *Steeves and Colpitts: Pioneers of the Upper Petitcodiac.* Vancouver: Tangled Roots Press, 1988.

Hocker, Edward W.. *Germantown, 1683-1933.* Germantown, Philadelphia, Pa.: Author, 1933.

------. *Genealogical Data Relating to the German Settlers of Pennsylvania and Adjacent Territory: From Advertisements in German Newspapers Published in Philadelphia and Germantown, 1743-1800.* Baltimore: Genealogical Publishing Company, Inc., 1981.

Hodges. Henry. *Artifacts: An Introduction to Early Materials and Technology.* London: John Baker Publishers Ltd., 1976.

Hofmann, Peter. *Heimatbuch der Marktgemeinde Wertheim.* Steinfeld: Verlag-Druckerei Karl W. Goldammer, 1967.

------. *Die Ursiedlung "Werdheim" im Wandel der Zeit.* Wertheim: Rotadruck M. Weber, 1980.

Holder, Jean M.. *Nova Scotia Marriage Bond Index 1763-1864.* Publ. No. 14 of the Genealogical Association of Nova Scotia, 1997.

Holderle, W.. *Gottes Wort bleibt ewig: 700 Jahre Kirchengemeinde Hundersingen.* Dettingen/Erms: Evangelische Kirchengemeinde Hundersingen, 1987.

Huber, Eva, ed.. *Neuschottländischer Bote* (*Nova Scotian Messenger*), quarterly pub. in Halifax: Summer and Fall, 1997.

Hughes, Philip. *A Popular History of the Reformation.* Garden City, N.Y.: Image Books, 1957.

Irish, Donna R.. *Pennsylvania German Marriages.* Baltimore: Genealogical Publishing Co., Inc., 1982.

Jackson, Thomas, ed.. *The Lives of Early Methodist Preachers*, V. London: Wesleyan Conference Office, 1873.

Jefford, Andrew and the German Information Service, London. *Wines of Germany.* Mainz: Deutsches Weininstitut GmbH, 1993-1994.

Kapp, Friedrich. *Geschichte der deutschen Einwanderung in Amerika.* Leipzig: Verlag von Quandt & Händel, 1868.

Katcher, Philip. *Armies of the American Wars, 1753-1815.* New York: Hastings House Publishers, n.d..

Knapp, Hans. "Warum sie ihre Heimat verließen." *Viernheimer Auswandererbuch.* Ed. G. Franz Eckard. Darmstadt: Verlag des Historischen Vereins für Hessen, 1984, 11-32.

Knaurs Kulturführer Deutschland. München: Droemersche Verlagsanstalt, 1985.

Knittle, Walter Allen. *Early Eighteenth Century Palatine Emigration.* Philadelphia: Dorrance and Company, 1937.

Köpf, Ulrich, ed.. *Die Hungerjahre 1816/17 auf der Alb und an der Donau.* Ulm: Arbeitsgemeinschaft der Heimatmuseen im Alb- Donaukreis, 1985.

Körner, Günter. "Ein Birkenauer 'Komplott' wegen des Hirtenlohns (1705)." *Birkenauer Geschichtsverein,* 56-59.

Kohn, Hans. *The Mind of Germany.* New York: Harper & Row, 1960.

Krüger, Arndt A.. "The Image of Germany prior to World War I: Canadian Scholars and Germany." *German-Canadian Yearbook,* XIV. Toronto: Historical Society of Mecklenburg, Upper Canada, 1995, 41-60.

Kulischer, Eugene. *Europe on the Move:* War and Population Changes, 1917-1947. New York: Columbia University Press, 1948.

Langguth, Erich. "Büchsenmacher und Büchsenschifter -- alte Handwerkskunst in Wertheim." *Messebeilage der Wertheimer Zeitung.* Wertheim, Sept. 29, 1995, 1-6.

------. "Häcker und Bauern- Höhefelds Einwohner um 1600." Ein sozial- und familiengeschichtlicher Beitrag zur Orts- und Grafschaftsgeschichte, *Wertheimer Jahrbuch 1981/82.* Wertheim: Verlag des Historischen Vereins Kreuzwertheim e.V., 1983, 27-84.

------. "Peter Herrschaft, seine Ämter und seine Familie." *Historie in Kreuzwertheim, 400 Jahre Peter Herrschaft-Haus.* Kreuzwertheim: Geschichts- und Heimatverein Kreuzwertheim E. V.-Verlag, 1994, 6-23.

------. *"Wertheims Geschichte in neuer Sicht." Wertheimer Jahrbuch 1981/82.* Wertheim: Stadtarchiv Wertheim, 1982, 15-30.

Langguth, Otto. "Auswanderer aus der Grafschaft Wertheim." Sonderdruck aus den *Familiengeschichtlichen Blättern,* 30. Jahrgang, Heft 3. Leipzig: 1932, 1-24.

Larracey, Edward W.. *Chocolate River.* Hantsport, N.S.: Lancelot Press Ltd., 1985.

Lee-Whiting, Brenda. *Harvest of Stones: The German Settlement in Renfrew County.* Toronto: University of Toronto Press, 1985.

Lehmann, Heinz. *Immigration, Settlement and Culture*. Trans., ed., and intro. Gerhard P. Bassler. St. John's, Nfld.: Jesperson Press, 1986.

------. *Zur Geschichte des Deutschtums in Kanada*, Bd. I: *Das Deutschtum in Ostkanada*. Stuttgart: Ausland und Heimat Verlags- Aktiengesellschaft, 1931.

Liddell, Peter. "The First Germans in British Columbia." *German-Canadian Yearbook*, VI. Toronto: Historical Society of Mecklenburg Upper Canada, 1981, 74-77.

Lorraine Berceau des Tritz, Lothringen, Die Wiege der Tritz, Lorraine Cradle of the Tritz. Issues of the Tritz Family Publication, 1986-1990.

Luther, Martin. *Three Treatises*. Philadelphia: Fortress Press, 1960.

MacFarlane, W. G.. *Fredericton History: Two Centuries of Romance, War, Privation, and Struggle*. Reprint: *St. John Sun*, 1893. Woodstock, N.B.: Non-Entity Press, 1981.

Machum, Lloyd A.. *A History of Moncton: Town and City, 1855-1965*. Moncton, N.B.: City of Moncton, 1965,

McLennan, S.. *Louisbourg: From its Foundation to its Fall, 1713-1758*. Reprint: London: Macmillan, 1918. Halifax: The Book Room Ltd., 1996.

Magnusson, Magnus and Hartmann Palsson, eds.. *The Vinland Sagas*. The Norse Discovery of America. Toronto: Penguin Classics, 1965.

Magee, Joan. "John Dulmage (c. 1740-c. 1814): A Loyalist of Palatine German Origin." *Loyalist Mosaic: A Multi-ethnic Heritage*. Ed. Joan Magee. Toronto and Charottetown: Dundurn Press, 1984, 173-190.

------. "Peter Etter (1715-1794): A Loyalist of Swiss Origin." *Loyalist Mosaic: A Multi-ethnic Heritage*. Ed. Joan Magee. Toronto and Charlottelown: Dundurn Press, 1984, 101-122.

Majka, Mary and David Christie, eds.. *Still the Gentle Breezes Blow: Essays on the History of Harvey Parish, Albert County, New Brunswick*. Albert, N.B.: Harvey Parish Bicentennial Committee, 1984.

Marschalk, Peter. *Deutsche Überseeauswanderung im 19. Jahrhundert*. Stuttgart: Ernst Klett Verlag, 1972.

Martynowych, Orest T.. *Ukrainians in Canada: The Formative Period, 1891-1924*. Edmonton: Canadian Institute of Ukrainian Studies Press, 1991.

Maxwell, Lilian M. Beckwith. *The History of Central New Brunswick*. Sackville, N.B.: The Tribune Press, 1937.

Medick, Hans. *Weben und Überleben in Laichingen: 1650-1900.* Göttingen: Vandenhoek & Ruprecht, 1997.

Memminger, H.. *Beschreibung des Oberamts Münsingen.* Stuttgart: 1825.

Mennonite Historian. Pub. by the Mennonite Heritage Centre of the Conference of Mennonites in Canada and the Centre for Mennonite Brethren Studies of the Canadian Conference of Mennonite Brethren Churches. Eds. Ken Redding and Abe Dueck. Winnipeg, Man.

Merz, Johannes Helmut. "Johann Leonard Kratz, 1756-1829: A Hessian Soldier's Story of Hardship and Love." *German-Canadian Yearbook,* VIII. Toronto: Historical Society of Mecklenburg, Upper Canada, 1994, 245-262.

------. *The Hessians in Upper Canada.* Hamilton, Ont.: German-Canadian Historical Book Publishing, 1997.

Mitcham, Allison. *Prophet of the Wilderness: Abraham Gesner.* Hantsport, N.S.: Lancelot Press, 1995.

Mönckmeier, Wilhelm. *Die deutsche überseeische Auswanderung: Ein Beitrag zur deutschen Wanderungsgeschichte.* Jena: Gustav Fischer Verlag, 1912.

Moore, Christopher. *The Loyalists.* Toronto: MacMillan of Canada, 1982.

Müller, Helmut M. *Schlaglichter der Deutschen Geschichte.* Mannheim: Bibliographisches Institut, 1986.

Mühlenberg, Melchior. *Journals of Henry Melchior Muhlenberg, In Three Volumes,* II. Tran.. Tappert, T. G. and Doberstein, J. W.. Philadelphia: Evangelical Lutheran Ministerium and Muhlenberg Press, 1955.

Murphy, Peter. *Together in Exile.* Saint John, N.B.: Peter Murphy, 1990.

Norbye, Jan P.. *The Complete History of the German Car: 1886 to the Present.* New York: Portland House, 1987.

O'Driscoll, Robert and Lorna Reynolds, eds.. *The Untold Story: The Irish in Canada,* 2 Vols.. Toronto: Celtic Arts of Canada, 1988.

Orlow, Dietrich. *History of Modern Germany, 1871 to Present.* 3rd ed. Englewood Cliffs, New Jersey: Prentice Hall, 1995.

Osterloh-Gessat, Elke. *Von Erd bin ich gemacht.* Karlsruhe: Info Verlagsgesellschaft Karlsruhe, 1996.

Pahlow, Hans. *Deutsches Namenlexikon.* Frankfurt/Main: Suhrkamp, 1967.

Papers of Benjamin Franklin, XII, Jan. 1765-Dec. 1765. Cambridge, Mass.: Yale University Press, 1961.

459

Pendleton, Philip E.. *Oley Valley Heritage: The Colonial Years: 1700-1775*. Birdboro, Pennsylvania: Pennsylvania German Society, 1994.

Pennsylvania German Society Proceedings and Addresses. *Pennsylvania German Church Records of Births, Marriages, Burials*, etc., 3 vols.. Baltimore: Genealogical Publishing Co., Inc., 1983.

Pesch, Heinrich. "Waidwerk und Wild in herzoglicher und königlicher Zeit." *Münsingen: Geschichte, Landschaft, Kultur*. Eds. R. Bütterlin & V. Götz. Sigmaringen: Stadt Münsingen, 1982, 509-520.

Petryshyn, Jaroslav. *Peasants in the Promised Land: Canada and the Ukrainians, 1891-1914*. Toronto: James Lorimer and Company, 1985.

Philippovich, Eugen von. *Auswanderung und Auswanderungspolitik in Deutschland*. Leipzig: Verein für Sozialpolitik, 1892.

Pinson, Koppel S.. *Modern Germany: Its History and Civilization*. Prospect Heights, Ill.: Waveland Press, 1989.

Pincombe, C. Alexander and Larracey, Edward W.. *Resurgo*, I. Moncton: The City of Moncton, 1990.

Pipes, Gail Bonsall, ed.. *Loyalists All*. N.p.: United Empire Loyalist Association of Canada, New Brunswick Branch, 1985.

Ploetz: *Große Weltgeschichte*. Darmstadt: Wissenschaftliche Buchgesellschaft, 1986.

Pritzker-Ehrlich, Marti. "Michael Schlatter (1716-1790): A Man-In-Between." *Yearbook of German-American Studies*, XX. Lawrence, Kansas.: Society for German-American Studies, 1985, 83-95.

Province of New Brunswick Crown Land Grant Index. Fredericton, N.B.: Natural Resources and Energy, 1988.

Punch, Terrence M.. "Hessian Auxiliary Troops in North America: Auxiliaries, Not Mercenaries." *German-Canadian Yearbook*, XIII. Toronto: Historical Society of Mecklenburg, Upper Canada, 1994, 230-244.

Raff, Dieter. *Deutsche Geschichte: Vom Alten Reich zur Zweiten Republik*. München: Max Hüber Verlag, 1985.

Ramsay, Bruce. *A History of German-Canadians in British Columbia*. Winnipeg: National Publishers, 1958.

Raddall, Thomas H.. *His Majesty' Yankees*. Halifax, N.S.: Nimbus Publishing Ltd., 1942.

Ratz, Alfred E.. "Frühe Kulturarbeit deutscher Herrnhuter in Labrador." *German-Canadian Yearbook*, II. Toronto: Historical Society of Mecklenburg Upper Canada, 1975, 50-69.

Rawlyk, George, ed.. *New Light Letters and Spiritual Songs, 1778-1793*. Hantsport, N. S.: Lancelot Press, 1983.

------. *The Canada Fire: Radical Evangelicalism in British North America*. Kingston and Montreal: McGill-Queen's University Press, 1994.

Rayburn, Alan. *Geographical Names of New Brunswick*. Ottawa: Surveys and Mapping Branch, Department of Energy, Mines and Resources, 1975.

Raymond, W.O.. "Colonel Alexander McNutt and the Pre-Loyalist Settlements of Nova Scotia." *Transaction of the Royal Society of Canada*, Section 11, 1911, 23-115.

------. "Appendix: Some Notes Regarding Peter Fisher," in Peter Fisher, *The First History of New Brunswick*, 1825, reprint. Woodstock, N.B.: Non-Entity Press, 1983, 123-133.

Reim, Hartmann. "Zur Besiedlung der Münsinger Alb in vor- und frühgeschichtlicher Zeit." *Münsingen: Geschichte, Landschaft, Kultur*. Eds. R. Bütterlin and V. Götz. Sigmaringen: Stadt Münsingen, 1982, 464-475.

Rempel, John I.. *Building with Wood*. Toronto: University of Toronto Press, 1980.

Reuter, Claus. "Kanada und die Braunschweigischen Truppen, 1776-1783." *German-Canadian Yearbook*, XIII. Toronto: Historical Society of Mecklenburg, Upper Canada, 1993, 265-287.

Reynolds, Helen W.. *Dutch Houses in the Hudson Valley before 1776*. Dover Reprint, 1965.

Richey, Mathew. *A Memoir of the Late Rev. William Black*. Halifax, N. S.: William Cunnabell, 1839.

Richter, Manfred. "Deutsche Mundart von Lunenburg County, Nova Scotia." *Annalen*, 4, 1978, 19-30.

Riedel, Walter E.. "Exiled in Canada: Literary and Related Forms of Cultural Life in the Internment Camps." *Yearbook of German-American Studies*, XXIV. Lawrence, Kansas.: Society for German-American Studies, 1989, 73-88.

461

Riedesel, Friederike Charlotte Luise, Freifrau von. *Die Berufsreise nach Amerika*. Berlin: Haude und Spener, 1800.

Rimrott, F. P. J. and Eichenlaub, W., eds.. *"Was du ererbt...."* Toronto: Deutsche Sprachschulen, 1978.

Rippley, La Vern J.. *The German-Americans*. Lanham, MD, New York, London, Engl.: University Press of America, 1984.

Ritter, Alexander, ed.. *Deutschsprachige Literatur im Ausland*. Göttingen: Vandenhoeck & Ruprecht, 1985.

Roan, Nancy. "Nineteenth and Twentieth Century Pennsylvania-Mennonite Foodways." *From Pennsylvania to Waterloo: Pennsylvania-German Folk Culture in Transition*. Eds. Susan M. Burke and Mathew H. Hill. Kitchener, Ont.: Joseph Schneider Haus, 1991, 97-108.

Roe, Frederick B. *Atlas of the Maritime Provinces of the Dominion of Canada with Historical and Geological Descriptions*. Saint John, N.B. and Halifax, N.S.: Roe Brothers, 1879.

Roeber, A.G.. *Palatines, Liberty, and Property: German Lutherans in Colonial British North America*. Baltimore and London: The John Hopkins University Press, 1993.

Rosch, D.. *Über die Noth in Volke, die Unzufriedenheit und die Auswanderung*. Nürnberg: Zeh'sche Buchhandlung, 1838.

Rosenberg, Louis. *Canada's Jews: A Social and Economic Study of Jews in Canada in the 1930s*. Montreal & Kingston: McGill-Queen's University Press, 1993.

Rupp, Israel. *Chronologisch geordnete Sammlung von mehr als 30.000 Einwanderern in Pennsylvanien aus Deutschland, der Schweiz, Holland, Frankreich und anderen Staaten von 1717 bis 1776*. Hildesheim: Gerstenberg, 1975.

Rupp, August. *Pfälzische Kolonisation in Nordamerika*. Stuttgart: Eugen Wahl Verlag, 1938.

Ryder, Huia. "History of Handicrafts." *Arts in New Brunswick*. Eds. R.A.Tweedie, Fred Cogswell, W. Steward MacNutt. Fredericton, N.B.: The University of New Brunswick Press Ltd., 1967, 229-260.

Sack, B.G.. *History of the Jews in Canada*. Montreal: Harest House, 1965.

Sautter, Udo. "Ein deutscher Geistlicher in Neuschottland: Johann Adam Moschell (1795-1849)." *German-Canadian Yearbook*, I. Toronto: Historical Society of Mecklenburg Upper Canada, 1973, 153-159.

Scheuerbrandt, Arnold. "Die Auswanderung aus dem heutigen Baden-Württemberg nach Preußen, in den habsburgischen Südosten, nach Rußland und Nordamerika zwischen 1683 und 1811." *Historischer Atlas von Baden-Württemberg*, XII, 5. Stuttgart: Kommission für geschichtliche Landeskunde in Baden-Württemberg, 1983, 1-46.

Schloezer, August L.. *Vertrauliche Briefe aus Kanada und Neuengland vom J. 1777 und 1778: Aus Hrn. Prof. Schlözers Briefwechsel* [Rpt. of Göttingen edn., 1797]. Ed. Lothar Zimmermann. Toronto: German-Canadian Historical Association, 1981.

Schmeisser, Barbara M.. Information Sheet on John Eagleson, Parks Service Atlantic Region, Halifax, N. S., 1996.

Schneider, Manfred. "Weinbau in Kreuzwertheim: Eingefangener Sonnenschein." *Historie in Kreuzwertheim, 400 Jahre Peter-Herrschaft-Haus*. Kreuzwertheim: Geschichts- und Heimatverein Kreuzwertheim-Verlag, 1994, 98-123.

Schultz, John, ed.. *Writing about Canada. A Handbook for Modern Canadian History*. Scarborough, Ont.: Prentice-Hall Canada Inc., 1990.

Schultz, Karla Lydia. "At Home in the Language: The Cases of an Exile and an Immigrant." *Yearbook of German-American Studies*, XX. Lawrence, Kansas.: Society for German-American Studies, 1985, 125-132.

Selig, Robert A.. "The Price of Freedom: Poverty, Emigration and Taxation in the Prince-Bishopric of Würzburg in the Eighteenth Century." *Yearbook of German-American Studies*, XXVI. Lawrence, Kansas.: Society for German-American Studies, 1991, 105-126.

------. "The Idea and Practice of *Ius Emigrandi* in the Holy Roman Empire from the Reformation to the French Revolution." *Yearbook of German-American Studies*, XXVII. Lawrence, Kansas.: Society for German-American Studies, 1992, 15-22.

Sieveking, Karl. "Unsere Auswanderer aus dem unteren Werretal -- Ihre Gründe, Wege und Ziele --." *Beiträge zur Heimatkunde der Stadt Löhne und Bad Oeynhausen*. Löhne, Bad Oeynhausen: Verlag Hermann Brackmann, 1985.

Simmons, R. C.. *The American Colonies: From Settlement to Independence*. New York: David McKay, 1976.

Sloan, Eric. *A Reverence for Wood*. New York: Ballantine Books, 1973.

------. *A Museum of Early American Tools.* New York: Ballantine Books, 1973.

Sprotte, Bernhard. *Der Wertheimer Mainübergang.* Wertheim: Verlag E. Buchheim, 1982.

Stanley, George F. G.. *Canada Invaded, 1775-76.* Toronto: Hakkert, 1973.

Steeves, Helen Harper. *The Story of Moncton's First Store and Storekeeper.* St. John, N.B.: J. & A. MacMillan Ltd., 1924.

Steeves, Maimie. *Fundy Folklore.* N.pl.: Albert County Historical Society Inc., n.d..

Stenger Frey, Katharine. "The Danube Swabians in Canada: They Call it Their Land, Too." *German-Canadian Yearbook,* VI (Toronto: Historical Society of Mecklenburg Upper Canada, 1981), 78-83.

Stine, Eugene E. *Pennsylvania German Dictionary.* Introd. by Rev. Willard W. Wetzel, Editor, and Dr. Glenys Waldman, Librarian and Curator, Grand Lodge of Pennsylvania. Birdboro, PA: The Pennsylvania German Society, 1996.

Strasburger, Ralph B. and W.J. Hinke, eds.. *Pennsylvania German Pioneers,* 2 vols.. Norristown, Penn.: Genealogical Publishing Co., 1934 & 1966.

Soucoup, Dan. *Historic New Brunswick.* Lawrencetown Beach: Potterfield Press, 1997.

Surette, Paul. *Colonisation et destruction (1731-1755).* Moncton, N.B.: Les Editions d'Acadie,1988.

------ et la Société historique de la vallée de Memramcook. *Histoire des Trois-Rivières.* Dieppe: la Société historique de la vallée de Memramcook, 1985.

Sutherland, Maxwell. "Case History of a Settlement." *Dalhousie Review,* XLI. 1961-1962, 65-74.

Taubert, Sigfred. "The First German Printers in Canada," *German-Canadian Yearbook,* I. Toronto: Historical Society of Mecklenburg, Upper Canada, 1973, 71-76.

Taylor, George. *A History of Salisbury, 1774-1984.* Moncton, N.B.: Barnes-Hopkins Ltd., 1984.

Temperley, Howard, ed.. *Gubbins' New Brunswick Journals 1811 & 1813.* New Brunswick Heritage Publications, Fredericton, N.B., 1980.

Tratt, Gertrude. "Eagleson, John." *Dictionary of Canadian Biography*, IV, 259-259.

Trautz, Fritz. *Die Pfälzische Auswanderung nach Nortamerika im 18. Jahrhundert*. Heidelberg: Carl Winter Universitätsverlag, 1959.

Trenholm, Gladys, Norden, Miep, Trenholm, Josephine. *A History of Fort Lawrence, Times, Tides and Towns*. Edmonton: Sherwood Printing Ltd., 1985.

Treude, Erhard. "Eskimoische Landabtretung in Nordlabrador im 18. Jahrhundert." *Polarforschung*. Deutsche Gesellschaft für Polarforschung, 47. Jg., Nr. 1/2. Münster: 1977, 61-71.

Trueman, Howard. *The Chignecto Isthmus and Its First Settlers*. Toronto: William Briggs, 1902.

Tweedie, R. A., Cogswell, Fred, and MacNutt, W. Stewart, eds.. *Arts in New Brunswick*. Fredericton, N.B.: University of New Brunswick Press, 1967.

Ullmann, Christiane. "The Early German Societies in Halifax, N.S.: 1786-1871." *German-Canadian Yearbook*, X. Toronto: Historical Society of Mecklenburg, Upper Canada, 1988, 1-10.

Vagts, Alfred. *Deutsch-Amerikanische Rückwanderung*. Heidelberg: Carl Winter Universitätsverlag, 1960.

Voisey, Paul. *Vulcan: The Making of a Prairy Community*. Toronto: University of Toronto Press, 1988.

vom Grafen, Jürgen. *Begleiter durch die Martinskirche Münsingen*. Münsingen: VG Public Relations, n.d..

Wade, Mason. *The French Canadians (1760-1967)*, 2 Vols.. Toronto: MacMillan of Canada, 1968.

Walker, Mack. *German Home Towns: 1648-1871*, Community, State, and General Estate. Ithaca and London: Cornell University Press, 1971.

------. *Germany and the Emigration: 1816-1885*. Cambridge, Mass: Harvard University Press, 1964.

Walling, H.F.. *Topographical Map of Westmoreland and Albert Counties*. New York: W.F. and A.A. Baker, 1862.

Wasseem, Gertrud. "Die Fahrt nach Nova Scotia: Zur Vorgeschichte der Gründung Lünenburgs, N.S.." *German-Canadian Yearbook*, III. Toronto: Historical Society of Mecklenburg Uppper Canada, 1976, 53-59.

------. "Deutsche Einwandererschicksale in der Grüderzeit von Nova Scotia." *German-Canadian Yearbook*, VII. Toronto: Historical Society of Mecklenburg Upper Canada, 1983, 40-48.

Waterman, T.T.. *The Dwellings in Colonial America*. Raleigh: University of North Carolina Press, 1950.

Watson, Allan. *The Germans, Who are they now?* Illinois: Carol Stream, edition q, inc., 1993.

Webster, John Clarence. *The Forts of Chignecto*. Shediac, N.B.: J.C. Webster, 1930.

Weissenborn, Georg. "The Germans in Canada: A Chronological Survey of Canada's Third Oldest European Ethnic Group from 1664 to 1977." *German-Canadian Yearbook*, IV. Toronto: Historical Society of Mecklenburg Upper Canada, 1978, 22-56.

Weller, Karl and Arnold. *Württembergische Geschichte im südwestdeutschen Raum*, 10th edn.. Stuttgart: Theiss Verlag, 1989.

Wenzel, Hermann. "Familie und Kindheit im 16. und 17. Jahrhundert." *Münsingen: Geschichte, Landschaft und Kultur*. Eds. R. Bütterlin and V. Götz. Sigmaringen: Stadt Münsingen, 1982, 269-294.

Wertheim und Umgebung in Graphik und Malerei. Ausstellung 1973. Wertheim: Kulturkreis Wertheim e.V., 1973.

Weyer, Robert van de, ed.. *The Harper Collins Book of Prayers*. New Jersey: Castle Books Edison, 1997.

Whelpley, J.. *The Problem of the Immigrant*. London, Engl.: Chapman & Hall, 1905.

Wilson, Bruce J.. *Records of Our History. Colonial Identity: Canada from 1750-1815*. Ottawa: National Archives of Canada, 1988.

Wright, Esther Clark. *Samphire Greens*. Kingsport, N.S.: Clark Wright, 1961.

------. *The Petitcodiac*. Sackville, N.B.: The Tribune Press, 1945.

------. *The Saint John River*. Toronto: McClelland & Stewart Ltd., 1949.

------. *Planters and Pioneers*: Nova Scotia, 1749-1775. 2nd rev. edn.. Hantport, N.S.: Lancelot Press, 1978.

------. The Steeves Descendants. Wolfville, N.S.: Self publication, n.d..

Yoder, Don. *Pennsylvania German Immigrants: 1709-1786*. Baltimore: Genealogical Publishing Co., 1980.

------. *Discovering American Folk Life: Studies in Ethnic, Religious, and Regional Culture*. Ann Arbor, Michigan: UMI Research Press, 1989.

------, ed.. *Rhineland Emigrants: Lists of German Settlers in Colonial America*. Baltimore: Genealogical Publishing Co., Inc., 1985.

------. "The 'Dutchman' and the 'Deitschlenner': The New World Confronts the Old." *Yearbook of German-American Studies*, XXIII. Lawrence, Kansas.: Society of German-American Studies, 1988, 1-18.

------ and Thomas E. Graves. *Hex Signs: Pennsylvania Dutch Barn Symbols and their Meaning*. New York: E.P. Dutton, 1989.

Wolf, Stephanie Grauman. *Urban Village: Population, Community, and Family Structure in Germantown, Pennsylvania 1683-1800*. Princeton, New Jersey: Princeton University Press, 1976.

Zimmermann, Lothar, ed.. *Annalen/Annals/Annales, 8: German-Canadian Studies in the Nineties, Results and Projects*. Toronto: German-Canadian Historical Association, 1993.

Zimmermann, Wolfgang. "Geschichte-Münsingen." *Der Landkreis Reutlingen*, Bd. II. Sigmaringen: Landesarchivdirektion Baden-Württemberg, 1997, 128-135.

Appendix A

Letter written by Capt. John Hall to William Smith & Co. on June 13, 1766:

Courtesy: Historical Society of Pennsylvania, Philadelphia

Deare Sir: We Landed safe at Petitcodiac
the third Day of June and Our people was
well pleased with the Land but most tired
out with a Long passage. & have Eate
up 2 Barrels of flower on Borde which
I Bought of Corronabe Dickson or tha must
a Broke up the Bed stid, or a sufferd I
Like wise got a hoghead of petatoy for
them to plant as tha told me theirs was
hurt & some had none for our Depender
must be on what Petatoy we Can Rase
& I believe tha are all planted by this time
Our Chance for Buck wheet is not
great for the grass is So Long & green
that it will not Burn & the Dead grass
a mouunght the green mahes it Bad moing
Our only Chance is for Rye after Buck
wheet Comes off & some we shall so with
Buck wheet, for it is not possible to get
it in aney tollarable Order: with the Best
plowes & horses Pencilvania can aford, for it
is so tuff: or if we had the good lock to
a got their as Soue as you Expected it might
have altered the Case: how ever You may Depend
on our Doing Every thing in our power
for the Best: we Desine to try for turnup
Our Land is Strong anough Even for hemp
for the Inglish grass is above our Reefe & is
pasture anough for to fatten a 1000 head
of Cattle: as for rye we have some Sead
But not a Nough But if it possible I Get some
but that Cannot help us till havest Comes a year
Sir I have told you Our Case & I mahe
no Dout but you will Do what Ever
Apears to be Best: I have gone Contrary
to my Orders about the Oxen in Stide of
Buyiny 2 Yoah I bought but one but tha
are the Best I Could get At the price of the
others or a Little more I Bought 3 fine Cows
& 2 Calfs the Company or my Stock, first Cont

469

to my Buying Cows. for heard is a fine
place for Cows. & you cannot hire a milk
Cow under 7 or 8 Dollers a year or season
I got what young Cows I Could: for tha said
they should not go Idle, but worke as well tha
& give milk two. I have Drawn on
Mr Hughs & you for seventy Eight pounds
ten shillings in 2 Bills one for £58:7 & the
Other £20:5:0 Dated this Day thirty pounds
a 11= & 3 is for Freate which in part will
some what surprise you, but I have sent
you a Copey of his Accompt & then
you can Do as you pleas I have
Inclosed a Letter to my wife & some
Others which pleas to forward I
should Be glad to heare from you &
Aney thing you Candirect or advise
shall Puntualy Done I Life the Land
well and am willing to be my part
if it was as much again. My Best
Complaments to Mrs Smith & Famaley
And am;

June 13: 1766   Sir Your humle Sert
                        John Hale

N:B Mr Hughs. has Ordred me
to Buy a Cow and Calf for Each of
his sellers which is Done & a mare
and Colt But I Bought a fine
young Bull in stid of them. &
he will Be Vsfull amoungst the
Cows & will worke well for I bought
him out of the Geers I Expect
to take Mr Huston a Long with
me as I Return home

Capt. John Hall's letter of June 13, 1766 reporting on the safe arrival of the settlers on June 3, 1766.

Transcription of Capt. Hall's letter:

Deare Sir: We Landed Safe at Petitcoodiac the third Day of June and Our people was well pleased with the Land but most tired out with a Long pasage & have Eate up 2 Barrels of Flower on Borde which I Bought of Corronal Dickson or tha [they] must a [have] Broke up the Bed Stid or a sufferd. I Like wise got a hoghead of petators for them to plant as tha told me theirs was hurt & Some had none for our Dependas Must be on what Petators we Can Rase & I believe tha are all planted by this time.

Our Chance for Buck wheat is not Great for the grass is so Long & green that it will not Burn & the Dead grass a mou nght [naught/not?] the green makes it Bad moing. Our only Chance is for Rye after Buck wheat Comes off & some we Shall so[sow] with Buck wheat, for it is not posible to get it in aney tollarable order: With the Best plowes & horses Pencilvania can aforde, for it is so tuff: or if we had the good lock to a got their as sone [soon] as you Expected it might have altered the Case: howeverYou may Depend on our Doing Every thing in our power for the Best: we Desine to try for turnup. Our Land is Strong a nough Even for hemp for the Inglish grass is a bove our neese & is pasture a nough for to fatten a 1000 head of Cattle: as for rye we have some seed But not a Nough. But if it posible I Get some but that Cannot help us till havest Comes a year.

Sir I have told you Our Case & I make no Dout but you will Do What ever apears to be Best: I have gone Contrary to my orders about the oxen in St'de [instead] of Buying 2 Yoak I bought but one but tha are the Best I Could get & for the price of the Others or a Little more. I Bought 3 fine cows & 2 calfs the Company or my foks first con[sented] to my Buying Cows for heare is a fine place for Cows & you cannot hire a milk Cow under 7 or 8 Dollers a year or seasen. I Got what young Cows I Could: for tha said the should not go idle, but Worke as well as tha & give milk two. I have Drawn on Mr. Hughes & you for Seventy Eight pounds ten Shillings payable to Charles Dickson [f]or 1 order in 2 Bills one for £58:5 & the Other £20=5=0 Dated this Day thirty 2 pounds a 11=&3 is for Frate which in part will some what surprise you, but I have sent you a Copey of his Account & then you Can Do as you please. I have inclosed a Letter to my wife & some Others which

471

Pleast to forward I Should be Glad to heare from you & Aney thing you Can direct or advise Shall Puntualy be Done I Like the Land well and am willing to be my part fully if it was as much again. By Best Complaments to Mrs. Smith & Famaley And am:

	Sir Your humbl. Sert.
June 13: 1766	John Hall

N: B Mr. Hughs has orderd me to Buy a Cow and Calf for Each of his setlers which is Done & a mare and colt   But I Bought a fine Young Bull in Stid of them & He will Be use full amoungss the Cows & will worke well for I bought him out of the Geers [garrison?] I Expect to take Mr. Huston a Long with me as I Return home.

[In the left hand margin on the second page of the letter is a partially obliterated sentence beginning with] "my Desine is to Lot Every famely ...."

NOTE: The letter by Captain John Hall was discovered by Mrs. Muriel Lutes-Sikorski in 1983 in the William Smith Papers among documents regarding Nova Scotia, Historical Society of Pennsylvania, Philadelphia.

Appendix B

Joseph Gray's Petition (1775/1783 Hillsborough Census)

A ... number of inhabitants &c that has been settled in the Township of Hillsborough in the County of Cumberland and ...

Return of Souls—&c. abstracts in the township of Attleborough, in the County of Cumberland, Jan. 1, 1783.

Names of Heads of Families	Religious		Children			Remarks
			Of Age		under age	
			Male	Female		
Abstract of those who are Heads of Families, with specifying those of them who ... in all Probability will be Heads of their own for the ensuing year.						
Joshua Attingburham	wife	Joshua Gilbert and his Maidservant only one				
John Gilbert	wife	John Gilbert and wife				1
Robert Law	wife	Robot — and wife				1
William Sutton	wife	William Sutton and wife			2	Saint Kennekis Maid Sirvan
Joseph	wife	Joseph and wife			5	
John Hoffer	wife	John Hoffer and wife			5	Saint Kennekis Maid Sirvan
John Miller	wife	John Miller and wife			1	his Maidservant &c no further upto
Thomas Briggs	wife	Thomas Briggs and wife			3	his maidservant &c no further upto
Christopher Shuman	wife	Christopher Shuman and wife			3	
John Badius	wife	John Badius and wife			6	
Emanuel Badius	wife	Emanuel Badius and wife			4	
Gregory Zidies	wife	Gregory Zidies and wife, & 1 Son, 1 Daughter of age & 1 under age	1		3	
Corina Zidies	wife	Corina Zidies, also John Berger and wife				
Samuel Wilkam	wife	David Wilkam and wife			2	
Stille Stila	wife	Samuel Wilkam and wife			6	
Jacob Robideau	wife	Nathaniel Stila and wife, 2 Sons and 1 Daughter of age, 1 under age	2	1	4	
Jacob Rodin	wife	Jacob Rodin and wife, & 2 Sons and 2 Daughters of age, 1 in the make	2	2		
Peter Lees	wife	Peter Lees and wife and 1 Daughter of age		1	1	
James Smith	wife	James Smith and wife, & 1 Son & 1 Daughter of age		1	2	
Joseph Bihara	wife	Joseph Bihara and wife and one Daughter—of age			2	
Charles Meyer	wife	Charles Meyer and wife			4	
Joseph Elshare	wife	Joseph Elshare and wife			5	
Amiable Robin	wife	Amiable Robin and wife			1	
John Debry	wife	Jacque Debry and wife and 1 Daughter of age			2	
Michel Herrin } Lewis Herrin	wife wife	Michel Herrin and wife, Lewis Herrin & Son & 1 Daughter of age	4	1		Thay of ... field and all the rest
Pierre nu	wife	Pierre and wife ...		4	...	Li....
Michael Lees	wife	John Stave and wife	4		4	two fields ...
Henry Lots	wife	Michael Lots and wife and four sons of age				
Jacob Stave	wife	Henry Lots, Son of Michael Lots, & young man				
Widow Olive		Jacob Stave and wife			5	
		Widow Olive with a large family of black & a ... Amount			3	

Index

abois d'eau, 167

Acadian(s), 1, 32, 154, 155, 159, 160, 163, 164, 165, 169, 180, 185, 197, 198, 207, 209, 239, 257, 259, 261-263, 265, 266, 278, 296

Adams, John, 326

Albert County, 12, 159, 209, 257, 268

alcohol consumption in New Brunswick in 1825, 336

Alemanni, 84, 85

Allan, Benjamin, 330

Alline, 33, 242-244, 246, 247, 250

Allinite, 243, 250

Alsace, 4, 23

American War of Independence, 12, 25, 32, 135, 199, 207, 208, 227, 280, 318, 322

Amherst, 5, 206, 244, 247, 290, 326, 330, 338

Amherst, Geoffrey, 5

Anabaptist, 26, 28-31, 135, 252, 254, 255

Angst, 2

Anse-des-Larosette, 180

antinomianism, 242, 243, 247

"Articles of Agreement", 44, 47, 68, 145, 179, 184, 270

Augustin, 100, 103, 104, 107, 108

Austria, 21, 23, 31, 36, 37, 83, 87, 152

Baker, Charles, 189, 192-195, 198-200, 231, 232, 262, 285, 296

"Bald Marsh", 270, 285, 330, 336

Baltimore, 160, 169, 193, 198-200, 241, 296

Baptist(s), 26, 29-31, 137, 176, 242, 243, 245, 250, 252, 253, 254, 255

Barbarossa, 56, 59, 85

Barren Hill, 135, 142-145, 180

Basel, 59

Bay of Fundy, 154, 157, 159, 167, 174, 180, 205, 208, 318

Beck, Adam, 6

Beck, Martin, 6, 201, 207, 260, 283, 334, 342, 344

Belliveau, Pierre, 1, 257, 263

Bend, The, 170, 203, 261, 278, 280, 286, 297, 330, 334

Bentley, John, 185, 268, 278, 280, 334

Berczy, 6

Bernard, Hans, 4

Black, William, 30, 203, 206, 207, 242-247, 250, 324

Botsford, Bliss, 172, 280

Bouquet, Henry, 144, 157, 165

Bowser, John, 297, 331, 333, 336

Brackman(n), Joseph, 170, 204

Briar Island, 326

Bronnbach, 61, 62

Brown, Mary, 284

Brüdergemeine, Herrnhuter, 6, 239, 253, 326

Bulkley, Richard, 240

Burgoyne, John, 5, 324

Burksdorf, Frederick, 6, 160, 170

Calhoun, Thomas, 159, 160, 162, 164, 165, 167-169, 184, 193, 199, 206, 252

Calhoun, William, 165, 166, 169, 170, 184, 196, 200, 241, 261, 263, 286

Calvin, John, 28, 97

Cape Breton, 5, 152, 154, 157

Carleton, Sir Guy, 321

Carleton, Thomas, 292, 342, 323

Catherine the Great, 2

Catholic(s), 4, 26, 28-32, 60, 61, 77, 83, 87, 88

Caton & Co., 174, 185, 188
Chandler, E.B., Esq., 336
Chappel, Eliphalet, 330
Charlemagne, 2, 59, 83
Charles II, 4
Charleston, 193
Charters, Elizabeth, 283
Chestnut Hill, 137, 144
Chipman Papers, 160, 170
Chipoudie, 180
Clarkson & Co., 155, 185
Colpitts, Robert, 330
conditions on board ships, 36, 128
Cook, Captain James, 4
Copple family, 137, 183, 185, 186, 194, 195, 199, 229, 231
Copple, John, 179, 185, 195, 199, 229, 268
Copple, Judith, 229, 231
Cornwallis, Governor, 36, 152
Coverdale, 270, 271, 282, 290, 332, 334, 343, 344
cow cabbage, 262
Cowes, 34, 128, 131
Cross, Jacob, 160
cuius regio, 31, 31
Cummings, Robert, 163, 193, 196-200, 204, 254, 265, 285, 296
Cutler, Ebenezer, 179, 278, 284
Daigle, Hans, 4
Daniels, "Dimas", 286
Daniels, William, 163
Delaware, 135, 142, 172, 175
Delesdernier, Moses, 169, 193, 196, 197, 207, 232, 262
DesBarres, Frederick, 157, 160, 161, 163
deutsche, 8, 135, 170
Dick, John, 34-36
Dickson, Charles, 206, 231
Dieppe, 1, 180
Dieskau, Baron von, 4

Digby, 180, 322
Donkin, Alexander, 330
Dorchester, 180, 270, 278, 284, 326, 330, 333, 343
Dunkers, 253, 320
Dürer, Albrecht, 59
Dutch, 12, 26, 45, 47, 126, 135, 144, 170, 207, 209, 241, 243, 244, 286, 323, 347
Eagleson, John, 30, 170, 180, 181, 183, 192, 196, 199, 200, 203, 240-242, 246
Early, William P., 250
Eberhard im Bart, 86
Eddy, Jonathan, 326
Eddy Rebellion, 207, 209, 241
Edict of Nantes, 90
Edict of Revocation of Fontaine-bleau, 23
eius religio, 31
Emigration fever, 74, 77, 97
Emmerich, 125
Endorf, 45
Erb, 7
Erickson, Leif, 3
Etter(s), 7, 269, 326
Etter, Peter, 44, 341
Etter, Peter, Jr., 326
Eugene of Savoy, 31
Father of Confederation, 288
Fisher(s), 7, 326, 340
Fisher, Peter, Jr., 326
Fort Beauséjour, 161, 322
Frankfort, 7, 31, 43, 54, 59, 135, 179, 186, 188
Franklin, Benjamin, 154, 171, 173, 175, 192, 196, 239, 326
Francklin, Michael, 161, 169, 186, 196, 207-209, 232, 233, 239-241
Frankfurt, 31, 43, 54, 59, 135

Franklin & Co., 155, 171, 179, 183, 196
Frank(s), 55, 85, 294, 324
Frederick the Great, 22
Geldart, Joshua, 232, 292
Gerhart, Matthias, 160
German-Canadian Yearbook, 9, 25, 157, 166, 324, 326
German Brook, 7
German Creek, 7, 159
German Society, 347
Germantown, 7, 131, 159, 160
Germantown Lake, 159
Germantown, N.B., 6, 12, 141, 144, 155, 157, 159, 163, 164, 166-170, 175, 184, 192-194, 196, 198, 199, 204, 206, 207, 239, 252, 263, 267, 268, 296, 342
Germantown, PA, 131, 135, 137, 139, 141-145, 159-162, 253, 269, 320, 346
Germantowner Zeitung, Die, 253
Germany (settlement), 1
Gerrish, Joseph, 169, 196, 198, 201, 207, 232
Gesellschaft, Hochteutsche, 347
Gesner, Abraham, 7, 261, 323, 326, 330, 346
Gesner, Henry, 326
Gesner, Konrad, 326
Gesner, Solomon, 326
Glackemeyer, Heinrich, 6
goose tongue, 262
Goreham, Joseph, 209, 241, 326
Grand Manan, 265
Grass, Michael, 6, 323
Gray, Joseph, 159, 170, 185, 201, 203, 208, 209, 229, 269, 292
Gray's Island, 209, 281
Greiner, Andres, 180, 188
Grimmer, 7, 323
grindstone sales, 167, 168, 336, 337
Grosseilliers, Sieur des, 4
Grove, Frederick Philip, 6

Gubbins, Joseph, 47, 73, 161, 195, 196, 205, 254, 255, 265, 268, 270, 282, 283, 323, 331, 336, 337, 340
guilds, 18, 20, 68, 86, 91, 105
Habsburg, 2, 23, 31
Häcker, 62, 72, 73
Haldimand, Frederick, 157, 160, 162-164, 167, 168
Halifax, 34, 144, 147, 152, 154, 155, 160-162, 164, 169, 174, 175, 181, 183, 196, 208, 228, 241, 252, 324, 333, 347
Halifax, Lord, 34, 152, 154
Hall, John, 1, 170, 180, 181, 183-185, 188, 257, 260
Hall's Creek, 179, 184, 194, 231, 296
Hammond River, 320
Hand, John, 160
Hanover, 21, 33
Harper Ledgers, 170, 283, 290, 331, 337, 345
Harper, William, 331, 337, 338, 340, 341
Hasenclever, Peter, 157
heart motif, 278
Heidelberg, 8, 23
Heimat, 20, 82
Herckheimer, Nikolaus, 5
Herrnhut, 6, 27
Hessian(s), 5, 25, 55, 166, 321, 323, 324
"Hex" sign, 263
Heyse, Paul, 32
Hillsborough, 6, 26, 32, 44, 81, 108, 142, 155, 159, 169, 170, 188, 192-201, 203-209, 227-229, 232, 233, 239-242, 244-246, 250, 255, 266-269, 280, 283-285, 288, 290, 292, 330, 332-334, 336, 337, 342-345, 347

Hiltz, 7
Hoffenthal, 6
Höhefeld, 60, 62-64, 74, 79, 87
Holy Roman Empire, 19, 75, 85
Honau, 84, 104-106, 262
Hoops, Adam, 144, 157, 159, 160, 162-164, 166-169, 193, 196, 199, 227, 233, 322
Hopewell, 157, 159, 160, 162, 168, 169, 255, 286, 343
Horsman, Christopher, 176, 344, 345
Howe, Sir William, 321
Hudson River, 32
Hudson's Bay Company, 4
Hughes, 145, 171-176, 179, 181, 183-186, 189, 192-194, 196, 205, 260, 285
Huguenot(s), 23, 26, 31, 157, 262, 319
hunt(ing), 22, 75, 87-89, 93-95, 108, 257, 259, 262, 263
Huss, Johannes, 27
Hutterites, 252
ius emigrandi, 31
Johnson, John, 4, 320
Johnson, William, 4
Jonah, Peter, 197, 344
Jones family, 229, 286
Jones, Catherine, 250, 285
Jones, Charles, 67, 155, 183, 184, 194, 195, 228, 229, 285, 286, 323, 344, 345
Jones, Henry, 195, 228, 246, 286, 343
Jones, John, 163, 195, 233, 285, 286
Jones, Margaret, 194, 278, 285, 286
Karrer, Regiment de, 5
Kartoffelklöße, 265-267
Keefer/Kieffer, Thomas, 6
Kelly, James, 2, 290, 338, 341
King George I, 4, 33
King's Road, 179
"King's Stores", The, 183
Klein, Jacob, 180, 188
Knapp, (Titus), 7, 81, 323, 341, 342

Kocherthal, Joshua, 35
Krefeld, 135, 269
Kreuzwertheim, 54, 56, 58-64, 67, 68, 71, 72, 75, 77, 79, 124, 125, 139, 141, 145
Krieghoff, Cornelius, 6
land, scarcity of, 1, 2, 21, 92, 108, 157
Lawrence, Governor, 154
Leibhuhn, 86
Lentz, Matthias, 180, 188
Lewis, Ichabod, 184, 278, 330, 331, 337, 338
Lewisville, 179, 330
Lorraine, 4, 23, 51, 52, 87, 319
Louis XIV, 2, 21, 23, 26, 31, 61, 93
Louisbourg, 5, 34, 75, 143, 152, 157, 169, 322
Löwenstein, 62, 75, 78, 86
Loyalist(s), 6, 8, 12, 33, 44, 152, 170, 171, 185, 209, 254, 261, 268, 278, 280, 296, 297, 318-326, 330, 331, 340-342, 345-347
Lüneburg, 37, 147
Lunenburg, 6, 8, 32, 34, 37, 98, 127, 137, 144, 146, 147, 152, 154, 157, 239-241, 247, 255, 324, 326, 347
Lutes Mountain, 7
Lutesville, 7
Luther, Martin, 18, 26-28, 30, 59, 86, 87, 255
Lutz family, 18, 60, 62, 67, 68, 83, 124, 139, 141, 194, 204, 233, 282-284, 290
Lutz, Georg, Michael, 60, 63, 64, 204, 207, 232, 284, 294
Lutz, Henry, 141, 204, 207
Lutz, John, 72, 270, 284, 286, 294, 332, 333, 336, 338, 343, 344
Lutz, Margaretha, 137

481

Lutz, Peter, 68, 199, 200, 203, 204, 207, 232, 233, 269, 284, 290, 331-333, 337, 341, 343, 344
Lutz, Thomas, 54, 63, 79, 83, 145
Lutz, William, 284, 341
Machias, 206, 227
Magnetic Hill, 288, 290
Main River, 55, 58, 59, 61, 71
Mainz, 55, 59
Mann, James, 7, 250, 250, 323
Mannhurst, 7
Mann Mountain, 7
Marlborough, Earl of, 31
Maryland, 5, 198, 319, 321, 322, 326
Mathias, Peter, 160
Mauger, Joshua, 209
McNutt, Alexander, 146, 154, 155, 172-176, 180
Melanchthon, 67, 86
Memel, 7
mercantilism, 2, 25, 33, 73, 74
mercantilist, 97, 98, 106
Methodism, 250, 254
Miigmag, 261-263
Mi'kmaq, 261
Mill Creek, 176, 180, 194, 207, 278, 285, 290
Millidge Report, 194, 195, 228, 229, 231, 233, 292, 333, 345
Mills, Reuben, 185, 330
Mittelberger, Gottlieb, 128, 169
Mohawk River, 32
Monckton, 108, 143, 145, 147, 155, 163, 169, 170, 172, 174, 176, 179, 184-186, 188, 189, 192-197, 203, 204, 206, 207, 209, 227-229, 231-233, 241, 244, 255, 260, 261, 268, 271, 278, 283-286, 290, 292, 296, 322, 326, 333, 336, 343
Moncton, 1, 26, 44, 139, 159, 172, 179, 180, 231, 233, 239, 265, 267, 268, 270,
271, 280, 286, 290, 292, 294, 295, 326, 330-333, 336-338, 341-345
Moravia(n)(s), 6, 27, 29, 31, 239, 252, 253, 326
Morris, Charles, 159
Mühlenberg, Melchior, 143-147, 154, 172, 239, 240, 254, 255
Müller/Miller Valentin, 143-145, 180, 188
Münsingen, 30, 47, 81, 84-88, 90, 91, 93-95, 98, 100, 103-106, 108, 109, 229
Münster, 6, 45, 254
Myers, Charles, 170, 188, 204
Napoleon, 2, 338
Neuländer, 35, 36, 73, 74, 78, 97, 98, 108, 125, 126, 129
New Brunswick, The First History of, 326
New Brunswick, Sketches of, 340
New York, 4, 32, 146, 173, 295, 319-326
Newlander, 35
Newlight, 30, 241-243, 246, 250, 252
Niedaltdorf, 51, 52
North Joggins, 280
Nuremberg, 59, 81, 82
Nürnberg, 108
Oriskany, 5
Osnabrück, 30, 83
overcrowding, 3, 37, 88
Palatinate, 4, 8, 21-24, 32, 33, 47, 52, 54, 61, 86, 324, 326
Palatine(s), 4, 5, 8, 21, 23, 24, 32, 34, 35, 92, 99, 128, 154, 319, 320
Panaccadie Creek, 180
Peace of Utrecht, 152
Peasant Wars, 62, 87
Peck, Abiel, 169, 184, 199, 206, 284
Peck, Rachel, 206

Penn, William, 4, 33, 135, 269
Pennsylvania(n), 1, 4-6, 8, 10, 12, 19, 21, 26, 30, 32, 34, 35, 37, 47, 54, 63, 73-75, 77, 79, 95, 97-99, 104, 106-108, 126, 131, 135, 137, 139, 141-144, 147, 152, 154, 157, 159, 160, 163, 167, 170-173, 175, 185, 186, 188, 189, 193, 204, 205, 246, 252, 253, 254, 255, 259, 261-263, 266-269, 271, 278, 283, 285, 286, 319-324, 326, 344, 347
Pennsylvania German jurors, 62, 342-344
Pennsylvania German town officials, 95
persecution, religious, 26, 32, 33, 44, 143, 322
Petitcodiac, 1, 27, 30, 55, 63, 64, 84, 88, 97, 108, 145, 147, 155, 159, 171, 172, 174, 175, 180, 188, 192, 201, 205, 231, 240, 242, 244, 246, 247, 255, 266, 267, 269, 278, 280, 283, 284, 295, 296, 318, 326, 333, 334
Petitcodiac German(s), 6, 19, 26, 30, 31, 37, 43, 45, 52, 54, 62, 63, 67, 81-83, 100, 104, 131, 132, 135, 137, 141, 144, 147, 169, 170, 172, 188, 194, 196, 197, 198, 200, 204-206, 209, 227, 229, 231, 233, 239-247, 250, 252-255, 257, 260, 261, 265-267, 269, 278, 280, 283, 286, 288, 294, 295, 296, 318, 323, 325, 326, 331, 333, 336, 337, 338, 340-345
Petitcodiac River, 1, 8, 12, 19, 44, 144, 145, 155, 170, 171, 176, 180, 184, 189, 194, 196, 206, 243-245, 257, 268, 270, 271, 278, 285, 334, 340
Philadelphia, 1, 30, 34, 36, 37, 74, 81, 104, 106, 107, 126-128, 130, 131, 135, 137, 139, 141-147, 155, 157, 163, 165-167, 170, 172, 174, 175, 180, 181, 186, 188, 192, 197, 205, 208, 227, 228, 231, 255, 286, 320, 321
pietism, 95, 97, 135, 143, 252

pietism, German, 253
pietist, 31, 97, 135, 143, 252, 253, 255, 345
pirate raids, 206, 209
Point de Bute, 228
poutine râpée, 265
poverty, 24, 63, 68, 74, 78, 79, 90, 92, 108
Près d'en Haut, 245
Prince-Lewis House (renamed in 2000 to "Treitz Haus"), 179, 184, 196, 268, 271, 278, 326
Prince, Thomas, 278, 290, 297, 330, 334
Protestant(s), 6, 8, 23, 26, 28-34, 60, 61, 77, 87, 88, 90, 95, 97, 144, 154, 176, 179, 184, 196, 241, 250, 255, 266, 320, 322
proto-industrialisation, 91, 92, 97, 108, 269
Prussia, 21-23, 36, 37, 83, 152, 323
Quakers, 4, 35, 135, 154, 252, 321
Queen Anne, 31-33, 319
Radisson, Pierre Esprit, 4
redemptioner(s), 37, 131, 132
Reformation, 27, 31, 58, 87, 252, 254
religion, 12, 23, 26, 31, 78, 87, 97, 243, 245, 252, 254, 255
religiosity, 97, 252
réunion, 23
Reutlingen, 88, 98, 104, 262, 266
Rhine, 23, 24, 29, 32, 35, 45, 54, 59, 124, 126, 319
Ricker family, 44, 334
Ricker, Jacob, Jr., 43, 44, 193, 195, 197-200, 203, 204, 207, 228, 229, 233, 269, 290, 331, 332, 334, 344
Ricker, Jacob Sr., 43, 44, 186, 194, 195, 203, 207, 228, 229, 231, 268, 271, 285, 334

Ricker, Mary, 200, 283
Ricker, Michael, 203, 229, 233, 290, 331-334, 337, 338, 340, 341, 343
Ricker's Point, 7, 203, 207
Ricker, Rosanna, 195, 271, 278, 285
Riedesel, Baron von, 5, 6, 324
Rindisbacher, Peter, 6
Rochefort, 60, 61
Rotterdam, 34, 74, 98, 124-126, 131
Roxborough, 135, 139, 144
Royal Fencible Americans, 170, 326
Royal Greens, 5
Rupert, Prince, 4
Russia, 2, 4, 29, 36, 83, 152
Saarland, 8, 47, 51, 52, 54
Sackville, 159, 168, 184, 185, 198, 231, 241, 334, 343
Saint John River, 159, 176, 179
Samphire, 9, 30, 137, 141, 170, 172, 188, 199, 207, 227, 229, 231, 250, 257, 260, 262, 269, 270, 283, 285, 286, 343
Sauer, Christopher, 137, 253, 255, 320, 321, 323, 346
Schlatter, Michael, 143-146
Schnitz, 137, 259, 263
Schultheiß(e), 62, 68, 77, 91, 95
Schwerdtfeger, Samuel, 6
Seißen, 106, 108, 125
Schuylkill, 135, 172, 346
Seven Years' War, 37, 152, 157
Shepody, 155, 157, 159, 160, 167, 169, 170, 201, 265, 281
Shirley, Governor, 34, 152
Sikorski, Muriel (Lutz), 290
Sinton, William, Esq., 283
Smith, William & Co., 155, 170, 174, 179, 180, 188
Society for the Propagation of the Gospel, 239, 240
Somers Creek, 180
Sommer family, 142, 145, 200, 239, 280, 290

Sommer, Andrew, 142, 195, 203, 207, 233, 290, 332, 333, 337, 338, 342-344
Sommer, Anna Catharina, 142, 188, 200, 290
Sommer, Matthias, 139, 142, 144, 145, 180, 183, 188, 203, 228, 231, 252, 338
Sommer, Rachel, 142, 246, 282, 283
Sowers, 320, 323
Spanish War of Succession, 23, 92
Spätzle, 267
Spessart, 45, 54, 56, 124
Stahlecker, Regina, 84, 104, 105
Stamp Act, 174, 192, 196
Steadman, William, 184, 278, 297, 330, 331, 333, 336, 337
Steeves colony, 209
Steeve, Henry, 142, 197, 203, 229, 332
Steeves, William Henry, 283, 288
Steeves Mountain, 7, 296, 325, 326
Steeves Settlement, 7
Steveston, 288
Stieff Bible, 81, 108, 247, 270
Stieff family, 10, 22, 30, 83, 97, 104, 105, 107, 108, 183, 200, 247, 255, 257, 266, 267, 280
Stief, (Birkenau), 83
Stieff, Catharina (Lutz), 269
Stieff, Christian, 185, 194, 200, 207, 243, 244, 250, 254, 267, 271, 285, 297, 325, 332, 341-344
Stieff, Frederick, 142, 145, 331, 334, 344
Stieff, Heinrich, 11, 88, 228, 270, 283
Stieff, Henry, 201, 207, 250, 337
Stieff, Jacob, 141, 200, 207, 268, 280, 282, 341, 343
Stieff, John, 207, 232, 270, 280, 282, 284, 332, 333

Stieff, Lewis, 338
Stieff, Matthew, 207
Stiles, Reuben, 285
Stoney Point, 175
Strasbourg, 23
Stultz, Henry, 326, 330, 336, 337, 341, 342, 344
Summersett, 193
Swabian(s), 23, 84, 85, 89
Swabian Highlands, 84, 92, 269
tax, 23, 63, 73, 75, 87-89, 91, 141, 192, 342, 343
Terre Rouge, 180
Theresia, Maria, 59
Thirty Years' War, 2, 19, 20, 22, 23, 25, 31, 45, 51, 59-61, 71, 82, 83, 87-89, 92, 94, 99, 103, 135, 165, 252
Treaty of Aachen, 152
Treaty of Westphalia, 2
Treitz family, 52, 60, 334
Treitz, Abraham, 176, 185, 194, 196, 207, 231, 244, 286, 297, 331, 336, 338, 343, 344
Treitz, Christian, 47, 184, 185, 268, 270, 271, 278, 285, 297, 330, 331, 333, 334, 336, 340, 343, 344
Treitz, Elisina, 285
Treitz, Jacob, Jr., 185, 195, 267, 271, 278, 285, 343, 344
Treitz, Jacob, Sr., 179, 185, 228, 229, 231, 233, 271, 278, 285, 330, 342
Treitz, Rosanna, 188, 199, 200, 254, 262, 267, 283, 285, 286, 330
Trites, Elizabeth, 330
Turenne, Marshall, 22, 61
Turks, 2, 23, 29, 31
Tyrkir, 3
Upper Merion, 186, 193
"Village", 176, 196, 244, 245, 326, 331
Village-des-Allemands, 5
Village-des-Blanchard, 180
Village-des-Lacouline, 180

Villars, Marshall, 23
Viniculture, 71, 72, 88
Vinland, 4
Virneburg, 60, 61
Virginia, 155, 173
Waldo, Samuel, 5, 73, 75, 98, 144
Waldoboro, 5, 75
Wallace, Hugh, 157, 167, 169
Watson Esq, James, 176, 341
Watson, J. Thomas, 228
Wayne, Anthony, 163, 171, 172, 174, 175, 181, 186, 197
weather, 20, 24, 25, 32, 71, 166, 261, 262
weaver(s), 89, 90, 97, 98, 159, 204, 268, 269, 331
weaving, 11, 88-90, 92, 97, 100, 104, 108, 137, 198, 203, 204, 269, 270, 295
Wertheim, 18, 54-56, 58, 59, 61, 62, 68, 71-75, 77-79, 86-88, 97, 98, 108, 124, 139, 145
Wethered, Joshua Winslow, 181, 183, 185, 189, 192, 193
Wießler, Anna Walpurgis, 67
William of Orange, 23, 26, 31
Wilmot, Governor, 154, 155, 157, 170
Wilmot, Malcolm, 338
Wilson Cemetery, 176, 338
Wilson, William, 229, 233, 268, 343, 345
Wissahickon, 135
Wood, commodity of freedom, 340
Wortman family, 44, 204, 292
Wortman, Georg, 45, 47, 179, 185, 195, 204, 207, 228, 229, 232, 292
Wortman, Jacob, 233, 292, 294, 343
Wortman, Margareth, 330
Wortman, Mariah, 292
Wortman, Martin, 233, 292, 294
Wright, Alexander, 297

Württemberg, 8, 11, 21, 23, 47, 84, 86-93, 95, 97-100, 103, 104, 108, 252, 255, 262, 266, 267

Würzburg, 55, 59, 60, 62, 71

Yorkshire, 207, 209, 297, 330, 331

Yorkshire settlers, 330, 331

Ziegler, 91, 100, 104, 108, 270

Zimmermann, Heinrich, 4

Zwingli, Ulrich, 28, 87